SOCIOLOGY
STUDYING
THE HUMAN
SYSTEM

SOCIOLOGY
STUDYING THE HUMAN SYSTEM

Jonathan H. Turner
University of California, Riverside

Goodyear Publishing Company, Inc. 83-1106
Santa Monica, California

Library of Congress Cataloging in Publication Data

Turner, Jonathan H.
  Sociology: studying the human system.

  Includes bibliographies and index.
  1. Sociology. I. Title.
HM51.T79   301   77-21142
ISBN 0-87620-814-6

Current printing (last digit):
10 9 8 7 6 5 4 3 2

ISBN: 0-87620-814-6
Y-8146-6

Art Direction: Vinje & Reid Design Studio
Illustrations: Kathy Philpott
Photo research: Genoa Caldwell
Supervising Editor: Sue MacLaurin

Printed in the United States of America

Thank you, Alexandria Maryanski

CONTENTS

PART I

THE SOCIOLOGICAL PERSPECTIVE 1

1

THE SOCIOLOGICAL IMAGINATION 2

PART II

BASIC ELEMENTS OF THE HUMAN SYSTEM 38

Contents   38
Preview   38

2

THE SCIENCE OF SOCIETY: THEORY AND METHOD IN SOCIOLOGY   18

3

IN THE BEGINNING: THE EMERGENCE OF HUMANS   40

4

HUMAN CULTURE: THE SYMBOLIC WORLD 68

5

INTERACTION: THE BASIC SOCIAL PROCESS 98

6

SOCIAL ORGANIZATION: THE CREATION OF SOCIAL STRUCTURE   118

7

PERSONALITY AND SOCIALIZATION: THE CREATION OF HUMANS   140

8

SOCIAL CONTROL AND DEVIANCE 172

11

FORMAL ORGANIZATIONS   240

12

FLUID ORGANIZATIONS: PATTERNS OF COLLECTIVE BEHAVIOR 268

13

HUMAN COMMUNITIES 300

14

STRATIFICATION   326

PART IV

15

RACE, ETHNIC, AND MINORITY RELATIONS 358

BASIC HUMAN INSTITUTIONS 382

16

FAMILY AND KINSHIP 384

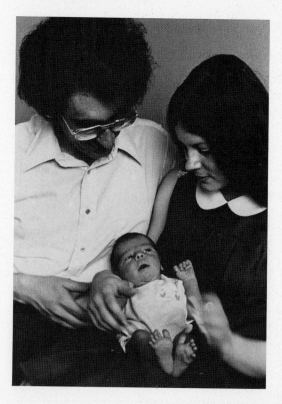

17

RELIGION   414

18

THE ECONOMY   440

19

GOVERNMENT 470

PART V

CHALLENGE AND CHANGE IN THE HUMAN SYSTEM   516

21

ECOLOGY AND THE HUMAN SYSTEM   518

22

POPULATION AND THE HUMAN SYSTEM 536

23

CONTINUITIES IN THE HUMAN SYSTEM 550

PREFACE

Each book has its own rationale, and perhaps mine is no better than others! But I have sought in this text not only to cover the traditional sociological topics but have also tried to illustrate the reasons why sociologists study these topics and to demonstrate how these topics "fit into" a larger intellectual scheme of things. Let me elaborate.

I have sought to communicate that sociology is the study of *the human system*. This system is composed of people and their creations: culture and diverse patterns of social organization. These creations are maintained and changed by certain crucial social processes. The task of an introductory text is, I believe, to demonstrate that sociology, with the tools of science and the use of intuition, can understand how humans relate to each other and how they create, maintain, and change their cultural and social patterns. I have tried to do this in several ways:

First, sociologists have often lost sight of the fact that we are animals. Admittedly, we are very unique ones; nonetheless, we evolved from primal animal ancestors. We came from somewhere and retain certain biological attributes. I do not want to overemphasize these attributes, because humans are unique by virtue of their symbol using abilities and their capacity to construct complex social relations. And yet, neither should we ignore completely our biological and evolutionary heritage.

Second, humans create artifacts, symbols, and structures which are all interrelated. Freeways and poison tip spears are the result of knowledge (a form of symbols) and certain unique patterns of social organization. Thus, I have sought to organize the chapters into sections that give students a sense for how culture is created, what kinds of social relations it allows, and how people have constructed diverse forms of social organization.

Third, the chapters reveal a logical progression. The first two chapters expose students to the sociological orientation—what we study and how we study it. The next section of chapters deals with the basic elements of the human system: our emergence as a species, our reliance on culture, our symbolic forms of interaction, our diverse forms of social organization, our unique way of socializing ourselves, our tendencies to deviate and to control, and the changing nature of gender and sex roles. The next section deals with the diverse patterns of social organization, or social forms, that humans have created. Groups, formal organizations, fluid organizations, communities, stratification, and ethnic subgroupings are thus examined. The third section of chapters explores the nature of basic human institutions: kinship, religion, economy, polity, and education. These embrace other social forms and resolve basic human problems. And the fourth section deals with master trends in the human system, most particularly trends in population, ecology, and human organization.

Fourth, in organizing the materials this way, an over-all theme becomes evident. We are a species which first evolved biologically, and then with this biological heritage, evolved culturally and socially. Through the basic processes of adaptation to the exigencies of our environment and interaction with each other, we have elaborated culture and diverse social forms. Cultural components and social forms did not all appear simultaneously. They have emerged over time and now constitute a fantastically complex system—the human system. Sociology must study the history of this system as well as its current profile. And we must study the human system at all its levels—from the first moments of one of its members' lives to the giant institutional complexes of the most advanced society. All the topics of sociology are covered in the pages to follow, but they are presented in an order and context which allows students to see how the human system emerged, how it grew, and how, in all its complexity and majesty, it is maintained and changed through certain fundamental processes.

In the pages to follow, then, I hope to cover the field comprehensively, but with more coherence—a coherence that stems not from intellectual dogmatism, but from the recognition that the human system in its present forms has been created by people over thousands upon thousands of years. Our job as sociologists is to uncover the uniqueness as well as the regularities in this creation.

Jonathan H. Turner
Riverside, California

ACKNOWLEDGEMENTS

I wish to thank several individuals for assistance in preparing several chapters: Michael Werthman co-authored with me chapters 3, 4, and 5; Douglas Brooker provided assistance for chapters 7, 9, and 11; and James Crawford helped prepare chapter 12.

The suggestions of the following reviewers helped guide the rewrite of the manuscript, and I would like to thank them: Joan Huber, Burton Wright, Joel Best, and Michael Brooks. Other valuable comments and contributions were made by Charles Palazzolo, Robert Sherwin, Philip Knowles, and Joyce De Ridder.

I would also like to thank Clara Dean, who for eight years has been typing all my work. She has provided invaluable help in correcting my spelling and grammar for this and many other projects. But most importantly, she is to be commended for learning to read my handwriting.

SOCIOLOGY
STUDYING THE HUMAN SYSTEM

THE SOCIOLOGICAL PERSPECTIVE

CONTENTS

PREVIEW

In these two short chapters, we will become oriented to sociology. What is sociology? What do sociologists study? How do they study the world? These are our guiding questions. However, we should remain aware that these chapters provide only a general introduction. They are intended to alert and sensitize you to sociology. The sociological perspective can only be truly appreciated at the book's end, but we can begin now, at least, to look at the world sociologically.

THE SOCIOLOGICAL IMAGINATION

PROLOGUE

Guiding Questions: What is sociology?
What does it study, and how? How did the
field emerge? What is the book about?

Chapter Topics

WHAT
IS
SOCIOLOGY?

Ancient people probably gazed at the sky and the land, wondering about the nature of the universe. They were probably awed and humbled by the power of nature and by the vastness of the universe. Slowly, as they came to grips with the world around them, they began to unravel some of these mysteries of nature. People in Europe, Asia, and the Americas developed calendars to record the regular movements of sun, moon, and earth. Early mariners learned how to navigate from the positions of the stars and sun, and during the Renaissance, astronomers began to theorize about the orbits of the celestial bodies. Eventually, Isaac Newton was able to explain many of the mysteries of the world through mathematical laws, and Albert Einstein was to expand and refine this knowledge, explaining some of the basic relationships among matter, energy, light, and time. The quest for further understanding goes on today.

Just as people have thought about the physical world around them, they surely must have wondered about themselves. Who were they? Why were they here? What was the purpose of life? Must things always be done the way they have always been done? Indeed, it may have been more difficult to ponder these matters than questions about the physical world. Thus, it may have taken them longer to ponder the nature of social life. Eventually they did, although, just when, where, and how can never be known.

We are, in a sense, "outsiders" when looking at the earth and heavens; we can see the stars, moon, sun, plants, animals, rivers, and lakes as separate from our body and mind. But we are "insiders" when it comes to viewing ourselves

and our social world. How do we stand back to view ourselves? Can we even perceive of a social world when our daily lives, thoughts, and actions are so involved in it? Once we begin to ask what our place in the world is, why we must do certain things, and why we live our lives the way we do, we begin to develop a sociological imagination. For in answering such questions, we come to see ourselves as involved in social relationships with other people. These relationships bring joy, happiness, jealousies, frustrations, resentment, and other human emotions. But we have achieved the critical insight: our lives are greatly influenced by the social relationships around us.

Sociology as the Study of Social Relationships

Sociology is the study of human **social relationships.** Sociologists do not study people who live in isolation, they study people who are in contact and communication with others—people in social situations. Many human relationships are direct. We have personal friends with whom we talk, and in whom we confide. For much of our lives, we look to our parents for affection, guidance, and discipline, but even when they are not present, we often use them as a symbolic frame of reference.

Much of our social world, however, is more remote. We are part of a college or university that constrains what we do: we go to classes, take notes, subject ourselves to exams, defer to the authority of instructors, and allow our minds to be influenced. The actual number of people whom we know and contact is small: a few friends, classmates, instructors, and an occasional administrator. Yet, we can feel and sense that there is a "system of relationships" beyond our more personal contacts. It constrains and controls, and although we are part of it, much of it exists as an external reality beyond our immediate experience and control. What is true of a college or university is also true of other social worlds—the economy, the government, and the community, for example. We are part of these social worlds: we have jobs, we vote and know that government regulates our lives, and we have places in which to reside. Yet, we also know that the economy, government, and community extend beyond our personal experience. They involve relationships, often numbering into the millions, with which we have no contact or familiarity.

Thus, when we say that sociology is the study of social relationships, we mean much more than our personal relationships; we mean all social relationships, in all their complexity and majesty. We are interested in understanding how and in what ways social relationships among individuals, groups, governments, corporations, communities, nations, or other social units are created, maintained, or changed. In other words, we are interested in **the human system**—the types and forms of social relationships we have created in the course of our existence on earth.

Let us take a concrete example from our daily lives: the college or university. For an individual, the college reveals only a general structure: buildings, courses, requirements, class schedules, and the like. Much of a person's actual behavior is more personal: lunch

The human system is composed of various social relationships, ranging from small gatherings such as that pictured below to large urban, industrial societies.

with friends, friendly exchanges with fellow students, a question for the instructor, a chat with the instructor after class, for example. Sociologists look at this world much differently. They view it as a structure of relationships among positions, not among people. They see the classroom as composed of two positions—instructor and student—and these positions have certain rules governing behavior for both the student and the instructor. The class is viewed as a *social structure*. It is, however, a subunit within a much larger system, which is composed, most generally, of different types of positions: administrators, faculty, and students, for example. But these positions vary in such matters as duties and power. The same is true of faculty, and is even true among students. Sociologists attempt to study the important relationships among individual positions and any important subunits; they examine power, rivalries, conflicts, cooperation, and other social processes. The college itself might be viewed as a subunit within a larger system of higher education.

What we can see, then, is that sociologists do not focus on people, per se, but on the potentially complex relationships among positions and different social units in which people participate. But do sociologists lose sight of people? Certainly not, because sociologists are most interested in what happens to people in social units, such as colleges and universities. They seek answers to the questions of how the college experience affects people's personalities and adjustment and how people see and define their situation. Most importantly, sociologists want to know how the actions of people change the system of relationships.

Let us take another example: the family. For us, the family is a series of personal relationships with mothers, fathers, siblings, and children. For sociologists, the family is a system of positions, governed by rules, existing within other systems of relationships such as the economy and the community. Although sociologists are certainly interested in individual relations of family members, they are even more interested in how these relations reveal common patterns among families in response to economic conditions, for example. In this system of relationships, too, the thrust of the sociological imagination is to see daily life in relation to larger networks of social relationships. People do count, of course, because they are the creators of these networks and because these networks only have life and vitality by virtue of people's thoughts and actions.

Thus, the study of sociology deals with how, why, and in what ways people form and change social relationships and with the consequences of these relationships on people themselves. Sociology is a very broad subject, attempting to study the wide diversity of relationships that typify the human system. We should examine the relationship between sociology and other social sciences, if only briefly. There is naturally much overlap for such a broad field; but there are differences in emphasis, and we should be aware of these.

Sociology and Economics

Economics studies the production and distribution of goods and services. Sociology also studies these matters, but sociologists study them with a somewhat different purpose.

Whereas economists study the flow of goods and services among economic units and sectors, they do not study extensively the nature and attributes of these economic units, whether they be individuals, corporations, or government. Sociologists, on the other hand, are not only concerned with general economic relationships among units but also with social relationships within these units and the psychological states of individuals in economic contexts. They are interested in how people feel, what their attitudes and opinions are, how a corporation operates, and how governments and corporations form relationships.

Sociology and Political Science

These two fields are beginning to converge on the general question of how power is used and distributed in society. Traditionally, political scientists have studied international relationships among nations and the administration of government within nations. In contrast, sociologists have rarely studied international relations, and when studying the administration of government, they have been primarily interested in how it illustrated the more general problem of bureaucracy. Moreover, sociologists have studied many topics that only recently have attracted political scientists: political attitudes, social backgrounds of leaders, social class, and other factors that influence people's political behavior. Now, sociologists study intersocietal relations, and political scientists study a wide range of forces that influence political behavior, attitudes, and organization. Thus, the concerns of political sociology and political science are likely to be much the same in the near future.

Sociology and Psychology

Psychology is the study of behavior. Behavior, however, is defined broadly and includes thinking, learning, perception, emotions, motives, and increasingly, the physiological (organic) as well as the social causes of behavior. Sociology and psychology overlap in an area known as **social psychology** which is the study of social factors that influence people's behavior—their cognitions, emotions, attitudes, decisions, and actions. Psychologists usually concentrate on understanding the actual behavior, whereas sociologists are more likely to study the social situations that produce certain behaviors. Perhaps the greatest overlap occurs in the study of personality—the traits and attributes of people—but, here again, psychologists are more likely to study the structure and processes of personality, per se, whereas sociologists are usually more interested in how types of social relationships have produced certain personality characteristics.

Sociology and Anthropology

Anthropology and sociology have common intellectual roots. Anthropology is divided into several specific areas: cultural organization, linguistics, archaeology, and physical anthropology. Sociology and anthropology overlap primarily in the area of cultural organization, although sociologists are becoming more attuned to the biological or physical facets of human behavior. Within cultural (or social) organization, the major difference between the two disciplines is in the type of societies studied. Anthropologists tend to concentrate on primitive or traditional systems and sociologists on more modern societies. Yet, a curious shift is taking place: just as sociologists are becoming more aware of traditional societies, anthropologists are beginning to study more modern systems. As we will see in the following chapters, the two disciplines have much in common.

Sociology and History

History is the study of societal events of the past. Historians seek to chronicle what occurred and to offer some clues as to why one set of events led to another. Some of the earliest sociologists performed historical analysis, but there was a difference between sociologists and historians which persists to this day. Sociologists attempt to generalize from historical events; historians concentrate on the unique features of each event. For example, historians might give a detailed account of events leading to the French Revolution to demonstrate that this revolution was the culmination of a sequence of specific processes in French society; sociologists, however, would tend to view the French Revolution as an example of revolutions in general. They would try to see how the events leading to this revolution could be considered, along with evidence from other revolutions in different times and places, as examples of the general conditions that cause all revolutions. For the most part, historians stay with the particulars; sociologists try to discover the general conditions that such particulars illustrate.

Sociology and Social Work

For a long time, people outside sociology and social work considered the two areas synonymous. Such an association is an incorrect one. Social work is a profession for helping people, and as such, it draws upon knowledge from all the social sciences as well as from the individual social worker's intuition. Of course, many social workers have received sociological training, for sociology is a highly relevant discipline. But sociologists try to understand why certain situations—for example, crime and poverty—exist. Sociologists do not usually try to intervene in the social world; rather, they attempt to provide the knowledge for those who do intervene. There is, however, considerable disagreement among sociologists over their proper role and responsibility. Should they be detached, or should they be activists and try to change human affairs? The answers tend to vary for each sociologist.

We can see from these comparisons that sociology is a very broad discipline, covering almost every facet of human affairs. It overlaps and converges with other social sciences and even with some disciplines in the humanities, such as history. Indeed, nowhere is the convergence more evident than in the history of sociology. Few of sociology's founders called themselves sociologists. The discipline is young—no more than 150 years old—and those scholars who contributed most to the sociological imagination were interdisciplinary in outlook. Only with the emergence of sociology as a distinct discipline does their work, in retrospect, become sociological. Therefore, we should briefly review the emergence of the sociological perspective. Much of what follows in this book was inspired by the genius of these "first sociologists."

THE EMERGENCE OF SOCIOLOGY

Auguste Comte

Sociology emerged in Europe in the early 1800s. The French social philosopher Auguste Comte (1798–1857) was the first to use the word, *sociology,* and to argue for a "science of society." He called this **science** "social physics," which underscores his view that society could be studied in much the same way as could other aspects of the universe. He divided sociology into "social statics" and "social dynamics"—the traditional distinction in the physics of his time. With this distinction, Comte emphasized that humans form social

Auguste Comte (1789–1857) was the titular founder of sociology.

relationships that reveal a *structure,* or degree of stability, over time. But he also recognized that in the process of dealing with each other, humans are constantly in motion. They continually restructure, rekindle, and rework their relationships.

Comte was not a highly original thinker; in many ways, he consolidated and gave forceful expression to ideas that were prevalent in his time. Nonetheless, his contributions were important: (1) he gave sociology its name; (2) he emphasized the scientific, as opposed to the religious, philosophical, and moral analysis of society; and (3) he emphasized the nature of the human system as both structure and process. For this, present-day sociology is in Comte's debt.

Herbert Spencer

Early sociology flourished in England and Germany as well as in France, and by the end of the nineteenth century it began to prosper in America. Many events occurred simultaneously in these countries, but we will discuss them sequentially. In England Herbert Spencer (1820–1903), a social philosopher and biologist, was attempting to synthesize all the sciences. Spencer's genius has been frequently obscured because he was often a political apologist for causes that are now unacceptable to the sociological community. But he almost discovered the theory of evolution before Darwin, and it was he rather than Darwin who introduced the phrase, "survival of the fittest." Unfortunately, Spencer sought to apply this doctrine to human affairs, arguing that people should be left free to compete so that the most

Herbert Spencer (1820–1903) was the first English sociologist.

he borrowed from Comte, but he forced the recognition that human societies must be viewed as elaborate structures of parts. Society was not the sum of individuals; it was an organism with a life and vitality of its own. Second, Spencer developed a theory of social evolution, arguing that societies were much like growing organisms. They went from simple to more complex states, from homogeneous masses to highly differentiated complexes.

Spencer's ideas were enormously popular and were widely read outside academic circles. But his real contribution to sociology may have been in what he stimulated in the French sociologist, Émile Durkheim. Spencer had an enormous impact on Durkheim: Durkheim rejected almost all of Spencer's questionable assumptions about "survival of the fittest," but he extended and refined Spencer's ideas about how the "social organism" was maintained and changed. Spencer is hardly read any more, but Durkheim continues to inspire the sociological imagination, as we shall see throughout this book.

Émile Durkheim

Émile Durkheim asked a simple set of questions: What holds society together? Why are people willing to form and abide by social relationships? His answers have become sociology's first principles: Humans create ideas to regulate their affairs. They hold values, beliefs, doctrines, and dogmas; they regulate their conduct with norms and rules; and they come to see these ideas as compelling truths and to invest them with great emotion.

able could find the best niches. Such arguments supported rather well the interests of those who wanted to keep the masses impoverished and working for low wages. They could also support discrimination since the failure of people to be "equal" was the result of the operation of a "natural law." Spencer thus tainted his analysis with what he thought "ought to be."

Spencer's contribution to sociology can be seen in two forms. First, he sought to view society as a type of organism—as a system of interrelated, functional parts. In this analysis,

Émile Durkheim (1858–1917) built upon Comte and Spencer, becoming one of the early intellectual giants of sociology.

Durkheim's insights seem simple, but they had far-reaching implications for sociology: (1) Social order is governed by symbols—by ideas, values, beliefs, and norms. (2) These symbols can become a part of people, a part of their personalities—that is, of their needs, desires, or perceptions. Social order is thus maintained by ideas becoming an aspect of people's personalities, ruling them from within. (3) Complex social relationships are also governed by negotiations between parties. Problems of order in complex societies increase because the power of symbols lessens and is replaced by exchanges of goods and services among people.

Durkheim's vision of what holds society together was buttressed by a concern with developing sociology as a science. He was the first sociologist to test his theories about society with systematic data collection and statistical analysis. In so doing, he sought to implement Comte's vision of a science of society—a topic to be addressed in the next chapter.

But Durkheim, like Spencer, recognized that societies move from simple to more complex forms. Ideas—or the "collective conscience," as he termed the matter—have less power in more complex forms. They become more general and abstract; they can no longer regulate human affairs in great detail. Social relations become based increasingly on exchanges of mutual interest and benefits. People work for pay rather than for moral duty to the society. Because people do not always work out their exchanges clearly or smoothly, their frequent lack of consensus over ideas can create disorder and deregulation and cause problems of order for the human system.

Karl Marx

Our history of sociology now turns to Germany, where we must first look at Karl Marx (1818–1883). Marx was, of course, an advocate of revolution. He saw the misery of workers and peasants in early industrial Europe, and he devoted his life to advocating the revolution that he believed would better their lives. In advocating this revolution, Marx achieved some enduring insights into society. He saw society as held together not so much by consensus over ideas, but by power. Those with

Karl Marx (1818–1883) was the first sociologist to explore the dynamics of power.

power could force and manipulate others to do their bidding. Power came from property—from the ownership of the means of production on which the economic system and people's survival exists. Those who own the land in agricultural societies have power; those who own factories in industrial societies have power; and their power is immense. They coerce; they manipulate ideas; and they convince people that exploitation is for their benefit.

Marx emphasized that societies reveal natu-ral and inevitable sources of conflict and tension. Order and stability are always subject to countervailing forces of disorder and change. The unequal distribution of power makes this conflict inevitable; each type of economic system—slavery, feudalism, and capitalism, for example—reveals a different set of power relationships between those who own property and those who do not. And thus it is inevitable that those who do not have power seek to gain it; and once they have power, others attempt to take it from them.

Marx opened new fields of study for sociologists. How are resources distributed? How are resources used to manipulate people and classes? What tensions and conflicts are likely to emerge? How do these change society? Marx provided new insight into the social forces of power and inequality. He held that societies were not stable social organisms, governed by democratic rules and mutually beneficial exchanges. The rules were imposed by those with power, and the exchanges were one-sided. Marx's analysis corrected Comte's, Spencer's, and Durkheim's overly consensual and orderly view of society and social change. We will return frequently to Marx in other chapters.

Max Weber

The other great German sociologist was Max Weber (1864–1920). Weber still influences a wide variety of topics in sociology: social change, religion, stratification, bureaucracy, power, and almost any area of inquiry pursued by sociologists. We will refer to Weber's insights frequently, for it is in his specific analysis of particular topics that his contribution to sociology resides.

Max Weber (1864–1920) presented sociology with insights into the social forms and dynamics of modern society.

Weber's approach to sociology is perhaps as important as his actual conclusions about events. He emphasized that sociology must understand the causal relationships among important facets of social life. How does religion influence economic change? How does bureaucracy shape a society? What kinds of inequalities and divisions in society are important in understanding other features of that society? Weber sought to answer such questions by employing two major techniques: (1) ideal-type analysis, and (2) historical analysis. To understand why a social structure exists, it is necessary to know the features of this structure that make it a unique form. For example, if bureaucracy is an important social phenomenon, what distinguishes it from other forms such as the family? Weber constructed an "ideal type" of this form—that is, a list of the basic and distinguishing features of bureaucracy, or of any other social phenomenon. *Ideal* was perhaps a bad choice of words; *pure type* may be a more appropriate description.

Weber then engaged in historical analysis to find the causes of the social form or event under study. The causes of bureaucracy, for example, were found in those events preceding its emergence. But Weber did more than merely record historical causes; he was interested in bureaucracy, in general, or in its pure form. He was not interested in bureaucracy in Germany, France, England, or in some specific place, but rather, he would try to use his historical analysis to *generalize* about what makes bureaucracy emerge in all societies at all times. This emphasis on defining a social phenomenon of interest with a clear ideal-type description, and then discerning the general causes of this phenomenon, gave real substance to Comte's cry for a science of society.

Weber also provided an important qualification to his work. Sociologists must not only look at how social events influence each other, they must also look at what events mean to people. How do people define the world? What are their interpretations? What, for example, do bureaucracies mean to those who work in them? This kind of understanding at the "level of meaning" is essential to the sociological imagination.

European sociology of the nineteenth and early twentieth centuries left an important mark. It sought to create a science of society, and it tried to explore the nature of society. All major European thinkers viewed society as a system of parts, interrelated to form a social whole that transcends individuals. Each provided a way of analyzing this emergent social whole, and each provided an insight into its workings. Yet, they tended to concentrate their thinking on society *as a whole*. Although Durkheim realized that moral rules become part of people's personality, although Weber recognized the importance of understanding people's meanings and definitions, although Spencer emphasized individuals in combat and competition, and although Marx stressed the importance of power in exploiting people, they all soon left the individual person behind. Totally consumed by the big picture of society, they all failed to indicate *how* society "gets inside people" or *why* people are willing to participate in society. These were the questions that concerned the first American sociologists. Their insights provided an important "missing link" in the sociological imagination.

Early American Sociology

At the turn of the century, early American sociologists asked some fundamental questions about individuals and society. How does society become a part of individuals? Why are people willing and able to be members of society? Their answers, which will be explored in detail in later chapters, were that through communication and interaction with others, people learn to become members of society. Without this learning, society could not exist.

The social philosopher, George Herbert Mead, codified this line of thought into a coherent perspective. He saw the capacity for thinking—to weigh, consider, define, and reflect on matters—as a social product. *Mind*, as he termed it, evolves out of interaction with others. With "mind," individuals develop a conception of themselves as certain kinds of people. This "self" gives their actions stability and predictability. People also learn how to anticipate each other's responses—to imagine what others might or must do. In this way, they learn to cooperate and to maintain social relations. People begin to see themselves and their actions from a broader perspective—from a "community of attitudes"—and thus begin to see the world in similar ways and to conform to generally accepted practices. All of these learned social products help facilitate the creation and maintenance of social relations—that is, of society itself.

What Mead did was to sensitize sociology to what seems like an obvious fact: society is created by people. Its existence depends on people learning certain capacities. However, the reverse is also true: humans depend upon an existing society. What makes us human is our participation in society. Society and the individual are seen as different sides of the same coin, and sociology must seek to understand the processes by which society and the individual make each other possible.

THE SOCIOLOGICAL PERSPECTIVE

Our review of these early sociologists has allowed us to see how sociology emerged and to appreciate the issues and concerns of early sociology. These concerns still remain—in greatly altered and amplified form. Because they are the essence of the sociological perspective, we should review them once more.

First, sociology defines itself as a science. We will examine this fact closely in the next chapter. Second, sociology views social relations as structured—as constituting a reality that transcends individuals. Third, sociology is concerned with how this structure is created, maintained, and changed. Marx emphasized power. Durkheim stressed consensus over moral rules. Spencer advocated competition as the essential process. Weber gave us a method of examining the causes and forms of these structures. Mead provided a framework for visualizing the processes through which society shapes individuals and through which individuals create social structure, or society. All these concerns constitute an element of the sociological perspective, and each will be examined in the chapters that follow.

For our purposes, we must recognize that sociologists study individuals and their creations: social relationships. These relationships become very complex and elaborate, taking on diverse forms. However, we must never forget that people are involved. These forms, no matter how elaborate, are maintained by the actions of people. Yet, as we also must remember, people are influenced by the very social forms that they create. These matters are the essence of the sociological perspective.

PLAN OF THE BOOK

This book is divided into five sections. Part I, "The Sociological Perspective" is short, as the goal is to orient you to sociology. Chapter 2 shows how sociologists study the human system.

Part II, entitled the "Basic Elements of the Human System," gives an overview of the sociological perspective. Chapter 3 deals with our emergence as humans and with the forces that helped us develop into unique creatures. Chapter 4 examines the symbolic world of this unique animal: culture. Humans use culture to guide the formation of social relationships. Chapter 5 examines the basic social process: interaction. It is through symbolic interactions that the human system has been created. Chapter 6 examines the products of culture and interaction: patterns and forms of social organization. These patterns will only be previewed, because the chapters of later sections examine each in more detail. Chapter 7 explores human personality. In this chapter, we will see the reciprocity between individuals and society. In chapter 8 the conflicting tendencies for and deviance social control are explored. Here, we will see why and how people have tendencies to deviate and observe the ways that such propensities are controlled. Chapter 9 examines a final key element in the human system: gender. Our analysis will explore the consequences of sexuality for the way humans interact and organize themselves.

Part III is titled, "Basic Forms of Human Organization." The chapters of this section each deal with a unique pattern of social organization. We start with groups in chapter 10, and then in chapter 11, look at formal organizations. Chapter 12 explores fluid organizations—crowds, mobs, panics, crazes, and other temporary social patterns—Chapter 13 examines human communities—their emergence, history, and trends. Chapter 14 focuses on inequality and human hierarchies—classes, castes, and other products of humans' tendency to distribute unequally what is valued. Finally, chapter 15 explores the creation and maintenance of racial and ethnic blocks in society.

Part IV is titled "Basic Human Institutions." Institutions are the ways by which we use various social forms to meet our basic needs. Chapter 16 examines the first human institution—family and kinship, chapter 17 deals with religion, chapter 18 concerns the economy, chapter 19 focuses on politics and government, and chapter 20 deals with education.

Part V consists of three chapters on trends in the human system. Our intent in these chapters is to explore how the elaboration of the human system has created fertile areas of study. Chapter 21 concerns the impact of the human system on the ecological system. Chapter 22 deals with the study of population and its explosion, and chapter 23 summarizes the trends of the human system since its inception, and offers clues to what can be expected in the future.

In these 23 chapters, we will see what the human system is like and will come to understand how sociologists study it. We will have received only an introduction, however, for topics in each chapter usually constitute a special area of sociological inquiry. But it is hoped that your sociological imagination will have been stimulated by exposure to the sociological perspective.

SUMMARY AND PREVIEW

In this chapter, we have tried to get a "general feel" for what sociology is, what it studies, what distinguishes it from other disciplines, and what thinkers were instrumental in its development. We began with a definition of sociology as the study of social relationships and then explored briefly the fuller implications of this seemingly simple definition.

We examined the convergence and divergence between sociology and other related disciplines: economics, political science, psychology, anthropology, history, and social work. We reviewed the emergence of sociology as a discipline, briefly mentioning the importance of such figures as Auguste Comte, Herbert Spencer, Émile Durkheim, Karl Marx, Max Weber, and George Herbert Mead. It is from these giants of our past that the sociological perspective first became coherent.

Part of this coherence stems from sociology's definition of itself as a science. Not all sociologists accept this definition, but most do. It is to the exploration of *what science is* that we now turn in the next chapter. We will define science, examine *theory*, and review the methods that sociologists use to gather information about the human system.

Key Terms

Sociology: the scientific study of social relationships—from their simplest to their most complex forms

Social Relationships: social bonds that emerge among humans as they communicate and interact. These bonds can range from simple friendships to large urban regions and institutional complexes

Social Structure: social relationships which reveal some degree of stability and continuity over time

The Human System: the entire complex of social relationships created by humans

Social Psychology: the study of the relationship between individuals and the human system

Generalize: the practice of viewing specific events as instances of more generic processes

Science: the use of objective and verifiable methods to test, or to create, generalizations about processes and events

Review Questions

1. What does it mean to say that sociologists study social relationships?
2. Why don't sociologists study people, per se?
3. Can you point out the similarities and differences between sociology and:
   economics
   political science
   psychology
   anthropology
   history
   social work
4. Who first used the terms listed below? What is the significance of each?
   social statics and social dynamics
   survival of the fittest
   social organism
   collective conscience
   power
   ideal type
   historical causes
   mind and self

Suggested Readings

Berger, Peter. *An Invitation to Sociology: A Humanistic Perspective.* New York: Doubleday, 1963.

Mills, C. Wright. *The Sociological Imagination.* New York: Oxford, 1959.

Inkeles, Alex. *What Is Sociology: An Introduction to the Discipline and Profession.* Englewood Cliffs, N.J.: Prentice-Hall, 1964.

Shostak, Arthur. *Sociology in Action.* Homewood, Ill.: Dorsey, 1966.

Nisbet, Robert. *The Social Bond.* New York: Knopf, 1970.

THE SCIENCE OF SOCIETY: THEORY AND METHOD IN SOCIOLOGY

PROLOGUE

Guiding Questions: How do we understand the world around us? How does science help? What is science? What are the goals of science? How do sociologists conduct scientific inquiry?

Chapter Topics

THEORY AND SOCIOLOGY

Why do we study the human system? The answer is that we are curious about ourselves and the social world. We want to know more, and we want to understand and comprehend as much as we can. But how are we to know, understand, and comprehend? How do we learn about the social world? How do we accumulate knowledge?

Such questions led to the development of *science*. Science is a way of accumulating knowledge about *why* events occur. Speculation about the social world has gone on for millennia, but only recently have the procedures and tools of science been applied to the study of the human system. Our goal in this chapter, therefore, is to understand what science is, what it makes possible, and how it is used in sociology.

Science involves two related activities: (1) accumulating knowledge and (2) collecting data or information. These two activities are usually termed *theory* and *methods*, respectively. **Theory** is how we accumulate knowledge and make sense of the world. **Methods** are procedures for looking at the world. The two are inseparable; methods are involved in the collection of data, or information, that needs interpretation, or theory.

We emphasize these points because this chapter is divided into two main sections: theory and methods. We need to understand how these two activities are conducted and what they allow us to do. We will examine theory first, and then explore the methods of sociology.

What Can Theory Do?

We are accustomed to thinking of theory as something dull and as something to be avoided. This is really a tragic error on students' part, for just the opposite is the case. Theory allows us to understand and to see clearly what we only vaguely perceive. Let us take some concrete examples in order to appreciate what theory can do.

We can begin with some seemingly disconnected observations. During World War II there was great unity in the United States. Patriotism ran high. People made sacrifices, often the ultimate one of "giving their life for their country." This was true not only in the United States; it is frequently true whenever two nations go to war: nationalism and patriotism increase. When two football teams are about to take the field for the start of a game, we can observe that there is much hand-slapping, rear-end patting, cries of emotion, huddles where emotion is released. The "bigger" the game, the more of this activity we are likely to observe. Two street gangs in a large city are about to engage in a "rumble." There is much talk, gang members feel close, and ready to "go at it." In another city, somebody has just shot a policeman. Police become intense; they coordinate their efforts as never before "to get the cop killer." Two fraternities have a traditional rivalry. The rivalry extends into many areas: intramural sports, debates, which gets the best over-all grade average, and which has the best parties. When this rivalry surfaces, as it often does, the members reveal sudden comradeship. In ghetto riots of the 1960s, residents often felt a sense of brotherhood in the face of police and troop actions. If only temporarily, they felt as one, united against an "enemy."

*Conflict against a common enemy creates group
solidarity, as Georg Simmel's theory predicts.*

We could list similar examples, and in looking at them, we might get a sense that they have something in common. We have phrased them in a way so that commonality is more evident than it might otherwise be. We can view these examples as *data* —as information collected on what goes on in the social world. A theory seeks to explain these data, to find the connecting thread that binds them together. If such a thread can be found, we will have achieved a new level of understanding about our world.

Is there a theory that can explain these events? German sociologist Georg Simmel (1858–1918) presented a theory, which is not always true, but see what it does for the small mass of data that we have accumulated (Simmel 1908).

*The greater the degree of conflict between
social units, the greater the respective degrees
of internal solidarity of these units.*

Perhaps, standing alone, this theoretical statement seems obscure and dull, but when applied to the diverse events, it has definite meaning. We have an understanding of why citizens during wartime, football teams before games, gang members before a fight, police after a killing of their own, fraternity members in a rivalry, and rioters in the midst of a confrontation all act the way they do. Not only has this theoretical statement helped us understand our data, it offers a prediction of what will likely happen in the future when individuals, groups, organizations, or entire nations enter into conflict. Thus, if we have any curiosity about the social world, it is hard to see how a statement that organizes our experience and that would help us make predictions about the future is dull. Theory can help us answer the question, *why?* Why do people act the way they do?

Of course, Simmel's theoretical statement is only suggestive and is not true in all situations. But it illustrates the potential of theory for understanding the human system. This brief theoretical statement can also be used to illustrate the characteristics of all theory. These characteristics give theory the power to bestow understanding and insight into human affairs.

Characteristics of Theory

Abstractness. The theoretical statement above is *abstract*. This is what makes theory seem dull; it is detached from our everyday world and seems remote. But this abstractness is a virtue. Abstractness means to pull away from specific events in particular times and places. Thus, rather than address a specific conflict, our statement is capable of saying something about them all; it could only do this if stated abstractly.

The first characteristic of theory, then, is abstractness. If theory is to inform us, to help us seek the similarities of events in the world, and to explain why these events occur, it must transcend particulars and details. Of course, these details are what give social life its uniqueness and fascination. But too much concern with detail can prevent us from seeing the whole. We should view theory as a new source of excitement: a medium or tool that will help us understand, comprehend, know, and predict. Abstractness is necessary for us to be capable of realizing this source of intellectual excitement.

Components of Theory. Our theoretical statement appears simple, but it is constructed from a number of components. A theory must be built this way so that it can be useful. If constructed improperly with poor components, theory loses its power to inform and explain. The basic components of theory are: (1) definitions, (2) concepts, and (3) propositions. Let us explore each of these and view their relationships to each other.

Propositions. Our statement on conflict is a proposition. A **proposition** states relationships among events. In our case, the relationship is between "conflict" and "internal solidarity." The more conflict there is, the greater the internal solidarity of those involved in the conflict. Without propositions, we would not see relationships in the world; the world would consist of unconnected events. A proposition points to important relationships that can help us understand the world.

Concepts and Variables. Our statement is composed of several concepts: "conflict," "internal solidarity," and "social units." A **concept** denotes some aspect of the world; it points to an event or phenomenon and sensitizes us to its existence. In our example, the concept of "conflict" points out some events, while ignoring others. The concept of "internal solidarity" does the same thing: it highlights some states while excluding others. Similarly, the concept of "social unit" focuses attention on social groupings of people that reveal some characteristics, while ignoring other characteristics of people's relationships.

Concepts tell us what a theory is about. In our example, the concepts inform us that the theory is about conflict among groupings of people and what one consequence of this conflict—internal solidarity—will be for these people. The theory does not address many matters; additional concepts would be required to do this.

A **variable** is a kind of concept, which, as its name implies, denotes events that vary and reveal different degrees of some property. For example, the concept of "cat" merely denotes a particular type of animal; it says little about variations in cats. "Cat size" is a variable concept because it allows us to visualize cats of different sizes.

Variables are a critical type of concept in the creation of a theory. Propositions, as we already know, state relationships among concepts denoting events, and they usually take the form, "the more of this event, the more of some other event," or "the greater the degree of this phenomenon, the greater the degree of something else." The concepts in such propositions are variables—degrees of one phenomenon are related to degrees of another. In our proposition on conflict, for example, the concepts are stated as variables: The *degree* of conflict, the *degree* of internal solidarity. Much of what sociologists do, therefore, is to isolate and define variables that mutually influence each other. A world that reveals differences, degrees, and change must be described by concepts that can capture these and other forms of variability.

Definitions. Concepts are constructed from definitions. A **definition** is a statement that indicates something's existence and properties. In our example, a definition of conflict might be action on the part of social units that is directed at preventing the other units from attaining their goals. Such a definition says: "This process of mutually frustrating each other's goal attainment exists and is part of a process called conflict." Each concept, then,

must have at least one definition. Concepts have meaning only through definitions.

The relationship among these three components of theory can be stated as follows. Propositions establish relationships among events or phenomena denoted by concepts, especially variables. Concepts, in turn, are constructed of definitions that specify what exists in the world, at least for the purposes of theory. In our example, the proposition relates the concepts of "conflict," "social units," and "internal solidarity" to each other. The definitions specify what "conflict," "social units," and "internal solidarity" are.

Figure 1: The Components of Theory

Theory = Relationships among propositions

↑

Propositions = Relationships among abstract concepts

↑

Concepts and Variables = Relationships among definitions that denote properties of the world

↑

Definitions = Relationships among symbols on which people agree, such as words or mathematical notations

Theory is the goal of science. Theory is composed of propositions, concepts, and definitions. Definitions are constructed from symbols, the meaning of which people agree on. Concepts are constructed from definitions, and a proposition is built from concepts. A theory can be one proposition, but most theories are constructed of a number of propositions that are systematically related to each other.

In theory, it is critical that definitions of concepts be clear. At this stage of the theory-building process ambiguity makes it difficult to know what the theory is about. Concepts could not denote those features of the world to be covered by a theory. Propositions must state a clear relationship among concepts. If the relationship is not spelled out, then it is difficult to explain, understand, or predict what occurs, or will occur, in the world.

The goal of science is to develop theory. Theory unlocks the mysteries of the physical and social universe; it tells us *why* things happen. However, theory must be tested against the facts. It is one thing to construct an abstract proposition as we have done, but it is quite another matter to have this statement hold up against the facts. Theories must be tested again and again before we can accept

them as plausible. Theory is tested by comparing what it says should occur with what actually occurs. To conduct such tests requires a set of proper methods, which when used to test theories or to gather the facts necessary to build a theory are termed the *scientific method*.

We can now see that methods have a purpose: to test a theory, or to help construct one. The goal of all science is to build theory, but theory must stand up to tests. Moreover, sometimes we must gather facts and information before we can think up a theory. These facts must also be collected carefully through the scientific method. Thus, methods are important in both testing and creating theory. For this reason, we should examine the procedures by which sociologists collect information about the world.

Figure 2: The Relationship of Theory, Methods, and the Real World to Each Other

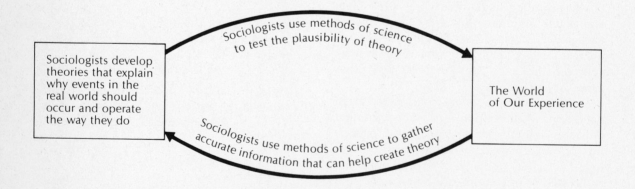

THE SCIENTIFIC METHOD AND SOCIOLOGY

All scientific research must be conducted in accordance with the scientific method. The **scientific method** is a sequence of procedures that are to be followed if accurate knowledge about the world is to be secured. Moreover, by following an established rigorous set of procedures, other researchers can repeat or replicate a particular study. In this way, information or data can be checked or verified any number of times. Without valid and reliable information, a theory cannot be tested; conversely, if data are used to build theory, the theory must be constructed from factual information.

The scientific method is usually divided into a series of steps that are somewhat artificial and that are not always followed in a precise order. Yet, they do give us a general feel for the scientific method. These steps are: (1) stating a problem that needs to be studied, (2) formulating an hypothesis or proposition that resolves this problem and can be tested, (3) constructing a research design or plan for collecting data that can test the hypothesis, (4) analyzing and summarizing the data and drawing conclusions about the plausibility of the hypothesis, and (5) revising, reformulating, or affirming the hypothesis.

(1) Stating a Research Problem

Our curiosity about the social world must become translated into a testable **research problem.** Some problems cannot be tested and thus are not a part of the scientific realm. For example, the question of whether or not God exists is one that cannot be answered.

Research problems can be stimulated by a number of forces. First, an existing theory might dictate that certain issues be explored. Our earlier example of a theory might lead us to ask what happens to corporations that find themselves in intense competition. An answer to such a query would have implications for the plausibility of our theory. A second source of research inquiry are previous research findings. For example, it may have been reported that during the 1960s residential segregation of blacks and whites had not decreased. Whether or not this holds true in the 1970s might be a question of interest to researchers. Note, however, that this statement does not owe its origin to any well-articulated theory. A third stimulus to a research question is human curiosity that does not follow from theory or previous research. For instance, a researcher might just be interested in why people prefer private cars to public transportation.

Thus, science begins with a well-formulated research question. The best **scientific questions** are those that have relevance for testing or creating theory. However, there are other reasons for collecting information. We may have to make a political decision about intergration or mass transit and have to collect accurate data on these matters. Thus, the methods of science can be used to achieve nonscientific goals.

(2) Formulating a Hypothesis

In science, we must state *what we expect to find* within the domain specified by a research problem as a **hypothesis,** which is a proposition stating relationships that we expect to discover in a particular research setting. In contrast to the propositions of theory, a hypothesis is not abstract; it is specific.

Many hypotheses are logically derived from an abstract theory and are used to test the plausibility of a theory. For example, the hypothesis, "the more intense the competition between corporations, the more tightly organized they become," tests the plausibility of our more abstract theoretical proposition, "The greater the degree of conflict between social units, the greater the respective degrees of internal solidarity of these units." The hypothesis brings the level of abstraction down to a specific social unit (corporations), a particular type of conflict (competition), and a specific form of solidarity (tight organization). Now, we are in a position to focus the collection of data.

Naturally, not all hypotheses are derived from a well-developed theory. Yet, the logic of hypothesis formation is the same: We need to know about something, which is the prediction provided by the hypothesis. Without this prediction, we would not know what information to collect. We would waste precious energy gathering useless information. Nontheoretical problems also require hypotheses. For example, residential segregation has not declined in the 1970s, and people will prefer to drive their cars and use mass transit only as the last resort are two hypotheses about which the collection of information can be focused and efficient. We know what it is we want to discover.

How do sociologists develop hypotheses? In its present state, sociological research often proceeds without a hypothesis. Naturally, this means that considerable energy is wasted and that much useless information is collected. Yet, much of sociological research is an expedition into the unknown. It is only recently that the methodologies and statistical techniques of sociology have become sufficiently developed to allow deep exploration into the human system. Sociologists often do not know what regularities to look for; they simply have a hunch that certain matters are important, and they try to collect information in order to get a preliminary picture of an area of inquiry. With this preliminary picture, they then begin formulating hypotheses and testing their plausibility.

In a science without developed theory—and sociology is such a science—research is often geared to discovering the regularities that might stimulate the development of theory. Unfortunately, at times this necessity has become an excuse in sociology for what is known as "shot gun" research in which any and all information is gathered, analyzed, and reported without much concern for testing or developing theories. In these cases, the methods of science can be used to avoid the goals of science—that is, the development of theory. One of the most persistent controversies in sociology is over the issue of the purpose of research—to test and create hypotheses and theory or to sharpen data analyzing techniques.

(3) Constructing a Research Design

Each science has its own ways of conducting research or collecting data. Physicists use linear accelerators, cloud chambers, and vacuum tubes to gather information. Sociologists obviously could not use these means for collecting information about the social world. They must employ other techniques, which, generally speaking, can be grouped in three ways: (1) experiments, (2) observations, and (3) surveys.

Experiments Design. Research must yield accurate information. It must allow the researcher to examine the influence of events upon each other, while controlling for, or taking account of, the impact of other events. The classical way to do this is with the **experimental design.** In such a design, two matched groups of subjects are selected. One group—the **experimental group**—is subjected to the influence of a particular stimulus situation, and the other group—the **control group**—receives no such stimulus. For example, one group might be asked to compete (the stimulus), and the other group be left to conduct its affairs as it normally might. Changes in the experimental group—for example, the formation of group solidarity—could then be attributed to the influence of the induced competition. Figure 3 outlines this kind of research design.

Figure 3: The Experimental Design

STEP 1	STEP 2	STEP 3	STEP 4	STEP 5
Two matched groups are selected:	Measurement of relevant properties of groups are recorded	A stimulus is introduced to the experimental group	Another measurement of relevant properties of both groups is taken	Differences in groups A and B are viewed as caused by the stimulus
Group A	Group A	Experiences stimulus	Changes in group A, if any, are recorded	Group A is now different than earlier
Group B	Group B	Does not experience stimulus	Changes in group B, if any, are recorded	Group B is unlike group A

The student guards in Zimbardo's experiment soon became like their counterparts in an actual prison—revealing that the structure of persons rather than the "personality" of guards caused repressive, and at times, brutal, behavior on the part of the guards. This is what experiments are designed to do: isolate the influence of variables and control for the effects of other factors.

Why do we perform this seemingly elaborate procedure? The object is to isolate the effects of variables and see their impact on each other. In our example, we want to observe the impact of competition on a group. To do this, we compare a group that experiences competition with one that does not, and we can make reliable and accurate inferences about the impact of competition on solidarity.

In actual experimental work, this classical design is often modified. However, the goal remains the same: to isolate the impact of some variables and to neutralize the effects of those that could potentially contaminate this impact. For example, some experiments are performed without a control group. In one experiment, a researcher wanted to test the effects of prison structure on the behaviors of guards and prisoners (Zimbardo 1972). Rather than go to an actual prison where the impact of many forces could not be controlled or accounted for, the experimenter created a prison setting. He recruited student volunteers and put them into matched groups; he then made one half of them "guards" and the other half "prisoners." Prisoners were confined in "cells," and guards were responsible for keeping order. After only a few days, intense hostility developed between guards and prisoners. Guards became abusive, if not somewhat brutal; inmates became resentful and yet were resigned to their fate. It was possible to draw conclusions from this experiment. Since prisoners and guards were matched at the beginning of the study, the differences in their behaviors can be attributed to the structure of the prison situation—confinement, the need to keep order, and the resentment of those confined. Such an experiment is informative about real prisons in the actual world. There is something about the structure of prison life—not the personality of guards or inmates—that creates many of the inmate/guard problems of the modern prison.

Good experiments isolate the impact of key variables—in this example, the structure of inmate/guard interaction—and control for, or hold constant, potentially contaminating variables—in this study, the backgrounds and personalities of the guards and inmates who were "matched" or the same. Moreover, a good experiment has relevance for theory or for social policy. This experiment was relevant for two reasons: it could easily stimulate theoretical propositons about coercive interaction settings and it has implications for solving "prison problems."

In the real world, however, it is not always possible to match groups of subjects, to introduce stimuli systematically, or to make sure that other stimuli do not influence the experiment. For example, finding two corporations exactly alike would prove difficult. Even if we found two that were similar to each other, we probably could not induce competition for one of the corporations (sociologists do not have this kind of power). Moreover, we could not keep other events, or unwanted stimuli, from intruding into either or both corporations over a period of time.

Since most matters studied by sociologists are examined in the natural world where one cannot find matched groups, systematically introduce stimuli, or control for the impact of other, extraneous stimuli, how do sociologists record the impact of those variables or events in which they are interested? There are a number of techniques employed in selecting subjects and analyzing the data. Recognizing that many research problems can only be examined in nonexperimental situations, sociologists em-

ploy two other prominent research designs: observations and surveys.

Observations. Early American sociologists became particularly adept at *observations*. By systematically observing events and recording them, these scientists gained insight into the actual processes of the real world. The goal of observation, especially **participant observation,** in which the researcher is also an active participant in the events being studied, is to obtain intimate knowledge of the events and how people in these events feel, think, and define their world. As you will recall from the last chapter, such a goal is consistent with Max Weber's emphasis on understanding social action at the level of its meaning to actors. It is also consistent with George Herbert Mead's and his early American colleagues' concern with how individuals construct their social worlds through their capacities for self-reflection and thinking.

A number of sociology's classic studies were conducted with a participant-observation format and yielded enormous insight into human affairs. Such studies often present a number of problems, however. First, they are rarely guided by theory and hypotheses; investigators just become involved in a setting, hoping to observe regularities that can stimulate theory. As a result, observations are often random, unfocused, and unproductive. Second, it is difficult to remain unaffected by events when actually participating in them. How, then, does one yield unbiased observations? How do participants sort out their feelings and emotions from the actual events that are occurring? Third, a researcher is typically an intruder as well as a participant in a social setting. How do researchers know that they have not interrupted the natural flow of events that they wish to observe?

Despite these problems, there can be no substitute for familiarity with the social world. For this reason participant observation is a valuable research method. It allows us to see people in their natural settings, to "get inside their heads," and to observe how they view their settings. At its best, observational research provides insights that can stimulate more controlled research, or it can supplement more controlled research by seeing what events mean to actors. The problems of observational research make it controversial, but its advantages also make it an essential methodological tool. For example, although the inmate/guard experiment is insightful because it removes the influence of confounding factors, it is still not a substitute for observations in a real prison. Only in this way can sociologists actually understand and appreciate the dynamics of the inmate/guard interaction.

Surveys. Another way that sociologists gather information is by asking people questions in real social situations. This tack is known as survey research and it uses questionnaires, interviews, or a combination of both. **Surveys** are probably the most frequently used tool in sociology. There are many reasons for this, but most investigators would probably include the following advantages. (1) Questionnaires or interviews are comparatively easy to administer. (2) They allow a lot of information to be gathered in a short period of time. (3) They can eliminate many sources of bias in unstructured observations. (4) The data collected are highly amenable to statistical manipulations.

How do sociologists conduct surveys? They must first have a research problem because questions must be directed at an area. Surveys are conducted for a wide variety of reasons. Public-opinion pollsters use survey techniques to gather information about public attitudes and feelings about certain issues. The national census is a survey designed to gather information on the characteristics of the population. In addition to these applications, surveys are also used to test hypotheses derived from theory. We can see, then, that surveys are used to solve a variety of research problems and to gather different kinds of information.

After a problem is selected, a measuring instrument is constructed. This involves creating a questionnaire to be mailed or otherwise distributed to subjects. Another variant is to construct an interview schedule—that is, a series of questions that an interviewer will ask subjects.

These measuring instruments may be pretested on a preliminary group of subjects in order to make sure that the respondents understand the questions and that the questions yield the information desired.

The next step is to distribute the questionnaire or to send interviewers out into the field. At this stage, a **random sample** of the population of interest is usually taken. A **sample** is a smaller or limited number of people drawn from a larger population who will actually be asked questions. A random sample is a sample of respondents selected by chance. Each person in the population has an equal chance of being selected; selecting a sample by chance means that the sample will more likely be *representative* and reflect the composition of the general population. There are other sampling techniques to assure representativeness, or even nonrepresentativeness if it is the researcher's goal, but the general goal of sampling is to secure a smaller group of subjects to question or interview. For example, public-opinion pollsters have become so adept at securing representative samples that they require only 2,000 people in a sample that can, in most cases, reflect the distribution of sentiments of the entire nation.

The problems with surveys revolve around the issue of what they measure. If we ask people questions about their beliefs, values, opinions, or about the facts of their life (how old are you? for example), will they give accurate and truthful answers? Moreover, are the categories of responses provided in the survey questions those that the subjects themselves use, or are they fabrications of the sociologist's mind? Finally, the extensive reliance on surveys limits what sociologists, or any researcher, can examine. What about all those social phenomena that cannot be measured by asking people questions? Are we ignoring these because surveys are easy to conduct? Despite these problems, however, survey research methods are a valuable tool for conducting sociological research. They give quick, and for certain problems, reasonably accurate information about some events occurring in the human system.

Once data are collected, whether through experiments, observations, or surveys, the researcher turns to data analysis. What does the information tell us about our research problem or hypothesis?

(4) Analyzing the Data

Once the data are collected in accordance with the procedures of the research design, they must be subjected to a variety of manipulations. These can become very complicated and usually involve the use of statistical techniques. But the general thrust of data analysis is to summarize the findings in a way that has relevance for testing a hypothesis, or if there is no hypothesis, for creating a proposition that can become a hypothesis in a subsequent research effort.

Much of what we will discuss in the remaining chapters is the end result of research and data analysis. An introductory sociology book reports what sociologists know about the human system. This knowledge can be communicated verbally, but it is also necessary to present the data in numerical form. There are a wide variety of data analyzing techniques, but data are usually presented in two ways: (1) as **correlations** among events and (2) as **tabulations** of phenomena. Both ways of presenting analyzed data are intended to communicate information efficiently. The following two boxes show two basic ways in which data are analyzed and presented.

What is
a Correlation?

A correlation states a relationship be-tween variables. As one increases (decreases), then the other increases (decreases). The *strength* of a correla-tion ranges from .00 to 1.0—.00 means that there is no correlation; 1.0 means a perfect correlation. Any increase in one event is associated with a propor-tional increase in another. For our purposes, we will visualize correlations as a graph that plots the relationship between two variables.

In this example the solid line indi-cates a perfect correlation between

variables, 20% increase in nonagri-cultural workers is associated with 20 degrees of industrialization, 40 by 40 degrees, and so on. This correlation could be expressed as a number 1.00. The dotted line indicates a less-than-perfect—that is, less than 1.00—correla-tion, but it is still a correlation between these variables—that is, greater than .00. When we express this correlation as a number, it is .55—a

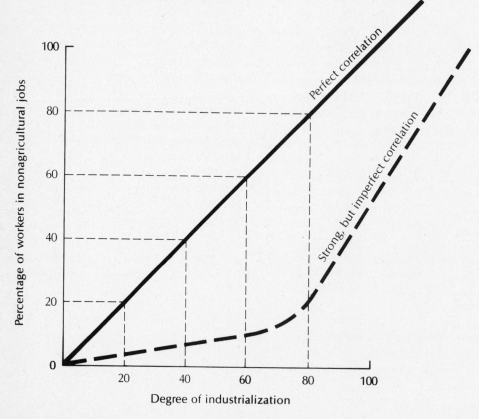

strong correlation. Most correlations in the social sciences are less than .55 because many variables usually influence a particular event. For example, the percentage of workers in non-agricultural work is influenced by more than industrialization—for example, government, schools, and other social forces. Sociologists try to sort out these various influences, discerning the impact of each one or their combined impact.

For our purposes, we need only know that correlations can be expressed graphically, and we will have occasion to do this. What a graph communicates is simply the pattern of relationship among events.

What is a Table?

A table summarizes data by indicating the frequency, amount, percentage, or other measure of an event in relation to some other phenomena. Examine the table below:

Economies and Composition of Work Force

Percentage of workers in various occupations	Economy Type		
	agrarian	industrial	post-industrial
farm	97%	20%	5%
blue-collar	2%	60%	35%
white-collar	1%	20%	60%
Total	100%	100%	100%

This data is similar to that in the graph in the previous box. But we can see that we learn different things when presenting data in table form. First, read the title of the table; it can give a first clue as to what the table is about. In our sample, the title says that the table provides information on the composition of the work force in different types of economies. Second, read the two headings that label the variables on which data are to be presented. One heading is almost always on the top; the other is on the left side (as in our table) or at the top at the far left. In our table, one heading refers to the percentage of work force in various occupations and the other to types of economies. Third, then examine just how each variable labelled by headings is broken down. In our case, percentage of workers is divided into three categories: farm, blue-collar, and white-collar, type of economy is also broken down into three categories: agrarian (agricultural), industrial, and postindustrial. Fourth, make sure that you understand in what numerical form the data are being presented. In this example, the data are in percentages. Fifth, by reading the data draw a conclusion about what these data communicate. What is it that they say? In our example, the data show that the percentage of the work force in white-collar jobs increases as economies become industrial and postindustrial, whereas the proportion in agriculture declines.

If this table is clear, then all tables reported at various places in the text should be easily understood and interpreted. It might be worth coming back to these examples, however, if you encounter difficulty in interpreting a table at some point in the text.

(5) Revising, Reformulating, or Affirming the Hypothesis

If the data support the hypothesis, then the plausibility of the theory from which the hypothesis was derived is increased. To use an earlier example, if a group that has been subjected to competition increases in its degree of internal solidarity, then the general theory about the relationship between conflict and solidarity becomes more plausible. However, the data often do not unequivocally support a hypothesis. In this case, the hypothesis must be rejected and the theory thrown into doubt. If, for instance, the group subject to competition does not show increased solidarity, we must reject the hypothesis and hold our theory about conflict and solidarity as suspect. Frequently, we may want to reformulate the theory in order to suggest new hypotheses. Thus, we might want to conclude that competition is not a very severe form of conflict and therefore infer that the theory applies only to "intense conflict" among "social units." We would then begin the research procedure again—restating our problem, reformulating the hypothesis to apply only to more intense conflicts, reconstructing a research design, and analyzing the new data.

It is this constant interaction, or dialogue, between theory and research that increases our knowledge. We constantly test our theories with the facts. We reject, revise, and reformulate. Then, we test again. If a hypothesis stands up to repeated testing, we gain more confidence in our theory and feel more confident that we "know" and "understand" something about the world around us.

SUMMARY AND PREVIEW

In summary, the scientific method gives us knowledge in which we can have confidence. It allows us to move beyond mere speculation and to see if the world does indeed operate the way that we think it does. This method applies to all science—physical, biological, and social. However, each discipline has its own techniques for implementing the scientific method. We have observed that sociology confronts problems of dealing with events embedded in their natural, and confounding, circumstances. Moreover, sociologists are in the position of studying phenomena like themselves—that is, people involved in social relationships. Our subject matter can think, reflect, question, and resist efforts at probing in ways that a rock, solar system, or cell cannot. Thus, sociology develops its own way to secure reliable and valid information. Sociologists experiment, observe, and survey. These tools are the way sociologists test and create theories—that is, knowledge and understanding about the human system.

In this chapter, we have sought to learn what science is, and what it does. As we have discovered, science is composed of two interrelated activities: theory and research. Theory explains and increases our understanding; research tests, and helps create, theories. Most sociologists—though many still disagree—view sociology as a science, as a discipline that seeks to build and test theory with research. Sociologists thus tend to follow the dictates, within broad and flexible limits, of the scientific method when conducting research. Three principal techniques for collecting data are experiments, observations, and surveys. Collected data are often analyzed statistically and presented as correlations or tabulations.

In many ways, this chapter can be read at the beginning or end of the book. Our goal has been to communicate how sociology operates as a science. The 21 chapters that follow summarize much of what we know about the human system by virtue of the application of theory and methods. This chapter gives you a clue as to why and how information in the following chapters was assembled. You might have a better appreciation for the science of society after the book has been completed, and yet, in fairness it is perhaps best to alert you very early as to how the information about the human system has been collected and interpreted. We now direct our attention to the study of the nature of the human system as revealed by the "science of society."

Key Terms

Science: the use of theory and methods to understand the events of the world

Theory: the use of abstract concepts, incorporated into propositions to understand and explain the events of the world

Methods: the procedures used to examine the events of the world

Abstractness: the situation where a statement is not tied to specific referents in a particular time and place

Proposition: a statement of relationship among events denoted by concepts or variables

Concept: statements that isolate, point to, or denote some feature of the world

Variable: a type of concept that denotes the variable properties of phenomena in the world

Definitions: statements that indicate what is or exists in the world and that are used to formulate concepts

Scientific Method: the established procedures of science by which accurate and verifiable data are collected and used to test or create theory

Research Problem: a question about events that is to be the subject of scientific inquiry

Scientific Questions: research problems that are designed to test or create theory

Hypothesis: a proposition that states an expected relationship among events in a particular research setting

Experimental Design: the procedure by which at least two matched groups are used to collect data. One is exposed to a stimulus, whereas the other remains unexposed to the stimulus

Experimental Group: the group in an experimental design that is exposed to a stimulus of interest to the researcher

Control Group: the group in an experimental design that is unexposed to a stimulus of interest to the researcher

Obervation: the research technique in which the researcher collects data through personal observation of events

Participant Observation: the research technique in which the researcher actually participates in, and then observes, the events that are being studied

Surveys: the research technique in which samples of subjects are asked to respond to prepared questions

Random Sample: a sample in which subjects are selected by chance, with all members of a population having an equal chance to be selected

Sample: a smaller group of a larger population selected for study

Correlations: statistical techniques that summarize the relationships among variables

Tabulations: a means for presenting data on events in a table

Review Questions

1. Why do humans use science?
2. What are the characteristics of science?
3. List the steps of the scientific method.
4. What are the components of theory?
5. What is the goal of science?
6. How do sociologists collect data?

Suggested Readings

Cole, Stephen. *The Sociological Method.* Chicago: Rand McNally, 1976.

Labovitz, Sanford, and Hagedorn, Robert. *Introduction to Social Research.* New York: McGraw-Hill, 1971.

McCain, Garvin, and Segal, Erwin M. *The Game of Science.* Monterey, Ca.: Brooks/Cole.

Mullins, Nicholas C. *The Art of Theory Construction and Use.* New York: Harper & Row, 1971.

Reynolds, Paul. *A Primer on Theory Construction,* New York: Bobbs-Merrill, 1973.

Richter, Maurice N. Jr. *Science as a Cultural Process.* Cambridge, Mass.: Schenkman, 1972.

TenHouten, Warren D., and Kaplan, Charles D. *Science and Its Mirror Image.* New York: Harper & Row, 1973.

BASIC ELEMENTS OF THE HUMAN SYSTEM

CONTENTS

PREVIEW

In this part we will learn how sociologists approach the study of the human system. Chapter 3 will examine the roots of human antiquity. We will explore where we as humans came from and how our ancestors developed the human system. We will begin to understand that we are animals and that much of what we are and do is the result of our biological heritage. In chapter 4, however, we will come to appreciate ourselves as unique animals who have become liberated from our biological heritage. For no other animals can develop culture or the capacity to guide their affairs with symbols—values, beliefs, stored knowledge, religious doctrines, and language, and the like—to the degree that we can. We will thus emphasize that it is our ability to use symbols that makes the human system possible. In chapter 5 we will examine how our symbol using abilities allow for interaction. Interaction is the basic process underlying all facets of culture and patterns of social organization; hence, it is the process that enables us to construct the elaborate and complex structures that have come to dominate the human system. Chapter 6 examines social structures as they emerge out of the use of culture and symbolic interactions. We will come to understand how humans build the structures in which they live and how they conduct their affairs. In chapter 7 we will examine how we become human. We are not born human; we must learn through interaction how to participate in society. This process of interaction is termed *socialization*, and through its study we will learn to recognize what makes each of us a unique personality and, at the same time, a part of the human system. In chapter 8 we will explore social control and deviance. Humans are not robots; they often deviate from accepted practices, and they frequently become subject to efforts of control by other individuals and agencies in society. We would not understand the human system without knowledge of the dual processes of deviation and social control. Finally, in chapter 9, we will examine an obvious but important fact of human existence: sexuality. In no society are males and females treated identically, thus forcing us to explore the way in which gender enters into, and alters, the nature of the human system.

Part II, then, presents an overview of the sociological perspective. We will see what makes sociology a distinctive discipline; at the same time, we will acquire the concepts and intellectual tools for developing further insight into the human system.

IN THE BEGINNING: THE EMERGENCE OF HUMANS

PROLOGUE

Guiding Questions: Where did we come from? What shaped our destiny? Why were society and culture created? What forces in the biology and the enviroments of our primate ancestors conspired to create human organization?

Chapter Topics

THE EMERGENCE OF HUMANS

In a geological time frame, humans have not been on earth very long. Even if we go back to our first primate ancestors, our presence in a world that we seem to control has been short. Yet, despite the appearance of control, the way we organize ourselves is constrained by our biological nature as it has evolved over millions of years.

In this chapter, we will not explore early American society, early European, or any society with which we are familiar. We will seek the origins of human societies. To do this, we must go back to our first ancestors as they tentatively descended from the trees and entered the hostile world of the African savannah. By starting the study of human interaction and organization at its beginning, perhaps we can come to see the human system in a new light.

Our families give us many basic things: our names, the color of our eyes, hair, and skin, and our general body shape. But we also belong to a family that encompasses far more than our parents, brothers and sisters, and close relatives. That wider family also contributes significantly to what we are. We are animals, not plants, and so are related—to some degree—to all other animals. The animals to whom we are most closely related are the **primates,** a group including all monkeys and apes. A human being is, in fact, a very special sort of evolved

Chimpanzees are humans' closest primate relative. Note similarity between humans and chimps in arms, hands, eyes, ears, and other features.

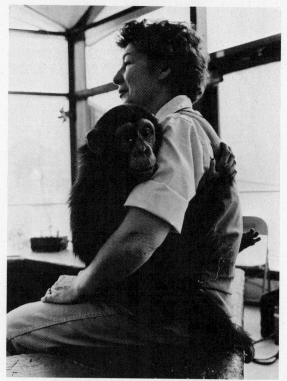

ape. In its simplest form, human evolution is the story of the general development of primates and of the particular factors that separated humans from their ape cousins millions of years ago.

The Process of Natural Selection

As have all living things, we have evolved our particular characteristics in response to a process called **natural selection** (Darwin 1859). The survival of any species depends on its ability to adapt to its environment, to prosper in a niche within that environment, and to reproduce its kind. If a species' characteristics permit it to exploit its surroundings, it will survive and increase its numbers. If conditions change so that the species is no longer suited to its environment, it must change to new circumstances, find another suitable niche, or face extinction. This is how natural selection works: species are selected for survival if what they are fits the world in which they must live or if they are flexible enough to exist in a changed world.

As the world changes—usually in minor ways, but sometimes quite drastically—living things are altered as they try to fit themselves into changing conditions. Such alteration is the basis of natural selection. It takes place because certain plants or animals have characteristics enabling them to cope with new environmental demands. They perpetuate the adaptive traits of their kind by reproduction. In this way, new environments produce new species and those unable to adapt perish.

Natural selection is clearly a life-and-death matter involving very subtle and complex

Charles Darwin provided biology with the basic principle of the natural selection—the process that created humans and their system.

processes. But it is also as simple and direct as what happens to a fish out of water. Fish are suited to life in the water; out of it they die. Evolution will permit even fish to survive on dry land, but only if nature allows some species of fish enough time to develop the ability to breathe air. The species that evolves such an ability through natural selection will have characteristics unlike its ancestors or any other fish; it will have become something entirely new, and it will survive.

It was the transforming power of natural selection that produced our earliest original ancestor—the primates. Much of what we are was determined by what the first primates were and by what later primates became.

Natural Selection
and Life in the Trees

The world of the first primates was a universe of trees. Some 75 million years ago, most of the earth's surface was covered by jungles and forests. Primates developed the very special characteristics that allowed them to survive and prosper in an arboreal (tree) environment. Since humans do not live in the trees, it may seem strange to concern ourselves with our tree-dwelling ancestors. But what we are biologically, and thus what we could be socially and culturally, was shaped by the adaptations of primates to the trees (Pfeiffer 1969; Pilbeam 1972).

The earliest tree-dwelling primates were **prosimians** (premonkeys). They were descendants of creatures that had been forced by natural selection to give up living on the ground, probably because they were unable to compete for food and space with more aggressive and faster-breeding rodent species. Their primate characteristics enabled them to exploit the food resources in the trees. Just as natural selection had driven them from the ground, so natural selection shaped and molded them into animals ideally suited to an arboreal existence in the forests.

For any living things to be successful, they must achieve a balance between what they are and what their environment offers them and demands of them. What was it about life in the trees that so favored primate exploitation of that niche? What were the biological and be-havioral characteristics that ultimately made primates such remarkably successful inhabitants of the trees?

The most obvious difference between living in a tree and living on the ground is that one can fall out of a tree. Consequently, animals with traits that lessen the risk of falling will have a better chance of surviving as individuals and as a species. Primates had such an adaptive trait: hands and feet with prehensile digits that enabled them to hold onto a limb or branch with relative ease. This was no small matter. It gave the early primates a distinct advantage over animals that could climb trees only by digging in with their claws and do little more than hang on, literally for dear life. It permitted primates to move freely through the trees, feeding, sleeping, and breeding. Because it increased the chances for survival in the arboreal habitat, natural selection favored primates with that grasping trait and continued favoring those who further developed and refined that characteristic.

All primates have the grasping ability in some form or other. Over tens of millions of years, evolution has produced primate species, including human beings, with vastly improved prehensile capacities, steadily replacing claws with fingernails on flat, sensitive fingertips (Napier 1962).

As important as prehensile hands are, they are not, by themselves, all that is required for successful arboreal life. Living in trees makes tremendous demands that can be met only by creatures with traits unlike those of all earlier, ground-dwelling animals. To move about and feed in the trees, an animal must be able to see extremely well—to see, in fact, in an entirely new way. To progress swiftly and surely from

These contemporary prosimians are relatives of the first mammals to ascend the trees and are distant ancestors of all primates, including humans.

branch to branch, one must see each branch clearly; it must stand out from the background of other branches and leaves. This ability requires three-dimensional eyesight. Over many generations, natural selection gave a survival advantage to primate species that developed such stereoscopic vision as a result of having their eyes placed closer together in the front of their heads. Prosimians, like present-day lemurs, possess only the beginnings of stereoscopic sight. But monkeys, apes, and humans see both in three dimensions and in color.

Beings that have stereoscopic color vision have great advantages over those that lack these traits. If an animal's eyes are at the sides of its head, it sees everything as a flat, two-dimensional picture; if it cannot distinguish colors, it has considerable difficulty picking out individual objects lost in a panorama of black, white, and grays. Its visual sense will be alerted only by moving objects, so it must depend on its smell and hearing to warn it of possible danger or to lead it to food.

On the ground, animals do quite well without seeing in three dimensions and in color; after all, grazing animals have only to keep their faces near the ground to smell out a meal, and sharp ears will warn them of predators. But tree dwellers do best if they can pinpoint everything within their habitat, regardless of whether it moves or not and regardless of its color. Primates' vision gives them this ability; with it they can find a wide variety of foods, and they move securely among the branches with unrivaled confidence.

Moreover, the combined use of their marvelous eyes and hands allowed primates to hold and examine various objects with a degree of skill unmatched by other creatures. This vastly increased their chances of finding all the food about them and surviving to perpetuate their kind.

By favoring primate species that developed the grasping ability and stereoscopic color vision, natural selection enabled them to prosper in the trees for millions of years. But the possession of these traits also triggered the development of other features that would characterize and shape the destiny of all more highly evolved primates, including human beings.

Evolving primates took new forms, better suited to exploitation of various arboreal niches. No longer relying so much on smell, their faces became flatter because they did not need snoutlike noses. Their teeth also changed over the generations to match the more generalized diet they found in the trees. The foxlike muzzles of lemurs reflect what prosimians looked like before these changes took place; the heads of monkeys show the effects of the changes. However, the most important changes took place inside the heads of developing primates: their other traits encouraged the evolution of a larger and very special kind of brain (Tobias 1971).

Brains had to evolve in order to process all the information supplied by the primates' ability to see and handle so many objects. Their senses gave them access to a larger and more complex world, and the growing primate brain reflected the size and complexity of that expanded environment. By about 35 million years ago, when they became the dominant arboreal primates, **monkeys** had the capacity to experience and make sense of more of their surroundings than any previous life forms. This ability to gain a wider and more accurate view of physical reality set them apart from prosimians and other less-evolved animals. If a species was to compete with monkeys for survival, it had to develop additional adaptive skills, including yet larger brains.

Monkeys were, and still are, unexcelled in making use of most of the arboreal environment, but the niches they cannot occupy are open to other creatures. Because monkeys are basically four-legged animals who scamper and jump along the tops of branches, they have trouble getting food hanging well below a branch or way out on a limb too light to bear their weight. However, **apes** are able to hang or swing from branches and reach out for food while holding on with one or more of their other hands or feet. Natural selection favored the evolution of apes with such abilities to exploit those food sources beyond the reach of monkeys.

Apes evolved alongside monkeys, sharing certain important primate characteristics and developing others totally unique. Because primate skeletons are fairly generalized—that is, because they have not become as specialized as, say, birds or snakes—it was a natural evolutionary step from monkeys to apes. Apes were able to evolve in slight, but critically new ways that gave them their particular adaptive traits. Apes split away from their four-legged monkey kin by developing the ability to swing through the trees. This form of locomotion, called *brachiation*, enabled apes to move their arms in a wider arc, giving them the appearance and capacities of two-legged creatures. Apes had even better manual dexterity than monkeys, and they evolved considerably larger and more intricate brains to handle the additional information flow.

Despite their longer, more mobile brachiating arms, more dexterous hands, and improved brains, early apes still possessed basic primate features needed for survival in the trees. Like monkeys, they relied on their stereoscopic color vision rather than on their sense of smell, so they had fairly flat faces with a relatively generalized primate dental structure. Like all primates, apes were gregarious, living in groups with patterns of interaction that reduced the sorts of conflict that might be permitted among ground dwellers but that could be disastrous in the trees. Ape survival has always been dependent upon their getting along with one another in groups, and this rule of evolution applies equally to humans.

The nature of primate families is of the utmost importance in the survival and evolution of primate species. Primates do not give birth to large litters; they usually have only one infant at a time. Survival in the trees, where primates evolved their special traits, makes it unlikely that more than one infant could be cared for adequately. Natural selection did not encourage the birth of more than one primate infant at a time. There were several reasons for this. It simply is too hard for a mother to carry more than one baby around through the trees. Furthermore, because there are far fewer pre-

Human and chimp mothers with their children.
Note the similarity in the ways that each relates to
its child. Many of our behavioral tendencies are
the products of our primate heritage.

dators in the trees than on the ground, primates did not have to bear large litters to ensure the survival of their kind; one at a time was sufficient. That one received unusually close and careful attention.

Primate young are more dependent on their mothers for a longer period than are other animals. They are born in a less-developed state, and it takes months or even years before they are able to feed and care for themselves. Because primates rely so much on specialized arboreal skills, many of which have to be learned, they must have the time to learn them from their mothers. And because primates' survival depends on the survival of their groups, the young must be socialized within their group, they must learn what behavior is expected of them, which takes time. The result is that each young primate who survives infancy has had the time to acquire the skills that increase the likelihood that it, its group, and its species will survive. These factors make primate family life very important (Lancaster 1975).

Obviously, primates are admirably suited to life in the trees. But do all those wonderful arboreal adaptations have any significance for human beings, who are, in fact, primates but who do not live in trees? They are of the greatest importance, because we also possess most of those special characteristics. They were transmitted to our early human ancestors by primates who left the trees forever. How primate traits, which evolved in response to the pressures of arboreal existence, were adapted to survival on the ground is the story of the emergence of our own species.

Natural Selection
and Life on the Ground

Just as the pressures of natural selection forced the earliest primates into the trees, so, too, were certain species encouraged to seek a new life on the ground. Competition in the trees was difficult for apes; in fact, many species of smaller apes became extinct trying to live among well-adapted monkeys. But a few larger forms of apes survived. Their size and strength gave them advantages. Eventually, some of the largest found it hard to find sufficient food in the trees. They began to do some foraging on the ground, spending less and less of the time in the trees, perhaps only to sleep and to say out of the reach of predators, much as chimpanzees still do.

In order to cope with the new opportunities and new problems presented by life on the ground, the apes who left the trees had to find new ways of doing things; they had to adapt. Fortunately, their characteristics were quite flexible and served them well in the terrestrial habitat. But those traits had evolved over more than 50 million years, and despite modifications for ground living, the apes retained their basically primate character. The future evolution of the ancestors of human beings, who were to evolve from these first ground apes, was circumscribed by this primate heritage.

A Human Shadow on the Land. Human beings did not evolve in the trees. They arose from humanlike primates who learned to survive on the ground. We lack positive evidence of what was involved in the process because, despite many important recent discoveries, the record remains fragmentary and unclear (Pfeiffer 1969). Much of what we believe about the creatures from which we are evolved is based on inferences from such uncertain findings. We are not entirely sure which of these prehuman beings are our direct ancestors or even what they looked like because our knowledge is based on the few remains of them we have uncovered, remains millions of years old. We are particularly uncertain about how they lived and what their society was like. Behavior and social organization, as we will see in all the chapters of this book, are very complex and are often left unrecorded in the archaeological record.

We do know that about 25 million years ago the world was changing in ways that opened a place for primitive, ground-dwelling prehumans. The almost endless stretches of forest that had encouraged the development of monkeys and apes were contracting, leaving large expanses of grassy plains or savannahs. Prehumans and early humans steadily adapted to, and were shaped by, life on the savannah. Human evolution was the result of the interaction and modification of basic primate characteristics in our savannah-dwelling ancestors.

Life on the savannah was far more dangerous than arboreal existence. Predators, such as the great cats, found prey among herds of grazing animals and were prepared to kill and eat terrestrial primates they could catch. The primate eyesight of prehumans held them in good stead in their struggle to stay alive. Lacking the developed sense of smell of most ground animals, they had to rely on their keen vision. With it they could see stationary or slowly moving predators far more easily than animals lacking their ability to see in color and three dimensions. Their superior eyes also allowed them to identify likely food sources at a distance.

As descendants of brachiators, prehumans were basically two-legged and became accustomed to standing erect. This permitted them to gaze out over the savannah grasses and further increased their chances of recognizing dangers and locating food. It has also been theorized that two-legged creatures are less likely to be attacked by predator cats who are used to pouncing on the backs of four-legged prey. Moreover, an erect prehuman may well have been somewhat frightening to predators.

Having the arms and hands of brachiating apes, prehumans could pick up things and throw them. This skill is a most advantageous one, because when they stood erect and threw rocks, sticks, or bones, prehumans could frighten most enemies. The ability to throw things was ultimately to make them successful hunters.

Prehumans were indeed hunters. Survival is primarily a matter of finding sufficient food. On the savannah, our ancestors, possessing the generalized primate teeth that enabled them to eat almost every sort of food, probably consumed seeds, roots, and other vegetable matter. But they had also developed a taste for meat. As large primates with large brains, they required considerable quantities of protein, which meat supplies in abundance. At first they probably ate only what meat they could find— scavenging the remains of animals killed by predators, or capturing young, very old, or sick beasts. But their primate characteristics steadily developed to make them skillful hunters. With an erect walking gait and with eyes that could find all sorts of prey, they could catch and kill animals with weapons held in their hands or even thrown. Because they could use, and ultimately make, weapons and tools, they found it comparatively easy to eat the animals they killed because they could skin and butcher them (Lee & DeVore 1968; Service 1966).

Primate gregariousness was also a survival factor on the savannah. Prehumans were relatively small and slow creatures who by themselves would have had a difficult time getting along. But primates do not live alone; it is their nature to band together, a characteristic that was especially advantageous given the dangers of ground dwelling. We know virtually nothing about the form of prehuman social organization, but we can infer certain basic things about the character of prehuman bands and their social interactions from what we know about all primates. Such speculations are vital if we are to understand the basis of human organization. For it was prehuman organization into groups, coupled with the biology of being primates, that enabled them to survive. Without organization, the human system could never have existed.

No species survives for long unless its young survive, and because primate young are dependent on their mothers for so long, their survival and that of their species requires a form of social organization centering on the protection of infants and mothers (Lancaster 1975). Prehumans—like their ground-dwelling primate cousins, the chimpanzees, gorillas, and baboons—must have organized themselves to provide sufficiently secure surroundings in which their slow-developing young could grow; and while they grew, they learned. Prehuman youngsters surely had more to learn than any young primates before them. They

Baboon "family" engaged in grooming, the basic form of warm, personal interaction among non-human primates. Humans' need for each other is yet another reflection of our primate heritage.

had to be taught all the survival skills required to live on the savannah; they had to learn what foods were good to eat, where to find them, and how to obtain them; they had to gain an awareness of the dangers around them, and—perhaps most important for survival as terrestrial primates—they had to learn to get along with other members of their band. By watching their mothers and other adults, and then as they played together, young primates learned to control their emotions and discovered their place in the social structure of their band. It was an enormous amount to learn, but learning

it allowed them to survive because natural selection favored those best able to learn and teach their own young.

To thrive on the savannah, our ancestors had to range over ever-wider spaces, learn more and more skills, and teach them to their young. This expansion of experience encouraged the evolution of increasingly larger and more complex brains. With bigger brains, prehumans could fashion more elaborate tools, undertake more complicated tasks, and engage in more intricate social interactions. All these activities had to be taught to their offspring. Natural selection favored the continuing development and enrichment of prehuman experience and capacities. Selective pressures operated in this circular manner, encouraging the growing complexity of their lives, which in turn prompted the further evolution of yet bigger and better brains. Eventually the line between prehuman to human was crossed, and beings emerged who were like us in most important ways.

Becoming Human. Precisely when the most primitive human first appeared is not yet established. Anthropologists examine every new bone fragment or artifact, debating whether or not it is evidence of the earliest humans. For the purposes of this book, which is concerned with the nature of human society, it is not necessary to detail all the points of interest to anthropologists. It is sufficient that we agree on what features characterize humanity and that we recognize that certain of the evolving forms uncovered by anthropologists probably manifested those features.

Humanlike beings are classified as **hominids,** a group comprising modern people and various extinct forms that are our ancestors or near relations. There is some evidence that the earliest hominid, known as **Ramapithecus,** lived as much as 15 million years ago, although some experts hold that it was little more than an advanced ape. Most agree that more than 5 million years ago a true hominid, **Australopithecus,** appeared, and some very exciting new discoveries support the idea that almost that long ago not just relatively primitive hominids but members of the genus *Homo* existed. This is the genus to which all modern people, *Homo sapiens*, belong. Each of these types of near-humans ventured out into the savannah, and in adapting to life there, one or all of them developed characteristics we would recognize as human. The most human of the creatures was probably our direct ancestor.

What were savannah hominids like? They were bipeds, whose pelvises, hips, legs, and feet were designed to allow them to stand erect, walk, and perhaps even run easily. They probably used tools and may even have made stone implements to dig up roots and bulbs, to defend themselves from attackers, and to kill and cut up animal prey. Bipedalism and tool use reinforced one another, because as their highly manipulative hands were used to carry and handle things, hominids found it more and more advantageous to walk erect, which in turn freed their hands for additional and more involved tasks. It is not clear which developed first, but it is certain each facilitated the evolution of the other. Using tools and walking erect prompted a dramatic increase in brain size and complexity, because erect, tool-using hominids go farther, see and do more, and must learn so much more—all of which requires additional brain capacity to accommodate all the memories, thoughts, and ideas such rich experiences generate.

The larger hominid brains became, the harder it was for the heads of their babies to pass through the female pelvis at birth. A mother's pelvis could not be too broad or she would not be able to move as a true biped. This meant that young hominids had to be born before their heads were very fully developed; as a result, hominid infants remained helpless for much longer, and their mothers had to care for them for the several years it took them to gain self-sufficiency. Extended hominid infancy forged a powerful bond between mother and child, a bond that influenced the character of all aspects of their society.

The mother/child bond and the increased length of hominid childhood turned out to be central to survival on the savannah. It was during their extended childhood that hominids acquired the vast quantities of basic information needed to make them functioning members of their band, and because breeding females were burdened with infants, they had to be protected and provided for by others. This called for the creation of a hominid social system more supportive of its members and far more like that of contemporary humans.

Hominid society differed in several important ways from those of other ground-dwelling primates. Baboons also live on the savannah, but their biological and social adaptations have trapped them in an evolutionary cul-de-sac. Baboon bands are defended by highly aggressive males who are much larger than the females, and because usually only the most dominant of these males mate, their characteristics are perpetuated. Consequently, baboons were condemned to remain four-legged monkeys, living the same way forever because their social organization was so inflexible. At the other extreme, chimpanzees and gorillas have a fairly flexible society and also spend much of their time on the ground, but they live in fairly lush forests and have not been pressured to evolve further by the need to find food and defend themselves against savannah predators. Hominids felt such pressure acutely and in response survived and evolved both physically and socially, producing an adaptable society that was highly supportive of all its members.

Because hominid society was designed to provide for all within it, the obtaining of food was organized in a novel way. Unlike animals who all find their own food, seldom sharing with others, hominids divided the task of finding sustenance. While males hunted for meat, females gathered vegetable matter to eat; each shared with the others. This division of labor was intensified over time as male hominids improved their hunting skills and had to range farther and farther to find adequate game. They learned to operate from a sort of home base, where the females and infants stayed, and they would return, hopefully burdened with their kills, because as highly developed social primates their existence was focused on life within their group.

Hominids were linked to one another by extremely strong ties not unlike those that bind modern humans within their social structures. The long period of a hominid infant's dependency forged a lasting mother/child bond. The close associations with playmates, which developed during their extended childhood, typically lasted into adulthood. And, perhaps most important, bonds between adult males were intensified by the requirements of the hunt, and the ties between adult males and females were strengthened to an unprecedented degree by the evolution of female hominid sexual behavior. Instead of being sexually active only during certain estrus periods, females came to be sexually receptive at all times. This encouraged the development of the beginnings of genuine family ties, which were intensified and reinforced by the ongoing social pattern whereby male hunters brought back food for their mates and offspring and could share in what the females had gathered.

For several million years hominids were evolving a way of life recognizable as human: they were large-brained and walked erect; they used and made tools, and they had a stable, yet flexible social organization with rudimentary families and homes in which they tenderly trained and nurtured their slow-developing young. The complexity of their lives was matched by the increased capacity of brains that allowed them to mentally re-create the richness of their experience and ultimately to share their thoughts and feelings with others of their kind. This generation and sharing of ideas was the first step toward the creation of human culture—that is, a world mediated by symbols, and although hominid culture was immeasurably simpler than our own, it was culture nonetheless—a thing of the mind and spirit. It comprised all the memories, knowledge, signs, symbols, rules, and traditions that accumulated over generations of hominid life on the savannah.

It is important to understand that hominid survival and their future evolution into true humans increasingly depended on the acquisition of cultural skills by successive generations. But it is of equal significance to remember that the evolutionary path hominids had already traveled had been determined by the characteristics they inherited from their primate forebears. They had only those primate traits to work with if they were to survive on the savannah; they could not abandon their primate heritage by becoming something totally different from what they were; they could not evolve into tigers or lions; and they could

not remain unevolved primates. So they accentuated, through natural selection, those primate features that would serve them best. They made more and better use of their hands and growing brains by using and making tools, by creating a complex social system and culture with which all their young learned to live. As a result, they encouraged the gradual evolution of better minds and bodies with which to act. Their evolution firmly set the course of the development of the more advanced humans who followed and replaced the hominids starting some one and a half million years ago.

True humans built on the biological and behavioral foundations hominids had established in the span of perhaps 15 million years. All human evolution after the hominids is really an elaboration of tendencies already set, of patterns already shaped—a change in quality and dimension, not in kind. Although the hominids lived without such enormously important things as fire, language capable of transmitting the full symbolic content of thought, and all the features of civilization, they lived in a very human way and by their living enabled us to achieve our humanity.

We are humans because our ancestors were hominids and because their ancestors were primates. Our nature, actions, thoughts, society, culture, and destiny were inescapably shaped by the eons of progress from arboreal primates through terrestrial hominids to space-age men and women.

Within the Human Measure. The path of human evolution made a critical turning about one and a half million years ago. Evidence forces us to speak of our ancestors from before that time as prehuman or humanlike. In their form and behavior these primitive beings undoubtedly had begun to develop human characteristics and tendencies, but their physical, mental, and cultural equipment was still too limited to permit them to achieve full-fledged humanity. Then, perhaps 1.3 million years ago, *Homo erectus* emerged.

Homo erectus was not just a little more advanced than less-evolved hominids such as Australopithecus. This species was the first of our ancestors whose traits and capacities fall within the human measure—the first about our size and build and with more similarities to us than differences from us.

Homo erectus was able to elaborate upon the biological and cultural tendencies of earlier hominids because it possessed such truly human characteristics as a greatly enlarged and improved brain.

Some *Homo erectus* people obviously had brains as large as those of many modern humans. Moreover, there are scientists who maintain that even a 750 cubic centimeter brain, if it is sufficiently human in its internal structure, should function much as our far larger ones do. From what we know about *Homo erectus* behavior, their brains seem to have been both big enough and complex enough to permit identifiably human thoughts and actions.

What did they do with their more developed brains? They employed them in the unending day-to-day struggle for survival; in the process they found some remarkable, even revolutionary, means to increase the chances that they and their descendants would survive and prosper.

Homo erectus' most dramatic discovery was fire. Fire is a terrifying force from which all creatures flee. But some individuals must have overcome their fear because they had the curiosity and intelligence to approach and attempt to control naturally occurring fires. From fires started by volcanic eruptions, lightning, or other natural forces, they may have snatched up burning sticks, the flames of which could be contained and put to use. We lack evidence that these early people ever learned to make fires, but we are certain that they found ways to keep their campfires burning over very long periods and probably figured out how to carry flaming torches or glowing embers when they moved. Mastery of fire separated *Homo erectus* from all other animals, who still live in fear of fire. The use of fire is uniquely human, and it gave *Homo erectus* a strong claim to human status.

Knowing that all other animals fear fire, *Homo erectus* could use it to frighten away even the most ferocious predators. Fires could be set to stampede even the largest herd animals into places where hunters could kill them. Thus, controlled fire provided a new degree of security and vastly increased sources of food. In addition, by using fire to cook meat, these early people could more readily digest large quantities of high-quality protein. Cooking saved much of the time and effort that was required in chewing raw meat and waiting for their basically vegetarian primate digestive systems to process a meal. Thus, by reducing the need for all that chewing, the use of fire encouraged the evolution of smaller teeth and less massive jaws. These, in turn, led to less brutish looking faces and the gradual increase in the size of skulls and brains, which were also increasing in response to other influences.

Figure 1: The Family Tree of Humans

Prosimians   Monkeys   Apes   Humans

Modern humans (40,000 years ago)
Neanderthals (100,000 years ago)
Homo erectus (1 million years ago)
Australopithecus (6 million years ago)
Ramapithecus (20 million years ago)

Common Ancestor

Fire brought new power and security, spurred human evolution, and encouraged the exploitation of new environments. Although *Homo erectus* emerged in the tropics of Africa and southeast Asia, fire freed them to migrate northward over thousands of years into colder areas of Asia and Europe. Because their tropic evolution included loss of most of the body hair that had been typical of their ancestors, they probably could not have survived in the north without campfires to warm them. But survive they did—for hundred of thousands of years.

Whereas animals cannot survive in an ecological niche that does not fit their physical makeup, human beings can. Their survival does not depend solely on finding environments for which their biological evolution has prepared them. They can also rely on cultural evolution, on such learned skills as the use of fire and the fashioning of tools, weapons, clothing, and artificial shelters. *Homo erectus* survived by developing some, or possibly all, of these skills and in so doing became more and more human.

Even fairly primitive hominids before them were hunters, but these earlier hunters could hardly have been deemed mighty. Their weapons and their hunting tactics were too crude to permit them to catch any but the smaller species or the old, sick, or young of larger forms. Yet hunting remained a basic part of life throughout the millions of years of hominid evolution, and *Homo erectus* inherited the hunting tradition, refined it, and became a systematic hunter who could kill even the biggest game. Big-game hunting had a profound impact on fundamental aspects of human behavior and evolution (Pfeiffer 1969).

The most obvious advantage of bagging big game is that far larger quantities of food can be taken at one time. This means that more people can be sustained for longer periods from the efforts of a single hunt. It means less time has to be devoted to finding food than when people must spend most waking hours chasing down great numbers of small game, such as rabbits and lizards. But the value of big-game hunting is not only in the catch.

Hunting bands survive through cooperation, by having all members learn and carry out various tasks. First, the hunters must cooperate, because no one hunter can track down and kill something as large as an elephant. Several must work in concert, planning the hunt, assigning responsibilities for who will set fires behind the prey, who will wait in ambush, which hunters will go in for the kill. Next, females who are not part of the hunt itself must be assigned such tasks as caring for infants and the sick or injured, tending the campfires, and gathering vegetable food near camp to sustain the band if the hunters return empty-handed—which must have happened rather often. Such sexual division of labor had its beginnings earlier in hominid evolution and persists, out of habit rather than necessity, in some degree for most societies today.

A successful hunting life required cooperation and refinements in social organization, which, in turn, depended on improvements in human communication. To locate sufficient game, *Homo erectus* hunters had to operate over rather large areas and be away from their camps for extended periods. They had to develop powers of communication subtle and specific enough to guide their planning of a long hunt and to inform the women when they could be expected back or where to meet them. All such information, including all the details of hunting techniques, had to be communicated to each new generation. Much of this communication probably relied on sign language, but it is very likely that the rudiments of spoken language emerged in *Homo erectus* times. Their survival depended on increased cooperation and the reduction of ambiguity, and spoken language facilitates both.

The development of language influenced, and was influenced by, human physical evolution. Individuals who communicated best were most likely to survive and pass their abilities on to their descendants. Natural selection steadily favored those with bigger brains able to handle the increased use of language and with the vocal equipment best suited to speech. The result was that brains got larger, and people probably made increasingly effective use of language.

Hunting activities and the development of language inspired the creation of the first true societies. The *Homo erectus* band became a human society because its members had to rely on one another and interact with one another in more complex and meaningful ways. Their hunting life gave them a great deal to talk about as they gathered around protective hearths at their home bases to share food and stories, increasing their social cohesion. Their

care and concern for one another must have also increased as genuine families emerged. Whereas Australopithecus adults probably had sexual contacts with each other, it is likely that *Homo erectus* males and females chose regular mates, perhaps for life. Because their hunting prowess provided large amounts of food, they could ensure the survival of sick, old, or injured individuals who would have died in less organized groups. By constructing such a sharing and caring society, *Homo erectus* achieved a level of social complexity of which only real humans are capable.

Homo erectus social organization was not confined to single bands of 25 or so individuals. Cooperation among these great hunters extended to regular coordination of activities with other bands. This made it possible to catch more big game; it encouraged improved communication skills; and it forged social bonds between several hunting groups. Ideas and experiences were shared, mates were obtained from other bands, genetic qualities and knowledge were exchanged, and the social and biological heritage of all concerned were strengthened.

The success of these early humans placed limits on the direction of human evolution. Their survival depended on the use of fire and language, on their ability to teach their young to make spears and other improved stone implements with which to kill big game, and on the transmission from generation to generation of the rules of social organization that preserved their way of life. Later human beings, if they were to survive, would have to inherit not only the biological advantages of larger brains and speech faculties but also the

cultural traditions of their *Homo erectus* fore-bears. The recipients of this biological and cultural heritage were the first *Homo sapiens*—people much like ourselves—whose evolution was determined by the struggle and accomplishment of *Homo erectus*. The physical form of modern humans and even the basic components of our societies follow the profile of development outlined hundreds of thousands of years ago by *Homo erectus* people.

Homo erectus, on the left, was the first human-like hominid. They wandered over the earth for a million years. About 100,000 years ago, Homo erectus gave way to the Neanderthal, pictured on the right. Neanderthals closely resembled modern humans; in fact, they had larger brains.

HUMANS AND THEIR FIRST SOCIETIES

The Neanderthals

Homo erectus survived more than a million years. But a more advanced form of human evolved to cope with the new challenges that environmental changes began to present. About 200,000 years ago, the climate of the northern hemisphere grew much colder, and a long period of glaciation started. In this ice age game became scarce, which required advanced hunting techniques and improved weapons. Evolution answered the need by producing the earliest *Homo sapiens*. As early as a quarter of a million years ago, people with larger brains than *Homo erectus* emerged, and about 100,000 years ago a very advance type of human—*Homo sapiens neanderthalensis*, the Neanderthals—appeared.

Neanderthal fossils were among the first discovered in modern times, and theories about them gave these people a very bad image. Crude scientific analysis led people to believe that Neanderthals were big, apelike, and stupid creatures. This popular stereotype lasted until quite recently. Evidence has now been gathered to prove that Neanderthals had brains as large or larger than our own, and though they were relatively squat and small in stature and enormously strong, they were probably every bit as bright as most modern people. Although their heads lacked the prominent high foreheads of modern men and women, Neanderthals—dressed and groomed in contemporary fashion—would easily blend into a modern crowd and be recognized as fully human.

Neanderthals contributed to the evolution of human beings by achieving a cranial capacity within the modern range and by elaborating social structures basic to human existence. It is believed that they had more tightly regulated family relationships than did *Homo erectus*, and the entire Neanderthal band was probably more structured as well. This is understandable in light of the greater reliance that had to be placed on social organization for the hunt and for survival in an increasingly inhospitable environment.

Neanderthals in more temperate areas lived much as *Homo erectus* did. But the greatest evolution—culminating in the appearance of **Homo sapiens sapiens,** or modern humans—took place in the colder northern regions that challenged Neanderthal intelligence, ability, and organization. Challenge brought adaptive change and natural selection favored the emergence of more advanced individuals.

On the frozen tundra or in icebound mountain valleys, Neanderthals lived in relative isolation, relying on the adaptability of their bands. Men stalked and killed great beasts like the woolly mammoth, and the entire band butchered the animals and carried the meat home, where it was stored in ice crevices for later shared consumption. People were forced to rely on each another to a high degree, to learn to take orders from the best hunters, and to take great care in teaching hunting techniques and the methods of making new tools to the young. This system improved the chances for survival and ensured that cultural and social achievements would be passed on to aid in future survival. Such social interactions made Neanderthal bands the first identifiably human communities.

Regulation of the size of the population may also have been necessary, to make certain that there would not be too many mouths to feed and that there would be enough hunters to obtain the food. Because there is evidence that Neanderthal groups usually included more males than females, it is believed that some female babies were allowed to die. Such infanticide is hardly admirable by modern moral standards, but the fact that it may have been practiced is testimony to the Neanderthals' common sense and self-conscious understanding that even such drastic means must be employed to assure the survival of their kind.

Neanderthals did not confine the employment of their intelligence to pragmatic matters of survival. They also engaged in activities indicating that they thought about the nature of their existence, the beginnings of what we call philosophy and religion. The Neanderthals were the first people to bury their dead. This is enormously significant, because it means they thought about the difference between life and death, that they felt life had a special meaning, and that each individual—alive or dead—was worthy of being remembered and of receiving ceremonial attention. Neanderthals' burial rituals mark them as people who paid as much attention to matters of the mind and spirit as they did to demands of the body, which sets them apart as truly human.

They may also have had hunting rituals, which involved marking their bodies with magical symbols to increase the chances of a successful hunt, and the possibility that they engaged in ritual cannibalism indicates they may have hoped to obtain the knowledge, skill, or luck of a deceased comrade whose brain or flesh they consumed.

The biological makeup and the cultural activities of Neanderthals make it possible for us to consider them the first beings to achieve fully human status. In them, we see our immediate ancestors.

The First Modern Humans

Homo sapiens sapiens—people like ourselves—replaced Neanderthals about 40,000 years ago. Just as *Homo erectus* was replaced by Neanderthals who had superior tools, bigger brains, and better social organization, Neanderthals gave way to modern people. *Homo erectus* and Neanderthals were both apparently too static in their ways to produce the improved techniques needed to survive and to compete with better-endowed people. Despite the great brain size and intelligence of Neanderthals, they lacked some of the refinements that gave modern humans distinct survival advantages.

The modern brain evolved the high-domed shape it still exhibits. In those new portions of the brain, which Neanderthals lacked, were areas devoted to functions involving greater foresight, creativity, and imagination. This new structure made modern people more adaptable, more able to plan complex activities and devise better ways to live and prosper.

Although the first modern humans were hunters and gatherers like their predecessors, they refined all aspects of their behavior. They created far better tools and weapons, which enabled them to catch a far wider variety of game. They learned to cooperate with other bands and came to rely on their relationships outside their own bands. Marriages between members of different bands linked them through kinship ties until bands became clans or tribes. Where Neanderthals usually lived in bands of about 25, modern humans became accustomed to operating in groups of as many as 500 individuals. It became necessary to develop a social system that could regulate the behavior of such large numbers.

The rudiments of a political system may have emerged to control increasingly complex interactions. Rules were probably established based on taboos about who could marry whom among the closely related members of the tribe. Tribal laws had to be enforced by leaders of some sort of tribal government that was recognized by all.

The beginnings of religion seen among the Neanderthals were elaborated by modern tribes. Early modern people, such as the **Cro-Magnons,** decorated their caves with fine artwork, which was part of their rich ceremonial life. Drawings, sculptures, and ceremonies were employed to aid in the hunt, to honor the reproductive role of women, to commemorate birth, death, and the entrance into adulthood. Because there was enough surplus food to feed even the older, nonproductive members of society, they may well have been assigned roles as ritual leaders or priests. This may have been the start of organized religion.

For about 30,000 years modern people prospered, populating all parts of the world. They remained hunters and gatherers—much like existing tribes in primitive areas today—following herd animals, practicing their ancient rituals, and passing their traditions along to their children. They had emerged in a very short time, in terms of evolutionary history, and their marvelously innovative minds brought about changes that in an even shorter period completely altered the life of humanity.

Farmers, Cities, and Modern Societies

About 10,000 years ago, people in the Middle East discovered that wild grains could be regularly nurtured and harvested and that certain animals could be domesticated. This discovery is termed the **Neolithic Revolution,** and it profoundly modified the way human societies were organized because it freed people from their reliance on a wandering life in pursuit of animals to hunt. It created a stable economic base with sufficient food for large numbers of people who could live off what could be produced by a few people in a relatively limited area.

Agriculture did not cause biological evolution, but when farmers replaced hunters, social evolution was accelerated as new forms of behavior were needed to handle new living situations. Population in certain areas grew until tribes could be counted in the thousands, which demanded the establishment of clear political structures to regulate all aspects of life. After millions of years of groups in which all members enjoyed relative equality, agricultural communities began organizing themselves into classes, with social stratification distinguishing one sort of people from another; plenty and security brought inequality.

The importance of land on which food was produced made people more concerned about the protection of their territory. This led to the persistent conflicts between groups contesting claims to fertile land. Human aggression increased and warfare became typical; humans established themselves as the only species that regularly kill their own kind. The evils of war seemed to be one of the prices of the good created by agricultural abundance.

SUMMARY AND PREVIEW

Such abundance also prompted the development of uniquely human social structures. Urban communities, using the wealth generated by farming to build cities, grew up in farming areas; and within those earliest cities, some 5,500 years ago, all the elements of modern human society began to emerge. Social stratification and inequality between classes became more pronounced. Specialization of tasks became the rule: some people farmed; some worked as artisans creating pottery, metal tools, and weapons; some made wine or baked bread; and other served as scribes who used the new invention of writing to keep records. Urban communities became states with laws and governmental regulations controlling the fate of all within society. Civil, military, economic, and religious authority was exercised by kings, priests, and full-time warriors who took upon themselves the power to determine how the resources of society would be distributed.

The emergence of the human system was the culmination of perhaps 15 million years of human evolution. From the time the earliest hominids ventured onto the savannah, humans had developed increasingly complex ways of doing things. They progressively improved their social structures and enhanced their ability to survive in hostile environments. However, it was not until the invention of agriculture 10,000 years ago and the creation of civilization shortly after that they succeeded in reversing the process. Thereafter, humans characteristically used their culture—their tools and idea system—to gain mastery over nature itself.

The discovery of simple agriculture marked a revolution in the human system.

This chapter uncovers our heritage as biological beings. We saw how our prosimian ancestors clawed their way into the trees. Later, monkeys evolved to take advantage of this new found niche, and still later, apes emerged and developed many of those biological characteristics that typify humans. Eventually, as the forests receded, some apes and monkeys ventured onto the African savannah. Through adaptive changes in their anatomy, and most important, through their patterns of social organization, they led the way to the development of *Homo sapien sapiens*—humans. With the biological and sociocultural legacy of our ancestors, the pace of human evolution was greatly accelerated. This acceleration resulted from the liberation of evolution from physiological change. Humans possessed cultural and social organization, and these were to prove more flexible and easily changed. Thus, human evolution now involves changes in cultural and social patterns. It is the nature of these cultural and social patterns that interests sociologists.

Yet, we must not forget that human beings are products of a dual evolution—biological and cultural. Despite our elaborate social and cultural structures, we are still evolved primates, animals with biological traits that limit and control much of what we are capable. Our cultural and social organization developed as solutions to survival problems, and in surviving and continuing to develop them, we created our most uniquely human characteristics. Although there are broad variations in our responses to different circumstances, scientists maintain that it is unlikely that certain biological tendencies that also regulate our behavior have not been programmed into all of us. This matter is still the subject of serious debate, but it is valuable to speculate about certain aspects of this biological programming so that we may take all possibilities into account when examining our nature and the nature of human society. Thus, in the following chapters we will describe how the pattern of human behavior and organization *might* reflect biological propensities within very broad limits and with great capacity for variability. This area of inquiry is known as **sociobiology,** and it promises to be an interesting and provocative supplement to our analysis of human culture, interaction, personality, and organization.

The thrust of a sociological analysis, however, is on *created* patterns of culture, organization, and personality. As we have seen, we are unique because we have invented these patterns in efforts to adapt to the environment. The task of sociology is to understand the products of human creation that influence how we live. In reviewing the evolution of humans as a species and their social and cultural creations, we have placed ourselves in a better position to appreciate why a social or cultural pattern emerged and why we respond to it the way we do. It is to the task of unraveling the complex world we live in that we now turn. This system has a past that we would do well to remember as we proceed to review the field of sociology.

Key Terms

Primates: the order of mammals to which prosimians, monkeys, apes, and humans belong

Natural Selection: the process whereby those traits that facilitate adaptation to the environment are retained in a species, because members possessing those traits are more likely to survive and reproduce

Prosimians: a mammal (premonkey) who ascended the trees and became the first primate

Monkeys: a species of the primate order that evolved for life in the jungle forest after the prosimians

Apes: a species of the primate order that emerged after monkeys and from which humans evolved

Hominids: that order of apes who are humanlike and who can be classified as the ancestors, or close relative of the ancestors, of humans

Ramapithecus: the first hominid, it is believed, who lived on the savannah some 15 million years ago

Australopithecus: a hominid that emerged some 5 million years ago and that was the first member of the genus *Homo*

Homo erectus: the first true humans who emerged 1.3 million years ago and who belonged to the family of *Homo. sapiens*

Neanderthals: the last early relative of humans who lived up to about 100,000 years ago

Homo sapien sapien: modern humans

Cro-Magnons: the first modern humans who emerged about 40,000 years ago

Neolithic Revolution: the discovery of agriculture about 10,000 to 12,000 years ago

Sociobiology: the study of how human biology interacts with the way humans organized themselves in society

Review Questions

1. For what biological characteristics did life in the trees "select"?

2. What new niches were open to monkeys? Why?

3. What new niches were opened to apes? Why?

4. For what biological *and* cultural traits did survival on the savannah "select"?

5. What significance did the evolution of culture have for the pace of human evolution?

Suggested Readings

Brace, C. Loring, and Metress, James. *Man in Evolutionary Perspective.* New York: Wiley, 1973.

Dolhinow, Phyllis. *Primate Patterns.* New York: Holt, Rinehart & Winston, 1972.

Jay, Phyllis. *Primates.* New York: Holt, Rinehart & Winston, 1968.

Kratz, Solomon. *Biological Anthropology: Readings from Scientific American.* San Francisco: W. H. Freeman, 1974.

Kummer, Hans. *Primate Societies.* Chicago: Aldine, 1971.

Lancaster, Jane. *Primate Behavior and the Emergence of Human Culture.* New York: Holt, Rinehart & Winston, 1975.

Pfeiffer, John E. *The Emergence of Man.* New York: Harper & Row, 1975.

Poirier, Frank. *Fossil Man: An Evolutionary Journal.* St. Louis: Mosley, 1973.

Quiatt, Duane. *Primates on Primates.* Minnesota: Burgess Publishing, 1977.

Weiss, Mark, and Mann, Alan. *Human Biology and Behavior: An Anthropological Perspective.* Boston: Little, Brown, 1975.

HUMAN CULTURE: THE SYMBOLIC WORLD

PROLOGUE

Guiding Questions: How does culture make
humans unique? What is culture? How does
it shape our lives and the society in which we
live? Why is culture the "cement" of human
organization?

Chapter Topics

THE CREATION OF CULTURE

Modern human beings came into existence because biological evolution favored the survival of our ancestors. Chapter 3 outlined the process whereby the characteristics we call human developed steadily over thousands of generations. The pressure of natural selection encouraged people to become fully erect, gave them greater ability to manipulate objects with their hands, and, most important, spurred the evolution of bigger and more complex brains. With those advanced brains, humans gained the capacity to create unprecedentedly successful ways of ensuring that they and their descendants would survive.

Whereas all other animals have had to rely primarily on physical attributes, instincts, and other strictly biological factors to protect and sustain them, humans have been able to fashion their own survival mechanisms. Humans were able to free themselves from total reliance on biological evolution, to arm themselves in the struggle for survival with far more than what they received as their genetic heritage. Their brains enabled them to make tools, devise intricate patterns of organization, conceive and communicate ideas, and to invent solutions to new problems (Simpson, 1952). These abilities were passed on to their young through instruction. This has meant that human survival and development could depend on cultural evolution as well as on biological evolution, and the human capacity to create culture has led to the emergence of human societies in their present intricate forms.

Humans have used their large brains to create elaborate social patterns, such as complex urban structures.

In contrast to humans, insects such as the bee are programmed at birth to create certain social patterns.

Modern culture has built upon the achievements of primitive culture, which probably began with tool use and eventually involved making and refining tools for more and more complex tasks (Garn 1963). It can be seen in the discovery of the use of fire for such purposes as hunting and cooking, protecting campsites, and providing a warm place around which people might gather and share their experiences. Culture developed as people improved their techniques both for action and the exchange of information. Therefore, hunting contributed to cultural evolution by requiring that people learn to work together, plan their joint efforts, divide responsibilities between those who hunted and those who stayed near the camp to care for the young and gather plant food, and by teaching people to share both food and ideas. By such cooperation, the chances of survival were increased, and the effectiveness of cooperation required increasingly effective communication. The need for better communication skills stimulated the development of language, which, more than anything else, inspired the evolution of human culture (Pfeiffer, 1969).

As early humans improved their capacity for language, they greatly enriched their cultural potential; they increased the scope of their activities and enhanced their ability to transmit their cultural patterns to succeeding generations (Hewes 1973; Hill 1972). For example, animals do not bury their dead, but humans do. This cultural activity shows that humans care in very special ways about one another and that they think in unique ways about the nature of life and death. However, burying the dead does not represent a great cultural advance. But exchanging the ideas touching human burial inspires the continuation of the

THE SOCIOLOGICAL STUDY OF CULTURE

practice and the elaboration of ideas attached to that activity. Eventually, such rituals lead to the development of a pattern of thoughts and actions we might call religious practices. Likewise, the fact that humans organized themselves into families, bands, and tribes meant they had to rely increasingly on language to communicate to all members of those groups what was appropriate behavior. Thus, human social organization involved not only actions, but shared ideas about right and wrong actions. Such ideas, including taboos, beliefs, and values, were cultural components of evolving human society. Modern societies are also the products of such ideas, because without the system of ideas that comprises culture, human organization would be impossible. It was the creation of culture that led to human social life as we know it.

Culture is the "cement" of human organization. Unlike animals whose groups are held together by instinct, humans organize themselves by means of cultural patterns of their own creation. Culture, then, is a very important topic in the study of humans and their system of social organization. For that reason, it is imperative that we give careful attention to the nature of culture.

In the real world, society and culture occur together, for one could not exist without the other. But the two must be artificially separated for purposes of analysis if we are to fully comprehend ourselves and our organization. In talking about culture as an abstraction—as if it were something apart from actual people in a concrete society—we can get closer to the workings of culture and uncover basic characteristics that might otherwise be obscured if viewed amid the distracting complexities of society. This same method is used by biologists to study living things and by physicists to explore the nature of energy and matter (Kroeber & Parsons 1958). They, like all scientists, must sometimes concentrate on an abstract concept if they are to gain a degree of certainty about how the real world operates.

The term *culture* is used in many ways by various people, often without being defined at all. In fact, it has already been used in this book without precise definition, because in the contexts in which it was mentioned you could apply your own generalized understanding of the concept. Now, as our examination of the human system becomes more detailed, so must our definition of such a fundamental concept (Singer 1968).

Not all social scientists, not even all sociologists, define culture in the same way (Kroeber & Kluckhohn 1963). Some sociologists define it as "the patterns of living of a people." This definition is also employed by some anthropologists and even by many nonscientists. This usage is far too broad for the kind of close analysis we intend. We need a far more precise definition to help us see all that culture is and how it works.

Many people, experts and nonexperts alike, often speak of culture as "the higher things of life," as refined taste in art, music, literature, and similar pursuits of the rich or well educated. These things are, of course, part of culture, but such a definition ignores all the interesting and important "lower things of life." Therefore, this definition must be rejected as inadequate for a clear sociological perspective.

A Sociological Definition

A more sociological definition is: **culture** is a system of meaningful symbols that people in a society create, store, and use to organize their affairs. It requires, of course, elaboration and amplification (Parsons 1951; Kroeber & Parsons 1958).

Let us examine in more detail some of the critical terms of this definition: (1) symbols, (2) systems of symbols, (3) meaningful symbols, and (4) stored symbols.

What are Symbols? A **symbol** represents something else. Understanding the relationship between a symbol and what it stands for requires the mental powers of big-brained animals. Symbols are literally everywhere. The words on this page are symbols representing ideas and things that readers can identify because they have learned how to read the English language. A badge is a symbol of authority; it is not authority itself. A medal is symbolic of courage; it is not, itself, courage. Flags are symbols of nations. To Christians, bread and wine are symbols of the body and blood of Christ. Even certain types of clothing can be symbolic: uniforms, a judge's black robes, and a wedding dress all symbolize specific functions or situations.

Systems of Symbols. Symbols are organized into systems, which carry meanings for those who create or use them—often very complex meanings that entirely escape people outside the group using the symbols. Language is an obvious example; unless one has knowledge of a language, written or spoken, the words printed in that language are little more than meaningless marks on a page and the spoken words are an unintelligible babble. Religion is another common example of **systems of symbols.** If one has no knowledge of Christianity, for instance, the cross is nothing more than a shape, and those who are not Jewish may have difficulty in finding meaning in the Star of David. But to members of those religious groups, such symbols are rich in historical and devotional meaning and inspire great emotional, intellectual, and behavioral reaction. When symbols are combined into systems, they bind the members of the group together and help them organize their actions and affairs.

What is Meaning? Meaning refers to what symbols "say" or "communicate" to the people. The more meaningful the symbols are, the more they contribute to the courses of action among members of the symbol-sharing group. Culture guides action by providing meaning, but it is also the product of the interaction among people. As people seek to form relationships, they create and use symbols to help them organize their affairs.

Culture is Stored. Culture can also be seen as a "storehouse" of meanings. It is the sum total of meanings that people can use and draw upon in organizing their lives and their society. The concept of storehouse is meant to emphasize that meanings are gathered and stored in people's memories or by artificial means such as writing, and can be retrieved later. Both material and nonmaterial things can be found in the storehouse of culture; that is, culture is not only the repository of meanings about such nonmaterial aspects of human life as patterns of behavior, notions of right and wrong, and similar customs and ideas, but it also contains knowledge of material things, what they are, how they are used, and how to make them. The storehouse is filled with all a people's skills in fashioning every object they feel is important to their existence—from tools and weapons to, perhaps, a perfect omelet.

The cultural storehouse is constantly being modified and expanded as people cope with new situations and new problems. Older parts of the culture are replaced when they no longer fit the way people live, when no one has use for them any longer, or when better ideas, methods, or devices are developed. In this way, the belief in magic may give way to trust in science, and the skills of the witch doctor are forgotten when the modern physician takes over the tasks of healing.

It must be remembered, however, that any existing storehouse of culture has been built up from what went into it long before. Many basic ingredients are never really lost. On the material side, knowledge of the wheel was used to create everything from clocks to cars, and the prehistoric mastery of fire was necessary before the art of cooking could develop to its present manifold state and before the first metals could be turned into the implements with which humans ended the Stone Age. There are numerous similar examples. The nonmaterial components of every culture have emerged from earlier symbolic systems regulating how people were to behave and treat one another. The ideas underlying social interaction remain in the cultural storehouse, from which they are drawn upon as people seek better ways to organize their affairs in response to altered circumstances.

It is in the nature of human existence that circumstances continually change. Change can result from the impact of natural forces and, probably more often, as an outgrowth of human creativity. Humans never seem to rest in their generation of ideas that can alter the shape of social interaction. Such ideas either operate directly by changing people's attitudes about how they should behave or indirectly by creating material objects that influence people's way of life and their conceptions of how to live. For example, if a group believes it is wrong to eat meat, their way of life will be critically altered if most of them decide meat eating is acceptable. A tribe of headhunters would behave differently toward their neighbors if they came to believe that taking heads was wrong or meaningless. A society in which people adopt the precepts of a major idea system, such as Christianity or communism, will be marked by significant changes in the way people think and act about their lives.

Creative additions to the material ingredients of a culture also can have profound effects. Think of the influence of the telescope. Once people were able to see the universe more

CULTURE AND HUMAN ORGANIZATION

closely and clearly, they realized the earth was not its center. This realization changed basic ideas about the importance of humanity; it undermined faith in human religions that had been based on the idea that the earth was the center of things, and opened the way for a complete overhaul of culture during the Renaissance and during the industrial and scientific revolutions. The widespread use of automobiles has led to the construction of highway and freeway systems, which, in turn, have given people the opportunity to move out of urban centers in great numbers. People's expectations have changed because of autos and good roads; they have come to expect to be able to live in comfortable suburbs; they are ready to spend large amounts of money on large and powerful cars and devote the largest single part of their nation's energy resources fueling their cars. Even their status in society has come to be marked by whether they have a small economy model or an expensive sports car. The telescope and the automobile are but two examples of the tremendous number that might be cited to show how ideas can lead to the invention of material objects and ways of using them, which, in turn, can influence people's basic ideas about organizing their affairs. There is, in fact, considerable feedback between changes in material and nonmaterial culture, each influencing the other and the people of whose lives they are part.

Our definition of culture allows us to view it as a resource for human interaction and social organization, to see that it actually permits interaction and organization, and to see that it shapes and directs the formation of society. But to do this, culture must be more than a neutral resource, more than merely a storehouse; it must also be an active shaper of the direction of most human interaction—of people's perceptions, of their loves and hatreds, and just about everything else they sense, experience, and think.

In studying culture, then, we must be alerted to two of its facets: (Parsons 1951): (1) Culture can be viewed as a *resource*, as a tool or capacity that allows interaction and organization among humans to occur, and (2) culture should also be seen as an active *constraint*, as a set of symbols that also shape and guide the course of interaction and patterns of social organization.

Culture as a Resource

As a resource, culture provides people with many ways to store and transmit meaningful symbols, knowledge, and skills. A prime example of this aspect of the human cultural system is language. Language has the power to convey richly varied meanings. It is a cultural resource equally capable of explaining the scientific complexities of such theories as relativity or prompting emotional responses when used in a love poem or a letter from home. All members of a society who know and use a particular language draw upon it throughout their lives.

Language enables them to learn all they must know to master specific tasks, provides them the means whereby they can make their needs and desires known to others, and makes possible all social relationships and contacts. When language is preserved in writing, it becomes a resource that can be transmitted through the centuries. Ideas conceived 2,500 years ago have been written down so that when one reads Plato today, it is almost as if that ancient Greek were here to share his inspiration with the modern reader. Language is truly a potent cultural resource on which we all can draw not only for spiritual or emotional nourishment and intellectual enrichment, but also for dealing with others in the social world around us.

Moreover, language was a cultural resource even before writing was invented, and it still relies on more than words, written or spoken. The way language is used can be as important as the words themselves. Inflection can also be a symbolic resource. Think about the difference between the way we express a question and a statement. Notice that in a question the last word is emphasized differently than it is in a statement (Farb 1973). Thus, there are two different meanings in these same words: "I am to blame." "I am to blame?" The richness of language as a human cultural resource can also be seen in the way that people use their entire bodies for expression. Smiles, frowns, glares, hand gestures, even posture contribute to meaning (Shibutani 1961). In our culture shaking the head means "no," and nodding it means "yes." Words are secondary or supplementary.

Gestures—words, voice inflections, hand movements, body posture, and the like—all carry symbolic meaning. Language thus involves more than words.

In fact, such body language is more important than the words—for example, when someone says no while nodding in affirmation or says yes while giving a negative shake of the head.

Body gestures as language can have highly significant, even sexual, implications. Julius Fast's popular book, *Body Language*, has detailed some of the provocative aspects of this form of human communication. He reminds us that we "say" things—impart meanings to others—even by the way we position ourselves in relation to another person. If we move close, we communicate a higher level of desire for interaction than if we hang back. By making eye contact, assuming an open and available expression, perhaps even parting our lips, we clearly are inviting more intimate interaction than if we coldly stare in the opposite direction from a person in whom we are sexually interested. People who exhibit bodily grace, confidence, aggressiveness, and receptivity to contact are constantly communicating meaningfully without saying a word. Such body language is not as central to the development of culture's storehouse as is verbal and written language, but it demonstrates that people learn to draw upon every cultural resource that serves or fulfills them.

The Origins of Culture: Language among Chimpanzees

Culture depends upon the capacity to create, use, combine, and recombine symbols. Language is the primary means for such symbolization, and culture cannot exist without language. A value, belief, norm, technology, or religious doctrine could not be created or be used to guide our affairs without language.

It has often been said that we are unique because we can use language and create culture to mediate our interactions and regulate our organization into societies. But are we? Recent studies indicate that chimpanzees have a rudimentary capacity to use language. Chimps are probably very much like our primal ancestors who left the trees and began living on the savannah, and thus, the abilities of chimps can perhaps be viewed as "evidence" for what our ancestors' initial capacities for developing culture might have been.

The first recognition that chimpanzees could learn the rudiments of language came from a husband and wife who raised a chimp named Washoe using only the sign language used by deaf mutes. Washoe could not only label objects in her environment, but she could also build crude sentences, like "out open, please hurry" or "drink sweet, please hurry." Other chimpanzees have been taught language in other ways. A psychologist took a chimp named Sarah and taught her to use plastic shapes to represent objects and acts, such as "give" and "take," and then to construct crude sentences, like "Mary (her caretaker) give apple."

Recent evidence indicates that chimps can use language outside the purview of humans. For example, Washoe was placed in a natural setting with other chimps who did not know sign language. When a snake appeared, all of the chimps screamed, and scrambled into the trees. All except one to whom Washoe in sign language said, "Hurry dear—danger." Another study has discovered a chimp mother who is now teaching sign language to her offspring. Thus, chimpanzees can do much more symbolizing than once thought.

Humans' and chimps' ancestors once had a common ancestor. In their evolution, chimps did not have to use language or develop their brains to acquire greater symbolizing capacity, because they were—and are today—well adapted to their niche. However, our ancestors were forced to live in a hostile savannah environment, and the rudimentary culture-using capacities that we see in chimps had selective value for adjustment to this environment. Adaptation was increased by the ability to label, to construct sentences—no matter how crude and simple—and to talk to each other. Our

A chimp in an experimental laboratory uses symbols to "talk" with humans and to communicate its needs.

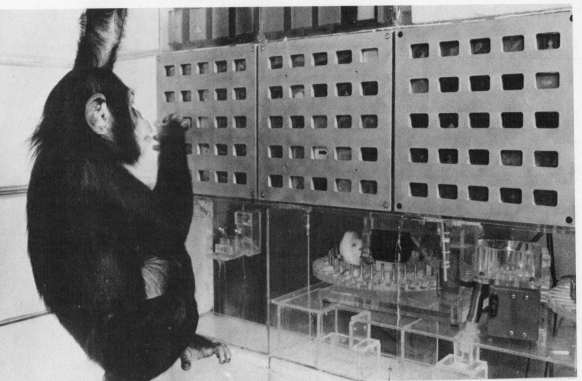

hominid ancestors could warn and help each other—the beginnings of social organization mediated by culture. Since symbolizing and the creation of culture had selective value, larger brains, or at least more complex brains, that could allow greater symbol-using capacity had selective value. So brain size, brain organization, and the emergence of our "unique" ability to use language and thereby create culture evolved.

However, we should not forget that our distant cousin, the chimp, has the rudiments of that ability. The chimp provides us with a speculative glimpse at what prehumans were like and what they could potentially be as they began to live on the African savannah.

Sources: Hewes 1973; Hill 1973; Lawick-Goodall and Fouts 1974

Culture as a Constraint

Cultural resources are symbol systems that allow interaction and organization. They also carry messages that shape and guide social action because the messages convey ideas constraining human perceptions and options.

The studies of Edward Sapir and Benjamin Whorf have shown that language is far more than just a medium for transmitting symbols that reflect the nature of a culture (Whorf 1940, 1956; Carroll 1956). The character of a language in reality sometimes compels people to comprehend their experiences in a certain way; language can mold the way we think about things. This is because we do not simply experience the world, we translate our impressions by means of thoughts organized according to the structure of our language. Whorf used the example of the difference between the way English-speaking people and Hopi Indians conceive of time in their thoughts and speech. He reminded us that English relies on tenses, on a keen sense of past, present, and future, whereas the Hopi language has no tenses. This means that English-speaking people experience the world in terms of progressions through time, according to identifiable stages through which all life and action move. The Hopis conceive of all things as part of an unbroken, continuous movement in which everything is forever becoming and nothing is thought of as being or having been. Other peoples have similar special ways of seeing things and thinking about their lives, ways that arise from the nature of their language. To illustrate this point we can note that our language views *time* as a noun that can be manipulated and controlled. We can "cut," "save," "spend," "lose," "gain," "waste," and *do* other things to time. Thus, we are likely to perceive of the world as manipulatable and to act on this assumption. In other human systems with different symbols, such thoughts and actions do not exist or are seen as highly inappropriate (Hall, 1959).

The power of a cultural medium to shape our perceptions and to limit our options can be demonstrated even without comparing our language to that of other peoples. Our own language conveys important messages above and beyond the actual meaning of the words it contains, and those messages are usually received and acted upon without our ever noticing them because they are camouflaged by our instinctive acceptance of the language as it is. Yet how we act and, more important, how we treat one another can depend on such messages, so it is necessary for us to learn to separate the messages from the medium if we are to improve the clarity of our thinking and the quality of our social interactions.

One of the best examples of the power of hidden linguistic messages is the way our language tends to perpetuate the notion of male superiority and dominance. Most Western languages are products of male thought, and even the most self-conscious feminists can find themselves using their language in sexist ways. The following test should give you a good idea of how language makes your mind work, and it may surprise even the least male chauvinistic readers.

Read these sentences and supply the pronoun—*he* or *she, his* or *hers*, or whatever—that you most immediately think is best with the noun used.

The surgeon knew——could save the patient.
The detective's gun was in——left hand.

The scientist smiled graciously as they awarded——the coveted Nobel prize.

No matter what the spy did,——could not get away from——pursuers.

For the following sentences, no nouns are supplied, so all you must do is furnish pronouns—as above—that you think best fit the situations or activities depicted.

——was always strong and confident.

——was the most intelligent student in law school.

——pleaded with——to help——fix the car.

After——cleaned the house,——did the shopping.

Everyone knew——was afraid to be alone.

——always prepared the income tax returns because

——was too easily confused by all those figures.

——was silly and scatterbrained, but pretty.

In the first list, unless you tried to overcome your first reactions, you probably used masculine pronouns with the nouns describing people with skill, power, ability, daring, or competence; and in the second list, even without typically masculine nouns to trigger your response, you may well have used masculine pronouns to fit situations requiring dominance, knowledge, or ability and supplied feminine pronouns where inability, helplessness, household chores, or submission was described. You are not a bad person, even an insensitive one, for having done so. The language compels you to match certain words, to think of things in certain ways. Reality is not only in what is, but is what our culture constrains us to think it is. Little wonder that it is so hard to change the way men and women interact and to liberate people from the controlling messages that are built into a system of symbols.

Another example of the power of a cultural resource to shape what can occur in society is found in the way various types of technology can influence what thoughts and actions are possible for people in a given society. The development of knowledge—a system of symbols—about how to plant and cultivate the land provided enormous new benefits for humans, but at the same time, it placed limits on the future direction of social interaction. By applying this technology or knowledge to their lives, farmers could not be nomads; they had to stay close to their fields and flocks. The application of agricultural technology produced plenty of food; but that abundance made possible the growth of population, the specialization of labor, the growth of cities with rigid class distinctions, and the emergence of governments to regulate what the farmers and everyone else did. In itself, the technology of agriculture seems applicable solely to economic pursuits and seems to have a meaning largely for farming groups. But this technology also changes the way people act and think about life because it transforms the relationships among people.

A modern example of technological influence is the advance of electronics. Radio, television, calculators, and computers are developed from the application of knowledge, or technology. Once this cultural knowledge is applied and used to create electronic devices, it alters a way of life and changes attitudes and behavior. Television makes all who watch it aware of the wealth and abundance of their society; it makes them want all the products and services advertised; it makes them aware of the actions of their leaders and, perhaps, of their inability to influence events. Television is not just a box filled with circuits, not just a

medium of communication, it is a transmitter of values and aspirations that influences what people desire, believe, and trust. It shapes how we perceive much of our world by guiding our thinking.

Thus, the use and application of symbols can shape our lives, either directly by constraining our thoughts and actions or indirectly by allowing for the development of material things, such as televisions, calculators, and freeways, which then constrain and shape our actions in the world. All human thought and activity is constrained by the symbolic systems constituting culture. These systems tell us how to act, shape what we see, and condition the way we experience life. The constraint is never complete, however, and we are often able to liberate ourselves from various aspects of our culture. But if we become too liberated and insist on acting too unconventionally, we will be labeled deviants and will be subject to what can often be severe sanctions. Most of us, of course, stay pretty much in line and willingly operate under the cultural constraints of our society—sometimes knowingly and other times unconsciously. So the nature of those constraints and the symbolic systems exercising them is of immediate interest to us.

The conceptualization of culture as constraints is often defined as the impact of ideas or idea systems on human thought, perception, and action. The definition takes into account a kind of circular and interdependent process. Symbolic systems are created and then stored in all, or most, of our minds; but once stored, they have a tendency to feed back on us and thus shape how we think, perceive, and act. In many ways we are captives of our creations, of our ability to have ideas and make symbols;

Cultural ideas—communicated in many diverse ways—and cultural products shape and constrain social life.

but it is necessary that we remain captives to some degree because without the constraints of our idea systems, social interaction and meaningful organization could not proceed. Constraint would be replaced by chaos.

Imagine interactions in which people did not share at least some of the same assumptions, in which they did not "see" the same things, in which they believed conflicting forms of behavior were appropriate. What would happen? The Biblical story of the Tower of Babel is a well-known example. When the thousands of people trying to build a tower into heaven were robbed of their common language, they became incapable of any concerted, efficient action because none could understand the other. A less dramatic example is what happens when people from different cultures share the same experience but see it from different perspectives. This can be as simple as the differences between the way one culture treats personal space and how individuals from another culture respond. In some societies it is customary to deal with other people close up, to touch them a lot, perhaps even hug or kiss them in moments of excitement. Americans, however, usually like to operate at greater distance, feeling better if there is some space between them and their companions. It is an intrusion to get too close, and Americans will probably be embarrassed by the close physical contact of some foreigners. Consequently, if they are in exactly the same situation, two people will experience two entirely different realities and have conflicting responses. If the American moves away as the foreigner makes friendly advances, the American will have offended that person by rejecting both the individual and the culture in which such advances are customary. If the foreigner persists, the American will become uncomfortable and confused.

Such cross-cultural conflicts are common and are especially pronounced when those from modern, industrialized countries encounter people in simple, tribal societies. Eskimos see offering their wives to a visitor as courtesy; outsiders see it as outrageous. Tribes that have long practiced headhunting consider it correct behavior, perhaps even believe it to be central to the stability of their way of life. People from Western cultures see it as murder.

Without mutually recognized and understood cultural constraints, life within a given society becomes a schizophrenic nightmare in which all the inmates hear different voices, experience separate realities, and act not as their culture has taught them but according to their own ever-changing lights (Shibutani 1961).

How do sociologists conceptualize, visualize, or describe the systems of ideas that constrain, guide, and control our thoughts and interactions? Typically they are categorized as: (1) **values,** (2) **beliefs,** and (3) **norms.** Different sociologists may label each somewhat differently, but the phenomena described are the same.

Values. These are abstract ideas or conceptions that members of a society or group share about what is appropriate, inappropriate, good, and bad (Williams 1970, 1969). Values carry considerable emotion, and people feel strongly attached to them. Values do not apply to any one situation but are instead general, abstract, and meaningful without reference to any particular event or circumstance. All human organizations reveal values, but of course, they vary from society to society.

Some examples of American values can help us understand what they are. *Activism* is one American value emphasizing devotion to work and action, especially if it is directed toward manipulating and mastering the environment. *Achievement* is an important American value stressing the importance of winning, being successful, and doing well in all things. *Materialism* or pursuit of "the good life" is another prominent value in the United States. *Progress* is yet another value, stressing the importance of constant betterment of people's lives. The values of *efficiency* and *practicality* in all pursuits are also prized. Despite the limitations placed on many individuals within our society, *equality* and *democracy* are important values; *freedom* is extolled as a basic value despite the reality of forces tending to restrict it. A related value is *individualism*, and a seemingly contradictory one is *conformity*, yet both are parts of American culture. Americans consider themselves generous and caring, and they value *humanitarianism.* They pride themselves on their high sense of *morality*, seeing many issues in absolute terms of right and wrong (Williams 1970, pp. 438–500.). These values are clearly related in many ways, reinforcing and, in some cases, undermining one another. We will discuss how they interact when we discuss cultural integration and conflict.

Beliefs. These are systems of symbols or ideas that pertain to specific situations. Unlike values, they do not transcend all social contexts and spheres but apply to particular aspects of social life, such as work, family, school, recreation, and other concrete spheres of activity. Some beliefs say what *should exist* in a situation, expressing people's specific expectations or sentiments. Religious doctrines are systems of belief designed to guide behavior in certain situations. Political ideologies also rely on beliefs, in this case beliefs about what should occur in the political arena. Such beliefs might be termed **evaluative beliefs** (Turner & Starnes 1976).

Evaluative beliefs give people the intellectual and emotional tools for envisioning and interpreting specific events and situations. Thus, those who hold communistic beliefs have faith that the problems of class conflict and the just distribution of wealth and power will be solved if a society adopts Marxist doctrines. People who believe that the best of all possible worlds is one based on the values of the traditional family are convinced most problems arise from the breakdown of family ties, from divorce, and from children's loss of respect for their parents. On the other hand, there are people who believe that the family itself causes many important problems in society and maintain that society will be improved and individuals freed of their emotional difficulties only when new and better ways to raise children and conduct sexual relationships are found. They advocate alternatives to marriage, creative divorce, or such arrangements as communal living.

A second type of belief concerns what *actually exists* rather than what should exist. Such beliefs are often mistaken and inaccurate, but they still shape the perceptions of the people who hold them and who are convinced of the truth of what they believe. These idea systems can be called **empirical beliefs** (Turner & Starnes, 1976).

Examples of empirical beliefs might include racist notions, according to which some people sincerely believe that individuals of one race are inherently inferior or superior to those of another. The beliefs that certain drugs are unquestionably bad or good similarly characterize the believers as people whose concepts of what is true are controlled by their beliefs as much as by facts. But there are also people who hold empirical beliefs that are true or

largely true. Scientists have a degree of belief in their conclusions, but they are continually altering those beliefs in response to new research and hypotheses. This is not true of those who trust in such pseudosciences as astrology, who believe that the position of the planets actually influences the future life of particular individuals.

All of us hold some evaluative and empirical beliefs. To a considerable extent, our thoughts and actions are shaped by what we would like to see exist or what we are totally convinced does exist in a concrete situation.

Norms. These are highly specific expectations about what people are supposed to do in a particular situation (Blake & Davis 1964). They are sets of rules—sometimes written, perhaps in the form of laws, but more often unwritten and implicit—about how people are supposed to act, what they are expected to do in various situations. There are norms about the proper dress for a wedding or a beach party, about which side of the road to drive on and how fast. Some norms, rules, regulations, and laws can be violated with impunity; others are enforced stringently. The social norm that people should not eat with their hands can usually be violated with little more than stares and perhaps rude comments from one's tablemates. The rule against killing can lead to life in prison if someone kills another and the deed is considered murder. The rule can be suspended for soldiers who must follow the norms of military discipline and kill under orders.

Clearly, the relationship among norms and between norms, values, and beliefs is complex, often conflicting, and sometimes confounding. Yet these components of culture are what allow society to function as effectively as it does. A world without values, beliefs, and norms would be chaos. People could not interact and organize themselves; therefore, these aspects of culture are studied extensively by sociologists.

Relations Among Values, Beliefs, and Norms. Different types of ideas are never entirely isolated; they are interrelated. Values constrain beliefs; beliefs influence norms; norms reflect values; and so on. Widespread and concerted violations of norms can lead to their disappearance and to the weakening of the values and beliefs that inspired them. Changing norms tend to create pressures for modification of beliefs, and, of course, the ongoing conflicts among values, beliefs, and norms can make life interesting as well as complicated.

We are all familiar with conflicts between values and beliefs—we may even exhibit some of them in our thoughts and action. As good Americans, most of us will attest to our devotion to the value of equality; yet we may have strong objections to such things as school busing or racial quotas for jobs because we hold evaluative beliefs contradicting our faith in equality or because we hold empirical beliefs that integration does not promote equality. We see actions to give others equality as a threat to our valued individualism, freedom of action, and the pursuit of success and the good life. Then again, some of us may simply hold racist, sexist, or religious beliefs that justify our unequal treatment of people unlike ourselves. The conflict of idea systems involves contradictions among the values and beliefs individuals adhere to and the norms they follow. It also arises from differences between the ideas held by various groups within society.

Figure 1 shows the interplay of idea systems.

**Figure 1:
Culture and
the Person**

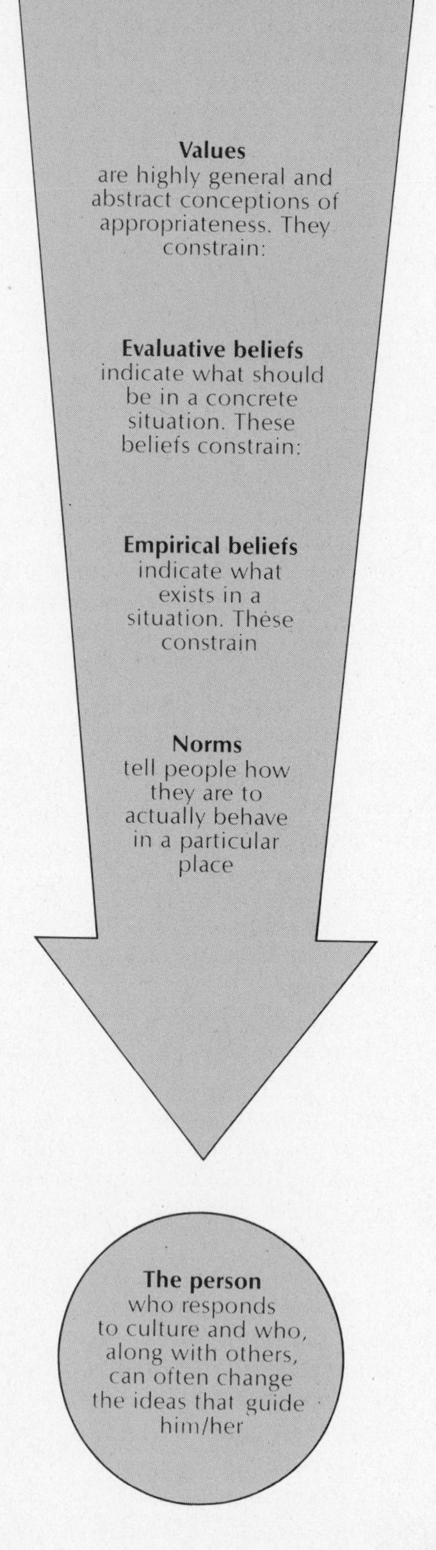

Values
are highly general and abstract conceptions of appropriateness. They constrain:

Evaluative beliefs
indicate what should be in a concrete situation. These beliefs constrain:

Empirical beliefs
indicate what exists in a situation. These constrain

Norms
tell people how they are to actually behave in a particular place

The person
who responds to culture and who, along with others, can often change the ideas that guide him/her

VARIATIONS IN HUMAN CULTURE

Variations Between Cultures

We know that languages are characterized by basic differences; hence, we know that the symbolic resources stored for any particular people will vary from those of any other. We also know that the cultural resources used to facilitate social interaction carry messages constraining the shape and direction of that interaction. Different languages, for example, allow people to see things in certain ways and force them to predicate actions on different premises (Hall 1959).

Yet, people often think and act as if all cultures should be like their own. This behavior is called **ethnocentrism.** Ethnocentrism is the conviction that the way things are done in one's culture is the best, most civilized, most progressive, most right and good. Sociologists and anthropologists usually counter the claims of ethnocentrism with the concept of **cultural relativity,** which holds that each society must be measured only in terms of that society itself. They hold that claiming that all people should adhere to particular values and cultural traditions is unscientific, at best, and racist, at worst. Still, ethnocentrism persists, working like a form of intellectual imperialism to impose one set of customs and beliefs on another people whose heritage is entirely different. It is inherent in the growth and perpetuation of culture for the members of a society to take pride in their own ways, and it is, perhaps, inevitable that people operating within different cultural storehouses will try to press their traditions on each other.

Cultural Variations Within a Society

Not only do different societies use different cultural storehouses, but within most societies, and unquestionably within any large and complex one like the United States, there are **subcultures** the members of which share values and beliefs and abide by norms that are, to varying degrees, different from those held by the majority (Yinger 1960; Miller 1958). There are American subcultures among racial and ethnic groups, among economic groups, and among people engaged in the same occupation. There are youth subcultures, subcultures of the old, of hippies, the poor, and of prison inmates. Each group's members are part of the main society, but much of their behavior is shaped by somewhat different symbolic systems unique to their immediate grouping. Subcultures develop because members of a group are somehow set apart from the majority of society. The factors that distinguish the group are usually apparent to outsiders and are what make insiders aware of their separate, special character.

The racial or ethnic background of people can be the foundation of subcultural traits. Racial and ethnic groups quite often have marked physical differences, such as the color of their skin, and because of their unique biographies and because of discrimination, their life-style and outlook on life often vary considerably from that of the majority. For instance, although most Americans today eat some of the same foods—hamburgers, fried chicken, pizza, Chinese food, or frozen, packaged dinners—only blacks prepare, consume, and enjoy "soul food" on a regular basis.

Likewise, Americans of Latin and Indian descent eat a lot more of their own traditional dishes than do any people outside their subculture. Despite the fact that in certain large cities and resort areas lox and bagels, corned beef, and pastrami have become favorites, only those with a Jewish background regularly prefer such foods to others and prepare numerous related dishes known to them and to few outsiders. Not just in food habits, but also in language, family life, political and religious views, and many other basic aspects of living, members of subcultures choose these unique cultural traditions, which may be just a little different from those of the general society, or almost completely unlike them.

For example, there are religious groups, such as the Amish and the Hasidic Jews, who follow their beliefs so closely that they are actually societies within our society. All their members wear one kind of clothing, cut their hair a certain way, do not send their children to public schools, usually live in entirely separate communities, and seldom, if ever, involve themselves in the social and political life of the rest of the nation. Yet religious differences need not lead to such total separation and differentiation. Many Protestants who consider themselves as devout as the Amish and many Jews who adhere to their religion without taking the extreme position of the Hasidim, look and act like most other Americans. The degree to which any factor will support subcultural distinctions depends on how important that factor is to the members, on how big a part it plays in their lives.

Subcultures and conflict between subcultures is a prominent feature of modern social life.

What encourages the development of a subculture is often beyond the control or choice of its members. This is usually true of subcultures based on age and economic necessity. Old people, for instance, often find themselves forced to live in ways different from those they lived when younger. Their beliefs and actions are, of necessity, shaped by the fact that they no longer have jobs, that they live on fixed incomes, that their families may no longer have a place for them, and—most important— that physical changes of aging have curtailed their activity. The subculture of the elderly thus may include the segregation of older people into neighborhoods having housing they can afford. Their political views will feature demands that Medicare be extended, inflation controlled, and public services be offered at reduced rates; even individuals who may have at one time opposed social security may, as senior citizens, share the attitude of their new subculture and call for larger social security benefits.

Various groups of young people may also be members of subcultures because of their age. Teen-agers are usually heavily influenced by the values of their subculture. Instead of thinking about what the adult world expects of them, they are more likely to try to meet the standards of their adolescent friends. They will be keenly aware of what clothes are "in," will try to choose the right hair style, and know all the latest hits by the current music superstar. If they are out of high school, they will still be influenced by the age group with which they spend most of their time. If in college, they will encourage each other to be political activists,

seek social popularity and membership in a fraternity or sorority, or became nonactivist dropouts. Young people care more about what those in their group think than about the opinions of their parents or society in general. They seek acceptance within their age group and so share the subcultural values and beliefs of that group—hoping to be liked, accepted, and respected. The process takes place generation after generation; the particular features may vary, but the pressure to conform to the standards of a youth subculture is fairly consistent.

As economic circumstances change (or if people find themselves trapped by economic reality), one's economic subculture assumes tremendous importance. Poor people obviously have a life-style quite unlike that of the rich. Although everyone may share, for example, the general American value of success and achievement, the impact of that value in people's lives will depend to a great extent on their economic position and power. For skid-row vagrants, success can mean panhandling enough change to buy some cheap wine. For those on welfare, success can mean getting all the public benefits to which they feel they are entitled or receiving the training needed to find a well-paying job. For people whose income is strictly limited, supplying themselves and their families with enough food, clothing, and a decent place to live is a great achievement. The meaning of economic factors clearly depends on the perspective that one's relative affluence creates. Consequently, the subculture of the so-called "jet set" reveals beliefs and norms far different from those of less well-off people and from most of society in general. For the jet setters, it is not enough to own a car, one must have an expensive, unique touring machine. Wearing fine clothes alone does not bring acceptance; one's apparel must come from only the most fashionable clothing designer. Group members are judged by what they do, how they do it, whom they know, and with whom they are seen. The wealthy are not any freer than the poor when it comes to the pressure exerted upon them by their own subculture. They simply hold different cultural standards to which they conform.

Most of everyday life is played out within the framework of subcultures. Because people spend so much time at their jobs, occupational subcultures take on great importance. As a result, the way police officers spend their time—even off duty—and whom they have as friends, will be influenced by the cultural storehouse that emerges while on the job. Their attitudes toward such things as conformity, authority, drug use, and political activism will be quite different from the outlook of, say, doctors, lawyers, trade unionists, or college instructors, whose occupational subcultures give them different beliefs and values.

People who are physically separated from the rest of society develop subcultures with characteristics sharply different from the rest of society. Prison inmates must learn to behave partly in response to the rules of the institution and even more in terms of the pressures of other inmates, who enforce their standards by rewards and punishments that are inescapable in the close confines of the prison. Likewise, inhabitants of a small town must follow the standards of their community—wherein every-one knows almost everything about everybody else—or be excluded from many meaningful experiences. Local subcultures are common as are regional subcultures, such as those in the South, certain parts of New England, and the Midwest. When some people belong to a special group, like the military, the ministry, or professions with limited membership, they will spend most of their time with others like themselves and will tend to act and think more like those people than the typical members of American society at large.

When a subculture actually exhibits values, beliefs, and norms directly opposed to basic social expectations, the subculture might be termed a **counterculture** (Yinger 1960). For example, people who are part of the drug traffic, which includes heroin, whether as dealers or addicts, are members of the drug counterculture and probably the criminal counterculture. Those who set up communes with group marriage are following the standards of a counterculture because they refuse to organize their lives according to the values of most people in society.

Subcultures provide options for members of society; they permit people to live their own way, with ideas and beliefs that suit the nature of their background and experience better than society's general standards. But subcultures, and especially countercultures, can at times be forces pulling society apart, challenging cultural integration, and creating conflict among members of society. Therefore, subcultures, are part of the fundamental problem of all societies trying to achieve integration of behavior and values in the face of built-in conflicts.

CULTURAL INTEGRATION AND CONFLICT

The existence of subcultures is only one factor influencing the integration of a culture. The other concerns the degree of compatibility and consistency among a culture's components. Compatibility is never perfect among values, beliefs, and norms. A fully integrated culture would be one in which all members of society agreed on the meaning of all important terms, shared respect for all central ideas, and tried not to violate any fundamental rules. This comes close to achievement in some simple societies, but in large, complex societies like ours, people must learn to live with a degree of inconsistency. Because humans have such intricate brains, they are able to tolerate inconsistent beliefs. They employ mental defense mechanisms to keep things straight—rationalizing their conflicting ideas and segregating their feelings about some things they think or do from their responses to contrary beliefs or behavior.

We are all familiar with people who claim to believe deeply in freedom, equality, and democracy. But those same people will resist the efforts—even by people they love—to achieve equality and freedom from discrimination based on sex. Many people will energetically oppose attempts to integrate their neighborhoods or schools but will say that other people's resistance to racial integration is wrong. Incompatibility among values, beliefs, and norms is quite common, and people must struggle to find reasons for following one set of ideas that run counter to another they also want to support. Yet there is also a high degree of cultural integration at work in our society.

The following example is just one that might be presented to show how integrated cultural elements strengthen the foundations of a society. It deals with the way our cultural resources and ideas influence the ways we deal with the environment.

Because our language is an active one, it encourages us to think about the environment in active, manipulative terms, to see the environment as something to be used and exploited. We talk about nature as something to be overcome, controlled, figured out, and defeated in a great test of power that we must win. We think of the earth as an inexhaustible source of materials for our use—we change its face, plow it up, mine into it, change it with our creations. Our language is structured in ways that allow us to see the world as manipulatable. Values similarly allow this orientation toward the environment: activism, achievement, progress, pursuit of the good life and related elements of materialism, all stress controlling and manipulating the environment for human purposes. Beliefs, like the notion that economic growth is good, are evaluations about how things should be and prompt us to use the environment to achieve economic growth at the expense of serious depletion of resources and potential ecological disruption. The empirical belief that science and technology have virtually limitless power to control the environment encourages us to attempt, or approve the attempt, to achieve that control. We trust that more and bigger machines will solve problems created by machines used in the past. We have faith that polluting technology can be corrected by the development of antipollution devices. Even norms in specific contexts encourage manipulation and exploitation of the environment, nature, and our own personal resources. We establish work roles that perpetuate the idea that people should work hard, be industrious, thrifty with time, energy, and money. We give up a great degree of our freedom in our jobs, willingly subordinating our efforts with the assembly line, the time clock, or production deadlines. We see it as right and good to add our labor to that of all others altering the shape of the world in the great human campaign to produce more goods and services. Finally, we organize our society capitalistically, producing an economic system based on affluence, high rates of production, and access for the majority to the material goods produced through manipulation of the environment.

Of course, the purpose of this example is to emphasize the compatibility of the elements of our culture as they apply to this one aspect of reality—the way we approach the environment. On such individual matters, there may well be significant integration among our cultural resources, our values, beliefs, and norms. Such integration can give our social structure stability and continuity, but incompatibility and conflict are often equally influential in the everyday aspects of a culture.

For example, we can try to follow the norms of working hard and saving; and yet, in trying to acquire the material goods we associate with the good life that we all value, we can spend too much, get in debt, end up working to little purpose in an endless struggle to keep up. Our belief in the power of technology can break down in view of the reality of pollution, de-

humanization, and the tendency for the products of technology to start controlling people as much as they are controlled by them.

The other basic problem of cultural integration involves trying to fit subcultures into the society as a whole, despite the fact that they are always a potential source of conflict and disintegration. Sometimes it is possible to deal with subcultures by segregating them in time and space; that is, the society permits them their differences so long as their variant behavior is confined to places outside the main stream of social life or limited to times when people are not expected to be devoting themselves to activities approved by most of society. Thus, the subcultures of the young or very old are tolerated because they operate before or after those periods in the life cycle when people are supposed to follow the standards of general society. Communes will not be attacked as dangerously deviant if they operate out of sight of most people. Totally incompatible subcultures or countercultures, however—like those of criminals or even religious groups whose beliefs outrage general society—are likely to be massively repressed.

The threat of subcultures can sometimes be met by denying their differences and conflicts with the rest of society. In this way, the homosexual subculture is tolerated because people take the attitude that gays are not really different, they are just temporarily sick or misguided. And those who refuse to work, marry, or otherwise assume social responsibilities, can be treated like otherwise conforming people, and their conflict with society can be denied by saying they will eventually take jobs and settle down. This sort of social blindness is a com-

Conflict between subcultures often leads to efforts by the dominant culture to control the various subordinate cultures.

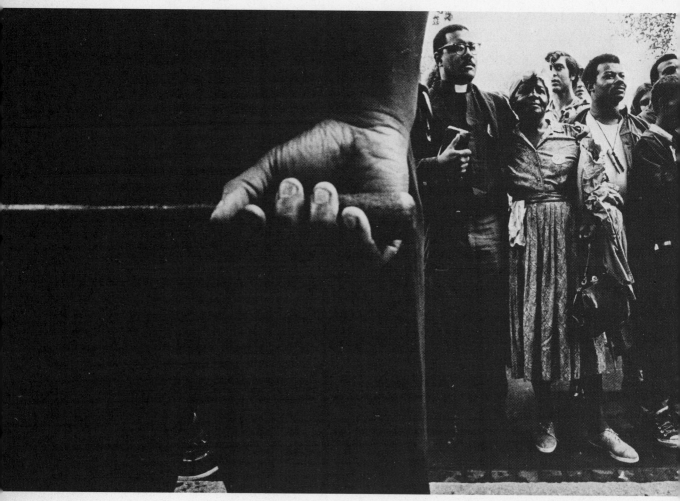

mon and seemingly necessary characteristic of those who wish to avoid facing the reality of cultural conflict. But on some occasions, the conflict can neither be ignored nor avoided.

When student radicals challenged the establishment in the 1960s and early 1970s, the actuality of their refusal to conform to com-

mon values was undeniable. They refused to serve in the armed forces, closed down major universities, demanded—and in many cases were given—a voice in the making of university policy, and in innumerable ways proved they were unwilling to follow the standards of behavior set for them by their elders. The great civil-rights struggle of the 1960s is a similar example. Despite massive action by police in

SUMMARY AND PREVIEW

communities maintaining those laws, and despite beatings, burnings, and murders to intimidate them, the black civil-rights advocates and their white supporters continued their resistance and demonstrations. The result was that they forced the society in general to recognize that the standards of one dominant part of society destructively conflicted with the values of the society as a whole. The civil-rights subculture challenged the white segregationist subculture, and the conflict was not diminished until the general society faced the implications of that conflict. The issue is far from being resolved, but neither is it ignored or denied.

Similar conflicts between subcultures and the dominant culture continue everywhere in America. Youth gangs pit their standards of right and wrong against rules the police must enforce. Women trying to get jobs for which they are qualified struggle for acceptance by men who try to maintain their traditional dominance of such professions as law, medicine, and college teaching and such occupations as fire fighting, construction work, and white-collar management.

At no one time will all aspects of a complex society be entirely integrated. There will always be conflicts between basic values, because belief in such values as progress are bound to conflict, at times, with values like freedom and equality, and individualism is bound to collide with the expectation that everyone should conform. Values, beliefs, and norms operate inside people to produce conflicts as well as compatibilities, and, of course, they also produce subcultures that by definition reveal differences that can inspire conflict.

It is humans' big brains that have, over millions of years of evolution, allowed them to create culture. Culture gave otherwise weak humans the capacity to adapt to their environment.

Although people use the word *culture* in numerous ways, and even sociologists have several definitions for it, the most useful definition views culture as a system of meaningful symbols that people in a society create and use to organize their affairs. This meaning encompasses two cultural systems: resources, such as language and technology, and constraints, including values, beliefs, and norms. The two systems interact and feed back on one another to produce different patterns of social organization. People draw upon cultural resources to fashion social organizations, and individuals and organizations are guided and controlled by ideas.

No two cultures are identical because they each have different resources in their cultural storehouse and each uses them in different ways. There are significant cultural variations within any given society because members of a society will use its cultural resources and be guided by its values, beliefs, and norms in various ways. This means that cultures must constantly struggle with the problem of cultural integration and conflict. Integration allows society to exist, but conflict is an ever-present fact of social life, especially in big and complex societies like the United States, where numerous subcultures provide behavioral and intellectual options to people.

In this chapter we have sometimes talked about culture as if it existed outside of people. We did this to make analysis of the concept more manageable, to permit us to see what culture is actually like without the distractions of examining it in actual situations. This is the approach that scientists must often use. Of course, if we look at the real world of actual people coping with life, we do not see a "thing" called culture floating over their heads constraining them. As our many examples have shown, culture guides and controls people because it is part of their mental imagery, and much of it is understood by them without their having to be told what it is. It is so thoroughly and completely bound up into human affairs that its power and influence often go unnoticed. This is why we have separated it and looked at it as if it existed outside human affairs. But it must be remembered that culture is created, altered, and maintained in society through concrete interactions between people and between groups of people.

It is the elaboration of culture that allows these interactions to occur. Culture is the cement of human social organization. Without culture we are like all the other animals who must depend on biological characteristics and instincts to guide behavior. Without it, the way we live would be impossible. Culture thus permits us to organize ourselves into societies; it holds us together through networks of learned behaviors and systems of ideas that influence the ways we act, feel, and think. The social organizations made possible by culture are the subject of sociological investigation and analysis. Most of this book is devoted to discovering the nature of such organizations and how they work in our lives. The following chapter deals with the ways basic social interactions create and sustain uniquely human social forms.

Key Terms

Culture: a system of meaningful symbols that people in a society create, store, and use to organize their affairs

Symbol: a sign that humans emit and use to represent ideas, objects, and others in their world

Systems of Symbols: symbols that are interrelated with each other and that give meaning and the capacity to interpret and make sense of objects or events

Meaning: what is capable of interpretation and over which a grouping of humans share common interpretations

Values: ideas or conceptions that people in a society share about what is good and bad or appropriate and inappropriate

Beliefs: ideas or conceptions that people hold about what should exist or what *actually does exist* in a *particular* social situation or context

Norms: expectations about what people are supposed to do, or how they are supposed to behave, in a particular social position or situation

Evaluative Beliefs: ideas or conceptions that people hold about what *should exist* in a *particular* social situation or context

Empirical Beliefs: conceptions that people hold about what actually *does exist in a particular* social situation or context

Ethnocentrism: the practice of viewing other societies and cultures in terms of the standards of one's own culture

Cultural Relativity: the scientific recognition that the values, beliefs, and other systems of symbols and patterns of behavior of a culture and society must be assessed in their own terms and that scientists must not impose their own values, beliefs, and other cultural components when examining a society

Subculture: a group of people who share certain common systems of symbols that distinguish them from the majority of people in a society

Counterculture: a group of people whose behavior and culture rejects that of the dominant society and culture

Review Questions

1. What makes humans unique as an animal species?
2. What is culture? What components of culture do sociologists study?
3. What are the dominant values of American society?
4. Why are there subcultures in large societies?
5. What are some of the problems of cultural integration and conflict that all societies must confront?

Suggested Readings

Becker, Howard. *The Outsiders*. New York: The Free Press, 1963.

Benedict, Ruth. *Patterns of Culture*. Boston: Houghton Mifflin, 1961.

Chagnon, Napoleon A. *Yanomamo: The Fierce People*. New York: Holt, Rinehart and Winston, 1968.

Farb, Peter. *Word Play*. New York: Knopf, 1973.

Fouts, Roger. "Language: Origins, Definitions and Chimpanzees." *Journal of Human Evolution* 3 (1974):475–482.

Lewis, Oscar. *The Children of Sanchez*. New York: Vintage Books, 1961.

Williams, Robin M. Jr. *American Society*. New York: Knopf, 1970, pp. 438–500; 580–609.

Yinger, Milton J. "Contraculture and Subculture." *American Sociological Review* 25 (October 1960): 625–635.

INTERACTION: THE BASIC SOCIAL PROCESS

PROLOGUE

Guiding Questions: What makes society possible? How do humans create culture and complex social systems? What is the process of interaction and how does it influence the course of our daily lives as well as the course of human affairs?

Chapter Topics

THE SIGNIFICANCE OF INTERACTION

In a species organized by cultural symbols rather than by instincts, interaction assumes new importance. We must actively construct our world and work at its maintenance or its alternation, and we must recognize, assess, and anticipate the responses of other people if we are to cooperate, or even come into conflict, with them. Unlike the lives of many animals programmed by instincts from birth, human life is possible because of the way we construct a world from our interactions; thus, interaction is the basis of culture and human organization. Without it we would be autistic, isolated, and dead, for it is through the construction of organization and culture from interaction that the human system is created, maintained, and changed.

Interaction between individuals can most simply be defined as *the process whereby individuals mutually influence each other and, in so doing, create, maintain, change, or terminate a pattern of joint action.* This means that people begin to interact with others soon after they are born. As needs are communicated through crying—or even more fundamentally just by carrying on natural infant functions that demand attention—adults interact with their young by picking them up, comforting them, feeding them, or changing their diapers. The child, as any parent knows, influences them and they influence the child, initiating a lifetime of interaction.

Interaction becomes increasingly complex and meaningful as people mature and become more aware of the world around them. As their perceptions sharpen and their ability to communicate improves, they are better equipped to inform others of their needs, desires, or intentions, to determine others' needs, wants, or intentions, and to respond appropriately to this communication. Consequently, in mature interaction individuals are conscious of their capacity to influence and be influenced by others, and they try to act in ways that will produce reciprocal responses that will benefit them most. Moreover, because interaction involves the joint action that underlies social organization, the more people interact the more familiar they become with what is expected of them as members of various social organizations (Stryker 1961; Shibutani 196).

Because humans are social animals, living with and depending on many other people, interaction is enormously important. It directly

THE PROCESS OF SOCIAL INTERACTION

and inescapably influences the quality of life; it determines how people will be treated, limits what they can do, makes them happy or keeps them from what they desire, fills their lives with joy and achievement or darkens it with sadness, inhibition, and defeat. Obviously, interaction is of major personal significance to each of us, but this is only part of what makes it "the basic social process." It is essential because society itself is built, maintained, and modified by social interaction, and society and culture could not exist without interaction (Blumer 1969).

As people interact, they forge the bonds that hold society together. As networks of such bonds are extended, strengthened, and perpetuated, the society and the cultural patterns of that society are given stability because people learn to act within, and according to cultural premises inherent in the varied social organizations that constitute society (Warriner 1970).

Each of us contributes to this basic process; we influence society and culture and are, of course, influenced by social and cultural forces that shape and direct our interaction. Thus, society depends on interaction, interaction depends on us, and we depend on interaction for our involvement in society and for the fulfillment of our needs and desires. The process is undeniably basic, and our understanding of it is central to building our knowledge of the human system.

Interaction is the basic social process and we, as interacting individuals, are the basic units in that process. Yet, even though we interact during most of our waking hours, we are so involved in the process that we seldom realize just what is happening. Our main interest, after all, is the outcome of interaction, not the process itself; that is, while we are interacting with others, what we really care about is getting a date or a job, impressing another person with our charm or intelligence, showing we are capable, worthy, confident, or attractive, and achieving whatever goal we sought through the initiated interaction. But as students of the human system we must somehow get outside ourselves and step back to look at the process; we must take the scientifically objective perspective that will allow us to discover the nature of interaction. This knowledge can supply us with important insights into what we are and what we can become in the social world we occupy.

We can begin to understand the process of interaction by looking at one of the most common interactions, one celebrated in song and story and familiar to almost everyone—boy meets girl. It can happen on a city street, in a classroom, at a party, anywhere—even in one's dreams. In the simplest terms, what happens?

Two people meet. They may be introduced by a third person or accidently make eye contact. Once they have seen each other, they make a conscious decision to continue the interaction; otherwise the encounter would end right at the start. Now they attempt to communicate in some way. One smiles, the other smiles back. They exchange names. She asks what his major is (or how he makes a living, or where he is from, or some other typical small-talk question), and he responds. Seeing that things are warming up, loosening up, one may move a little closer to the other. The communication continues—in words, gestures, facial expressions, body posture, and even physical contact—as they try to inform one another of how they feel and what they intend. Such communication can be subtle and quite reserved, never getting much beyond the stage of polite introductions. It can also be blatant and abrupt and develop quickly into a sexual encounter.

The interaction now requires that each try to figure out what the other is really after, to interpret the mutual communication. Obviously, if they have stated their intentions outright, little interpretation is called for. But usually people have to read intentions that are still hidden. They do this by mentally putting themselves in the other person's place to see what the other may be thinking. He might wonder if he is making a good impression, asking himself if she is really interested in him or just being courteous and cordial. As she listens to him, evaluates his expressions and actions, she tries to determine what he might do next. They watch each other carefully, both thinking about what they should do and attempting to understand what the other will do.

Before the interaction can go any further, the two people must decide what their behavior will be, and their decisions must be based on their reading of the other's communication and their evaluation of the other's intentions. So now each considers alternative lines of action, which takes the form of an imaginative rehearsal of what might happen. That is, each

constructs a series of mental images depicting the possible results of various forms of conduct.

For example, she might see herself staying with him for the next several hours, perhaps even spending the night with him, and believe that such involvement is justified by her attraction to him and her belief that he is sincerely interested in her. She might envision a lasting relationship filled with happy scenes, or she might feel he is worth getting to know better, but doubts that he really finds her attractive. So she will begin to rehearse mentally how she will break off the interaction. She might imagine the worst, seeing herself giving him her time and affection and coming away with nothing but disappointment if she lets the interaction go any further. These and, perhaps, other scenes will be played out in her mind before she decides how she will act. She will juggle her own feelings and her estimates of how he feels to produce a mental image with which she is comfortable.

He must also rehearse alternative lines of action. He might interpret what she has said and done so far as signs that she desires a long-term involvement. His mental images may include pleasurable moments in her company, leading to some permanent association, or he may be afraid to do anything that will lead to a strong commitment because he distrusts her, himself, or the durability of emotional relationships. Then again, he may only be interested in the fun that can be extracted from a single evening's contact and will picture the two of them enjoying the short-term intimate interaction. A variation on that image, however, could

*In counting relationships, the full range of
gestures—verbal and non-verbal—are used in the
process of interaction.*

involve his belief that she would want to extend the relationship over time, and so he may decide not to do anything that would get him tangled up in her emotional life. He, too, must mentally rehearse many alternative possibilities before making his next move.

The actions each will take involve how each has interpreted the other's communication and how each has evaluated the imagined results of various lines of conduct. They will act in ways that they hope or expect will produce re-

sponses by the other that will bring about the form of continued interaction they desire most.

For instance, he may decide that she has been reacting positively toward him, but he will adjust his response in accordance with what he wants or expects to happen next. He may merely ask for her phone number and say he will call her soon; he may invite her out for dinner later that week; or he may act immediately on her apparent interest in him by suggesting they go back to his apartment that night. It all depends on how eager he thinks she is, on how well he believes things will turn out, and on how involved he wants to get. He may be getting a negative reaction from her and simply say, "It was nice to meet you." The two would then part company, probably forever, and seek interactions elsewhere.

Her response will similarly be adjusted to what he has said and done and to what she thinks he feels and intends. If her desires do not mesh with her estimate of his plans, her response may well be to break off contact. But if they are both confident of mutual interest and attraction, the interaction will continue, be followed by more communication and responses adjusted to that communication, and a relationship will have been developed. The initial, basic interaction will have become a pattern of joint action built upon the physical contacts and mental evaluations of both parties.

This sort of interaction happens quite rapidly, and if it does not end with the decision to break off contact, the process starts over again and may be repeated many times, resulting in increasingly illuminating and meaningful responses. People have the ability to run through the entire process of a single episode of interaction in a matter of seconds. In fact, as they get to know one another better (and especially if they are close relatives or have known one another for a long time), the process becomes virtually automatic and almost instantaneous. What accounts for the speed of the process? What, in fact, is at the heart of the interaction process?

Interaction is a mental as well as a physical process, and its mental dimension is a reflection of the unrivaled capacities of the human mind. Other animals interact on a primitive level by responding to physical cues and in accordance with their biologically programmed instincts. When it is time for them to mate, they mate; they do not decide to do it because they really have no choice. The element of choice requires mental, rather than instinctual, control. Human beings have mental control because they are uniquely endowed with brains that allow them to interpret communication, to mentally rehearse alternative lines of conduct, and to adjust their responses in terms of their desires and their estimations of other individuals' feelings and intentions (Mead 1934; Dewey 1922). The basis of interaction, then, is the power of the human mind, and sociological analysis of interaction has been built on the scientific examination of how the mind contributes to interaction. The man who laid the foundation for the exploration of the relationship between mind and interaction was George Herbert Mead. A brief discussion of his central theory will amplify our understanding of the process of social interaction.

THE GENIUS OF GEORGE HERBERT MEAD

Mead (1863–1931) was one of sociology's early theorists. A philosopher by training, he developed a body of concepts for describing the relationship between society and the individual. He asked two of sociology's most fundamental questions: How does society shape the individual? And, conversely, how do individuals create and maintain society? He began his analysis with these questions, and the answers he found and the work of others who built upon his basic discoveries will be referred to in later chapters because his theories influenced many facets of sociological thought (Mead 1934, 1938).

One of Mead's central concepts is the notion of **role-taking** of "taking the role of the other." For centuries, scholars tried to figure out what enabled interacting individuals to adjust their behaviors in order to cooperate. Mead made the critical breakthrough in solving the problem with his concept of role-taking.

Mead observed that all humans use **gestures;** that is, they communicate information about their internal states (feelings, attitudes, wants, intentions) through signs or signals. All humans who are physically and mentally unimpaired are able to interpret these gestures. Thus, every person is constantly using as well as reading gestures. By reading and interpreting other people's gestures, individuals can put themselves in another's place; they can assume the perspectives, attitudes, dispositions, and other internal states of those with whom they are to interact. Likewise, by using gestures, they can inform others of their internal dispositions; they can communicate what they feel, need, desire, or intend. Without this capacity to take the role of the other, which allows people to adjust their responses by taking other peo-

George Herbert Mead (1863–1931) synthesized currents of thought into a coherent picture of the relationship between individuals and society.

ple's viewpoints into account, humans could not interact.

Role-taking gives conscious control and direction to human interaction; people do not interact like so many living billiard balls that bounce randomly off one another. They are able to steer and aim themselves in their contacts with others. This ability is a natural outgrowth of their primate heritage. Human brains, eyes, hands, and erect posture have given them highly evolved mechanisms of perception and understanding. Whereas animals

Our patterns of interaction are shaped by our primate heritage. Note the similarity between human and chimpanzee interaction.

interact by following the irresistible dictates of their instincts, which have been programmed into their genes, humans construct and control their interactions. This "taking the role of the other" puts people in a position to adjust their responses so they can cooperate, interact, and establish patterns of joint action (Turner 1962, 1968).

The social and cultural evolution of early humans depended upon the mutual reading of gestures, role-taking, and adjusted responses that permitted them to work together to survive as a species. Mead labeled these and related mental capacities **mind.** Mind is a dis-

tinguishing human characteristic and is at the heart of the interaction process. In our earlier discussion of the human ability to use and understand symbols (language, gestures, and other organized systems of meaning) we saw the mind at work. To Mead, symbolic communication and role-taking combine with the capacity ""to imaginatively rehearse alternative lines of conduct" to produce the process of adjustment that underlies social interaction.

More than any other animals, humans can weigh various alternatives. They can do this quickly, quietly, and covertly in their minds, which enables them to anticipate the likely outcome of each conduct, especially the reactions of others with whom they are role-taking, of those whose viewpoints they are considering during interaction. Such **imaginative rehearsal** of the possible results of each course of action permits them to make **adjusted responses** to others by selecting that conduct that they hope will achieve a desired response from others and a favorable resolution of the interaction.

As a species lacking specific genetic, instinctual programming to direct our actions, we must have alternative mechanisms for interaction and cooperation. Mead was the first to adequately conceptualize the most fundamental mechanism of human interaction. He identified it as mind operating through mutually understood symbolic communication, role-taking, and imaginative rehearsal of behavior to produce an adjusted response. Building upon Mead's profound insights, sociologists have examined the intimate relationship between interaction and social organization. They have come to realize that to understand society one first must understand the nature of interaction among individuals. Mead's theories give us a starting point for the systematic exploration of interaction.

EXPANDING ON MEAD'S THOUGHT

Let us begin with a few simple facts: interaction occurs over time; it is an unfolding process. At each point in this process, cultural, social, psychological, biological, and ecological forces influence what occurs or will occur as the interaction proceeds.

It should be obvious that in our boy-meets-girl interaction example the process seemed to run through stages and was subject to many influences. Now, by carefully examining the stages of interaction and the forces influencing interaction, we can expand and enrich the simplified picture we have already drawn of the process.

The Stages of Interaction

Interaction is a process: events are followed by other events. To analyze this process, we must impose some concepts that highlight certain of its stages. In so doing, we must recognize that with our concepts we are simplifying and imposing a sense of discrete stages in what is actually a continuous flow of events. Yet, this imposition can help us better understand this flow.

Interaction can be seen as moving through five general stages:

1. *Mutual awareness*—at least two, and perhaps more, people become aware of each other's presence and decide to interact or to avoid contact.
2. *Attempts to communicate*—these mutually aware individuals signal their intentions and dispositions and give clues to how they will act by using gestures (through language, facial expressions, posture, movements, and the like).

3. *Mutual reading of gestures*—each person actively tries to figure out what the other wants and intends. By making an effort to take the role of the other, each is better able to understand the other's gestures and to get a clearer idea of that person's internal disposition. Role-taking helps reveal how that person will act and what reciprocal actions are expected or desired.

4. *Covert, imaginative rehearsal of alternative conduct*—on the basis of their reading of gestures and role-taking, both individuals think about, imagine, and rehearse what will result from various forms of action they might take.

5. *Adjusted response*—from the options examined in imaginative rehearsal, the interacting individuals select a course of action and offer a response that they believe will achieve the desired form of interaction by eliciting appropriate responses from the other.

Some interactions show these stages more clearly than others. In comfortable situations in which one has been with the interacting individuals before, the stages are less discrete and tend to blend smoothly into one another, and individuals are unlikely to be conscious of these mental operations. An old married couple is one of the best examples of this unconscious process. They read each other's gestures almost before the gestures are made. The slightest grunt or mumble can have enormous significance, although only for them. Each knows the other so well that they are both aware of every possible course of action the other may take; each has become so accustomed to the other's needs and desires that each is almost constantly taking the other's roles. Although not all their adjusted responses provide both with results entirely to their liking (marital discord and the high divorce rate attest to such results), they have found ways of interacting that sustain their continuing joint action.

In contrast, the stages stand out most and individuals become keenly aware of the process of interaction when they encounter one another for the first time. We can return to the boy-meets-girl example to illustrate.

They are strangers; they only become aware of one another when someone else introduces them or when they happen to come into contact. Once they are aware of each other's presence and have decided to interact, they enter the communication stage.

Attempts to communicate begin as both use gestures that provide the other with clues to their feelings and intentions. Communication continues into the stage where mutual reading of gestures takes place. Had they been old friends, each would have had a pretty good idea of what the other had in mind. But, as strangers, their initial interaction depends on careful reading of gestures and role-taking.

She has to put herself in his place to get some idea of the nature of his interest in her. Is he simply on the make—a cool, smooth operator who views her as just another potential conquest—or is that gleam in his eye the first sign of sincere interest and affection? He must do likewise. Playing her role, he tries to figure out how he appears to her and what is in her mind. Is she cold and aloof? Is her seemingly warm smile a practiced gesture holding no particular meaning for him, or is it the earliest sign of genuine feeling? Neither knows for sure what the other is really thinking, which makes this stage of interaction so important. The mutual reading of gestures and role-taking give them something to go on, breeding confidence in their ability to interact so as to achieve desirable goals.

They enter the fourth stage of interaction as they begin rehearsing, in their minds, conduct that seems appropriate in view of the gestures they have read and the perspectives they have acquired through role-taking. If he has come to believe she is eager to know him better, his covert imaginings are likely to include thoughts of him asking her for a date, of her accepting, and of the two of them spending more time together in the immediate future. She might have become convinced he is hustling her, and her covert images of the outcome of their interaction might be filled with pictures of an active and energetic romance ending quite soon. She might find this appealing, or she can rehearse such a scenario only as a way of comparing it to others she likes better. In any case, in this stage of interaction, both will be running mini-motion pictures of things they think could be but that, for the moment, exist only in their minds. Whether or not these covert images can be translated into reality will depend on their adjusted responses in the final stage of interaction.

Adjusted response completes this episode of interaction. Of all the conduct alternatives they have covertly rehearsed, they both select their own course of action, one they believe will bring the most desirable results, the one that will best fit their intentions and that will prompt the other to respond most fittingly.

If they have read each other's gestures correctly and have successfully taken each other's roles, this instance of interaction will end favorably. They will have increased their awareness of each other; they will begin another round of interaction; and this time they will be able to communicate more precisely about their internal dispositions and intentions. Their reading of additional gestures will be easier; each will be able to take the other's role with greater ease and certainty; their imaginative rehearsal of alternative conduct should be more accurate; and their future adjusted responses are likely to mesh better with their mutual desires and needs. Each succeeding interaction will comprise all five stages, but the participants will run through them more quickly and less self-consciously than they did in their first encounter.

The Parameters of Interaction

The process of interaction as described may appear somewhat mechanical and inescapable, but it is not. True, if people were no more than physical objects completely subject to the laws of interaction, they might well have no choice but to experience each interaction as a series of inevitable stages. But every interaction is subject to variable forces that shape and direct how people interact. Some of these forces are largely outside human control, but others are introduced into the process by the individuals themselves. Because these forces influence interaction in so many ways, they give people numerous options about what they can and will do. The nature and operation of these different influences obviously play a critical part in interaction, and understanding them can greatly enrich our appreciation of the meaning of social interaction.

Every stage of interaction is subject to psychological, social, cultural, biological, and ecological forces; they shape and direct the behavior of each interacting individual. The exact nature of their influence depends on their combined impact, and no two people should be expected to respond identically to them in similar circumstances.

Ecological Parameters. Ecological forces are readily identifiable. The physical arrangement of things must always be taken into account during interaction. For example, one cannot interact with someone who, because of distance and spatial arrangements, is simply too far away. Similarly, at a crowded political rally, intimate interaction with the speaker on the rostrum is not possible. Ecological forces can encourage or inhibit interaction insofar as they throw people together or keep them apart.

Biological Parameters. Biological forces can also aid or interfere with interaction. We are biological creatures with drives and instincts, with specific abilities and limitations. All living beings have basic needs for food, drink, sex, adequate space in which to live, and, usually, the company of others like themselves. These instincts inspire many interactions and influence what we become aware of, how we communicate, and how we respond. Moreover, our interactions depend on the biological equipment we possess. Our keen eyes, sensitive hands, and erect posture influence how and to what degree we become aware of the world

and each other. They are our tools for interaction; and, of course, our special mental skills allow us to use those tools and direct every move we make during interaction. Most important, our brains give us the capacity for language and the manipulation of symbols, without which our interactions would resemble many encounters among animals—devoid of imagination, role-taking, true sympathy, and the freedom to choose what we wish to do.

It is important to remember that the ecological arrangements and biological forces are important. They are fairly easy to identify: we know whether we are hungry or driven by sex; we know that on a crowded subway train interactions are likely to be quite different from those at a quiet dinner for two. Although ecological and biological influences are always at work and impossible to ignore, they are not what makes human interaction special. After all, every animal is also subject to them, and, in fact, all interaction except that between humans and perhaps a few other animals is controlled by ecological and biological forces. Other, purely human forces influence the way we interact, and it is with them that we must be particularly concerned. It is the psychological, social, and cultural forces that are of greatest significance to sociologists and students of the human system.

Psychological Parameters. Psychological forces involve personality traits: motives, self-conceptions, personal styles, and the like (Hewitt 1976). Everything that makes each of us unique individuals can play a part at each stage of every interaction. Personality is what makes people different and special, and it enters into all encounters with others whose own personalities it must contend with if the interaction is to proceed (Goffman 1959).

Social Parameters. Human life means living in a world of other people, a world of groups, rules, regulations, power relationships—that is, in a world of composed social forces. Most interactions must be played out within social structures such as kinship and organizations. How people interact is influenced by their position in these structures, by their status, age, sex, experience, and, especially, by their relationship to those with whom they interact.

Cultural Parameters. Cultural traits set humans apart from all other beings, and cultural forces are uniquely influential in regulating our interactions. How we interact is largely determined by the idea systems of our culture—by the values, norms, and beliefs. The humanness of our interactions is based on our possession of language and the ability to manipulate symbols that are resources of our culture. Culture gives us the capacity to interact meaningfully with others who are also equipped with ideas and the power to process information. But in giving us this capacity, it constrains how we interact and is thus another parameter of interaction.

Figure 1 provides a simple, diagrammatic picture of the influence of these three critical forces on each stage of interaction. By referring to this diagram and by considering the following examples, we can better visualize the way psychological, social, and cultural factors shape the course of interaction.

Returning to the example of the boy and girl meeting for the first time, we can ask: What are some of the ways psychological, social, and cultural forces might influence the stages of the boy-and-girl interaction?

If either's personality is dominated by shyness, the interaction may never begin at all, because although they become aware of one another, the shy one will decide to avoid contact. Similar psychological forces, however, can ensure that the interaction will begin. For instance, if he sees himself as a ladies' man, he may be compelled to strike up a conversation. If she is self-assured and enjoys the give-and-take of such intersexual encounters, she will welcome his advances.

Social forces will also play a part in the process. Obviously, if they are brother and sister, the nature of their kinship relation will strictly control how they interact. Likewise, if they are part of the same organization—if one is the boss and the other the subordinate—whether they begin the interaction and how far and in what direction it will go must take that relationship into account. Power relationships and social status can facilitate or prevent smooth interaction. If the individuals are of equal status, they will have, by definition, much in common and should get along rather well. But say she is Princess Grace and he is a student traveling in Monaco. They are unlikely to meet, would probably not become mutually aware of one another, and even if they did, he would have a very hard time taking her role to figure out what her intentions are.

Cultural forces have an equally great impact. If she has been raised to believe certain behavior is not appropriate, then certain of his advances may force her to respond by ending the interaction. If he believes that there are only

Figure 1: The Process of Interaction

**FORCES INFLUENCING
THE COURSE OF INTERACTION**

STAGES OF INTERACTION

psychological
social
cultural

1. Mutual awareness:
individuals become aware of each other's
presence and decide to interact or to avoid
contact.

psychological
social
cultural

2. Attempts to communicate:
individuals use gestures—language, facial
expressions, posture, etc.—in an effort to present
their intent and dispositions.

psychological
social
cultural

3. Mutual reading of gestures:
individuals seek to put themselves in the other's
place—to take the role of the other—as part of
the process of trying to see and understand other
people's gestures and to figure out their
intentions and internal dispositions.

psychological
social
cultural

4. Covert, imaginative rehearsal:
individuals think about, imagine, alternative lines
of conduct on the basis of their role taking and
reading of gestures.

psychological
social
cultural

5. Adjusted response:
individuals select and emit a response which
they hope or expect will achieve the desired form
of interaction by eliciting appropriate responses
from the other.

"good" and "bad" women, who can be distinguished by how they respond during intimate interaction, then her eagerness to interact may be taken by him to mean she is "easy," when in fact she is simply polite or just liberated. The cultural values and beliefs they possess will determine how—indeed whether or not—they take each other's roles and select the appropriate responses to make their interaction mutually meaningful.

Interaction Among Chimpanzees: Speculations on Our Primate Heritage

In Chapter 3 we noted that chimpanzees could learn to use language. In their natural habitat, however, they do not appear to employ language. Although they may have the rudimentary capacity for language, their environment places no pressures for the development of the more elaborate patterns of social organization that the use of language allows. Yet, chimps and all other primates communicate with gestures. We might be advised to review briefly some of the communication processes among chimps, if only to provide speculation on what our ancestors might have been like as they lived on the savannah. By comparing our gesturing capacities with chimps, we can see how unique human interaction is and why it reveals the form that it does.

In these pictures we can see a few examples of the many gesturing patterns of chimps. Note the heavy

reliance upon facial, vocal, and arm-body movements. Humans use facial and arm-body movements to communicate their internal states and to take roles—a clear debt to our primate heritage. Imagine, for example, how it would be to interact with someone who used no gestures, but words. It would be *unhuman* interaction, much like interacting with a robot. Our complex vocal and language abilities are the only form of gesturing not seen in chimp interaction. Language apparently had selective advantage on the savannah as more closely organized bands were needed to deal with predation and the need to coordinate hunting activities. Without these selective pressures for language, interaction as we know it and the creation of elaborate patterns of human organization would not have been possible.

Chimpanzees do not use verbal language in the human sense, but they employ gestures in much the same way as humans. Note the reliance upon hand, facial, and vocal gestures in these pictures. Humans employ the same gesturing techniques.

SUMMARY AND PREVIEW

It would be impossible to talk about society and culture if individual interactions did not take place between millions of people in all sorts of settings. There would be no society if people did not interact to forge the basic bonds that connect them to one another and that make social organizations work. There would be no culture if people did not use their powers of symbolic communication and did not create, and then depend on, values, beliefs, and norms. It would be impossible to study the obvious manifestations of society and culture, such as families, political systems, laws, communities, social classes, religions, unless we understood that this basic process of interaction—this common yet remarkably complex phenomenon—is at the heart of all we do as social creatures.

In Chapter 3 we saw how certain biological attributes of primates, and especially human primates, made possible social and cultural elaborations. Our brains, hands, eyes, erect posture gave us what we needed to move from apelike to humanlike to fully human. Humans survived biologically by evolving socially and culturally, which depended on developing interaction skills.

In Chapter 4 we spoke of culture as the cement of human social organization; we can now see that interactions are the bricks. Here we have concentrated on the smallest bricks, interactions between individuals. But larger units—groups, institutions, communities, organizations, even nations—also interact and are subject to the same influences affecting the interacting individuals who constitute the membership of all such social units. Ecological, biological, psychological, social, and cultural forces constrain and direct interaction at all levels, and that interaction, in turn, influences our ecological, biological, psychological, social, and cultural destiny.

Society is an imposing edifice. We have now examined the interactional processes that go into the making of complex patterns of social organization. We are now ready to begin our exploration of those larger patterns. In Chapter 6 we will identify the basic forms of social organization. We will learn what makes such complex social patterns possible by studying the fundamental components of social systems. We will see how people, over time, create and modify social organizations to meet their personal and group needs. In Chapter 7 we will find out what makes people more or less willing to participate in these intricate arrangements of their own creation. And in Chapter 8 on deviance, we will examine how and why people sometimes have difficulty adjusting to patterns of social organization.

Key Terms

Interaction: the process whereby individuals (and other types of social units) mutually influence each other and, in so doing create, maintain, change, or terminate a pattern of joint action

Role-taking: the process whereby actors mutually interpret each other's gestures, putting themselves in each others' places and interpreting others' dispositions to act

Gestures: signs or signals—verbal, facial, bodily—that people emit and use as a basis for interpreting others' dispositions and intentions

Mind: the capacity of humans to designate each other, mentally constuct alternative lines of conduct, inhibit inappropriate responses, and select a desired response

Imaginative Rehearsal: G. H. Mead's term for describing the process of imagining the consequences of alternative lines of conduct

Adjusted Responses: actions of individuals that occur after role-taking and imaginative rehearsal and that lead to cooperation among actors

Review Questions

1. Why is interaction the basic social process?
2. What are the stages of interaction?
3. What important insights did George Herbert Mead have about the interaction process?

Suggested Readings

Goffman, Erving. *Interaction Ritual.* New York: Doubleday, 1967.

———. *The Presentation of Self in Everyday Life.* New York: Doubleday, 1959.

Shibutani, Tamotsu. *Society and Personality.* Englewood Cliffs: N.J.: Prentice-Hall, 1961.

Warriner, Charles K. *The Emergence of Society.* Homewood, Ill.: The Dorsey Press, 1970.

SOCIAL ORGANIZATION: THE CREATION OF SOCIAL STRUCTURE

PROLOGUE

Guiding Questions: How is society created? How does interaction result in diverse social forms? What are the basic social forms of the human system? How are they related to each other?

Chapter Topics

Interactions create and maintain social bonds among people. The bonds are sometimes very simple and constitute little more than friends informally enjoying each other's company, but they often become complex in modern societies. Human have created giant cities, huge bureaucracies, industrial economies, and other monolithic structures that impinge upon our lives. We can see, then, that humans organize themselves into different types of social forms. However, even the most complex is maintained by interactions, and we will require new concepts to comprehend the diversity and complexity of the social patterns that emerge from, and are maintained by, these interactions.

We are all familiar with social organization, although many of us probably do not have very clear ideas about its structure and how it affects us. It influences us throughout our entire lives, affecting virtually every thought and action. Our participation within this organized social matrix occurs in a variety of ways. We are members of families; we become assimilated into various peer groups; and we are involved in different school systems. Even the observance of various laws constitutes a way social organization affects our lives. Although it acts as a constraining force upon people, channeling their behavior patterns, their values, and their personalities, it is also a resource. The evolution of social organization is what enabled our early primate cousins to survive on the African savannah, a new and potentially hostile environment (see Chapter 3). By developing a different mode of social organization, they were able to adapt to the enormously different conditions of life that the African savannah presented.

This chapter will outline the concepts sociologists use in trying to understand human patterns of social organization. It describes the majesty, complexity, and diversity of social organizations, which is what distinguishes human beings from all other animal forms—not culture alone, but what culture has allowed us to do: create incredibly complex ways of organizing ourselves socially.

THE BASIC "BUILDING BLOCKS" OF SOCIETY

Social organization is a general term used to describe the structure of human social relations. As the term **structure** implies, social organization must be "built" from more elementary "pieces." Sociologists have developed three interrelated concepts to denote these more elementary units that, when combined, describe social structures: *statuses, roles,* and *norms.*

Statuses

Imagine yourself in a situation in which you are able to observe a fair number of people in a detached, largely objective way—as a spectator, in other words. The situation could be anything: a school classroom, a club meeting, or even a party. In any of these social situations, you can observe many different details about the interactions that are taking place. In the classroom, for example, the professor interacts with the students in a very distinctive way. Posture, gestures, and tone of voice will all convey somewhat implicitly the status of professor. The students will also demonstrate their own status as students. For example, they might dress in an academically casual manner, whereas the professor might be expected to dress in some style befitting to his or her own status. These are all popular stereotypes, of course, but they are useful in describing the clues we use to determine a persons' position in a particular social context.

What exactly is status, then, aside from those social clues that help us to perceive them? **Status** can be defined as *a position in society, integrated within a network of positions, in which individuals are able to see where they fit into the social scheme.* Although the word *status* connotes something elevated or privileged, in sociology it is stripped down to refer only to that position an individual holds in a social system.

The concept of status has many implications. We have already touched on the fact that people tend to manifest their status by what they say and do and how they express themselves in more subtle ways. For example, a high-level business executive will show patterns of behavior that conform, to a greater or lesser extent, to what most of us might imagine: $300 suits, a booming, decisive voice and a strikingly well-tailored figure, a bone-crushing handshake, and other intimidating gestures. By contrast, a lower-level, white-collar employee in the very same business environment will show quite a different set of gestures: deference and respect. In general, relationships to other employees will be considerably different from those of the executive in a position of power.

Another implication is the nature of a relationship among status positions. Many positions are highly interrelated—that is, they derive meaning only in relation to another. A father, for example, could never *have* that status unless he had a child; there is no husband without a wife. The position of, say, a supervisor in a factory is made so by the fact that the rest of the workers take orders from that person. *There is almost no status position that one can occupy that does not bear some relation to another status position.* The statement strengthens our definition in which we said each status position exists in a network of positions.

How does one attain a status position? We can easily describe two polar ways, recognizing that there are many gradations between these extremes: a status position can either be as-cribed, or it can be achieved. **Ascribed status** positions include sex, race, and religion—any factor with which we are born that determines the status we can occupy. The principal ele-ment in an ascribed status is that we are more or less *born into it.* An **achieved status** comes through personal effort; that is, an individual works to attain a particular position. Most occupations in industrial societies are achieved, with the exception, perhaps, of the young man who becomes the president of a company because his father owns it. Nepotism notwithstanding, such positions as banker, pol-itician, artist, writer, doctor, lawyer, and sol-dier are, in general, *achieved.* People en-deavored in some way to occupy these posi-tions, to make them integral to their lives. The methods employed to achieve a desired status can vary as much as the human personality. One might take a highly systematic approach because it might be absolutely necessary, as in the case of becoming a physician. A would-be physician must plan a rigorous regimen of education. Other approaches might be less than systematic, perhaps even chaotic and illogical. Many artists and writers sometimes have to suffer through jobs and other distrac-tions before they finally start to make their living through that status position to which they have been aspiring.

Most people, of course, usually hold a num-ber of status positions simultaneously. A man can be a son, a father, a husband, an engineer, and a member of a community club. Some of these positions are ascribed, some achieved. Some of the achieved positions can be deter-mined, or thwarted, by those which are as-cribed. For example, a woman may be denied a promotion to a position of managerial power because she is a woman. People usually call

attention to the fact that an ascribed status po-sition might not jibe socially with a particular achieved status position. If a man is a lawyer, we call him, simply, a lawyer. But if a woman has that position, we usually think of her as a *woman* lawyer, as though the word *woman* is needed to call attention to what some might consider a social anomaly. Age, too, can act as an ascribed status necessary to become in-volved in an achieved status position. One has to reach the age of 18 to have the status position encompassed in the right to vote. The legal drinking age, also, fits into this category; most states designate 21 as the legal drinking age, whereas others have lowered it to 18.

Thus, we can see that the concept of status denotes where we are located within the larger social scheme. The concept allows us to visual-ize the links between people and society. As such, it is fundamental to understanding peo-ple and the larger patterns of social organiza-tion in which they are implicated.

Roles

If status indicates where we are located, then the concept of **role** can be defined as *the aggregate of those gestures, manners of dress, and other patterns of behavior that are man-ifested by those in a particular status position.* For example, a job can be seen as a status position, whereas the actual performance of work is the role. A role is the way people behave in a given status position. (Linton 1936; Davis 1948).[1]

---

[1]For a somehat broader definition of role, see Ralph H. Turner (1962, 1968). For comprehensive over-views of role analysis, see: Biddle and Thomas (1966); Gross, Mason, and McEachern (1958); Nei-man and Hughes (1951); Sarbin (1954).

Thus, our discussion of the clues that help us to perceive differences in statuses among people was actually a discussion of the roles we play in each status position. The student who listens to the professor, takes notes, asks questions, and sits quietly throughout the lecture, is playing the *role* associated with the status of student. In the same way, everything that the professor does in the context of the classroom is playing the role of that status position. Role is the *dynamic* element of statuses.

It is possible for one status position to carry with it several roles. For example, a lawyer would fill one role in relation to his or her client, as well as roles differing in certain ways in relation to colleagues or judges. An array of different roles that cluster about one basic status position is called a *role set* (Merton 1968, pp. 422–423). The existence of multiple roles associated with a single status has alerted sociologists to the possibility of **role conflict** in which the enactment of one role prevents obligations of other roles from being met. For example, a working mother with young children is often placed in role conflict. She must assume the status of worker and perform in this role, and while she works, she may violate, at least in her mind, her wife and mother roles. A related problem is **role strain** (Goode 1960). This concept refers to a situation in which a person has difficulty in coping with the various demands of a particular role. Such a situation can occur in the family, on the job, or anywhere in which there is a network of statuses. A good illustration is found in work roles, such as a foreman who must stand between higher management and lower employees. He is expected to represent the objectives and wishes of management, yet at the same time keep on

good, close terms with those employees under him. In this situation a classic conflict of interests can arise, causing role strain. Role strain, then, occurs when those expectations normally associated with a status position become ambiguous or self-contradictory. Role strain can also occur if an individual is simply unable to meet the demands of the role behavior of a status position. Any failure in life exemplifies this: a failed marriage, the loss of a job because of incompetence, or an estrangement between friends.

Norms

Much of what we engage in as individuals is idiosyncratic. Since every personality is unique, many actions and types of behavior displayed by different people are also unique. Indeed, existence would be dull if the social world were not invested with a high level of human diversity. However, in order for social organization to remain intact and for the humans as a species to survive, we still must be willing to adhere to **norms** (Williams 1970). As we indicated in Chapter 4, norms are rules that people follow. In effect, norms are simply patterns of *expected behavior, behavior accepted by a consensus as being the best way people should act in a given situation.* People must be able to anticipate or count on consistent and predictable responses from others in various social situations; and although a certain flexibility in society is perhaps necessary, a good measure of stability is also required. Norms provide one source of stability.

Norms are evident in the most mundane activities of life. In simply making a telephone call, we follow norms by modeling what we say along the lines of accepted telephone etiquette and courtesy. We abide by norms in such situations because if interaction is to be rewarding and socially useful, it must follow marginally familiar patterns of expression. Without the existence of basic norms, which invest interactions with this kind of familiarity, we would never know what to expect from other people, what to anticipate, and society would run on fear and distrust rather than on fundamental human understandings.

However, norms can vary considerably from one culture to another. In the Greek and Roman civilizations, homosexuality was practiced openly and with complete social approval. But in our culture norms generally dictate that these activities are deviant and abnormal.

Different norms also vary in different social contexts. Thus, they conform to the nature of a particular situation. It would not be normative behavior, for instance, to be laughing at a funeral or to be having sex in a public place. Thus, we have established norms: there is a *particular* time and a *particular* place to express certain kinds of behavior.

Norms also vary over time. For example, in the 1960s, long hair on men was symbolically feared as representing a radical, revolutionary movement. Now, more than a decade later, nobody really pays much attention to long hair, or at least people no longer stigmatize a long-haired male as a "hippie" or "revolutionary" to the extent that they did in the past.

Norms also vary in intensity. Some are more strictly enforced than others. For example, certain sexual taboos such as incest are dealt with by society with relative severity. Other norms pertaining to sexual behavior have been relaxed, such as the notion that a girl should remain a virgin until she gets married.

Not only do norms vary in intensity, they also vary in terms of their power to influence our feelings and perceptions. For example, we can feel guilt or remorse if we have transgressed a norm, such as committing some crime or behaving inappropriately in a particular situation. A death in the family almost always evokes sadness and depression for the other members. Similarly, norms tell us we should not stare at a crippled or physically deformed person; we are to perceive them as though they are no different from anyone else.

Perhaps the most remarkable aspect of normative behavior is how relatively unconscious or automatic it is. Naturally, if a norm is so strong that it creates a real moral dilemma for a person, then there is hardly anything automatic about dealing with it or enacting it. But in most instances, such as raising one's hand in a classroom before speaking or eating dinner with silverware instead of one's hands, behavior is almost automatic. We do not *think* about the norms, we simple conform to them. Such is the power of norms over us. Because of their power, some degree of stability and orderliness is possible in the human system.

Working backwards over these basic concepts, then, we will briefly redefine these three building blocks of society and show their relations to one another. Norms are rules or guidelines about expected patterns of behavior. Roles are the aggregate of gestures, manners of speech and dress, and other patterns of behavior manifested by people in a status. And finally, statuses are the social positions that people occupy in a social system.

THE CREATION OF SOCIETY:
the organization of statuses, roles, and norms

In a sense, we can visualize society as the sum total of all the possible combinations and permutations among statuses occupied by individuals, the roles they play to realize or express those statuses, and the norms that regulate and guide how a role will be enacted. However, to do so would inhibit our understanding of social organization; for in reality there are so many different combinations of statuses, roles, and norms involving the almost numberless status positions, so many different shades and nuances of each role enactment, and so many variations in normative standards that to limit ourselves to these three would ultimately confuse rather than clarify.

Statuses, roles, and norms describe the most basic units of society. But by themselves, they are not very useful in telling us about the patterns, types, forms, and levels of social organization that are constructed out of these units. To do this, we must invoke additional concepts that will enable us to shift our perspective and to visualize the larger forms of human organization. These additional concepts will represent larger parts operating within an even larger social whole. Just what a larger social whole refers to depends upon our purposes of analysis. It could be a bureaucracy within which smaller units—divisions and groups, for example—operate, or it could be a city, state, or nation. The ultimate social whole would be the world.

Taking this perspective, some of the basic questions for sociologists thus include: What holds a particular social system together? What are the basic forms or patterns of organization that distinguish the human system from other social systems? Which forms are important for understanding how and why human beings behave the way they do?

Forms of Human Organization

To get a clear conception of the human system, we must now discuss its different forms. In some textbooks, levels of social structure are merely divided into two different realms: the microlevel and the macrolevel. But for our purposes this is too simplistic. A division of that sort is too rough and does not adequately illustrate the gradually expanding dimensions of various forms of organization, from small groups of individuals to entire societies. We must try to do more than delineate the polarities or extremities of society without delving into the vast middle area of social organization.

Our discussion in this section, therefore, will seek to isolate basic forms. We will begin with a form of social organization with which the individual has the most tangible contact, then examine larger forms which, from the individual's point of view, will become increasingly abstract and distant, until we have run the gamut of human organization (Olsen 1968).

Groups. Probably the most elementary social form studied by sociologists is the group. Groups are relatively small social units and can be distinguished in terms of such variables as size, differentiation of statuses, and purpose or goals. Sociologists often make a distinction between *primary* and *secondary* groups. Primary groups are smaller in size, involve face-to-face contact, reveal minimal differences in status positions, evidence strong emotional ties

Primary groups are smaller and more intimate than
secondary groups.

among members, and reveal highly constraining norms. In contrast, secondary groups are larger in size, involve less face-to-face contact, and evidence few strong ties among members. The most obvious example of a primary group is the family; a group of workers on a construction site would serve as an example of a secondary group. Sociologists also make other conceptual distinctions between groups, but these will be discussed in greater detail in Chapter 10, dealing specifically with social groups. At this point, we can limit ourselves to just acknowledging that people's involvement in groups probably has the most profound impact on the development of their character and other personality traits, because they are the smallest form of social organization, and because groups are in a closer, more direct, and more intimate position to affect our feelings and perceptions.

Formal Organizations. Formal organizatons have larger dimensions than groups. In many cases, a formal organization will subsume several different groups of varying size and purpose. They are typified by these general attributes: (1) clearly differentiated statuses arranged in an authority hierarchy, (2) clear rules, policies, and procedures regarding how people are to conduct themselves within the organization, (3) a high degree of formality and a specificity of function in role behaviors, and (4) an explicit set of organizational goals or objectives. Bureaucracies and corporations are probably the best examples of formal organizations. Formal organizations are the topic of Chapter 11.

Communities. Communities are geographical units in which people work, live, and carry out other necessary functions. They include towns

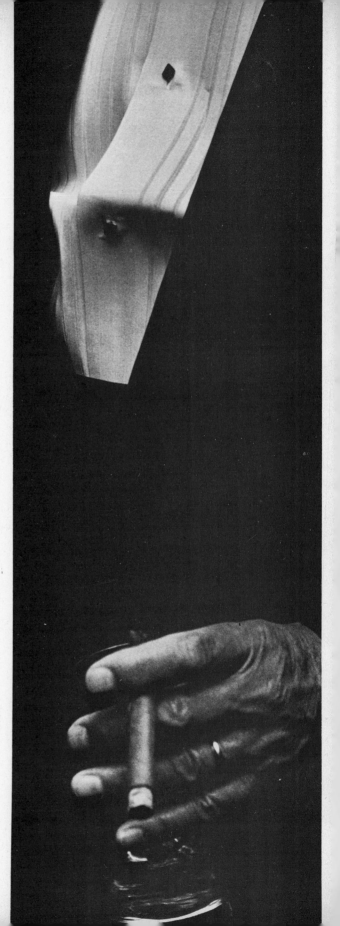

and cities that are politically self-governing, although they have relations with larger political bodies. Usually groups and formal organizations exist and function within communities, but there are instances in which a large corporation or a particular industry can effectively "take over" a town or community. There are coal-mining towns in which that industry employs practically every male resident. In other small towns a single large factory might have the same approximate relationship with the population. There is much diversity in how they are planned (or unplanned), how they are governed, what their demographics are, and what consequences they have for the individual in choosing to live in one as opposed to another. One community might have a population numbering not much more than a good-sized group, whereas another is teeming with millions of people. Communities will be studied in Chapter 13.

Strata and Classes. Most groups, organizations, and communities reveal an unequal distribution of resources, such as money, manifestations of power, material effects, prestige, or anything that people define (in accordance with social values, beliefs, and norms) as valuable or desirable. A social class is therefore defined by its degree of access to such resources, as well as by factors that serve to somehow limit or expand this access, such as religious beliefs, ethnicity, race, occupation, and income level. Sociologists are often interested in how a population within a community or even an entire society becomes ranked according to the access to scarce resources that people have (Turner & Starnes 1976). When people with a given degree of access to re-

People's life-styles are profoundly shaped by their access to scarce resources.

The small family farm and the frantic crush of a stock market highlight the diversity of structures embraced by a social institution like the economy.

sources reveal common behavior and cultural patterns—voting, life-style, beliefs, values, and other common characteristics—this aggregation is called a *social strata* or *class*. When these strata can be ranked from high to low in terms of their share of all resources, this ranking constitutes what is called a *stratification system*. Such systems have typified human affairs since the dawn of agriculture and now represent one of the most pervasive forms within the human system. They will be studied in detail in Chapter 14.

Social Institutions. Social institutions are pervasive patterns of organization that embrace other units or forms of organization, such as those we have been discussing up to this point—groups, formal organizations, communities, and social classes. They determine the way people resolve some of their basic problems, such as securing food from the environment, rearing children, regularizing sexual relations, organizing societal resources in the

pursuit of goals, and, in general, just dealing with the problems of life and survival as a species. Thus, institutional structures are complexes of social units involved in the resolution of certain problems facing all human populations. The economy encompasses all other forms of social organization and deals with problems of the gathering, producing, and distributing of goods and services to the rest of society. Another institution—the family—resolves other problems, such as regularizing sexual relations and providing for the care and rearing of children. Religion embraces many of those structures dealing with problems arising from the uncertainty and anxiety of social life. Government deals with problems of allocating human and material resources for realizing societal goals and with the issue of maintaining social order. In modern societies, education becomes an important new institution and deals with the problems of preparing and allocating people to crucial statuses. Thus, social institutions are complexes of other social units that resolve and deal with the most fundamental problems facing humans. Their importance for the human system is so great that we will devote an entire group of chapters to their study in Part III of this book.

Race and Ethnic Groupings. As human populations evolved, they developed minor variations in skin color, facial features, and body size. Yet, these minor variations are often used to distinguish people in terms of race: whites, blacks, orientals, or browns, for example. In point of fact, however, biologists and physical anthropologists have difficulty distinguishing races from each other in terms of clear biological attributes. For this reason, sociologists often distinguish segments of a population in terms of their ethnicity. Ethnicity refers to the distinctive culture—values, language, beliefs, and norms—and social patterns—family and religion, for instance—of a subpopulation within a society. Frequently, people use imprecise biological criteria—black, white, brown, for example—to classify people as a member of an ethnic group, and frequently in human affairs, the distinctive cultural and social patterns of an ethnic group often arise from discrimination by the majority of a population against those with identifiable biological characteristics, such as skin color. For example, black Americans constitute a distinctive ethnic grouping by virtue of past patterns of discrimination.

The key point is that in many societies people are classified by others and come to see themselves as members of ethnic groups. These groups can cut across the entire society and become an important force in the society. For example, communities in the United States could not be comprehended without knowledge of the distinctions between whites and blacks or among whites, blacks, and browns. Ethnicity is thus a major principle of social organization, as will be explored in Chapter 15.

Societies. Sociologists usually define societies in much the same way nonsociologists do, as a geopolitical organization of an entire people with a distinct culture(s). As such, societies embrace all those forms of organization we have discussed. A society is the number, size, pattern, form, and nature of all the interrelationships among all its constituent social units. In most cases, a society is synonymous with a nation, the boundaries of which enclose a large geographic region. Some have highly distinctive characteristics developed through centuries of adaptation to the world.

Systems of Societies. Recently, sociologists have begun to recognize that societies have social relationships and that some of these relations have profound implications for events in the world. OPEC, or the Organization of Petroleum-Exporting Countries, is such a system of societies. Other systems of societies are organized by politics or ideology rather than by economic ties, such as the Communist Bloc and NATO. Recently, smaller and generally underdeveloped nations have begun to band together, at least in the diplomatic context of the United Nations, to form what has been termed the Third World countries. Because of these developments, sociologists are now beginning to expand their analysis to systems of societies and investigate the properties of such systems and their consequences.

SOCIAL ORGANIZATION AND CULTURE

We have talked about the basic building blocks of society: statuses, roles, and norms, and we have seen the patterns of social organization made from statuses, roles, and norms. At this point it is necessary for us to recognize that the organization and operation of these social units are circumscribed by culture. Therefore, it can be said that *each social unit* will, to some extent, have its own distinct culture, be it a group of three or four friends, a square-dancing club, the FBI, a military battalion, or a political party. Yet, each unit will usually be a variant of the culture of the larger society or system of societies.

As we learned in Chapter 4, culture is a resource and a means for creating patterns of social organization. The values, beliefs, norms, language, and other symbol creations of humans are, as we noted earlier, the cement that allows social units to exist. In studying any social form—whether it be a group, formal organization, social class, community, ethnic grouping, society, or system of societies—we must remain alerted to the fact that culture is intimately involved in these patterns of organization. Culture enables people to interact, and it provides the symbolic resources neges-sary to guide and maintain the continuity in all social forms. To a very great extent, the elaboration of the human system into complex forms is the result of the expansion of the cultural storehouse of values, beliefs, technologies, and other symbolic systems.

SOCIAL ORGANIZATION AND THE INDIVIDUAL

As a sort of natural progression, we must now discuss the ways in which *individuals* affect social organization. Indeed, it is people occupying statuses, playing roles, and recognizing the norms that become organized. We have said that culture, in itself, exerts a considerable, and in some ways, an independent force in determining how we organize ourselves, and giving all social units, large and small, a relative wholeness of entity distinct from others. We have an idea of what culture is, but where is it couched? Through what medium is it tendered to pervasively influence the levels and overall structure of society? The answer is quite simple: the medium is the individual. All individuals harbor within them the basic effects of culture. Their motivations, values, moral obligations, emotional responses, and other personality traits might effectively be analogized as a "society" of traits. For without the complex, multilayered, and multifaceted nature of the human personality, which will be examined in the next chapter, social organization could never exist. It is important to recognize this, for the relationship between society and the individual is not a one-way street; we are not simply *controlled* by cultural forces. If this were the case, the kind of human existence as described in Aldous Huxley's *Brave New World* would result: total and utter stability, but at the cost of human creativity and innovation on the individual level. The force that individuals exert to influence social organization is the principal reason why society *has* not only a semblance of stability and order but an elasticity as well, a capacity to figuratively "roll with punches" and display a remarkable degree of flexibility.

SOCIAL ORGANIZATION AND BIOLOGICAL FACTORS

We have talked a lot about aspects of people and society as being crucial to the survival of our species. Survival can therefore be considered probably the single most important *motivating force* behind why humans have created what they have. From this point of view, then, we can see that social organization and social behavior are not phenomena that can be judged as purely intellectual constructs—that is, as though our evident preoccupation with social systems were no more than a highly elaborate game to complement our highly elaborate mental processes, a way of fending off boredom, as it were. Social organization is a fact of life because it is, quite literally, a necessity. It is a means of survival, and in recognizing that survival is the basis for much of what we do, it is logical to infer that biological factors play a major part in not only having initially *caused* the early rudiments of social organization, as we saw in Chapter 3, but in maintaining and influencing it as well.

Why, for instance, should we band together in different types of groups such as family units? The question is almost ridiculous. Certainly, one brief incident of sexual intercourse can result in the birth of an infant, a member of a new generation to supersede the old. But if both members of the sexual union, after that single act, immediately go their separate ways—indeed, if *all* ostensibly going their separate ways, and *all* of them existing in virtual shells of solitude—how can that infant, or any infant, survive for more than perhaps a few days or weeks at best? The mother, alone, cannot possibly perform all the necessary tasks needed to keep both her and her baby alive. She could not leave the baby for as long as it would take to simply secure enough food for a day or two. Thus, this biological factor of survival has determined that the family, either as we know it or in some other functional form such as the former Mormon practice of polygamy, serves a pivotal part in adaptation to the contingencies of life. A father and mother together are much better able to confront the demands imposed by the environment in successfully rearing the children they have. But even the family, if left in relative isolation cannot easily survive. The need for more elaborate organization is often necessary to ensure survival of the species. Thus, groups of families band together, easing further the strain of simply staying alive. Communities are formed for the same reason. In modern social organization, various forms have made unnecessary the earlier, almost universal individual activities. Not many of us have to hunt for food any more in order to feed ourselves; formal organizations such as large food manufacturing companies and retail food chains make it no more difficult than getting to the grocery store by some modern means of transportation. Modern social organization does not just allow us to survive, however; it allows many of us to survive so well that we cannot even *think* of it in terms of survival, as though some struggle were involved. But this is only true in nations with highly industrialized and technologically advanced societies. A portion of the world's population is still, sadly enough, mired in despairing conditions of life in which famine and disease claim many lives. For them, literal survival is a very real, very palpable accomplishment, and whatever forms of social organization they employ are sure to play a large part in saving them from complete demise.

In more specific ways biological factors can operate as the impetus behind the creation of certain forms of social organization. For example, the basic solidarity of kinship is grounded in fundamental and organic blood ties. Sexuality, too, is a major biological influence by drawing two members of the opposite sex together as marital partners, after which children, who will perpetuate the species, usually follow.

Thus, we must never forget that humans are biological entities who, like all other species, must survive in the world around them. Culture, social organization, and, as we will see shortly in the next chapter, personality are all created in response to the need to survive. Moreover, as we have discussed in Chapter 3, and as we will illustrate in all the chapters to follow, our primate heritage has shaped the direction and form that the human system has taken.

Variations in Social Organization Among the Primates

Interactions create, maintain, and change patterns of social organization. As we have noted, however, there are parameters to social organization, such as previous social patterns, personality characteristics, ecological/biological factors, and of course, existing values, beliefs, technology, and other cultural forces. Although chimpanzees are our closest primate relative, they did not have to live and evolve on the African savannah. They evolved in the lower parts of the trees next to the savannah. They could thus take refuge in the trees when danger presented itself. However, a very distant relative—the baboon—did evolve on the savannah under conditions similar to those facing our ancestors. The differences in chimp and baboon social organization reflect, to some degree, the different environments in which they evolved. But more than this is involved: baboons are monkeys with smaller brains and with less capacity to brachiate, or swing with their arms, than chimps (who are apes). Baboons thus entered the savannah with a much different biological legacy, which certainly influenced the evolution of their social patterns. But we might compare chimp and baboon "societies" to appreciate some of the differences that ecology, biology, and perhaps, personality make in the evolution of social organization.

Chimps are highly vocal, baboons are much less vocal. Chimps reveal very loose, free-floating social relationships. Baboons show clear patterns of male dominance and authority. Chimps are much less sexually dimorphic—that is, they reveal fewer differences in size and strength between males and females—than baboons—male baboons are much bigger and stronger than females. Chimps move about in a somewhat chaotic fashion; baboons move in "formation" with dominant males at the front, back, and sides of the troops, encircling females, children, and nondominant males. Chimps flee, in an "each-chimp-for-itself" fashion, when danger presents itself, whereas dominant male baboons are more likely to stand and collectively attack aggressively a dangerous predator. Chimps are sexually promiscuous, engaging in sex regularly and easily—for example, males have been seen to "line up" and "wait their turn" for access to a receptive female. Dominant male baboons aggressively protect "their females," although females often "sneak off" to mate with lower-ranking males.

The contrasts between baboons and chimps show the impact of varying ecological, biological, and personality forces. Since we are closer to our ape cousin—the chimp—than we are to the baboon, and since our ancestors were forced to live under similar conditions to those facing the baboon, how did our ancestors' more "care-free" personality, "loose" patterns of organization, greater arm mobility, and most importantly, big brains interact on the savannah to produce the human system? The baboon's solution to survival problems was order, structure, male dominance, and aggressiveness. Our ancestors' solution appears to have been bipedalism (walking upright), tool use (throwing, for example), increased brain size, language and culture, and more fluid social patterns. Our present social patterns thus reflect the biological heritage that our ancestors brought from the trees to the same environment that faced the ancestors of the baboon.

CONFLICT, INTEGRATION, AND CHANGE IN SOCIAL ORGANIZATION

Social organization, like the entire organization of biological life on earth, is subject to disharmonies brought on by degrees of stress from both internal and external sources. This stress is represented by various conflicts and tensions that are the natural result of those somewhat opposed tendencies of both people and society: stability versus flexibility. It is hard to visualize a world devoid of conflict. Indeed, as an abstracted notion, it is a major preoccupation of humankind. The very essence of most art and literature centers around depictions of conflict and stress inherent in the human condition. So although it can make life difficult and even despairing or painful, it also makes life extremely interesting, in many ways representing the seed of our capacities for creativity, innovation, imagination, and true genius.

How do conflicts and disharmonies occur in the framework of social organization? In the first place, all forms of social organization, by way of their very structure and design, have a *potential* for conflict and disharmony. This predisposed potential can and does exist in every element and level of social organization discussed thus far, residing in our individual enactments and responses to the basic building blocks of statuses, roles, and norms, as well as between entire organized entities such as groups, formal organizations, societies, and so forth. This is largely because involvement with the entire matrix of society, by individuals as well as by forms of social organization, is described by myriad desires and expectations that are sometimes at odds with one another.

Sometimes the resolution of such conflicts can be relatively simple, with a minimum of disruption to the ongoing fabric of society. Others result in such devastating consequences of global magnitude that the conditions of human life can be substantially altered, as was the case with both world wars of this century.

On a smaller scale, conflict and stress in social organization often originate in statuses, roles, and norms. Earlier in this chapter we talked about the terms *role strain* and *role conflict*, both of which represent conditions that can lead to different degrees of conflict and stress. These concepts reflect *basic discontinuities* that characterize human social existence. Furthermore, discontinuities are built into the process of socialization, the process that enables us to acquire our distinctively human personalities. Socialization will be the major subject of our next chapter, but for now we can use it to illustrate what we mean by discontinuity.

Socialization can be characterized by the fact that we all grow up and mature. This means that what was once relevant when we were young children may no longer be relevant to us as adults. For example, when we were children, a typical day might have consisted of various fun and games, but entry into adulthood usually marks the emergence of new pressures, obligations, and responsibilities. This transition can often be very rough with anxious and fretful consequences for the individual—a fact that underscores the potential discontinuity in life. Humans are continuously shedding old statuses and taking on new ones—for example, we become one year older than the year before, or we suddenly marry after years of bachelorhood, or we were promoted to a new position within a corporation. Thus, various degrees of stress are a fact of life. Most people are usually able to sufficiently weather different discontinuities in life. But some of us are not as well prepared to face these exigencies. The reason for this can be termed as inadequate role preparation, which simply means that an individual may not have been sufficiently socialized to confront new obligations and responsibilities as they naturally occur at different times in maturity. For example, the "momma's boy" may grow up to be a child in an adult world, or the emotionally neglected boy may grow up unable to express emotions.

Conflict can also exist between forms of social organization, such as groups, formal organizations, and social classes because different groups, organizations, and societies will often have priorities, objectives, values, or even ideological precepts that reflect conflicts of interest. Conservation groups, for example, are always battling the industrial "progress" of business concerns and other bureaucratic organizations. Violent conflicts between religious factions have contributed to many of the wars throughout recorded history. Thus, we can see that social conflict exists, either in a potential or realized state, in every element and layer of social organization, whether it involves an individual coming to terms with the expectations embodied in statuses, roles, and norms, or the larger entities of social organization.

SUMMARY AND PREVIEW

In this chapter we have sought to communicate that humans are organized into many diverse social forms. These forms are created from, and are maintained by, interaction among people occupying statuses, playing roles, and recognizing cultural symbols, particularly norms.

In many ways, we have offered a table of contents for much of this book, which embraces much of what sociology is: the study of the structurae and interaction processes within and between diverse types, forms, and layers of social organization. Of course, we will also study other matters in the sections to follow: crowds, mobs, publics, riots, revolutions, and other fluid forms of organization as well as population dynamics and the ultimate parameter of the human system—ecology.

Before we venture into a detailed discussion of the structure and processes of social forms, however, we must discuss other major elements in the sociological perspective, Human personality and its genesis through socialization is one such element. Our biological heritage has allowed us to evolve highly complex personalities, which, as we will come to see, emerge out of our interactions in various forms of organization. Without personality, people could not play roles or deviate from normative expectations. Without personality, human life would be like that of ant and bee societies: devoid of variety, uniqueness, and creativity. Personality is thus a critical ingredient in the human system; for in the end, it is people who occupy the statuses, play the roles, and conform to, or deviate from, the norms from which the imposing edifice of society is constructed.

Key Terms

Structure: relatively stable patterns of interaction among social units

Status: a social position within a larger network of positions

Ascribed Status: positions that individuals inherit at birth

Achieved Status: positions that people assume by virtue of effort and performance

Role: behavior that is manifested by persons occupying status positions

Role conflict: a situation in which enactment of one role prevents, alters, or hinders the enactment of other roles

Role Strain: a situation in which a person has difficulty meeting the requirements of a role

Norms: expectations about how people are supposed to behave

Review Questions

1. What are the basic "building blocks" of society?

2. What is "built" from them?

3. How does culture influence social organization?

4. What is the relationship between the individual person and social organization?

5. What influence do biological factors have?

6. Why are patterns of social organization rife with conflict and change?

Suggested Readings

Butler, Edgar. *Urban Sociology*. New York: Harper & Row, 1976.

Duberman, Lucile. *Social Inequality: Class and Caste in America*. Philadelphia: Lippincott, 1976.

Kramer, Judith R. *The American Minority Community*. New York: Crowell, 1970.

Olmsted, Michael S. *The Small Group*. New York: Random House, 1967.

Olsen, Marvin E. *The Process of Social Organization*. New York: Holt, Rinehart and Winstone, 1968.

Presthus, Robert. *The Organizational Society*. New York: Knopf, 1962.

Parsons, Talcott. *The Social System*. New York: The Free Press, 1951.

Turner, Jonathan H. *Patterns of Social Organization: A Survey of Social Institutions*. New York: McGraw-Hill, 1972.

Wallerstein, Immanuel. *The Modern World-System*. New York: Academic Press, 1974.

PERSONALITY AND SOCIALIZATION: THE CREATION OF HUMANS

PROLOGUE

Guiding Questions: What makes us individually unique? What is personality? How is it acquired and maintained? What consequences does personality have for the individual and society?

Chapter Topics

SOCIETY AND PERSONALITY

Some societies are maintained almost entirely by instinct, such as those among bees and ants. At birth the young "know" their place, their role, and their obligations, but they do not "know" in the same way that humans do. Indeed, they are incapable of symbolic thought and are biologically programmed to behave in certain ways. Other animals, including the primates, must learn how to behave. Although instincts may govern much of their activity, they must be taught, or learn through the "hard knocks" of experience, what they must do in order to survive.

As a general rule, the larger and more complex the brain of an animal, the more it must be taught how to survive. Moreover, the larger-brained animals are likely to have a prolonged period of depending on others, since the brain is slow to grow and mature. Thus, there is a dual reason for the prolonged "childhood" of larger-brained animals: (1) they must learn how to survive, and (2) they must be given time to mature biologically.

Humans carry these reasons to the extreme. We cannot participate in society without a prolonged period of learning, and we take a considerable period to mature biologically. We must learn and wait to become human, and through our experiences over a period of years, each of us comes to acquire a uniqueness. Other animals reveal a distinctiveness, as anyone who has had a favorite pet can testify. But humans reveal a complex cluster of traits that give them an even more unique character—a personality.

Much of what makes human life interesting and exciting revolves around personality. Getting to know someone, or falling in love, are but obvious indications of how we deal with other people's personalities. For all its uniqueness and fascination, however, we must not lose sight of a central fact of life: the acquisition of personality is what enables humans to become a part of society. Every culture and all patterns of social organization require certain things of their participants. People must be willing to occupy crucial positions; they must be willing and able to play roles and to abide by cultural symbols, such as norms and values. They must be able to share the same assumptions and definitions of situations. However, social life is not a beehive or anthill. People often clash, argue, and fight. They often cannot, or will not, play roles. But if a majority of people could not assume statuses, play roles, and recognize cultural symbols, the human system would not be possible.

Personality is thus a crucial element in the survival of society and the human species. Deviance, hate, dissension, alienation, and other indications of people's unwillingness or inability to fit into, or accept, existing social patterns all document that personality can be a force for change and alteration. But personality can also be a force for order and stability. The acquisition of personality through socialization enables humans to be human and allows society to persist over time.

In this chapter we will examine the acquisition of personality through our lifelong interactions with others. Those processes of interaction that influence our psychological characteristics, or personality, are termed **socialization.**[1] Our task is not to explore what is unique about people, as fascinating as this topic might be; our goal, as students of sociology, is to see how personality develops and how it is a critical element in the human system.

To visualize how critical an element personality is, visualize humans raised in isolation without conventional socialization experiences. Let us examine a few cases in which by accident and malice this has occurred. Children who are raised in these isolated or near-isolated conditions are termed *feral children*.

One of the classic cases of a feral child was "Anna of the Attic" (Davis 1940, 1947, 1948). Anna was an illegitimate child, and this displeased her grandfather very much. To show his displeasure, the grandfather kept Anna confined in a small dark attic where she remained for the first six years of her life. She received enough minimal care to keep her alive, but nothing more. When Anna was discovered by social workers, her clothing and bedding were filthy, and it became apparent that Anna had been completely isolated from all human contact, receiving no education or training whatsoever. She could neither walk nor talk, and initially it was thought that she was also blind and deaf. When Anna was placed in a special school, however, it was discovered that she was not handicapped by deafness, blindness, or congenital mental retardation; and with special care and training

from other human beings, she showed marked improvement in learning how to coordinate her body and to communicate with others. Unfortunately, Anna's life was shortlived as she died only four and a half years after she was discovered, having learned to do such things as string beads, identify colors, and use language in a limited way, mostly in the form of fragmentary phrases. She had begun to walk well and could even run somewhat. But because of her early death, it could not be learned how far she might have progressed.

Isabelle was another case (Davis 1940, 1947). She, too, was an illegitimate child and was isolated for that reason, just as Anna was. She was approximately six and one-half years old when discovered. Isabelle's mother was a deaf mute, and the two of them shared a dark room. Like Anna, Isabelle never had any opportunity to learn language because she was never exposed to normal human communication. The only mode of communication she had developed with her mother was through gestures, and instead of speech the only vocalizing she did consisted of guttural, croaking sounds. She was thought to be deaf, but when she was examined, it was discovered that she could hear. Nonetheless, specialists who worked with Isabelle thought she was "feeble-minded." After only two months of systematic and intense training, however, she began making substantial progress. She could construct sentences, and after only nine months could even identify written words and sentences. She learned to use numbers somewhat, and developed the ability to retell a story after hearing it. After 16 months, she had a working vocabulary of 1,500 to 2,000 words, and by the time

[1]For basic references on socialization and personality, see Clausen et al. (1968); Elkin and Handel (1972); Erikson (1950); Goslin (1969); Heise (1972); and Wallace (1970).

A wolf boy about nine years old, discovered in India.

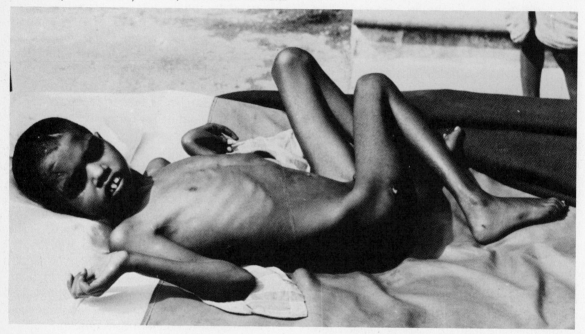

Isabelle had reached the age of eight and one-half, specialists concluded that she had overcome the consequences of her years of isolation and had miraculously attained an educational level considered normal for a girl of her age.

Although having reached the age of six or slightly more, both girls were considered virtual infants in terms of their social development. Their levels of intelligence and muscular coordination were severely deficient. The logical explanation for this is that because they were isolated from a human environment, they never had an opportunity to "learn" how to be human through the normal process of socialization. Although Anna remained at a somewhat deficient level even after several years of training, Isabelle was able to progress to the point where she made up for all her years of isolation and reached a level of social and physical development considered normal for her age. Therefore, Isabelle's case demonstrates that even though someone has been isolated for over six years and has subsequently failed to acquire a means of communication through language, it is possible to become a "normal" member of society.

These cases, and others, illustrate the acquired nature of our personalities and point to the significance of the process of socialization. As humans, we do not come by personality innately. Our growth as human beings is not an unfolding of traits or characteristics biologically determined at birth, but a process of social growth.

Wolf Children: The Learned Nature of Human Personality

The account below, offered by Roger Brown (1972), documents the degree to which the biological heritage is influenced by learning experiences:

Kamala and Amala. Since 1850, at least, there have been constant reports of wolf-children in India. Some of the Indian people have a superstitious reluctance to kill wolves and there has also been a practice of exposing unwanted children. Most of those carried off have certainly been killed, but occasionally the child is taken to the wolf den and survives for a time as an extra cub.

In 1920 the Rev. A. L. Singh was told of a *manushbhaga*, a man ghost, haunting a certain Indian village. The ghost had been seen in the company of wolves going in and out of a giant dead anthill, which the animals presumably used as a den. Singh had a shooting platform built over the hill. He and some natives watched there one night and saw a procession of mother wolf and cubs, two of which looked human though they went on all fours and had long matted hair. The local natives would not dig out the hill, but Singh brought in some more willing workers. The mother darted out to attack the invaders and was killed. In the den itself they found a monkey ball of four little creatures clinging together—two cubs and two little girls.

Kamala was about eight years old and Amala only one and one-half. They were thoroughly wolfish in appearance and behavior: hard callus had developed on their knees and palms from going on all fours. Their teeth were sharp edged. They moved their nostrils sniffing food. Eating and drinking were accomplished by lowering their mouths to the plate. They ate raw meat and, on one occasion, killed and devoured a whole chicken. At night they prowled and sometimes howled. They shunned other children but followed the dog and cat. They slept rolled up together on the floor.

From Roger Brown, "Feral and Isolated Man On Language," edited by U. P. Clark et al. New York: St. Martin's Press, 1972.

WHAT IS PERSONALITY?

There has been considerable disagreement over the definition of personality. Much of this disagreement is simply a matter of emphasis. Most social scientists, however, recognize that all humans who have lived in society develop a series of characteristics that both distinguish them as individuals among other people and yet make them able to participate in society.

For our purposes, *personality* is the product of interaction with others in a variety of social units—from the family to school, and finally to job. It consists of all those traits and characteristics that (1) organize people's feelings about themselves, (2) organize the way they are prepared to act or behave in various interactional situations, and (3) organize the ways in which they finally *do* act and behave in those situations. It is thus a clustering of traits that describe a sort of "tendency system" within a particular individual and makes him or her likely to reveal relatively consistent and predictable patterns of behavior that can be recognized by others. All of us can think of friends or relatives who behave consistently and predictably in this fashion, setting them apart from others. We might distinguish someone as being generally hot tempered most of the time, whereas another might be apathetic or undemonstrative, and still another might be extremely gullible. If John is known for his fondness of liquor, gets drunk during a party, and behaves in some embarrassing ways, his friends will doubtlessly comment. "Well, that's John for you . . . always getting smashed and acting like a jerk." They have, in effect, recognized his own "tendency system" for "getting smashed and acting like a jerk."

Of all the fantastically complex and intricate traits that determine a person's tendency system, sociologists tend to focus on some while ignoring others. The reason for this selective emphasis is that sociologists are primarily interested in the ways that personality influences people's adjustments to one another through interaction, and hence, the ways that it affects, and is affected by, patterns of social organization.

Components of Personality

The components of personality that sociologists typically study include: (1) biological heritage, (2) self, (3) motives, (4) role playing skills, and (5) cultural directives.

Biological Heritage. Toward the end of the nineteenth century, when most people overcame the shock and outrage of Darwinism and the theory of natural selection, the scientific community came to accept the proposition that humans were indeed animals. Therefore, they must share with all other members of the animal kingdom inherited or innate instincts, except perhaps on a more elaborate and complex level. It followed that personality traits, then, could be traced back to basic instinctual drives. The many wars throughout history, for example, could be attributed to an innate belligerence or aggressiveness. The fact that we organize ourselves into highly complex societies could likewise be seen as a manifestation of a herding instinct. Our proclivity for acquiring and owning property of various sorts could be explained by a fundamental acquisitive instinct. The same reasoning was applied to differences in personality. It was generally thought that almost every aspect of human behavior was biologically determined at birth, and the process of maturing was only a matter of having these traits come to the surface, independent of any other environmental conditions.

However, Russian physiologist, Ivan Pavlov, was one of the first to demonstrate that personality was not so simple. His experiments with dogs showed that even with certain lower animals, some forms of behavior were *learned* rather than the product of pure instinct. His experiments involved the pairing of various stimuli to produce the same reaction. For example, Pavlov observed that a hungry dog would salivate at the sight of food. By pairing the stimulus of the food with the ringing of a bell, eventually the dog would salivate when the bell rang, regardless of whether or not any food was about. This dispelled the notion that personality and behavior were genetically determined and not subject to any other influences.

Today, many scientists believe that people's personality characteristics are influenced to some unknown extent by **biological heritage** (Clausen 1967; Mazur & Robertson 1972; Eysenck 1970). Biological factors include such things as a person's physical appearance, hormonal balances, and intelligence. This genetic "blueprint" will play a part in determining the "broad lines" of an individual's participation in society. Individuals who are physically attractive may acquire self-confidence and self-esteem because of the extra attention they receive. People born with congenital defects may develop into unhappy or maladjusted individuals because their condition increases the likelihood that they will be rejected or spurned by other members of society.

However, no single biologically determined characteristic can be considered alone. Furthermore, almost any disadvantage that is genetically inherited can be overcome by favorable socialization. A fat person, for example, might not feel self-conscious about the condition if the immediate family or early friends in school never call derisive attention to the condition. At its simplest level, biological heritage simply involves a person's set of general strengths and weaknesses, which serve as guidelines in terms of how that person will participate in society. A frail boy, aware of the limitations of his physique, will not seriously pursue a career as a professional football player. The more important idiosyncratic features of an individual's personality are gained from the processes of socialization.

Self. Human beings have a unique capacity for self-awareness (Mead 1934). *Self* refers to the feelings and attitudes people develop about themselves based almost entirely on the "feedback" they receive from others around them—that is, what they "perceive" others to think of them. This self-concept usually develops into a highly elaborate system of sentiments concerning who and what individuals feel themselves to be, and it profoundly influences various patterns of behavior in different social situations.

How does a person arrive at a self-concept? The process is a gradual and complex one that continues throughout a person's life. It comes through interaction with other people, and the family is usually the first and greatest influence. Suppose a young boy is complimented by his father because he shows some early athletic prowess, which might come through playing catch with a football in the back yard. The boy immediately perceives the compliment as an approval and works to further develop his athletic skills. By way of more compliments and other reinforcing agents, the boy begins to think of himself in terms of his physical strengths and talents, and his thinking becomes a major aspect of his self-definition. Likewise, if children are given no encouragement in any direction or if disapproval is shown, then their self-concept will be affected. A loss of self-confidence can result, creating low self-esteem. How people view themselves influences their behavior. A person with low self-esteem will act differently than one with high self-esteem. Thus, people's feelings about themselves as certain kinds of beings, with particular assets and liabilities, influence how they participate in society. These feelings are acquired through experiences with others, which emphasizes the importance of socialization in the development of human personality.

Motives. Those processes that "energize" a person toward a particular course of action are called motives. Inherent skills and talents as well as self-concept play a large part in determining why people will be motivated to do one thing rather than another. Motives develop concurrently with self-concepts, mainly because the two are often closely related. People's conception of what they are and what they can do will shape their propensity to engage in certain activities and avoid others to some extent.

Motives are acquired through socialization, but they are often related to biological functions. For example, those motives residing more distinctly in biological processes would include the sex drive, appetite, and elimination.

Role-Playing Skills. As children mature, they are forced to play different roles. In so doing, they begin to acquire techniques for playing roles in society. Some children are able to develop a vast repertoire of **role-playing skills,** others are less adept. Probably the best and usually earliest example of role-playing comes when children engage in "playing house." A little boy will dress up according to what he has perceived as an adult and, perhaps, will act out the role of the father. A little girl will do the same, but since the mother exerts the most influence in a child's early development, she will play the role of mother, mothering a doll, changing its diapers or clothes, cuddling it, and feeding it with a bottle.

The significance of this kind of activity is that children are acquiring role-playing skills, not just those necessary for mother and father roles but for other roles as well. As children play one role, they develop general skills of interpreting norms, reading each other's gestures, and adjusting their responses in order to cooperate. Through such rehearsals and through growing participation in other roles, children acquire a *level of skill* and develop *a style* of role-playing that comes to typify their interactions with others. Other personality traits, such as self, motives, and biological factors, obviously influence the role-playing style of individuals. But their skills are also acquired from early experiences and eventually reach a level so that, when coupled with other personality traits, they result in a typical role-playing strategy, a unique manner and approach to social interaction (Goffman 1959).

Cultural Directives. We have discussed how culture "gets inside people's heads" in earlier chapters. The concept of **cultural directives** as a component of personality emphasizes this fact. It concerns culture as a whole and the force it exerts on individuals in channeling perceptions, thoughts, and actions in certain ways (Parsons 1951). It concerns the moral machinery we acquire through socialization, filtering these perceptions, thoughts, and actions through conceptions of right and wrong or good and bad. It is the judgmental part of our personality, directing our behavior to conform to certain established ways defined as appropriate by the symbols of a culture.

Lawrence Kohlberg (1967, 1971) investigated the development of cultural directives by presenting children of varying ages with a moral problem. He described the following situation as an example: a man's wife is dying, and he learns that there is only one drug that will cure her. The problem is that the drug is very expensive, costing $2,000. Since the man is not able to raise the money in time, he asks the druggist if he can have the drug now and pay later. The druggist refuses. Finally, the man goes back to the drugstore and, breaking in, steals the drug, thus saving his wife's life. Kohlberg then presented a question to the children: was the man right or wrong in stealing the drug? He presented this and similar moral dilemmas to children, not only of different ages but of different cultures as well: the United States, Mexico, China, and Turkey. His conclusion was that the manner in which people develop their moral consciousnesses—that

is, cultural directives—is not limited to their cultural surroundings, which might dictate a different conception of what is right or wrong; but like other gradual processes involving emotional growth or the acquisition of cognitive skills, it is something that develops in "stages." Kohlberg divided these stages into three discrete levels: the preconventional level, the conventional level, and the postconventional level. At the preconventional level, the child is able, by acquiring skills in role-playing, to behave well but has no understanding why that behavior is good in moral terms. Children do as they are told simply because they fear punishment rather than because they recognize that it is morally right to obey elders. Children tested at this stage tended to react to the hypothetical moral problem in favor of the man stealing the drug, mostly because it was practical insofar as he could not afford the cost of the drug and needed it to save his wife's life. When children reach the conventional level, they begin to take on an increasing interest in what other people think of them. As a result, they are more likely to behave in ways that will gain overt approval, because they begin to recognize that what they are doing is somehow good. At the conventional stage, the moral problem is more truly a problem. There are more ramifications involved in deciding whether or not the man was justified in stealing the drug. Finally, in the postconventional level, when children have begun to move increasingly away from the family sphere and are interacting with more people with ideas different from their own, their conceptions of good and evil become more complicated. They develop general principles about such matters as justice and come to accept nicely succinct dictums like the Golden Rule. Children at the postconventional

Figure 1: Society, Biology, and Personality

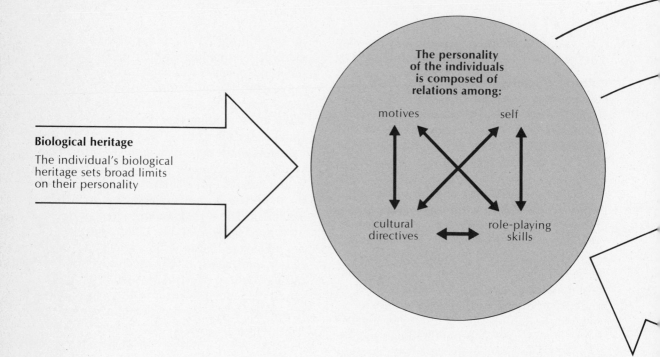

Biological heritage

The individual's biological heritage sets broad limits on their personality

The personality of the individuals is composed of relations among:

motives   self

cultural directives   role-playing skills

level had the most difficulty deciding whether the man was truly justified in stealing the drug. Although in doing so he was saving the life of his wife, he could be considered to be clearly in the wrong in terms of the larger community. If this man were right in stealing, would it not encourage others to steal? If so, it would be to the detriment of society.[2]

---

[2]Jean Piaget's work (1932) also documents the stages in the development of moral conscience in children. For an excellent review and summary of Piaget's work, see Flavell (1963).

Society & Personality Components. Figure 1 illustrates how complex and interrelated all these different components of personality are. People are given a biological or genetic history, which provides them with a crude "blueprint" of basic attributes, such as facial features, general attractiveness or unattractiveness, hormonal balances, and physical and mental strengths. As the result of experiences with others, a sense of self and eventually a self-concept begin to influence behavior. People

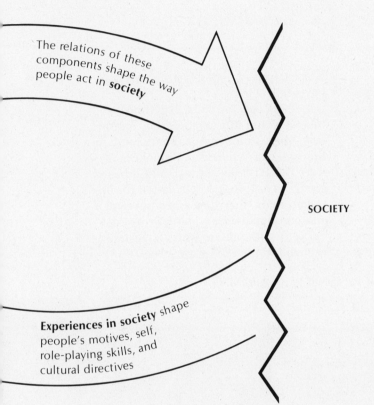

The relations of these components shape the way people act in **society**

SOCIETY

Experiences in society shape people's motives, self, role-playing skills, and cultural directives

also begin to acquire generalized motive states or propensities to mobilize their energies in certain directions. As role-playing skills develop, they give people levels of competence and styles of acting in the world. Finally, cultural directives give people a common way of evaluating and viewing the world. All of these components, which act on others while simultaneously being acted upon, give people an "action tendency," a way of viewing themselves, and a manner of approaching others. Without personality, people would not be

"human," and society would not be possible. If we imagine a world populated by Annas and Isabelles, we can see that social organization would not be possible without the components of personality that we have discussed. It is for this reason that the process of acquiring personality—that is, the process of socialization—has been extensively studied by sociologists.

Infant Needs: Evidence from Our Primate Relatives

We can see how close chimp and baboon infants stay to their mothers. This mother/child bond appears to be critical to the normal development of infants into adults. Although the mother/child bond might be replaced by any adult/child bond, the evidence is clear that infants require physical contact with a parent or an adult. If socialization is to be effective, physical contact must be the first interaction establishing the warmth and trust from which more symbolic interactions can develop.

A series of laboratory experiments by Harry and Margaret Harlow on infant Rhesus monkeys is illuminating in this context. When infant monkeys were denied body contact with other monkeys and raised in isolation for up to five years, they developed physical and emotional abnormalities; they did not play with others; when attacked, they did not defend themselves; they

Baboon infant and father. Note the emphasis on physical contact.

did not mate or have offspring. In other experiments the Harlows constructed different types of surrogate mothers for infants raised in isolation. One type was made of wire mesh; another was a wire mesh body with a feeding apparatus attached; another was a sponge and cloth mother without a feeding device; and still another such mother had a feeding device.

A monkey with its mother surrogate. Note that the infant prefers the clothed surrogate to the wire one.

Monkeys developed strong attachments to the cloth mother, regardless of whether or not they were fed by the experimenters, the wire-mesh mother, or the sponge and cloth mother. Apparently, the contact with the warm soft "body" provided needed comfort to the deprived monkeys. The Harlows observed that even monkeys raised in complete isolation developed strong attachments to the cloth lining on the bottoms of their cages.

What do these studies show about humans? First, we have strong biological needs, originating from our primate heritage, for physical contact with each other. Second, the quality of our initial contacts with others influences the personality that we will develop. Third, a society that would deny its infants contact with adults would soon perish, for its young would not be able to play necessary and critical roles as adults.

Source: Harlow (1959); Harlow and Harlow (1962a, 1962b)

THE PROCESS OF SOCIALIZATION

With this general understanding of what personality is, we can now begin to approach the question of how personality is acquired and what consequences it has for human organization. Humans acquire personality through a process called *socialization*. As we stated earlier, socialization can be defined as that process of interaction whereby people's personalities are acquired and concomitantly altered through interaction with other people in different social contexts. It is through this lifelong process of interaction with others in a wide variety of contexts that our biological heritage, more pliable in human beings than in any other animal form, is molded and supplemented to form a unique personality for every human being—unique in its idiosyncratic dimensions, yet almost infinitely duplicated as the fundamentally "human" element.

The concept of socialization has evolved over the last 100 years in the theoretical works of many scholars. The works of these thinkers can give us key concepts that can help us gain further insight into this most important process. Our first step in understanding socialization will be to examine the divergent and convergent opinions of various scholars.

George Herbert Mead

George Herbert Mead wrote: "The self . . . is essentially a social structure, and it arises in social experience. After a self has arisen, it in a certain sense provides for itself its social experiences, and so we can conceive of an abso-lutely solitary self. But it is impossible to conceive of a self arising outside of social experience." (Mead 1934, p. 140).

The question Mead is addressing is primarily concerned with which came first, society or the individual, but not in the sense of absolute genesis—that is, not in tracing humankind's development to the very "dawn" of creation as if it might be possible to pinpoint that moment. But rather his concern is with how society leaves its indelible mark on the individual, and what the consequences are for both the individual and society.

Logically enough, Mead theorized that the commencement of self-awareness began with the mother/child relationship. Every human being's mother is typically the first object of the interaction process. As a child grows and matures, of course, interaction with others proliferates considerably, but the whole process is initiated in mother/child interaction.

In order to survive, infants must depend on others around them. They must learn to communicate their desires so that they can get fed when they feel hungry or get hugged and cuddled when they want comfort and security. An important aspect of infants' growing facility for communication is their recognition of *significant others*. A **significant other** is a person who has the first and most important relationship in a child's early life. One's mother, of course, is usually the first significant other in any person's life. By identifying significant others, the infant establishes patterns of communication that facilitate adjustment to the social world. In this process of adjustment, the infant begins to recognize which gestures are effective in communicating specific desires; the mother, in turn, learns to react to those gestures in terms of the infant's needs or desires, thus reinforcing the infant's correct use of conventional gestures and words.

As the infant and its mother communicate, the infant learns not only to use gestures that allow it to communicate its needs, but it learns to read the gestures of significant others. In our discussion of Mead's thought in Chapter 5, we called this process of reading other's gestures and then using this reading to understand the other's dispositions *role-taking*. This capacity to role-take marks a significant breakthrough in a child's development, for then it is possible to cooperate—in a crude and rudimentary way—with others. For example, children "help" their mothers to wash or dress them. They also begin to inhibit responses that make their mothers angry and repeat behaviors that make their mothers respond favorably.

As young children read the gestures of others, particularly those in their immediate families who are of most significance, they begin to do more than read these gestures so as to cooperate. Children begin to interpret gestures to determine whether they are good, bad, competent, or incompetent; they begin to see themselves as objects of evaluation by others, and they begin to have feelings about what others think of them. It is through this process that the earliest foundations for a self-concept are laid.

A contemporary of Mead, Charles Horton Cooley (1864–1927), termed this process the **looking-glass self** (Cooley 1964, republication). The gestures of others are a "mirror" or "looking glass" in which we see ourselves reflected. We interpret what is reflected from the gestures of others. We assess how we appear to others; we evaluate how they judge us; and we have feelings about who and what we are in light of these assessments and evaluation of others.

By gazing into the looking glass that exists in all interaction settings, these self-evaluations become stabilized over time into a more enduring self-concept. The first images from significant others—usually mothers and fathers—are the most important because they come first and imprint themselves on a comparative "blank page." But as the child's interaction networks expand, other images supplement those received from parents and begin to influence who and what children believe themselves to be.

As the self begins to emerge and take form with age and growing experience in the world, children begin to role-take—that is, assume the perspective—of not just specific others in the environment but also of a *generalized other* or, as Mead termed it, *a community of attitudes*. By the age of eight or nine, children begin to evaluate themselves rather consistently and to regulate their actions by the general beliefs and values about what is good and appropriate. Mead's *generalized other* is thus what we earlier called *cultural directives*.

Children at this stage of development role-take with specific others and with more general ideas about what is appropriate. They can play roles and cooperate with others, but they also acquire a sense of self, a concept of who and what they are. This **self-concept** will begin to influence how and what roles a person plays. Eventually, people's concept of themselves begins to act as a filter or screen over the looking glass when interpreting gestures in terms of their self-concept. For example, a girl with little self-esteem might interpret gestures of males in her class much differently than one who views herself as competent and desirable. It is this selectivity that gives people's actions a continuity; it is the initiation of action in terms of a self-concept that allows us to predict how people will behave and react. When we can predict people's behavior, we can cooperate with them more readily. Thus, self provides individuals with a key trait of the personality, but it also allows society to run more smoothly.

This dual aspect of self was one of Mead's great insights. The process of role-taking allows people to cooperate, but it also creates a self-concept that gives people their uniqueness and yet allows for more predictable behavior. Mead's vision of how the capacity to role-take emerges, and what consequences this has for both individuals and society marks a lasting contribution to the social sciences.

Sigmund Freud

Sigmund Freud (1856–1939) needs no introduction. Although sociologists tend to be a bit suspicious of his notions of motivation, they do acknowledge his contribution to our understanding of how cultural directives "get inside us and rule from within" (Freud 1938). We are already familiar, through the analysis of personality, with how these cultural directives motivate, channel, and direct human action. Although Mead's concept of the generalized other describes how people role-take and make use of a community of attitudes to guide their behavior, it was Freud who achieved the earliest insight into the extent to which internalized cultural ideas direct human action, even against what he saw as powerful forces to the contrary.

According to Freud, the **id** is the energy that propels people to act. It does not respect rules, regulations, or any notions about morality, and it causes us to strive heedlessly and mindlessly toward the satisfaction of our drives. Ideas about good or evil have little significance; they are shunted aside and left in the wake of passionate debauchery.

The **super ego** is the id's "enemy." It is comprised of our general feelings about morality, about what is right as opposed to wrong, and about higher ideals about humanity. It develops through impingement of cultural directives on our consciousnesses as they have been acquired through agents of socialization such as the family and school. Freud viewed the id and superego as being so diametrically and violently opposed, that in attempting to reconcile the two the individual often fails and thus suffers from some form of mental disturbance.

Sigmund Freud (1856–1939) provided much initial insight into the dynamics of human personality.

The **ego** tries to reconcile the warring id and superego within us. It attempts to deal with the maniacal impulses of the id by substituting the "reality principle" for the "pleasure principle." "The ego represents what may be called reason and common sense, in contrast to the id, which contains the passions. . . . its relation to the id is like a man on horseback who has to hold in check the superior strength of the horse" (Freud, *The Ego and the Id,* p. 15). Conversely, the ego deals with the superego from the same base of the "reality principle," perhaps reconciling an unpleasant juxtaposition of what

"ought" with what "is." It can be compared to a sort of demilitarized zone within an individual, where contradictory elements of one's personality are molded together and tempered and where the requirements of social reality are allowed to impose themselves.

Freud's main contention was that the failure to achieve adequate reconciliation between these forces results in anxiety and unhappiness, which have a profound effect on self-concept and which affect one's skills and styles of role-playing as well as one's ways of dealing with the demands of society. This volatile conception of the inner workings of the personality is what sets Freud apart from Mead. From Freud's point of view socialization is not the gentle merger between the individual and society that Cooley and Mead saw. Rather socialization is something *forced* on people very much against their will, triggering innumerable conflicts and tensions. The result is that the individual is forced to repress desires originating from the id and to rechannel them according to social norms and cultural directives.

Freud's emphasis on motivation is a topic often ignored by sociologists. Its study has been left primarily to psychologists. Instead, sociologists simply assume that the need to maintain a self is one important source of motivation; that is, people are motivated to maintain their self-concept. Moreover, sociologists typically assume that once internalized, cultural directives become needs in themselves—in other words, we come to *want* to abide by various values and dominant evaluative beliefs. Freud's view of motivation and conformity provides a sense of more volatile and precarious relationship between society and the individual.

THE STAGES OF SOCIALIZATION:
Erik H. Erikson

Erik H. Erikson, one of Freud's greatest students, crystallized what sociologists have come to recognize about the process of socialization: it occurs in stages. Mead delineated stages in terms of recognition of the significant other role-taking and the emergence of self. Freud outlined a similar set of stages based on the development of the id, the ego, and the superego. Erikson, however, took a slightly different and very interesting approach.

In his book, *Childhood and Society* (1950) Erikson set forth his "Eight Ages of Man," which describe eight different stages of human development. In passing from one stage to another, the individual is seen as having to encounter problems relating to shifting social perspectives brought on by aging. The passage is often filled with a great deal of uncertainty for the individual, resulting in anxieties and pressures. These come from suddenly not having a clear idea of who and what we are, precipitating in what Erikson called an "identity crisis." There are both positive and negative elements in weathering these crises. If things go relatively well, a person can get through each of these crises; a person can begin to rebuild a slightly altered but stronger version of self or identity.

Stage 1: Trust vs. Mistrust (Infancy). In the first year of childhood, infants are completely dependent on adults for survival, most notably on their mothers. The crisis at this stage is in developing a sense of trust toward the adult environment. Everything is unfamiliar and unpredictable to infants, even their own sensations of comfort and discomfort. Mothers who respond warmly and consistently to the needs of their infants will create a sense of *basic trust* in their children. The more consistent the care and attention given by a mother, the more reliable and "safe" the immediate world becomes to her infant, thus creating a general sense of comfort and certainty. Conversely, if a mother is erratic, neglectful and somewhat unresponsive in her behavior toward her baby, a crisis develops in which the infant cannot count on anyone to alleviate its discomforts or give it a feeling of well-being and security. The critical area is in the quality of maternal care. It plays a large part in determining the basic adjustment of human beings toward themselves and other people.

Stage 2: Autonomy vs. Shame and Doubt (Early Childhood). The development of muscle control and coordination in children during the first two years of life becomes most time consuming. Children will spend an endless number of hours trying to coordinate their body actions. As they reach the age of three, children's muscles and nerves have developed to the point where they soon do a variety of things; they can walk, grasp objects, and even begin to control elimination processes. All these accomplishments are very rewarding for children, but the relative autonomy they experience in acting on their environment and achieving some degree of mobility can be a frightening experience, raising serious feelings of doubt or shame. Through their explorations, children might hurt themselves by falling over objects and bumping their heads. The pain of the experience will cause them to be more fearful about their new-found freedom, creating self-doubt about their ability to deal with the environment. Likewise, shame can result if toddlers wet their pants and are reprimanded by their parents. Children learn that the self-

The beginnings of a human's effort to achieve a sense of autonomy.

control they were just beginning to take for granted is not as reliable as they had thought.

If the parents of the children at this stage allow them to develop more or less at their own pace, the children are more likely to gain confidence in their ability to govern themselves and their actions—Erikson terms this *autonomy*. However, if a child perceives parental supervision as an indication that it is not able to fend for itself, the child may develop self-consciousness, losing the desire to explore and learn on its own for fear of punishment or ridicule from the adults. Children who are undisciplined and often neglected may also have problems, because their parents are never available to keep them from getting into situations in which they might get hurt in some way. To develop self-confidence properly, Erikson suggests that the children must be encouraged "to stand on their own two feet" but that the parents should always be ready to intervene to protect them from experiences that can cause shame and doubt.

Stage 3: Initiative vs. Guilt (The Play Stage). When they are four or five, children become more motivated toward role-playing as they develop a greater sense of self and a "feel" for manipulating their material environment in a limited way. They learn the ways and manners of others around them, both in the adult world and among their peers, and engage in games that imitate them. In short, they develop their role-playing skills. These skills enable them to objectify themselves, to gain a new perspective of what they are and how they fit into the general scheme of things. Much of their time is spent in the world of make believe. Through this process children begin to develop a sense of initiative. They *initiate* activities on their own for their own purposes or goals. Before this stage children are limited to a minimal exploring of the world around them, and role-playing is at a much more primitive level.

Initiative in children can be greatly affected by gestures of either approval or disapproval by adults. At this age, their sense of self-worth is based to a large degree on the respect they receive or do not receive from adults. If children are ridiculed or even ignored, they will develop doubts about the value of the limited goals toward which they are striving. Without encouragement or approval for even the smallest endeavor, such as drawing a picture with crayons or winning some trivial game, children will assume that what they are doing is simply not worth the effort and consequently will fail to develop confidence in making decisions. Moreover, they will develop a sense of guilt,

which can stop them from engaging in self-initiated activities. Erikson urges parents with children at this stage to display some kind of favorable gestures toward their children concerning those activities.

Stage 4: Industry vs. Inferiority (School Age). At this stage children move out of the home and into the expanded interactional arena of school. It is a critical moment for children, since the personal relationships at home are supplemented by a new environment, full of strange people impersonally commanding them to do this or that. They are rudely awakened to the reality and complexity of society with its rules and regulations. Going to school represents an initiation of sorts. Children begin to acquire the skills through education that will prepare them for status positions in the adult world.

Ideally, children will respond positively to these demands, deriving self-satisfaction through involvement in new games and learning new things. They learn the competitive nature of society by measuring their skills against others through the grading system. However, if children are not prepared to deal with the immensity of this new setting compared to family life, serious consequences can result. A child might not perform well compared to other students and might develop feelings of inferiority. A child might even find that family background—race, ethnic group, income level—is a social liability. A child's clothing might be inferior to the clothes worn by others, resulting in ridicule. These factors can destroy a person's self-esteem later on in life by creating an inferiority complex, causing an individual to never attain his or her poten-

Children learn to play roles and to manipulate their environment—Erikson's "Play Stage."

tial. Such an inferiority complex can also work to cause an individual to destructively reach beyond his or her real capabilities later in life, trying to overcompensate for feelings of inferiority during the first years in school. Erikson thus emphasizes that teachers must recognize those children who might be having difficulties adjusting to the new environment and give them special attention and encouragement in order to prevent them from developing serious feelings of inferiority. In this way children can learn to take pride in the industry employed toward any achievement.

Stage 5: Identity vs. Role Confusion (Adolescence).

This stage marks the transition from childhood to adulthood. Adolescents suddenly become very concerned about their identity—that is, who and what they are and what these self-perceptions mean in terms of others around them. At this time, it is important for individuals to have relatively clear ideas about their beliefs, values, and other moral considerations shaped and formed by various cultural directives. Some adolescents may have succumbed to the various rigors of the previous stages, acquiring deficient social skills, reinforced by other adverse experiences, and enter this stage with extreme confusion as to what their role is in society. They have no idea what is expected of them or how they should go about giving their lives some kind of direction. This time is one when they should begin developing clear ideas about what they are going to do with their lives, such as choosing a career. If they do not, the result can be a stultified and haphazard entry into adult life, governed by nebulous chance and desperate situations.

Stage 6: Intimacy vs. Isolation (Young Adulthood).

People desire and need the companionship of others. During young adulthood individuals learn of their ability to acquire friends or lovers and hold onto them. A young man and woman may enter into a relationship and marry, fully confident that their relationship will endure, only to discover a short time later that they are stifling one another. Jealousy of a very destructive nature may intervene and destroy the relationship, or they might simply become vastly bored with each other. Individuals may find themselves alone and lonely,

Young adults seeking intimacy with the opposite sex, hoping to avoid the potential isolation of young adulthood (stage 6).

having relationships with members of the opposite sex that are fraught with tension and anxiety and lasting only a short time. These same sorts of problems can affect conventional friendships of a platonic type. A person might seek out new acquaintances only to be shunned by subtle avoidance or direct rejection. Erikson explains that in seeking intimacy with others, one always risks the consequences of vulnerability, of rejection, of being hurt, of having a relationship that was so good in the beginning turn sour in the end. Most people reject and are rejected at one time or another. By gaining a balanced perspective, people can learn compassion and sympathy and lead fairly normal emotional lives. In contrast, people who are continuously rejected can develop serious problems. Likewise, people who have supreme self-confidence can suffer from the silent envy and hatred of others. Most people desire a lasting commitment of friendship or love from those with whom they develop emotional ties. They have outgrown their dependency on their parents, and they are prepared to take their own places in society as adults. Thus, based on their varying capacities for expressing or communicating love toward others, people establish emotional bonds.

Stage 7: Generativity vs. Stagnation (Young Adulthood and Middle Age). By this age most people have found respectable niches in society that give them feelings of security. The most important, but also the most exciting, decisions have already been made: choosing and pursuing a career, finding someone to settle down with, and other social adventures of youth. At this stage, feelings of stagnation can begin. People can feel that they are not "growing" any more, that they are not moving in a useful or gratifying direction in life. A man may find himself "stuck" with a job that is not very demanding, interesting, or fulfilling. A woman may find herself saddled with the drudgery of housework, equally unfulfilling and unrewarding, alleviated only partially by hobbies. This kind of middle-aged stagnation can be overcome with considerable effort and

imagination. The individual breaks out of old habits and forges a new sense of what Erikson calls "generativity." Often the appearance of an infant in the family can be the impetus for this new direction. Erikson describes this as a person's "need to be needed." An infant can satisfy an adult's needs by demanding care and attention, while the adult in turn satisfies the infant's need by giving care and attention.

The risks in fending off stagnation involve vulnerability again. Social stagnation at this time of life, however much pain it causes, is still a form of security. People hang on desperately to obsolete ways of life and habits simply because they provide an identity or self-image. Shedding those personalized effects leaves them vulnerable. In passing through this stage people must be resilient and willing to confront that uncertainty until the identity crisis is over and an altered identity is assimilated to meet the future.

Stage 8: Integrity vs. Despair (Old Age). This last stage involves a person's ability to overcome those attributes commonly associated with old age: a sense of uselessness, the reality of physical decrepitude and invalidism, and the problems of confronting death. Individuals are relegated to reflection and evaluation. Old people will often survive by memory alone, reliving past triumphs and defeats. In achieving integrity at this stage, Erikson means that people are able to evaluate both the good and bad times, feelings of adequacy and inadequacy, and arrive at a higher level of self-acceptance. Individuals come to accept the course of their lives and derive satisfaction from having had the unique experience of being human. Despair can come if the past seems only to be represented by a series of failures and missed chances. Individuals can

The aged often live in memory, suffering, and despair, and attempt to relive past triumphs.

be overcome by crippling and debilitating diseases, after having led an energetic and vital life. Since the elderly often rely so heavily on events in the past because of despair, many younger people believe that dwelling on the past is a "typical" trait of the aged. Attitudes like this, suggests Erikson, reinforce elderly people's feelings of constantly "being in the way" or causing members of their family unhappiness at their very existence. The elderly have much to contribute in terms of experience and wisdom, yet if they are made to feel as if they are an encumbrance to both family and society, the loss of integrity will bear out the self-image they feel others are projecting upon them.

MEAD, FREUD, AND ERIKSON:

An Overview

These three theories of the socialization processes are complementary. Each theorist provides important insights, but the combined concepts of Mead, Freud, and Erikson give us even more insight into how human personality emerges. Mead visualized the basic dynamic of personality acquisition as the interpretation of gestures through role-taking with ever widening others and audiences, culminating in role-taking with the generalized other. Out of this basic process self and the ability to cooperate with others emerge. Freud emphasized that there is always a tension among the requirements of society, internalized cultural symbols, and people's biological and socially derived needs. Society and person often collide, and personality is the arena for this collision. Erikson's analysis took us through the critical stages in people's lives. His work emphasizes the identity, or self-definition, problems of people as they cope with new dilemmas at various stages of their lives. He recognizes, much like Freud, that personality is an arena of discord, but like Mead, he also sees adjustment to the social world as mediated by people's self-conception, or identity.

These theories have given us a way of conceptualizing socialization. Now, our task becomes one of examining the specific agents of socialization—that is, the social contexts through which the processes described by Mead, Freud, and Erikson are activated.

AGENTS OF SOCIALIZATION

Individuals

During the first year or two of life a human infant is totally dependent on adults for survival, and thus, individuals are the first tangible **agents of socialization.** However, it must be emphasized that individuals, as agents, represent norms, beliefs, and values in the culture of a society. For an adult individual is also a social product, and the forces that shaped that individual will influence how socialization of others will occur.

Parents are the first agents of socialization. The infant is nurtured by the mother and through this initial form of human interaction learns to "trust" others by virtue of depending on her (Rheingold 1969). The world of the family eventually becomes a cast of significant others as members respond to the infant's gestures. In so responding, the infant eventually learns to use and read gestures, which will not only facilitate adjustment outside the family but which will also influence the emergence of self.

When a human being enters early childhood, parents and other members of the family exert a growing influence on the development of self-concept by approving or disapproving of its activities. This comes through the looking-glass process, as Cooley termed it, in which the child starts to perceive how it looks to others. Am I good? Am I bad? Does Mommy like what I drew? The child relies on the "feedback" it gets to find the answers to these important questions.

Eventually, the child branches out from the family, and new individuals become agents of socializaton. They might include a teacher, various friends of the same age, or even cartoon characters on television. How they occur and where become increasingly diverse: home, school, playground, corner grocery store, or anywhere. Children desire more and more to be respected and approved by these individual agents of socialization and model their behavior accordingly. In these contexts, children see themselves reflected in the looking glass and thus further define themselves as certain types of people. Moreover, the cultural beliefs and values that these new others personify also come to serve as a means for evaluating but also for absorbing basic cultural directives (Bowerman & Kinch 1959; Coleman 1961).

Groups

The older a person gets the more *groups* of people act as agents of socialization. The family can even be viewed as having group influence. As a person matures, the family becomes more of a single unit, influencing and shaping self-images and moral judgments within the individual. The mother often personifies the family, individually symbolizing it as a whole because of the strong influence she has early in a person's life.

Peers also play a large part as group agents of socialization. This is particularly true in high school when different peer groups become more discernibly established. In these larger, rather amorphous peer groups, stereotyped characteristics are often imitated by speech patterns, a style of clothing, hair styles, and a general mode of behavior (Coleman 1961).

However, group agents are more often in the form of smaller, cliquish circles of friends, acquired from the earliest years in school on up through adulthood. The group agent will act on a person to behave a certain way in order to be a part of that group. It is because of people's desire to "belong" to something and identify with certain groups that groups can have such a strong influence over the way those people behave, what opinions they will have, how they will dress, and other facets of their person.

This process continues into adulthood. However, there is more diversity in what characteristics are shared by members of a so-called "group." The group might consist of people brought together by shared alcohol or drug inclinations, or the group might consist of people with more conservative life-styles. The important thing is that the group, even on its simplest level of just a circle of friends, pressures people to conform to its cultural norms, beliefs, and value premises. In order to remain a member, the person must often be willing to accept, perhaps implicitly and unconsciously, this fact of social life (Brim 1968; Brim & Stanton 1966).

School children not only learn the three R's in school; they also learn how to play roles as adults in bureaucratic organizations.

Organizations

The first organization to influence children is the school. When they first enter school, children usually view it as a lot of strange new faces, but soon school begins to shape their understanding of the basic structure of society. By enforcing various rules and regulations, school is the first organization that hints at the kinds of complexities individuals must confront in dealing with other people in society as

whole. Children start to understand what others expect, both singly and collectively. School provides a sort of society in miniature, initiating individuals into a social setting of expanding dimensions, far beyond those of the family (Parsons 1964).

Throughout life, however, organizations influence people's personalities. Participation in clubs or work settings continue to shape and mold people's selves, motives, and beliefs— although not to the degree that an impressionable child's first participation in school organizations does.

Media

As agents of socialization, various forms of media can have profound effects on individuals. In the United States as well as in other modern cultures, children are especially influenced by television (Liebert & Povlos 1972).

Different types of shows display a variety of interaction situations that can give children early exposure to social settings outside the family. Some shows might be purely entertaining, such as cartoons and other shows produced especially for young children. However, young children might also inadvertently watch soap operas, a genre of television dealing, for the most part, with melodramatic adult social situations. In viewing shows of this type, children can be exposed to a much wider variety of roles, which can influence their developing skills in role-playing even though the shows are produced for adult audiences. The commercial aspect of television also has a great impact on children. They respond to the selling techniques of commercials, which shape their material desires, by telling one or both parents that they would like to have a toy they saw advertised. Commercials have the same effect on adults as well, although by the time people reach adulthood, they are usually less impressionable and more likely to exercise better judgment in discriminating between various products.

People often feel "changed" after viewing a particularly affecting film, changed because they might have just witnessed a group of characters on film "acting" in parts that communicate plausible yet different values from their own, causing them to make changes in their own values. Books also have this effect, as do other printed media such as magazines, newspapers, and the like. What all media have in common is the ability to influence people's thoughts and actions by synthesizing an array of different ways people interact with each other, different value systems and mores from other cultures, and different roles that people play in society.

Socialization is a continuous process occurring in relation to different agents of socialization. We have emphasized children's socialization, because the first contact with individuals, groups, organizations, and media is likely to have the most lasting impact on people's self-concepts, motive states, role-playing skills, and internalized cultural directives. Personality thus becomes *relatively* stable by late adolescence. Of course, change still occurs since people are usually affected by their experiences with other individuals, by their participation in groups and organizations, and by their exposure to the media. But their styles and basic response patterns are more often than not, stable and coherent. Therefore, people "seem the same" even when we have not seen them for some time. Stability is more common than change, but change does occur and we should not lose sight of this fact.

PERSONAL STABILITY AND THE SOCIAL ORDER

Personality gives people a stable foundation from which they organize their responses to other people. We can implicitly use this notion of personality to predict the behavior and actions of others and thus cooperate with them. Although it is possible for a person to change his or her personality in some willful way, it is rare. Examples of such change are found in individuals who are exposed to different cultural directives, such as a person who abandons the conventional family mode of living by joining a commune, or a person who has a deeply moving religious or spiritual experience that completely changes his or her sense of self in society. Under these circumstances radical changes can occur.

The relative rarity of such events is what makes society possible. Without the consistency and predictability that the human personality has, society would not be possible; interaction would be awkward and enormously time consuming if people's personalities were constantly in flux, as changeable as wind direction. In many ways the very survival of humans hinges on our capacities for stable and consistent behavior.

Adult personality is thus often difficult to change. There are several reasons for this. First, people tend to interact selectively and to assume statuses and play roles in those situations that meet their existing needs, confirm their self-concept, avoid taxing their role-playing skills, and abide by their beliefs and values. People who are thrust into situations for prolonged periods of time that tax their role-playing skills, violate their self-concept, frustrate their needs, or go against their values suffer severe stress and are likely candidates for a mental breakdown. Second, people selectively interpret situations in ways that confirm their existing "tendency system." They filter the images from the looking glass; they redefine situations in ways that conform to motives and values; and they fail to see role-playing inadequacies. Third, with age people appear to have a growing cognitive rigidity. They appear to have difficulty redefining themselves, reordering their values, altering motive states, or improving their interpersonal skills. Because we are pliable early in life, our early socialization has the most impact. Seemingly, this impact is difficult to escape. The lack of dramatic success in changing people's selves and motives in therapy attests to this rigidity, although various group experiences, such as encounter, training, and efforts at group-induced change, do appear to have some capacity to alter beliefs and values as well as to improve role-playing skills. Thus, self and motives have proven more difficult to alter than cultural directives and role-playing skills.

SUMMARY AND PREVIEW

In this chapter, we have examined the emergence of human personality. Personality is one of the key elements in the human system; it gives each of us a unique character, and yet it is the basis for stability and order in society. Without the willingness and capacity to occupy statuses, play roles, and recognize norms, human society would not be possible. Such willingness and capacity depends on people's motive states, their sense of self, their role-playing skills, and their internalization of critical cultural directives. These personality traits are acquired through interaction with others in a wide variety of contexts, individual encounters, groups, organizations, and media. Early interactions have the most impact on what people's personalities will be, giving humans consistency in the way they approach and deal with each other.

Socialization and the emergence of personality is thus one of the basic processes of the human system. A sociologist once described the process of birth as an "invasion of barbarians" into society. Socialization tames these "barbarians" and makes them ready and able to participate in society.

Of course, we must also remember that humans are rarely robots. Bees, ants, and many other species are genetic robots who behave in ways ruled largely by their genes. Humans learn most of what they must do through socialization, but personality can be fluid and creative. People are not socialized to the same degree that ants are genetically programmed, which means that individuals can change social patterns through innovation, brilliance, luck, or even obstinacy. Socialization of personality thus allows for both the perpetuation of society as well as for its change and alteration. This fluidity and flexibility is what makes humans, and their creation of culture and society, fascinating and exciting.

In the next chapter, we will explore another key element in the human system: deviation and social control. People do not always conform; they often deviate from norms; and they often hold contrary beliefs and contradictory values. Socialization can prove ineffective for some, and they deviate. People can also become socialized into groups and subcultures that, as a whole, deviate from society in general. Few societies are highly tolerant of deviation. Efforts at social control of deviance prevail, and one of the most fascinating tensions in society is between deviants and the agents of social control.

Key Terms

Personality: all people's traits and characteristics that organize their feelings about themselves, their orientations to situations, and their tendencies to act

Socialization: those interactive processes with others in society that lead to the acquisition of a personality

Biological Heritage: all those genetic characteristics with which a person is born

Self: the capacity to view oneself as an object and to develop attitudes, dispositions and feelings about oneself

Motives: those processes within individuals that "energize" and propel them to act in certain ways

Role-playing Skills: the level of skill and the typical style with which a person plays roles in society

Cultural Directives: the process in which cultural symbols guide and direct a person's perceptions, feelings, and actions

Significant Other: a concept used by George Herbert Mead to denote those individuals who are particularly important in a child's, and later an adult's social world

Looking-glass Self: Charles Horton Cooley's concept to describe the process whereby people use other people as a frame of reference for viewing and evaluating themselves

Self-concept: that stable cluster of attitudes that people develop about themselves as objects

Id: Sigmund Freud's concepts to describe the energy and motives that drives individuals to act in certain ways

Ego: Sigmund Freud's concept used to describe those processes which reconcile situational expectations, a person's motives, impulses, and cultural values and beliefs in ways that allows the person to act in the social world

Agents of Socialization: those persons, groups, organizations, media, and other social forces that are involved in shaping the emergence, persistence, and change in a person's personality

Review Questions

1. What is personality? What are its components?
2. How does personality emerge?
3. What are prominent stages in the emergence of personality?
4. What are the key agents in the emergence of personality?
5. What consequences and implications for society does the emergence of personality have?

Suggested Readings

Brim, Orville, and Wheeler, Stanton. *Socialization after Childhood.* New York: Wiley, 1961.

Coleman, James S. *The Adolescent Society.* New York: Free Press, 1961.

Elkin, Frederick, and Handel, Gerald. *The Child and Society: The Process of Socialization.* New York: Random House, 1972.

Erikson, Erik. *Childhood and Society.* New York: Norton, 1950.

Eysenck, Hans J. *The Biological Basis of Personality.* Springfield, Ill.: Thomas, 1970.

Heise, David R. ed. *Personality and Socialization.* Chicago: Rand McNally, 1972.

SOCIAL CONTROL AND DEVIANCE

PROLOGUE

Guiding Questions: Why do humans deviate? What forces seek to control deviance? What forms does deviance take?

Chapter Topics

In the preceding chapters, we have portrayed a somewhat utopian picture of the human system. We use culture to interact and to create patterns of social organization. Social structures, such as groups and organizations, shape and mold our actions, thereby making society orderly and predictable. We acquire through the socialization process the basic cultural directives, motives, interpersonal skills, and self-concepts that push us into key status positions and compel us to behave appropriately. These elements are all basic to the human system. Without them, social life as we know it would be impossible.

Yet, if all people shared the same values and beliefs, if all interacted smoothly and effortlessly, if all status, roles, and norms were unambiguously ordered, and if all personalities were perfectly matched to the requirements of the social world, human life would be dull. It would be orderly, safe, and predictable, but it would be dull. It would be like ant, bee, or termite societies in which all individuals have their place and know from birth their social function.

Of course, as we all know, human social life is often punctuated with deviation. People do not always do what they are supposed to do. They violate norms; they resist efforts to bring them into conformity; they flaunt social conventions; and they rebel against tradition.

This fact of social life requires us to examine another basic element of the human system: deviation and social control. Social life is a kind of dynamic tension between forces driving us away from conformity to established practices and counterforces seeking to bring us back into the fold. It is this tension that makes human life interesting and exciting; and it is what distinguishes the human system from that of other animals who are programmed from birth by their genetic heritage.

In this chapter, we will learn more about the opposing forces of deviance and social control. We will divide our discussion into three major areas: (1) the nature and types of deviance, (2) the process of social control, and (3) the causes of deviation.

THE NATURE AND TYPES OF DEVIANCE

What Is Deviance?

Generally, **deviance** is defined as behavior that violates significant and widely held social norms and that is thereby evaluated, and reacted to, negatively by the members of a society.[1] This broad definition, however, obscures a number of important issues: (1) Which norms are violated? (2) Who is violating them? (3) How visible is the deviation? (4) Who decides if a violation has occurred and who imposes the negative evaluation. Answers to these questions can give us considerably more insight into the nature of deviance.

Which Norms Are Violated? Which norms are violated makes a great deal of difference to the members of a society. If people violate unimportant norms, the deviation is more likely to go unnoticed and to be tolerated. Jaywalking, fudging a bit on one's income tax return, speeding, and exaggerating to impress a date are all examples of deviation from accepted norms that often go unnoticed and that, in most cases, are not severely punished. In contrast, killing another person, taking sexual liberties with one's daughter or son, destroying another's property, and physically assaulting an individual are all acts that violate norms over which there is wide consensus and strong emotional commitment in American society. These deviations are likely to be noticed because they disrupt the flow of normal interaction and conduct; and when noticed, violators are likely to be evaluated negatively and severely punished. As a general rule, then, acts that violate norms that are essential for maintaining a given social order and that reflect dominant values and beliefs will be noticed and punished.

Who Are the Violators? Not only must we consider violation, but we must also know just who is violating the norm. In no society are deviants treated equally. A doctor's child and the child of a ghetto resident in American society are likely to be treated much differently on the same drug-use charge. A rich person is unlikely to be put on death row for a murder, whereas a lower-class minority individual is. A large corporation that makes illegal political campaign gifts in a national campaign is not likely to be as severely treated as a small company that does the same thing at the local level. Drug use and abuse is defined as a crime when the drug users are lower class and young (heroin users), whereas drug use and abuse among older, middle-class populations is seen as a medical problem (alcoholism and over-use of barbiturates).

Thus, we can conclude that, in general, those who are wealthy and who possess social power will be treated differently than those without these attributes.

How Visible Is the Deviation? Many deviant acts are hidden from view and thus subject to a less severe reaction. For example, "white-collar crimes," such as employee theft, income-tax

---

[1] For general references on deviant behavior, see Bell (1971); Becker (1964); Clinard (1974); Cohen (1966); and Gibbons and Jones (1975).

evasion, medical malpractice, embezzlement, and consumer fraud are less visible than "street crimes," such as robbery and assault. As a result, white-collar crimes are not as vigorously prosecuted as street crimes in our society. Part of the explanation for the difference in treatment, of course, stems from the fact that white-collar criminals tend to be more affluent and powerful than the typical street criminal. Yet, the visibility of a deviant act operates to increase the negative evaluation and harshness of the reaction.

Who Decides and Who Reacts? Just what is defined as deviant is often a matter of who has the power to impose the definition. For example, for many decades, the Bureau of Narcotics imposed its definition of marijuana as an addictive drug and its view that marijuana users should be prosecuted as "hard" drug addicts. Only recently and only in some states has this inaccurate definition and disproportionate reaction been challenged and changed. Similarly, for many years, homosexuality was defined by the American Psychiatric Association (APA) as a "mental illness," and homosexuals were labeled "mentally ill." Recently, homosexuality was dropped from the APA's list of illnesses, thereby encouraging a different view of this form of deviation.

In sum, just what is defined as deviance is influenced by other social and cultural forces. The nature of the norms, the persons, groups, or organizations committing the deviance, the visibility of the deviance, and the power of those who define and react to the deviance all operate to determine what is and what is not deviant in a society. All people violate norms; humans are not robots. But just which acts become *defined* and *reacted to* as deviant is often determined by social forces.

Not only do social conditions determine what is labeled as deviant at a given time, but just what is considered deviant changes with time. Marijuana use is no longer considered *as* deviant as it once was, although it is still considered by a majority as aberrant behavior. Women smoking in public was once deviant, but is now "normal" behavior. Medium long hair on males was highly deviant in the early 1960s, but in the 1970s it is considered normal, even among otherwise conservative business people. Norms change, and reactions to violations also change. Thus, it is sometimes difficult to determine distinctive types of deviance, since definitions of, and reactions to, behaviors shift over time. Yet, we should at least seek to understand the *general* types or forms of deviation in the human system.

Types of Deviance

Table 1 shows the most frequent response to the question, "What is deviant?" If we asked a similar question in a non-Western, nonindustrial society or if we could put the question to members of a past society, the answers would vary. However, although different behaviors are labeled deviant by members of

The Pervasiveness of Criminal Deviance

Most people commit deviant acts, and most never "get caught" and suffer the pressures of external social control. In an early study James Wallerstein and Clement Wyle (1947, p. 110) asked a sample of New York City area residents to indicate those crimes that they had committed. The table below summarizes their findings. We should caution, however, that the sample was not systematic and that many "acts" were reported as crimes by respondents when, in fact, the authorities might not define them as crimes. Yet, as can be seen, criminal deviance was widespread.

	PERCENT OF RESPONDENTS ADMITTING TO OFFENSE	
Offense	Men (N = 1,020)	Women (N = 678)
Malicious mischief	84	81
Disorderly conduct	85	76
Assault	49	5
Auto misdemeanors	61	39
Indecency	77	74
Gambling	74	54
Larceny	89	83
Grand larceny (except auto)	13	11
Auto theft	26	8
Burglary	17	4
Robbery	11	1
Concealed weapons	35	3
Perjury	23	17
Falsification and fraud	46	34
Election frauds	7	4
Tax evasion	57	40
Coercion	16	6
Conspiracy	23	7
Criminal libel	36	29

Source: From James S. Wallerstein and Clement J. Wyle, "Our Law–Abiding Law Breakers," *Probation* (1947), pp. 107–114. Reprinted by permission.

different societies, we can begin to visualize at least five general types of deviance (Cohen 1966; Spencer 1976, p. 145): (1) deviant acts, (2) deviant habits, (3) deviant personalities, (4) deviant groups and organizations, and (5) deviant subcultures.

Table 1: Most frequent responses to the question "What is deviant?"

Rank	Response	Per cent
1	Homosexuals	49
2	Drug addicts	47
3	Alcoholics	46
4	Prostitutes	27
5	Murderers	22
6	Criminals	18
7	Lesbians	13
8	Juvenile delinquents	13
9	Beatniks	12
10	Mentally ill	12
11	Perverts	12
12	Communists	10
13	Atheists	10
14	Political extremists	10

Source: Adapted from J. L. Simmons, "Public Stereotypes of Deviants," Social Problems 13 (Fall 1965), p. 224. Reprinted by permission.

Deviant Acts. All deviance involves behavior or action that violates norms. When we speak of a deviant act, we are referring to deviant behavior that forms a discrete unit. Deviant acts have a point of initiation and termination, or in other words, they constitute a distinct act.

Most crimes are deviant acts. Assault, robbery, rape, embezzlement, and fraud are discrete units of behavior that violate formal laws about appropriate conduct. A criminal may be a slavish conformist in all respects, except that he or she occasionally robs a bank or defrauds a client. Much sexual deviation reveals a similar pattern; it is a discrete act that violates normative stands of appropriate sexual conduct. Call girls and homosexuals may live non-deviant lives, except in their sexual behavior, which goes against dominant norms. Deviant acts represent a distinctive type of deviance that, as we will see shortly, often invokes strong efforts at social control.

Deviant Habits. A deviant habit is much like a deviant act, except that the behavior is not sporadic but habitual. We usually also view the behavior as compulsive, as lying outside the person's ability to control it. For example, drug use and addiction can become a deviant habit when it leads people to violate accepted norms. Alcoholism is by far the most pervasive instance of a deviant habit, although addiction to other drugs often results in deviant habits. Another example of a deviant habit is compulsive gambling in which a normal activity is carried to such extremes that it causes people to deviate in their normal activities. Many compulsive gamblers lose all their possessions, incur large debts, and forsake their families.

Deviant habits often lead to lives
of despair and failure.

Deviant Personalities. A considerable amount of deviation stems from personality disorders in which, for a wide variety and for often unknown reasons, people are not able to effectively interact with others and play normal roles. For example, almost one in ten Americans will spend some time in a mental hospital, and many more will seek professional outpatient care. The distinctive feature of deviant personalities is that the person is unable to play a wide variety of roles and has difficulty in creating and maintaining social ties. For example, severe psychotics simply withdraw from normal social interaction and enter an imaginary world of people and forces that cannot be understood by others. Such withdrawal renders the individual psychotic incapable of normal interaction and participation in the human system.

Deviant Groups and Organizations. Not all deviance involves individuals acting alone. Deviants are often organized into clear structures, such as groups, communities, and organizations. For example, the Amish of Pennsylvania are organized as a community the members of which engage in behaviors that are deviant by modern American standards. Small collective communes also represent the organization of people whose behaviors are deviant. Juvenile gangs that roam ghetto and slum streets can also be viewed as deviants who are organized into group forms. Organized crime represents yet another form of deviant action, which resembles a modern corporation. Thus, within the broader patterns of a society, especially large and complex ones like that in the United States, we can often find deviants who are organized into different social forms.

A Mennonite community which lives in isolation from a broader society.

Deviant Subcultures. A subculture is a population that shares distinctive cultural traits, such as unique beliefs, values, and language (see Chapter 4). A deviant subculture is a population whose distinctive cultural traits violate, and are at odds with, those of the majority in a society. Members of subcultures are often members of deviant organizations, as is the case, for example, with some communes who form small groups whose values and beliefs run counter to those of the majority. But the organization of deviance does not necessarily create a deviant subculture. Many members of organized crime syndicates, for instance, adhere to most dominant American values and beliefs. Moreover, a deviant subculture can exist without high degrees of organization. Drug addicts, skid-row alcoholics, and homosexuals have traditionally constituted deviants who share certain cultural traits, but who have not been highly organized.

However, members of deviant subcultures sometimes become more organized. For example, the gay liberation movement represents an incipient social organization among large numbers of deviants who share certain cultural components. Although male homosexuals have revealed some degree of organization—gay bars and "hang outs"—they have, until recently, been more of a deviant subculture than a deviant group or organization. Such an organization often emerges as an effort to resist sanctions and control by the dominant society.

These types of deviance are not always mutually exclusive. Habitual drug users, for instance, often constitute a subculture or tight-knit group. Criminals have been observed to abide by a distinctive cultural code of conduct. But by isolating these types of deviance, we can get a better view of the variety of patterns that deviation in the human system can take.

As we stressed at the beginning of this chapter, there is a constant tension, or dialectic, between the processes of deviation and social control. We now have some understanding of what deviance is and what forms it takes. We are now ready to examine those forces that seek to control and eliminate deviance.

THE PROCESS OF SOCIAL CONTROL

Social control is the process whereby conformity to norms is maintained in a society. Without social control, society and the human system would not be possible. We can see instances of social control by simply calling attention to everyday, taken-for-granted events around us. Your professor shows up each day at approximately the correct time. So do you. Most students sit quietly in class. Most are polite and follow the proper procedure for asking questions. We all drive on the right side of the road, stop at red lights, and use our turn signals. We go to the bank and we are sure that people will be there to help us; similarly, we know that the check-out clerk at the grocery store will ring up our order. These are commonplace events, but they are what makes society possible. Despite tendencies for deviation, most people, most of the time, are willing to occupy key status positions, recognize relevant norms, and play appropriate roles.

It is only when people do not do what we expect or what is required that we become aware of the process of social control. For the most part, social control operates quietly and outside our consciousness, but with deviation, social control becomes apparent; people frown, they call the police, they scold, and they reject offenders. To feel the pressure of social control, all that is necessary—if you have the courage—is to consciously violate a norm: speak out in class without raising your hand and interrupt the professor with a hostile question. What prevents most people from behaving this way, and what happens when someone does? Mechanisms of social control—an angry glance from the professor, an annoyed inflection of the voice, and unbelieving stares from classmates, and our own "reluctance"—all operate to shape conformity to classroom norms or the norms of other important social settings.

Social control is a vital element in the human system. Therefore, we should seek to understand its different mechanisms. At the most general level, we can isolate five such mechanisms (Parsons 1951): (1) socialization, (2) social sanctions, (3) group pressure, (4) organizational confinement, and (5) institutionalization.

Socialization

We saw in the last chapter that much of what makes us human—that is, what gives us a distinctive personality—occurs through the process of socialization. Through socialization, we acquire important values and beliefs, the interpersonal skills necessary to perform roles, the basic motives that commit us to occupy key statuses and to play roles, and a conception of self that hinges on evaluations of others. As we acquire the values and beliefs of our culture, we begin to see and perceive the world in the same way as others. We share the same assumptions and agree on what is right and wrong. As we learn basic role-taking skills, we acquire the capacity to anticipate the responses of others and to adjust our behaviors to get along with them. As we acquire motives, we feel driven to behave in certain ways, to channel our energies in socially acceptable directions. And as we acquire a conception of ourselves as an object, we come to depend upon the positive evaluations of others and upon conformity to cultural standards in order to "feel good" about ourselves.

It is in this way that socialization makes us willing, able, and dependent upon participation in society. Although socialization gives us all a unique personality, it also makes us similar in that we possess the desire, capacity, and need to occupy statuses and play roles in the human system. As such, socialization is one of the most important mechanisms of social control in society. If socialization processes are not effective, then deviance is likely to occur.

Social Sanctions

Social sanctions are actions on the part of others in a society that provides rewards for conformity and punishments for nonconformity. Sanctions can be either *informal* or *formal.*

Informal Sanctions. Most sanctions are informal in that we emit and receive them in the course of interaction. A frown, a grimace, a curt tone in the voice, a cold stare, and other gestures that people use can serve as *informal negative sanctions,* as a way of subtly punishing inappropriate behavior. In contrast, a laugh, a warm twinkle in the eye, a smile, a relaxed and friendly manner, a pat on the back, and other gestures operate as *informal positive sanctions,* because they provide rewards from others.

Most social sanctions are informal. In the ebb and flow of interaction people use gestures not just to communicate but also to control. We often do this unconsciously, and at other times, we may consciously manipulate our gestures in order to "bring somebody down" or to "bring them into line." Without this capacity to mutually sanction each other informally as we interact, the human system would not be possible. We would have to endure indignities, and if we did not want to suffer such indignities, we would have to pull out a gun, call the police, or use our fists. Yet, at times, informal social sanctions are inappropriate or ineffective, which necessitates formal sanctions.

Formal Sanctions. Social life is often punctuated with formality—a fact which will be discussed in greater detail in Chapter 10. Formal sanctions are patterned and organized ways of bestowing rewards and punishments. A medal or award, a college degree, a testimonial dinner, a bonus for a job well done, or a promotion are examples of *positive formal sanctions.* In contrast, a parking or speeding ticket, confinement to a prison or mental hospital, a demotion, and the imposition of a fine are *negative formal sanctions.*

Negative formal sanctions become necessary when socialization and informal sanctions are insufficient to ensure conformity. Societies that must rely upon the extensive use of negative formal sanctions are likely to be experiencing considerable internal conflict and turmoil. In more stable societies socialization and informal sanctions are, in most instances, sufficient to maintain the social order. But in unstable totalitarian regimes, the police, army, and prisons become the major forces of social control. Even more stable societies, like the United States, often resort to the extensive use of negative formal sanctions to control and punish deviants.

Formal sanctions often involve coercion of deviants by agents of social control.

Group Pressure

As we will explore in the next chapter on groups, much social interaction occurs in small groups—family, peers, friends, classmates, fellow workers, and the like. We need groups, and this fact gives groups great power to control our behavior. Informal sanctions are most effective in those groups in which we value membership highly. But groups exert pressure independently of open sanctions. We want to conform to group norms, because membership in the group is important. We often fear or anticipate sanctions from close friends or important others in groups, with the result that we conform to expectations.

For example, why is it that you do not stand up and shout your true feelings to the sociology instructor during class? One reason is the anticipated consequences: a bad grade and strange looks from classmates. This is **group pressure.** No overt sanctions have been emitted, but fear of them pressures conformity.

Organizational Confinement

Deviants are sometimes "put away" or confined to special organizations. Prisons and mental hospitals are the two most common organizations in modern societies for controlling deviants. They are an extreme type of negative formal sanction and are used to protect others, to punish the deviant, and in some instances, to resocialize the deviant so as to reduce future deviation. Organizational confinement occurs when other social control processes no longer work. They are an admis-

Organizations for the confinement of deviants are usually unpleasant places to reside—as is evident in this operating prison.

sion of failure to control a person in society.

Because **organizational confinement** is a sanction of last resort, it must deal with those considered "highly deviant," and the success of organizations in resocializing deviants is rather low. For example, most criminals who enter a prison will return, and, in fact, confinement to prison may increase criminal tendencies. Table 2 shows the percentage of those released from prison in 1972 who were rearrested within four years.

Table 2: Percentage of Criminal Repeaters for Different Crimes

Type of Crime	Percent Rearrested Within Four Years
Burglary	81
Robbery	77
Motor Vehicle Theft	75
Rape	73
Assault	70
Stolen Property	68
Forgery	68
Larceny/Theft	65
Narcotics	65
Murder	64
Weapons	64
Fraud	63
Gambling	50
Embezzlement	28

Source: From *Crime in the United States: Crime Reports* (1975, p. 45). Reprinted by permission.

Institutionalization

The term **institutionalization** refers to the patterning, or structuring, of interaction. When interaction occurs in systematically organized status positions with clear norms and when expected role behaviors are unambiguous, then we can say that interaction and social relationships are institutionalized. Much social life is institutionalized—home, school, work, and even recreation. It is patterned and structured; We know when, where, and what we are supposed to do.

In a general sense, institutionalization can be viewed as a mechanism of social control because it makes clear what is to occur and because it separates in time and space potentially conflicting activities. For example, work roles are separated from family roles in American society since different and incompatible motives, orientations, and skills are required. At home we are to be warm, loving, and relaxed, whereas at work we are to be hard driving and efficient. These roles are potentially incompatible; hence, they are separated. We leave the home to work; we rarely work with kin; and we are supposed to "leave" our job at the office. Institutionalization thus patterns activities in ways that specify what is to occur in a given situation, while segregating incompatible activities. In this way, considerable tension and strain, which could cause deviation, is eliminated.

In sum, then, we can visualize five general mechanisms of social control: (1) socialization, (2) social sanctions, (3) group pressure, (4) organizational confinement, and (5) institutionalization. These five mechanisms operate to control deviation. Yet, as we have emphasized, they are never completely effective. Deviation pervades all human systems, and its pervasiveness has led sociologists in search of its causes. Part of the cause certainly resides in the failure of the mechanisms, such as socialization, to control people. But sociologists have come to recognize that deviance is endemic to broader patterns of human organization. There is "something" about human organization that assures the emergence of deviance. We should thus close our analysis of deviance and social control with a discussion of various theories about what this "something" is—that is, what causes deviance in the human system.

THE CAUSES OF DEVIANCE

Why do people fail to conform to norms? There are a number of ways to answer this question. Some people may be born with a chemical imbalance that causes schizophrenia or hyperactivity, which can result in criminal acts. Others may endure a difficult period of socialization, thus creating anxiety, insecurities, and aggression that cause deviance. Instead of looking to these possible causes, sociologists are concerned with how social conditions cause deviance among biologically and psychologically "normal" people and how these conditions channel the deviant acts of people who do reveal biological and psychological impairments. Not all deviants are "abnormal personalities"; many are psychologically healthy. Thus, the sociological approach must explain why certain forms of deviance emerge in society and not seek refuge in questions of the individual psychology of the deviant.

There are three general approaches to the sociological search for the causes of deviance: (1) anomie theory, (2) cultural transmission theory, and (3) labeling theory.

Anomie Theory

The concept of **anomie** was introduced to sociology in 1893 by the French sociologist Émile Durkheim. For Durkheim, the concept denoted a situation in which social norms are weak, conflicting, ambiguous, or nonexistent. The result is that people are unsure of what to do, unable to share common goals and perspectives, and unable to control their wants and desires.

Robert K. Merton (1938) adopted Durkheim's concept of anomie in an effort to explain the cause of different rates and types of deviance in society. In adopting the concept, Merton modified its meaning somewhat. Merton's explanation for the causes of deviant behavior has become known as anomie theory.[2]

For Merton, anomie exists when cultural values extolling certain desirable goals and the structural means or avenues for achieving these goals are out of balance. For example, if the values of culture dictate a strong concern with acquiring material goods and possessions, while the means for acquiring goods are not available to all, then anomie can be said to exist for those who do not have access to means. A society like the United States, Merton argues, will experience high rates of deviance because it has powerful values emphasizing success goals but does not give all segments of the population opportunities to realize these goals.

Merton thus locates the causes of deviance in cultural and social arrangements. Deviance is caused by disjunctions between cultural values and patterns of social organization. Merton then attempts to explain different types of deviance in terms of the nature of the disjunction between cultural values and structural means. Table 3 shows Merton's typology of deviance forms in terms of his means/ends scheme (Merton 1968, p. 194).

---

[2]For further discussion and use of anomie theory, see Clinard (1964); and Cloward and Ohlin (1960).

Table 3: Merton's Typology of Deviant Behaviors

| Type of Deviant Response | RELATION BETWEEN CULTURAL GOALS AND STRUCTURAL MEANS | |
	Accepts Cultural Goals	Accepts Legitimate Structural Means
Conformist	yes	yes
Innovator	yes	no
Ritualist	no	yes
Retreatist	no	no
Rebel	no, creates new goals	no, creates new means

Conformity is, of course, nondeviance and is that situation in which individuals accept cultural goals and legitimate means for achieving these goals. Most of you who are reading this book accept cultural goals of success in American society and are using one of the legitimate means to achieve success, higher education. You are, therefore, "conformists."

Innovation is likely when people accept cultural success goals but do not have access to legitimate means. Most lower class criminals fall into this category; they accept goals of success but do not have access to, or refuse to use, legitimate means. They are thus "innovators" in that they invent new, illegitimate means for realizing material success. Merton would predict that American society would have high rates of criminal deviance, since material success is a prominent cultural goal, but opportunities to achieve this goal legitimately are often limited for those in the lower socioeconomic classes.

Ritualism is likely when people lose sight of cultural goals, but adhere rigidly to the means for realizing these abandoned goals. Merton is not clear on exactly why people lose or abandon cultural success goals, but he appears to argue that success-striving generates anxiety and that many people cope with this anxiety by becoming obsessed with the ritual enactment of the means. A good example of a ritualist is the bureaucrat who is obsessed with rules and regulations to such a degree that the goals the rules were designed to meet are but a distant memory. One need not look beyond their university or college to find ritualists who have lost sight of educational goals in the interest of rigid conformity to, and obsession with, rules and regulations.

Retreatism occurs when both cultural goals and accepted means are abandoned. Drug addicts, alcoholics, hobos, and skid-row bums are good examples of people who do not accept either the success goals of American society or means for achieving goals.

Rebellion occurs when individuals actively reject goals and means, while substituting new and highly disapproved-of goals and means. Violent street gangs are a good example of rebellion, for the members of these gangs have rejected traditional American success goals and means in favor of new success goals—toughness and the creation of fear—and illegitimate means—violence and physical intimidation. Members of such gangs are typically lower class, slum residents who have no hope

of achieving goals and little possibility of using legitimate means. Hence, they reject both and develop goals and means that are within their grasp.

Merton's anomie theory has stimulated considerable research and speculation. Its prime virtue is that it views deviance as a response to cultural and social conditions. It does not explain all deviance in all societies, but it represents an important sociological insight into the sources of deviant behavior.

Cultural Transmission Theory

Two University of Chicago researchers, Clifford Shaw and Henry McKay (1929), made an interesting discovery during the early decades of this century. Although different ethnic groups moved in and out of neighborhoods, high crime rates persisted. This finding led them to speculate that deviant behavior must be learned and that newcomers to the neighborhood learn deviant patterns. Deviant patterns, particularly delinquent gang activity, were being *transmitted* from generation to generation.

Edwin Sutherland (1939), who also studied Chicago at this time, developed the **differential association theory** in an effort to understand how this transmission of deviant patterns occurred. His basic hypothesis was that "a person becomes delinquent because of an excess of definitions favorable to violation of the law over definitions unfavorable to the violation of the law." In other words, people are exposed to ideas that stress both conformity and deviance. When the number of ideas advocating deviance exceeds those stressing conformity, then deviance is likely to occur. In poor, high-crime areas, many young are exposed to criminal definitions as they interact with others. Thus, they are likely to perceive that criminality is legitimate for them.

Sutherland's theory stresses a number of factors that will determine the impact of deviant or conformist definitions on a person. One factor is *intensity* of involvement with others; definitions of close friends and family are more influential than those given by less intimate acquaintances. *Priority* refers to how early in life a child is exposed to conforming or deviant definitions of proper conduct. The earlier a definition is received, the more impact it will have. Another factor is *duration,* or the length of time that a young person is exposed to a definition. Still another factor is *frequency* or how often a person is exposed to conforming or deviant definitions. A last factor is the *number* of contacts with persons espousing either deviant or conforming definitions.

For Sutherland, then, deviant behavior, particularly criminal behavior, is learned in much the same manner as conforming, noncriminal behavior. Depending upon the number, priority, intensity, duration, and frequency of contacts with conforming or deviant definitions of proper conduct, people will have a ratio of criminal to conforming definitions that either favors deviant or conforming behavior. In high-crime areas it is likely that interaction with family and friends will produce an excess of criminal definitions, thereby increasing crime rates in that area. The reverse is true in low-crime areas.

Sutherland's differential association theory is less an actual theory than a description of how children raised in environments showing high rates of deviance will be more likely to be deviant than those raised in areas of low rates. The nature of interaction with others and the subtle definitions about what is appropriate conduct that accompany such interaction determine whether or not deviance and conformity will occur. Sutherland has given us a view of the process of how deviant traditions are transmitted from generation to generation. His "theory" does not explain how these traditions emerged in the first place—perhaps anomie theory does this—but it does inform us as to why they are likely to persist.

Labeling Theory

A more recent explanation for deviance than either Merton's anomie theory or Sutherland's differential association theory is **labeling theory.** This perspective was first developed by Edwin Lemert (1951) and expanded upon by a number of scholars (Becker 1963, 1964). The labeling perspective argues that people constantly engage in deviant acts, but most of these go unnoticed. Adolescents frequently engage in homosexual play with friends; a good many Americans "cheat" on their taxes; children and adults sometimes experience "strange feelings" and hallucinations; people get angry and hysterical; young and old alike experiment with illegal drugs; many people shoplift; and so on. Lemert calls such deviance **primary deviance.** The deviance is unnoticed by others and is not defined by those engaging in such acts as deviant.

At times, however, people are "caught in the act" and are labeled deviant. A youth is caught experimenting with LSD; a businessman is convicted of income-tax evasion; or a pair of adolescent boys are interrupted during homosexual play. The person so exposed is called "dope fiend," "crook," "queer," or some other degrading label. Once publicly labeled, people begin to act toward the person *as if* he or she were, in fact, deviant, and in this way a cycle is set in motion: the labeled person is treated as deviant; when treated as deviant, the person begins to be thrust into a deviant role; in turn, further deviant actions "confirm" the labels. Lemert calls these further deviant actions **secondary deviance.**

If this labeling process results in people's redefining themselves as deviant, then they begin to exhibit deviant behaviors that further label and stigmatize them. Over time, this process can result in the pursuit of a deviant career in which the only options available to them are to interact with other deviants and to assume a deviant role as a way of life.

An effeminate boy, like all other boys, may not have strong sexual preferences in the sixth grade, but if others label him gay and begin to act toward him *as if* he were "different," then the label may become a part of his identity. If this happens, then the boy may develop like-sex preferences and assume a homosexual career, seeking comfort in the company of other gays.

Much of the labeling process occurs in formal organizations. For example, many young minority children are labeled "retarded" by school officials because they cannot perform well on standardized tests (usually because English is a second language or because standard English is not used in their environment). They are then put into special programs in which they are treated as retarded, which further labels them. Eventually, they come to define themselves as mentally deficient and to "act retarded."

Less dramatic labeling processes occur with former prison inmates and mental hospital patients. Once incarcerated, they become "suspect" and carry the label "former prison inmate" and "former mental patient." The result is that their behaviors become interpreted and labeled as an instance of their deviance. For example, most of us who are not "former mental patients" can get away with being emotional and hysterical at times, but a person called a "former patient" cannot. Such behavior becomes confirmation that the person is "not really cured," and people begin to act *as if* that person were "sick." On a more formal level, employers are reluctant to hire former inmates or mental patients, which places enormous stress on them often forcing them back to criminal activity or to emotional disruption.

Labeling theory has provided new understanding of how deviance can emerge and persist. It serves as a way of understanding how some—but not all—deviant careers may be set into motion inside and outside formal social contexts. It provides sociologists with yet another set of tools for understanding why deviance emerges.

The Causes of Deviance:
The Great Unknown

Each of these three perspectives offers insights into why deviation occurs and why it persists. Yet, we must be frank and admit that sociologists and psychologists alike do not understand deviance very well. Just why it emerges is not always clear. The theories presented here are three of the more plausible, but it is certain that taken alone, all are inadequate. As with many features of the human system, sociologists have much to learn.

SUMMARY AND PREVIEW

In this chapter we have examined the last of our basic elements of the human system: the tension or dialectic between deviance and social control. We have seen that deviance is the violation of norms, but we have also seen that the nature of the norms, the nature of violators in question, the visibility of the transgression, and the nature of who decides an act is deviant all shape what is considered "deviant" in a society. Deviance is thus relative, varying over time and in different systems.

The relativity of deviance makes difficult its classification. We sought to isolate only general types: deviant acts, deviant habits, deviant personalities, deviant groups and organizations, and deviant subcultures. These are not mutually exclusive categories, but this classification can give us a feeling for the range of deviance in the human system.

Social control is the process that seeks to reduce the amount of deviance and disharmony in the human system. Social control is never completely effective, but all systems reveal mechanisms operating to maintain the social order. The most prominent of these include: socialization, social sanctions, group pressure, organizational confinement, and institutionalization.

Finally, we have sought to unravel some of the ways that social conditions can cause deviance to emerge and persist. Anomie theory, differential association theory and labeling theory were offered as examples of the three most promising sociological approaches.

We can now visualize the human system as a constant dialectic between control and deviation. Many such dialectics exist in human affairs. The final basic element of the human system often creates tensions, while at the same time, it is the cornerstone of society. Perhaps this element is the most basic dialectic. Humans are divided into two sexes and this fact has profound consequences for how we interact and organize ourselves. This basic element is examined in the next chapter.

Key Terms

Deviance: behavior which violates important social norms

Deviant Act: a distinct unit of behavior that violates a norm

Deviant Habit: persistent behavior that violates a social norm and that interferes with conformity to other norms

Deviant Personalities: deviance that appears to be caused by disorders of personality

Deviant Groups and Organizations: those situations where individuals are organized collectively to pursue deviance

Deviant Subcultures: a population whose distinctive cultural traits violate, and are at odds with, those of the majority in a society

Social Control: those processes that attempt to maintain conformity to existing norms

Social Sanctions: actions on the part of others in a society that provide rewards for conformity and punishments for non-conformity

Informal Sanctions: sanctions emitted in the ordinary course of interaction

Formal Sanctions: patterned and organized ways that rewards and punishments are bestowed

Group Pressure: the process whereby people perceive group expectations to exert pressures for conformity

Organizational Confinement: the segregation and isolation of deviants in specialized organizations

Institutionalization: the patterning of social interaction in ways that reduces the possibility for tension, conflict, and deviance

Anomie: a state where norms are unclear, non-existent, or in conflict

Differential Association: the ratio of definitions favoring deviance or conformity that a person receives in interaction with others

Labeling: the process of an act being designated as deviant by those with whom one interacts

Primary Deviance: deviant acts that go unnoticed and unperceived by those emitting them as deviant

Secondary Deviance: deviant acts that have been labeled, with the labels further channeling actions into a deviant role

Review Questions

1. What does it mean to say that there is a tension between forces of social control and deviation?

2. What forces affect the definition of deviance in a society?

3. What are the general types of deviance?

4. What are the general mechanisms of social control in the human system? Which are most important?

5. What are the causes of deviance?

Suggested Readings

Becker, Howard. *The Other Side: Perspectives on Deviance.* New York: The Free Press, 1964.

Bell, Robert R. *Social Deviance: A Substantive Analysis.* Homewood, Ill.: The Dorsey Press, 1971.

Clinard, Marshall B. *The Sociology of Deviant Behavior.* New York: Holt, Rinehart and Winston, 1974.

Cohen, Albert K. *Deviance and Control.* Englewood Cliffs, N.J.: Prentice-Hall, 1966.

Gibbons, Don C., and Jones, Joseph F. *The Study of Deviance: Perspectives and Problems.* Englewood Cliffs, N.J.: Prentice-Hall, 1975.

GENDER: THE MALE AND FEMALE ELEMENT

PROLOGUE

Guiding Questions: In what ways are males and females really different? What consequences have sex differences had for the human system? What influences will the male and female element have for the human systems of the future?

Chapter Topics

9

SEX AND GENDER

Humans are either male or female. This seems obvious, but until recently in sociology, the existence of two sexes has been given scant attention. Sociologists have, of course, studied courtship, marriage, family, divorce, labor force participation, and other social patterns where sexual differences are involved. Yet, they have typically ignored the fact that virtually all facets of the human system are punctuated by sexuality, by the existence of two sexes. Social interaction, patterns of social organization, cultural symbols, socialization practices, and processes of deviance and social control all involve a sexual component. Sex and gender are thus a basic element of the human system—one with which we must deal before examining the elaboration of culture and social forms in the chapters of the next sections.

At the outset, we should make a simple, but important distinction between sex and gender. **Sex** refers to differences between males and females that are of an organic or physiological nature. **Gender** denotes the social and cultural distinctions that humans make between males and females. Sex and gender are interrelated but separate issues. Some people are biologically of one sex, but are defined, or seek to be defined, as members of the opposite sex. Others are biologically ambiguous, but come to be defined, and to view themselves, as one sex or the other. For example, as we noted in Chapter 7, hermaphrodites (children born with the organs of both sexes) who were raised as males developed relatively normal male social attitudes, behaviors, and sexual preferences; those reared as females exhibited female attributes (Money and Ehrhardt 1972; Ellis 1945).

Other case studies can provide further insight into the interaction of sex and gender. In one case (Stoller 1968), a young boy who had been born without normal male sex organs developed a male sense of identity. In another case, a seemingly normal girl who had external female sex organs and who had been reared as a female underwent a male voice change at puberty. A closer medical examination revealed that "she" was chromosomally a male with a normal male prostate gland, despite the existence of external female organs. Informed that she was a male, she "went home, took off her girl's clothing and became a boy, immediately beginning to behave like other boys" (Reynolds 1976:125). In another case, a child with male genitals reared as a boy developed female characteristics at puberty. The adolescent became extremely withdrawn and hid this fact until age 17, but at age 20 "he" underwent surgery to transform his male genitalia into those of a female. What is interesting about this case is the later discovery that the subject had secretly been taking female hormones since puberty to deliberately change sexual identification. Such a case points to the fact that persons can desire to be one gender, while biologically being another.

Studies of transsexuals and transvestites are providing new insights into the complexity of human sexuality. *Transsexuals,* for example, have the biological organs of one sex but self-concept, behavioral patterns, and dress of the opposite sex. Most transsexuals are men who want to be women; and as in the case cited above, they undergo surgery to alter their sex organs. *Transvestites,* on the other hand, share with transsexuals the desire to be the opposite sex, but they do not desire to change their sex organs, seemingly content to masquerade as a pseudo-member of the other sex.

Such cross-gender changes are not confined to modern, urban societies. For example, Bogoraz (1907) reported that among the aboriginal Chuckchee Indians, shamans at times persuaded themselves that they were of the opposite sex. Apparently, when the "spirits" called for a man to become what was termed a "soft man," behavioral and dispositional changes ensued. At first, only the hair was braided and arranged in the female manner. Then, female dress might be adopted. Later, all male pursuits were abandoned and those of women were assumed. His lance, rifle, lasso, and harpoon were discarded in favor of the needle and skin scraper of the female. His speech changed, his strength was lost, and he became fond of small talk with gatherings of females; he even undertook the care of small children. Outwardly, such a person was and

Gender-identity is a social product and is created by the social roles that children play.

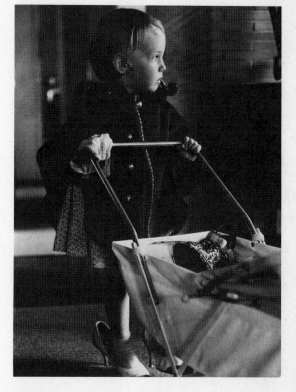

remained a member of the male sex, but in all important social respects, a transformation of gender from male to female had occurred.

These case studies emphasize that human sexuality is not simply a matter of biology. Sexual action and interaction are intimately connected to personality, culture, and patterns of social organization. People are not merely "driven" by their hormones; they are socialized into a gender-identity. And it is on the basis of this identity that they become cognizant of certain cultural directives and assume certain positions in society. Thus, from a sociological viewpoint, it becomes crucial to understand how sex and gender interact and operate to shape the human system.

SEXUAL DIFFERENTIATION

All societies divide their members into males and females. Each is viewed as a distinctive sex; and most important, males and females are required to assume different positions, play different roles, and reveal the typical attributes of their gender. There is considerable variation in *how* this differentiation occurs, however. For example, in a classic study of sex and temperament in three primitive societies, Margaret Mead (1935) observed vast differences in male and female behavior. In one tribe, the Arapesh, males and females acted in ways that Americans might define as feminine. Both sexes were passive, warm, and affectionate, with aggression and competition being discouraged for both males and females. Tasks were, to some extent, differentiated for males and females, but not nearly to the degree typical of most societies. Two tribes—the Mundugumor and Tchambuli—stood in marked contrast to the gentle Arapesh. Among the Tchambuli, there were clear-cut differences in gender, but these were the reverse of those that, until recently, might be associated with males and females in American society. Tchambuli women were assertive and were the major economic providers while Tchambuli men, in contrast, were highly nurturant, expressive, and somewhat gossipy. The third tribe, the Mundugumor, revealed extremely aggressive social patterns. Both sexes were assertive and violent. Women dreaded pregnancy and after childbirth all but rejected their children. Men were aggressive warriors and headhunters, and both sexes were cannibalistic.

Mead's tribes represent extreme cases, but they do emphasize that differences between male and female actions are shaped by social organization, cultural symbols, socialization experiences, and patterns of social control. Yet, despite the malleability of gender-linked attitudes and behavior, there are certain general patterns of sexual differentiation. First, there is usually some division of labor between the sexes. Males perform some tasks, females others. Second, males politically dominate in all societies, even in societies where females control the individual household. We should emphasize, however, that there is much variability in the human system as to just *how* these broad patterns of sexual differentiation are actually practiced.

We must, therefore, seek to answer the questions: What forces shape sexual differentiation? What significance does sexual differentiation make for the operation of the human system? We will approach these questions by first exploring the biology of gender, and then by examining the social and cultural influences on gender.

THE BIOLOGY OF GENDER

In order to assess the impact of gender on the human system, we must have some understanding of the biological factors that distinguish the sexes. We can classify these biological factors as (1) **genetic,** (2) *hormonal,* and (3) *anatomical.* We should not view these as separate biological forces, however, since they are highly interrelated.

(1) The Genetic Basis of Gender

All humans possess 23 pairs of chromosomes, except for occasionally abnormal persons. These chromosomes are exactly alike for males and females, but for one pair—the sex chromosomes. Females have two similar chromosomes in their pair (labelled XX), while males have dissimilar chromosomes in their pair (XY). Thus, a female's egg always contains an X chromosome, while a male's sperm can embody either an X or a Y chromosome. If a Y sperm fertilizes a female egg, then a male (XY) will develop in the mother's womb. If an X sperm fertilizes the female egg, then a female (XX) will develop.

Initially, (approximately 12 weeks) the sexes are undistinguished in their development. But after twelve weeks, the secretion of hormones begins to differentiate the fetus as either male or female. These hormones, as we will examine shortly, are responsible for not only the initial sex differentiation, but also for the development of secondary sex characteristics at puberty.

The male's lack of an X chromosome appears to make him, in some respects, the weaker sex. Males are more likely to be stillborn or malformed; they are subject to more hereditary disorders; and throughout their lives, they have higher rates of mortality. This is underscored by the fact that at birth, 106 males are born for every 100 females, but by young adulthood this ratio is even. With each decade beyond the mid-20s the sex ratio dramatically increases in favor of females.

(2) The Hormonal Basis of Gender

A **hormone** is a chemical substance secreted into the bloodstream by the glands. It operates to activate or retard other chemical processes. There are three principal sex hormones: estrogen, progesterone, and testosterone. Estrogen and progesterone are secreted by the ovaries in females, while testosterone is secreted by the testes in males. All three hormones are present in each human, but it is the relative concentration of hormones that influences the sex of an individual.

The concentration of hormones is crucial at certain stages in human development. The first stage is initial sexual differentiation of the fetus in the womb. The secretion of testosterone, as it is regulated by the XY chromosome pair, causes the development of male sex organs. The secretion of progesterone and estrogen causes the development of female sex organs at birth. The importance of critical concentrations is underscored by experimental findings. If large amounts of testosterone are injected early into a chromosomally female fetus, it will develop male sex organs. Conversely, if the secretion of testosterone is inhibited, a genetic male will exhibit female sex organs. With birth and the existence of differentiated sex organs (ovaries in females; testes in males), the regulation of appropriate concentrations of the sex hormones ensues. These concentrations can, of course, be altered through artificial injections of hormones.

The next critical stage is puberty. The increased secretion of testosterone in males influences the development of sexual drives and secondary sexual characteristics, such as body hair, voice, and muscle development. The converse is true for females at puberty. By the end of puberty, sexual differentiation between males and females is complete.

(3) The Anatomical Basis of Gender

Males and females possess somewhat dissimilar anatomical structures. The concept of **anatomy** refers to those structural features of the body that distinguish an individual, or as is our purpose here, that differentiate the sexes.

The anatomy of the sexes differs somewhat. Aside from the obvious distinctions between sex organs and secondary sex characteristics, there are differences in muscular development as well as in skeletal size and structure. But these differences are not nearly as great as Americans sometimes believe. The relative levels of athletic activities among boys and girls, and the encouragement of "masculinity" in boys and "femininity" in girls, has greatly accentuated dissimilarities between males and females with respect to size, weight, and strength. A casual glance at more traditional peoples where women perform much physical labor reveals much less **sexual dimorphism** (bodily differences between the sexes) than is evident among Americans.

How great are the anatomical differences between males and females? The childbearing and rearing functions of females represent one significant difference. Another major difference is in size and strength. Men are, *on the average*, about fifteen percent larger and stronger than females. This relatively slight difference has no doubt been a factor in the male's political dominance in the human system. Within any population, some females will be larger and potentially stronger (with full physical development) than men, but the strongest members of the population will likely be males, thus giving them the capacity to exert physical coercion over females (and, of course, over other males).

Another purported difference between males and females is more ambiguous. Are men more aggressive than females? Margaret Mead's findings reveal that females in a society can evidence more aggression than males. Testosterone does appear to increase aggression somewhat, but other factors—both genetic and socio-cultural—influence aggression even more. Thus, without any compelling evidence, we should hold in abeyance any assumptions about innate differences in sexual aggressiveness between males and females.

What, then, can be concluded about the biology of gender? First, there are genetic, hormonal, and anatomical differences. Second, these differences revolve around childbearing functions of women and around dissimilarities in average skeletal size and strength. These two biological differences are the most critical. What is most important, if we are to understand the impact of sexual differences in the human system, is the elaboration of these differences. Cultural beliefs, symbolic interaction, patterns of social organization, socialization practices, and mechanisms of social control have all operated to embellish these two critical differences. In other words, other basic elements of the human system transform issues of sex to questions of gender.

Sexual Dimorphism Among Primates

We have seen that humans reveal relatively little sexual dimorphism. Despite cultural beliefs in America about female "helplessness and weakness," males are only slightly larger and stronger than females. Much of the apparent dimorphism is the result of the American female's reluctance to realize her full physical potential. Such is the power of cultural beliefs and social organization.

There is wide variation in the degree of sexual dimorphism among our fellow primates. Some primates, such as the gibbon, reveal no differences between males and females in size or strength. Our closest primate relative, the chimpanzee, evidences only slight dimorphism. In contrast, the baboon, which evolved on the African savannah under conditions similar to those facing the ancestors of humans, is highly dimorphic. What accounts for these variations? What forces cause high or low degrees of dimorphism in primates? Answers to these questions can help us understand the comparative lack of dimorphism among our hominid ancestors, and hence, among present-day humans.

The answers lie in several interrelated factors: (1) the mating system of primates, (2) the ecological or environmental conditions under which a primate evolved, and (3) the nature of social organization of a primate. A primate will reveal high degrees of sexual dimorphism when *all* of the following conditions are met: the system of the primate is polygamous (especially when males mate with numerous females); the ecological conditions faced by the primate pose high predator threat; and the social organization of the primate does not involve the use of tools. The baboon fits these conditions. Baboons are polygamous monkeys who evolved on the savannah where there were extreme predator dangers. Large and dominant males had selective advantage for defensive purposes, and since the strongest males hoarded females, their offspring would also serve as effective defenders. As a monkey, the baboon does not have the necessary brain size or complexity to use tools, and thus, tight social organization of the troop, defended by large males, served to protect the baboon on the savannah.

Chimpanzees are closely related to humans. They are highly promiscuous, with males and females freely and casually engaging in sexual relations that do not result in enduring bonds. Chimpanzees are capable of using tools for gathering food, but they do not need to use tools for defense. They live in trees on the edge of the savannah, frequently wandering onto the grassland. At the first sign of danger, however, they flee to the safety of the trees. For the most part, then, chimps do not live under ecological conditions that pose great threat. They do not, therefore, meet our three conditions, and thus are not highly dimorphic.

We can now see why humans do not reveal high dimorphism. While our ancestor's environment posed grave threats, the ape anatomy (see Chapter 3) of our ancestors allowed them to evolve larger brains, to develop tools for defense, to become monogamous (permanent bonds between one female and male), and to organize cohesive troops in order to cope with dangerous savannah conditions. Hence, there was not a great need for large, aggressive males to defend the troop. Tools, cunning, and social organization increasingly served the ancestors of humans. During our human ancestors' early evolution, larger males may have had selective advantage. But large brains (and all that this implies), tool use, monogamy, and troop organization proved more effective in dealing with savannah conditions than did large, aggressive males who may have proved mal-adaptive, since they could disrupt troop organization and the stabilizing bonds between males and females. Thus, there was probably strong selective pressures against sexual dimorphism, and by the time *Homo sapien sapien* emerged (modern humans) some 40,000 years ago, little sexual dimorphism remained.

THE SOCIAL BASIS OF GENDER

We can see now that gender is a social product, and only secondarily a biological imperative. Humans learn their sexual identity through socialization, and this identity is reinforced by their participation in patterns of social organization. Thus, to understand the sociological basis of gender, we must explore how the other elements of the human system—culture, interaction, social organization, socialization and personality, and social control—operate to make and enforce gender distinctions. Conversely, we should be aware that gender distinctions feed back upon and shape the other elements of the human system. Cultural beliefs, as well as patterns of interaction, social organization, socialization, and social control will all reflect the kinds of gender distinctions made in a society. For example, if the gender of women in a society is viewed as passive, nurturant, and submissive, then cultural beliefs are likely to stress the appropriateness of "femininity," social patterns are likely to exclude women from roles requiring assertiveness, socialization practices are likely to stress passivity and nurturance, male interaction with females is likely to be somewhat condescending, and sanctions are likely to be levied against women who are too aggressive. The converse could be true in a society where gender is viewed differently.

The critical point is that gender makes a difference in the human system. Biological differences between males and females are elaborated, and once stable gender differences exist, they influence the operation of a society. Naturally, if gender distinctions are in a process of re-definition, then we can expect that the conditions creating these distinctions have changed. Moreover, we will find that the re-definition of what is masculine or feminine in a society will influence the profile of cultural beliefs as well as patterns of interaction, social organization, socialization, and social control. As we will come to see, such appears to be the case in the United States where gender is undergoing a process of re-definition—a process that promises to change the profile of the American system.

Since gender is intimately tied to the other basic elements of the human system, we should explore how each element influences gender, and in turn, is influenced by sex definitions. To do this, we need first to introduce the concept of **sex roles.** As reviewed in Chapter 6, *role* pertains to patterns of behavior associated with a given status position. A sex role, then, is behavior associated with the position of being a female or male in a society. What is it that females or males in society are supposed to do? How are they to behave? How·are females or males to be treated? What other positions in a society, in light of their status as women or men, are they allowed to assume? These are sex role questions and they will occupy our attention as we explore the sociological basis of gender in the human system.

Social Organization and Sex Roles

Social organization is the general term used to describe the ways that status positions, roles, and norms are structured in a society. We discussed this basic element in Chapter 6. The most important facet of social organization for understanding sex roles is what is termed the **division of labor.** How are tasks in various social spheres divided among males and females?

Sex Roles in Traditional Societies. As we reviewed in Chapter 3 on the emergence of humans, it is likely that females and males played the same roles as do members of present day hunting and gathering societies. Females do most of the work: They gather roots, berries, and fruits; they prepare and cook meals; and they tend and care for children. Males, in contrast, lead a less vigorous existence: They hunt or fish; they assist females in gathering activities; and they play many leisure games. However, in some societies, such as the traditional Eskimo and some nomadic tribes of American Indians, males perform hard labor, since the society is dependent upon a successful hunt or catch.

This original division of labor was, no doubt, influenced by the facts of childbearing and rearing. Since it is the female who carries the child and since the newborn is helpless and must receive considerable attention, it has typically been more convenient to have females remain near a camp or home base and perform household and economic tasks around the camp. Since men are free from childbearing, they could wander in search of game. We should emphasize that this is only the typical pattern among hunters and gatherers; there are deviations and variations. Yet, the need to bear and raise children and to gather as well as hunt necessitated a sexual division of labor.

The development of agriculture some 10,000 years ago created a new economic system and altered the division of labor. With hunting no longer a major economic activity, agricultural and household labor needed to be divided. Among traditional agriculturalists, no clear pattern between the sexes is evident, although there is a tendency among present day non-

Table 1: The Division of Labor by Sex in Traditional Societies

Role	Number of Societies In Which Activity Is Performed By:				
	Men Always	Men Usually	Either Sex Equally	Women Usually	Women Always
Pursuing sea mammals	34	1	0	0	0
Hunting	166	13	0	0	0
Trapping small animals	128	13	4	1	2
Herding	38	8	4	0	5
Fishing	98	34	19	3	4
Clearing land for agriculture	73	22	17	5	13
Dairy operations	17	4	3	1	13
Preparing and planting soil	31	23	33	20	37
Erecting and dismantling shelter	14	2	5	6	22
Tending fowl and small animals	21	4	8	1	39
Tending and harvesting crops	10	15	35	39	44
Gathering shellfish	9	4	8	7	35
Making and tending fires	18	6	25	22	62
Bearing burdens	12	6	35	20	57
Gathering fruits, berries, nuts	12	3	15	13	63
Gathering fuel	22	1	10	19	89
Preserving meat and fish	8	2	10	14	74
Gathering herbs, roots, seeds	8	1	11	7	74
Cooking	5	1	9	28	158
Carrying water	7	0	5	7	119
Grinding grain	2	4	5	13	114

Source: From George P. Murdock, (1935)

industrial agriculturalists for men to clear the soil, with men and women dividing or sharing the tasks of planting, tending, and harvesting the crop. Moreover, women almost universally perform child-care functions and prepare meals, although this burden is often assumed by other female relatives, such as a grandmother, who live in the large households of traditional agriculturalists. Again, this division of labor reflects the need for females to bear children. It may also reflect the slight differences in short-run exertions of strength between males and females, since tilling is the most difficult and taxing of agricultural tasks.

Yet, the labor performed by females is also arduous, and so we cannot draw any definitive conclusions about the way differences in musculature between males and females influenced the division of economic and household labor.

Table 1 presents a summary of male and female involvement in various economic tasks among traditional peoples. As can be seen, there are clear patterns in the sexual division of labor.

With respect to political power, we can speculate that the strength advantage enjoyed by males has been decisive. In all traditional societies, whether they be hunters and gatherers or agriculturalists, men are the political leaders. In some agricultural societies of the past, females have inherited leadership, but the day-to-day administration of inherited power and the enforcement of political dictates has been performed by males. The strength advantage of males may not have been the only factor in their political dominance. The fact that warriors must leave the household or that political administrators must work outside the household has made it easier for males, who do not have to bear or nurse children, to assume political roles.

Thus, we can see that the biological functions of childbearing and nursing, coupled with anatomical differences between males and females, become elaborated in traditional societies into a division of household, economic, and political labor. With the advent of industrial society, this division of labor has been preserved not so much out of biological necessity, but out of tradition. For as we will examine in a later section on the culture of sex roles, once beliefs about the "proper" roles of males and females emerge, they become an impediment to change.

Sex Roles in Modern Societies. During early industrialization in Europe, and today in the Third World, both men and women often must work in the factories. Yet, women almost universally will be strapped with the additional burden of household labor and child rearing. This situation reflects traditional beliefs about what is proper for men and women to do. Moreover, males typically refuse to perform household and child-rearing tasks, and with the inability of the average wife to coerce her husband into domestic tasks, the burden falls upon her. Subtle pressures of social control exerted in traditional societies also work to burden the female worker: Those females who do not work in factories apply subtle, interpersonal sanctions against those who seek male assistance in the traditional female role; and conversely, men who do perform domestic tasks are ridiculed by their peers for their lack of masculinity. An additional impediment to change in the sexual division of labor is the unwillingness or inability of poor, male-dominated political systems in industrializing nations to provide child care and other facilities which would relieve females of their domestic roles.

Among more advanced industrial nations, however, dramatic changes in the sexual division of labor are occurring. In some societies, such as the Soviet Union, Sweden, and China, the government has initiated deliberate policies to encourage female participation in the labor force and to reduce the domestic burden on females. Sweden is perhaps the most advanced in this area, for it is not uncommon to have the male perform most of the domestic chores when he is not working.

In other countries like the United States, female participation in the economy has become an economic necessity for many poor and working class citizens or a means for the more affluent to escape the boredom and stigma of being "just a housewife." Yet, even with one-half of all women in the United States participating in the labor force, many females, who cannot afford domestic help or child-care assistance, must assume a full load of household burdens, despite the fact that they work. It is only among the more affluent, and childless couples, that we see evidence of an equal division of household tasks.

Even with growing female participation in economic roles in industrial societies, they do not, on average, have parity with males. For example, in the United States, women are more likely to serve as adjuncts to male dominated roles: secretaries to "bosses"; nurses to doctors; prostitutes for pimps; or teachers for male administrators. Moreover, college educated women tend to be confined to certain professions: teaching, social work, library work, and nursing. And there are certain types of non-professional jobs toward which female wage workers are channeled: cashiers, child care, and clerical. Women tend to be excluded from high prestige and high paying professions, such as medicine, law, and engineering (Turner 1976).

Some modern societies reveal less partitioning of male and female work roles. In Russia, England, and France, greater proportions of doctors are female. However, in Russia where 76% of all doctors are women, the ascendance of the female doctor has been accompanied by a decrease in prestige for the medical profession—again attesting to the fact that, even in a totalitarian system, old cultural beliefs are not easily changed.

In the political sphere, women do not fare as well as they do in the economic world. For example, in the United States there are no women Senators, there is one female governor of a state, there is not one female Supreme Court Justice, and there is only one female mayor of a large city (San Jose, California). While this extreme pattern is not as evident in other modern societies, American females are dramatically under-represented in the halls of political power (Turner 1976).

Sex Roles and Inequality. The positions that people assume, especially their economic position, in a society greatly influence the scarce resources that they receive: income, power, and prestige. We will, of course, have much more to say about this topic in later chapters. But before closing our discussion of the division of labor, we should dwell upon the issue of inequality.

Female roles, in general, receive less money, prestige, and power. The role of the housewife is an unpaid one that involves no real political power outside the household and that is increasingly held in low esteem. Other female roles—teacher, librarian, social worker, cashier, and secretary—are similarly undervalued. Such a situation places women in a position of inequality: They are more likely to receive less money, power, and prestige for performance of their roles.

This degree of inequality has not always existed in the human system. The tasks performed by females in hunting and gathering as well as in simple agricultural societies are valued. Women receive respect and prestige. It is only with the advent of large agrarian and early industrial societies that women have been placed in a situation where they receive low prestige for their economic and household contributions. More advanced industrial societies show a trend toward increasing equality between the sexes, but this is only an incipient trend. As we will come to see, many of the dynamics of modern societies like the United States are the product of sexual inequalities.

Cultural Beliefs and Sex Roles

All enduring social relations in the human system are legitimated by cultural beliefs. That is, they are made to seem right and proper. The sexual division of labor, and resulting inequalities, is but one example of how cultural beliefs operate to reinforce a social pattern.

Each society, revealing its own division of sex roles, evidences a somewhat different set of beliefs. Thus, few cultural universals exist when it comes to the actual content of belief systems. Each society contains its own culture. We can, however, illustrate how beliefs legitimate sex roles by examining those that exist in American society.

Three general beliefs are used to legitimate the sexual division of labor in American society. These beliefs highlight presumed differences between males and females—making gender distinctions in America appear to be the "natural order of things." The three beliefs are (Turner 1976:314):

(1) Women are "naturally" more expressive, emotional, and affectionate than men.
(2) Women are "naturally" less aggressive and more submissive and dependent than men.
(3) Women are not as physically strong as men, and therefore, they cannot perform hard labor.

There is, of course, no evidence in the biological literature to support beliefs (1) and (2). Belief (3) is partly true in that there are differences between males and females in their capacity for feats requiring short-term strength. But it is also true that females have more long-term endurance than men. Moreover, there are very few jobs in industrial society in which strength differences are relevant to job performance. For example, few jobs in modern societies are as physically taxing as those that women perform *each day* in the agricultural fields of Third World nations. We can see, then, that people's convictions about "what is" and "what exists" are often inaccurate. Yet, these beliefs make it seem "proper" to exclude females from roles that require assertiveness or physical exertion, while confining them to roles in which their "natural" expressiveness, emotionalism, and affection can be used to good advantage. These latter roles tend to be low both in prestige and pay.

These beliefs are now under attack by the organizations of the women's movement in America. Furthermore, Civil Rights legislation has now been extended to females, forcing employers to hire qualified females for traditionally male-dominated jobs, such as construction and repair work. And with the growing participation of women in athletics, beliefs about their passivity and weakness may recede. Yet, cultural beliefs are altered only under enduring pressures for change, and thus, it will be decades before beliefs supporting non-discriminatory gender-typing of females will come to prevail in American society.

Thus, we can see that sex roles are not merely a phenomenon of social structure.

Cultural beliefs are always involved in the maintenance of an enduring social pattern. And gender distinctions are particularly influenced by cultural beliefs. This is true in American society as it is true in all human systems.

Socialization into Sex Roles

Socialization is the process by which cultural directives, motives, role-playing skills, self-concepts and other aspects of personality are acquired. We reviewed this process in Chapter 7. When a child is born, only its external sex organs distinguish it as a male or a female. Yet, those in the infant's social world soon begin to act toward the child *as if* it were male or female. And throughout the child's life, he or she will be responded to by others on the basis of sex. A child's motive states, the values and beliefs that guide its actions, the nature of his or her self-concept, and the style of its role playing will all reflect the gender to which he or she has been assigned.

Family Socialization. The first significant others for an infant are its parents. When a newborn baby is pronounced to be male or female, parents will tend to invoke the cultural beliefs and traditional socialization practices "appropriate" for a member of its sex. In American society for example, girls will be dressed as females and will be encouraged to play with dolls and to imitate feminine roles, such as housewife and nurse. In contrast, boys are likely to be channelled into more assertive games and to be encouraged to play male roles, such as doctor, fireman, and policeman. And with such channelling into different roles comes a whole set of expectations about what

In American society, males are socialized to be assertive and aggressive, while females are taught to play nurturant roles.

"men are" and what "women are." These expectations continue to be imposed throughout a child's life in the home, but they are further reinforced by non-familial agents of socialization: the school, peers, and the media.

School Socialization. Gender distinctions are maintained in schools. In America, for example, boys play competitive sports involving physical contact; girls more typically play less competitive sports involving less physical contact. Girls become class secretaries, cheerleaders, and members of home economics clubs. Boys become varsity players and mem-

bers of math and science clubs. Boys take shop, girls take sewing and cooking. Girls are often counseled into English and humanities; boys are encouraged to develop their math, science, or vocational skills. These and many other practices shape gender identity. Girls are encouraged to play less assertive and less competitive roles, while acquiring domestic skills. In contrast, boys play active and competitive roles, while learning occupational skills.

These experiences in American schools are often reinforced by the content of textbooks.

Several studies document clearly that texts portray males as active, assertive, and combative, while girls are seen as passive and dependent. For example, in a study of pre-school books, Weitzman and Eifler (1972) found that nearly all prize-winning books present a highly stereotyped view of males and females. Males were represented in pictures ten times as often as females, with one-third of the books having only male central characters. When females did appear in the other two-thirds of the books, they were usually subordinate to the male hero.

Peer Socialization. Patterns of family and school socialization tend to be reinforced by peer associations. In the United States, formal clubs are often divided by sex: girl scouts vs. boy scouts, YMCA vs. YWCA, girls' sports vs. boys' sports, homemaking clubs vs. car clubs, and so on. More informal peer interactions are likely to further channel gender identity: girls shop together, sew together, experiment with make-up and clothing together; boys rarely do such things. Rather, they play sports, "shoot the bull," or "cruise" in cars together. Other peer traditions also reinforce gender-identity: Boys rather than girls ask for dates; boys drive the car; boys open doors; boys decide where to go; and so on. All these experiences condition the young into a gender identity, complete with gender-linked motives, beliefs, and role-playing styles.

Media Socialization. In modern societies like the United States, the mass media—books, television, comics, magazines, radio, records, and films—are major agents of socialization. On the whole, these support gender stereotypes in America. Girls' magazines emphasize fashion and appearance; boys' stress activities, projects, and sports. Television portrays highly stereotyped versions of mother and father, hero and heroine. Comics have Super*man*, Spider*man*, and Aqua*man*.

We can see, then, that children face many obstacles if they wish to avoid gender-typing. Socialization influences motives, values and beliefs, concepts of self, and role-playing styles before there is much awareness on a person's part as to what has occurred. Such is the power of socialization to mold gender in the human system. Often, only through therapy, counseling, and consciousness-raising groups can males and females overcome the impact of their socialization experiences. However, those

who do seek to re-define for themselves what is masculine and feminine face strong forces of social control.

Social Control and Sex Roles

As we observed in the last chapter, social control is the process whereby some degree of conformity to dominant norms is maintained. Through formal and informal mechanisms tendencies toward deviation are held in check. Deviations from dominant beliefs about gender and from traditional sex roles are thus likely to encounter resistance and to invoke efforts at social control.

The most important mechanisms inhibiting violations of traditional sex roles are informal. Males who assume female roles, and females who seek entrance to male roles, are often subject to interpersonal sanctions—ridicule, rejection, and negative stereotyping. For example, in American society, a husband who stays home, cares for children, and performs domestic chores while his wife works is often ridiculed and rejected by other males and females, and is subject to negative stereotyping as effeminate and lazy. Similarly, females who seek entrance into male-dominated positions are also likely to be sanctioned negatively. If they attempt to compete with men, they might be labelled "men haters." Or, more likely they are considered to be masculine and overly aggressive.

This tendency to label unfavorably those who enter "the man's world" is illustrated in two studies conducted by Matina Horner (1968, 1969). Male students were asked to make up a story in response to the following sentence: "After first term exams, John finds himself at the top of the medical school class." Stories by males were positive about John, although the stories of women were much more ambiguous. When females were given the same sentence with the name "Anne" substituted for "John," the stories were much less positive and often predicted unpleasant consequences for Anne. When males were given the sentence with "Anne" as the medical student, reactions were negative. They often viewed her as unfeminine or as compensating for physical handicaps or mental problems. More recent efforts to replicate Horner's findings, however, have shown a much less negative reaction (Katz, 1972)—suggesting that beliefs about sex roles are undergoing change in America.

While informal, interpersonal sanctions are important in maintaining sex roles, we should not forget that formal sanctions, such as prohibition against women in certain traditional male roles, can also operate to maintain gender distinctions. Women in traditional societies, for example, are often prohibited from engaging in certain male activities, such as hunting and special religious ceremonies. Or, as has been the case in America, females have been formally prevented from joining combat units in the armed forces.

In sum, then, we can visualize how gender distinctions are maintained by the other basic elements of the human system. Patterns of social organization always reveal a male-female division of labor. Socialization practices, cultural beliefs, and mechanisms of social control then operate to maintain this division of labor. Yet, as we can observe in the United States, gender can undergo re-definition, creating pressures for changes in cultural beliefs, the division of labor, and socialization practices. Such changes lead us to the question: Are gender distinctions inevitable in the human system, and most particularly, in modern societies?

IS GENDER INEVITABLE?

Gender definitions appear to change with advancing industrialism. Many of the reasons for this will be explored in the chapter to follow as we begin to analyze the human system in more detail. We can, however, provide a brief view of the forces reshaping gender definitions and redefining the "proper" role of men and women in society. We will use the United States as our example, but what we say is also true of other post-industrial societies.

In modern societies, the family loses many of its traditional functions to other institutions, while its size progressively decreases. Thus, the motherhood role and the associated domestic tasks become less burdensome and essential, especially among the affluent who can hire others to perform many domestic tasks. The diversification of the modern economy which deals in services as much as commodities tends, in the long run, to undermine the sex-based division of labor. As non-physical jobs increase, the old belief that women cannot work becomes increasingly untenable. The expansion of education, especially higher education, to a citizenry further undermines gender definitions. Well-educated women are likely to want to use their skills and to realize the rewards that come from occupational achievement. And as women work, the males' claim to being the sole "breadwinner" becomes less credible, and they are forced to help in the domestic chores of the household.

These forces have increasingly required a reassessment of traditional gender-definitions and sex roles. This re-assessment has been encouraged by the Women's Movement and the political pressure that it has brought to bear on government and industry. Lawsuits, political lobbying, and financing of political campaigns by women's organizations have created a new sensitivity to sexual discrimination,

SUMMARY AND PREVIEW

resulting in the enforcement of Civil Rights laws for women as well as minorities. Moreover, the existence of women's organizations, and the publicity that they generate, encourages a kind of "consciousness-raising" among traditional women to assess their situation and to begin to alter their view of the "proper female role."

Such pressures for change are, of course, going to encounter heavy resistance. Many males are not likely to give up their favored position easily. And women, who have been socialized into traditional beliefs, will find it difficult to support changes in, and a further devaluation of, their sex roles. Yet, these forces for change are, in the long run, greater than the barriers to change.

Thus, in the future, we can expect considerably more equality in sex roles. We can expect that gender will become re-defined so that women are viewed as capable of competing equally in "a man's world." For in a technological society, where great feats of strength are rarely required and where child-care facilities can, if given the desire, be made available to all, biological differences between males and females become less critical in the organization of sex roles. This simple fact will lead to pressures for change in the roles of men and women in the human system of the future.

In this chapter, we have sought to introduce a final element into the human system: gender. Sex is a biological concept, pertaining to physiological differences between males and females. Gender is a sociological concept, denoting the way people define sexual differences.

We first sought to outline the biological differences between males and females. Such differences are genetic, hormonal, and anatomical. The only substantial differences were seen to be the childbearing function of the female and the slight size and strength advantage of males.

These differences have not been trivial, however. They have become elaborated into clear gender-definitions and sex roles in all societies. We then reviewed how patterns of social organization, dominant cultural beliefs, established socialization practices, and mechanisms of social control operate to maintain gender distinctions. We closed this review with a recognition that in modern societies the childbearing responsibilities of females and the strength advantages enjoyed by males need not any longer be viewed as critical determinants in the roles that males and females play. At one time in the human system, sex roles may have been necessary, or at least they were the most efficient way to organize activity, but in modern societies, such is not necessarily the case. Thus, gender re-definition will be an important element in human systems of the future.

We are now at the close of Part II of this book. In addition to our discussion of the emergence of humans, we have reviewed each basic element of the human system: culture, interaction, social organization, socialization, deviation and control, and gender. The next two sections of chapters will examine how these basic elements have become elaborated into different social forms: groups, formal organization, patterns of collective organization, communities, strata, race and ethnic populations, and social institutions. With an understanding of the basic elements, we are now in a good position to see and appreciate (a) what has been created in the human system, (b) how these creations operate, and (c) why they change or remain the same. These will be our goals as we approach the study of basic social forms in Parts III and IV.

Key Terms

Sex: differences between males and females that have a biological or physiological basis

Gender: the general term used to denote masculine and feminine, or male and female, distinctions made by members of a society

Genetic: those factors pertaining to genetic structure of humans, particularly to the alignment of genes on chromosomes

Hormone: chemical substances secreted into the circulatory system that influence bodily functions

Anatomy: those factors pertaining to the bodily structure of humans

Sexual Dimorphism: differences in the size, strength, and other relevant features between males and females

Sex Roles: those behaviors in a society that are assigned to, or assumed to be related to, being either male or female

Division of Labor: the differential allocation of tasks and functions to different members of society

Review Questions

1. Why do sociologists distinguish sex and gender? Explain.

2. Is there evidence for a distinctive female or male personality? Why or why not?

3. What social and cultural forces operate to maintain sex roles?

4. Is there a biological basis for sex roles in modern societies? Why or why not?

5. How have biological differences become elaborated into gender distinctions?

Suggested Readings

Friedan, Betty. *The Feminine Mystique* (New York: Dell, 1963).

Huber, Joan, ed. *Changing Women in a Changing Society* (Chicago: University Press, 1973).

Maccoby, Eleanor, ed. *The Development of Sex Differences* (Stanford: Stanford University Press, 1966).

Stoller, Robert. *Sex and Gender* (New York: Science House, 1968).

Whitehurst, Carol. *Women in America: The Oppressed Majority* (Santa Monica: Goodyear, 1976).

Yorburg, Betty. *Sexual Identity: Sex Roles and Social Change* (New York: Wiley, 1974).

BASIC FORMS OF HUMAN ORGANIZATION

CONTENTS

PREVIEW

In this part we will explore how the "elements" discussed in Part II "fit together" in building a variety of social forms. Humans organize and reorganize themselves in a wide variety of ways. Our goal is to capture a sense of the structure and dynamics of human organization.

In Chapter 10, we will seek to understand the most basic social form, the group. Most of our activities are carried out in groups, and we must understand how groups operate and how they influence us as individuals as well as the society and culture as a whole. Chapter 11 deals with a comparatively recent form of social organization: bureaucracy. Social life in modern societies is increasingly conducted in a bureaucratic context—giving human affairs a formal character. Thus, we must explore the structure and operation of formal organizations if we are to understand their impact on our lives and on society. Chapter 12 examines fluid patterns of

III

social organization. Although human affairs are often formal, they are also fluid and subject to violence, impulse, contagion, and chance. We will therefore try to provide an overview of fluid social patterns: mass behavior, public opinion, crowds, riots, mobs, and social movements. Many of the dynamics of the human system are to be formed in these fluctuating and fluid social forms. Chapter 13 concerns how and where we live. Humans are located in a place when conducting their affairs. When this place is relatively permanent and comprised of a number of interacting persons, it constitutes a community. Much of human social life is influenced by the residence, work, and activity patterns dictated by community. Thus, communities influence both our individual lives and the character of the society at large. Chapter 14 will focus on inequality and how it creates more or less enduring rankings of members in the human system. Humans form social hierarchies in terms of who gets the money, prestige, and power in almost all

social settings. Our emphasis will be on societywide hierarchies and what these mean for the individual and society. Chapter 15 explores the creation and maintenance of large, societywide race and ethnic groupings. Patterns of group, class, and community organization in many societies operate in ways that create and maintain large subpopulations that are distinguished by a unique cultural heritage. The dynamics and structure of society is often influenced by the patterns of interaction among these subpopulations.

In this group of chapters, then, we examine the social forms that comprise the human system. The field of sociology is, to a very great extent, organized around the study of processes and structures in these social units. Much of what sociology "is" can be gleaned from a careful reading of Chapters 10 through 15.

SOCIAL GROUPS

PROLOGUE

Guiding Questions: What is a group? How do groups influence our lives? How do groups help shape our personalities and patterns of social organization?

Chapter Topics

THE GROUP BASIS OF SOCIAL LIFE

We cannot live in a social vacuum. We depend upon others and our creation of culture and patterns of social organization for survival. Probably the most basic of these social patterns are **groups.** From the moment we begin to perceive other people around us and ourselves through the looking-glass process as Cooley called it, we work toward integrating ourselves as individuals into the vast web of society. Society can sometimes be a terrifying entity, overwhelming in its huge dimensions and complexities if viewed from a solitary and disenfranchised perspective. We work ourselves into the structure of society through participation in the more personal structure of social groups. Groups help us to establish feelings of comfort and security in the world and to perpetuate the macrocosmic dimensions of society itself.

The overall manner in which society is organized can be compared to the atomic structure of matter. Without the miniscule and seemingly independent movements of atoms and the way they are bonded together in physical systems, the "matter" that they ultimately describe could not exist. Such is the case with social organization. The whole (society) could not exist without an organized system of particles (social groups).

In Chapter 7 we briefly discussed the impact of such groups as the family, peers, the school classroom, private clubs, and occupational groups on our lives. Interactions in each of these groups involve different degrees of emotional involvement. People's relationships with their parents in the family are much different than those relationships acquired later in work and peer groups. Thus, it is difficult to imagine human lives devoid of emotional involvement in groups. We would not be human; we would be like Anna and Isabelle, the feral children, or like the Rhesus monkeys raised in isolation. Recall Anna and Isabelle. When discovered, they literally behaved like nonhumans. They moved about on all fours and could not communicate with language or gestures except on a rudimentary level; they were less human than a one-year-old infant.

The POW experience during the Korean War provides another grim example of how important group participation and identification are. The common procedure of the Chinese toward prisoners of war usually consisted of total isolation from peers, or at best, confinement to very small groups. Even prisoners in these small groups were frequently shuffled about in order to prevent the emergence of cohesive group bonds. Perhaps the most significant feature of POW's treatment was that the Chinese were able to "brainwash" their captives. Alone and disoriented, the prisoners were slowly ground down to whimpering, sluggishly obedient creatures. One prisoner might find himself alone in a room, facing a group of interrogators shielded by a screen, hearing coldly authoritative voices but seeing nothing, and being told that he should divulge any important information that he might have because all of his friends and comrades were already "informers." The interrogators might also tell prisoners that their government had abandoned them and their government had given up the war and was not interested in their welfare or fate. Given the social vacuum the Chinese had contrived along with various means of torture, it was not difficult to "break" the POWs and to get them to believe or say anything in total contradiction to former beliefs and values. Without the peer group in close proximity, nor any vestige of any other social reinforcement, a prisoner's system of values and beliefs could be reshaped (Clifton 1961).

The POW situation in the Vietnam War was somewhat different. The brainwashing tactics employed by the North Vietnamese were not nearly as effective or successful as those that had been employed in the Korean War. New training of soldiers stressed that (1) the POW must, wherever possible, endeavor to keep in contact with other POWS and (2) that the POW must always obey the senior American officer present. Although the conditions of the POWS' confinement by the North Vietnamese often made these orders difficult to follow, the training apparently helped sustain morale under difficult conditions. The successful maintenance of this proportionately higher level of morale among POWS in the Vietnam War compared to the POWS in the Korean War was particularly remarkable in light of the fact that public opinion in the United States was so violently divided over the legitimacy of the war itself. These divisions at home were constantly parlayed by the North Vietnamese to undermine the POWS' morale, but with comparatively little effect in changing their attitudes and beliefs.

The effort to train military personnel to specifically work at maintaining strong group ties exemplifies the importance of the relationship between the individual and a group. Should group ties of a strong and cohesive substance be sundered, the individual commences to lose his or her sense of identity, an identity built out of an association in groups (Little 1964; Shils & Janowitz 1948).

If we are to have a more precise understanding of our behavior, perceptions, aspirations, and other aspects of our thought and conduct, we must become aware of our experiences in different groups, whether these experiences reside in the past, the present, or the future. Groups implicitly set the rules we follow, whether we are conscious of them or not. Some people—indeed most individuals—find comfort, security, and solace in group membership, and thus, they embrace its rules and thrive on conformity. Others develop a more disparaging, even hateful attitude toward groups. Henry David Thoreau, no lover of social conventions, once wrote: "Wherever a man goes, men will pursue him and paw him with their dirty institutions, and, if they can, constrain him to belong to their desperate oddfellow society." This rather harsh indictment reevokes Freud's contention that society, armed with social groups as its personified henchmen, forces us to "toe the line" and adhere to established norms even against our will.

Thus, we can see that the study of groups is vital to gaining insight into ourselves, into who we are and why we think and act the way we do. Moreover, in shaping our thoughts and actions, groups operate to maintain society and culture. By providing us with a place to live and act, as well as with common symbols to share, groups give social life continuity and stability. They make possible the human system. But groups also provide conflict and change; they often clash; they often place conflicting obligations upon us; and as Freud emphasized, they often constrain us. Thus, the dynamics of the human system frequently occur within social groups.

In this first chapter on the diverse forms of the human system, we will examine this most fundamental of social units. Our purpose will be threefold: (1) to outline the properties of social groups, (2) to indicate the many ways they influence our thoughts and actions, and (3) to show some of the ways that the structure of various social groups differ.

The Group Imperative

As we noted in Chapter 3, our hominid ancestors could not have survived on the African savannah without social organization and culture. It was our ancestors' ability to form viable social groups for food gathering, reproduction, and defense that enabled them to survive. Group organization was probably carried from the forests out onto the savannah some 20 million years ago.

Present-day primates provide us with some evidence of what these former inhabitants of the savannah were like. Our closest cousin, the chimpanzee, is a group-oriented animal. However, chimp groups tend to be fluid, with members coming and going. In contrast, baboon groups are much tighter in organization, and members of one group are often likely to view baboons from another group suspiciously. Gorillas are also group oriented, with small groups wandering through the thick brush forest of the low and high mountain regions of Africa.

It is likely that our hominid ancestors entered the savannah with propensities for group organization like that of the chimp, but because they faced severe conditions, they became increasingly more tight knit in organization, perhaps approximating baboon organization. We will never know, of course, exactly how group oriented our original ancestors were. But it is clear that social groups were the first form of societal organization. With group organization, and subsequent new technologies, more elaborate social forms became possible, culminating in our present complex social systems. But none of this would have been possible had we not first created group bonds. For it was in the context of group living that true humans emerged and were able to survive.

Source: Lancaster (1975).

WHAT
IS
A GROUP?

Like all social structures, sociologists view groups as networks of status positions, filled by role playing actors who take cognizance of norms. The number, nature, and structure of status positions, of course, vary from group to group. Norms also vary and so do the nature of incumbents and their enactment of roles. For example, the organization of statuses, contents of norms, and role-playing actions of members in family groups are different than those in work groups. Therefore, we must discern their diverse forms. To do this, we must first discover what a *group* is and how it can be seen as a distinctive form of human organization.

First, *groups* are relatively small social units and are composed of a fairly narrow range of status positions. For our purposes we can say that most groups rarely exceed a few hundred people, but they are usually much smaller. A group, at its maximum size, might be best exemplified by a large academic lecture in which a hundred or more students have been gathering over the course of a term in one room. Status positions are few: student, instructor, and, perhaps, a teaching assistant or exam reader. In American society a group such as the family represents a smaller social unit, numbering rarely more than six people. Again, status positions are very few: the father, mother, and child.

Second, for each status position in any group there are norms. For example, certain patterns of behavior are expected from both the instructor and his or her students. Similarly, different norms apply to different members of a family unit. Sometimes, depending on the group or the idiosyncrasies of the individuals holding status positions, these expectations can be un-

clear and ambiguous, but in most cases, the norms are relatively clear. If they are not clear, the members of a group will usually make efforts to clarify the norms. The persistence of ambiguous or obscure norms within a group usually result in considerable conflict, perhaps leading to the disintegration of that group.

Third, status positions and norms in a group are often reciprocal; that is, they derive their significance and meaning only in relation to each other. The status position of a father, for example, is defined by the existence of a son or daughter; an instructor is also defined by the body of students attending the lecture. The norms of status positions are also interconnected. What is expected of a father corresponds in some minimal way to what is expected of a son or daughter. Students "expect" an instructor to deliver a lecture, just as the instructor expects the students to listen and take notes.

Fourth, groups usually have some means of exerting social control to ensure that, to some minimal and yet constraining degree, each incumbent playing a role conforms to normative expectations. Social control in this sense is most typically performed by informal sanctions: words and other gestures or symbols designed to induce a uniformity of norms. For instance, a father reprimanding his child for misbehaving is a form of social control. By so doing, he reminds the child what patterns of normative behavior he expects.

THE POWER OF GROUPS

Fifth, groups usually show some degree of flexibility and a potential for change. People in face-to-face interaction within the group often renegotiate their expectations for each other. Groups have means of exerting group control— usually through the use of informal sanctions— to ensure that role behaviors reflect normative expectations. Yet groups are capable of change; they can be flexible and conducive to innovation and alteration.

With this provisional understanding of what a group is,[1] what its physical boundaries are, and how its internal structure is organized, we can now begin to examine the scope and range of *influence* that groups exert on human thought and action.

---

[1]For some basic references on the structure and processes of groups, see Cartwright and Zander (1968); Hare (1962); Hare, Bates, & Borgatta (1965); Homans (1950); Mills (1967); Olmstead (1959); Rogers (1970); and Shepard (1964).

A boy is "busted" for possession of marijuana. Bailed out, and on his way home, his parents ask with disappointment, "What made you get into this kind of trouble? Why have you done this to us?" The boy fidgets; there does not seem to be an adequate explanation, except for: "I don't know . . . like, you know, all my friends are into it . . . I don't know." The parents might go on, in a lecturing tone, about the effect of "peer pressure" in pejorative terms, adjuring that he should not have succumbed to smoking marijuana just because his "friends" are "into" it. This example not only illustrates one case of how groups can influence us to engage in activities from which we might otherwise refrain, but it also points to the inherent problems of moving from adolescence to adulthood (Eisenstadt 1956; Coleman 1961). In this transition, patterns of behavior expected by the family unit are often in conflict with expected patterns of behavior in other groups, such as peer groups. The boy's arrest marked such a conflict. The influence of his family's values and moral sense conflicted with the increasing influence of his peer group.

When the expectations of different groups conflict, we can become acutely aware of their influence. But throughout life, groups perpetually influence the way we think, what we say, what we believe, and how we act in the world around us. In a sense the total number of groups in which people participate *are* their world (Simmel 1955). Although technological breakthroughs in media such as television give us access to other worlds, the most salient reality for most people is their web of group affiliations.

Group Influence On Behavior

Interesting studies have been conducted that show the power groups have over us. The most notable of these was a pioneering study conducted at the Western Electric Plant of the Bell Telephone Company (Landsberger 1958). In one set of experiments, six women, whose work consisted of assembling telephone relays, were chosen to be set apart in a "test room" from the rest of the workers in their department. The test room was set off from the regular work area by an eight foot high partition. One immediate change in the women's working conditions was the lack of close supervision by superiors; the workers were watched from an adjacent room by a team of investigators. Steps were taken earlier to measure the women's rates of productivity prior to their being placed in the test room so that the investigators would know their average output before a series of changes in their work environment were introduced. The crux of the experiment resided in trying to find how working conditions, if changed in some way, would have an effect on employee attitudes and performance.

Once placed in the test room, the women did what they had always done, assembling telephone relays, with no discernible change in their working conditions except for the obvious fact that they were set apart from the rest of the plant and no longer under direct company supervision. After about two weeks, the investigators began to implement gradual changes, which they termed "periods." Each successive period was marked by an improvement in their working conditions over those in the past. Rest periods were initiated twice daily

in one, five minutes each. Then they were lengthened to ten minutes. Later on, six five-minute rest periods throughout the day were used. Still later, the company began providing free lunches for them and letting them go a half an hour earlier. As was expected, productivity rose steadily with each improvement in the work environment.

However, the investigators suspected that some other factor was involved in this dramatic rise in output. Therefore, in the 12th period, the working conditions were returned to what they had been at the outset: no breaks, no getting out early, and no more free lunches. The rates of output did decline somewhat, but did not approach the level of productivity registered in the beginning. The conclusion was inescapable, "Something was happening which could not be explained by the experimentally controlled conditions of work." (Homans 1958, p. 585).

The investigators surmised that the women had developed group bonds that turned out to be unconsciously conducive to higher output. "Each (woman) . . . said that the increase had come about without any conscious effort on her part." One of the main factors turned out to be the absence of any supervisory control. Although they worked very closely to each other, the women were not allowed to carry on conversations with one another under normal working circumstances. Although the observer watching the women initially attempted to enforce this rule in the test room it was eventually abandoned for fear that their cooperation in the experiment would be lost. "Talk became common and was often loud and general." It was observed that "the character and purpose of the supervision were different and were felt to be so." In this absence of normal supervision, the development of a cohesive social group became more evident as well as recognizable group attributes, such as self-appointed leadership and an overall sense of common purpose. During separate interviews with the women at the end of the experiment, all of them showed disparaging attitudes toward the regular shop department compared to the test room. "They felt relief from some form of constraint, particularly the constraint of supervision."

In other experiments involving male workers, the organization of informal social groups in the work environment was found to play a primary part in causing the failure of a wage incentive scheme. Under this type of plan, a worker's wage was to become proportionate to his level of productivity: the more he turned out, the more money he would make. Management felt that this scheme would induce workers to produce more. But such was not the case:

> [Workers] shared a common body of sentiments. A person should not turn out too much work. If he did, he was a "rate-buster." The theory was that if an excessive amount of work was turned out, the management would lower the piecework rate so that the employees would be in the position of doing more work for approximately the same pay. On the other hand, a person should not turn out too little work. If he did, he was a "chiseler"; that is, he was getting paid for work he did not do. A person should say nothing which would injure a fellow member of the group. If he did, he was a "squealer." Finally no member of the group should act officiously. (Homans 1958, p. 591)

If it were to succeed as management wanted, the incentive wage scheme could only have done so on an individual basis—that is, if the work environment was an "everyone-for-him/herself" type of situation. But in a large plant where many of the workers were engaged in the same type of work, this could not be the case. Initially workers were simply together by virtue of the physical conditions that surrounded them, but over time, emotional ties began to emerge as workers talked about the problems regarding their surroundings. In the work groups studied, these bonds created normative expectations about what constituted "a good day's work" and came to regulate group member's behaviors, even though these behaviors decreased their earnings. Thus, in subtle, yet powerful ways, the group influenced and controlled how these workers performed their jobs.

In other occupational contexts group control of this sort operates in different ways. For instance, police officers observe an unwritten norm that one policeman should avoid testifying against a fellow officer in court. The implications toward the power of groups in this kind of situation are indeed profound, for police officers serve the specific function in society of preserving and enforcing law and order. Yet the norms within their group dictate that they should break the law from time to time. For example, one study of the police in a Midwestern city asked officers to respond to a hypothetical situation: if they were aware that their partner had stolen $500 from a drunken prisoner, would they report him? They were also asked if they would testify in court as a witness against him, provided the prisoner

Even highly formal and routine situations frequently cannot prevent the formation of group bonds.

brought formal charges. The results were almost unanimous: Only one officer answered "yes" to both of the questions, and that officer was a "rookie." Every member of the police force was aware of the consequences of perjury: suspension or dismissal. Yet more consideration was given to the consequences of being labeled a "stool pigeon" and ostracized and harassed by fellow officers (Westley 1956). The nature of police work is probably the prevailing factor in causing this overwhelming response. To survive the kind of dangerous assignments that the police are often required to confront, policemen must be able to rely on each other. In addition, for police to work effectively in various criminal provinces, they must frequently maintain "shady" liaisons with the underworld and even resort to illegal tactics, creating a situation in which almost any police officer might be vulnerable to prosecution.

The close, fraternal type of cooperation that groups often extract from their members is probably most evident in wartime military units. In combat situations and the inevitable stress associated with such situations, group influence on individual behavior can be powerful. For example, studies of "war heroes" have documented that they are rarely exceptional people, but individuals caught in situations in which their close group ties force them to do extraordinary feats. To leave a "buddy" to die, for instance, would expose a soldier to group sanctions; therefore, despite fear and a desire to flee, some soldiers make the dramatic rescues of their fellows. Again, we can see the power of group norms in forcing actions that individuals in a nongroup context might not perform (Marshall 1947; Shils & Janowitz 1948).

Groups and Perceptions

Involvement in groups can influence more than just behavior; it can cause people to interpret or perceive a single situation in significantly different ways. Several studies in many different contexts demonstrate this phenomenon. One such study concerned the perceptions of spectators during a football game in 1951 between Princeton and Dartmouth (Hastorf & Cantril 1954). It was a close game and one fraught with an inordinate number of penalties on both sides. At one point in the first half of the game, the battle had become so fierce that a Princeton star, who was in the running for All-American honors, had to leave the game with a concussion. The roughness of the game continued into the second half, with a Dartmouth player having to be carried off the field with a broken leg. After the game many charges were made by both sides that there had been "dirty" football. A week later students from both schools who had attended the game were asked to fill out questionnaires regarding how they felt about the results of the game, and how "fair" it was. All of the Princeton respondents described it as "rough and dirty" especially in reference to the sportsmanship of the Dartmouth players. Of the Dartmouth respondents, however, one-tenth thought the game to be "clear and fair," a third described it as "rough and fair," and the rest agreed that it was indeed "rough and dirty." Nine-tenths of the Princeton respondents felt that the dirty play in the game was instigated by the Dartmouth players; but of the Dartmouth respondents, only one-third responded this way. The rest held both sides guilty in equal terms. Later, the students were shown movies of the game and asked to make further evaluations of the many infractions and penalties: the Princeton students saw twice as many violations as the Dartmouth students and also cited them as being more "flagrant." All these students, of course, were in the same stadium watching the same game. Because of their separate group affiliations, however, their perceptions of what had gone on were markedly divergent; of course, the fact that Dartmouth had won influenced these perceptions.

Of a more controlled nature were experiments conducted by S. E. Asch (1958). The specific nature of these experiments involved studying the effect of group pressure on the possible modification of people's stated perceptions. The experiment was contrived so that an individual would be confronted with a unanimous opinion concerning a perception by a group, varying in size from perhaps three to fifteen people. The problem for an individual in these groups was that the perceptions voiced by the overwhelming majority were jarringly incorrect. The point of the experiment, then, was to examine how much the "test" individual would modify his or her opinion according to the sway of the group. The so-called "majority" was, of course, collaborating with the experimenter.

The experiment was devised in this way: Each member of the group was told to judge a series of perceptual relations; they were instructed to match the length of a given line with one of three other unequal lines. The choice that each member made had to be announced publicly. In the "contrived" tests, an individual could begin to find that his or her perception was in contradiction to the aggregate group perception. The errors of the majority were usually very large, too, forcing the "test subject" to feel at variance with the majority opinion. The overall results pointed to a marked movement toward the majority by the test subject. About one third of all the estimates by the test subjects were either identical with or leaning toward the distorted estimates of the majority. However, it was observed that the effect of the majority was far from complete; there were subjects whose responses remained independent of the majority without exception. The differences in the emotional reactions among the critical subjects were equally striking. "There were subjects who remained completely confident throughout. At the other extreme were those who became disoriented, doubt-ridden, and experienced a powerful impulse not to appear different from the majority" (Asch 1958, p. 177).

Variations on this experiment produced different effects, such as varying the size of the group. If the group size was only two—that is, consisting only of the test subject and one other person—the "majority" effect was totally nullified. In a group of three—that is, a majority of two against one—subjects began to show marked signs of yielding. In group sizes of four or more, the incidence of yielding by subjects stabilized at a more or less constant rate of one-third. The influence of a divided majority was also studied in which a "true partner" would emerge from the group and side with the subject. Having an ally caused a higher rate of independence among subjects.

These studies demonstrate quite graphically how much we can be influenced by groups. Even our perceptions, or at least our willingness to state our perceptions, are influenced by the group context in which we interact.

Group Influence on Feeling

Groups can have a powerful effect on our emotions or feelings. In our discussion on socialization we saw how the concept of self is necessarily shaped by the "feedback" we get from other people. In the same way groups represent a source of feedback and are capable of shaping feelings about ourselves and others. A dramatic example of the power of groups to influence what we feel comes from the work being done in drug rehabilitation by a group called Synanon. Synanon is involved basically in helping drug addicts "kick their habit." When someone new is admitted to a Synanon house, he or she is forced to go through withdrawal on a living room couch in the presence of other members of the household. The withdrawal from a particularly addicting drug like heroin is usually stereotyped as an excruciating experience, one in which a person becomes violently ill, suffers convulsions, passes in and out of states of delirium and dementia. Contrary to this stereotype, a new member of a Synanon house going through withdrawal is comparatively placid and suffers a minimum of physical discomfort. The reason for this is that withdrawal from heroin is partly psychological, and the physical discomfort can be allayed by the kind of group environment that Synanon offers. Members of Synanon houses are all ex-addicts and can therefore offer the kind of sympathy that helps alleviate the pain of withdrawal by simply offering emotional support since they have "all been through it." Having to "kick the habit" alone, or confined to a cold, impersonal jail cell, is what makes withdrawal an ordeal. Thus, groups have the power to alter our feelings.

Beliefs acquired in a group context are more readily learned and retained. Even the distracted young cannot escape the group influence.

Group Influence on Beliefs

Our beliefs are the product of socialization. Groups have a great influence in controlling and shaping what beliefs we hold, because they are major agents in the process of socialization. For example, our religious, political, economic, and other beliefs reflect those of the groups in which we have participated. Numerous studies have documented that offspring tend to hold political beliefs similar to those of their parents, primarily because the family is an early group influence on an individual. Religious beliefs are similarly acquired in the family, and if church attendance is frequent, they are reinforced in church groups. People's beliefs about the "best economic arrangements" are influenced by their participation in economic groupings. The beliefs of a member of the Chamber of Commerce, for instance, are likely to be much different than those of someone active in the affairs of a labor union. Thus, what one believes is likely to be a reflection of the dominant beliefs associated with those groups in which a person values membership.

Groups and Identity

We have already extensively discussed in Chapter 7 how *self* is influenced and takes on recognizable patterns and characteristics through socialization. We also know that in most cases the family unit is the first group to influence, and hence has the greatest impact on, the formation of the self. Approval or disapproval, reward or punishment, and encouragement or neglect from members in key groups, such as the family, is critical in determining how we view ourselves as people.

A unique study of sexual inclinations emphasizes this kind of group influence. All people have the rudiments of the sex organs for both sexes; normally, chromosomal information is transmitted during the embryonic development of a child so that either the male or female sex organs will physically predominate upon birth. There are rare cases, however, of people in whom the sex organs for both male and female are developed to an unusual degree. Medically these people are termed *hermaphrodites;* others are termed *pseudohermaphrodites.* The distinction is slight: pseudohermaphrodites can be classified biologically as either male or female, but they still possess the sexual apparatus of both sexes. (Ellis, 1945).

The study of these sexually indeterminate people focused on the development of their erotic interests in adult life. The general hypothesis was that if sexual inclinations depend on the secretion of particular hormones, then it would follow that the objects of sexual expression would be contingent on somatic structure rather than on the way a person might be reared by his or her parents. A review of the medical literature on the subject, however, revealed that 87% of the pseudohermaphrodites raised by their parents as "males" developed heterosexual relationships. The rest had no apparent sexual interests at all and lived celibately. Of those who were raised as females, 73% of them were attracted by men, 11% were sapphic or lesbian, 7% professed bisexuality, and the remaining 9% had no erotic interests.

The evidence demonstrates that groups, the family unit especially, have a great effect in influencing self definition. Although biological heritage has an undeniably great effect in determining sex roles, this study shows that sexual *identity* can indeed be very malleable, subject to the forces of group agents of socialization to a much larger degree than we might initially think.

In sum, then, groups have power. They can create a war hero out of one who might have wanted to run; they can make us lie to ourselves about what we perceive; they can make us give up earnings; they can require us to break the law; they can evoke emotions and feelings; they can make us believe or disbelieve; finally, they make us what we are—that is, what we *think* we are. Their power to influence us in an incredible variety of ways is not only pervasive, but inexorable. Humans are dependent upon groups for their survival as a species and for their individual identity. This dependency gives groups enormous influence over almost every aspect of our lives—our behaviors, perceptions, feelings, and sense of self. This power is rarely explicit; it works on us in subtle and often unconscious ways. Something that has this kind of power over humans is worthy of further study.

THE
STRUCTURE
OF
GROUPS

It is time to pursue a more systematic perspective of social groups. Our task will be to provide a skeletal overview of the structure of groups that clarifies our earlier definition and discussion of their properties. We should understand, however, that there is not complete agreement among sociologists on just what a group is. We need only review other introductory textbooks on sociology to discover how widely the definition of social groups vary. Some authors contend that *all* social units of organization are groups regardless of size. Others are more delimiting, as we have seen. As a caution, then, we must be aware that there is not a complete consensus on our topic.

Primary and Secondary Groups

Charles Horton Cooley was one of the earliest social thinkers to recognize the significance of differences in group structure (Cooley 1909). The main thrust of his recognition involved distinguishing **primary groups** from what we now term **secondary groups.**[2] Cooley observed that relationships within either of these groups varied in terms of the degree of intimacy, permanence of relationships, complexity of relations, goal directedness, and emotional expressiveness.

Primary Groups. In primary groups we establish more intimate contacts with the other members and get to know them on a more individual basis. This intimacy comes through constant, face-to-face interaction on a fairly regular basis. Primary groups are typically small, enhancing the chances for intimacy of the relationships. They often have a more to-

tally emotional impact on us, taking up more of our time, energy, and involvement. Cooley typified this greater involvement as arising out of a "we feeling" in which members possess a high degree of group identification, and from Cooley's perspective it is through interaction in primary groups that a person's self is formed.[3]

The family unit is probably the most obvious primary group. American families are usually small, the members numbering not more than five or six in most cases. Close affectionate ties are evident. Families in America are more relationship oriented, for members of a family exist for each other's benefit rather than for organizing effort toward clearly defined goals or tasks. Peer groups also exhibit primary relationships. Peers form bonds because they have common interests, because they feel that they can "relate" to one another, and because they simply like each other's company. They can be described as cliques or circles of friends, varying in size depending on the social skills of the members. Introverted, shy, and somewhat quiet people will tend to have or form a relatively small circle of friends, whereas those who are outgoing and socially active will have more members in their peer group or will have multiple peer group membership.

Secondary Groups. The relationships among members in secondary groups are more impersonal and less enduring. Interaction is more formal, limited, and infrequent. Thus, group identification is less apparent and less influential on one's patterns of behavior outside the group. Members of secondary groups are less interested in each other as people and are more

[2]Cooley never employed the term *secondary groups,* but this term is consistent with the thrust of his analysis.

[3]For basic references on primary groups, see Cooley (1909); Faris (1932); Gross (1953); and Warriner (1956).

likely to view each other as functionaries pursuing some explicit goal or task.

Examples of secondary groups abound in modern societies: work groups, unions, country clubs, schools, even football teams. They are usually larger than primary groups, but in some instances they can involve interaction between only two people, such as in the case of a customer making a purchase from a salesperson in a store. The functions of the group members are emphasized rather than the degree of intimacy. For the most part, the salesperson is only interested in making a sale and taking the customer's money in exchange. Likewise, the customer is primarily interested in receiving goods and getting a receipt. Although cordialities are often exchanged, they are given reflexively and involve little emotion. But secondary groups are usually large, involving large numbers of persons organized for some explicit task. A lecture hall or college classroom are good examples. Although everyone is somewhat aware of who is in the class, relationships are impersonal as people assemble for the explicit task of hearing the lecture. In smaller classes, however, more informal relations sometimes emerge over the course of a semester, indicating that secondary relations can sometimes become more primary.

Cooley emphasized this distinction between primary and what is now called secondary groups, for he, like so many other social commentators of his time, noted the increased impersonality associated with industrialization, urbanization, and bureaucratization of modern social life. All of us, at one time or another, complain about the impersonal structure of society: how we are seen as statistics rather than as people and how we seem to have our efforts at more personal interaction

thwarted. This observation caused alarm among the social thinkers of Cooley's period, but they captured a basic truth about modern society: much of our participation in groups, once we leave our families, involves secondary relationships—in school, on the job, and proliferating into myriad clubs and organizations. In modern societies only the family and close peer groupings are prominent primary groups.

Although insightful, Cooley's conception of primary and secondary groups is probably too simplified. His analysis forced the recognition that groups differ and vary in their structure and that these differences have varying consequences for the individual. Societies composed predominantly of secondary groups have much different characteristics than those in which primary groups are the dominant form. In primitive systems, for example, primary group formations dominate interaction. In a village of no more than 50 to 100 people, everyone knows everyone else on a personal basis. In modern society such a situation hardly exists. Human beings fit into much more highly specialized niches. Specialization has made secondary groups more important because they enable the human system to carry out more complex activities.

Cooley's distinction between primary and secondary groups thus alerts us to variability in groups by positing two polar types. We can visualize this distinction in terms of our definition and conception of groups offered earlier, varying along the lines of different dimensions and characteristics. Group size, for example, is usually smaller in primary groups than secondary. Membership tends to be longer lasting in primary relationships. The normative structure is typically more formal and constraining in secondary than in primary groups, and secondary groups are more likely to be task oriented than are primary groups.

In-groups provide a basis for a "we" feeling.

In-groups and Out-groups

William Graham Sumner (1840–1910), an American sociologist, was the first to use the terms, *in-group* and *out-group* (Sumner 1906). They relate to an individual's perspective of group involvement and the consequences of such involvement. People belong to groups such as families, churches, and cliques. These are their **in-groups,** because they derive a sense of "we" or "consciousness of kind" through affiliation. All people are able to perceive that

for various reasons they do *not* belong to some groups; these are their **out-groups.** They are outside of them, and will remain so, unless they aspire to assume positions, play roles, and abide by norms that might enable them to secure membership.

Through the use of these terms—*in-groups* and *out-groups*—we can see more clearly how such a phenomenon as stereotyping can occur. Persons who come in limited contact with their out-groups often develop limited and inaccurate appraisals of the behavioral characteristics of out-group members. We are all guilty of this at one time or another, perhaps occasionally referring to another as a "typical" Jew, a "typical" black, a "typical jock," or "typical something else." If we make exceptions, after learning something more personal about an individual, we still cling to the stereotype as a point of reference, perhaps commenting, "Funny, he doesn't *act* like a Jew." Stereotyping of out-groups can reach particularly cruel and prejudicial levels with minority groups. According to Sydney Harris, minority group members basically know that they are usually judged by their radical member(s) who may only comprise 10 percent or less of the whole group. These radical members make a name for the group, whereas the other 90 percent mind their own business and their minority status goes unnoticed.

Another interesting aspect of in-groups is that their members often develop a "consciousness of kind," which can enable individuals who have never met to have much in common upon meeting for the first time. Political movements can often generate this kind of consciousness, as can distinctive occupations, because members share many common experiences. Similar majors taken by different students in college can serve as an example. Two English majors meeting for the first time would have much to talk about because of their shared interests within their in-group. An English major and an engineering major, on the other hand, might have comparatively little to say to each other.

Thus, the concepts of in-groups and out-groups are useful in making us recognize the way we organize our individual perceptions of groups around us, both those to which we belong and those to which we do not.

Reference Groups

One of the most intriguing concepts describing individual relations with types of groups is that of **reference groups.**[4] The concept of reference groups was anticipated by George Herbert Mead's concept of the generalized other (see Chapter 7). For Mead saw that people use generalized perspectives as points of reference for evaluating themselves and selecting actions. In essence, they use a "community of attitudes" among others who are not actually present in a situation. This initial insight led to the recognition that people often use different types of groups with which they have differing relations to evaluate themselves and shape their conduct. Thus, groups not only influence the way we enact a role because we are presently members in them, but groups can also influence our perceptions and behavior even though we may not be members or interact with any of their members. We simply use their norms and other cultural symbols as a frame of reference for guiding our actions. Because we can invoke reference groups from the past, present, and future and because almost any group can be used symbolically as a frame of reference, the understanding of a human being's behavior and actions can become a confusing endeavor. For example, our parents or past friends can act as a frame reference for our present behaviors.

The capacity to invoke reference groups has stimulated attempts to describe various types of relationships to these groups. The most obvious relationship is one involving *membership* in which we use the perspective of a group

---

[4]For basic references on reference groups see Kuhn (1964); Merton (1968); and Shibutani (1955).

Reference groups can influence the way we dress. This college student is not likely to need his "overalls" after graduation.

to which we belong as a frame of reference in guiding our thoughts and actions. Another type of relationship is one of *aspirations* for membership in which people use the normative standards of groups to which they aspire to belong as a yardstick for evaluating themselves and guiding their behavior. Thus, graduate students will often begin to emulate the attitudes, orientations, and behavior patterns of professors—a status they aspire to reach. Still another type of relationship is one of *identification* in which people identify with some aspect of a group to which they do not belong and use this aspect to guide their behaviors. For example, in the 1970s middle-class students in colleges and universities often affected a "farmer" appearance, wearing overalls, or they donned "hippie" garb and speech patterns, even though pursuit of a college degree is antithetical to the goals of that counterculture. A final example of various types of relationships with reference groups is one involving *negation* or *reaction formation* in which people's negative orientation to a group leads them to show the opposite behaviors from those dictated by the norms of the negatively evaluated group. For example, most hippies come from middle-class backgrounds, apparently rejecting the quest for material well-being.

The use of reference groups is the result of our big brains. We can symbolically invoke any standards to guide our thoughts and conduct, and we can thus use groups in which we are not interacting and to which we do not belong in selecting our actions. This capacity gives human thought and action a flexibility and fascination. But it also makes understanding of why people behave more complicated.

SUMMARY AND PREVIEW

In this chapter we have examined the group basis of social life. Much of what we are and how we behave is determined by our participation in groups. Not only are we, as individuals, shaped by groups, but the profile of society is revealed by the nature, number, and types of social groups. Groups provide humans with a locus and with behavioral guidelines, and in so doing they give the human system a necessary degree of continuity.

We have come to recognize that groups have power over our thoughts, actions, beliefs, senses of identity, and other facets of our behavior and being. We participate in varieties of groups, ranging from primary to secondary, and recognize out-groups. Perhaps most fascinating for students of human behavior, we use different groups in varying ways as frames of reference for guiding our thoughts and actions.

However, groups are often implicated in larger, more inclusive social forms. For example, a work group is often a part of a large organization, such as a factory or office complex. The nature and form of a group is thus influenced by the larger social units of which it is a part. Thus, we must begin to look beyond groups to understand the human system more completely. In the next chapters, therefore, we will examine other social forms to see how they influence our lives and the nature of the human system. In the next chapter, we will examine formal organizations, or bureaucracies, as we often call them. These forms of organization are different in their structure and operation, but like all the social forms to be discussed in the chapters of this section, they exert enormous influence over us and over the way society operates.

Key Terms

Groups: those relatively small social units, composed of few statuses and clear norms, in which individuals enact roles

Primary Groups: those groups that are small and that involve frequent and intimate interaction

Secondary Groups: those groups that involve impersonal interaction and that do not reveal a high degree of intimacy or affect among their members

In-groups: those groups in which individuals perceive themselves as like-minded in relation to external events and forces

Out-groups: those groups in which individuals perceive themselves to be nonmembers

Reference Groups: any group, social entity, or perspective that individuals use to assess themselves and guide their conduct

Review Questions

1. What does it mean to say that the individual enters society through membership and participation in groups?

2. In what ways do groups have power over the individual?

3. What are the various ways that people can relate to groups?

Suggested Readings

Eisenstadt, S. I. *From Generation to Generation.* New York: The Free Press, 1956.

Hare, A. Paul. *Handbook of Small-Groups Research.* New York: The Free Press, 1962.

Homans, George C. *The Human Group.* New York: Harcourt, 1950.

Mills, Theodore M. *The Sociology of Small Groups.* Englewood Cliffs, N.J.: Prentice-Hall, 1967.

Rogers, Carl C. *On Encounter Groups.* New York: Harper & Row, 1970.

FORMAL ORGANIZATIONS

PROLOGUE

Guiding Questions: How do humans deal with large-scale tasks? Why does social life sometimes seem impersonal and formal? What is a formal organization? What impact do they have on the individual and society?

Chapter Topics

THE FORMALITY OF MODERN LIFE

As most of us realize, modern social life has become more formal. We participate in a wide variety of contexts that are impersonal and less emotionally involving. Job, school, clubs, and the myriad of organizations in which we are involved reveal certain common features that can be subsumed by the term *formal*. We often decry this formality; we romanticize the "simple life" in which personal bonds take precedence over bureaucratic imperatives. But few of us would be willing to give up the material well-being and luxuries that the formalization of social life has brought.

As with all patterns of social organization a **formal organization** is composed of interrelated statuses, roles, and norms. But in contrast to the group forms of organization discussed in the last chapter, the organization of statuses, roles, and norms is much more explicit in formal organization. We know our place; we understand what is expected; and we carry out these expectations with less emotional involvement than we have in small groups. In schools, in dealing with government, in our jobs, in stores, and in organized recreation, roles are frequently enacted with an impersonality, efficiency, and detachment that makes our comparatively few small-group contacts even more meaningful. Since so much of our time is spent in these types of social units and since they so pervasively dominate the structure of modern societies, it is important that we understand: (1) the reasons for the emergence of bureaucracies; (2) the nature and form of their organization of statuses, roles, and norms; and (3) their consequences for the individual and for society.

THE STRUCTURE OF FORMAL ORGANIZATION

Max Weber's Ideal Type

As one of sociology's "founding fathers," Max Weber (1864–1920) has had a profound impact on contemporary sociological thought. Throughout our discussion of many topics, we will note sociology's indebtedness to this great thinker. Nowhere is this indebtedness more evident than in his discussion of bureaucracies. One of Weber's favorite methods was to construct an **ideal type** of a prominent feature of the social world. Such ideal types accentuated important features of a phenomenon, highlighting them and giving us some tools for their understanding. Weber presented a classic example of his ideal-type method in his analysis of **bureaucracy.** No single organization corresponds exactly to the ideal type, but the features of this ideal are what make formal organizations a distinctive social unit.

Weber's basic model can be characterized by five points of emphasis, each describing unique properties of bureaucracies (Gerth & Mills 1946). These five characteristics can be used as an index of comparison with which we can measure the realities of formal organizations as they actually exist.

1. Division of Labor. "The regular activities required for the purposes of the organization are distributed in a fixed way as official duties" (Gerth & Mills 1946, p. 196). Weber is referring to specialization and its important function in the organization of small, specific tasks each person carries out within a bureaucracy. Its importance is based on the notion that by having people specialize in a defined task, the overall effect will be to increase efficiency in total production.

2. Hierarchical Statuses. Another very important feature of bureaucracies is the fact that the statuses of formal organizations are arranged in a hierarchical order. Without this feature, integration of all the divisions of labor would not be possible. There would be general confusion, and workers would not have a clear idea of their specialized functions within the larger framework of the organization. As Weber put it: "The organization of offices follows the principle of hierarchy; that is, each lower office is under the control and supervision of a higher one" (Weber 1946, p. 331). Through supervision by officials in a downward and usually widening chain of command, bureaucracies are able to operate smoothly, with every member of the organization having a clear idea of his or her functions and responsibilities—much like a pecking order. At the top, individuals make decisions and give orders to those just below. All positions between the top and the bottom layer of the hierarchy have a dual purpose: they are subordinate to superior positions, while occupying a position of superiority in relation to positions under them. These middle positions usually assimilate orders from above and discharge them in some appropriate way to subordinates. The chain of command is very strictly circumscribed by this system of descending status prerogatives, and the discharge of authority or power by each position is delimited by its hierarchical relationship to the others. Interpreted in the ideal sense, this means that although individuals in certain positions of authority will have certain powers to recommend a promotion or a firing, they have no control over how another individual conducts his or her personal life, as long as it does not interfere with the job or function being performed. In reality, however, this delineation is not entirely the case. Weber's principle of hierarchy predicated this limitation of control on the depersonalized nature of the structure. In modern corporations, however, most conform to standards that both invade and pervade their private lives. For example, if a man is to "get ahead," he may be expected to not just have a wife, but a "corporate wife." An employee might also be expected to conform to political leanings, to dress a certain way, and to affect many other subtle elements of demeanor. Weber felt that the principal advantage of statuses arranged in a hierarchy was the corresponding reduction in interpersonal friction. Subordinates merely have to accept their salary levels, their privileges, responsibilities, and accountability to their superiors in order for work to be carried out smoothly and efficiently.

3. Codified Norms. The norms of a formal organization are always explicit, clear, and written down. This system of codified norms helps each status incumbent know what is expected and how tasks are to be carried out. They help render complex activity more predictable, methodical, and precise.

4. Disinterested Role Enactment. "The ideal official conducts his office . . . (in) a spirit of formalistic impersonality . . . without hatred or passion, and hence without affection or enthusiasm" (Weber 1946, p. 340). Weber felt that personal detachment in the enactment of roles allowed for action to be rational and geared toward achieving the goals of the organization. By suppressing personal feelings, incumbents could overcome passions and other emotions that might impede the efficient operation of the organization.

5. Technical Competence. This final characteristic of Weber's ideal type is bureaucracies' emphasis upon technical competence in hiring, retaining, and promoting employees within the organization. By specifying an impartial basis for assessing qualifications and performance, greater efficiency and rationality is achieved.

As we mentioned earlier, Weber's "ideal" model of a bureaucracy works more as a definition of exactly what it is and how it *ought* to operate. It should not be taken as an example of how formal organizations really *are*. Indeed, various studies of governmental, business, and other organizations indicate that actual bureaucracies do deviate in some respects from Weber's ideal type. Yet, we can say that in most cases Weber's model is highly useful in describing the salient features of bureaucracies. But we must remember that these features are usually "contaminated" or "enriched" by the human element. No matter how "depersonalized" conditions in an organization, humans will form personal bonds and will have a potential for reaching somewhat partial or biased decisions. In fact, some characteristics of formal organizations cause people to exhibit behavior patterns at variance with what is supposed to occur. For example, the emphasis on moving up the organizational hierarchy can make people anything but impersonal, fair, or rational. Jealousies, irrational decisions, power brokering, and other dysfunctional behaviors can render formal organization less efficient.

Weber recognized such contradictions, but he felt formal organizations to be superior to other social forms in "getting things done." For despite their dehumanizing impact on society and the individual, Weber viewed formal organization as a "technically superior" method of social organization. Needs for more personal bonds and for a less competitive environment could be met by other social forms, such as primary groups. Indeed, this is how most of us actually cope with the relative degree of impersonality of formal organizations: we work to form close group bonds both inside and outside of our involvement with bureaucracies in an effort to compensate for the lack of intimacy so important to our needs as human beings. We saw in the previous chapter how close group ties among women working in factory conditions actually improved individual output under experimental supervision. Weber's principal insight was in recognizing the superiority of formal organizations in terms of precision, efficiency, and unambiguous organization. But his "ideal" model was developed before the word *bureaucracy* had become something of an epithet. Although he recognized and regretted that a fairly high degree of impersonality would result for the individual, Weber felt that the advantages outweighed the disadvantages.

THE RISE OF FORMAL ORGANIZATIONS

For most of human history, formal organizations did not exist. Social life was carried out in more intimate group and community contexts. Formal organizations are human creations for dealing with human problems. Although they create new complexities and problems for people and society, they often enable humans to do what could never have been imagined by the first bands of *Homo sapiens sapiens.*

Historical Forces Behind Bureaucratization

One of the fundamental reasons behind the emergence of bureaucracies is that they enable large-scale tasks to be performed. Without the complex and yet systematic organization a bureaucracy can provide, we could not accomplish much of what we now take for granted. Thus, the emergence of formal organizations can be traced back to the early societies that began to undertake social projects and tasks of increasingly larger proportions and dimensions. (Blau & Meyer 1971).

Egypt can probably be credited with the "invention" of the bureaucracy. This human system was one of the first to have conditions that naturally gave rise to formal types of organization. Projects such as the building of the pyramids and the construction of irrigation projects throughout the country could not have succeeded without the basic characteristics of bureaucracies—the specialized division of labor, formal norms coordinating role behaviors of large numbers of workers, and the hierarchical arrangement of statuses for a more efficient chain of command.

Later, in other countries bureaucratic systems were born out of a desire for an organized military defense against aggressors. Most countries were "fair game," and whoever had the power and military might could undertake an invasion. In order to protect themselves, humans used bureaucratic methods of organization to create, maintain, and use a large and effective army to guard open frontier regions.

One of the most important developments favoring the emergence of formal organization was the introduction of a money economy (Weber 1946, Blau & Meyer, 1971). Money, like bureaucracy, is a comparatively recent invention by humans, but it lays the basis for an entirely new type of social relation: the payment of wages for work performed. Work was previously performed out of duty in small groups, by the capturing of slaves, or by barter. But with a money economy, workers can be induced to give their labor and can be organized into large-scale enterprises without the problems of social control created by slaves or the inefficiencies of barter over unlike goods. For example, imagine the problems of organizing large-scale tasks by joining unpaid families to work, by maintaining order among disenfranchised slaves, or by paying each worker in food and clothing. Of course, slavery was an early technique for performing large-scale tasks, as the building of the pyramids

testifies or as the American plantation system demonstrated. Yet, money exchanged for labor proved more efficient and thus allowed for the creation of even larger bureaucracies organized for engaging in even more complex tasks.

Capitalism was also a major factor in the general advancement of the bureaucracy. Early capitalistic systems required an unregulated competitive market in which money, work, and goods and services could be exchanged in pursuit of economic gain. Capitalism also encourages large-scale enterprises, since in capitalist economies large corporations came to dominate the market. Such large scale enterprises can use the incentive of wages to draw workers into increasingly more complex tasks, thus requiring bureaucratic organization.

Religion has also been an impetus behind the development of bureaucracies. The organization of the Catholic Church, which sought to extend its influence to larger and larger masses, encouraged the creation of church bureaucracies. Later, the emergence of Protestant religion, as Weber documented in another classic work, *The Protestant Ethic and Spirit of Capitalism* (Weber 1964), stimulated the acceleration of capitalism, which, as noted above, encouraged the formation of rational, profit-seeking organizations.

Structural Conditions Behind Bureaucratization

Although these historical factors give some insight into the general trend toward formal organizations over the centuries, they do not fully explain why some organizations are highly bureaucraticized, and others are less so. Therefore, we must examine certain structural considerations that help account for why these variations exist.

Population growth has had a great influence on the need for more efficient methods of social organization. Bureaucracies meet these kinds of demands. Since we have experienced such an exponential growth in population, especially in the last two centuries, it has been necessary to use formal types of organizations to control and supervise these larger masses of people in an effort to deal more efficiently with the problems that larger masses of people confront. For example, the provision of adequate food supplies and the creation of activities to keep people occupied are two such problems that bureaucracies help resolve. Since formal organizations create many status positions and are able to orchestrate these statuses toward the completion of goals, they represent one answer to the problem of socially absorbing greater numbers of people. Without their development, we probably would never have witnessed the present population explosion, because famine and general social disorder would have resulted and thus kept the population explosion under control. (In this case, then, bureaucracies have proved to be a mixed blessing.) Moreover, increases in

Large-scale tasks, such as the building of pyramids, required formal organization, since many diverse tasks among large numbers of workers needed to be coordinated.

Formal Organization Among the Primates: The Baboon Troop

population, as a matter of logic, involve an increase in the size and scope of tasks being undertaken. From an economic perspective alone, it becomes necessary to produce enormous quantities of goods and services because of escalated consumer demand.

In a larger sense, the creation of bureaucracies themselves has often required other bureaucracies to supervise and control them. The activities of governments can be viewed in this context, for much of what government does is supervise the interaction and relations among other bureaucracies. The United Nations represents the greatest extension of this function by supervising the relations among all the nations of the world, or most of them, although its power over the member-nations is admittedly limited. But its existence nevertheless symbolizes a progressive use of formal organizations to mediate massive struggles among other social units.

These are not all of the historical and structural forces behind the emergence of formal organizations. However, these forces give us a sampling of reasons for the dominance of bureaucratic forms. Bureaucracies met certain needs that, at the time of their inception, powerful people defined as important. Once created, bureaucracies generate their imperatives for further bureaucratization of social life. Formal organizations are now among the most conspicuous features of the human system, and we must explore the properties of this social form in more detail.

Formal organization is a recent development in human history, having been initiated by the Egyptians. Yet, we can see the ability to develop formal structures among our distant primate cousins, the baboons. Most primates groupings, especially those like the chimp, are loosely structured, but baboon troops are more tightly and hierarchically structured. Why?

The answer resides in the conditions facing many baboon troops: open savannah where predators abound. Baboons are not as smart as chimps. Nor can monkeys—and the baboon is classified as a monkey—rotate their arms to use tools or weapons as well as an ape like the chimp can (see Chapter 3). Thus, our ancestors may have been able to use tools and their greater cognitive skills to maintain a defense and still be somewhat informal in their organization. But the ancestors of baboons did not possess these cognitive or physical skills. Thus, they evolved a more formal structure for dealing with savannah conditions—a testimony to the fact that primates, when required, can create patterns of formal organization.

The formal baboon troop is organized around a hierarchy of adult males. Usually one or two males dominate the group. The males form a perimeter defense and "march" across the savannah. When "en-

A baboon troop marching across the savannah. Note the leader and his lieutenants flanking the troop.

camped," the authority hierarchy is observed, with dominant males attempting to control access to females. Other males give submissive gestures to these dominant males—much as middle and lower level bureaucrats might do to "the boss." The hierarchy is not always a clear pecking order, however. Coalitions of males sometimes occur, and they collectively assert their dominance over other males who might be stronger than any of the individuals in the collective. Yet, there is a clear "boss" who does not belong to such "middle management" cabals.

Not only do nondominant males show deference, but dominant males exhibit threat behavior, such as dramatic displays of their canine teeth. In this way, the underlings and females are kept in line.

Thus, although the baboon troop is a long way from constituting a formal organization, some of the elements of organization are present: hierarchy, a clear protocol of gestures among males in the hierarchy, regimented spacing of members on the march, and a formality and distance of hierarchical social relations.

TYPES OF
FORMAL
ORGANIZATIONS

As was emphasized by Weber's ideal type, formal organizations have certain common features. Yet, the operation of organizations is obviously influenced by their functions and goals. In this section we will provide a general overview of variations in the structure and operation of formal organizations. We all have an implicit familiarity with these variations, and our goal is to make them more explicit and thus enable us to understand more clearly this fundamental pattern of social organization.

Voluntary Organizations

The main distinction between **voluntary organizations** and other types of formal organizations revolves around how members are recruited (Etzioni 1961). Participation in voluntary organizations is, as the name implies, voluntary. Individuals join of their own accord, and they are usually not paid for their activity. In fact, members are sometimes required to pay dues or other fees to belong to the organization. Another distinguishing characteristic of voluntary organizations is that people are typically involved on only a part-time basis, although a small, full-time staff may be employed to discharge the administrative duties of the organization. A third feature of voluntary organizations is that people characteristically join them for personal reasons, perhaps to augment an interest in political movements, to pursue a hobby, to realize religious convictions, to participate in sports, to become involved in community affairs, or to seek social companions. Examples of voluntary organizations are skydiving clubs, country clubs, PTAs, tennis organizations, the Peace Corps, and even colleges or universities. Churches are usually not categorized as voluntary organizations; nonetheless, membership is usually fully voluntary.

Voluntary organizations vary in their size and location. Some, like the PTA of a given community, are limited to a comparatively small group of people and are geographically restricted to the school district. Other voluntary organizations have millions of members and are national, or even worldwide, in their scope. For example, Rotary International, the Freemasons, the National Rifle Association, and the Republican and Democratic parties have large numbers and cover broad geographical areas. In these larger organizations, membership is still completely voluntary, and individuals are free to withdraw at any time. But because of their large dimensions, some full-time, paid employees perform the administrative work necessary to keep the affairs of such large organizations running smoothly.

American society could by typified by the high rate of involvement in voluntary organizations. We acquire this propensity at a very early age, as can be seen by school systems' emphasis on "extracurricular" activities, such as the student council, language clubs, sports, debate teams, pep clubs, cheerleading, and the other activities in which students are encouraged to participate. The premise behind school-system emphasis on participation in such activities is that extracurricular activity provides a more "well-rounded" character and better prepares students for involvement in organizations as adults. Although this premise may or may not be generally true, it helps account for the general propensity of our citizens to be "joiners," thereby encouraging further proliferation of formal organizations in America.

Voluntary organizations often provide people with a basis for social identification and with a vehicle for expressing beliefs.

Coercive Organizations

Membership in **coercive organizations** is not voluntary. Coercive organizations are the opposite of the voluntary organizations. An individual simply has no choice but to join such an organization and participate in its activities (Etzioni 1961). Common types of coercive organizations include the army in times of military conscription or the prison systems. As might be expected, most coercive organizations are not popular since freedom of choice is severely restricted. Yet, some coercive organizations are not commonly viewed as coercive because they are so endemic to normal social life. For example, our system of education forces participation in school organizations. We all have to go to school, but most of us do so without much thought as to its coercive nature. The pressures exerted by the process of socialization make us respond with an almost automatic willingness to participate in school, from the elementary level on up through high school. The military draft has operated this way, as in both world wars of this century when many men entered the armed forces because it was the "right thing to do." The Vietnam War, however, highlighted the coercive nature of the draft. Because a large segment of the population, especially young people, viewed the war as "immoral," draft resistance was very commonplace and is still the subject of much controversy.

Even schools can be viewed as a form of coercive organization.

Utilitarian Organizations

Utilitarian organizations—by far the most common—tend to lie on a continuum between voluntary and coercive organizations. They are best exemplified by business firms, corporations, governmental agencies, or other practical organizations in which we might be employed. Although we are not physically coerced to participate in them, we become involved in order to make enough money to live (Etzioni 1961). Indeed, almost every adult male is expected to hold a job, and thus, an individual's occupation is the most common point of contact between people and utilitarian organizations in modern societies.

Utilitarian organizations pursue explicit goals, providing goods or services in exchange for money. Almost every type of private business and industry in America is a utilitarian organization, and all have probably the most common organizational form in modern societies. Indeed, conditions of general poverty or prosperity in the nation can usually be traced to the prosperity of utilitarian organizations, emphasizing their significance in determining basic standards of living.

Mutual Benefit Organizations

Mutual benefit organizations are established to provide the benefits for both the organization as a whole as well as its members (Blau & Scott 1963). Utilitarian organizations, as well as some coercive organizations such as schools and even (ideally) prisons, can be viewed as mutual benefit organizations. Utilitarian organizations, however, often benefit their owners more than their members. Churches and labor unions, on the other hand, are more expressly interested in furthering the specific needs of their members. Ideally, they are typified by more emotional involvement by members, since the benefits derived are of a more individually personal character. This distinction between mutual benefit organizations and other types of organizations is, of course, a matter of emphasis, but the concept is useful in delineating those formal organizations that, ideally, *give* more to their members than they *take*.

Client-Centered Organizations

Client-centered organizations are ones that deal with people on an individual basis (Blau & Scott 1963). Schools lie under this heading as well as under the utilitarian one because they are concerned with the education of each and every student. Other examples are hospitals, various social agencies such as welfare organizations, and more specialized organizations such as Synanon, which serves the needs of people with drug problems. These organizations are focused toward the particular needs or problems of an individual client, and we use the term *client-centered* to designate them. They usually serve important humanitarian functions in society by helping those who for one reason or another are not able to help themselves. Their basic problem is the maintenance of administrative efficiency. For example, the welfare system has been characterized by inefficiencies and inequities almost from the beginning. State-run hospitals are also often poorly managed, in debt, and inefficient in the delivery of services to their poor clients. Nevertheless, client-centered organizations meet important needs of individuals, and their number and impact on social life in modern societies is increasing dramatically.

Commonwealth Organizations

Most **commonwealth organizations** are local, state, or federal in governmental contexts. As such, their existence is for the benefit of the public at large, which distinguishes them somewhat from client-centered organizations. Commonwealth organizations enact policies that affect public life without becoming as *directly* involved in the affairs of individuals as client-centered organizations (Blau & Scott 1963). Therefore, most governments can be viewed as examples of commonwealth organizations, for what they do is supposedly for the common good of its citizens. More specific examples can be found in various government agencies, such as the Internal Revenue Service, the Food and Drug Administration, and almost any law enforcement agency. They "regulate" various aspects of public life for the benefit of the general public, at least hypothetically. More controversial forms of commonwealth organizations are the Federal Communications Commission and various censorship boards, such as the one in the motion picture industry, which determine how a movie might be rated

or whether a particular show is morally suitable for television. Though commonwealth organizations may operate with the best of intentions, they can also be guilty of the most flagrant violation of individual rights. Recent allegations concerning covert operations by both the Federal Bureau of Investigation (FBI) and the Central Intelligence Agency (CIA) are a good example of abuse by commonwealth organizations. Illegal breakins and searches as well as "bugged" telephones are often difficult to defend as being in the "public's best interest." Thus, because of their more general "public goals" and because of their bureaucratic structure, commonwealth organizations can overlook individual human rights (Blau & Scott 1963, pp. 40–58).

We should emphasize that many of the distinctions among these types of bureaucracies depend upon a member's position. A student attending a university, for example, may see the institution as a voluntary or mutual benefit organization, whereas a professor or other employee might perceive it in more utilitarian terms. To most of us, a policeman is a representative of a commonwealth organization; but to the policeman himself, the police force is a utilitarian organization. Thus, the distinctions offered in this section are not definitive. They simply point to a range of organizational forms in modern societies. Sociologists have yet to develop clear concepts for classifying distinct organizational types; and yet, all of us who have participated in the proliferating world of formal organizations can recognize that these distinctions capture much of our experience.

BUREAUCRACIES IN PROCESS

In their actual operation formal organizations depart from many of the classifications offered thus far. Human personality, various historical forces, and current structural pressures all contribute to make formal organizations lively and vibrant social forms, for despite their formality, they are filled with human drama. Humans thus "adulterate" formal structures, making bureaucratic organizations something less than rigidly formal and impersonal monoliths.

The Reality of Formal Organization

The Informal System. In all social contexts, humans seek more personal bonds with each other. This basic human need is often realized, even in the midst of structures established to limit personal involvement and the emotions that such involvement can engender. Recall our discussion of work groups in the last chapter, for example. The women isolated in the experiment at the Western Electric plant developed informal social bonds that regulated their output. So did the men who evolved norms about what constituted "a good day's work." A more general conclusion is that *informal* relations among people within formal organizations are inevitable. Because they often work in very close proximity to one another, they interact; and as they interact, they form social bonds (Landsberger 1958).

What exactly do we mean by the informal system within a formal organization? It was not mentioned in the definitive characteristics of bureaucracies listed in Weber's ideal type. Nor do many business firms or factories place emphasis on attaining an informal structure of human relations. For our purposes, we can say that the informal system is a series of more personal, primary relations that emerges within and influences the structure of a formal organization. Some of the formal prescriptions of organizations are unrealistic with regard to the way humans actually behave. Moreover, to follow many of the rules and regulations within a formal organization without "bending" them can result in a hopeless tangle of formal steps, and thus, defeat the purposes of the organization. In many cases, efforts to break up friendship ties and other intimate groups has had the effect of impairing an organization's overall efficiency by undermining employee morale. The wisdom of management, therefore, must reside in addressing two main concerns: (1) maintaining a basic formality to increase an organization's effectiveness, and (2) providing satisfactory "human" conditions in the work environment so that members of an organization harbor favorable attitudes toward the organization and a willingness to work efficiently and enthusiastically for the attainment of its goals. These concerns must be delicately balanced, and it is a rare organization that achieves a perfect balance.

In white-collar bureaucracies, the informal system meets human needs for friendships, but it often does more. Through informal relations, individuals can gain considerable insight into which positions carry the most influence, apart from the authority with which a position is formally imbued. It is possible for the president of a business firm, for example, to have

*Within the formal organization, informal
relations usually develop.*

less authority or influence than the vice-presi-dent. This situation may have resulted from the vice-president's having established more rap-port with people in other statuses that, on an aggregate level, gives him or her the ability to get things done because more employees are on his or her side. In sum, the informal struc-ture within any formal organization can result in a status position with more authority or influence than the formal description of the position would indicate.

In blue-collar working conditions, informal groups' ties are more important in relieving the monotony of the tasks. Automobile factories, for example, are notorious for the depressingly "hypnotic" tasks workers are required to per-form. Workers often cope with the drudgery by implementing their own largely unsanctioned informal work practices. One such practice is that of "doubling up," in which a worker takes on two jobs so that a friend can take some kind of unscheduled break. Without these informal structures, it is easy to visualize how worker morale would drop, and production, in terms of both quantity and quality, would fall off (Howe 1972).

Another social reality that bureaucracies must face is change. Based on the descriptions of formal organizations, the often sterile formality of their structures almost suggest a timeless, changeless, and eternal rigidity. Of course, this rigidity does not exist. Formal organizations frequently must change in accordance with changing conditions in their environment. This change can be accomplished in many different ways. The existence of an informal structure is often responsible for implementing change, mainly because it is more amenable to needs for flexibility or for new directions in policies and procedure. Sometimes radical changes in personnel are necessary to accomplish this change, based on the notion that "new blood" in an organization will have an invigorating effect—perhaps doing away with old, outmoded methods for attaining organizational goals. Thus, although bureaucracies depend enormously on formal methods of organization, they still must have the capacity to change and to demonstrate a resilience after such changes are made.

Organizational Tendencies in Bureaucracies

The Expansion of Bureaucratic Structure. The influence of bureaucracies extends to almost every sphere of social organization. Our primary group relations in the modern society are often subsumed under the vast umbrella of formal organizations. Part of the reason for this is that bureaucracies have a tendency to increase their size and scope; they are expansion-oriented. Thus, they permeate almost every aspect of social life. This predisposition for expansion is sometimes the factor contributing to a formal organization's expiration. Most empires of the past have overextended to the point of collapse; the Roman Empire and Hitler's grisly war campaign are examples. In the business world organizational expansion is evidenced by a general tendency for certain businesses within a particular type of industry to merge and become large industrial conglomerates. General Motors is such a conglomerate; at one time all of the separate model divisions—Chevrolet, Pontiac, Oldsmobile, Buick, and Cadillac—were separate corporations. Other large corporations, such as ITT and Summa Inc. encompass a wide diversity of industries. The trend is thus clear. Bureaucracies tend to reach out further and further until it is no longer physically or legally possible to extend. Often they overreach and fall apart.

The Iron Law of Oligarchy. Another trend in bureaucratic organizations is what Robert Michels termed the iron law of oligarchy. An oligarchy is an organization controlled by a small group. Michels (1915) thought that over time bureaucracies develop a small oligarchy that continues to perpetuate its influence, even to the detriment of the organization. Michels' insight was intended as a criticism of Weber's implicit contention that promotion to top positions in an organization is democratic and occurs in terms of merit and competence. On the contrary, argued Michels, organizations are often run by elites who are skilled at acquiring power, but who may be less competent at running the organization efficiently on a day-to-day basis.

In some sociological quarters, Michels' dictum has been criticized as being too "fatalistic." The fact remains, however, that the tendency toward oligarchy is strong in formal organizations. They can develop in any bureaucratic organization, almost regardless of type or size. Formal organizations tend toward oligarchical forms for two interrelated reasons: (1) ambition for power by elites and (2) indifference of the rank-and-file members of the organization. As long as rank-and-file members enjoy some benefits from the organization, they are unlikely to be terribly concerned about the perpetuation of certain leaders in positions of power. Thus, under some conditions, formal organizations can evidence anti-democratic and authoritarian tendencies.

The Peter Principle. One of the more humorous, and yet important, tendencies in bureaucracies is described by the "Peter Principle"—named after its founder (Peter & Hull 1969). The Peter Principle is: "In a hierarchy every employee tends to rise to his or her level of incompetence." The rationale behind this principle is that promotions in bureaucracies are given, for the most part, on individual merit. A person does well at one job, and is promoted up the hierarchical ladder to the next job and so on, until that person ultimately reaches a status plateau at which he or she has reached a "level of incompetence." According to Dr. Peter, everything that is accomplished with any measure of efficiency or competence is done by the scores of people who have not yet reached their level of incompetence. This principle is truer of white-collar than blue-collar organizations, largely because positions tend to be more diversified and promotions more vertical in white-collar than in blue-collar organizations. Thus, bureaucracies can become inefficient because they can, at times, employ large numbers of incompetent personnel. The Peter Principle is, of course, only a potential tendency. It operates only part of the time and only for some organizations. Yet, the principle does call our attention to an interesting process.

Our experiences probably "confirm" the operation of these tendencies for the spread of formal organizations, the creation of elite oligarchies, and the promotion of people to positions beyond their talents. We all have complained about the impersonality of social life, the unresponsiveness of leaders and those with power, and the incompetence of "bureaucrats." Yet, we should not overemphasize these processes. They occur, but not in all cases and at all times. One of the most fascinating fields in sociology—the study of complex or formal organizations—is currently trying to determine the conditions under which these events are most likely to occur.

BUREAUCRACY AND THE INDIVIDUAL

Bureaucracies are a fact of modern life. We must participate in them if we are to realize the benefits of modern societies. Although many people have chosen not to participate, few of us escape completely involvement of some kind in bureaucracies. The ability to participate in bureaucracies, however, does not emerge overnight. It must be acquired. Imagine, for example, how the members of the society pictured would respond to bureaucratic structures.

Our ability to play roles in a wide variety of formal organizations is learned. Moreover, we often pay a "psychic price" as we learn to become incumbent in formal statuses, play roles, and conform to highly circumscribing norms. As you read this book, you are playing such a role in a formal organization. Therefore, we should learn more about how we come to acquire the ability to participate in bureaucracies and what it costs us as people.

Socialization and Bureaucracy

Early Socialization. The development of "the generalized other," as propounded by George Herbert Mead (see Chapter 7), is probably the first tangible step we take in conforming to the increasingly impersonal character of social life. By seeing ourselves in a more "generalized" way—that is, as a single entity among many others—we are able to perceive that we are expected to enact roles and patterns of behavior that are more formalistic. The generalized other is a necessity because interaction would be difficult without conformity to certain general norms.

*Some individuals in modern societies have
sought to escape the formality of organizations.*

For most of us, school is the force that first marks our perception of the more impersonal and formal world of organizations. For the first time we are confronted with a largely impersonal figure of authority: the teacher. For the first time we are required to obey rules and regulations that are decidedly more explicit than those within the family unit. In short, for the first time, we are forced to become involved with a bureaucracy, though on a somewhat miniaturized scale (Eisenstadt 1956; Parsons 1964; Turner 1972).

School not only prepares us for a lifetime of participation in formal organizations but also for dealing with the realities of informal relations in organizations. We become accustomed to the persistence of primary-group ties within bureaucracies. We learn how they can be used to undercut the ponderous formality and impersonality of formal organizations, many times in favor of increased efficiency as well as more felicitous emotional environments. In addition, the learning process itself exposes us to the varying types of formal organizations. We begin to understand not only those aspects that are present in *all* bureaucracies, but also those that distinguish one type from another, such as the basic differences between a utilitarian organization and a coercive or voluntary organization.

Although early exposure to the systematic structure of primary schools is usually our first taste of formal organizations, the process continues through secondary schools and into college. It is necessary to become prepared for the specialized statuses and roles that will mark adulthood.

Training for Work. In the past 20 years, there has been a general trend in businesses and government agencies to require undergraduate or graduate degrees for positions in their organizations. Although there are exceptions, most formal schooling, even at the university level, does not really prepare an individual to do the specific job he or she will be doing for a particular organization. A bachelor's degree in most academic areas gives a person a general orientation to a field of endeavor, but it does not usually train people to fill particular statuses in specific organizations. Therefore, training programs within organizations are necessary. Our training in how to live in a bureaucratic world thus moves from the acquisition of a general orientation in schools to the acquisition of specific job skills.

Training often involves more than just learning the bare essentials of a particular skill or job. Newcomers in organizations are usually supervised and evaluated on how well they can relate to others in the organizational structure. Thus, most organizations observe the realities of bureaucracies: personal adjustment for each employee in terms of fitting into the human environment is just as important as how well he or she performs specific tasks.

Some organizations demonstrate particularly effective methods of indoctrination (Whyte 1957; Shapiro 1973); one such organization is IBM. As a commentator observed:

> IBM is a religion, a very successful religion, more so than most. It really indoctrinates people. . . . Those who can't stand the discipline leave. . . . Ultimately, the vast majority of IBM'ers stay put, giving the company a low turnover rate, a high *esprit de corps* and lots of people who will say they're "proud to be a small part of IBM." (Shapiro 1973, p. 35)

These comments illustrate the importance of bureaucratic training programs that supplant what we learn in academic organizations. Yet, despite intensive efforts to mold humans to "fit into" an organization, problems do emerge, for ultimately, organizations must come into conflict with human personality and with other roles that we all play outside the organization. There is always a tension between people and the roles that they must play. This fact makes life exciting, but it also creates real and disturbing problems for both the individual and the organization.

Personality and the Organization

Role Strain and Conflict. We are now more familiar with the concepts of role strain and conflict. For example, an excellent teacher may be promoted to an administrative position that proves stressful. In this new position, the former teacher may find that the new role is so radically different from what he or she had previously performed that a serious tension develops for both the teacher and organization. The work may be boring compared to the immediate gratifications of teaching students, or it may be full of unforeseen complications that cause feelings of futility, to emerge. Under these conditions the teacher-turned-administrator can become a liability to the organization, because crucial tasks are not being adequately performed. This type of example could also be applied to the Peter Principle.

In other situations, serious role conflicts may supplement these role strains. For example, for those who must still play teacher roles, administrative roles can cause a severe role conflict. The job of administrator may conflict with the teacher role, placing the teacher-administrator in a highly conflicting situation.

These kinds of conflicts, strains, and tensions can place a heavy burden upon people's personal stability. Depending upon the situation and the characteristics of the person, a wide variety of adjustments are possible to the pressures of formal organizations (Merton 1968). We should examine some of these, if only briefly.

Ritualism. Ritualism describes an attitude an employee may develop to fight off the endless complexity of a particular position within a bureaucracy. Without exception, the employee will "go by the book" in all matters and situations, strictly adhering to rules and regulations, sometimes losing sight of an organization's goals. Imagination and intuition, often important factors in making various decisions or carrying out other duties, are increasingly lost in the ritualistic employee. Although it is one way of coping with role conflict and strain, this "solution" can pose problems for the organization: rigidity, inflexibility, and inefficiency. We have all encountered ritualistics—people who will not bend a rule or flexibly deal with a complex or unique set of circumstances. It is one of the tragedies of bureaucracies that they often drive their incumbents to this state.

Alienation. Alienation is a situation in which employees become blasé or indifferent to all but the most important functions of their positions. Alienation is most evident in blue-collar jobs, where the work is so routine and oppressively boring that the worker takes only a minimum of interest in what is being done. However, sometimes this general state of indifference can be sprinkled with periodic acts of rebellion, such as taking longer and longer breaks or "forgetting" to perform some essential task. For example, workers operating the fork lifts that are used to move finished automobiles about sometimes "drop a car" and claim that the incident was an "accident" but they are silently venting frustrations.

Constructive Conformity. This adaptation is probably the best for both the individual and the organization. Constructive conformity is where employees will (1) minimally conform to the requirements and expectations of a position, (2) not lose sight of organizational goals, (3) evidence personal initiative, and (4) maintain personal integrity. Individuals will make constructive use of the informal structure and will bend rules to meet the broader goals of the bureaucracy and to serve the needs of their personalities.

Most people show a combination of these three basic patterns of adjustment. Often, the mode of adjustment will be situational. In some instances, we may be ritualists, unable to break out of the rules even when organizational goals are best served by such a break. At other times, we can become alienated from the organization, if not rebellious of its encroachment on our individuality, integrity, and freedom. At at still other times, we are able to balance conformity to rules with the need to "get things done." Probably the only possible generalization about which mode of adaptation will dominate is that alienation and ritualism are greatest among long-term, lower-level employees who are at the bottom of the authority structure in routine jobs and who have few prospects for advancement, whereas constructive conformity is likely to be greatest among higher-level employees and among those who have less routine jobs and who still have hope for advancement in the bureaucracy.

SUMMARY AND PREVIEW

In this chapter we have sought to understand the nature, operation, and impact of formal organizations. We have come to recognize that, despite our protestations about their dehumanizing impact, they are an integral part of the modern human system. We could not enjoy the benefits of modern life without bureaucracies. Yet, as with most social forms, they present a contradiction: the regulation of our lives and the imposition of strains and tensions.

We have seen that although Max Weber's ideal type portrayal of bureaucracy is useful as a starting point for understanding bureaucratic structures, this ideal type does not expose the human dynamics or dilemmas of formal organizations. Thus, we have tried to visualize: (1) some of the forces creating bureaucracies as a social form, (2) the wide variety of shapes that formal organizations can take, (3) the internal processes of this social form, and (4) the complex dialectic between organizational structure and the individual.

However, we must remember that in the absence of some kind of radical and catastrophic change in social organization, we can safely say that bureaucracies will continue to dominate many aspects of our lives. Despite many of its problems, bureaucracies are still the only way to efficiently perform large-scale tasks, and in a world that is now characterized by large-scale demands, bureaucracies are currently the only viable answer. Particularly in the United States, we have come to not only depend upon, but *expect*, most of the benefits attributable to formal organizations. Our extensive dependency on materialistic concerns makes the absence of bureaucracies inconceivable. To do without the structured organization of the bureaucracy would be to do without much of what we now largely take for granted. Unless we radically alter our values and general standard of living, bureaucracies will continue to be a prominent part of the human system.

Nevertheless, we have shown in this chapter that bureaucracies are capable of changing with the times. Organizations can and do respond to current needs or problems that confront them. This change comes through a constant process of reform or new methods of organization. The truly "rigid" bureaucracies actually only poses a temporary threat, for without an essential element of fluidity, they become the earliest bureaucratic casualties and with good reason. The future of bureaucracies is therefore bright as long as they continue to demonstrate a dual responsiveness to the needs of humans, to provide the organizational savvy for accomplishing the large-scale tasks needed to satiate humans' voracious material appetite, and to respond to the emotional needs of human beings.

Despite the formalization of social life with bureaucracies, we must remember that we are emotional beings. We are not robots, programmed by instinct. We exhibit a spontaneity and responsiveness to the world. Therefore, it is appropriate that we follow this chapter on formal organizations with an analysis of more fluid social patterns. In this way we can resist the temptation to view the human social system as overly structured, devoid of the flexibility that characterizes *Homo sapien sapien*.[1]

---

[1]For more detailed overviews and analyses of formal organizations, see Asumi and Hage (1972); Bennis (1970); Blau and Meyer (1971); Blau and Scott (1963); Caplow (1964); Croziere (1964); Etzioni (1961); March (1965); March and Simon (1958); and Presthus (1962).

Key Terms

Formal Organization: the organization of status, roles, and norms in ways that involve explicit relations among status positions, clear norms, and highly standardized role performances

Ideal Type: Weber's strategy of analytically accentuating the most salient features of a social pattern. His ideal type of bureaucracy is one of his most influential works

Bureaucracy: another term to designate formal organizations

Voluntary Organizations: those formal organizations in which membership is voluntary and unpaid

Coercive Organizations: those formal organizations in which membership is involuntary

Utilitarian Organizations: those voluntary organizations in which membership is paid and induced by financial and other rewards

Mutual Benefit Organizations: those organizations that are established and run to provide benefits and services for their members

Client-Centered Organizations: those organizations that provide services and benefits for individuals outside the organization

Commonwealth Organizations: those public or governmental organizations that provide services and benefits to the society as a whole

Informal System: those more personal, informal, and affective ties that develop among individuals in formal organizations

Iron Law of Oligarchy: that process whereby a small clique perpetuates its control of an organization

The Peter Principle: that process in formal organizations whereby people are promoted to, and then frozen in, those positions in which their level of competence is exceeded by the demands of the position

Ritualism: that process in formal organizations in which employees strictly adhere to formal rules, even if such conformity decreases flexibility and prevents attainment of organizational goals

Alienation: that process whereby actors cease depositing emotional energy in their roles

Constructive Conformity: that adaptation in a formal organization in which workers conform to the rules, maintain knowledge of organizational goals, evince personal initiative, and keep their personal integrity

Review Questions

1. What are the prominent features of Max Weber's ideal type of bureaucracy?

2. What are some of the causes for the emergence of formal organizations?

3. What are the various types of formal organizations?

4. What is the informal system and what consequences does it have for formal organizations?

5. What are some prominent trends in bureaucracies?

6. In what ways must we be socialized in bureaucracies?

7. What are some of the problems that humans encounter in bureaucracies?

Suggested Readings

Asumi, Koy and Hage, Jerald. *Organization Systems*. Boston: D. C. Heath, 1972.

Bennis, Warren G. *American Bureaucracy*. Chicago: Aldine, 1970.

Blau, Peter M., and Meyer, Marshall. *Bureaucracy in Modern Society*. New York: Random House, 1971.

Blau, Peter M., and Scott, Richard. *Formal Organizations: A Comparative Approach*. London: Routledge & Kegan, 1963.

Etzioni, Amitai. *A Comparative Analysis of Complex Organizations*. New York: The Free Press, 1961.

March, James G. ed. *Handbook of Organizations*. Chicago: Rand McNally, 1965.

March, James G. and Simon, Herbert A. *Organizations*. New York: Wiley, 1958.

FLUID ORGANIZATIONS: PATTERNS OF COLLECTIVE BEHAVIOR

PROLOGUE

Guiding Questions: Why do riots occur?
What drives people to express themselves
collectively? Why do fads and fashion prevail? What influences public opinion? Why
do the civil rights, the feminist, and other
large-scale social movements have in common?

Chapter Topics

WHAT IS COLLECTIVE BEHAVIOR?

Most modern societies reveal a spontaneity and fluidity. Fads, fashions, riots, mass demonstrations, sudden shifts in public opinion, and pressures for social change punctuate social life. These fluid social forms are termed **collective behavior.** We have all been caught up in collective behavior. The clothes that we wear change with fashion trends. We sometimes participate in crowds, demonstrations, and rallies. We can become involved in movements for change; civil rights and feminism are two recent examples.

Collective behavior gives social life some degree of unpredictability. However, sociologists seek to remove the mystery behind collective behavior. They desire to isolate its various forms and to predict the conditions under which it is likely to occur. Sociologists have yet to unravel all the mysteries of fluid organization, but in this chapter we can get a sense for this most fascinating feature of the human system. We will first define collective behavior. Then we can view some of the general conditions stimulating its occurrence. Finally, and for the bulk of the chapter, we will analyze four basic forms of collective behavior: mass behavior, public opinion, crowds, and social movements.

Although the distinction is not absolute or categorical, sociologists refer to collective behavior as patterns of behavior that are relatively fluid, unstructured, unpredictable, and sometimes violent. Beyond this, however, sociologists rarely agree on what collective behavior is. However, we can view four basic characteristics that typify all forms of collective behavior. These characteristics will help us get an idea of the nature of collective behavior as a general social form and will facilitate our understanding of the specific types to be discussed later in the chapter.[1]

First, *forms of collective behavior are unstructured in comparison to other patterns of social organization.* In riots, mobs, panics, and other highly volatile forms, a permanence of structure is not evident. People mill about in an aimless and often agitated way. Restlessness precludes stable structure or organization, with the result that statuses, roles, and norms are less clearly defined.

People often lose individual identity and become "faceless" during participation in some form of collective behavior. However, some structure usually emerges with the passage of time. For example, the "milling" effect often sensitizes people to each other, producing a common mood or sense of "collectivity." Still, in the initial stages of most forms of collective behavior, very little recognizable structure or organization is evident (Blumer, 1957).

---

[1]For basic references on collective behavior, see Blumer (1957); Brown (1954); Lang and Lang (1961); Marx and Wood (1976); Milgram and Toch (1968); Smelser (1963); Turner and Killian (1972).

*Collective behavior embraces transitory
and fluid social patterns.*

Second, *the fluid or somewhat tenuous structure that does exist can often be volatile and unpredictable.* When a precipitating event has set a mob or riot into violent motion, many different things can happen. Thus, conditions existing at the beginning of some form of collective behavior are usually not an accurate guide to what will happen in the immediate future. For example, the violence and confusion of a riot may subside, only to be rekindled by an inflammatory rumor of some kind. Thus,

once a mass or a crowd is stimulated toward some pattern of collective behavior, there is no easy way to predict what will emerge, or how long it will be maintained.

Third, *most forms of collective behavior are less enduring than other basic forms of social organization.* Some forms of collective behavior last only a few hours, some for a few days, and still others for perhaps an entire year. An audience gathered to view a film or play, for example, is engaged in that type of collective behavior only for as long as the show lasts, usually two or three hours. A financial panic, on the other hand, may consume a week or more. Clothing fashions and certain fads sometimes last much longer, perhaps conforming to annual cycles during which an article will be "in" for one entire year and "out" the next. But even these forms are relatively brief when compared to such basic forms of social organization as groups, organizations, social classes, communities, and ethnic groupings. Thus, the comparative lack of structure is the main reason that collective behavior is relatively unenduring.

Fourth, *participation in various forms of collective behavior can often consume a great deal of an individual's emotional energy.* The intensity of emotional involvement is great in mobs and riots. Although intensity of emotional involvement is high, participation in fads, fashions, or crazes channels energies in a different way. For example, a participant in a riot or mob is prone to violent and destructive acts, whereas someone participating in a fad or a craze is emotionally characterized by an obsessive or passionate feeling for an object, a movie star, or, perhaps, an activity. Social movements also consume much emotional energy, but in a less violent or obsessed way. Participants in social movements expend energy more evenly. This is largely because social movements often reveal more structure, predictability, and endurance than other forms of collective behavior; and as we will come to see, they are distinguished by the fact that they often reveal other types of collective behavior during different stages in their development.

Thus, collective behavior can be defined as those social forms that reveal comparatively less structure, evidence a less predictable profile, endure for shorter periods of time, and yet often consume considerably more emotional energy than other social forms. They are most typical in modern societies, although the history of any society is marked by many instances of collective behavior. As long as certain conditions are met, this social form is likely to emerge.

Primate Riot!

Many animals exhibit collective behavior. A herd of animals may flee in response to the threat of a predator. Our primate relatives, however, reveal a more human form of collective behavior. Our distant cousin, the baboon, often shows our primate tendency to evince collective behavior. For example, baboons are typically "tense" animals who are easily mobilized to deal with any danger. It does not take much to release this tension, and frequently, actions within the troop, rather than those of potential predators, send the troop into a collective outburst. For example, two dominant males initiate a fight. Fear, emotion, and excitement immediately spread through the troop. Some mothers drop their children and run. Others do the opposite. Younger males suddenly attack each other. Some low-ranking males grab young, holding them to their breasts, and pretend to be females. Great screaming, noise, and general confusion reigns among the normally quiet, disciplined, and highly organized troop.

Then, just as suddenly as it began, the collective frenzy stops. Quiet, order, and discipline return. Children and mothers unite. Males stop fighting and resume their normal posture. All is again normal, and the troop is ready to deal with the outside, hostile world.

Other primates, most notably our ape cousin the chimpanzee, also exhibit collective outbursts. In fact, chimps often engage in collective frenzies, but these are not as intense and bizarre as those among baboons. These examples suggest that we may have a biological potential for collective behavior; we may have a generalized biological tendency to react to frustration and emotion in a contagious way under the right conditions, such as those outlined by Smelser in the following section. At the very least, our primate relatives often riot. We humans are thus carrying on a long primate tradition.

Source: Lancaster, 1975.

THE PRECONDITIONS OF COLLECTIVE BEHAVIOR

The structure of modern society embraces many of the elements stimulating collective behavior. Societies such as ours are rife with social diversity and are experiencing rapid change. These forces create tension, strain, and conflict in society. It is just such general conditions that result in many of the more volatile forms of collective behavior. For example, the unequal distribution of various resources resulting in basic social inequality has been the primary cause of many urban riots and various social movements. Other conflicts arise simply out of the fact that modern societies harbor such a wide variety of values and beliefs among people, many of which are in conflict with one another.

The mass media of modern societies also play an important part in shaping collective behavior. Before the advent of mass communication systems, people rarely went outside their local communities, and most social interaction took place within primary groups. Now, through technological advances in this area, we know of myriad social affairs in all parts of society. Mass media have expanded our capacity to *know* and be *aware of* the society and world, making various forms of mass behavior, such as fads, fashions, and crazes more likely. Media can also expose the inequalities in a society. When low-income people compare their status to that of the more affluent, their sense of deprivation is increased. Such deprivations are a precondition for collective forms such as riots. Mass communication systems, however, have not only increased the likelihood of collective behavior, but have also increased the rate at which it takes place. Information can be disseminated at incredible speeds through such media as television and radio. Madison Avenue has taken full advantage of the increased capacity to transmit information, ideas, and attitudes rapidly and simultaneously to many people. By exposing people to various products through advertising in the mass media, they are able to literally create markets. In the process of doing so, advertisers—if they are highly successful—also create such forms of mass collective behavior as fads or even crazes such as the hoola hoop.

There are other preconditions of collective behavior, however. Probably the best model of these preconditions has been advanced by Neil Smelser (1963). He suggests that there are six essential determinants for collective behavior: (1) structural conduciveness, (2) structural strain, (3) a generalized belief, (4) precipitating factors, (5) mobilization for action, and (6) operation of social control.

Structural Conduciveness

Structural conduciveness refers to certain social factors that must be present to permit a particular type of collective behavior to take place. Thus, for a financial panic to be possible, the society must have an economy in which assets can be exchanged freely through such expedients as banks or the stock market. Similarly, no race riot can happen unless two large racial groups are within close physical proximity to one another. Structural conduciveness thus refers to the social elements in society that make collective behavior possible. But these structural conditions alone cannot determine when collective behavior will occur, only that it can.

Ghetto conditions are an example
of structural conduciveness.

Structural Strain

Structural strain can be any kind of structural conflict or ambiguity that generates frustration and tension in people. For example, high levels of unemployment, blatantly racist patterns of discrimination, or sexist organizations in a society can be sources of structural strain. The form of collective behavior that begins to emerge from this strain will be influenced by the nature of other conditions discerned below.

A Generalized Belief

When people begin to interpret tension and strain in the social environment in a meaningful way, then they have begun to develop generalized beliefs. People develop a need or desire for some kind of "answer" to the conditions causing strain. For example, the generalized belief of the feminist movement interprets certain arrangements in economic, political, educational, and familial structures as discriminating and in need of change. Generalized beliefs, however, do not have to be accurate. Indeed, they are often based on misconceptions or outright myths. For example, an innocent man may be lynched by a mob on very flimsy or utterly false evidence. In such a case, the mob may have formed a generalized belief merely as a pretense to vent racial hate or some other type of prejudice. Thus, generalized beliefs are ideologies, attitudes, beliefs, or any other shared system of meanings that allow actors to interpret and to achieve a sense of understanding about events and conditions.

Precipitating Factors

Once conduciveness, strain, and a generalized belief have been established, collective behavior is not inevitable. Some precipitating event must occur to trigger the beginning of a collective response. Such an event might appear to be, by itself, trivial or insignificant. But given the existence of the preceding three conditions, it can serve to "precipitate" the onset of some form of collective behavior. Many race riots during the 1960s were triggered by routine police arrests of ghetto residents. But because of the tense conditions and growing discontent among residents in these urban centers, such as Watts and Detroit, these "routine" procedures sparked tremendous violence and property damage. Whereas the previous conditions set the stage for collective behavior, precipitating factors confirm people's anger, suspicion, and uneasiness and prompt them to act.

Mobilization for Action

The only necessary condition remaining now is for participants to respond to a precipitating event by mobilizing into action. Sometimes, as in the case of a riot, a crowd may mobilize spontaneously, swept into motion by common feelings. In other cases, such as social movements, participants may have to be exhorted and organized into action through the systematic behaviors of leaders or groups of leaders. Whatever the source of mobilization, we can say that when participants are successfully mobilized into action, then collective behavior is evident.

MASSES AND MASS BEHAVIOR

Operation of Social Control

Social control refers to any action taken before or during a form of collective behavior to prevent or suppress it. Such action can originate in efforts by police, government leaders, or others in positions of influence or power, and it can take such widely different forms as a war-on-poverty program or the use of curfews. Thus, social control is actually a counterdeterminant of collective behavior; it seeks to preclude, interrupt, deflect, or inhibit a collective action. If social control fails, however, the collective response or activity can continue unabated; and sometimes, efforts at social control can encourage and inflame collective behavior, such as when police actions enrage rioters who then escalate their behavior to even higher levels of violence.

We are now familiar with what collective behavior is as well as what general conditions determine it. Our next task is to explore both where and how it actually occurs in modern society. The remainder of this chapter will be devoted to this undertaking. First, we will examine four social contexts within which all forms of collective behavior fall: (1) masses, (2) publics, and (3) crowds, and (4) social movements.

What Is a Mass?

A **mass** is "a relatively large number of persons, spatially dispersed and anonymous, reacting to one or more of the same stimuli but acting individually without regard for one another" (Hoult 1969, p. 194).

Moreover, a mass typically exhibits no clear-cut statuses, roles, customs, or traditions. Nor are there any organized sentiments or strong emotional ties among members. Finally, there is little, if any, direct interaction (Blumer 1969, pp. 86–87).

It is relatively easy to see, then, that mass behavior will have some characteristics that distinguish it from collective behavior occurring in, say, crowds. For example, a mass differs from a crowd in three basic ways. First of all, a mass is a scattered aggregation of people with little or no physical contact with one another, whereas crowds are collections of people with comparatively close physical contact. Second, since masses are so scattered, almost no interaction occurs, whereas in crowds interaction has a much better chance of occurring depending on the type of collective behavior. Lastly, members of a mass make individually selected responses to stimuli not confined by a particular time or space, whereas the responses of members in a crowd are more collective and limited by time and space.

Masses also differ from crowds in that often they are creations of the mass media. Since masses are so spatially dispersed, only advanced communication systems as we now have could provide the means by which individually selected responses are possible over large geographic areas.

Masses include a wide variety of groups. For example, people who simultaneously read and respond to a newspaper advertisement for a clearance sale at a department store constitute a mass. People who participated in the California gold rush were also a mass. Even people who allow their sideburns to lengthen or shorten according to the dictates of a particular fashion are a mass. Thus, almost any grouping of people imaginable can constitute a mass.

As members of a large, modern society, we are also members of a *mass society*. Characteristics of mass societies include a greater emphasis on secondary-group relationships, specialization of role and status, and less individual reliance on traditional mores or values for making decisions or choices. Thus, much of our social involvement in the mass society is characterized by anonymity and impersonality. Although many have lamented this trend, as we noted in Chapter 11 dealing with formal organizations, these characteristics reflect changes in social organization that are important to keep modern societies as large and complex as our own operating smoothly and efficiently.

Mass Behavior

Mass society produces particular forms of collective behavior called **mass behavior.** Mass behavior is unstructured, unorganized, and individually selected. However it occurs, it represents the sum total of many individual responses. It is distinguished from other types of collective behavior because certain factors,

such as the mass media and social mobility, have caused people to be more detached from traditional cultural and social moorings. As we now know, these factors operate to create masses and, more generally, the mass society. The following terms refer to different types of mass behavior: *fads, fashions, crazes, hysterias, and panics.* Although each of these terms generally describes a distinctive type of mass behavior, we should be aware that an almost infinite variety of actions by participating members can occur.

Fads and Fashions. All of us participate in fads or fashion. They are the pursuit of a particular interest, often somewhat trivial, usually done briefly and capriciously, and usually with an exaggerated sense of devotion or zeal. For example, choosing a particular mode of dress, hair style, or general pattern of behavior are all such faddish interests. The use of certain slang expressions, such as "dig it," "far out," or "outta sight," are also fads.

Fads usually disappear because their innovative possibilities have been exhausted. However, other fads usually follow immediately. Thus, although particular examples of fads and fashions usually have very brief life spans, people's needs and desires for them, as well as economic interests in making money from them, appear to be insatiable and inexhaustible.

Crazes. Although similar to fads and fashions, people's obsessive emotional behavior is the distinguishing feature of crazes. In a craze, people may hold in abeyance many other routine activities in which they usually participate. For example, the recent, somewhat cultish following in consciousness movements such as

"Streaking" is an example of a fad that was short-lived. For a brief period, it was commonplace. Now it is rare to see a streaker.

TM (Transcendental Meditation) or est (Erhard Seminar Training) are also crazes, although these have certain characteristics qualifying them as more enduring social movements.

Some crazes involve frantic or dishonest financial investment schemes. For example, people may be induced to invest in spurious stocks and bonds. Real estate schemes also "con" people into buying plots of land that they have never seen. People think the investment is "sound," having been assured that the value of their land will double or triple in only a few years, but they discover that their property is located in a desert or on inundated land and has no present value and little likelihood of any future value.

Crazes thus sometimes represent the discovery of what appears to be limitless opportunity. A craze is usually maintained by a distorted perception of the situation. This factor, too, distinguishes a craze from fads or fashions, for the latter usually reflect people's tastes and beliefs rather than a glamorized distortion of facts.

Panics. The preceding forms of mass behavior have involved movements toward something. In contrast, behavior in **panics** often involves a mass rush to escape something. Waves of fear or extreme distortions of the actual facts often result, and sometimes symptoms of physical illness may be present among the participants. Some forms of panic behavior, however, may not involve fear or phobic dread, but rather, overwhelming feelings of what could be termed "hysterical euphoria." For example, people at evangelistic revival meetings are often overcome by what they feel is the "power of God." They will weep, and at times, even

collapse. Similarly, during performances by popular musicians—the Beatles and Elvis, for example—many teen-age girls have to be carried from the concert halls because they have fainted.

True mass panics have been fairly rare in history. The best known to us is probably the financial panic of 1929 that precipitated the Great Depression. Natural disasters, such as earthquakes, tornadoes, and hurricanes, can also cause short-lived panics, until people are able to regroup and deal with the disaster. On rare occasions a panic can be responsible for loss of human life. For example, 500 people died in a Boston nightclub in 1942 when a fire engulfed the building. The crowd numbered over 1,000, and in a desperate, chaotic, and disorganized scramble to escape, they jammed the revolving front door. (Turner & Killian 1972, pp. 121–22).

In looking back on masses and mass behavior, we should emphasize one point. Some of these types of mass behavior may *appear* to be trivial, such as fads and fashions, but we must remember that even these seemingly insignificant or frivolous types are the result of powerful economic forces. The fashion world, for example, is "big business," as are any number of industries that satisfy people's various faddish desires. Thus, all mass behavior, in all its varied forms, has important consequences not only for us as individuals but also for the structure of modern society. We must recognize this fact since mass behaviors have a direct, and sometimes indirect, bearing on all our lives.

PUBLICS AND PUBLIC OPINION

A public is a scattered aggregation of persons who share some interest in, and are perhaps divided over, a common issue or concern. As with masses, physical proximity is not a necessary condition. **Public** is thus the general term that sociologists use to denote a wide range of groupings of varying social significance, such as magazine subscribers, voters, consumers, or stockholders, who focus on an issue or concern. Each public often develops its own symbols, vernacular, and means of communication. Since publics are not highly organized, it is difficult to determine how much social power or significance they have. Most sociological analysis of publics has concentrated on public opinion, since the influence of public opinion on social affairs can be observed (Katz et al. 1954; Lang & Lang 1961).

Opinion Formation

It has always been difficult to grasp the exact process by which **public opinion** is formed (Berelson & Janowitz 1966). Of course, mass media play a major part, and dominant cultural values contribute to the formation of public opinion. But several sociological studies have supported the idea that the ground level of opinion formation is shaped and directed by social backgrounds and group affiliations (Blumer 1948, pp. 542–549). For example, American blacks usually have an interest in issues involving inequality in society. Similarly, participation in groups or organizations, such as the American Legion, the Rotary Club, the Women's League of Voters, religious sects, and political parties, all profoundly influence members' public opinion.

The mass media carry considerable weight in public-opinion formation. Newspapers, television, and radio not only report news but *make* news as well. Publics would never even have the opportunity to form opinions on pressing issues such as abortion, capital punishment, or certain social movements without the mass exposure that various media provide. Publics also tend to put great trust in what they read or hear in newspapers or television. To this extent, the mass media have great power and influence in forming and creating public opinion. Although social backgrounds and various group affiliations probably have more importance, mass-media systems provide, at the very least, an arena in which all members of society can be exposed to a vast plurality of issues.

Leaders also play a large part in forming public opinion. Leaders in business sectors, religions, labor unions, social movements, and governments all affect public opinion. Besides often being the *subject* of much public opinion, they also stand for the opinions, beliefs, and attitudes that generally describe a particular public. When leaders make adequately explained and justified decisions on certain issues, constituent publics usually modify opinions accordingly.

Public opinion can also be shaped by reference groups. A reference group is any group providing perspective and standards shaping an individual's behavior, regardless of whether or not the individual is an actual member of the group. A reference group for a business administration student, for example, would be the business world at large. Although not presently a member of the "business community," the student still uses it as a frame of reference. It conditions and shapes the student's thinking on certain issues, often influencing the relative importance of one issue over another.

Sociologists' understanding of opinion formation is far from complete. But they recognize the importance of certain forces: the media provides both the medium and a message. Backgrounds of people are also important, especially as they have created commitment to values and beliefs. Group affiliations and group leaders also influence opinion, and orientations to reference groups can supplement the influence of other forces. However it is formed, public opinion is a powerful force in modern societies. Political leaders, for example, would do well to recognize people's views, or as is often the case, to take care in manipulating these views for political purposes. The central part played by publics and public opinion in modern social life has led to much concern about how to measure public opinion.

Measurement of Public Opinion

Decisions that leaders make are often based on attitudes and opinions already present in the public domain. This is made possible by the public-opinion poll. Although a fairly recent development in modern societies, the art of measuring public opinion has in itself become a science, achieving remarkable accuracy in recent years.

In the typical opinion poll, which is a form of survey research discussed in Chapter 2, a small number of people who represent a cross section of the general public is sampled. This sample is composed of people from different classes and social backgrounds, all in correct proportion to how they are represented in the total population (Rosenberg 1968). A pollster gives these respondents a set of questions on a public issue, political candidacy, or some other specific topic. The questions are prepared and designed so that each respondent can provide clear answers that can be reported as "yes" or "no" or grouped into a small number of categories. If successful, a reasonably accurate measurement of public opinion results.

However, there are many pitfalls that can undermine the validity of opinion polls. One general problem is the fluctuating nature of public opinion. In some cases respondents may express opinions regarding certain issues that they know nothing about. In addition, the questions may be phrased so that they are misleading or ambiguous. Another problem arises in trying to predict the "undecided" element of a response to public-opinion polling. The most famous miscalculation of this sort was in the Dewey-Truman presidential election in 1948. A landslide victory was predicted for Dewey, but many of the "undecided" ended up casting their votes for Truman. Also, much of the support for Dewey indicated by the polls simply did not materialize. Those who might have supported him stayed home, thinking the results would be the same with or without their electoral support.

Opinion Manipulation

Much public opinion research has emphasized the manipulation of public opinion. Two manipulative methods sociologists pay particular attention to are propaganda and censorship (Katz et al. 1954).

CROWDS AND CROWD BEHAVIOR

Propaganda has come to mean an underhanded attempt to influence beliefs and attitudes of citizens. Formerly, propaganda referred to the teaching of information or doctrines pertaining to some branch of knowledge or religion. Now, however, it refers to efforts by governments or organizations to create a climate of public opinion favorable to these organizations or governments. Propaganda is thus a kind of selective education. It is able to manipulate ideas and opinions because of a limited, selective, or even false presentation of the facts.

Censorship is the withholding of any information from the public. Essentially it is used to prevent collective behavior from occurring that might encourage social change. All governments practice some degree of censorship over their citizens. In the United States, censorship is usually exercised in sex-related areas. For example, censorship of movies, television, books, and magazines is practiced in many communities. Censorship is not confined to governmental bodies, however. Businesses may withhold information concerning the inferiority or defective nature of a product; schools may withhold "facts" about the less desirable actions of national news; and parents may censor much information from their children. Censorship pervades all social institutions.

Of course, both censorship and propaganda are controversial. Whether the ends they serve justify them as means will always be debatable. With the growing complexities of modern societies and the extensive reliance on the media for information, the potential capacities for governments and businesses to employ propaganda and censorship is increased. Censorship and propaganda are thus likely to be a constant point of controversy in the human system.

Definition and Characteristics

We are probably more familiar with crowds than any other social phenomenon. Unlike masses and publics, crowds are limited by time and concentrated in space. Riots and mobs, for example, are usually located at a particular place and limited to only a few hours or days. Thus, we can initially define crowds as temporary gatherings of people reacting together to common stimuli.

This general definition does not capture the full flavor of this temporary and highly fluid form of social organization. Several other features are what make crowds a unique and fascinating topic of study. We will briefly review these.

Anonymity. As in masses and publics, there is anonymity of membership in crowds. But when people begin to form a crowd, a common mood divesting the participants of their individuality prevails. Participants are more likely to exhibit those behaviors in which they would not normally engage. In the lynch mobs of the past, for example, a crowd could commit atrocious, brutal, and barbarous acts. In riots, people may loot and steal with glee and abandon. In both of these examples people commit anonymously in the crowd what they would never do as individuals. Moreover, it is of interest to note that participants in such crowds as lynch mobs and riots frequently do not express any feelings of guilt or shame in the aftermath. Apparently, whatever the nature of the action, anonymity operates to shift moral responsibility to the crowd as a whole, rather than to individual members.

Suggestibility. Crowd behavior is comparatively unstructured and unpredictable. The anonymity that induces people to commit acts that they would probably not do individually also makes them highly suggestible. Suggestibility simply refers to a high potential for active responses to various sources of suggestion, such as the decisive or authoritative commands of a leader. A crowd may demonstrate suggestibility in the ebb and flow of its unpredictable actions, such as when people begin to participate in burning and looting in growing numbers during a riot.

Contagion. Contagion refers to the process whereby information and psychological states of participants travel through a crowd. Contagion usually develops during the members' common responses to various stimuli. As the responses intermingle, they increase in intensity and reverberate throughout the crowd. The term *interactional amplification* might best describe this phenomenon. Leaders are often important in generating contagion. For example, evangelists encourage their audiences to move down as close to the dais as possible before they begin. By getting people closely packed together in such a way, the potential for contagion is greatly increased. Another example of contagion comes from sporting events. Conditions of anonymity and suggestibility allow spectators to respond spontaneously and uninhibitedly. During a football game, for example, a touchdown is scored and the crowd immediately responds, either elatedly or disgustedly. Such an immediate collective response demonstrates how rapid the phenomenon of crowd contagion works.

Emotional Arousal. Extremely high emotional arousal is possible in crowds when people feel anonymous, are highly suggestible, and are subject to the rapid flow of information and emotions. It is the complex interactions among these forces—anonymity, suggestibility, contagion, and emotion—that makes crowds volatile and often frightening. As emotions are aroused, they enable people to lose inhibitions, to become more easily swayed to do things that they would otherwise resist, and to be subject to the emotions around them as well as to rumors and other fragmentary sources of information.

These are the common features of crowds. Different types of crowds will evidence different levels and combinations of these elements. Some allow less anonymity, suggestibility, contagion, and emotion, whereas in other crowds the opposite is true. Thus, we can distinguish between various types of crowd organization and behavior.

Types of Crowds

Herbert Blumer (1957) has advanced the most complete classification of crowds. He views crowds as falling into four basic categories: (1) casual, (2) conventional or neutral, (3) expressive, and (4) acting.

Casual Crowds. Casual crowds form spontaneously and for superficial reasons. Of all types of crowds, they have the least structure, the least interaction, and are the least enduring. Participants do little more than engage in a fleeting, passive observation of an event inspiring common interest, curiosity, or appeal. A casual crowd, for example, could be a small

A casual crowd responding to a mutual stimulus.

group of people stopping to watch a trio of musicians playing songs on a street corner. Another could be a group milling about the scene of a car accident. Thus, members of casual crowds tend to come and go, and the duration of the gathering can usually be mea- sured in minutes. In such crowds, emotions are not greatly aroused, suggestibility is low, contagion is unlikely unless circumstances change dramatically. Anonymity, however, is quite high.

Conventional or Neutral Crowds. Conventional or neutral crowds demonstrate more group structure than casual crowds. There are several reasons for this. First, members usually have a specific purpose or common goal for gathering, such as shoppers in a grocery store or members of an audience viewing a film. In addition, members are tacitly expected to behave according to established norms, and normative deviations may result in social censure. For example, loud, boisterous behavior would be completely inappropriate during the performance of an opera or symphony orchestra, and any persons acting in such a way would probably be asked to leave. Other conventional crowds include passengers on a bus or students gathered in a lecture hall after a class. Although in conventional crowds members share a common goal, there is usually little interaction, mutual awareness, potential for contagion and suggestibility, or emotional arousal.

Expressive Crowds. Expressive crowds are a variant of conventional crowds and are distinguished from conventional crowds in terms of their members' emotional involvement. As the term suggests, participants are more "expressive"; they tend to become less inhibited, they loosen up, and, perhaps, they exhibit behavior that would be judged inappropriate in many social settings. Each member's subjective experience is emphasized. People who attend rock concerts, disco nightclubs, religious revivals, or a Mardi Gras are all members of expressive crowds. Although high emotional arousals are common features of expressive crowds, chaos need not result. The huge rock festival at Woodstock, for example, was one of the largest expressive crowds ever assembled, and yet, it was relatively peaceful and orderly.

Acting Crowds. Acting crowds are the most volatile and potentially dangerous of the four types. They differ from conventional crowds because their members exhibit such high states of emotional arousal that they are often stimulated into action because of anger and indignation over repressive or inequitable social conditions. Collective action by an acting crowd may be precipitated by many types of incidents. But the crowd behavior that results can be violent, agitated, and turbulent, as was the case with many urban and student riots during the 1960s. Considerable property damage and human suffering are often left in the wake of acting crowds.

Because acting crowds can have such a powerful impact on the social order, we should examine some recent examples. No social event is more frightening and fascinating than those collective outbursts that threaten, if only temporarily, the patterns of order in the human system.

The Detroit Riot. In July 1967, one of the worst riots in our history occurred in Detroit, Michigan (Kerner 1968). Anger and frustration in the black community ran high, exacerbated by high unemployment among inner-city blacks, harrassment and abuse by police, and sweltering weather conditions. The city was transformed into a time bomb. Any seemingly insignificant event could set it off, and it was the police themselves who provided that precipitating event. Late on Saturday, July 22,

An acting crowd attacking the police
in Boston during that city's efforts
to integrate the schools.

1967, they raided five social clubs in the 12th Street area. The clubs were suspected of harboring illegal gambling and conducting the sale of liquor illegally after hours. A mass arrest ensued, which was the precipitating fac-

tor that touched off the riot. A great deal of friction already existed between residents of the area and the police. It had been rumored a month earlier that a prostitute was murdered by a member of the vice squad. When the last of those arrested during the raid were being taken away in a paddy wagon, a large restless crowd had already gathered, now early Sunday morning, July 23. A bottle crashed through the window of the last patrol car leaving the scene of the mass arrest, and the crowd continued to swell, both in number and anger.

By sunrise the situation had become serious, and the initial crowd of 200 now numbered 3,000. Beleaguered and outnumbered, the police tried only to confine the growing mob within a six-block area. Soon, small groups of blacks began breaking into shops and stores, carting away whatever they found and were able to carry. The 12th Street area became a carnival of unrestricted looting and stealing. Because the police were aware of the volatility of the crowd, they simply kept the area cordoned off and made no move to stop the looting. For a while, the apparent impotence of the law served to lessen the tension of the crowd. One black congressman entered the area in an attempt to stop the lawlessness, but he was rebuffed by hecklers.

Later in the day rumors that aroused the hostility of the crowd once again began to circulate. It was rumored that a black man was bayoneted to death only a few blocks away. This triggered the crowd into more violent action. They began hurling stones, bottles, and other missiles at the police stationed around the area and setting fire to many of the stores they had been looting earlier. Soon 800 state police and 1,200 National Guardsmen were summoned to quell the escalating violence and destruction. A curfew was instituted between 9 P.M. and 5 A.M. for all residents of the city as well as some of the outlying suburbs.

The rioting continued unabated through Monday despite the curfew and police rein-forcements. Finally, President Johnson issued an order to send in federal troops, the total number eventually reaching 5,000. Many of them had traveled several hundred miles and had no experience with mob control whatsoever. Once in Detroit, they were given only the hastiest instruction on how to handle riot situations and were sent out into the city in small bands to bring the looting and fire bombing under control. By that time, however, all they found were empty streets, not bristling and angry mobs. By Wednesday, July 26, much of the looting and arson had subsided only to be replaced by rumors of an increase in sniper activity. The atmosphere was one of calm compared to the preceding couple of days, but tension and concealed danger still existed. By the end of the week, when relative order had more or less been restored, 43 people had died (over 30 of them killed by police, national guardsmen, or federal troops), 7,200 people were in jail, and an estimated $22 million worth of property damage had resulted.

The report of the *National Advisory Commission on Civil Disorders* (Kerner, 1968) revealed many interesting facts about the nature of this riot and others, such as those in Watts, Newark, and other cities.[2] For example, it dispelled the notion that violent rioting in Detroit and other cities was conducted strictly by criminal types, commonly termed the "riff-raff theory." The basic core of rioters were regular residents of the city, fairly well educated, and involved in normal community affairs. Hence, the riff-raff theory does not explain the fact that a full 40% of the ghetto residents in Detroit either actively participated in the riot or were at least bystan-

---

[2]See Kerner (1968), but also Lieberson and Silverman (1965); Murphy (1966); and Turner (1976:245–251).

ders. In this riot and in other urban disturbances, all the characteristics of crowd
behavior were evident: anonymity, suggestibility, contagion, and high emotional
arousal. The study revealed that the Detroit riot
was far from being the result of outside agita-
tors, consisting ostensibly of vagrants, bums,
hoodlums, and the like; rather, it conformed to
basic patterns of collective behavior in acting
crowds.

Student Strike at San Francisco State. On October 31, 1968, the Black Students Union at San
Francisco State College officially announced
that they intended to conduct a student strike
commencing November 6. This was in response to the suspension of a black instructor
at the college, George Murray, who was a
member of the Black Panther Party. Murray's
suspension was the culmination of much controversy concerning the instructor's then-re-
cent trip to Cuba where he had made
inflammatory remarks about the "imperialis-
tic" involvement of the United States in Vietnam, saying that every soldier killed by the
Vietcong translated as "one agressor less" to
deal with here at home (Orrick 1969). Publication of Murray's remarks and other speeches
elsewhere in the United States in the San
Francisco *Examiner* caused general public uproar over his role as a member of the faculty.
This uproar was heightened by the fact that the
president of the university, Mr. Smith, renewed
his employment for the fall semester. Under
pressure by the board of trustees and then-
Mayor Alioto, the president capitulated and
issued orders to suspend Murray from his
teaching duties. This suspension, Murray's
supporters argued, had more to do with his

activities outside the campus than with his
competence as a member of the faculty. This
suspension was thus the precipitating event
leading to the student strike.

From the very beginning there was confusion as to what sort of strike it was to be—that
is, whether it was to be a one-day protest or to
be more prolonged. As it turned out, the strike
was longer. What is more, it escalated to a
point where one of the goals of the strikers was
the disruption of the entire process of education at San Francisco State.

On November 5, one day before the strike
would officially start, a black delegation made
a visit to President Smith with a formal list of
ten demands. The demands were described as
"nonnegotiable" and included the demand
that Murray be reinstated as a member of the
faculty, as well as demands ranging from im-
munity for those participating in the strike
(which was to go on whether or not the demands were met) to a minimum number of
blacks to fill full-time teaching positions in the
Department of Black Studies. On November 6,
the day of the strike, groups of blacks roamed
the campus, walking into classes in session and
asking students and faculty alike why they
were not supporting the strike. President Smith
closed the campus that afternoon, announcing
that he had heard reports of fires being started
and that a typewriter had been thrown through
the window of the business and social sciences
building.

The campus was reopened on November 7.
There was some scattered violence but not as
much as the day before. On Friday, November
8, however, the student militants accelerated
their guerrilla tactics, setting approximately 50
fires around the campus. Campus offices were
invaded, desks overturned and other office

equipment smashed and destroyed. All of this hit-and-run action made for an extremely unstable and uneasy mood at the college.

President Smith suspended regular student disciplinary procedures. A three-day, Veterans Day holiday intervened, then classes resumed on November 12. November 13 represented a turning point in the course of the strike. A confrontation occurred between the San Francisco Police Department's tactical squad and students. The result was termed a "classic pattern of escalation and the polarization of many previously uncommitted students" (Orrick 1969, p. 41). The campus was again closed due to the violence. President Smith was roundly criticized for his indecisiveness and his capitulation to the strikers' tactics. The rest of the month and early December were marked by frequent clashes between police and students. President Smith continued to be the object of sharp criticism. Governor Reagan called his on-again–off-again orders to close the campus "an unprecedented act of irresponsibility" (Orrick 1969, p. 45). Finally, on November 26, President Smith resigned his position at the college because of his "inability to reconcile effectively the conflicts between the Trustees and Chancellor, the faculty groups on campus, and political forces of the State" (Orrick 1969, p. 54).

The trustees immediately named as acting president, S. I. Hayakawa, a famous semanticist and part-time professor of English at the college. Hayakawa announced tough new guidelines for the reopening of the college, stating further that "as many police as necessary to enforce the rules would be used" (Orrick 1969, p. 62). Only eight days after Hayakawa took office, a major disturbance erupted. It was December 5. A rally at noon was scheduled to take place. Once enough student activists had gathered, a march was initiated. The demonstrators formed lines four and five abreast and marched down a 15-foot-wide asphalt esplanade running 250 feet between the administration building and the business and social sciences and humanities, language, and literature buildings (Karaguezian 1971, p. 11). They marched into the administration building, jammed the stairways, and filled the lobby of the building to capacity. Many of the demonstrators began brandishing crowbars, sticks, and metal pipes, and chanting: "We want the puppet! We want the puppet!" referring to acting-President Hayakawa (Karaguezian 1971, p. 16). There was a press of demonstrators at the very door of the president's office when six San Francisco policemen emerged from the police room, moving toward the head of the group. There was no resistance to the movement of the police, largely because of the initial shock at their presence. A tense standoff ensued for several minutes; the police were almost chin to chin with the demonstrators. Then one black demonstrator drew out a can of Mace, spraying its contents in the direction of the police. The police reacted by drawing their guns and waving them threateningly. The demonstrators made a mad attempt to scatter at the sight of guns, but because of the crowded conditions, escape was slow and difficult. The demonstrators regrouped in stairways and halls. The confrontation had caused high emotional arousal, and outside the administration building the marchers decided to move their attack to another building. Soon, the sound of breaking glass was heard. Finally, a line of San Francisco policemen moved in, cordoning off the building while the demonstrators moved away and gathered in the open space of the quadrangle. Not long after, Hayakawa began addressing the crowd over a public address system loaned to the campus by the California Disaster Corps. "I order you to clear the campus immediately," his voice boomed. "Leave the campus at once. There are no longer any innocent bystanders." The longer he spoke the more he was jeered and taunted by the demonstrators, some chanting, "Fascist Pig," and others sporadically shouting obscenities (Karaguezian 1971, p. 21). By the end of the day, 20 had been arrested and several demonstrators had been injured. The striking students considered the day a victory, having completely disrupted the college's normal activities (Karaguezian 1971, p. 26).

More disturbances and confrontations marred the rest of the semester at San Francisco State, but Hayakawa's determination to keep the campus open and his adamant stand not to give in to the guerrilla tactics of the strikers earned him wide approval from many, in the community and nation, although a large number of the students and faculty members at the college itself did not approve of his actions.

These two examples of collective behavior illustrate not only riot forms of crowd behavior, but also the preconditions necessary for collective behavior. Each of these riots revealed structural conduciveness, structural strain, the emergence of generalized beliefs, precipitating factors, mobilization for action, and efforts at social control. We can visualize these conditions by briefly reviewing their importance in the Detroit and San Francisco State riots.

Structural conduciveness existed in the Detroit ghetto and at San Francisco State. In the ghetto, widespread poverty, tense police/community relations, high concentrations of residents, many of whom were on the streets on hot nights, and visible signs of inequality, such as white-owned slum housing and businesses, were all conditions highly conducive to riot behavior. San Francisco State revealed a widely diverse student body—from ghetto blacks to upper middle class whites—in an urban area of a state, which, at that time, was headed by a conservative governor. These conditions could potentially produce collective outbursts and efforts at their repression.

Structural strains began to emerge in these highly conducive situations. For black residents in Detroit, the failure of the war-on-poverty program, which had raised hope and expectations, escalated black residents' sense of frustration about their social status and their dependency on the white community. At San Francisco State, the influx of large numbers of blacks onto the campus created many tensions as they confronted the structure of what has traditionally been a white, middle-class world. Academic practices appeared to be racist and to confirm the negative experiences of blacks in a white environment. White students, who had been annoyed by the formalities of large state universities, began to voice their frustrations and to join black students in opposing "their oppression."

Generalized beliefs soon began to emerge among ghetto residents and students. Residents in Detroit increasingly viewed their situation as the result of "white oppression" and the police, in particular, as "instruments of white oppression." In San Francisco black students codified their feelings into a list of ten non-negotiable demands.

The *precipitating factors* in both situations involved acts by the authorities who had become focal points of frustrations. In Detroit the mass raid and arrest on 12th Street prompted action by residents, whereas in San Francisco the suspension of black instructor George Murray initiated the student strike and riots.

In Detroit, *mobilization for action* started in and around 12th Street with rock throwing at police, later escalating to looting, fire bombing, and rumors of sniping. Among the students in San Francisco, mobilization started with the ill-defined strike and escalated to rallies, protests, and confrontations with police and administrators.

Social control in both situations appeared to escalate tensions and actions, but in the end, the massive application of force suppressed the collective outbursts. In Detroit the use of police, state militia, and the National Guard appeared to incite the riot, but eventually the rioters were crushed. At San Francisco State the activities of the police fed emotions and eventually encouraged many whites to join in the protest, but police actions also brought suppression of the demonstrations.

Riots thus bring into bold relief some of the conditions for more volatile forms of collective behavior. Other forms of collective behavior, such as mass actions and public opinions, appear to be less influenced by these condi-tions than crowds. Yet, fads and fashions, to some limited extent, also follow conducive conditions, strains, beliefs, and incidents. For example, something as "trivial" as lengthening of hair styles occurred in the 1960s during a period of the questioning of many structural arrangements by young people, during a long series of clashes between authorities and demonstrators, and during a period when many general beliefs about "loosening up" and becoming "less uptight" dominated. Public opinion was also influenced by these forces. Initially negative on alternative styles, student demonstrations, and other activities, opinion virtually reversed itself on personal styles and the Vietnam War, which had prompted many student demonstrations. Yet, because of their dispersion (a structural condition that is "conducive" to noncrowd behavior), action in masses and publics could not be mobilized in the same way as it was among those located together in a ghetto or on a college campus.

We are now in a position to begin examining the fourth form of collective behavior: social movements. They often grow out of the same conditions causing riots. Indeed, most social movements evidence all other forms of collective behavior: *mass behavior* such as fads, fashions, and even crazes; alterations of *public opinion;* and *crowd behavior,* ranging from mass demonstrations to riots. They are thus a major force in the human system.

SOCIAL MOVEMENTS

Social movements are persistent and fairly enduring efforts to effect or resist social change.[3] The goal or issue around which social movements focus usually has the following characteristics: (1) the issue affects a large segment of the population; (2) it arouses deeply felt emotions; and (3) it makes at least some people willing to devote the energy, time, and resources necessary for mobilizing and organizing publics, masses, and crowds.

Structurally, social movements often begin to take on many characteristics of formal organizations described in the previous chapter. Although rigid, formalization is not as necessary as in bureaucracies, some degree of organization is required to carry on and pursue goals effectively. Indeed, to mobilize publics and masses as well as to initiate effective demonstrations requires organization. For it is difficult to disseminate information, to reach publics and masses through media and by other persuasion techniques, and to assert goals with strategic demonstrations without some degree of bureaucratic organization. However, such organization does not immediately flower. Social movements tend to go through stages, increasing their degree of organization as the movement progresses. Therefore, we should try to understand these stages.

---

[3]For interesting analyses on social movement, see: Ash (1972); Cantril (1963); Gusfield (1970); Howard (1974); Killian (1973); Oberschall (1973); Roberts and Kloss (1974); Toch (1965); Wilson (1973).

Stages in Social Movements

Four stages have been designated as constituting the "life cycle" of most social movements (Dawson & Gettys 1935; Hopper, 1950): (1) the preliminary stage, (2) the popular stage, (3) the formal stage, and (4) the institutional stage.

The Preliminary Stage. In the preliminary stage discontent over some issue or social condition begins to emerge, but it is unfocused and immobile. All the conditions for a social movement are coming to the fore, but they fail to become sufficiently crystallized for organized efforts. Antagonism and frustration often result in isolated outbursts of violence or sporadic rioting. Leadership is not centralized or coherent; hence, there is no concerted path to follow in rectifying what has become defined by some as an intolerable situation.

The Popular Stage. Leaders now emerge, and shared discontent is communicated to the degree that members realize they constitute a sizeable faction. Leaders thus attempt to amplify discontent with rhetoric designed for the purqose of "consciousness raising"—that is, getting members increasingly aware of their common situation and of the need for some concerted effort toward change. Awareness at this stage is heightened, but the social movement still lacks clearly defined goals or the methods to attain these goals.

The Formal Stage. The formal stage is marked by a codification of ideals, beliefs, and goals, as well as by the emergence of formal organizations. Thus, an ideology is developed with which members can more solidly identify. A hierarchy of statuses and roles emerges among incumbents who will involve themselves with the movement on a full-time basis. In addition, leadership is less ideological and more pragmatic, concerned with how effectively to mobilize efforts toward the attainment of goals. These efforts are often strategically discharged on several social fronts, in such forms as public demonstrations, propagandizing, or efforts through legal channels to gain passage of legislation pertaining to the goals of the movement.

The Institutional Stage. At this point, at least partial success has been achieved, and the social movement moves closer to being a social institution to ensure that progress will continue to be made and maintained. The fervent activism of the first three stages no longer prevails, and members become even more rational and pragmatic. In effect, the "glamor" and excitement of the movement's salad days are over; the goals and objectives have been assimilated into society. In fact, the movement may no longer be recognized as such, since its goals have become established norms of the society (Hopper 1950).

Social Movements in Action

Social movements in practice reveal different characteristics. Therefore, we are required to categorize them. One basis for classification revolves around the degree of violent action by members. Another concerns the type, nature, and extent of change they seek to implement. Thus, we can distinguish types of social movements on the basis of varying degrees of volatility and on the extent to which they seek change.

Reform Movements. A reform movement seeks modification in some area of social organization rather than a top-to-bottom transformation of all existing conditions. Usually, such movements are confined to some single aspect of social life over which the public begins to express discontent. Feminism, slavery abolition, prohibition, and others are all examples of reform movements. Feminism, in particular, has come to the forefront of social consciousness in the last few years. It has had a long history in which it might be said the preliminary stage in its development lasted an inordinate length of time. As far back as 1792, Mary Wollstonecraft had protested the subordinate social position of women in society in her article *Vindication of the Rights of Women.* But it was not until the late nineteenth century and the early part of the twentieth that women finally began to achieve some unification, mostly embodied in the goal of women's suffrage. Once women achieved the right to vote, however, another long period of dormancy ensued. The growing frustrations over sexual inequality finally transformed women's liberation into a full-fledged, ongoing social movement in the 1970s. Feminist goals cover a wide

Efforts to achieve civil rights for black Americans are an example of a social movement.

range of reforms in the social structure but focus primarily on equal opportunities in education and employment. The movement consists of hundreds of subgroups and orders, some fairly conservative in approach, such as NOW (National Organization of Women) and some more militant or radical, such as WITCH (Womens International Terrorist Conspiracy from Hell) and WRAP (Women's Radical Action Project). Although a reform movement, feminism works for change in society that would alter some basic premises about male and female roles.

Revolutionary Movements. Revolutionary movements involve much more sweeping and often violent changes in society. Tremendous levels of discontent are evident. Although the term *revolutionary* is frequently used in a loose sense, for our purposes here it refers to movements that seek to completely undermine and overthrow the existing social structure. The New Left was such a revolutionary movement. Represented by groups and organizations such as the Students for a Democratic Society (SDS) and the Youth International Party (Yippies), their goal was to destroy the existing political, economic, and social structure of the United States. Other revolutionary movements grew out of racial discrimination, such as the Black Panther Party and the Black Muslims, although much of the civil rights movement was more reformist in nature. The most dramatic and effective revolutionary movements have, of course, occurred outside the United States in such countries as China, Russia, and Cuba, to name a few of the obvious examples. Thus, when a movement seeks to dismantle the existing social structure of a society, we can visualize it as revolutionary movement.

The American Nazi Party is an example
of a reactionary movement.

Reactionary Movements. Reactionary movements seek to halt social change. The Klu Klux Klan, the John Birch Society, and the American Nazi Party are all reactionary movements. They all oppose the social changes advocated by other movements. What both revolutionary and reactionary movements often have in common are extremist beliefs and collective actions. Moreover, at times they both are willing to use violence to initiate or inhibit change in the social structure.

Expressive Movements. Expressive movements are somewhat unique as a type of social movement. Few people involved with them are concerned with changing external conditions of society, but rather seek to modify their internal emotional reactions to better cope with the conditions of the world around them. Members of expressive movements are thus comparatively passive and resigned. Whatever is "wrong" with society is perceived as fundamentally inalterable. Therefore, change must come from within rather than without. Expressive movements are enjoying increased popularity, as evidenced in growing interest and membership in movements such as TM (Transcendental Meditation), est (Erhard Seminar Training), Arica, Esalen, and others. Similarly, the religious revival of the 1970s, especially among the young, represents another example of an expressive movement (see Chapter 17). Participation in any of these movements is a quest for internal peace of mind. People seek to achieve mastery over their feelings and emotions. By doing so, the impersonal and unsympathetic conditions of the modern society become less of a cross to bear.

SUMMARY AND PREVIEW

In this chapter we have tried to show the human system not as overly structured and rigid but as a fluid system. Social structural arrangements and cultural symbols often create tensions in humans that, under conditions just beginning to be understood, cause eruptions into more fluid forms of social action and organization. Our goal in this chapter has been to review the types of action usually studied under the rubric of "collective behavior."

As we have come to see, the study of collective behavior is a diverse field. It embraces the study of four distinct, and yet often interrelated forms: masses, publics, crowds, and social movements. We have examined each in detail, offering a description of the diversity of mass, public, and crowd behaviors as well as the variety of social movements evident in modern societies.

However, we must recognize that collective behavior occurs within a social and cultural context. It is not random action. If we understood more about collective behavior, we could perhaps predict with greater accuracy its likelihood of occurrence and its form. Just because a form of action and organization is fluid, and appears spontaneous, does not mean that it is not amenable to scientific understanding. We have some general understanding of the preconditions that cause collective action: structural conduciveness, structural strain, the emergence of generalized beliefs, emotional arousal, mobilization for action, and efforts at social control. In the future sociologists will seek to be more specific and to indicate more precisely what conditions will produce various forms of collective behavior.

In our study of crowd behavior in particular, we noticed how often inequality and perceived deprivations were a precondition to collective outbursts. We are now ready to explore this topic in more detail in the following chapter. As we will come to appreciate, almost every facet of the human system is influenced by inequality. We have seen how true this is for collective behavior, and we will see how true it is for other social forms. Thus, we have come to recognize the duality of the human system, in its fluidity and orderliness, and we can now continue to explore other prominent forms of organization. Community is one such form, and we can now turn our attention to this important topic in the next chapter.

Key Terms

Collective Behavior: those social forms that reveal less structure, evidence less predictable profiles, endure for shorter periods of time than most social forms, and consume their incumbents' emotional energies

Mass: a relatively large number of persons, spatially dispersed and anonymous, reacting to one or more of the same stimuli but acting individually without regard for one another

Mass Behavior: those behaviors that are unstructured, unorganized, and individually selected

Fads, Fashion: the pursuit of a particular interest, usually done capriciously and briefly, often with an exaggerated sense of devotion or zeal

Crazes: obsessive emotional behavior in which people hold in abeyance many of their routine activities

Panics: behavior in which people behave hysterically, either to escape or approach some stimulus

Public: an aggregation, group, or other plurality of people who are focused on an issue or concern

Public Opinion: the assessment of a public's attitudes and other feelings or cognitions about particular issues

Propaganda: efforts by organizations to create a climate of public opinion favorable to their interests and goals

Censorship: the withholding of information from the public

Crowds: temporary gatherings of people reacting to a common stimulus

Social Movement: persistent and often enduring efforts by people to effect or resist social change

Review Questions

1. What are some of the preconditions of collective behavior?
2. What different forms can collective behavior take?
3. How can masses, publics, and crowds all be involved in a social movement?
4. Why is collective behavior termed *fluid organization?*

Suggested Readings

Blumer, Herbert. "Collective Behavior." In *Principles of Sociology,* edited by A. M. Lee. New York: Barnes and Noble, 1957.

Brown, Roger W. "Mass Phenomena." In *Handbook of Social Psychology,* edited by G. Lindzey. Reading, Mass.: Addison-Wesley, 1954.

Gusfield, Joseph R., ed. *Protest, Reform and Revolt: A Reader in Social Movements.* New York: Wiley, 1970.

Killian, Lewis M. "Social Movements: A Review of the Field." In *Social Movements: A Reader and Source Book,* edited by R. R. Evans. Chicago: Rand McNally, 1973.

Smelser, Neil J. *A Theory of Collective Behavior.* New York: The Free Press, 1963.

Turner, Ralph H., and Killian, Lewis. *Collective Behavior.* Englewood Cliffs, N.J.: Prentice-Hall, 1972.

HUMAN COMMUNITIES

PROLOGUE

Guiding Questions: What happened when humans discovered agriculture? Why did communities begin to proliferate in the world? What kinds of communities have existed in the past? What kinds now exist and how do they shape our lives?

Chapter Topics

WHAT IS COMMUNITY?

Community is a familiar word to all of us. In general usage, it most commonly refers to a human group with unique interests, unique activities, or both. Our daily language allows us to speak of the "banking community," the "religious community," the "scholastic community," and so on. Moreover, with our increasing reliance upon newspapers, radio, and television, we have become aware of the community of emerging nations, the free-world community, and other communities of similarly vast proportions. Occasionally we hear of the world community, and future generations will see themselves, perhaps, as members of the galactic community or the universal community. In the meanwhile, many of us continue a search for community, or yearn for a sense of community. Thus, the term *community* has many connotations.

Sociologists define *community* in such a way that the meaning of the term becomes more precise and more narrow than in everyday usage. Our concern is with community as a social unit or form of social organization within which many vital processes occur. Although sociologists rarely agree upon definitions, we can best define a **community** as those patterns of action and interaction that are shaped by a people's daily activities in a relatively permanent place of residence. Let us amplify this definition. The place where people live influences many other facets of their lives. Residence largely determines where one works, what forms of recreation are available, how one seeks and obtains needed commodities, where children go to school, and how other activities necessary for living are carried out. Thus, much of our daily activity is directly influenced by the characteristic features of our permanent residence. The orderly pursuit of necessary daily activities often requires a government. Roads must be built so that people can travel efficiently from one place to another. Systems of taxation must be devised, administered, and enforced so that schools can be built and maintained. Zoning policies are needed to regulate how, when, and where residential, commercial, and other types of structures are to be built. Still other services are necessary to the public interest, such as law enforcement, fire prevention, health maintenance, and mass transportation. It is apparent, then, that community living entails much more than mere residence.

When groups of people settle in a place, take up residence, and begin to do what is necessary to live, they are pursuing the satisfaction of existing needs. But in doing so, they create new needs. Primary among these new needs is the

Communities in the human system take a variety of forms, from the simple rural village to the giant central city of the modern urban complex.

necessity of a new pattern of organization to facilitate and to control public activity. This new, emergent pattern of organization is known as a community.

Communities need not be complex. A few houses or huts near a place of regular work, simple paths or dirt roads to serve the people as they move about, and a basic means of governance are all that is necessary for a community to exist. In fact, throughout most of human history, communities have not existed, since early humans were nomadic hunters and gatherers. When communities began to appear they were exceedingly simple. We should review how this basic social form first emerged and how it has come to influence so much activity in the human system.

THE EMERGENCE AND DEVELOPMENT OF COMMUNITY

Early Humans and Problems of Community Formation

In the sense of our definition of community, early hunting and gathering societies probably did not have community-oriented lives. They were nomads, moving from place to place. They may have perceived territories to which they restricted their movements. They may also have had "home bases," to which they would periodically return. But their daily activities did not revolve about a permanent place of residence. Hence, they did not have community as a form of organization. The organization of their activities was determined by kinship patterns. Mother, father, children, and assorted relatives banded together and roamed in pursuit of whatever they needed in order to survive. Their skills were extremely rudimentary. Basically, they had practical knowledge of local fruits, berries, and roots, and they possessed rudimentary hunting techniques. This knowledge, however, was not sufficient to allow them to settle in any one place. If they settled, they would soon exhaust the plant foods and game of the area. They were persistently forced to move on and were forever in search of more fertile grounds. To these precommunity peoples, "settling down" meant death.

Inevitably, certain of these roving kinship groups found geographic pockets of fertility that could support the formation of communities. It is most likely that these areas were in the basins of major rivers or on the coasts of our oceans. An abundance of marine life could be reaped from coastal areas, and major river basins offered an unequaled abundance of plant and animal life. This picture, no matter how credible it may appear, is impossible to verify with certainty. We have very little infor-

mation about our hunting and gathering ancestors. We do know, however, that approximately 10,000 years ago a major new skill emerged: agriculture. The invention of agriculture changed the patterns of human living dramatically. During this time we see the proliferation of the community form of social organization (Childe 1952).

Agriculture and Early Communities

Until recently, it was commonly understood that the vast majority of the first communities came about because of the discovery and refinement of agriculture. The proposition is a sensible one. It is hard to imagine a permanent and well-populated settlement existing without the benefit of agriculture. Also, the fact that agriculture, by its nature, requires the grower to be in the same place for much of the year supports the credibility of this hypothesis. Nevertheless, there is another view on the matter. This view states that agriculture developed because of the appearance of communities. If communities came into existence for reasons such as trade or common defense, then agriculture would have to be invented to ensure daily survival. Whether agriculture or community came first will remain a point of contention for social scientists. Our purposes, however, will not be hindered if we assume that the two came into existence together.

The simultaneous emergence of agriculture and community had many repercussions. Most immediately, many segments of the human population were becoming compact, or dense. *Compact* is, of course, a relative term, and none of us today would consider that these early people were suffering from population density.

Territoriality Among the Primates

If our hunting and gathering ancestors did not reveal community forms, except in pockets of fertility around rivers and oceans, then we would not expect to find community among our primate cousins. Baboons, macaques, and gorillas all move about in broad territories, settling down only temporarily. Chimpanzees are more stationary and do seem to amass themselves into large groups. Yet, little is known about them, except the fact that there is considerable mobility of individual chimps between these groupings. However, we can learn something about how primates—perhaps including human primates—react when they do have territories. The gibbon provides us with this insight.

The gibbon is a distant ape cousin who lives high in the trees. It is the only monogamous ape, which means that a male and female form a lifelong bond, living in a small and well-defined territory in the upper branches of a tree. Resources are scarce since this small area can support only a limited number of inhabitants. When mature, gibbon couples drive their young from their territory. More interesting for our purposes, however, is the ferocity with which gibbons defend their territory. They will fight to the death to maintain their territory and the resources it provides. No other primate is so intransigent.

Gibbons live high in the trees in true families, who defend their territory.

As humans settled into communities, they, too, became territorial. They were willing to engage in war; they often would die before they would give up their settlement. Such territoriality is common in the animal world, but it is not common among primates. Humans and gibbons are the most territorial. Other primates will fight, but flee when defeat is certain. So will humans on some occasions. But beliefs and values often "program" them to stay with their community, even in the face of death.

Later Developments in Community Organization

Because of greater organization and the increased food supply provided by agriculture, some community members found the time and energy to express themselves in new ways. When they were not farming, building fortifications, trading, or housekeeping they expressed their feelings toward nature and a new-found life-style rich with possibilities through art and religion. Once the division of labor was well established, the expansion of agriculture was probably necessary to support growing and diversifying communities. Yet, the agricultural technology that provided the principal support for the first communities was neither powerful nor efficient by present standards, and the possibilities of hunting and fishing were limited. Therefore, the size and complexity of these communities were extremely limited; few communities could tolerate a population of more than a few thousand people.

The Emergence of Preindustrial Cities

Cities are a type of community. They can be roughly defined as communities in which a comparatively large and concentrated population lives and works, engaging in extensive trade of goods and services with each other as well as with their surrounding environment. Before industrialization, cities were large extensions of the earliest communities. They had a diverse population that was quartered into discrete districts or sections. Consistent with a successful division of labor, they supported a wide variety of occupations; aside from the ever-present government officials and religious elites, occupational groups such as metal-smiths, weavers, tailors, and saddlers were prominent. Cities engaged in extensive trade with agricultural people for their food and with other cities for a wide variety of "exotic" goods. These activities fit well within the limits of traditional community activity (Mumford 1961; Sjoberg 1960). However, there is a readily applied distinction between the city and the traditional community, which is well described by Gideon Sjoberg (1971), who stipulates that a large, densely populated , and diverse community cannot be called a city unless it possesses a distinct literary elite. This qualitative requirement is not without reason. The presence of a literary elite is significant. The stable and continuous presence of this group calls to our attention the existence of a highly developed and highly specialized technology in the immediate vicinity of the literary group. A stable and continuous group of literary elites does not exist because it has the ability to entertain itself. It exists because it can support complex systems of industry, trade, and government. Organized literacy in the support of other organized activities must be achieved in order for cities to survive.

It is difficult for us to know precisely when the first preindustrial city emerged. We know that the Mediterranean community called Jericho exhibited persuasively the beginnings of city around 8000 B.C. But from determinations based on recent archaeological findings we can reasonably assume that Jericho lacked a literary elite. Certainly, by 4000 B.C. preindustrial cities existed in Egypt and in other parts of the world. Today, because of the phenomenon of "overlapping development," we can see reasonable approximations of the basic preindustrial form in such cities as Mecca, Istanbul, and Hué.

Cities and the Industrial Revolution

Just as the technology of agriculture marked a dramatic change in the human system—for example, the emergence of community—so did industrialization. Industrialization radically transformed the shape of the human system and the nature of cities.

The efficiencies of new scientific technologies allowed cities to boom during the industrial revolution. The range of valuable services the city could provide was greatly increased. Industry, based on technological innovations, became much more productive, and the potential for production seemed limitless. The values of urban life shifted significantly from religion to the mechanics of production, distribution, and consumption. The novelty of industrial life, and the exciting new possibilities it seemed to offer were major causes of the massive migration to urban centers.

Rapid advancements were also made in the technologies of every sphere of human activity. Improvements in medicine, transportation, and manufacturing techniques were most important to the development of the industrial city. In turn, improvements in medicine and the manufacture of food, or agriculture, gave a boost to the growth of population. A larger surplus of food could be produced by a smaller population of rural people at a time when the rural population was increasing significantly. This was one side of the two-sided phenomenon of rural-to-urban migration. On the other side, several events were contributing to this movement. Most basically, the practical application of the scientific method had culminated, briefly, in the dramatic use of the steam engine. Although wind and water power had been used in preindustrial cities, the use of steam first demonstrated in a convincing manner the advantages of inanimate energy sources as opposed to animate energy sources such as oxen and people. The use of steam allowed tremendous increases in manufacturing. Further increases came about when the time-old practice of the division of labor was refined in the factory system. Burgeoning industrialization created a need for a massive labor force that encouraged the influx of people from rural regions to urban centers.[1]

---

[1] The happy circumstance of obliging interchange between rural and urban regions as outlined here should not be taken for granted. In many parts of the world today, large numbers of people are drawn or driven to urban centers, which demonstrates the potential for large-scale industrialization and modernization. Often, however, the agricultural techniques and food surplus necessary to support the urban region are lacking. This leads to massive settlements of poverty-stricken people on the outskirts of these cities. These settlements are known as "suburban squatter slums," and are prominent in Caracas, Calcutta, Hong Kong, and other major preindustrial cities of the world.

An early industrial city in America. Note the extreme congestion and crowding. It is thus little wonder that people left for the suburbs as soon as it became technologically and economically possible.

In general terms, then, we can envision the representative city of the industrial revolution: a noisy, bustling urban center, sometimes filled with the sounds of newly invented machinery pounding out the products of manufacture, always filled with the excitement and movement of new seekers of opportunity; mechanical trams, newspaper hawkers on every corner, and steamboats in the harbor; wide-eyed businessmen and financiers on the move to keep abreast, and the quiet, imperceptible retreat of established elites; frantic loadings at the rail station, and the unattached hauteur of a new raft of petty officials, filled with a vision of their importance in the order of government; the confusion of largely experimental mechanical devices in public breakdown and, eventually, the sputtering automobile.

Postindustrial Cities: The Giant Urban Region

For the first century of the industrial revolution the industrial city was a well-defined territory with discrete borders. The dominant postindustrial urban form, however, is the giant **urban metropolis region.** In very recent years, a newer form has appeared, called **conurbation** (in Europe) or **megalopolis** (in the United States). The conurbation or megalopolis is formed by the gradual merging of two or more urban areas into a single complex (Hall 1966). This process first occurred in Europe, where regional industrial cities with similar economies flowed into one another. The mining cities of the Ruhr region of Germany, for example, underwent this transformation. It is the general opinion among social scientists, notwithstanding the occasional dissenter (see Blumenfeld 1971, p. 53), that the eastern seaboard of the United States, between Boston and Washington, is becoming a megalopolis and that others will follow.

Two of the dominant characteristics of the giant urban region are especially consistent with the impending appearance of the megalopolis. First, there is the consistent phenomenon of population diffusion. Contrary to common understanding, and despite the appearance of ever more gigantic commercial towers, the population of central cities of the most advanced urban regions has not grown appreciably over the past two decades (Blumenfeld 1971, p. 50). Economic pressures forced the housing industry away from the central cities; these same pressures have more recently had the same effect on a large portion of the business and manufacturing sectors. In the case of the business and manufacturing interests, further refinements in the techniques of communication, transportation, and distribution made this outward move more palatable. The promotion of suburban life as a positive goal worthy of achievement has also been a factor in the lessening of population density in postindustrial urban regions.

Secondly, the economy of the giant urban region can be characterized as a service economy. In the United States, for example, over 50% of the total work force is involved in service activities, and this proportion has been maintained for several years (*New York Times Encyclopedic Almanac* 1972, p. 653). The United States was the first nation to develop a predominantly service-oriented economy, but other industrialized nations are rapidly following suit. In at least one respect, the emergence of a service economy depends upon the previous existence of a highly developed industrial economy. Modern industry engenders the concentration of a large labor force within a relatively limited area. It is when this dense population—which is also a dense market—is firmly established that a massive service economy becomes feasible (Davis 1955, 1971). There are additional factors that help the service economy to prosper. Many former industrial workers of every rank either drift or run to the service occupations when their traditional work roles are rendered obsolete by the application of automation techniques. Because they are generally much less "labor-intensive" then traditional industries, many major service

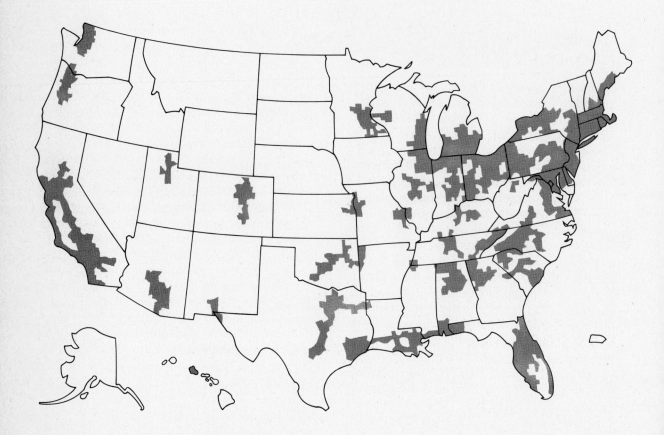

Figure 1: Projected Urban Regions: Year 2000

Dark areas mark projected urban regions & corridors

Source: Presidential Commission, *Population Growth and the American Future* (Washington, D.C.: U.S. Government Printing Office 1972).

occupations continue to do well in central cities despite the ever-skyrocketing costs of land use. Other sectors of the service economy do well in suburban and exurban areas. The continued success of a service economy depends upon its ability to market convenience at the expense of the consumer's self-sufficiency. In this sense it is very similar to the traditional industrial economy. However, the urgency with which this trade-off is proposed in many of the service occupations, plus the extremes to which the trade-off is carried, should advise us to withhold judgement concerning the ultimate wealth-generating capabilities of the service economy as a whole.

The postindustrial metropolis is also characterized by the consistent presence of the **suburb.** It appears likely that this trend toward suburbanization will continue in the world's urban regions, especially in the formation of massive residential and commercial corridors between major urban centers. Increasingly, suburban residents are able to find a suitable livelihood away from the central city upon which they once depended. Initially, this was possible only because changes in economic conditions and plant requirements were driving business and commercial interests away from the urban centers. Once started, however, this process reinforces itself; as residential suburbs and relocated industries come into contact with one another, the area of contact becomes more attractive to potential home owners and businesses. More local settlement takes place, and the area appears yet more attractive, and so on. Ultimately, the suburban area is vastly expanded; and in some cases, the birth of an urban corridor or a megalopolis is under way.

COMMUNITY TRENDS IN AMERICA

The Rapid Growth of American Cities

Perhaps the most noticeable characteristic of the city in the United States is its rapid development. By any standard, American cities matured very quickly. This rapid development, still evident today in its remains, reflects the spirit of progress of a new land in a new age, and creates problems for a newer age.

Many statistical reflections of this rapid growth have been developed. A look at a few of these will lend considerable texture to our understanding of the growth of urban America. Most graphic, perhaps, are the reported findings of A. Schlesinger (1951), A. L. Strauss (1961), and the U.S. Bureau of the Census (1970, p. 46). In its first official report the Census Bureau listed a total of 24 communities with populations in excess of 2,500, and two with populations in excess of 25,000. The year was 1790. In that year the urban population comprised 3.5% of the total population of the United States. According to Bureau statistics 100 years later, there were 160 communities with populations in excess of 25,000, and the urban population comprised 30% of the national total. Today, another 80 years later, the same source reports more than 800 communities with a population of 25,000 or more, and 40% of the national population within the boundaries of urban areas with populations in excess of 1,000,000. In 1800, no American city exceeded 100,000 inhabitants. But by 1860, New York City was the third largest city in the world, 800,000, and Philadelphia, with a population in excess of 500,000, had surpassed Berlin in size. At the same time, six other American cities had surpassed the 100,000 mark; and a mere 20 years later, there was a total of 20 American cities with a population in excess of 100,000 (Strauss, 1961).

The Spread of Urbanization

The first cities in the United States were commercial seaports on the eastern seaboard. The principal cities of this class were Boston, New York, Philadelphia, Baltimore, and Charleston. These early urban regions were important centers of importation of manufactured goods from Europe and exportation of agricultural surpluses.

Over time, new cities began to appear in more western regions, such as in Ohio and Indiana. The new cities in the West were almost exclusively inhabited by the sons of eastern urbanites. As these western cities appeared, the commercial profile of the seaports altered to include the manufacture of goods to be shipped west. More agricultural surpluses were received in return, which amplified further the import/export function of the coastal cities (Turner 1976, pp. 207–208).

At about the same time, industrial towns were beginning to make their appearance along major interior waterways, where the power source was plentiful and finished products could be easily shipped. For the first half of the nineteenth century, the major urban advancements were taking place on the shores of the Charles, the Hudson, the Susquehanna, the Ohio, and other rivers. Other major cities, such as Chicago, Erie, and Buffalo, were beginning to prosper on the shores of the Great Lakes.

During the 1850s and throughout the latter half of the nineteenth century, the urban development of the interior found a major catalyst in the railroad. As the railroad became a dominant mode of transportation, a city no longer had to be adjacent to a navigable waterway. It became more important in the newly opened areas of the West that an urban area be centrally located to provide a convenient and efficient crossroad for rail traffic. Chicago, already profiting from its position on Lake Michigan, became more important as a rail crossroads. St. Louis became an important rail city in addition to its role in Mississippi River traffic. Toledo and Kansas City also shared prosperity with the railroads. Following the completion of the Transcontinental Railroad in 1869, the importance of San Francisco, Salt Lake City, and other budding urban regions was greatly enhanced.

The effect of the railroad on the overall urban development of the United States has never been equaled. The greatest rate of urbanization in the United States occurred between 1860 and 1910 (Davis 1955), during the critical period of rail development. The timely invention of the automobile, the airplane, high voltage transmission of electricity, the telephone, mass food canning, electrical refrigeration, and other technological innovations have continued to support the rapid growth of American suburbs and the urban metropolis.

This fast rate of growth is summarized in Figure 2. The rural population of the United States outnumbered the urban population as late as 1910 (since only 46% were urban); this plurality was reversed by 1920. Now, of course, America is predominantly urban.

Figure 2: Percentage of Urban Residents in America, 1900–1970

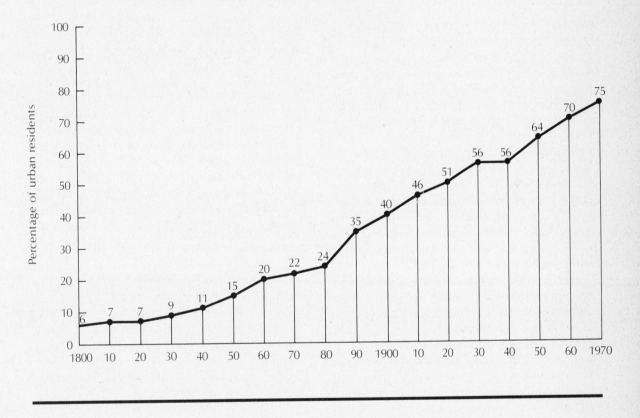

Social Conditions in the American City

These days, there is a strong inclination among "old-time" urbanities to decry the conditions of the modern city and to yearn for the old days when cities were more graceful, the air was cleaner, the pace was slower, and fine people strolled the avenues. Although the modern city has many serious problems, American urban regions have had many of the same problems for longer than the "old-timers" can remem-

ber. The ethnic ghetto was well established in American cities before 1900. When the rural southern blacks began to migrate north *en masse* between 1910 and 1930, there were incidents of racial violence to rival those of the past decade. Allen and Adair (1969) report, for instance, that there were 18 major race riots in the major cities of the United States between 1915 and 1919. Corruption in city government has always existed. In the absence of an income-tax program, the federal government

THE STUDY OF LIFE IN MODERN URBAN AMERICA

was largely unable to respond to the needs of the cities and the complaints of its residents. Moreover, the opportunity to help would most likely have been deferred by the federal government in the face of a strong and long tradition of local governmental autonomy. The city resident, especially in the ethnic neighborhoods, was entirely dependent upon the city's political machine and its local agent, the ward heeler, for relief from extraordinarily oppressive conditions. The ward heeler, in return for being a go-between for urban residents with no power of their own, demanded votes for the city machine, which was, in turn, largely free to exploit the general wealth of the city toward its own ends (Turner 1976, p. 210). The factories located in cities were not clean, and trains and cars polluted the air as much then as they do now. The poor were as pervasive then as they are today, as were the attendant slums and overcrowded conditions. In fact, the black ghettos of 50 years ago suffer by comparison with conditions in contemporary inner-city black "communities." It is too easy to forget that plumbing and waste disposal facilities were both more scarce and less efficient in the early industrial cities and that urban living in general was notoriously unsanitary. The conditions of urban decline had already solidified in American cities shortly after the turn of the century. Overcrowded conditions, slum dwellings, congestion, pollution, political corruption, racial segregation, racial tensions, and riots were no longer clearly evident to the urban dweller of 1910 (Turner 1976, pp. 210–211).

Early Studies: The Chicago School

The Chicago School is significant in the field of sociology for several reasons. Its members were the first modern social scientists to undertake a formal analysis of the purely social problems of city life. The epic proportions and serious nature of their efforts have since provided a standard for urban social analysis, and they pioneered in the application of ecological understandings to the analysis of urban society.

Early Studies of Urban Life. The Chicago School was so named because it was centered at the University of Chicago and because the main object of its study was the city of Chicago. The most notable member of this exceptional group is Louis Wirth. His essay, "Urbanism as a Way of Life" (1938), is a landmark in the field of social research and, in large part, is a summation of the efforts and findings of the Chicago School.

Wirth was preoccupied with the size and density of urban populations, and he thought that these factors, along with the heterogeneity of urban populations, largely determined most of the important conditions of modern urban life. For example, he determined that a dense population of sufficient size inevitably leads to a proliferation of secondary groups, a lessening of the intensity of personal interaction, and cultural heterogeneity. Wirth went a step further and reasoned that these occurrences led to the weakening of family ties, in particular, and to the subversion of traditional bases for social life—such as religion, common folklore, and common heritage—in general. Wirth found a

Louis Wirth was a central figure in the Chicago studies of urban life.

greater tolerance for individual differences among urbanites, but only at the sacrifice of relaxed, overall organization. Confusion and chaos were heightened in the city, and the city itself was continually altering its appearance and modifying its functional base (see Park et al. 1925).

The Biases of the Chicago School. The members of the Chicago School published many essays and findings structured largely on the basis of population size, density, and heterogeneity as parameters of analysis. The causal primacy of these population characteristics is

today a moot question, at best. The more serious objection to the great body of their conclusions centers on the rural bias of their interpretations. Consistently, the Chicago School evaluated urban life in ways that seemed to point to an essential, insoluble "badness" at the heart of the urban structure. This lent an editorial tinge to much of their work and, however well-intended, editorial evaluations are in violation of the principles of objective scientific inquiry.

This error on their part is understandable and is profitable to our understanding if we consider that the members of the Chicago School came from rural backgrounds. As we know, the rural population of the United States was proportionately much greater in the days of youth for these and other pioneering social scientists. It follows that many of the first social scientists carried with them a rural tradition that made it difficult to maintain objectivity and perspective when examining social problems. Today, this bias, if not altogether eliminated, has at least been balanced.

There were two other major reasons for the Chicago School's discouraging descriptions of urban existence. First, they tended to focus their attention on the poor and/or deviant citizens of Chicago, the overwhelming majority of whom were urban as a matter of necessity rather than choice. They rarely took into consideration the more affluent members of the community, who could afford the stability necessary for strong personal relationships and a meaningful family life, and who, at that time, had been city dwellers for a longer period of time than had most of the poor. Secondly, Chicago was not a representative city during the two decades of activity of the Chicago School. Chicago became famous as a model of stress, disorganization, rampant greed, and general chaos during the "Roaring Twenties" and the depression years. These conditions were reflected in the investigations of the Chicago School, as they should have been. Their rural bias, however, decreased the profitability of their work by allowing them to assume that this milieu was the rule, rather than the exception, of city life.

The Chicago School and Urban Ecology. The Chicago School is well remembered for other work that was not so easily influenced by a rural bias. They were among the first to study the urban ecology. Although ecology has enjoyed a recent popularity which leads many to believe that it is a new discipline, the origins of scientific ecology well predate the origins of sociology. The members of the Chicago School were willing to borrow ecological concepts from biology in their attempts to understand processes in urban America. Perhaps the most famous result of these efforts is the theory of *concentric zones*, put forward by E. W. Burgess (Park et al. 1925). Burgess proposed that the inexorable progression of economic land-use competition led to the organization of cities into concentric zones, the most central of which was held by the most moneyed interests of the day (see Figure 3, model 1). This central zone, Burgess held, is usually surrounded by a *transition* zone, which is poor and underdeveloped, and always threatened by the potential spread of the central business zone. Farther from the center are found zones developed into primary residence patterns. Although Burgess put forward the concentric-zone concept as a hypothesis, it was widely popularized as a finding of fact. More recently, other hypotheses of urban organization have been put forward. Homer Hoyt (1939) de-

Figure 3: Three Models of Urban Growth

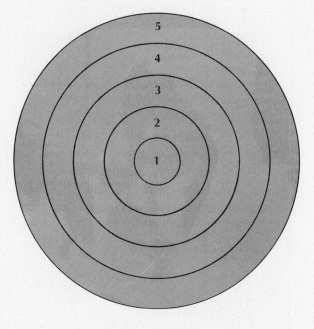

Model 1: The Concentric Zone Hypothesis
1. Central business district
2. Zone in transition
3. Zone of workingmen's homes
4. Residential zone
5. Commuter zone

Source: Adapted from Ernest W. Burgess, (1925).

veloped a *sector* hypothesis, which emphasizes the importance of railroads and highways in the organization of urban regions (see Figure 3, model 2). He proposed that different economic land-use areas in the central city grow outward along rail and highway routes, and remain distinct from one another. Chauncy Harris and Edward Ullman (1945) proposed a *multiple*

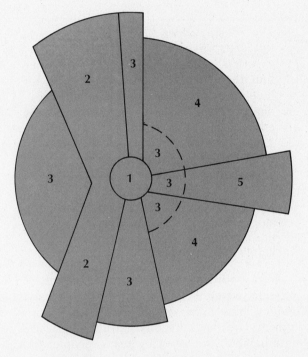

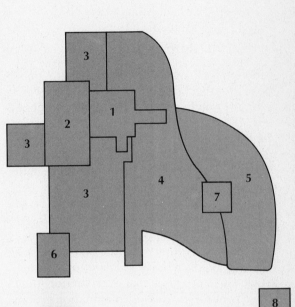

Model 2: The Sector Hypothesis
1. Central business district
2. Wholesale, light manufacturing
3. Low-class residential
4. Medium-class residential
5. High-class residential

Source: Homer Hoyt, (1939); (1943); and
Harris and Ullman (1945).

Model 3: The Multiple Nuclei Hypothesis
1. Central business district
2. Wholesale, light manufacturing
3. Low-class residential
4. Medium-class residential
5. High-class residential
6. Heavy manufacturing
7. Outlying business district
8. Residential suburb
9. Industrial suburb

Source: Adapted from Chauncy D. Harris
and Edward L. Ullman, (1945).

nuclei model of urban organization (Figure 3, model 3). This model is based on the assumption that the various urban land uses develop around separate nuclei. The locations of these nuclei, they said, are determined by a number of factors, some of which are general, whereas others are specific. A nucleus might develop in a specific location because of the facilities provided there, because other nuclei are specifically absent from the vicinity, or because the location is affordable. Harris and Ullman saw a growing number of separate nuclei as the urban area progressively grew and became differentiated.

More Recent Studies of Urban Life

Although sociologists do not pretend to ignore the real problems of urban life, many of which were accurately cited by the Chicago School, more recent studies have tended to deemphasize the negative aspects of city life slightly and to rephrase the strongly moral and evaluative elements of earlier interpretations of life in the city.

Urban sociologist Herbert Gans is in the forefront of this transitional process. His important essay, "Urbanism and Suburbanism as Ways of Life: A Re-Evaluation of Definitions" (1962), is representative of his efforts. In this article Gans proposes that every major American city nurtures five basic population groups, each with its own distinctive lifestyle:

1. *The "Trapped."* This group largely consists of old people, usually on pensions or public assistance, who cannot afford to leave the city. They tend to limit their existence to a single neighborhood, with which they identify strongly.
2. *The "Deprived."* This group includes the poor minorities, the aged, divorced mothers, and others. To the deprived, city life offers cheap housing, higher welfare payments than the rural poor enjoy, and increased opportunities for employment.
3. *The "Ethnic Villagers."* Usually a recent immigrant, the ethnic villager lives in a closed, almost independent community within the city. Ties with the rest of the city are usually weak. Kinship ties remain strong, and there is suspicion of those things beyond the boundaries of the ethnic community.

4. *The Unmarried or Childless.* Members of this group live in the city by choice, but experience little commitment to it. They find the city an advantageous place for meeting people. They tend to change residence frequently, and often leave the city entirely when they marry or have children.
5. *The "Cosmopolites."* This group is well educated and enjoys a high income. It is concentrated in the professions and the higher positions of industry, as well as the arts. Members of this group choose to live in the city largely because of its cultural offerings, but rarely have strong ties to a neighborhood.

From studies such as these, many aspects of city life, which were not clear to the Chicago School, have taken on greater clarity. For instance, it becomes obvious that, although a city is inhabited and used by many people, the number of those who identify with the city as a whole is relatively small—hence, the "alienation," seeming confusion (lessened by an appreciation of Gans' groupings), proliferation of secondary groups, and so forth. It also becomes clear that the general descriptions of urban life of the Chicago School and other observers from earlier days represented stereotypes rather than realities. According to more recent findings, intense primary-group activity does exist in the city, along with the deemphasis of economic and occupational roles. In fact, all of the virtues of an earlier and simpler form of life usually exist somewhere in most major cities. Scott Greer (1956) found that over half of his sample population from two Los Angeles neighborhoods visited their close relatives at least once each week. Other studies have yielded similar results. Apparently, kinship roles hold an important place in urban life, as they have traditionally in rural areas. Gans devoted a book, *The Urban Villagers* (1962), to a study of the manner in which the traditional agricultural life-style of rural Italians was adapted to an urban environment. Gans found that the rural life-style was not only discernible in a new form, but that much of its original structure was intact. This refutes the notion put forward by the Chicago School and others that urban life automatically destroys rural patterns when the two come into contact.

Studies of Suburban Trends in America

The Suburban Trend. The sociologist-demographer Phillip Hauser (1969) points out that suburbia accounted for 45% of the total growth of metropolitan areas between 1900 and 1950 and that this percentage was higher (61%) during the decade from 1940 to 1950, and then higher again (near 80%) during the 1950s.[2] An additional indication of the growing importance of the suburban area in modern life is illustrated by the fact that, within the context of a burgeoning urban population, the most dynamic growth during the past 70 years has occurred in cities with populations of less than 100,000. Since the U.S. Census Bureau's lower limit for urbanization status is 2,500, we may assume that much of this growth can be at-

[2]Although the emergence of suburbia is commonly thought to have begun about 30 years ago, the actual development of suburbs has been continuous, particularly in the United States, since the late nineteenth century. The well-known American suburb of Newport, R.I., underwent significant development during this period. Suburban developments had occurred sporadically for centuries before. For instance, the Palace of Versailles and its supporting elements could be considered an early suburb of Paris.

Table 2: Fastest Growing U.S. Metropolitan Areas Since 1970

Metropolitan Area	Percent Change April 1, 1970 to July 1, 1974
Fort Myers, Florida	46.4
Sarasota, Florida	32.0
Fort Lauderdale-Hollywood, Florida	30.1
Fort Collins, Colorado	28.0
Orlando, Florida	27.7
West Palm Beach-Boca Raton, Florida	27.1
Killeen-Temple, Texas	26.6
Tucson, Arizona	23.3
Colorado Springs, Colorado	22.7
Tampa-St. Petersburg, Florida	22.5
Tallahassee, Florida	21.3
Phoenix, Arizona	20.9
Austin, Texas	20.3

Source: Bureau of Census (1976:2).

tributed to the ascension of suburban communities.

In the growth of suburbia we can see the combined effects of personal, economic, and governmental factors. The federal government contributed greatly to the growth of suburbia by implementing informal housing policy through the Federal Housing Administration and the Veteran's Administration. The Federal Housing Administration, or FHA underwrote housing construction on a massive scale in the 1930s, primarily to stimulate economic growth. After World War II, the Veteran's Administration, or VA, performed similarly. One of the

Early suburbs have often become as crowded
and congested as the city.

effects of these federal programs was to make possible suburbs for millions of people who previously could not have afforded a home away from the central city. Suburbs had traditionally been the prerogative of the relatively well-to-do, but with the assistance of these programs blue-collar suburban communities began to appear in great numbers. After World War II, it was not uncommon for a blue-collar veteran to purchase a suburban home with a down payment of $200.

Early Studies of Suburban Life. The suburban phenomenon stands as the watershed between the past and the future of urban life in America. Appropriately, social scientists have paid special attention to American suburbs in the recent past. Also, as suburbs have increased in number, so have the number of sociological studies of suburban life. As with the studies of cities, however, the first studies of suburbia were contaminated with stereotypical attitudes. Early studies by A. C. Spectorsky (1955) and W. F. Whyte (1957), for example, contributed heavily to the common myths about suburbia. Whyte studied a Chicago suburb composed almost entirely of middle-level, white-collar "organization men"; Spectorsky happened to focus his attention on an upper-middle-class suburb dependent upon, but located far from, New York City. Both Whyte and Spectorsky found suburban life to be superficial. From their data, the most important concern of the suburban dweller seemed to be, to these researchers, the career of the husband in the supporting city. They found conformity to be rampant and hypocrisy as well. Appearance was very important, and social mores found enforcement in "gossip" and social blackmail. Conspicuous consumption was assumed to be

normal. Because of a frantic pace and formal social commitments undertaken to preserve false reputations, family life was disjointed. The consumption of alcohol and the undertaking of extramarital intrigues were found to be major preoccupations.

More Recent Studies of Suburban Life. Do these findings indicate general truths about suburban life? Recent research indicates that they do not. The problem with early studies was that they were heavily influenced by largely mythical impressions of suburban life. These impressions were further amplified by the choice of upper middle class, excessively upwardly mobile suburbs as subjects of initial investigations. Recent studies have given more perspective to our understanding of suburban life. The more suburban life is studied, the more familiar and nonreprehensible it becomes.

Gans (1962ab) found, for instance, that the behavior of people does not change appreciably upon their move to a suburban community. H. Laurence Ross (1965) studied two upper-middle-class white neighborhoods in New York City—one near the central city and one in the near suburbs—and found essentially no difference in their life-styles or their concerns. A Louis Harris poll in 1971 indicated that most of the surveyed suburban dwellers had lived in the same community for more than ten years, and that only 10% of the sample population rated their chosen community as "below average." Correspondingly, Farley (1964) found that suburbs retain their composition and character for longer periods of time than do urban neighborhoods. Wendell Bell (1958) found that suburbanites typically place a high value on the integrity and richness of family life. Not too surprisingly, Gans (1968) found that the quality of suburban life differs both from other suburban community life and from neighborhood life in the central cities largely on the basis of social class and the individual's position in the human life cycle, rather than on the basis of any general "conversion" to any preconceived suburban life-style. Bennett Berger's (1960) study of a blue-collar suburban community similarly revealed that its occupants "had not been profoundly affected in any statistically identifiable or sociologically interesting way." Again, Herbert Gans (1967) studied the famous suburb in Pennsylvania, known as Levittown, and found that, in general, its members were happy and enjoyed close kinship ties. Neighboring relatives were frequently visited, and neither status nor conformity were major concerns. A George Gallup survey in 1972 indicated that, among the people surveyed, fully 31% expressed a desire to live in a suburban community, whereas only 15% actually did. Apparently, an increased familiarity with the realities of suburban life, on the part of the social scientist as well as the layperson, has contributed a great deal to the erasure of earlier negative stereotypes.

American society has thus undergone a massive shift in its urban patterns. As a society, our community life has become more suburban. It is in these transitions from rural to city life, and now, from city to suburb that many problems reside. We should therefore close our discussion of community in America with a brief overview of the problems of urban America.

PROBLEMS IN CONTEMPORARY URBAN AMERICA

Financial Problems

The reports of the U.S. Census Bureau in 1970 made it official: the suburban community form had become the dominant form of organization in the United States. Census statistics in that year revealed that 74.2 million people lived in suburban areas, as compared to 62.2 million people in central city areas. Aside from the natural expansion due to births and immigrations, the suburbs also grew because of an influx of central city dwellers. The process of influx from the central cities can be seen as a self-reinforcing process, similar to the process, mentioned earlier, that is bringing about the creation of urban corridors. With the FHA and VA mortgage programs providing the initial catalyst, the success of the suburban form has bred further success. But, as in economics, the currency has to come from somewhere. As more and more people flee the central cities, the cities have experienced a serious erosion of their tax base. The "cream" of American taxpayers continue to make use of urban services and facilities during the work week. However, they no longer pay for these advantages in any significant way. This problem could have been largely avoided decades ago, when city governments were virtually unopposed in their determination of urban political boundaries, through incorporation of suburban communities into the city itself. However, at the time, suburban communities were viewed as a tax liability by urban politicians and advisors. Thirty years ago, the incorporation of the suburbs would have meant a loss of revenue to the existing city political body; the suburbs would have drained more revenue through services than they could have returned in taxes. By the time city government realized its lack of foresight, suburban communities had incorporated themselves into independent political entities, with the support of rural political influences in state legislative bodies. Therefore, the large body of the urban work force today resides in the suburbs, continues to make use of the central city, and pays virtually nothing for this use.

Governmental Problems

The fiscal problems generated by this phenomenon have only complicated and amplified the problems of central city government. As mentioned earlier, the great body of people who dwell in the central city do so for a variety of personal reasons, and few of them feel any essential allegiance to the city as a whole. Thus, it is difficult for elected officials to act from a unified base of political support or to refer to a consensual body of public political opinion. In the face of this situation, too many elected officials are forced to participate in *brokerage politics*. Government by brokerage involves efforts at appeasing various concerned secondary groups such as unions, corporate lobbyists, business affiliations, and ethnic-rights groups. The achievement of sound fiscal government is difficult in the face of an eroding tax base, and this problem is compounded when elected officials are forced to respond to diverse demands and often irreconcilable needs of different interests.

Sound city government is further impeded by unrestricted metropolitan growth. Current governmental structures are unprepared to deal with the problems of an extended metropolitan area. The question of responsibility among federal, state, and local governments is extremely difficult under present circumstances (Gans 1968). The New York City metropolitan area, for example, is composed of well over 550 independent political entities; yet, they share many of their problems in common—problems that demand common solutions. The recent fiscal crisis in New York City points out the difficulty of solving immediate problems when the question of prime governmental responsibility remains unresolved.

Segregation Problems

The FHA and VA housing mortage programs also gave indirect aid to another major urban problem: the perpetuation of racial ghettos. The FHA manual declared in 1950 that: "If a neighborhood is to retain stability it is necessary that properties shall continue to be occupied by the same social and racial classes." (Abrams 1966 523, 1969). Thus, the FHA continued, in policy form, the discrimination against upwardly mobile minority groups in housing. The most prominent example of enforced segregation involves the black minority, who compose an ever-larger segment of the urban population. From the beginnings of the migration of blacks from the South to the North, segregation against them has been enforced in one form or another. Often, blacks were forced by intimidation into inhabiting the most deteriorated urban housing because of threats of violence

SUMMARY AND PREVIEW

against them. Major violence in East St. Louis (1917), Chicago (1919), and Detroit (1943), amply discouraged blacks from seeking integrated housing (Allen & Adair 1969, pp. 31–37). In urban areas blacks typically pay more for housing that is equal in quality to the housing of whites. Taueber (1965, p. 140) reports that roughly 33% of black residents of urban areas spend more than one-third of their annual income on housing. Other ethnic groups typically pay less for housing of the same quality, although they realize more income.

Ethnic violence under these circumstances is no longer a mere potentiality, as we know (see Chapter 12). Currently, the racial violence that marked the late 1960s in Detroit, the Watts section of Los Angeles, and elsewhere has subsided. However, in a time when 80% of all urban blacks inhabit deteriorated central city areas and 90% of the growth of the black population is found in the central cities, the notion that further racial violence in our cities will not occur cannot be realistically entertained.

Thus, the problems of America's urban areas are severe and relate to the urban/suburban gulf. These problems are likely to intensify in the future, forcing alterations in the form of community organization.

In this chapter we have sought to understand how communities as a form of human organization first emerged. We have also gained some insight into their development in the past and how they now operate. As we have emphasized, communities became prominent with the development of agricultural technology. New economic patterns required new patterns of living and work. With the spread of industrialization, certain general trends in communities have become evident in all parts of the world: (1) growth of the city, (2) creation of suburbs, and (3) most recently, the emergence of urban corridors.

In American society we have seen that the pace and rate of these trends have been greatly accelerated. America's towns grew from small towns to large cities within 100 years. In this century the suburbs expanded, surrounding the central city and often joining to form urban corridors. The future will bring further suburbanization and the extension of these corridors in many parts of the country. This rapid growth and expansion has created a number of chronic problems, such as financial problems for the large, core cities, problems of political decision-making, and the entrapment of minorities in the decaying city cores.

Community is but one form of human organization. In the next chapter we will explore another social form—stratification—that, like community, was elaborated with the discovery of agriculture. Stratification is the form of organization that determines people's share of the scarce and valuable resources in a society. As people began to create economic surplus, problems of who gets what share intensified in the human system, and as societies developed, these issues of distribution became complex, leading to the elaboration of the stratification system.

Key Terms

Community: those patterns of action and interaction that are shaped by people's daily activities in a relatively permanent place of residence

Cities: communities in which a comparatively large and concentrated population lives and works, engaging in extensive trade of goods and services with each other and with the surrounding environment

Urban Metropolis Region: a large central city surrounded by smaller cities

Conurbation, Megalopolis: the merger of two or more urban regions

Suburb: a city, or group of cities, surrounding an even larger central city

Review Questions

1. Have there always been communities? What prompted their development?

2. What is the general trend in community development in the world?

3. What are some of the unique features of America's urban growth? In what ways does America's urban growth conform to worldwide trends?

4. What were some of the problems with early studies of city and suburban life?

5. What are the basic problems with America's urban system?

Suggested Readings

Abrahamson, Mark. *Urban Sociology.* Englewood Cliffs, N.J.: Prentice-Hall, 1970.

Butler, Edgar. *Urban Sociology.* New York: Harper & Row, 1976.

——. *The Urban Crisis: Problems and Prospects in America.* Santa Monica, Ca.: Goodyear, 1976.

Mumford, Lewis. *The City in History.* New York: Harcourt, Brace, and World, 1961.

Scientific American. Cities. New York: Knopf, 1971.

Sjoberg, Gideon. *The Preindustrial City.* New York: The Free Press, 1960.

Stein, Maurice R. *The Eclipse of Community.* New York: Harper & Row, 1964.

Strauss, Anselm L. *Images of the American City.* New York: The Free Press, 1961.

STRATIFICATION

PROLOGUE

Guiding Questions. Why do some people live in poverty and others in privilege? When did humans begin to distribute valuables unequally and why? What consequences does inequality have for the human system?

Chapter Topics

A look at American society confirms the existence of inequalities. Many people live in poverty; a few are very rich. A majority enjoy some degree of affluence, although most must scrape to make ends meet. A similar look at most societies will reveal inequalities. Whatever people value—money, property, power, health, prestige, or esteem—is distributed unequally. Some get more than others.

Inequalities have not always been a part of the human condition. Since simple hunting and gathering societies offer clues to our past, it is of interest to note that they evidence little inequality. In contemporary hunting and gathering societies, adults enjoy more prestige and authority than children, and some males perhaps have more prestige than others. But they all eat the same food, wear the same clothes, and shelter themselves under the same kinds of roofs. And so it probably was for at least 30,000 of our first 40,000 years on earth. Then, about 10,000 years ago, new technologies allowed humans to produce a surplus. As long as they could not produce and store a surplus, inequalities in property and wealth were not easily established. But once humans settled on the land, engaged in agriculture, and produced a surplus, it became possible for some to hoard more than others. As people accumulated wealth and the power, prestige, privilege, and other desirables that accompany wealth and were able to pass these possessions on to their offspring, a new social form emerged in the human system: stratification.

WHAT IS STRATIFICATION?

Before we can examine stratification in any detail, we should first give ourselves a working definition of the term. Although there are times when any definition of stratification is not wholly satisfactory, we may define **stratification** as those processes in a social system by which scarce and valuable resources are distributed unequally to status positions that become more or less permanently ranked in terms of the share of valuable resources each receives. To begin our systematic discussion of social stratification we will take a closer look at three key elements in our definition: (1) **scarce** and valuable **resources,** (2) unequal distribution, and (3) relatively permanent status rankings.

Scarce and Valuable Resources

It is a universal fact of social life that certain things, objects, or qualities are considered to be of special value. What these qualities or objects are differs from one society to another. Despite such variability and fluctuation, we can isolate three resources the value of which is socially universal. These are (1) power (2) prestige, and (3) wealth.

Power. We can define power as the ability to attain individual or group goals, even in the face of opposition (Weber 1957). Power may be thought of as existing in two basic forms. *Personal* power is essentially the power possessed by individuals that makes it possible for them to have the things they wish. *Social* power may be considered as the capacity to determine the direction of the social lives of others. Social power is usually, though not always, based on a position within a social unit of some kind.

Prestige. We can define prestige as the amount of esteem and deference that people receive from others. Prestige can exist in the absence of power and property, and it is highly valued in all societies. For example, the person who achieves commendable or heroic personal goals or who performs beneficial deeds attains prestige regardless of the amount of power or property he or she possesses.

Wealth. Typically, wealth is conceived of in terms of money, but money per se is only one of its forms, albeit its most liquid form. Any material asset that is defined as valuable by the members of a society can be viewed as wealth, such as cars, houses, stocks, spearheads, or arrows. Of course, wealth, like power and prestige, may exist alone or in combination with either or both of the three universal valuables. Although wealth does not guarantee power or prestige, its possession creates opportunities for the attainment of these other valuables. As one cynic once remarked: "Money isn't everything, but what it isn't, it can buy."

Max Weber and the Multidimensional View of Stratification

As we noted in Chapter 1, Max Weber was one of the founding fathers of sociology. One of his most important insights has implicitly guided our discussion and the general field of stratification. The specifics of Weber's analysis are less important than his general conclusions about the nature of stratification. Rankings of people are not unidimensional; within a society, one can see multiple sources of rankings. Prestige or "social honor" is one source of ranking, creating **status** groups. Wealth and property stemming from economic activities represent another source of ranking, leading to the formation of **classes.** Power is yet another valuable resource that is unequally distributed, leading to rankings in terms of **party.** Since Weber's penetrating analysis, sociologists have been alerted to the *multiplicity* of resources used to generate systems of rankings in a society. This is why we have emphasized three types of resources used to rank people in society: prestige, power, and wealth. As you can see, these roughly correspond to Weber's distinctions.

Unequal Distribution

The study of social stratification is largely the study of distribution of scarce and valuable resources. If the distribution of valuables was carried out in a manner such that valuables were received equally by all members of society, stratification would not exist.

As we attempt to gain knowledge about the processes underlying the unequal distribution of valuables, we should keep in mind that human social systems are not totally mechanical—they always include elements of chance, whimsy, or luck. We can find examples of this fact in the distribution of valuables. People win fortunes in lotteries. Many individuals "choose" the right parents. Often the accrual of valuables occurs as the result of a socially useful inspiration or invention, for which its creator can find no explanation. These occurrences have little value for scientific purposes, however. Social scientists are drawn to the study of unequal distribution because processes occur that systematically maintain the unequal distribution of valuables to individuals. It is these enduring processes that are of most importance in a sociological analysis of stratification. We will examine some of these when we explore the American stratification system in detail.

Relatively Permanent Status Rankings

One of the most basic consequences of the process of social stratification is the creation of relatively permanent rankings in terms of the proportion of valuables received. For instance, blue-collar workers differ from one another with regard to the valuables they each receive, but an overview of all blue-collar workers as a whole reveals a central tendency as to the amounts of valuables they receive. In other words, the income of blue-collar workers as a whole falls within a distinctive income range. This range tends to remain stable over time relative to the income ranges of other distinguishable income clusters. The upper and lower limits of the blue-collar income cluster fluctuate, of course, but these fluctuations are not enough to obscure the existence of the income cluster within the total range of income distribution within a society. The existence of several distinguishable income clusters within the total income range of a society is typical. Similarly, we can discern marked differences in the rankings of individuals with regard to other scarce resources, such as prestige and power.

Karl Marx's View of Class

Karl Marx provided a key insight into stratification. For Marx, people's *class* position was determined by their relationship to what he termed *the means of production*—that is, where they worked in the economy. He argued that societies tend to be divided into clear and conflicting interests: those who own and control the means of production using the labor of others to preserve their privilege, and those who own little, who work for wages, and who have an interest in changing the system so that they can receive a greater share of its resources. With their resources, however, the privileged can consolidate power to maintain their privilege and to preserve the class rankings in a society.

He then argued that, despite the power of the wealthy, the wage earners—or **proletariat**—would eventually become aware of their common interests and would unite in overthrowing the owners of the means of production—the **bourgeoisie.**

Marx's main insight was in recognizing that social stratification is maintained by the use of power by those who control the means of production. They control the distribution of resources and shape people's outlook and experiences in life. But, Marx insisted, the existence of social classes assures that all societies will eventually reveal conflict as those who do not receive resources by virtue of their economic position come into conflict with those who own and control the economic base of a society.

We can thus view stratification as composed of three elements: (1) a surplus of scarce and valuable resources such as power, prestige, and property; (2) the unequal distribution of these resources; (3) a degree of permanence or stability in this distribution so that some positions persistently receive more resources than others. All social units are likely to show stratification. A small group will have leaders who are accorded prestige, and perhaps, authority. Formal organizations are structured in ways that allocate power and authority unequally. Communities evidence inequalities in the distribution of income, wealth, housing, health, and power, as do most social units. However, sociologists have been particularly interested in *societywide* patterns of stratification. By examining society as a whole, we can raise several questions about stratification. Who gets what? For how long? With what result? In our discussion in this chapter, we will concentrate on societywide patterns of stratification. But we should remain aware that stratification is often a feature of other social forms.

STRATIFICATION:
Its Emergence and Profile in Different Societies

What trends in the distribution of scarce and valuable resources are evident? Why do different societies reveal varying degrees of inequality? Sociologist Gerhard Lenski (1966) raised these questions, and his answers give us a clue as to why stratification first emerged in the human system and why it takes different forms in the societies of the world.

For Lenski the process of stratification only comes into play in a significant manner when a *surplus* of valuables exists within a given society, especially material goods. A surplus of valuables can be said to exist when food, clothing, and other material resources and commodities are available above and beyond what is necessary to maintain the population at a subsistence level. Before a surplus of valuables exists, the array of functions and rewards within a society is relatively simple and homogeneous.

When a society attains a surplus of valuables, the surplus is unequally distributed to different segments of the society. Drawing on Marx's insights, Lenski argues that the unequal distribution of surplus occurs because different segments of the population vary in the degrees to which they use the power to effect control over the distribution of scarce resources. This distribution of valuables—usually wealth and property, initially—promotes the unequal distribution of other scarce resources, such as prestige and esteem. Often individuals find it possible to transform these resources into more power that they can use to divert the flow of other resources to their advantage. Thus, among those inclined to exercise power in this manner, a self-reinforcing process develops, as shown in Figure 1.

Figure 1: Lenski's View of Power and Privilege

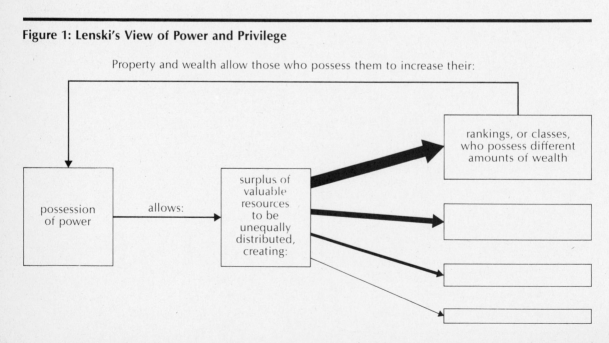

Property and wealth allow those who possess them to increase their:

possession of power   allows: surplus of valuable resources to be unequally distributed, creating: rankings, or classes, who possess different amounts of wealth

Lenski believes that many variables act to determine the amount and kind of surplus that exists in a society. These variables include:

1. the level of natural resources available to a society
2. the nature of the economy operating within a society including
   a. the size of the economy
   b. the productive capacity of the economy
   c. the features of the economic organization
3. the mode and level of technology and its application by the society.

In Lenski's system variable 3 is a significant determinant of variables 1 and 2. According to Lenski, it follows that the magnitude of surplus within a society varies directly with the level and application of technology. In turn, the degree of stratification varies directly with the magnitude of surplus. Thus, Lenski has hypothesized that technological factors should largely determine the nature and strength of stratification.

Lenski tested his hypothesis by examining a number of societies whose technological development varied greatly. He first examined the distribution of scarce resources in societies based upon *hunting-and-gathering* technology. In these societies people gather indigenous plants—fruits, roots, berries, and other available foods—and hunt animal life. Such a technology is simple; and as we emphasized in Chapter 3 on our beginnings as a species, we were for most of our existence on earth hunters and gatherers. There still exist such societies, but their numbers are rapidly declining. Lenski next examined what are called *horticultural*

societies in which people have learned how to plant seeds and to cultivate the soil with crude hoes and sticks. This discovery of gardening probably occurred 10,000 years ago, but it is still possible to find horticultural societies in the world today. Lenski turned next to *agrarian societies*, which are based upon advances in gardening technology. Whereas horticultural societies till small plots with only the hoe and the digging stick, agrarian societies use the plow to cultivate much greater tracts of land. Most people in the world today live in agrarian societies, although they are fast being transformed with industrialization. Finally, Lenski examined early and late industrial societies that increasingly use machines and factories to secure their necessary resources. England, France, Germany, the United States, Japan, and other nations industrialized many decades ago and are now *advanced industrial systems.* Other societies, such as many of those in Asia, South America, and Africa are now just initiating industrialization and can be termed early *industrial* societies. For a much more detailed discussion of these changes in the economic technologies of the human system, please consult Chapter 18 on the institution of the economy.

In examining inequality in these different types of societies, Lenski found consistent support for his hypothesis, to a point. He also found one surprise. According to his initial hypothesis, societies whose economic base is founded on advanced industrial technology would reveal the most inequality. Lenski found this to be true *except* within very advanced technological societies. In these advanced societies, Lenski discovered that the surplus of valuables is typically distributed somewhat more equally than in agricultural and less

Figure 2: Lenski's General Finding

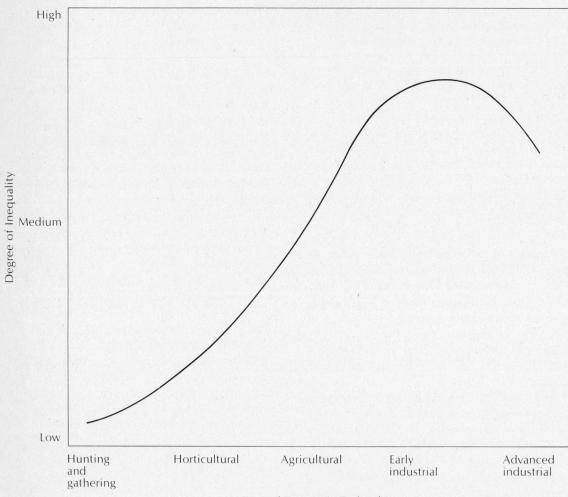

advanced industrial societies. Why should this be? Typically, sufficient excesses of surplus seem to provide the opportunity for organizations, such as labor unions and governmental departments, to exert themselves powerfully enough to alter somewhat the unequal distribution of resources.

Lenski's findings may give us a clue to the evolution of stratification in the human system. Our first human ancestors were hunters and gatherers, and over the last ten thousand years, humans have successively developed horticultural, agricultural, and industrial technologies. Hence, we might conclude that the curve shown in Figure 2 not only compares primitive, premodern, and modern societies of today, but also portrays the long-range trend in stratification since its emergence as part of the human system.

Stratification Among Japanese Macaques

We have observed some of the behaviors of the African baboon troop in the last chapter. A monkey that lives in Japan resembles the baboon but displays a somewhat different social order. Investigators have observed that the Japanese macaque is orderly like the baboon. One of the main principles of organization is an authority hierarchy. This hierarchy is not a true "pecking order," but those at the top are more likely to receive deference, and they are the least likely to be attacked. The typical pattern is for a troop to have one dominant, male leader and several subleader males. Other males are cast out to the periphery of the troop and are not allowed full participation. Alongside the male dominance hierarchy is a female hierarchy. Females will sometimes attack males, but in general, higher ranking males enjoy some degree of dominance over ranking females.

One interesting observation is that the top male is not always the biggest, strongest, or most aggressive. In fact, rank is rather weakly correlated with size, strength, and aggressiveness. Why is this so, especially since stronger males will usually retreat from attacks by weaker males higher up in the hierarchy? This pattern led observers to suspect that stratification processes are involved. Indeed, it was discovered that the sons of high-ranking females tended to become high-ranking males. Females were thus able to promote

Among the Japanese macaques, mothers appear to pass on their rank to their offspring in the stratification system.

run to the rescue of their young, with the result that the mothers then fight until one drives the other and her offspring off. One result is that offspring with weak mothers become fearful of those with tough mothers. Moreover, they seem to develop a "self-concept" of themselves as not terribly effective in combat. Thus, even as a young juvenile with a low-ranking female becomes stronger than his counterparts, he remembers the past and it appears to inhibit him. In this way, high-ranking females can pass their rank on to their weaker sons, and to a lesser extent, their daughters. This stability and permanence of rankings resembles what occurs in human stratification: Those who have resources—power, prestige, and wealth—can use these resources to maintain the position of their children, even though these young may not be as qualified as the children of lower ranking parents.

Occasionally, a strong and aggressive adult male of a low-ranking female can move up the dominance hierarchy by challenging and defeating higher ranking males in battle. But as with social mobility in human stratification systems, this is a difficult path to follow. It is fraught with danger, insecurity, and the potential for failure.

Source: G. Gray Eaton (1976).

the maintenance of power and privilege for their offspring. The process involved went like this:

Play among the young often erupts into fights. When this occurs, mothers

STRATIFICATION IN AMERICA

By examining stratification in America, we can see how stratification processes operate. Only in the specific processes of an actual society can we appreciate the degree to which stratification is a major social form influencing all of our lives.

In our review of stratification in the United States, we will try to answer these questions: (1) How unequally are wealth, power, and prestige distributed in America? (2) Can we discern permanent ranks? (3) How permanent are they and can we move from one rank to another?

The Distribution of Scarce Resources in America.

The Distribution of Wealth and Income in America. For the purposes of social research, measurement of wealth is done in terms of money. Because money is the universal medium for the exchange of material goods in modern societies, the accumulation of wealth can be best expressed in dollars. There are two basic descriptive measurements used by social analysts to determine the distribution of property within a society. **Income distribution** is determined by calculating the total earned income over a fixed period of time—usually one year. Once this total income has been calculated, the incomes of meaningful social groups or categories are calculated and then compared to the total income. When this is done, the total income within any chosen social group or category is expressed as a proportion of the total national income. This proportion may be expressed either as a numerical ratio or as a percentage. **Wealth distribution** is determined in much the same way, but wealth refers to the total assets—money, stocks, cars, homes, or any valuable commodity—that a given group or population holds in a given year.

A considerable amount of information exists concerning the distribution of income in the United States. The income distribution for the years 1929 to 1973 is presented in Table 1 (Turner & Starnes 1976, p. 51). As we can see, the table records the proportion (as a percent) of total income earned in a given year by five ranked income groups, or **income fifths**. How were these income fifths determined? What we have done is to rank every income earner in the United States from the highest to lowest. Then, we have taken the top 20% of income earners and called them the highest fifth. The next 20% of ranked income earners are termed the second fifth, and so on until we get the lowest fifth. Thus, what the table shows is the percentage of income earned in a given year by ranked 20% blocks of the income-earning population. The lowest 20% have typically received about 5 to 5.5% of all income; the top in recent years have received around 41%.

Table 1: Percentage Share of Money Income, Before Taxes, Received by Each Income Fifth

Year	Lowest Fifth	Fourth Fifth	Middle Fifth	Second Fifth	Highest Fifth
1973	5.5	11.9	17.5	24.0	41.1
1972	5.4	11.9	17.5	23.9	41.4
1971	5.5	11.9	17.4	23.7	41.6
1970	5.5	12.0	17.4	23.5	41.6
1969	5.6	12.3	17.6	23.5	41.0
1968	5.7	12.4	17.7	23.7	40.6
1967	5.4	12.2	17.5	23.7	41.2
1966	5.5	12.4	17.7	23.7	40.7
1965	5.3	12.1	17.7	23.7	41.3
1964	5.2	12.0	17.7	24.0	41.1
1963	5.1	12.0	17.6	23.9	41.4
1962	5.1	12.0	17.5	23.7	41.7
1961	4.8	11.7	17.4	23.6	42.6
1960	4.9	12.0	17.6	23.6	42.0
1959	5.0	12.1	17.7	23.7	41.4
1958	4.7	11.0	16.3	22.5	45.5
1957	4.7	11.1	16.3	22.4	45.5
1956	4.8	11.3	16.3	22.3	45.3
1955	4.8	11.3	16.4	22.3	45.2
1954	4.8	11.1	16.4	22.5	45.2
1953	4.9	11.3	16.6	22.5	44.7
1952	4.9	11.4	16.6	22.4	44.7
1951	5.0	11.3	16.5	22.3	44.9
1950	4.5	12.0	17.4	23.5	42.6
1949	3.2	10.5	17.1	24.2	45.0
1948	3.4	10.7	17.1	23.9	44.9
1947	5.0	11.8	17.0	23.1	43.0
1946	5.0	11.1	16.0	21.8	46.1
1945	3.8	11.0	17.2	24.0	44.0
1944	4.9	10.9	16.2	22.2	45.8
1941	4.1	9.5	15.3	22.3	48.8
1935–36	4.1	9.2	14.1	20.9	51.7
1929		(12.5)	13.8	19.3	54.4

Sources: U.S. Bureau of the Census, *Current Population Reports*, Series P-60, No. 85, Table 14 for the years 1947, 1950, and 1959–1971 (Washington, D.C.: U.S. Government Printing Office, 1972). Edward C. Budd, "Postwar Changes in the Size Distribution of Income in the U.S.," *American Economic Review* 60, 2(May 1970):247–260, Table 6, p. 255 for the years 1945, 1948, and 1949. U.S. Bureau of the Census, *Income Distribution in the United States* (a 1960 Census Monograph), by Herman P. Miller, p. 21 for the years 1929, 1935–1936, 1941, 1944, 1946, and 1951–1958 (Washington, D.C.: U.S. Government Printing Office, 1966). Data from the latter source were gathered by the Office of Business Economics.

Figure 3: Wealth Distribution in 1962

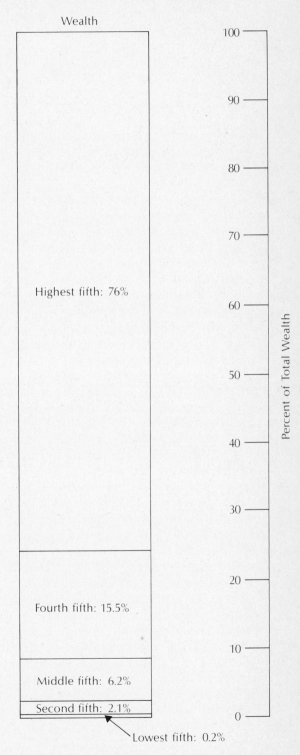

Wealth

Percent of Total Wealth

Highest fifth: 76%

Fourth fifth: 15.5%

Middle fifth: 6.2%

Second fifth: 2.1%

Lowest fifth: 0.2%

Source: Executive Office of the President: Office of Management and Budget, *Social Indicators 1973* (Washington, D.C.: Government Printing Office, 1973), p. 164.

Statistical data on the distribution of wealth—that is, all assets that can be converted into money—is not readily available. Wealth is more easily concealed, in general, than income; it is often difficult to assess wealth with reasonable accuracy, especially in those cases in which the wealth accumulation includes undeveloped real estate, precious stones, works of art, rare cultural artifacts, and the like. Moreover, the government has been reluctant to collect information on the distribution of wealth. The statistical information that exists indicates that the distribution of wealth in the United States is still more unequal than the distribution of income (see Figure 3). Although the information presented in Figure 3 is for 1962 (the only year for which data exist), this information is probably still true for this decade (Turner & Starnes 1976, p. 23). One obvious conclusion to be drawn directly from the data is the extreme inequality of wealth distribution in the United States. The top 20% of wealth holders, or the top **wealth fifth,** control 76% of all assets. Stated the other way around, 80% of the population control less than 25% of all assets or 60% control less than 9% of the wealth.

The Distribution of Prestige in America. In the United States, wealth not only promotes further wealth; it is often a direct source of power and prestige as well. Prestige springs from many sources, however. It is commonly believed that in the United States prestige is largely dependent on the nature of *how* one earns a living. In many cases the humanitarian, self-sacrificial, or otherwise morally valuable nature of an occupation will lend that position high prestige. In many other cases, the high prestige associated with an occupation largely reflects a public appreciation of the power, authority, or high income that comes with the occupation.

Because of the wide belief that occupation is a powerful determinant of prestige in the United States, a number of studies have been undertaken in efforts to understand the occupational dimension of prestige. Perhaps the most widely known of these studies was conducted by Robert Hodge, Paul Siegel, and Peter Rossi (1964) on behalf of the National Opinion Research Center. Their study compares the prestige rankings of 90 occupations according to public opinion surveys conducted in 1947 and 1963. The results are presented in Table 2. The inferences that can be drawn from the findings are seemingly endless and often amusing. Newspaper columnists would likely not appreciate a prestige ranking below that of a machinist, for instance. More serious and significant conclusions, however tentatively drawn, should be our main concern. One indisputable finding resulting from this study is the fact that the rankings from each year were found to have a .99 correlation with one another, which means that they were nearly identical. The most dramatic rating changes occurred in the scientific/technical occupational group. In that group, prestige ratings were almost invariably higher in 1963 than in 1947. Significant changes in the opposite direction were found for many occupations of a more "cultural" or "artistic" nature. The highest ratings were awarded to occupations in the fields of teaching, science, and public service. This seems to indicate that prestige is more likely to be associated with power, selflessness,

Table 2: Occupational Prestige Ratings, 1963 and 1947

Occupation	1963 Score	1947 Score
U.S. Supreme Court Justice	94	96
Physician	93	93
Nuclear physicist	92	86
Scientist	92	89
Government scientist	91	88
State governor	91	93
Cabinet member in the federal government	90	92
College professor	90	89
U.S. Representative in Congress	90	89
Chemist	89	86
Lawyer	89	86
Diplomat in U.S. Foreign Service	89	92
Dentist	88	86
Architect	88	86
County judge	88	87
Psychologist	87	85
Minister	87	87
Member of the board of directors of a large corporation	87	86
Mayor of a large city	87	90
Priest	86	86
Head of a state government department	86	87
Civil engineer	86	84
Airline pilot	86	83
Banker	85	88
Biologist	85	81
Sociologist	83	82
Instructor in public schools	82	79
Captain in the regular army	82	80
Accountant for a large business	81	81
Public school teacher	81	78
Owner of a factory that employs about 100 people	80	82

Occupation	1963 Score	1947 Score	Occupation	1963 Score	1947 Score
Building contractor	80	79	Plumber	65	63
Artist who paints pictures that are exhibited in galleries	78	83	Automobile repairman	64	63
			Playground director	63	67
Musician in a symphony orchestra	78	81	Barber	63	59
Author of novels	78	80	Machine operator in a factory	63	60
Economist	78	79	Owner/operator of a lunch stand	63	62
Official of an international labor union	77	75	Corporal in the regular army	62	60
Railroad engineer	76	76	Garage mechanic	62	62
Electrician	76	73	Truck driver	59	54
County agricultural agent	76	77	Fisherman who owns his own boat	58	58
Owner/operator of a printing shop	75	74	Clerk in a store	56	58
Trained machinist	75	73	Milk route man	56	54
Farm owner and operator	74	76	Streetcar motorman	56	58
Undertaker	74	72	Lumberjack	55	53
Welfare worker for a city government	74	73	Restaurant cook	55	54
Newspaper columnist	73	74	Singer in a nightclub	54	52
Policeman	72	67	Filling station attendant	51	52
Reporter on a daily newspaper	71	71	Dockworker	50	47
			Railroad section hand	50	48
Radio announcer	70	75	Night watchman	50	47
Bookkeeper	70	68	Coal miner	50	49
Tenant farmer—one who owns livestock and machinery and manages the farm	69	68	Restaurant waiter	49	48
			Taxi driver	49	49
Insurance agent	69	68	Farm hand	48	50
Carpenter	68	65	Janitor	48	44
Manager of a small store in a city	67	69	Bartender	48	44
A local official of a labor union	67	62	Clothes presser in a laundry	45	46
			Soda fountain clerk	44	45
Mail carrier	66	66	Sharecropper—one who owns no livestock or equipment and does not manage farm	42	40
Railroad conductor	66	67	Garbage collector	39	35
Traveling salesman for a wholesale concern	66	68	Street sweeper	36	34
			Shoe shiner	34	33
			Average	71	70

Source: Robert W. Hodge et al., "Occupational Prestige in the United States, 1925–1963," American Journal of Sociology, 70 (November, 1964), pp. 286-302.

and time spent in preparing for an occupation than with sheer wealth or property. Working with one's hands apparently fails to impress the public; electricians and machinists were the highest ranked manual technicians, 39th and 42nd on the list, respectively. The four occupations receiving the lowest prestige ratings all involve considerable manual labor.

The Distribution of Power in America. Unlike the distributions of property and prestige, the distribution of power is nearly impossible to measure accurately. Survey data on the distribution of power would only yield information concerning what was *thought* about power. We know that many people have power. We also know that many large institutions, foundations, and corporations have power. Certainly, our various governmental bodies have power. Still, it is difficult to know in certain terms the manner in which power is used. In fact, sociologists have long debated the issue of inequalities in the distribution of power (Dahl 1961; Mills 1959; Rose 1967). This debate has revolved around the following questions: How concentrated is power? Do a few hold it? Is it spread out among diverse and conflicting groups? In the absence of data, sociologists' answers to such questions follow from what they believe to be the case. Those who postulate the existence of "power elites" always seem to find them, whereas those who hypothesize "pluralistic centers of power" also seem to confirm their hypothesis.

Therefore, we can offer no conclusions about the distribution of power. We can only present a few guidelines for speculation and research on the issue. We can probably assume that wealth is well represented in the halls of power. Power and wealth can promote one another rather easily. Furthermore, if the wealthy have found their way to disproportionate power, we can reasonably expect that they will exercise their power as best they can to further increase their wealth. Of course, we know that not all wealthy people are powerful, and we can assume that many of the rich do not use their power exclusively in the pursuit of further riches. On the other hand, people rarely become rich through a dislike of money, and those who are fond of money will often use their available powers to increase their wealth. This can be done through the wealthy's ability to generate political influence. The same avenues of influence are open to the less affluent, and to the poor; but it is the wealthy who are especially equipped to use and maintain their power in the manner of their choice. To understand how the wealthy are best equipped in this regard, we should examine briefly the factors that determine the force of power and its availability for implementation through legitimate channels. To aid us in our examination, we will refer to Table 3, which will be the focal point of our discussion (Turner & Starnes 1976, p. 83).

In the column on the extreme left are the seven variables that we will consider to be most important in the determination of the availability and effectiveness of power. Of these, the

Table 3: Variables Influencing the Distribution of Power

	The Poor (bottom income fifth)	The Affluent (middle income fifths)	The Rich (portion of top income fifth)
(1) Size of population	large	quite large	relatively small
(2) Distribution of population	rural and urban, large mass in cores	urban, large mass in suburbs of large cities	rural and urban, relatively high degree of dispersion
(3) Level of organization	low, fragmented	high: unions, professional associations, corporations, and trade associations	high: corporations and trade associations
(4) Type of organization	fragmented, decentralized, loosely coordinated national confederations	highly centralized, tightly coordinated national confederations	highly centralized, overt and covert confederations
(5) Financial resources	meager	great	very great
(6) Lobbying tradition	short	long	long
(7) Established influence channels	few	many	many
Total power	little	considerable	great

most significant are financial resources, level of organization, and established influence channels. The column headings refer to rough income groupings: poor, affluent, and rich. From the perspective of scientific analysis, these are admittedly crude groupings, as are the verbal descriptions of the variable factors (1 through 7 in the first column) as they appear in the respective columns beneath these income groupings. Sadly, this reflects the "state of the art" of the analysis of power distribution.

Yet, by reading down the columns for the poor, affluent (including blue- and white-collar workers), and rich, we can see the varying capacities of people in these ranks to generate power individually or collectively through the organizations to which they belong. At the bottom of the table, the total power generated is summarized.

Social Class in America

Combining Marx's and Weber's insights, sociologists usually define **social class** as those members of a society who work in similar occupations, who share roughly the same degree of access to valuable resources, and who live a similar life-style by virtue of their share of resources. Distinguishing discrete classes in terms of our working definition is difficult in the United States. Although rough groups are discernible through the haze of dispersion, the class structure in the United States more resembles a continuum than a series of discrete levels. Yet for analytical purposes this continuum is often broken down into nominal groups, the number of which vary according to the purpose of the analysis. A hypothetical continuum and two modes of breaking the continuum for analytical purposes are shown in Figure 4.

Depending on their purpose, sociologists make varying assessments of how many classes exist. For instance, relatively intricate class breakdowns are more easily justified within the context of a study focused on a particular community; breakdowns of nation-wide classes are usually less detailed.

Part of the reason for the difficulties in isolating distinct classes resides in the different dimensions—wealth, power, and prestige—that can be used to rank people. At the national level, we can really distinguish only a few broad categories in terms of property or wealth: for example, the very rich, the large middle, and the poor at the bottom. Many of "the affluent," who hold blue- and white-collar jobs, would be accorded great differences in prestige. At best, we can say that the very rich and highly affluent have both property and prestige. The broad category of affluent embraces such a diversity of prestige rankings that it is difficult to distinguish people in terms of a combined wealth, power, and prestige ranking. The best that can be done is to distinguish among white- and blue-collar jobs; white-collar jobs usually carry more prestige and income, although there is much overlap in income. With respect to power—the most illusive scarce resource—the very wealthy have much power. White-collar or blue-collar ranks have power through their unions and professional associations and their sheer numbers, but the respective degree of power among these classes is difficult to discern.

These problems of distinguishing classes in terms of wealth, power, and prestige have led to much concern with "life-style" variables.[1] Are there differences in the way people spend their money and conduct their affairs? Do affluent blue-collar workers, for example, act, think, and organize their lives differently from white-collar workers who earn about the same? The answer to such questions is yes. Clear distinctions in the life-styles of white-collar and blue-collar categories are evident. The same is true of the wealthy and the poor. Thus, we can observe a number of divisions, or "classes" in terms of life-style—how money is spent, how people organize their lives, and what they value and believe in. As Marx recognized, these divisions are profoundly influenced by people's income and work.

---

[1]For example, see: Benser 1966; Bronfenbrenner 1958; Cohen and Hodges 1963; Duvall 1946; Gerstl & Rainwater 1961; Howe 1972; Kahl 1961; Kerckhoff 1972; Kohn 1963, 1969; Komarovsky 1964; Lewis 1965; McKinley 1964; Sennet and Cobb 1972; Shostak 1969; and Shostak and Gomberg 1964.

Figure 4: Different Ways of Viewing "Social Class" in America

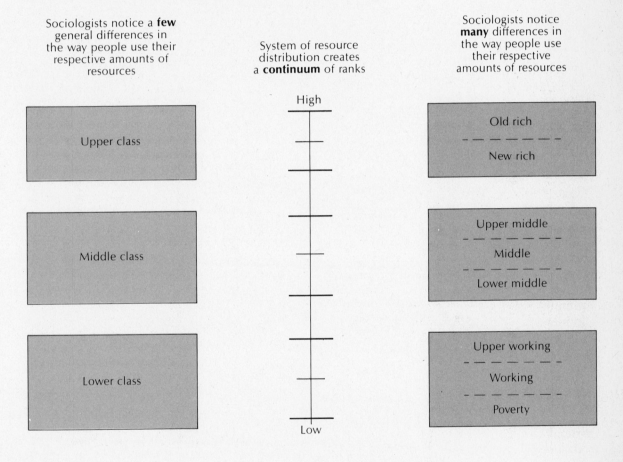

Variations in Life-Styles among Social Classes

In the brief descriptions below, "high-brow," "upper middlebrow," "lower middlebrow," and "lowbrow" refer to upper, upper middle, lower middle, and working classes, respectively. The descriptions are, of course, a bit cavalier. The purposes of the authors who developed them were somewhat different than our purposes here. Yet, by reading

	HIGHBROW	UPPER MIDDLEBROW	LOWER MIDDLEBROW	LOWBROW
How girl meets boy	He was an usher at her best friend's wedding	At college in the psychology lab	In the office by the water cooler	On the block
The proposal	In his room during the Harvard-Princeton game	In the back seat of a Volkswagen	After three drinks in an apartment he borrowed	In her home one night when mom and dad were at the movies
The wedding	In her living room performed by a federal judge	College chapel, nondenominational	City Hall	Neighborhood church
The honey moon	Mediterranean	Bahamas	Any Hilton hotel	Disneyland
Marriage manual	*Kama Sutra*	*Sexual Efficiency in Marriage*, vols. I and II	Van de Velde	None
Sex novels she reads	Jane Austen	*Lady Chatterley's Lover*	*Myra Breckenridge* and any novel by Harold Robbins	*Valley of the Dolls*
Sleeping arrangements	Double bed; orgasmic; female-dominated	King-size bed or twin beds with one headboard; affectional-sexual	Twin beds with matching nighttables; affectional-sexual	Double bed, for male's pleasure; reproductive
Sleeping attire	Both nothing	He: red turtleneck nightshirt She: gown with matching peignoir	Both pajamas	He: underwear She: nightgown
Background music	Ravi Shankar or the Beatles	Wagner	Dr. Zhivago	Jackie Gleason and the Silver Strings
Family structure	Individualistic, remarried couple, marriage for better only	Democratic, once-married couple, for better only	Democratic, for better or for worse, once-married	Hierarchal, for better or for worse, once-married

down the columns we can get a "sense"— and this is all that is possible in a short space—for the different ways that people in diverse social classes organize their lives.

Source: W. Simon and John Gagnon, in *Life Styles: Diversity in American Society*, ed. Saul Feldman and Gerald W. Thiebar (Boston: Little, Brown, 1972), pp. 86–87. Used by permission.

	HIGHBROW	UPPER MIDDLEBROW	LOWER MIDDLEBROW	LOWBROW
Husband and wife roles	Independent	Equal	Wife-dominated	Husband-dominated
Child role	Autonomous	Team member	Reflection of parents	Independent
Grandparent	Banished	Tolerated	Accepted	Needed
Goal	Personal happiness and independence	Happiness and getting ahead; service to the community	Conforming	Staying even
Divorce	Desirable if there is no personal happiness and sexual pleasure	Meaningful alternative	Tolerated	Sinful
Sex education	Ask the doctor, dear, when you see him tomorrow	Well, you see, daddy has something called a penis and mommy and daddy love each other very much	Daddy puts the seed in mommy's tummy	We got you in the hospital
Vacations	Europe in May. She takes the children to Cape Cod, he commutes weekends	Europe in July. Family camping in Yosemite	He hunts or fishes. She visits mother with the children	They visit brother Charlie in Des Moines
Who raises the children	English nanny, boarding school, analyst	Mommy and daddy, Cub Scouts, Dr. Freud	Mom and dad, the Little League, Dr. Spock	Mom, the gang, Ann Landers, good luck
Turn-ons	Pot	Champagne and oysters	Manhattans and whiskey sours	Beer

	HIGHBROW	UPPER MIDDLEBROW	LOWER MIDDLEBROW	LOWBROW
The schedule	Spontaneously, on an average of 2.5 weekly. That means 2 times one week and 3 times another	Twice a week and when the kids go to the Sunday matinee	Twice a week and when the kids go to Sunday school	Twice on Saturday night
Number of children	One each by a previous marriage; one together	2.4	3	As many as God provides
Anniversary celebration	A weekend in Mexico	He gives her a new dishwasher and she gives him a power lawnmower	Corsage and dinner out	Whitman sampler and dinner at Howard Johnson's
Quarrels	I don't care what your analyst says	I don't care if he is your brother	What do you think I'm made of?	Drop dead!
If the marriage needs help	He consults her analyst; she consults his	They go either to a marriage counselor or to a minister	He talks to his successful brother; she to her best friend	He talks to the bartender; she to her mother
The affair	But I assumed you knew	It was basically a problem in communication	It was bigger than both of us	Some things a woman shouldn't have to put up with
Financial arrangements	Separate trust funds	Joint checking account	She gives him a weekly allowance	He gives her household money

Social Mobility in America

Social mobility is the term used to denote the passage of individuals from one social class to another—assuming, of course, we can identify social classes. In sociological circles, the term also implies a relationship with time. Social mobility cannot be termed as "high" or "low" unless we consider the duration of time expended in the actualization of class transitions by individuals and/or families. In addition to the rate of mobility, we are also concerned with the direction of mobility. The major types of mobility are (1) **upward mobility,** (2) **downward mobility,** and (3) **horizontal mobility.**

As their names imply, class movements are largely viewed within the context of a hierarchical class structure. Upward mobility denotes an improvement of one's condition in terms of material well-being and increased sophistication in the art of integrating valuable accumulations in "tasteful," or socially appreciated ways. Downward mobility means the opposite of upward mobility. Horizontal mobility is a transition from one life situation to another, when both situations can be described similarly in terms of income or life-style.

How Much Mobility? The interest of those social scientists concerned with the processes of stratification is mainly devoted to studies of upward vertical mobility. This is especially true concerning studies of mobility in the United States, because the United States is considered to be the "land of opportunity." Sociologists have thus been interested in what enables people to move up the ranks of the stratification system. A number of studies have been conducted on this issue.

In a controversial study Seymour Lipset and Reinhard Bendix (1959) found that Americans have little more opportunity for advancement than do citizens of many other industrial nations. When they examined a survey population in terms of the percentage of manual workers who moved into nonmanual occupations, they found that 34% of Americans had compared to 32% of Swedes, 31% of British, 29% of French, and 25% of West Germans and Japanese had been mobile. According to this information, it seems that upward mobility in various Western industrial nations is relatively high and that the rate of mobility varies little from one country to another.

However, this study has met criticism from many quarters. Thomas Fox and S. M. Miller (1965), for instance, present findings that suggest that a great deal of the mobility found by Lipset and Bendix is misleading. They found that, in addition to educational attainments, one of the most crucial factors determining upward mobility is an advancing industrial technology. When levels and modes of production advance, many manual jobs disappear. They are partially replaced by jobs of a more technical, managerial, or clerical nature. Many of these new jobs, in turn, are filled by individuals who previously held the now-defunct manual positions. Thus, there is a degree of built-in **(structural)** upward **mobility** associated with an advancing technology of production. They argue that mobility from a blue-collar position to a position such as a file clerk does not necessarily represent significant upward mobility. (They might have added that, in an era of labor union preeminence, such a transition from blue- to white-collar work might in terms of income be considered downward mobility.) However, when they studied the mobility from working-class positions to professional and technical positions they found that this kind of significant mobility is somewhat more common in the United States than it is in other industrialized nations, although it occurs with much less frequency than the type of mobility studied by Lipset and Bendix. The movement from blue-collar positions to upper-level white-collar positions occurred among different nations with the following frequencies: United States, 10%; Japan, 7%; France and Sweden, 4%; West Germany, 1.5%. Although these findings indicate that significant upward mobility is more likely to occur in the United States than in other advanced industrial nations, the infrequency of significant mobility argues against the proposition that upward mobility is the predominant trend in American life.

What Causes Mobility? Another line of information comes from studies which seek to determine the causes of upward mobility. Peter H. Blau and Otis Dudley Duncan (1967), for example, articulated a complex pattern of influence of family and education on mobility. Generally speaking, they found the interrelationships to be not only complex, but also relatively insignificant compared to the influence of *unknown* factors on the dynamics of mobility. A graphic presentation of their findings can be seen in Figure 5. We can see that the strongest *known* determining factor of mobility is education, which operates directly and indirectly to determine both initial job status and mobility potential. More important, however, are unknown variables. For instance, Blau and Duncan indicate that unknown factors have more influence on a person's eventual career level than the combined impact of the first job, amount of education, parent's occupation, and the parent's education. Christopher Jencks (1972) has corroborated this conclusion that the influence of unknown factors is important in the determination of mobility dynamics and status achievement. He points out that many factors that are hard to measure operate powerfully. For instance, how do we measure an individual's love of money, of prestige, or of power and how much the individual is willing to sacrifice in his pursuit of property? How do we measure, before the fact, an individual's talents of persuasion or general personality? And, of course, we must acknowledge again the presence of that most pervasive and unmeasurable of social determinants: luck, serendipity, and discrimination.

Despite these obstacles and qualifications, we should pay serious attention to some of the more important identifiable—and sometimes measurable—determinants of social mobility: (1) structural factors, (2) differential fertility, (3) horizontal mobility, and (4) differential socialization.

Structural mobility is a very important factor in the determination of social mobility dynamics and statistics. At the same time, structural mobility operates to confuse our understanding of more basic social factors that operate to influence mobility patterns, such as

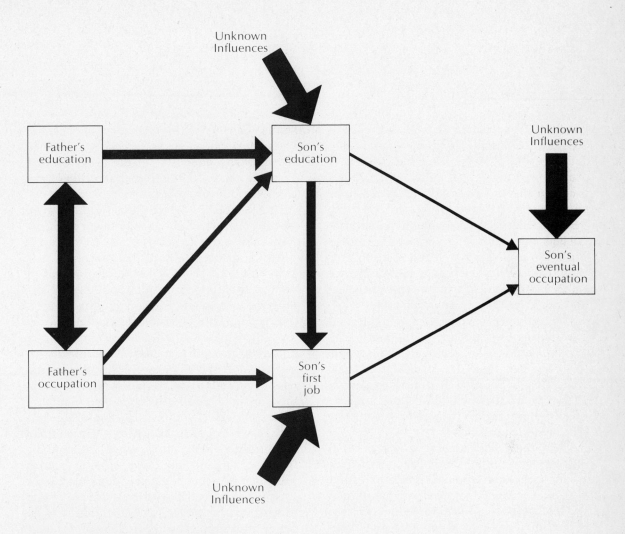

Figure 5: Some Causes of Mobility

Note: Size of arrows represents their relative influence.

Source: "Some Causes of Mobility," Blau and
Duncan, *The American Occupational Structure*
(New York: Wiley, 1967). Reprinted with
permission.

cultural, familial, and personal factors. We have already considered that much of the apparent mobility within American society is not so much a mobility of individuals as it is a change in the economic sphere as a whole. Moreover, mobility may appear to occur because our criteria for determining mobility are outdated. For example, a person who moves from a job as a street sweeper to a job as a county clerk or to a job as a salesperson of household necessities is, by present statistical measures, experiencing upward mobility. Yet, this transition may cost the person in question many thousands of dollars in personal yearly income. "White-collar" clerks and salespeople often earn less than the $15,000 to $20,000 annual income afforded to street sweepers in some urban areas of the United States. In these cases structural factors operate to confuse our analysis of social mobility.

Fertility rates differ among various occupational groupings. Kahl (1961) found that middle- and upper-class families tend to restrict their family size and that this trend has existed since the beginning of the nineteenth century. On the other hand, farm laborers and other occupants of the lower working-class strata have exercised this type of self-regulation to a markedly lesser degree. As a result, according to Kahl's findings, the professional classes do not reproduce sufficiently to replace their own members. He found the opposite to be true among the blue-collar and farming groups. These groups produced more progeny than needed to replace past generations of "lower" occupations. On the basis of these findings, it is easy to see that positions of supposedly higher status, which came into being largely because of an advancing technology, *had* to be filled by the sons and daughters of the lower classes. Thus, we can see that **differential fertility** rates can contribute to the phenomenon that we call "upward mobility." Differential fertility can be seen to operate automatically much as structural factors do.

At first glance, it seems that horizontal mobility has little relation to the phenomena of vertical mobility. Horizontal mobility, or the movement from one position to a similar position, is often ignored in sociological analyses of mobility. Yet, horizontal mobility operates as a powerful, though secondary, determinant of vertical mobility. More specifically, the willingness of an individual to undertake horizontal movements within his or her career is often a powerfully operating precondition of upward mobility. People who believe in their personal qualifications will often move horizontally from one organization to another if such a move can be seen to enhance their chances for eventual advancement. That people are willing to relocate is an indication of their desire to do better, and according to available data, their chances for upward mobility are indeed increased.

To a very great extent, people's desire to be mobile, and their perceptions of opportunities, are related to their socialization experiences. Two agents of socialization are regarded as critical: (1) family and (2) school. As the earliest agent of socialization, the family has the most important influence on the development of human personality. This we know from our discussion on socialization and personality in Chapter 7. This family influence can improve or limit chances for social mobility. Basic motives, beliefs, values, self-concepts, role-play-ing styles, and speech patterns are all important in social mobility. First of all, they are critical for doing well in school where crucial credentials are acquired, and they are highly influential in determining how well people will play occupational roles as adults. Moreover, the financial resources of parents will also shape a child's future prospects for mobility. The ability to live in neighborhoods with good schools, to finance special programs (lessons in art, music, and the like), and to afford a college education are all dependent upon the income of parents.

Because the attributes of the family are an important influence on what children can become, there have been a number of studies on the family structure of different social classes. Most studies concentrate on differences in blue-collar and white-collar families, although there have been a number of studies on poverty families (Lewis 1965). No conclusive studies exist on the family structure of the rich. The general findings of the studies document that white-collar families are structured in ways that increase the likelihood of their children acquiring those motives, values, beliefs, and speech patterns that will facilitate performance in school and in white-collar jobs. Blue-collar families are less likely to impart all of these traits, and poverty families are unlikely to be able to instill in their children those attributes necessary for mobility. Coupled with differences in financial resources of these families, we can see how family can operate to either improve opportunities for upward mo-

bility or to maintain people in a given class position. (For more details on class differences in family structure, see boxed material on pp. 346–348 and Chapter 16 on family and kinship.)

Education has increasingly become "society's gatekeeper"—a fact which we will examine in more detail in Chapter 20. For our purposes, we need only present the case that performance in school structures and the acquisition of "credentials" or diplomas will influence people's chances for securing well-paying and prestigious jobs. For those who wish to be upwardly mobile, then, acquiring an education is one important first step. In the past, people have often been able to start successful businesses and become "successful" without educational credentials. But the growing dominance of the economy by large corporations and government and their increasing reliance upon bureaucratic principles have made "educational credentials" more important in gaining access to the bureaucratic world (see Chapter 11 for details on why bureaucracies are becoming the arenas where social mobility occurs).

The Immobile Poor. Before closing our discussion of stratification in America, we should discuss the poor. Americans pride themselves on living in the most affluent land in the world. Yet, American society has one of the largest pockets of poverty—holding some 30 million people in its grip—in the modern world (Harrington 1962). Few of those in poverty are mobile. They are, in the words of Michael Harrington, America's "internal aliens."

Why are people poor, and what forces maintain their poverty? A number of sociologists

believe that a **culture of poverty** exists in the United States (Lewis 1965, 1971; Moynihan 1969). This culture of poverty hypothesis proposes that the life-style of the poor virtually guarantees that they will stay poor. The argument behind this hypothesis is presented in Figure 6. Poverty means that people have little income. In adjusting this sparse income, parents must live in slums and develop beliefs and values that emphasize the hopelessness of their plight. These beliefs and values, coupled with inadequate educational facilities in poor areas, prevent the young from aspiring and doing well in school. Without aspirations or education, their income earning potential is low; hence, they will remain in the same poverty situation as their parents.

Is this line of argument true? Some scholars think not; they argue that despair is not transmitted from generation to generation. Rather, individuals make a realistic adjustment of their lack of opportunities. The poor will take advantage of opportunities when they exist. (Rossi & Blum 1969).

Both of these arguments are plausible. They are probably each true for different groups of poor. It perhaps appears self-evident that the poor differ from one another in the same ways that the affluent do. Yet, this should be emphasized. Viewing the poor as a homogeneous group is as inaccurate as viewing all the affluent in America as all the same. Few know exactly what perpetuates poverty; in fact, sociologists know much less about poverty than they do about the general causes of mobility. There are, then, fertile fields of research for sociologists interested in the mobile affluent and the immobile poor.

Those who are born into poverty must face conditions that will make it hard for them to escape their impoverished situation.

Figure 6: The Poverty Cycle

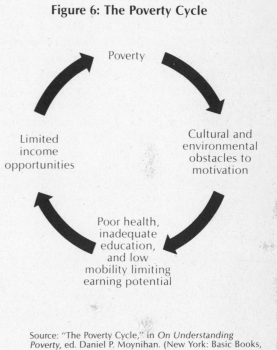

Source: "The Poverty Cycle," in *On Understanding Poverty*, ed. Daniel P. Moynihan. (New York: Basic Books, Inc., 1968). Reprinted with permission.

SUMMARY AND PREVIEW

Social stratification is an important social form. It touches all of our lives. We have defined stratification as the unequal distribution of scarce resources and the creation of relatively permanent ranks in terms of the shares of resources that incumbents in various ranks receive. We then examined the most basic resources: power, wealth, and prestige. These are what stratification processes distribute unequally. We saw that there has been a general trend toward growing inequality in the human system, although the most advanced industrial societies have reduced the degree of inequality somewhat.

We have discussed stratification in America in detail. We can view American society as a good illustration of how stratification processes operate. We have focused on the profile of distribution of scarce resources: wealth, prestige, and power. We have examined how unequal distribution results in relatively permanent ranks, or social classes. Since American society is viewed as "a land of opportunity," we also explored the forces that inhibit, and contribute to, social mobility. Finally, we noted the existence of a large poverty sector in "the most affluent land in the world."

If only by causal acquaintance with American society, we know that many in poverty are members of "minority groups." This fact calls to our attention another important form in the human system, racial and ethnic groups. We will explore this social form in the next chapter. However, we should not view racial and ethnic groups as merely a "social class." Although stratification and ethnicity are often interrelated social forms, especially in the United States, they are also distinctive. We should thus attempt to understand the more general dynamics of inter-ethnic and inter-racial interaction and how this interaction leads, in many societies of the world, to the emergence of a distinctive social form: race and ethnic groups.

Key Terms

Stratification: the unequal distribution of scarce resources in such a way as to create enduring rankings of positions that can be distinguished in terms of their respective shares of scarce resources

Scarce Resources: any material or symbolic object that is valued by members of a population

Power: the capacity of individuals or social units to impose their will, even against active resistance by other individuals or social units

Prestige: the bestowing of social honor to a person or social position

Wealth: all material possessions that are valued and viewed as assets

Status: Max Weber's term for rankings based on prestige or social honor

Class: Max Weber's and Karl Marx's term for rankings based on one's relationship to economic forces

Party: Max Weber's term for rankings based on the possession of power

Proletariat: Karl Marx's term for workers in capitalist societies

Bourgeoisie: Karl Marx's term for those who own the means of production in capitalist societies

Income Distribution: the term used to describe the distribution of total income in a society for a given year among various percentages of income earners

Wealth Distribution: the term used to describe the distribution of total wealth in a given year among various percentages of wealth holders

Income Fifth: a statistical category for describing 20% of income earners in a given year

Wealth Fifth: a statistical category for describing 20% of the wealth holders in a given year

Social Class: the concept used by contemporary sociologists to describe the existence of distinct populations who hold similar jobs, who share a given portion of scarce resources, and who evidence common experiences and life-styles

Upward Mobility: the process in which individuals move from a lower to higher social position in a system of rankings

Downward Mobility: the process in which individuals move from a higher to lower social position in a system of rankings

Horizontal Mobility: the process in which individuals move from one position to another without going to a higher or lower position in a system of rankings

Structural Mobility: the situation in which changes in people's social ranking can be explained by changes in the distribution of positions rather than by their attributes

Differential Fertility: the term used to describe the fact that different social classes have varying birth rates

Culture of Poverty: the concept used to describe the transmission of cultural values and beliefs among the poor that will inhibit their ability to perform well in crucial social spheres, and hence, to take advantage of opportunities for upward social mobility

Review Questions

1. Why are scarce resources distributed unequally?

2. What is a social class? How is it formed?

3. What are the trends in the distribution of resources?

4. Which is the most difficult scarce resource to measure? Why?

5. What is the profile of stratification in America for:
   a. the distribution of scarce resources?
   b. the formation of social classes?
   c. social mobility from class to class?

Suggested Readings

Beeghley, Leonard. *Social Stratification in America*. Santa Monica, Calif.: Goodyear, 1978.

Bendix, Reinhard, and Lipset, Seymour M., eds. *Class, Status and Power*. New York: The Free Press, 1966.

Bottomore, T. B. *Classes in Modern Society*. New York: Pantheon, 1966.

Duberman, Lucile. *Social Inequality: Class and Caste in America*. Philadelphia: J. B. Lippincott, 1976.

Lenski, Gerhard. *Power and Privilege*. New York: McGraw-Hill, 1966.

Mayer, Kurt and Buckley, Walter. *Class and Society*. New York: Random House, 1970.

Tumin, Melvin M. *Social Stratification: The Forms and Functions of Inequality*. Englewood Cliffs, N.J.: Prentice-Hall, 1967.

RACE, ETHNIC, AND MINORITY RELATIONS

PROLOGUE

Guiding Questions: Why do people treat those who are different in discriminatory ways? Why are there races and ethnic subcultures? What perpetuates them? What types of relations do ethnic populations reveal?

Chapter Topics

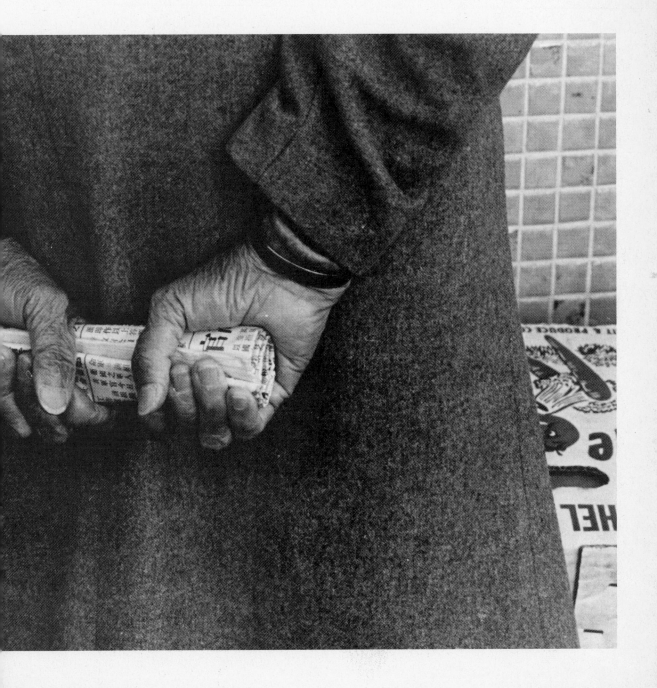

RACE
AND
ETHNICITY[1]

Race and Racial Populations

As the human system evolved, people radiated all over the earth. They settled in different environments, developed different cultures and patterns of social organization, and by virtue of their geographical, social, and cultural separation, they inbred and created distinctive differences not only in their culture and social patterns, but also in their typical height, weight, skin color, and facial features. It is for this reason that populations of humans are not exactly alike. They look different; they hold different values and beliefs; and they have different behavioral tendencies.

At some point in time, people with distinctive physical, cultural, and social characteristics began to encounter each other. Some migrated in search of a better life or to escape difficult conditions; others were conquered; and still others were captured and taken as slaves. The result was that humans of varying physical features, cultures, and social patterns interacted and created a new social form in the human system: racial and ethnic relations.

The interaction between minority and majority populations has rarely been harmonious. Interaction has been punctuated by tension, conflict, and oppression. These difficulties have often heightened differences among populations within a society, forcing people to live among themselves. It is these relations among different populations that will occupy our attention in this chapter.

Race refers to the superficial differences in people's physical appearance: body size, skin color, facial configurations, hair color and texture, height, and other traits. There have been a number of attempts to isolate and classify the different races of the world. One such classification is summarized in Figure 1. In this classification, there are three main racial populations, along with unclassified groups. Other investigators have reported 30 or more racial groups.

What does the fact of varying classifications signify? For one thing, as the biologist Dobzhansky (1962) emphasizes, "It should always be kept in mind that while race differences are objectively ascertainable facts, the number of races we choose to recognize is a matter of convenience." Thus, although we can observe biological differences, populations blend into each other, and the lines separating "races" are often arbitrary. They are drawn for particular purposes in order to take note of certain differences that are of interest to an investigator.

Sociologists examine "race" only when "it makes a difference" in the way people form social relations. Only if people respond to perceived biological differences does the concept of race take on sociological meaning. A biologist or population geneticist might make a number of distinctions among populations, but if the people of a society do not, then a separate "racial group" does not exist for sociological analysis. Conversely, people may make distinctions about presumed biological differences among populations that a biologist would

---

[1]For basic references on ethnicity and ethnic relations, see Bonacich (1972); Simpson and Yinger (1972); and van den Berghe (1972).

Figure 1: One View of the Races in the Human System

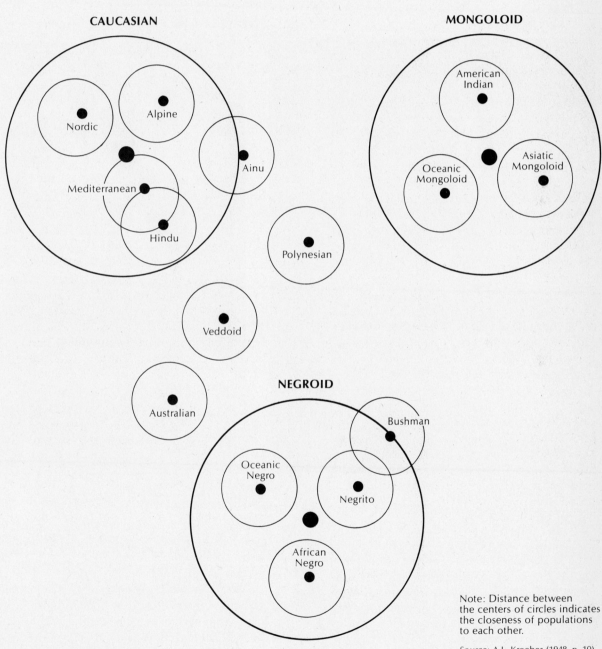

Note: Distance between
the centers of circles indicates
the closeness of populations
to each other.

Source: A.L. Kroeber (1948, p. 10).

Biological differences among the so-called "races" are not as sociologically important as cultural differences.

never make. For example, Jews have often been considered "a separate race" in some societies, but from a biologist's viewpoint, there are no significant biological differences between Jews and the general population. But the fact that in some societies Jews are "treated differently" and responded to *as if* they were different makes interaction between Jews and others important sociologically.

Ethnicity and Ethnic Groups

The fact that a subpopulation in a society develops its own cultural and social patterns or carries these patterns as it migrates to a host society, has led sociologists to the concept of *ethnicity*. An **ethnic group** is defined by sociologists as a population that is distinguished socially, that has developed its own subculture of beliefs, values, and norms, that has some distinctive patterns of behavior and organization,

and that has a shared feeling of "peoplehood" (Gordon 1964, p. 24). Thus, racial groups become significant to sociologists when the imputation of biological differences—imagined or real—to a population results in the formation of an ethnic group. Ethnic groups have cultural and social differences, and the nature of social relations in the human system is influenced by ethnic differences. Thus, blacks and Jews in America are ethnic groups because they have somewhat distinctive cultural and social patterns and because their relations with the larger population are influenced by their identification as "different." Just whether blacks are a "race" is for a biologist to answer. From a sociological viewpoint, biological factors only concern us when people act *as if* they were important, thereby forcing a population that has been labeled "different" to develop into an ethnic group.

DISCRIMINATION AND MINORITY POPULATIONS

Minority Groups and Populations

Minority groups are a type of ethnic group. They are a subpopulation within the broader population who share all of the characteristics of an ethnic group and who are singled out for unequal treatment. For example, blacks, browns, native Americans, Asians, and various white ethnics have been minority groups for varying lengths of time because they constitute a distinctive ethnic group *and* because they have been subject to unequal treatment.

Minority groups were first defined by the early American sociologist, Louis Wirth (1945), as "people who, because of their physical or cultural characteristics, are singled out from others in society in which they live for differential and unequal treatment and who therefore regard themselves as objects of collective discrimination." Minority groups are thus formed by a process known as discrimination.

The Process of Discrimination

Discrimination is a type of interaction involving actions against others that are designed to keep these others from enjoying the rights and privileges of a group, organization, or community. Discrimination should be distinguished from **prejudice,** which refers to negative, hostile, and inaccurate *beliefs* about another; discrimination involves overt *actions* against others. Robert K. Merton (1949) has proposed the typology reported in Table 1 for classifying the relationship between prejudice and discrimination.

Why do people discriminate? There does not, at present, appear to be a clear answer to this question. But several interrelated factors appear to encourage discrimination (Bonacich 1972; Vander Zanden 1972):

1. Populations which can be identified through distinctive physical, cultural, or behavioral traits are necessary for discrimination to create a minority population. Unless people can perceive differences between themselves and others, discrimination cannot be effective because targets of discrimination cannot be found.
2. Populations in a society must be unequal in power for discrimination to be effective. Without the power of one population to deny others access to resources and privileges, discrimination is impossible.

Table 1: Merton's Typology of Prejudice and Discrimination

	Discriminator	Nondiscriminator
Prejudiced	the prejudiced discriminator who actively implements prejudicial beliefs and who believes that not all should be treated equally	the prejudiced nondiscriminator, or "timid bigot" who is prejudiced against others but who is afraid to, or prevented from, enacting prejudices
Nonprejudiced	the unprejudiced who inadvertently discriminate, or who discriminate because it is convenient or because social pressures require discrimination	the unprejudiced nondiscriminator who accepts the belief that all should be treated equally

3. Competition, or potential competition, between identifiable populations for scarce and valuable resources is the final ingredient that results in discrimination. If groups compete for jobs, for example, and one group has more power than the other and the one without power is identifiable, then discrimination is likely.

Discrimination and prejudices that help make discrimination palatable result when populations with different degrees of power compete for scarce resources and when the population with less power is identifiable. Many examples can be offered that make this argument plausible. Working-class whites traditionally had the strongest prejudices against blacks, and through their unions and individual acts of violence, sought to exclude blacks from the mainstream of the job market (Bonacich 1972). The Chinese, who were originally brought to the United States to build the transcontinental railroad, suffered even more discrimination as they began to seek jobs in the broader labor market; and to a lesser degree, the early antagonisms among white ethnics such as the Irish, Poles, and Italians stemmed from members of each population perceiving the other population as potential competition for jobs and political power in the "political machines" of early big-city politics.

Yet, despite the plausibility of these factors, sociologists do not have complete understanding of why people discriminate. But once discrimination begins, it often strengthens people's ethnic ties and sense of identification, and it creates conspicuous minority populations within a society.

TYPES OF MINORITY/ MAJORITY RELATIONS

Discriminatory Social Relations

To the degree that members of a minority population are kept from equal participation with the majority in key social roles, we can say that a discriminatory social relation exists between the minority and majority. This discriminatory social relationship can take several forms: (1) segregation, (2) expulsion and (3) extermination.

Segregation. This type of social relation involves the separation of the majority and minority as well as the confinement of the minority to a limited range of roles. American blacks were, and still are, forced to live in neighborhoods that are separated from those of the white majority. Moreover, blacks have often been kept from assuming occupational positions that would allow them access to better-paying and skilled blue- and white-collar jobs. South Africa's policy of apartheid is perhaps an even more dramatic illustration of segregated social relations, although in this case a numerical minority segregates the majority. Blacks and whites are completely segregated, with whites receiving higher pay and the more important jobs.

Expulsion. At times, minority groups have simply been removed from a society. At one time, an American president of the last century contemplated the creation of a black state in Africa where free blacks in the postslavery era could be sent. In more recent times President Amin of Uganda simply expelled Asian residents who had lived in Uganda for many generations. Pakistan is a state created, in large part, in order that Muslims in India could have a place to go as they were pressured by the majority in India. Thus, expulsion can be both coerced or informal and "voluntary." At times, people are formally forced to leave, but a more frequent practice is to discriminate so intensely that minority populations "volunteer" to leave in search of a better life.

Extermination. Sometimes, minority populations are simply killed. The extermination of an entire population is known as **genocide.** A recent effort at genocide occurred between 1933 and 1945 in Nazi Germany, where millions of Jews were marched into gas chambers and killed. An even more recent effort at genocide occurred in Nigeria in 1966, where Ibos in the north and west were slaughtered by the ruling tribal group. Rarely is extermination complete, but in Tasmania, a small island south of Australia, English settlers completely destroyed the aboriginal population, often hunting them for sport and dog meat (Murdock 1936, pp. 16–18).

Of these three types of discrimination, segregation is the most common. In such relations the minority is "used" as cheap labor by the majority. Over time, however, the existence of a segregated minority creates pressures for less discrimination. If a minority population is "used," it has value to the majority, and with value it has some degree of power to force change in its social relations with the majority. Such has been the case with black Americans who, along with many white allies, have been able to force considerable change in their situa-

Jewish prisoners of the Buchenwald concentration camp as they were found in 1945. Most were dying of malnutrition.

tion. Yet, the existence of large black ghettos and the disproportionate unemployment rate and confinement of blacks to menial jobs should emphasize the present operation of discriminatory forces. However, as minorities exert pressures, less discriminatory social relations are likely to emerge.

Less Discriminatory Social Relations

Integration. When members of ethnic populations are given equal opportunities to participate in the same positions as the majority of a society, then we can say that the society is integrated. Thus, if we find that ethnic populations have the same work, residence, and income patterns as the general population, we can assume that the society reveals a high degree of integration. If, however, we discover that ethnic populations earn less money on the average than the general population, that they do not live in the same neighborhoods, or that they occupy a limited range of occupations, we can conclude that the society is not integrated. Indeed, it is segregated.

Integration as a type of nondiscriminatory social relation is often difficult to achieve. If a minority group has been subject to highly discriminatory practices in the past, it is difficult to undo the harm of past relations. For example, past discrimination confined black Americans to the slum cores of our large cities. Past discrimination confined black workers to menial jobs. Past discrimination excluded blacks from major colleges and universities. Past discrimination forced enormous hardships on families, creating a situation of high instability. It is difficult to change the impact of these past practices. To enact civil rights legislation, as was done in the 1960s, does not move children out of slums, give black workers new skills and work orientations, change attitudes about schooling, or dramatically alter family patterns. To integrate would require much

TYPES OF MINORITY ADAPTATIONS

more dramatic and expensive actions. Although a majority of Americans advocate integration, few are willing to incur the expense of slum clearance, relocation of blacks in the suburbs, massive educational aid, large cash subsidies to poor families, and other measures that would make opportunities really equal.

Cultural Pluralism. When ethnic groups are able to retain their unique character and when they are also able to participate equally in key roles, then a situation of cultural pluralism exists. Switzerland is perhaps the best example of a pluralist society that has no national language, and yet has national unity among a diversity of different ethnic groups. In contrast, American society has a large number of ethnic groups, but relations are not peaceful, nor are opportunities equal. Pluralism is thus a rather rare form of nondiscriminatory interaction. If differences are perceived to exist among populations, they typically become the basis for discrimination.

We can see, then, that discriminatory social relations between minority and majority populations are typical of the human system. Some societies have sought to integrate or to tolerate diversity, but such nondiscriminatory relations are difficult to implement in the wake of past discrimination. Moreover, competition for scarce resources among identifiable groups with different degrees of power will, as we noted earlier, constantly fuel antagonistic and discriminatory social relations. The difficulty of eliminating discrimination forces a variety of adaptations by minority populations to their subordinate position.

People react and adjust to situations. When confronted with discrimination, members of minority populations must adapt. They seek to make the best of a difficult situation. Depending upon the nature and magnitude of discrimination, as well as upon other social conditions, a number of adaptations are possible: (1) passive acceptance, (2) marginal participation, (3) assimilation, (4) withdrawal, (5) rebellion, and (6) organized protest. Different segments of a minority population may resort to several of these adaptations at the same time, or a population may pass through different patterns of adaptation. As we explore each of these adaptations, we should keep these qualifications in mind.

Passive Acceptance

If the power of the minority is small and the magnitude of the discrimination great, minority populations may have no choice but to accept their fate. For example, blacks during slavery were confronted with a situation in which it was virtually impossible to do anything but accept subjugation. Under these conditions, populations acquire interpersonal techniques for dealing with the majority while maintaining their sense of identity and dignity. The stereotypic slave, as portrayed in Harriet Beecher Stowe's *Uncle Tom's Cabin*, offers a vivid example of such techniques. Uncle Tom's bowing and scraping, and repeated use of the phrase, "Yes sir, yes sir," allowed him to gain favor with whites and to enjoy some degree of privilege. Passive acceptance, then, is often not passive, but active manipulation of a situation. Slaves were able to develop their own culture and to enjoy some of the basic pleasures of life through the appearance of "passive accep-tance." Of course, such a pattern of adjustment tends to perpetuate itself, since the minority population does not initiate change and since the majority is not pressured to cease its discriminatory practices.

Marginal Participation

At times, minority populations can find a niche where they can use their creative resources and prosper. For example, Jews have often been able to find business opportunities and to prosper in societies that actively discriminate against them. Chinese Americans were able to prosper in small businesses providing services to the Anglo majority. Such marginal niches are created when the majority is not inclined to enter a specialized field. Marginal adaptation tends to be most successful when the minority population is small and does not have to enter into areas dominated by the majority. It is probably for this reason that blacks and chicanos have been unable to find specialized niches; their numbers are too great.

Assimilation

Assimilation is the process in which the members of an ethnic minority become part of the broader culture and society, losing their distinctive character. The less identifiable a minority is biologically and culturally, the more readily it can be assimilated. Ethnic populations that can be readily identified, however, will have greater difficulty assimilating. It is for this reason that white ethnics in America, such as the Irish and Germans have become highly assimilated, although the large eastern cities have viable ethnic enclaves. Later migrants, such as Poles and Italians, have also tended to assimilate, although the East and Midwest have cohesive ethnic cultures of these populations. Blacks, on the other hand, have been prevented from assimilation because of their visibility and the resulting ease with which the majority can locate them as targets of discrimination.

Withdrawal and Self-Segregation

Another adaptation to discrimination is withdrawal and the creation of a self-sustaining "society" within the broader society. Such subsocieties create and support their own communities, businesses, schools, leadership, churches, and other social forms. For example, the early black Muslim movement in America advocated a separate black community, self-supporting and isolated from white institutions. Urban communities as well as rural communes were established and still prosper, although there has been a clear trend away from withdrawal and isolation among the black Muslims.

Self-segregation is a difficult adaptation to maintain. Opportunities are necessarily limited compared to those in the broader society. As a result, some begin to seek these outside opportunities. Moreover, economic, political, and social isolation is often difficult to maintain in urban media-dominated societies.

Rebellion

Minorities do not always accept, assimilate, withdraw, or marginally participate. They frequently rebel and challenge their oppressors. Such rebellion can take a number of forms. It can be translated into general hostility and aggressive behavior toward the majority. For example, few whites would feel comfortable walking through a black ghetto or a chicano *barrio*, because they "know" that there is some likelihood of intimidation and assault. The urban riots of the 1960s represent another example of minorities "striking back" and venting their frustrations.

Organized Protest

As our discussion of collective behavior in Chapter 12 emphasized, rebellious outbursts are often part of a larger social movement. Minorities frequently become organized and begin to make a broad-based and concerted effort to change patterns of discrimination. The civil rights movement represented one such effort. Beginning with sit-ins, freedom rides, moving through large-scale demonstrations and riots, and culminating in several national organizations that effectively changed many legal and social patterns, black Americans successfully challenged pervasive discriminatory practices. The movement has been far from completely successful, however, since neither integration nor cultural pluralism with regard to blacks is prominent in America. But when an ethnic population is large and organized, it can generate political power, and it can initiate some degree of social change.

The Civil Rights movement in America offers an example of how those who are deprived often organize and protest their continued subordination.

REDEEM THE
AMERICAN
PROMISE
LIFE, LIBERTY,
HAPPINESS
FOR ALL

ETHNICITY IN AMERICA

As much as any society in the world, the United States has enormous ethnic diversity. America is thus an excellent source of information on the dynamics of ethnic relations. Therefore, we should examine ethnic relations in America with an eye to what they can tell us about the process of discrimination, the establishment of minority/majority relations, and the varying patterns of minority adaptation.

Black Americans[2]

No other population has experienced the same degree of discrimination as black Americans. Blacks are America's largest minority, with some 25 million blacks able to trace their ancestry to slavery. As slaves, blacks had few legal rights: they were slaves for life; they were the property of others; children inherited their mother's position; marriages between blacks and whites were prohibited; blacks could not enter civil contracts, testify against whites, or engage in litigation; and until the end of slavery, blacks in the South could not acquire property. Blacks were thus kept out of the mainstream of the society: the economy, government, education, and community. Moreover, they were subject to highly prejudicial beliefs about their "inferiority" and "bestiality" (Turner & Singleton in press).

---

[2]For some basic references on black Americans see Blauner (1972); Farley (1968); Pinkney (1969); Turner and Singleton (in press); and Williams (1964).

After the Civil War abolished slavery, there was a brief period—known as Radical Reconstruction—when conditions improved. By the 1880s, however, blacks suffered severe legal, political, economic, educational, and community segregation. They lived in segregated areas, could not share public facilities with whites, were kept from the voting polls, were denied educational opportunities, and were kept in low-paying, unskilled occupations.

During World War I some blacks began migrating to the North to seek wartime jobs. In the North they met white violence and discrimination. They were confined to urban slums; and as in the south they were denied full economic, political, and educational participation.

During the Depression conditions worsened. But with the onset of World War II, new opportunities emerged. Blacks radiated all over the country to wartime industries. But as had been the case during World War I, blacks did not have equal opportunity in housing, jobs, schools, and politics. In the post-World War II period, when whites returned from the war, many black gains were nullified as they lost their jobs and were kept in the core of the large cities because of housing discrimination.

In the 1960s a number of important civil rights acts, plus the increasing militancy and political organization of blacks, eliminated much discrimination. But blacks have been limited in their capacity to enjoy these new "freedoms" because of informal discrimination, their confinement to the slums of the large cities, the poverty of their families and the resulting disorganization, the poor schools, and the lack of resources to pursue higher education. As a result, blacks are not much better off *relative* to whites than they were 20 years ago. They earn more money and advance further in school, but so do whites. Thus, blacks still lag far behind whites in education and income, and they are still segregated from whites in most American communities.

Blacks suffer from a clear lack of equal opportunities. They are an oppressed minority population; and their existence in a society valuing freedom and equality poses a severe contradiction and dilemma.

Chicanos[3]

The largest block of Spanish-speaking ethnics are Mexican-Americans, or chicanos. The first Mexican-Americans were small landholders in the Southwest. But the invasion of whites and large cattle interests resulted in their displacement from their land. The expansion of the railroad also encouraged the importation of Mexicans as cheap labor. Then, as large-scale agriculture moved to the Southwest at the turn of the century, Mexicans were brought over the border to be used as an agricultural labor force.

Today, there are over 5 million chicanos, although there may be well over a million illegal aliens who are not reported in government statistics. They are segregated into urban *barrios* or migrant farm camps. Because chicano children often do not speak English well upon entering school, they suffer severe educational discrimination. Because many are

aliens, they are often subject to search-and-identification procedures by police and border patrol officers. Although they have made important economic gains, chicanos are highly underrepresented in skilled blue- and white-collar jobs; they are less organized politically than black Americans; and thus, they have not been able to effectively alter many discriminatory practices.

Puerto Ricans

In 1898 the United States acquired the island of Puerto Rico, and in 1917 all Puerto Ricans became American citizens. In 1952 the island became a self-governing commonwealth. Over the last 30 years migration of Puerto Ricans to the American mainland has been dramatic. Now, there is rather frequent movement back and forth between the island commonwealth and a few large cities on the eastern seaboard. The young come in search of better economic and educational opportunities, whereas many old tend to return to the island.

Puerto Ricans arrive and locate in slum ghettos where work and educational opportunities are limited. Language problems further limit Puerto Ricans' job and educational chances. Furthermore, white prejudices against dark-skinned, Spanish-speaking persons with Latin cultural patterns are severe. As a result, the income of the close to 2 million Puerto Ricans in American cities is well below national averages. Educational attainment is also low. Puerto Ricans thus represent another large Spanish-speaking minority that has been segregated and denied equal opportunities.

---

[3]For some basic references on Mexican-Americans, see Burma (1970); Moore and Cuéllar (1970); and Stoddard (1973).

Asian Americans[4]

The two largest Asian populations in America are the Chinese and Japanese. There are approximately 450,000 and 600,000 persons of Chinese and Japanese descent, respectively.

The Chinese began their immigration in the middle of the last century, when they worked on the railroad and provided services, such as washing and cooking. When the railroad system was completed, the Chinese were subject to intense discrimination, primarily because they were perceived as potential competitors for jobs by the Occidental population. The Chinese were forced into enclaves in the coastal cities of the West, while being denied access to schools, jobs, and housing. In these enclaves, they developed enterprises for serving each other and for providing highly specialized services for the majority.

The Japanese came to America later than the Chinese. They settled on farms up and down the West coast where they grew fruits and vegetables for the dominant population. The Japanese have emphasized education and have been willing to abandon many of their ethnic traditions in an effort to assimilate. However, they have been subject to considerable discrimination as was dramatically evident during World War II, when they were rounded up, forced to abandon and sell their possessions, and "re-located" in camps. Yet, during the postwar period, the Japanese showed considerably more tolerance than did whites; they worked hard and made significant

---

[4]For some references on Japanese and Chinese, see Kitano (1971); Petersen (1971); and Yuan (1963).

"Chinatown, USA" underscores the degree to which the Chinese remain a separate ethnic group.

An internment camp during World War II.
Families were forced to liquidate their assets
and were shipped to rural areas where they were
crowded into small living areas.

achievements within educational and economic spheres.

Most Japanese are now almost completely
assimilated and, unlike the Chinese, many of
whom still retain their ethnicity in the "china-
towns" of America's urban areas, will not constitute a distinct ethnic population in several
generations. The process of assimilation
among the Chinese, however, will be much
slower, since strong ethnic patterns and considerable social segregation still exists among a
large segment of this population.

Native Americans[5]

The original settlers of the United States—the
Indians—now often live an impoverished existence, isolated and segregated from the
broader society and without the unity and
pride that can come from a viable ethnic culture.

[5]The following discussion taken from Brophy and
Aberle (1966); and Turner (1972).

Equality has not often been extended to the first Americans, who must endure dicrimination.

By 1871 all the various Indian tribes and nations had been conquered, and native Americans had been confined to reservations as wards of the government. Through exploitive, and often illegal, practices, Indians had close to two-thirds of their land—their most valuable economic asset—taken away. As a result, Indians must often attempt to live on land that is not capable of supporting their tribes. Many Indians are now leaving the reservations and migrating to urban areas where their lack of education and job skills, coupled with prejudi-

cial discrimination, limit their opportunities.

The federal government has contributed to the plight of American Indians. The Bureau of Indian Affairs has at times kept Indian tribes from developing their economic resources; it has inhibited their self-governance; it has provided for inadequate schooling on the reservations or forced the young to go to "Indian Schools" in urban areas; and it has rarely pushed for Indian rights in the courts. As a result, American Indians have lost much of their traditional Indian culture, their economic base, and their capacity for self-governance. Yet, they have been prevented from assimilating into American society.

White Ethnics[6]

America is predominately a land of immigrants from Europe. Close to one-half of the American population are descendants of people from the British Isles; another 25% have ancestors who emigrated from Germany. Italians, Poles, Russians, and French also represent a significant proportion of the population. Many white ethnics migrated to America during the latter part of the last century and the early part of this century. A typical pattern was for earlier migrants to discriminate against the newer

---

[6]For discussions of white ethnics, see Greeley (1974, 1975) and Novak (1972).

immigrants. The Irish were victims of harsh discrimination by whites who had arrived earlier. The Italians and Poles, who came to America after the Irish, were discriminated against by the Irish and previous immigrants.

These white ethnics often live within enclaves of large eastern and midwestern cities, although there is some evidence that the ethnic communities of white ethnics are breaking up with migration to the suburbs. Yet, there is considerable segregation of ethnic groups from each other in large cities. Table 2 offers one illustration of the segregation of ethnic populations. The numbers in the table are an index of residential segregation. If there was no segregation between any two groups, a zero would be recorded. Thus, the higher the number, the greater the segregation between populations. As might be expected from our earlier discussion, blacks and Puerto Ricans are the most segregated, with lower degrees of segregation for Irish, Germans, Poles, and Italians.

Table 2: Residential Segregation Among Selected Racial-Ethnic Groups in New York City

	Irish	Germans	Poles	Italians	Blacks	Puerto Rican
Irish	—					
Germans	33.3	—				
Poles	51.7	47.1	—			
Italian	48.0	45.6	52.7	—		
Black	80.3	80.6	79.7	80.5	—	
Puerto Rican	76.5	79.7	75.5	77.8	63.8	—

Source: "Residential Segregation Among Selected Racial-Ethnic Groups in New York City" in N. Kantrowitz, *Ethnic and Racial Segregation in the New York Metropolis* (New York: Praeger, 1973). Reprinted by permission.

Most white ethnics have achieved some degree of affluence (Greeley 1974, 1975; Turner 1977). They are above the median income and close to, or above, the median years of educational attainment. Thus, although some degree of residential segregation exists, this "isolation" is often by choice and has not prevented as many white ethnics as it has blacks and browns from having opportunities to share in the society's affluence.

Ethnic Populations and Relations: An Overview

We can see that ethnic populations represent an important social form in the American system.[7] Other societies reveal similar dynamics, but not to the degree evident for American society. We have observed that social relations among ethnic groups have tended to be discriminatory, usually involving segregation. More extreme forms of discrimination, such as expulsion and extermination, have been less frequent in America, although the mass killings of American Indians certainly attests to the use of more extreme discriminatory practices.

Even though American society is a land of immigrants, cultural pluralism is not pervasive. Those who are "different" have rarely been tolerated or allowed full participation in the society. Integration has occurred for many white ethnics and for such physically distinguishable populations as Japanese. But for those who can be readily identified by skin color, full integration is a long way off.

Minority adaptations to discrimination have varied. During slavery blacks passively accepted their situation. Indians fought until it was no longer possible. Blacks have rebelled, rioted, and organized themselves politically in recent decades. Asians, such as the Japanese, have sought assimilation, whereas the Chinese have shown several adaptations. Some have assimilated, others have engaged in marginal participation, and still others have withdrawn. Chicanos and Puerto Ricans have at times passively accepted their fate, but incidences of rebellion and movement toward political organization and protest are increasing dramatically. White ethnics have, on the whole, sought assimilation.

[7]For general references on ethnic relations in America, see Daniels and Kitano (1970); Dworkin and Dworkin (1976); Hughes (1970); Hunt and Walker (1974); Knowles and Prewitt (1969); Kramer (1970); and Vander Zanden (1972).

SUMMARY AND PREVIEW

In this chapter, we have examined ethnic and minority populations. In particular, we have been concerned with how discrimination creates that social form that we termed minority groups. Initially, we distinguished race and ethnicity, emphasizing that race only has sociological meaning when it influences social relations among members of distinguishable populations. Ethnic groups were defined as populations that can be distinguished in terms of identifiable cultural and social patterns. Ethnic relations are a most important form in the human system.

Minority groups are those ethnic populations that are subject to discrimination and that are thus denied equal participation in a society. Discrimination sets into motion various types of minority/majority social relations, including segregation, expulsion, extermination, integration, and pluralism. The existence of minority populations forces their adaptation to discrimination. A number of minority adaptations were explored: passive acceptance, marginal participation, assimilation, withdrawal, rebellion, and organized protest.

Finally, we turned our attention to ethnicity and minority groups in America. We first explored the ethnic composition of America and then some of the prominent ethnic populations, including blacks, chicanos, Puerto Ricans, Asians, native Americans, and white ethnics.

We are now at the end of this section of chapters on forms of social organization. We have examined groups, formal organizations, fluid organization or collective behavior, communities, stratification, and ethnic populations and groupings. The last basic form is social institutions. We will require a number of chapters in order to study the diversity of social institutions in the human system. All of the social forms studied so far are implicated in social institutions, and it is for this reason that we have delayed their analysis. But we are now ready to explore this last and critically important social form.

Key Terms

Race: The superficial biological differences among populations

Ethnic Group: a population that is distinguished socially and that has its own distinctive cultural and social patterns

Minority Group: ethnic groups that are the victims of discrimination by the majority in a society

Discrimination: a type of interaction in which the rights and privileges enjoyed by most are denied to others

Prejudice: negative and hostile beliefs about others

Segregation: the confinement of a minority group to a limited range of roles

Expulsion: the removal of a minority from a society through force or incentives

Extermination: the killing of members of a minority population

Genocide: the extermination of an entire ethnic population

Integration: that situation in which members of ethnic groups have equal access to the same roles as non-ethnics

Cultural Pluralism: that situation in which ethnic groups retain their uniqueness but are still given equal opportunities

Review Questions

1. Why is "race" only significant sociologically when a "race" can be seen as an ethnic group?

2. What is discrimination, what are its manifestations or forms, and how does it create minority groups?

3. In what ways do minority populations adapt to discrimination?

4. What are prominent ethnic populations in America? Which ones are currently minorities? Why?

Suggested Readings

Bonacich, Edna. "A Theory of Ethnic Antagonism." *American Sociological Review* 37 (October, 1972): 547–549.

Brophy, W. A. and Aberle, S. D. *Indians: America's Unfinished Business.* Norman: University of Oklahoma Press, 1966.

Daniels, Roger, and Kitano, Harry H. C. *American Racism: Explorations of the Nature of Prejudice.* Englewood Cliffs, N.J.: Prentice-Hall, 1970.

Knowles, Louis, and Prewitt, Kenneth, eds. *Institutional Racism in America.* Englewood Cliffs, N.J.: Prentice-Hall, 1969.

Simpson, George E. and Yinger, J. Milton. *Racial and Cultural Minorities: An Analysis of Prejudice and Discrimination.* New York: Harper & Row, 1972.

BASIC HUMAN INSTITUTIONS

CONTENTS

PREVIEW

In Part III we explored basic social forms. However, we did not discuss a last social form: social institutions. We have delayed addressing this social form, because to do justice to this complex topic will require several chapters.

What is a social institution? Like all social structures, human institutions are ultimately constructed from statuses, roles, and norms, and like all social forms, they are created and maintained through culture, symbolic interaction, patterns of organization, and socialization—the basic elements of the human system. Social institutions are, however, a unique social form because they are composed of other social forms: groups, organizations, collective behaviors, communities, and strata. They are soci-

IV

etywide social patterns, which often embody some or all social forms. They are thus congeries of group, organizational, stratification, and community forms. Institutions are distinguished by "what they do for" the broader society. Human institutions resolve some of the most fundamental problems facing humans and their organization, and different human institutions have different consequences for dealing with these basic problems.

When sociologists examine human institutions, then, they stand back and take a broad view. They examine how the basic elements and forms of the human system combine and collaborate to resolve fundamental problems, such as securing food and shelter, allocating responsibilities, maintaining order, preparing the young to participate in society, preserving culture, regularizing sex, and dealing with anxieties and un-

certainties. Social institutions help humans deal with these problems. But the content and structure of a social institution varies from society to society and from epoch to epoch.

Our task in this part will be to explore the five basic human institutions: family and kinship, religion, economy, government, and education. Each resolves a somewhat different set of problems, and over time, each has undergone profound alterations. Our goal in these chapters, then, is to understand the nature of these basic human institutions and how they have changed over the course of human history.

FAMILY AND KINSHIP

PROLOGUE

Guiding Questions: What was the first human institution like? What is the structure of kinship in different societies? What are emerging alternatives to kinship?

Chapter Topics

The first human institution was the family. The family was, no doubt, one of those inventions that enabled some of our species to survive and procreate. Organization of humans and prehumans into family structures resolved certain problems of survival. The family is thus intimately connected to our existence as a species.

In the abstract, we can conceive of life without a family. However, such thoughts have only recently crept into human consciousness. They are, perhaps, a luxury of modern life. But throughout most of our existence as a species on earth and for most people of the world today, social life was, and is, carried out in the family. It may be hard to visualize the confinement of virtually all social life to kinship, but for most of our history, kinship has been the basic organizing form. Economic, political, religious, educational, legal, and recreational activity has occurred within the boundaries of kinship. In our modern world, where work, schooling, politics, law enforcement, and recreation occur in separate institutional spheres, the pervasiveness of kinship seems hard to imagine. Yet, this pervasiveness existed, and it still does today in many places.

Because kinship was our first institution, which organized most of our group activities, other institutions have become separated from kinship over the last ten thousand years. In many ways the development of the human system has involved what is termed the *differentiation*, or separation, of institutions from kinship. Economic, governmental, legal, and educational systems are recent inventions and have become increasingly distinguishable from family life. This process of differentiation will be one of the themes in our discussion of all institutions. We will see how kinship has become transformed as other institutions have taken their place in the human system.

To understand social institutions, then, we must begin by analyzing kinship, the first human institution; and, of course, to understand ourselves and our lives, we must comprehend the first structure in which we, as individuals, participated. The structure and processes of kinship can thus provide us with insight into ourselves and the human system around us. In our discussion of kinship, we will have three primary goals: (1) to discover how kinship helped humans' survival and how it helps us resolve present-day problems, (2) to explore the different types of kinship systems of the past and in the world today, and (3) to examine the nature of the American kinship system in which most of us grew up and now live.

THE 'FUNCTIONS' OF KINSHIP

The family and kinship have helped humans resolve a number of problems. How are stable sexual relations to be established? How are young infants to be cared for? How are the infant young, who, as we noted in Chapter 7 on socialization, to become ready for participation in the human system? How are we to be assured of human comfort and companionship as well as relief from the anxieties of life? Such questions presented humans with obstacles— that is, with problems of survival. Kinship represented a solution to these problems. Those peoples who developed kinship in response to these problems were better adapted than those who did not. Thus, kinship as a way of survival emerged in the human species.

Kinship has proven to be such an adept way of meeting these problems that it remains a dominant institution. Although other institutions now resolve other survival problems once dealt with by kinship, the family still is the most efficient way of resolving certain problems. These can be termed the "functions of kinship" (Turner 1972, pp. 88–91).

Regularizing Sex and Mating

Sex drives are a wonderful, and yet, problematic phenomenon. They are necessary to get people together so that they can mate and perpetuate the species. But sex drives also pose problems. How are they to be controlled? How can sexual warfare and competition be minimized? How is sex to be prevented from disrupting the social bonds and groups upon which humans depend for their survival?

The answer to these questions is both simple and complex. The simple part is that humans

If sex were not regularized, the human system would soon become disorganized.

have developed norms or rules regulating how, when, and where sexual relations are to occur. They have developed particularly powerful norms for those sexual relations that result in the birth of a child. The complex part of the answer is that human societies have a diversity of norms over sexual matters, especially when children are involved. One of the tasks of sociology, as we will come to see in this chapter, is to understand this diversity of ways humans regularize sex and mating.

Biological Support

Human infants are helpless. Because of our large brains, we must be born before our heads become too large to pass through the cervix. The result is biological helplessness for the child and a period of incapacitation for the mother. If they are to persist, all societies must regularize this period of biological helplessness. If infants and mothers are left to die, the human species could not persist.

Not only are infants and mothers in need of biological support; so are the elderly and the sick. Although the elderly and sick can be left to die, it is only in a few societies or only under extreme circumstances that such practice is carried out. People develop attachments to each other and become willing to make sacrifices to preserve each other's health, even if it means that infants must be killed. Indeed, infanticide is far more common than other forms of population maintenance.

Thus, biological support is one of the critical functions of the family and kinship. Without such support, the human species could not have survived on the savannah, and even today in a world of medical wonders, it would seem impossible to support the species in structures other than kinship. Of course, it is possible but not very practical.

Social Reproduction

As the species that uses culture to organize itself, we are more liberated from our genes than others. But we have also created a problem: without instincts to program precisely our actions and social patterns, we must socialize each infant in order to perpetuate society. As we noted in Chapter 7, infants are "barbarians" who are asocial and a bit narcissistic. Through socialization, we acquire personalities, which make all of us unique but which also enable most of us to share the same culture, to be willing to occupy necessary statuses, and to know how to play roles. Although other institutions in modern societies, such as education, share the burden of socialization, it is still the family that is most crucial. Most of our basic personality characteristics are acquired through interaction with parents and siblings. Thus, not only is the family instrumental in our biological reproduction, it is also involved in social reproduction. The norms of kinship in any society provide guidelines for how this social reproduction is to occur.

Social Support

All animals experience emotion: anger, frustration, fear, uncertainty. With our big brains, however, we create a vast collage of emotions: hate, love, and jealousy, for example. As the inhabitants of mental hospitals testify, or as many who seek psychiatric help document, humans are psychologically fragile. We need social support, approval, esteem, and a host of other responses from others. As we saw in Chapter 10, people's identity is dependent upon group affiliations. Without a supportive group environment, humans quickly lose psychological stability and their ability to participate in society.

Family and kinship have proven an effective arena of social support. Surrounded by kinfolk, sexual partners, and children, we receive support in the face of frustrations, anxieties, and other potentially disrupting psychological states. In modern societies in particular, where so much of social life occurs in formal organizations, the family assumes increased burdens in dealing with the problems of coping with an impersonal world.

Social Placement

After years of socialization and biological maturation, the time eventually comes when people must assume adult status in society. Family and kinship are intimately connected to where people are placed. In simple societies placement does not imply inequalities in access to scarce resources. All share equally, and children become adults early and with little disjunction. But once inequality exists, placement becomes a more difficult issue. Social positions, such as one's occupation, will determine how much income, wealth, prestige, power, and other unequally distributed resources a person can receive.

In some societies, such as in the traditional caste system in India, social placement is directly determined at birth in terms of the caste position of a person's family. One's place as an adult is determined at birth by his or her parent's status. Occupation, religious affiliations, and legal rights are predetermined by kinship. Such a system is simple, for children know where they will be as adults and thus do not have to agonize over their future. Of course, the system is unfair in terms of Western values.

In other societies, such as in the United States, family is less directly involved in social placement. Yet, its influence is still profound. In most modern societies social placement occurs in terms of skills and performance. What people learn in schools and how they perform in their jobs determine their place in the society. The family is intimately involved in this process because family socialization influences those attributes that determine how well we do in school and how well we will perform on the job. Moreover, affluent families are better able to provide opportunities in schools and in the job market for their children than are the poor.

Thus, kinship and family influence social placement either directly or indirectly. What we become and where we end up in society are profoundly influenced by family. Such a system of placement is not always fair or equitable, but except in the simplest societies, it is a universal function or consequence of the family.

DEFINITION OF KINSHIP AND FAMILY

We have avoided defining the family until we could assess some of its important consequences for the human system. As we have already noted in the introduction to this section, human institutions can be defined in terms of the kinds of problems that they resolve. We now have some understanding of five such problems: (1) regularizing sex and mating, (2) biological support, (3) social reproduction, (4) social support, and (5) social placement. Kinship has evolved, and now operates, as a response to such problems.

As we have emphasized, all social structures are composed of statuses, roles, and norms. We already know that kinship involves norms that guide these five functions—that is, how sex and mating are to occur, how biological support is to be carried out, how social support is to be effected, and how social placement is to occur. The problem that we face in arriving at a definition is one of determining what statuses and role behaviors are to be included in the institution of kinship. As we will see, there are vast differences in just who is part of a kinship system. Each kinship system has its own definition of who is, and who is not, part of the family. The only generalization possible is that kinship systems specify who is related by blood and by marriage to whom. Such relationships are normatively determined, and there is no universal pattern of defining kinship systems. For example, in American society, norms indicate that marriage creates the focal family unit of husband, wife, and children. The parents of husbands and wives are given equal deference but very little authority over this small family unit. Aunts, uncles, and cousins may have

some importance, but this is usually determined by personal preferences of married couples. In contrast, some societies have much larger family units in which great-grandparents, grandparents, husbands, wives, children, plus aunts, uncles, and cousins may be intimately connected. Moreover, depending upon norms, these relatives are usually from only one side of the family, either the husband's or wife's.

Thus, in defining **kinship** we must be attuned to the vast differences in family statuses. With this qualification, we can provisionally define kinship as the institution that comprises those normatively specified statuses created by marriage and blood lines, which have still other norms for regulating role behaviors for at least the functions of sex and mating, biological support, social reproduction, social support, and social placement.

Of course, this definition is abstract. It does not capture the fascinating variety of kinship systems, but it can serve as a way of distinguishing kinship as a social institution from other institutions to be discussed in the chapters of this part and from other social forms examined in Part III. Let us now discover the variety of kinship structures in the human system.

THE DIVERSE FORMS OF KINSHIP[1]

In America, family life is simple. We get married; we have children; we live where we want or where jobs are available; and we enjoy our relatives but "live our own lives." Of course, there are complications and complexities that will be explored shortly, but in general the American kinship system is not elaborate. In other societies, however, kinship is complex, elaborate, and highly constraining. For much of human history and in less economically developed regions kinship has been the primary basis of social organization; it has been anything but simple.

For example, the Murgin aborigines of New Guinea are a simple and small hunting-and-gathering society (Warner 1937); they have an elaborate kinship system. As we will see, this system is rare among hunters and gatherers, but the Murgin can help us illustrate complexities of kinship when it is the principal basis of social organization. Social life among the Murgin is organized by kinship: where one lives, what one does, who one marries, and many other facets of life are determined by kinship rules. When a young man wishes to marry, he does not go out and "shop around," wining and dining potential mates. His choices are constrained. He must choose among the daughters of his mother's brother. He cannot marry his father's relatives, only those on his mother's side. He must bring his new bride to live in his father's household, and there, all the relatives on his father's side carry out fishing and other economic activities. Should our

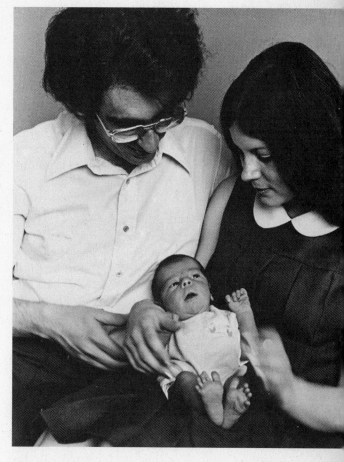

The nuclear family is the most elementary facet of the institution of kinship.

groom die, his wife automatically becomes the wife of his brother, even if the brother already has one wife. Thus, order is maintained by kinship. Everybody has a place, everybody knows what to do. People do not agonize as they do in America over "what they will do in life" and "what will they become." They know with a certainty that Americans rarely possess.

[1]For some basic references on kinship, particularly in a cross-cultural perspective, see Bell and Vogel (1968); Blisten (1963); Goode (1964, 1963); Nimkoff (1965); Stephens (1963); and Turner (1972).

Norms of Kinship

The differences in kinship systems reflect varying norms with respect to (1) size and composition, (2) residence, (3) descent, (4) authority, (5) activity, and (6) marriage and dissolution. These norms dictate which statuses are to be part of one's family as well as which role behaviors are most appropriate for status incumbents. By reviewing briefly the contents of these norms, we can better visualize variations in kinship, while having a sound basis for examining the American kinship system (Turner 1972, pp. 83–95).

Size and Composition. These norms indicate who is to be a part of a household. Potentially, all blood relatives and those acquired by marriage can be a part of a household, but obviously, this would be impossible. Thus, the peoples of the world have evolved norms that state who is to be included. Three general types are evident in the world's kinship systems, creating three different types of household units: (1) extended units, (2) polygamous units, and (3) conjugal/nuclear units.

The **extended family** is large and includes many relatives within the household unit. Parents, children, grandparents, great-grandparents, aunts, cousins, and others can be included in the extended unit. The **polygamous family** involves plural marriages and residence. The man or woman has multiple spouses who live together and form a household. The **conjugal family** (or **nuclear family** when children are included) is composed of only husband and wife (and children).

Although extended units are the most prevalent in the world, American kinship is dominated by the conjugal or nuclear pattern. We are a society of small somewhat isolated families in which parents and children seek their own way. It is even considered "unfortunate" or a "burden" if other relatives, such as the stereotypical "mother-in-law," must live with the couple and their children.

Residence. With marriage, a basic decision must be made: where are we going to live? There are three possibilities: (1) alone, (2) with the wife's relatives, and (3) with the husband's relatives. Most societies have patterns of **matrilocal** or **patrilocal** residence where married couples live with or near either the wife's or husband's relatives, respectively. In the United States and other industrial nations, however, a **neolocal** residence rule is more likely to dominate. Married couples are "free to live where they want," although subtle pressures are often exerted by parents to keep their children near. But too much pressure would be considered inappropriate, especially if one's job required a move.

Descent. At birth, people inherit two blood lines: their mother's and their father's. Most societies have rules about which is to be most important. Kin from one side of the family are thus excluded by a descent norm. In a **patrilineal system** the father's side of the family is most important, and a child will be under the authority of the relatives on the father's side. In a **matrilineal system,** the opposite is true.

Descent is perhaps the single most important facet of a kinship system. It determines who has authority, who is to be given deference, and through whom wealth and other resources are to be passed. Moreover, descent norms usually influence family size and composition as well as residence rules. Although there are exceptions, a patrilineal descent system will require extended families of a father's relatives and a patrilocal residence pattern. The reverse is true in a matrilineal system.

Such descent systems, however, are unfamiliar to Americans. We have a **bilateral system** in which both sides are treated equally. The only hint of patrilinearity is in the use of surnames in which the wife takes the husband's name. Even this tradition is showing early signs of breaking down as women are now often keeping their maiden names. A bilateral system can pose a problem: squabbles and competition among in-laws for the attention and favor of the married couple and their children. Such competition could be highly disruptive except for the fact that bilateral descent systems carry a norm specifying that the married couple should not come under too much influence from either side of the family. Thus, restricted bilateral descent systems are compatible with small conjugal or nuclear family units and neolocal residence. Were relatives to have control and authority over a young couple, the couple would feel uneasy about moving where they desire and about living in a separate household unit.

In America we rarely think about descent. It seems "obvious" that parents are to be treated equally, that children are to inherit their parents' wealth equally, that a married couple should be free from interference, and that they should live where they want. Such a system would be horrifying to many people; it would

scare them; it would seem morally wrong; and it would prove highly disruptive to their psychological well-being. The power of descent norms is such that those who are guided by them remain unaware of their power and those who view the descent norms of another people find them repulsive, if not frightening.

Authority. In all kinship systems, there are rules about which status positions are to hold authority. In extended families with many relatives, these rules become important in order to reduce friction among adults. In small conjugal families, less compelling rules are found, since the family is small enough to work out "agreements" over who makes what decisions. Norms of authority can be classified in three ways: (1) **patriarchal,** (2) **matriarchal,** and (3) **egalitarian.**

In patriarchal systems, the father of a residential unit makes decisions for that unit. But if descent rules and family size rules extend decision-making across units, then the eldest or most able male makes decisions for this larger grouping of kin. Matriarchal systems are rare, and it is typically not the woman, but the males on her side who actually make and enforce decisions. For example, a mother's brother, father, or grandfather is likely to be the authority figure in the household and to make decisions for the larger kin group. Matriarchal systems are almost always associated with matrilineal descent and matrilocal residence. Thus, a male brought into a household from another kin group must be willing to submit to the authority of the males in his wife's extended kinship unit and in his wife's descent line.

The third authority system is the egalitarian. Americans are more apt to have lived in households dominated by this authority rule. Mothers have authority in some spheres, fathers in others. Yet, in only the most "liberated" households does true egalitarianism prevail. Males typically are allowed to make the "important decisions," after "consulting" with other family members, and males are the ultimate "enforcers" of decisions. We will discover in our more detailed analysis of American kinship, however, that there are large social class differences in the *degree* of egalitarianism.

Family Activity. All kinship systems have norms about who does what and how. Rules tend to be most explicit in three major areas of activity: (1) household tasks, (2) child care, and (3) socialization of the young.

In order for humans to live and survive, certain household tasks must be performed. In simple societies these tasks are often economic. Women gather roots and berries or plant seeds for cultivation, while men hunt and help women in the planting and cultivation. Only in modern industrial societies do household tasks become defined as "chores" with little esteem and fulfillment attached to their performance. In more traditional kinship systems women's contribution to the household is equal to that of men, and in hunting and gathering societies it is often greater, since the women's gathering of roots, berries, and other plants provides more of the daily protein than the sporadic success of men's hunting activities. Of course, we will see that in American kinship changes are occurring in the division of household tasks. For the present, we should remain aware that there are usually clear understandings in kin units as to who does what in the household.

Child care and socialization vary enormously in the human system. The only universal is warmth and contact between offspring and their parents.

There are always rules as to how children are to be cared for in kinship systems. Feeding, clothing, and sheltering children are normatively regulated, with each society's kinship system having its own unique procedures. Not only are procedures dictated by norms, but just who is to do what aspect of child care is also specified. In extended families other relatives, such as a grandmother, aunt, or in-law, are required to carry out certain functions. Only in small conjugal units like those in the United States are mothers relegated most child-care activities.

All societies reveal their own unique way of socializing their young. In general terms, norms specify how children are to be raised and who is to perform what tasks. Other relatives in extended units are often involved, and within all family units there is typically a division of labor among adults over those aspects of child socialization for which they are responsible.

Marriage and Dissolution. Marriage establishes sexual and psychological bonds between males and females, while creating family units in the case of conjugal systems and subunits in extended and polygamous systems. Contrary to most Americans' experience, choice of marriage partners is not "free." Three types of norms have typically constrained freedom: (1) **incest taboos,** (2) **exogamy,** and (3) **endogamy.** Some kin, even some who are very distant, are often defined as taboo. People cannot, except under very rare circumstances, marry their sister, brother, aunts, uncles, mother, or father. Even cousins are often excluded in many systems. Americans, for example, feel "uneasy" about marrying a first or second cousin.

Other rules specify kin groups from which one must choose a partner (endogamy) or exclude kin groups as a potential source of marriage partners (exogamy). For example, the Murgin can only "choose" the daughters of his mother's brother—a very strict case of endogamy. Moreover, he cannot even consider someone for marriage or sexual play from his father's community of kin—a strict incest taboo but also a case of exogamy since, in this kinship system, one-half of the entire community is eliminated from consideration.

Dissolution of marriages is always governed by rules, since resolution of property and children must be made. Rules usually specify when and how dissolution can occur as well as how property and children are to be divided. Dissolution can be as simple as a wife moving her possessions out of her husband's hut or as complex as having to prove in court that a spouse has exhibited infidelity.

Kinship and Social Organization Among Primates

Chimpanzees reveal strong mother-child bonds which now appear to last for a lifetime and which become elaborated into complex kinship networks.

Many early field studies of primates were chauvinistic—they focused on male dominance. However, more recent studies have uncovered new insights: the importance of females and the bonds with her children in maintaining social order. Several facts have now emerged. First, primate young form enduring social relations with their mothers. They want to be around them; they groom them, sit with them, and otherwise "care for" their mothers. Second, there may even be incest taboos among primates. Among the highly promiscuous chimp—groups of whom often wait in line for access to receptive females—sons will not sexually address their mothers. Third, males often wander off, thus leaving their female siblings to carry on family traditions. This has created in many large troops what is termed the "matrilocal unit" in which a mother and her daughters, granddaughters, and great-granddaughters remain in contact. They groom each other and sit together. Thus, among the primates, we have the beginnings of a matriarchical, matrilineal, and matrilocal kinship unit.

Could such matrilocal units be our prehuman ancestor's first kinship prototype? It is impossible to know, of course, but the female and her children appear to be a vital principle of social organization in a number of primate societies.

Source: Lancaster (1975).

In sum, kinship norms regulate much human conduct. In simple societies most of the entire society is organized and governed by kinship norms. In modern industrial societies kinship no longer determines how economic, political, religious, legal, educational, and other social spheres are structured to the extent that it once did. Although it is always dangerous to generalize about kinship, we can summarize in broad terms some of the key differences between kinship in traditional and modern societies as shown in Table 1.

Recall our Murgin aborigine as an illustration of the traditional system. A male would live near or in his father's extended household; he would be acutely aware of the patrilineal descent system and of the authority of males on his father's side; he would have to choose a wife from a small pool of kin; and he and his spouse had clear understandings of what they were supposed to do in the household.

We must recognize that a modern system is not necessarily "better." The modern system is merely more prevalent in modern industrial societies. By simply recalling your childhood and by examining what you want (or now have) in the way of family life, a picture of the modern system can be constructed. Since the American family is so much a part of our lives, it is wise to pause and examine its features in more detail.

Table 1: Traditional and Modern Kinship Systems

Kinship Norms	Traditional Kinship	Modern Kinship
Size and Composition	extended polygamous	conjugal-nuclear
Residence	matri- or patrilocal	neolocal
Descent	patri- or matrilineal	bilateral and truncated
Authority	patri- or matriarchal	egalitarian
Family Activity	clear	ambiguous
Marriage and Dissolution	incest, endogamy, or exogamy; dissolution clear	incest, romantic love; dissolution in flux

THE AMERICAN KINSHIP SYSTEM[2]

The American kinship system has norms emphasizing small and isolated conjugal units of parents and children, neolocal residence, a deemphasis on descent, considerable free choice in marriage partners, a comparatively high degree of egalitarianism, increasingly ambiguous family activity norms, and greater ease in marital dissolution. This describes the basic profile of the family. We have to fill in this broad profile with more details, however. We can begin to do this by examining how family units are created through marriage, how the internal structure of these units operates and how it often reveals many internal conflicts, and finally, how the family is dissolved as a result of these conflicts.

Marriage in America

In America potential marriage partners are free to choose their spouses. Naturally, there are some constraints. Some people will never have a chance to meet because of class, regional, neighborhood, ethnic, and other differences. For example, a ghetto resident is not likely to interact with a daughter of a white doctor or lawyer. A rural southerner is not likely to meet an urban westerner. Moreover, there are differences in people's outlook—their values, beliefs, and other facets of their personalities—which make them unlikely partners. The daughter of right-wing Republicans, for example, is not likely to find a hippie an appealing mate—unless, of course, she has rebelled from her parents' beliefs. Finally, parents usually do make their preferences known, such as when a mother exclaims, "Why don't you bring home a nice boy, for once."

Yet, despite these constraints, much popular fiction documents how two people "in love" overcame these obstacles, or, if the story is to be considered more profound, how these obstacles came between "the love" of two people. These stories overemphasize the degree to which people from different backgrounds are likely to interact, and they underemphasize the extent of mutual revulsion when they do interact. But they reveal one of the most important normative systems in America: despite constraints, "love is to conquer all." People are to be free to choose their partners. They are to "fall in love." This emphasis on love would seem very strange to many people of the world where the choice of one's spouse is often dictated or where wealth, strength, and domestic considerations take precedence over "love."

We can label this normative complex the **romantic love** system. The basic tenets of romantic love norms are:

1. Selection of marriage partners is to occur in terms of "personality traits"—in terms of mutual attraction rather than in regard to wealth and social position.
2. Selection is to occur in terms of mutual attraction and compatibility, with life consisting of an unbroken sequence of compatibility. "Love" can overcome problems and troubles.

---

[2]For basic references on the nature of the American family, see Bell and Vogel (1968); Cavan (1969); Furstenberg (1968); Leslie (1976); Nye and Berardo (1966); Parsons (1954); Parsons and Bales (1955); Williams (1970); and Winch (1971).

The Romantic Love belief system emphasizes that the conjugal couple can be content with each other's company, isolated against the hardships imposed by the world.

3. Partners are to comprise a "oneness"—a sense of solidarity and psychological fusion which insulates the partners from the corrupting influences of the outside world.
4. Sexual bliss is inevitable between couples who reveal attraction and compatibility. [Goode 1963; Turner 1972, p. 103]

Stated in this way, these norms seem naive. But most Americans hold them. We may hold them in more sophisticated terminologies, hidden behind a "hip," "cosmopolitan," "cynical," or "worldly" veneer, but stripped of this veneer, these norms guide mate selection for most Americans. Attractiveness is emphasized, so is getting along. Sexuality is always present. An emphasis on the couple's isolation from others is dominant.

Such an emphasis on "love" is compatible with a kinship system emphasizing conjugal and nuclear units, neolocal residence, and the unimportance of descent. Since it is the couple who must live alone, it is perhaps appropriate for them to select each other on the basis of such nonfamilial and nonutilitarian traits as "love" and "compatibility." However, this selection also poses a severe problem: the romantic love complex of norms also sets up unrealistic and false expectations about what family life will be like. Coupled with the internal conflicts of the present American family, married couples can soon become disillusioned and unhappy.

The Internal Structure

The internal structure of the family is composed of the normative expectations and role enactments of incumbents in three status positions: father, mother, and children. At present, there appears to be growing confusion as to how roles are to be carried out. We can visualize the internal structure of the family and some of the problems this structure reveals by examining the expectations for each of these familial statuses:

Adult Males. In general, males are to be "bread-winners." They are to earn enough money to support the family. Yet, increasingly, wives are entering the work force to supplement this income or to realize the fulfillment that can come with nonfamilial roles. With two "bread-winners," other facets of the male role are thrust into some confusion (Blood & Hamblin 1968; Williams 1970, pp. 69–75).

For example, how much is the father to be involved in daily child care and in household chores? Who should change diapers, wash dishes, shop, transport children, and do the other activities that traditionally have been the female's? Presently, men appear to have avoided serious role conflict by allowing wives, even working wives, to perform the "domestic" tasks. Such a situation, as we will see shortly, has created enormous tension in the household.

Adult Females. Traditionally, females were to perform domestic chores: taking care of the house, caring for the daily needs of children, and other activities involved in keeping the household functioning. As wives have entered the work force and as they have begun to recognize the drudgery of much of housework, role conflicts have emerged. It is difficult to work full-time and to perform traditional mother roles. Yet, fathers have been resistant to performing "woman's work."

Children. One of the biological facts of life is that people grow and mature. Thus, nonadults pass through different stages of growth, requiring new role behaviors and new relationships with parents. We might visualize three distinctive stages in this process: (1) childhood, (2) youth, and (3) adolescence. In childhood, one is dependent upon parents for love, affection, approval, and guidance. The social world is limited to interaction with family members. It is a secure world, lacking the complexities that will mark life. With advancing age, greater participation in the neighborhood, and most importantly, enrollment in schools, childhood passes into youth. Although basic ties of affection remain with the family, youth assume many nonfamilial statuses, expanding their ties and learning to participate in the broader social structure. Childhood and youth pose comparatively few problems for the average family. It is during adolescence, however, that tensions begin to increase.

In childhood and youth, parents still dominate their children. Their word is to be taken unquestioningly; they are to be given respect; and they are the primary source of wisdom for the young. Adolescence is that awkward period when children have become, biologically at least, adults. Yet, in American society they are not ready to be "social adults." They do not have enough training, and their social and bureaucratic role-playing skills are insufficient to participate in adult roles.

Adolescent subcultures often emerge to insulate adolescents from the perceived constraints of home while the young await full adulthood. Adolescents are to be independent of parents, and yet parents represent major objects of affection, and of course, a principal means of support. They are to become heterosexually involved, but must postpone full involvement until they "mature." They are to learn about the world, and yet still be subject to parental authority.

Thus, adolescence poses built-in role conflicts. These conflicts are endemic to the family structure of a society that postpones full adulthood. In traditional societies adolescence is much less prolonged, but in a society that requires educational credentialing, dependency upon parents can extend well into young adulthood. It is inevitable, then, that parents and their biologically mature "children" will come into conflict. The young are gaining new experiences, which are often at variance with their parents'. Parents are having to adjust to transformed children, shifting their role behaviors to accommodate their growing offspring. Such adjustments can be particularly difficult if parents have yet to resolve their own conflicts about the "proper" roles of husbands and wives.

We can see, then, that sources of strain are built into the American family. This small, isolated conjugal unit must deal with these problems alone. Other kin are unlikely to be around to shoulder household burdens, to deflect emotions, to care for children, to counsel adolescents, and to otherwise help family members cope. It is perhaps a miracle that a family structure so filled with potential conflict does as well as it does in raising children and in proving an emotional base for its members. Yet, tensions often escalate to a point where dissolution is likely.

Divorce and Dissolution

In a small conjugal or nuclear family where role conflicts and tensions abound, it is inevitable that many marriages will be dissolved. At one time divorce carried enormous stigma, but beliefs have changed to accommodate the reality of marital and family tension. A divorce is now much easier to obtain, and it is less stigmatizing. Yet, many would claim that "divorce is out of hand" and that the "family is crumbling." We should examine carefully such statements. Is divorce out of hand, and is the family a less viable institution?

Divorce Rates. There is considerable confusion about divorce. Surprisingly, there are no accurate statistics on divorce. They are difficult to collect and interpret. Please examine the boxed material for some insights on problems with these statistics.

Your Chances for Marital Success: Fact and Fiction

The media frequently report that one in three or one in two marriages ends in divorce. People may decry the "crumbling of the basic cornerstone of the society" when they hear such reports. Others may have their faith in "romantic love" norms weakened. Such feelings are based upon incorrect statistics about divorces. For example, the "shocking trend" summarized below is usually what is reported:

Divorces per 100 marriages

1920	13.4
1930	17.0
1940	16.9
1946	26.6
1950	23.1
1960	25.8
1970	32.8
1973	40.6

These numbers are usually read as percentages—40% of all marriages end in divorce. The data do not say this; they do not indicate what your present chances for marital success are. They simply and arbitrarily compare divorces from *all* previous years of marriage to marriages in *one given year*. Perhaps your chances of success are only 60%, maybe they are 10%, 5%, or 40%. These data do not say. But the media and the public think that they do, and perhaps it is here that the "social problem" resides.

Table 2: Divorces per 1,000 Married Women, 15 and over for Selected Years

Year	Divorces per 1,000 Married Women
1920	8.0
1930	7.5
1940	8.7
1946	17.8
1950	10.3
1960	9.2
1970	14.9
1971	15.8

Source: National Center for Health Statistics, HEW, "Summary Report: Final Divorce Statistics," 1974.

The best statistics available—and these are not without problems—are summarized in Table 2. These data report the number of divorces in a given year as a proportion of all married females, 15 years old or older. These data do not reveal anything about a person's chances for a successful marriage. As the boxed material emphasizes, there are no data on such matters. The first thing that one notices is that divorces are increasing but are just approaching the "all time high" of 1946. Whether this rate is "too high" is, of course, a matter of personal assessment—a matter of whether or not divorce is "good" or "bad" in terms of your values. What the data do emphasize, however, is that there have perhaps been some exaggerations about "rising divorce rates."

Reasons for Divorce. To determine the reasons for divorces, we need some information on the length of marriages ending in divorce. The data reveal that most marriages end, if they are going to be dissolved at all, before the seventh year. But most divorces occur in the second year, which, because of the time lag involved in getting a divorce, indicates that most marriages really end in the first year. Apparently, the realities of marriage simply do not correspond to the expectations of "romantic love," and when conflicts over proper family roles surface, the tension leads the newly married to seek a divorce (Hetzel & Cappetta 1973).

We also need to know what happens to divorced parents. If people do not remarry, then this fact might signal a decline in the institution of marriage and family. But if they do remarry, this would indicate strength and vitality in the family. The evidence clearly argues for the attractiveness of marriage and family, since divorced partners, probably in accordance with "romantic love" beliefs, seek new marriage partners. As demographer Kingsley Davis (1972) summarized, "At such rates [of remarriage] the divorced population would soon be consumed if it were not constantly fed by newly divorced recruits." Thus, although people are more likely to seek a divorce, they are also more susceptible than ever to desire remarriage and the reestablishment of the family unit.

We also need to know which social groups and categories seek divorce if we are to find an explanation for increasing divorce (and remarriage) in America. One of the most important predictors of divorce is the age of the partners at the time of their marriage. The evidence is clear that the younger the age at which part-ners are married, especially if they are under 20, the higher the incidence of divorce (Hetzel & Cappetta 1973). The economic situation of a family also influences divorce patterns: the lower the income, the higher the divorce rate, regardless of age. Similar findings exist for the prestige of the male's occupation (which, of course, is correlated with income): the higher the prestige and status associated with an occupation, the lower the divorce rate. (U.S. Bureau of Census 1974) A final category for which there are data concerns the issue of previous marriage. If marriage partners have been previously married and divorced, then the new marriage is more likely to end in divorce, although the data on this matter are incomplete and should be interpreted carefully (Carter & Glick 1970).

We now have some clues as to why the divorce rate appears to have increased. For young married couples, who adhere to "romantic love" norms, the realities of family life, especially as they are exacerbated by conflicting male and female roles, can generate such frustration and tension that the partners immediately seek family dissolution. For the less affluent, financial problems can present additional tensions with which marriage partners have difficulty coping. Such tensions can be aggravated by the "working wife," whose income may lessen the financial burdens of the family, but whose *combined* work and household burden creates other sources of tension between spouses. Since the "working wife" is most likely in lower income families where husbands typically hold traditional beliefs about male/female roles and authority, the working-class wife is subjected to enormous pressure to perform both work and household roles. Under these conditions, maintaining a tension-free household apparently proves difficult.

The data on remarriage would indicate that people do not "learn from their mistakes." Apparently, divorced people seek remarriage in accordance with romantic love norms, but they also fail to alter their expectations and behaviors, or they fail to recognize them as a potential source of marital discord. Thus, many of the role and authority conflicts are repeated in second marriages, and when aggravated by economic circumstances, another divorce becomes increasingly likely.

In response to the inevitability of divorce in a society in which unrealistic romantic love beliefs, coupled with ambiguous and conflicting beliefs over male/female family roles, divorce has increasingly been simplified. These changes in divorce laws have no doubt encouraged people to seek the divorce option in an unhappy marriage.

Variations

We have made oblique references to differences in the family structure in America. For example, in the analysis of divorce we discussed working-class families holding traditional conceptions of the female role. We must expand, if only briefly, such topics. We must explore differences in the family, because although the "modern profile" discussed earlier describes the structure *in general*, each family is unique. Your family is not exactly the same as mine. More important for the sociologists, however, are unique characteristics that are associated with major structural dimensions of the society. Although the differences between any two families are interesting, the sociological imagination is stimulated when differences between classes, community types, or categories of people can be found. The most dramatic differences in family structure are those associated with social strata or class. We should review these briefly.

The differences among social class are most evident in regard to (1) size and composition, (2) residential mobility, (3) authority, (4) family activity, and (5) marriage and dissolution. The poor, who can least afford to, have the largest families. Birth rates are high and other relatives are more likely to live with a couple in an effort to pool resources (Rainwater 1900). They reveal less residential mobility than other classes. They have high male authoritarianism, but males are often absent, thus forcing mothers to perform all household tasks. Socialization of children is difficult for tired and discouraged mothers, or for unemployed or menially employed fathers and mothers. Obedience is stressed, but fatigue often makes it difficult to consistently enforce obedience. Dissolution rates are high, evidenced by high father absenteeism, but abandonment is often the alternative to divorce. Such a portrayal of the poor, however, emphasizes "negative" characteristics. A majority of the poor have stable nuclear units and do their best to raise children under difficult circumstances. It is the higher incidence of these more negative traits that distinguish the poor family from families in other social classes, and this is why we have emphasized these traits (Irelan 1966).

In contrast, the working-class, blue-collar family is smaller in size and more mobile. There is usually a clear division of labor, with males dominating the authority structure and females performing most domestic tasks

(Komarovsky 1964; Shustak 1969). Even working females perform these tasks, and thus, it is not surprising that a large majority of working-class wives would much prefer to be housewives than partial breadwinners. Socialization of children stresses obedience, getting along, and respecting authority. Working-class couples marry later than poverty couples, but earlier than those in the middle classes. The working class also has high divorce rates.

Middle-class, white-collar families are smaller than either poverty or working-class families. They tend to be highly mobile as husbands move in response to job advancement (Kohn 1969). Authority tends toward egalitarianism, with spouses having authority in different spheres. Family activity is less clearly structured: mothers perform most domestic chores, although fathers are also required to help. Women work more for self-

*America is a land of great contrasts in
terms of how well or how poorly people live.*

fulfillment and as a way of avoiding the drudgery of housework. Socialization emphasizes
self-reliance and independence, as children are
encouraged to achieve and do things on their
own (Bronfenbrenner 1958). Marriage comes
later than for either the poor or working class,
and rates of dissolution are lower than in the
other two classes (Kerckhoff 1972).

Little is known about the rich. Their family
patterns have not been subject to systematic
study, primarily because they are fewer in
number and because they are more isolated
and protective of their privacy. Thus, we cannot draw a profile.

As can be seen, money makes a great deal of
difference in the family life of the poor, working and middle classes. With money, there is
less strain and a more relaxed family life. Such
is the impact of stratification on this most basic
of social institutions.

THE CHANGING FAMILY AND EMERGING ALTERNATIVES

The modern family profile, as is illustrated by the American kinship system, emerged as a result of many social forces. Probably the most important was industrialization. As people left the farms to take advantage of jobs in industrial cities, they no longer "needed" large families of several generations of kin to farm the land. In fact, large families composed of non-wage earning members such as the elderly and aged become a liability to wage earners. As people move about from industrial city to industrial city, large families also become a problem: they are expensive to move and present problems in finding housing.

Other changes associated with industrialism similarly operate to change the family. The expansion of education, for example, will require expenses that would be difficult to meet in large families. Government social welfare programs also contribute to alteration of the family. With social programs to aid the elderly, the sick, and the indigent, couples are able to exclude their parents and other relatives, secure in the knowledge that they are being taken care of. Other relatives, of course, may prefer the sense of freedom afforded by "being on their own."

Finally, with industrialization and urbanism, a new trend of freedom is possible: the freedom to be alone, although this can mean freedom to be lonely. Although present-day Americans are fond of portraying the virtues of the large, multigenerational family, these portrayals probably underemphasize the repressed conflicts between generations and the sense of always being surrounded by kin. With freedom from the need for kindred as farm labor and as a means of social security, as well as the economic liabilities of kin, people are likely to see less advantage in maintaining extended families with powerful descent rules. This is particularly likely when, for the first time, they can experience freedom from kin supervision and a sense of personal intimacy with spouses.

For these and other reasons, then, the family moves from the traditional to modern profile summarized earlier in Table 1. Yet, as our discussion of the American family emphasizes, the conjugal or nuclear family unit can experience many problems. Moreover, as the general level of affluence in the society has increased, as people feel freer to experiment, as some become disenchanted by materialism, and as sexual freedom increases, many people seek alternatives to the current conjugal family. Just as the isolated conjugal family represented, at one time, a break from traditional kinship patterns, so present alternatives represent a departure from the conjugal or nuclear unit. Just whether or not these are future trends or merely experiments by more liberated people in a more tolerant social environment is difficult to assess. But we might close our review of family and kinship with a brief look at these emerging alternatives.

As we saw with divorce rates, there are few data on the family, and there are virtually none on alternatives. But we can see, at least impressionistically, three prevalent patterns: (1) childless marriages, (2) the unmarried couple, and (3) group living arrangements (Butler, in press).

Childless Marriages

At present, more married couples plan not to have children than ever before. Of course, whether or not these plans are adhered to can change, but there appear to be pressures favor-

*Increasingly, people are foregoing having children
in order to enjoy the freedom that non-parents have.*

ing an increase in childless marriages. First, women are beginning to seek professional careers equal to those of men. Second, there is less stigma attached to not having children, and third, a growing number of married couples prefer to spend their time together and their resources on travel, recreation, and non-child-related activities.

In childless marriages the functions of the family are altered. Biological support, social reproduction, and social placement functions are lost, whereas social support and sexual mating functions are, perhaps, increased. Not only are functions changed, but the internal structure of the family becomes more egalitarian, more isolated from kin, and more consumption oriented. An increase in this family pattern would thus mask a dramatic change in the institution of kinship in America.

Unmarried Couple

People live together out of wedlock; sometimes they also have children. There are no systematic data on unmarried couples but the limited information that does exist suggests the following pattern. The young are more likely to live together. The longer two people cohabitate, the more likely they are to eventually marry. Much cohabitation is short-lived, lasting only a few months. Children are not frequent in nonmarital unions, but their arrival usually makes a transition to a more enduring relationship, often involving marriage. Living partners typically play traditional husband/wife roles, despite the lack of legal obligations. At present, pressures for marriage are most likely to come from the female and her kin.

The unmarried couple, then, is much like its married counterpart. Limited finances or a desire to "get to know each other" are the most prevalent motives for forming nonmarital unions. Most couples desire to form normal marital and family relationships sometime in the future. Thus, the nonmarital union is more of an alternative to courtship in America—a way of finding out about married life and about life with a particular partner. Nonmarital unions allow people to enjoy social support and regular sexual relations, while avoiding the legal and moral complications often attending married couples.

Group Living

It is curious that in a society of small conjugal and nuclear family units, some people desire more extended living units. Group living often provides a practical alternative for resurrecting extended kinship groups. There are many diverse forms of group living, however. Some are more like small communities or *communes* in which groups of people seek to share their labors and the rewards of their work. Rural communes, for example, involve grouping of variously related people who seek to meet their needs through farming. Relationships among couples vary: some communes involve marriage and children and represent clusters of nuclear units. Others involve nonmarital units. Still others are composed of single individuals who shift their sexual and social attachments, and still others represent combinations of these. Urban communes show a similar variety of relationships, but these involve a pooling of earnings and the division of household tasks in terms of who is employed and unemployed. Most communes fail, however. The most successful are those that are rural, that have strict rules about membership and relations among people, and that have unifying beliefs—often religious—about their purpose. Thus, if communes can provide a sound economic base and the equivalents to kinship norms for regulating composition, authority, and member activity, then they can be as successful as traditional kinship systems in regularizing sex and mating, in providing social and biological support, and in socializing their new members and placing them within their community. Achieving these goals is often difficult, for it involves re-creating the equivalent to a kinship system that evolved from many generations and that involves interlocking ties of people related by blood and marriage.

There are other forms of group living that revolve around sexual liaisons. The addition of

Synanon House—a place where communal living, coupled with group encounters, has become an alternative way of life.

a third sexual party to an existing marriage is one common pattern. Mate swapping or groups of spouses who share and trade mates is another pattern. Groups of homosexual individuals can also be found. These sexual groupings tend to be highly unstable, but constitute a growing facet of family life in America. Many couples and unattached individuals do seek out, perhaps for only a short period, a wide variety of groupings that revolve around sexual and companionship activities.

SUMMARY AND PREVIEW

In this chapter we have reviewed the characteristics of humankind's first institution, family and kinship. Our emphasis has been on the varying functions and structures of this basic institution. We saw kinship as resolving five basic problems: regularizing sex and mating, biological support, social reproduction, social support, and social placement. A variety of norms were then viewed as emerging in response to such problems: Norms of size and composition, residence, descent, authority, activity, and marriage dissolution. We then discussed a traditional and a modern profile of kinship.

We examined kinship in America as an example of the modern profile: conjugal and nuclear units, neolocal residence, limited bilateral descent, a tendency toward egalitarian authority, an emerging ambiguity in the division of labor and socialization practices, and high rates of marriage and divorce. Social class variations were also examined, because they highlight the greatest differences in the American system.

Finally, we discussed three emerging alternatives to kinship: childless couples (that is, conjugal units), unmarried couples or families, and group living.

Early in our discussion, we emphasized that much of the evolutionary history of social institutions has involved a separation, or differentiation, of separate institutions from kinship. It is, of course, difficult to reach back into prehistory and know just what transpired among our relatives. But it appears that religion was one of the first institutions to become separated from kinship. For this reason, we now turn our attention to the study of religion in the human system.

Key Terms

Kinship: those normatively specified statuses created by marriage and blood lines that reveal still other norms for regulating role behaviors with respect to the functions of sex and mating, biological support, social reproduction, social support, and social placement

Extended Family: large families that include many relatives within the household unit

Polygamous Family: families that involve plural marriages in which either the husband or wife takes on several marriage partners

Conjugal Family: family units composed of only a husband and wife

Nuclear Family: family units composed of husband, wife, and their children

Matrilocal: a rule of residence specifying that a husband must live near or with his wife's relatives

Patrilocal: a rule of residence specifying that a wife must live near or with her husband's relatives

Neolocal: a rule of residence specifying that newly married couples are free to live where they choose

Patrilineal: a rule of descent in which the father's side of the family is defined as most important, with authority and inheritance residing in the male side of the family

Matrilineal: a descent norm in which the mother's side of the family is defined as most important, with authority and inheritance being calculated through the female side of the family

Bilateral: a descent norm, which indicates that both sides of a couple's family are to be treated equally

Patriarchal: a norm of family authority specifying that husbands are to have most of the authority within the family unit

Matriarchal: a norm of family authority specifying that the wife's relatives, usually her brother, is to have most of the authority in the family unit

Egalitarian: a norm of family authority specifying that a family unit is to share authority

Incest Taboo: rules that restrict sexual and marriage relations among specific members of the family

Exogamy: marriage rules specifying that marriage partners must be found outside a defined kin or other unit

Endogamy: marriage norms indicating that marriage partners must be chosen within defined kin or other units

Romantic Love Complex: norms of marriage selection indicating that a couple are to choose each other in terms of mutual compatibility and love

Review Questions

1. What are the functions of the family?
2. What are the differences between traditional and modern families?
3. What marriage and divorce patterns are evident in the American family?
4. What is the basic structure of the American family? What are some social class variations?
5. What emerging alternatives are evident in the American family?

Suggested Readings

Butler, Edgar. *The Family and Its Emerging Alternatives.* New York: Harper & Row, in press.

Cavan, Ruth S. *The American Family.* New York: Crowell, 1969.

Goode, William J. *The Family.* Englewood Cliffs, N.J.: Prentice-Hall, 1964.

———. *World Revolution and Family Patterns.* New York: The Free Press, 1963.

Leslie, Gerald R. *The Family in Social Context.* New York: Oxford University Press, 1976.

Parsons, Talcott. "The Kinship System of the Contemporary United States." In *Essays in Sociological Theory.* New York: The Free Press, 1954.

Winch, Robert F. *The Modern Family.* New York: Holt, Rinehart and Winston, 1971.

RELIGION

PROLOGUE

Guiding Questions: What problems do large brains create for humans? How have we dealt with the emotions created by our vast cognitive abilities? What is religion? Why is it a human universal? What is its form? How is it changing?

Chapter Topics

The evolution of large brains has given us the unique capacity to ponder the unknown and unknowable, to symbolically represent fears and anxieties, and to construct supernatural realms that influence our lives. We do not just react to events; we interpret them; we give meaning to them. Because life is filled with uncertainties, frustrations, imponderables, and much that we cannot understand, we create interpretations and explanations of problematic contingencies. We often do this with religion.

Homo erectus, our prehuman ancestor who lived one million years ago, may have sought religion for interpreting and explaining what could not be understood. Neanderthals certainly had religious beliefs about gods, the supernatural, and the sacred (Beals & Hoijer 1967, p. 82; Pfeiffer 1969). We can find evidence in their artifacts of religious services, rituals, and concern about the fate of their dead. So, too, were *H. sapien sapien* religious. Religion, then, has been a basic part of prehuman and human existence. As soon as brains were large enough to imagine worlds, entities, and universes beyond immediate experience, religion appears to have become a part of prehuman and human systems.

Religion was probably the first institution to become separated from kinship. From our knowledge of peoples of the past, and present-day hunters and gatherers, we know that religious statuses, roles, and norms are among the first to be distinct in time and place from kinship roles. Shaman, priests, witch doctors, and the like emerge before politicians, lawyers, and nonkin workers. Much of religion in early

Religion has been a part of the earliest human systems. Here, a somewhat idealized drawing depicts this fact.

human societies was conducted within the kinship unit, but as soon as a society became able to support "specialists," religious leaders were among the first to emerge. It is for this reason that we follow our discussion of kinship with a review of the institution of religion.

In our discussion we will focus on several topics in a sequence that will allow us to see diversity and similarities in religious institutions. First, we will discuss the basic elements of all religions. Then, we will turn to the functions of religion for the human system. We will examine different types of religious systems—from the simplest to most complex. Finally, we will explore religion in America.

BASIC ELEMENTS OF RELIGION

What is common to all religions? What makes religion a distinctive social pattern? We can isolate three basic elements of religion (Turner 1972): (1) a notion of the *sacred and supernatural,* (2) *beliefs and values,* and (3) *cults and ritual.*

The Sacred and Supernatural

Sacred is the idea that objects, events, or places have special significance beyond our control and understanding. What is sacred is the recipient of humans' most intense emotions. As such, the definition of some phenomenon as sacred involves a considerable degree of emotional arousal about the special qualities of that phenomenon. Indeed, humans have fought wars, migrated thousands of miles, and performed other spectacular deeds to preserve or find what is considered sacred.

Émile Durkheim (1912) was the first sociologist to examine the sacred systematically. He recognized that the sacred was a symbolic representation of people's religious sentiments and practices. The sacred personified and reinforced these sentiments and practices, and in so doing, it gave people a sense of order to the world around them, thereby promoting social cohesion.

Most religions embody the idea of the **supernatural.** There are some exceptions, but in general, religions postulate a realm beyond the reach of human senses, which is occupied by forces, spirits, beings, powers, animals, and persons who can shape and influence our world. The operation of the world around us is presumed to be controlled and guided by occurrences in this supernatural realm.

Rituals among different religious groupings vary. From (l) to (r): followers of Greek Orthodox, Jewish, and other Christian (Catholic/ Protestant) beliefs participate in rituals.

The supernatural and sacred are interrelated, but distinctive. The supernatural is a realm beyond our everyday world. The sacred are objects in our world that have powers, meaning, and other attributes that give them significance. Frequently, what is defined as sacred is assumed to be the result of the powers of forces and beings in the supernatural realm to bestow a unique quality on objects.

Beliefs and Values

Notions of the sacred and supernatural are a part of a more general set of *beliefs* and *values*. Beliefs define what is sacred and stipulate the composition of the supernatural. **Religious beliefs,** however, offer much more. They usually provide for an interpretation of the universe.

In providing this interpretation, religious beliefs emphasize certain matters. Typically, they posit levels of reality, moving from the everyday world of an average person to various supernatural realms. Moreover, beliefs usually spell out diverse realms of the supernatural—heaven, hell, nirvana, and the like. They often include a **pantheon** which is a kind of organizational chart or "who's who" among supernatural beings and forces. Pantheons contain hierarchies among gods: high gods, lesser gods, godlike persons, and the like. Frequently, there are myths about the history and origin of gods, about their power struggles and love affairs. Moreover, there are stories of their intervention in the worldly affairs of humans, which become codified in oral and written traditions—the Old Testament and the New Testament being the most obvious examples for Judaism and Christianity.

Religions also provide basic cultural **values** of what is right and wrong, appropriate or inappropriate. By investing values with the sanctions of supernatural beings and forces, they are given special significance. People violate the will of forces beyond their control when deviating from values. They also invite the sanction of these all-powerful beings.

Recall from our discussion of culture in Chapter 4 that values and beliefs were important components of the "cultural storehouse." We saw how they shaped and guided human thought and action, and now we can see that many of the beliefs and values in a society's cultural storehouse are provided by religious institutions.

Cults and Ritual

Ritual is a form of role behavior directed toward the supernatural and sacred that someone who is a member of a religious cult enacts. **Cult** is the general term used to describe the social unit embodying a religion. Cults can be very simple groups or complex organizations such as the worldwide Roman Catholic church. Cults, then, are the structural units within which ritual role behaviors occur.

There are common elements in all rituals in all societies of the human system.

Ritual behaviors address the supernatural. They are usually required and regulated tightly by norms and become stereotyped because there are precise ways, times, and places for their performance. Going to church, taking communion, and presenting an offering are typical rituals with which Americans are familiar. But rituals are highly varied in the religious

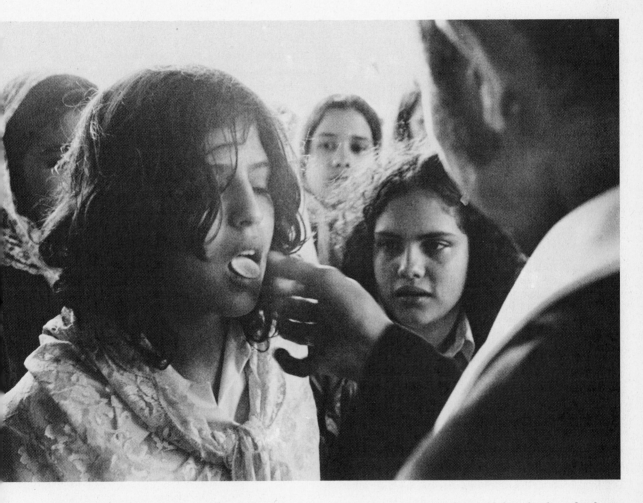

systems of the world, and most are more extensive and elaborate than those practiced in American religious cults.

Cult structures are composed of interrelated statuses, norms, and ritualized roles. Their structure varies enormously from a small group gathering of hunters and gatherers around the fire to the elaborate and ornate rituals of churches, such as the Roman Catholic and Russian and Greek Orthodox. The com-

mon features that make both of these gatherings cult structures are: (1) Those who are members of cults share common beliefs about the sacred and supernatural; (2) they share common values; (3) they practice common rituals; and (4) they have a "sense of community" or common membership in the cult.

THE FUNCTIONS OF RELIGION

What is the religion or religions of a society? Our answer would first make reference to cult structures. We might say that religion in America is composed of Jews, Catholics, and Protestants. Then, we would make reference to specific cults: Liberal or Orthodox Jews, Baptists, Presbyterians, Episcopalians, and the like. We might also refer to smaller cults such as the Black Muslims, the Bahai, Spiritualists, I Am, Hare Krishna, and so on until we had a catalogue of every group and organization that has common beliefs, rituals, values, and membership. Religion in America would thus be the combination of all these cult structures. In a simple society, however, our catalogue would be brief: the people believe in particular forces and gods; they organize their ritual activities within their kinship units.

In sum, then, the elements of all religions are: a conception of the supernatural and sacred, beliefs that specify the nature of the universe, particularly the various levels of reality and the pantheon of the supernatural, values that provide the basic premises for what is right and wrong, ritual activities directed toward the supernatural, and cult structures that organize religious statuses and that normatively regulate ritual role behaviors. Like all institutions, however, religion takes on meaning in reference to resolving problems that all societies face. It has helped people adjust to each other and the world around them. Just whether it still does this in the modern world is, of course, a hotly debated question. But religion is a universal; it exists in all societies. Thus, it must have functions for the human system. We should examine these consequences of religion for the human system.

Since religion emerged as one of the early elaborations of humans, it must have helped them meet problems of adaptation. Its persistence through the ages also indicates that it has been used to organize humans, although in new ways and forms. We can, at a very general level, visualize two universal functions of religion (Turner 1972): (1) reinforcing critical norms and (2) alleviating anxiety and tension. However, we must be cautious in not viewing the functions of religion as good or bad. Religion had been used by humans in certain ways that have had certain consequences. Whether these consequences are seen as good or bad is, of course, determined by one's own values. We must keep our analysis of the consequences in functions of an institution for society separate from our values of what "the good society" would be like. With this qualification, let us review the functions of religion.

Reinforcing Norms

Religious beliefs, values, and rituals reinforce crucial norms in other social contexts. By making norms appear as extensions of the supernatural order, they are given additional weight. People are less likely to violate norms that have been ordained by their gods. Again, the early sociologist, Émile Durkheim (1912), provided us with our first insights into this function of religion. He observed that ritual and other religious activities reinforced society. They were directed not just at the sacred and gods, but at society itself. In giving objects sacred powers and in possessing beliefs about the supernatural, people reinforced the social order—its values, norms, and networks of status roles—and gave it moral significance.

The Tikopian Islanders provide a geographic example of how religion reinforces other norms (Firth 1936). The Tikopia were a small island society in the South Pacific. Fishing was a crucial economic activity; it gave the Tikopia much of their protein. It was not surprising, therefore, that canoe preparation was also a religious ritual. Careful preparation of deep-sea fishing canoes was not just prudent, it was an obligation to the gods. The Tikopia can provide us with another example of religious reinforcement of critical social patterns. The Tikopia had a patrilineal descent system; that is, authority, wealth, power, and influence passed through the father's side of the family. Religious beliefs and norms required that the eldest male of a family maintain the temple where religious rituals to gods and ancestors were conducted. Moreover, women were excluded from many of these religious rituals. Although all this may seem like male chauvinism to moderns, such religious dictates reinforced the patrilineal descent system by investing important responsibilities in the eldest males and by excluding females from certain activities.

We can take yet another example of this consequence of religion from our cultural history. The genius of Max Weber, who figures prominently in almost all areas of sociology, provides us with this example. In a classic treatise Weber hypothesized that industrialization first emerged in Europe rather than Asia or some other continent because the religious beliefs of certain Protestant cults, particularly Calvinists, were conducive to capitalism (Weber 1904). By stressing this-world activity, hard work, thrift, and the accumulation of capital, Protestantism provided the critical push for economic development. People began to create, to invent, to accumulate, and to produce in accordance with religious beliefs. In Asia, which in many ways was more advanced technologically than Europe (knowledge of rocket power, advanced medical techniques, and developed mathematics), religious beliefs did not emphasize acquisitive striving to master one's fate—but just the opposite. Weber's thesis has been challenged and qualified, but there can be little doubt that Protestantism, at the very least, reinforced the emergence of the early capitalist economic systems of Europe and America.

Alleviating Anxiety and Tension

Imagine the fears, anxieties, and uncertainties of early humans: Would predators kill them? Would there be enough food tomorrow, next week, next year? Would one's mate die at childbirth? Would a person break a bone, become cut, or otherwise be injured and die? Social groups, of course, helped relieve much of this anxiety by providing companionship and support. But religious beliefs and rituals allowed humans to "do something" about their multiple and varied fears. They could pray to supernatural beings who controlled the earth. They could offer sacrifices. They could dance, sing, and exhort for help in dealing with the world. Religion thus allowed humans to release tensions and to sense that they had some control over the uncontrollable (Malinowski 1925).

DEFINING THE INSTITUTION OF RELIGION

Modern societies have eliminated some of the basic problems facing early humans. But modern societies have created new worries and anxiety: Will I get the promotion? Will I be laid off? What happens after death? People in more modern societies often have another problem: time and leisure. We have considerable time to ponder and embellish our mental life: What is life all about? What is the nature of humans and our place in the universe? Where is meaning and purpose to be found? What are the answers to the ultimate questions—life and death—of human existence. Humans have, of course, always thought about these questions, but modern people have the leisure time to ponder them extensively. For many, this pondering can create new anxieties and tensions that require an answer. Religion provides "answers" for many; it gives them a place to go, people to consult, and things to do in arriving at answers. Thus, it alleviates tensions for many people.

The religious revival among the young in America—born-again fundamentalists, Jesus Freaks, Hare Krishna, and other "new" religions—answer many questions and resolve many of the tensions for young people. In a society dominated by bureaucratic organizations, urban regions and corridors, and a constant striving for upward mobility, fervent religious involvement provides for some young a simpler way to deal with the complexities of modern life. Religion, then, still functions to alleviate anxiety and tension.

We are now in a position to define religion as an institution. We have seen that religion is composed of certain common elements: notions of the sacred and supernatural, beliefs, values, and ritual activities in cult structures. Religion has served throughout human history to reinforce critical norms and to alleviate anxieties and tensions. These features allow us to define the institution of religion as "that interrelated network of statuses, roles, and norms revolving around beliefs and rituals pertaining to the sacred and supernatural and organized into cult structures which have, at a minimum, consequences for reinforcing critical norms and managing variable sources of tension and anxiety in the human system" (Turner 1972, p. 349). This definition is, of course, an abstract one. It does not communicate the flavor, style, diversity, and intensity of religion in actual societies. But this definition does allow us to view religion in all societies as having certain common features. But we should begin to explore the diversity of religions in the world. Only in the general terms used so far are religions similar. In actual practice they vary, representing an important source of diversity in human systems.

Ritual Among the Mountain Gorilla

The existence of religion presupposes a large brain. It requires the ability to imagine realms, powers, and beings beyond the immediate, everyday world. It also involves beliefs, values, and normatively regulated rituals. Religion is thus exclusively human, and it probably became a part of the human system only after our ancestor's brains had reached the necessary size and complexity—perhaps one million years ago among those species we have termed *Homo erectus* (see Chapter 3).

Yet, we can observe the crudest beginning of ritual activity among some primates. Much like religious ritual, these stereotyped actions among primates appear to alleviate accumulated anxiety and tension. They are not religion because they are not directed at the supernatural or sacred. But they offer some clues about how primates—and we must remember that humans are primates—may be disposed to release tension.

The gorilla provides an example of an expressive ritual. Most of us are familiar with the spectacular chest beating of gorillas. But contrary to movie stereotypes, gorillas are not aggressive animals; indeed, they are rather quiet and passive compared to chimpanzees or baboons. Moreover, the chest beating is actually the climax of a more elaborate ritual. There are variations in the performance of the ritual, but it appears to be composed of a number of stages. It begins with hooting, a bipedal stance, a symbolic eating of a small piece of vegetation or the throwing about of leaves, kicking actions, and perhaps a brief run, and finally chest beating. The full ritual is thought to be performed only by older males, with females and younger males engaging in only certain of its elements. The young seem to learn many of the elements early, although not in the stereotypical sequence.

What does such a ritual do? First, for an animal as large as a gorilla, it scares would-be intruders. Second, it helps members of groups communicate and marks the presence of other gorilla groups. Yet, intimidation and communication are not its only "functions." The ritual is used in other contexts, and observers believe it to be a principal way to release tension—a way that is understood and respected by other members of the gorilla troop. It is not a far step to the animated religious dancing around open fires that marked our ancestor's first religious activity.

Source: George B. Schaller (1970).

THE DIVERSE FORMS OF RELIGION

Religion in Simple Societies: The Eskimo

Before its disruption by Western people and government, the traditional Eskimo system provided an example of religion in a simple society (Wallace 1966). Of course, although there was variation among Eskimo bands, their beliefs showed a common form. Beliefs in the supernatural consisted of a pantheon of spirits and gods. Some of the lesser gods were simply prominent humans and animals who had been accorded special status. Each individual, or a small group, had various minor spirits regulating their behavior. For example, a particular kin group might have its own ancestral spirits with whom they must reckon. Higher up in the pantheon were two primary gods—the Keeper of Sea Animals and the Spirit of the Air. The mythology about the life history and intervention into worldly affairs of these gods, however, varied from group to group. Moreover, the exact division of powers and hierarchy of control among these society-wide gods was somewhat blurred. Thus, religious beliefs among the Eskimo divided the universe into different realms, graduating from mortal humans through local spirits and ancestral souls to two higher gods.

---

[1]For basic references on the nature of religion in different societies, see Adams (1965); Bellah (1970, 1964); Berger (1967); Demerath and Hammond (1969); Glock (1973); Goode (1951); Lessa and Vogt (1958); Lowie (1948); Norbeck (1961); O'Dea (1970, 1966); Swanson (1960); Wallace (1966); and Yinger (1970).

Ritual activity was conducted primarily within kinship. Each Eskimo inherited "spirit helpers" through the patrilineal descent system—that is, from their father's side. These "helpers" guided and helped individuals in their daily lives. The wearing of little statuettes of walrus tusks, bags of pebbles, and small shells was required if one was to secure the help of these gods. Moreover, to get help, the person must refrain from killing the animals represented by these bodily adornments. A less individualistic form of ritual activity was required by the game-animal beliefs. People were required to observe certain taboos, such as not cooking land and sea animals together. Violations of taboos were to be confessed openly, and if an individual persisted in violations, banishment from the community ensued.

The only formal religious practitioners were part-time shaman. Shaman were to serve as intermediaries in calling upon the spirit helper for assistance. People who were suffering from ill health or fortune were assumed to have violated a taboo and to have offended a god, and thus, it was the shaman's job to find out which god had been violated or which taboo had been broken. Once the diagnosis was made, the shaman underwent a spiritual journey to rectify the situation.

In sum, the Eskimo have a form of religious organization that may resemble that of our hunting-and-gathering ancestors. Beliefs make only a few distinctions among supernatural realms and do not clearly specify relations among gods. Cult organization is coextensive with kinship, and ritual activity is individualistic and only sporadic. A number of taboos are observed, but these are not extensive. Such a religious system served the Eskimo well. It

*The traditional Eskimos revealed religious
patterns that fitted their simple economic system.*

helped alleviate anxiety by giving people a belief that "helpers" guided their lives and that consultation with the shaman could eliminate misfortune. It reinforced kinship norms and provided certain taboos which, in many cases, represented sound medical advice.

We can view the Eskimo religious system as a baseline. Other religious systems in more advanced societies reveal more complexity in their beliefs and in the organization of ritual activity. We should, therefore, briefly review the elaboration of religion in more complex human systems.

More Complex Religious Forms

There is a general trend in religious systems: a more complex belief system denoting clear supernatural realms and evidencing an elaborate pantheon of gods, more elaborate rituals conducted at specific times and places in clearly defined cult structures, and clear religious values dictating what is good and bad in human affairs. The complexity of religious beliefs and rituals appears to peak in traditional agricultural societies, after which a sudden reversal occurs: beliefs depict fewer gods and rituals become simplified. However, religious values remain explicit. Cult organization becomes highly complex, and by using new social technologies, it becomes bureaucratized. For example, the religions that now dominate the world—Christianity, Hinduism, Buddhism, Judaism, Confucianism, and Islamism—emerged out of, or replaced, religious systems with more elaborate pantheons of gods, myths of their feats, extended rituals, and tight-knit cult organizations.

Modern Religions

The trend in religious development over the last thousand years has been toward monotheism, or the worship of one god. For example, Islamism, Christianity, Judaism, and Confucianism clearly tend toward monotheism—Allah, God and the Trinity, God, and Tao, respectively, are the supreme powers in the supernatural realms of these religions. Hinduism and Buddhism, however, still have a more elaborate pantheon of gods. Religious mythologies have declined and are simplified in more contemporary religions. For instance, the myths concerning the activities of Krishna and Vishnu, the sequences of Buddhas, God and Moses, God and Jesus, Allah, the angel Gabriel, and Mohammed are very sparse compared to myths of earlier religions and to myths of religions in isolated pockets of traditional life. Compared to the jealousies, conflicts, rivalries, genealogies, and love affairs of earlier gods, the dominant religions of the world today are almost sedate.

Another critical difference between newer religions and those of the past is that, for the first time, beliefs emphasize that people have the potential for understanding the nature of both the everyday and supernatural worlds

(Bellah 1964, p. 367). For example, Hinduism not only holds out the prospect of better reincarnation in one's next life, but also the possibility of becoming a god. Christianity offers salvation after death. Islamism postulates paradise after death. Conversely, places in the supernatural realm are provided for those who are morally unworthy: hell, a poor reincarnation, and so on.

Values remain highly explicit in newer religions, for it is through conformity to values that people are able to qualify for access to supernatural realms. Thus, religious "codes of conduct" become a prominent feature of modern religions. The Ten Commandments, the sayings of Confucius, and the Noble Eightfold Path among Buddhists represent conspicuous examples.

Cult organization becomes more complex at the same time that pantheons, mythologies, and rituals are becoming simplified. The new social technology—bureaucracy (see Chapter 11)—is used to organize and extend religious influence. In nonindustrial societies this bureaucracy is often a powerful political force, and conflicts between political and religious leaders can become acute. With industrialization, however, this conflict declines as the political bureaucracy grows in power and separates the church bureaucracy from its sphere of influence.

The creation of bureaucratic organization in religions opens up new possibilities for conquering and conversion. Bureaucracies can mobilize resources toward explicit goals, and one of the goals of most modern religions is expansion. The result is that the world becomes dominated by relatively few religions as bureaucratically organized cults invade and displace more traditional religious practices.

Table 1: Membership in Dominant World Religions

	Millions of Members
Christian	900
Jewish	13
Moslem	500
Shinto	69
Taoist	54
Confucian	372
Buddhist	177
Hindu	436
Others, including traditional	900

The total religious membership in the eight religions is two and one-half times that of all other religions and is increasing. Such is the power of dominant religions to displace other religious forms.

Source: *Encyclopaedia Britannica Yearbook* (1974). Reprinted by permission.

RELIGION IN AMERICA[2]

Religion in America is a vast complex of cult structures. We can observe small cults or sects, such as various tent crusades, urban store-front churches, television ministries, one-church towns in rural America, and adaptations of Eastern religions like Hare Krishna, and other emerging cults. Dominating these smaller sects, however, are three large religious cults: Catholicism, Protestantism, and Judaism. This diversity of religious activity is the result of our unique history, and if we are to understand religion in America, we should briefly review this religious heritage.

The History of Religion in America

The first religions in America were, of course, those practiced by native Americans. The first settlers on America's shores were members of small Protestant cults (Herberg 1955; Williams 1970, p. 356). They settled in a religious vacuum, since there was no dominant religious system. Members of these cults were quite intolerant of other cults, despite the fact that they had often come to America to escape the very persecution that they were willing to practice on others. However, because the cults were small and because they were geographically dispersed, none could generate the resources and organization to eliminate the others. The

The small town church: symbol of religious activity in American communities.

result was the acceptance of religious diversity—an acceptance that was eventually codified into law.

These Protestant cults all revealed somewhat different adaptations of Protestant theology. But they did share one critical belief in common: there was to be a personal relationship between God and humans; each person was to "make peace" with God. The church

---

[2]For basic references on religion in America and the denominations that dominate religious activity in the United States, see Gallup (1974); Glenn and Hyland (1967); Glock (1973); Glock and Stark (1965); Herberg (1955); Johnstone (1975); Lenski (1963); Moberg (1962); Niebuhr (1957); Salisbury (1964); Stark and Glock (1968); Williams (1970, pp. 355–412); and Wilson (1969).

provided a place for common worship and ritual activity, but ultimately each person must actively come to terms with the supernatural. Such beliefs reinforced such dominant American values as individualism and activism (see Chapter 4). Individuals must be free to actively pursue their interests and to deal with the world around them. Thus, the Protestant cults of early America had beliefs that were to reinforce those values that, in turn, were to help stimulate industrial capitalism.

The rise of capitalism and the resulting urbanization of the American population encouraged much consolidation of religious cults. As we will examine shortly, Protestant cults became more bureaucratized on the national level, forming umbrella organizations for local church organizations. The expansion of industry also encouraged the migration of Europeans to this country in the latter half of the last century. With these European immigrants came the other two religious groups in America: Catholics and Jews.

Although early immigrants were subject to all manner of economic, political, and religious discrimination, the begrudging tolerance of Protestant cults for each other and the codification of this tolerance in the Constitution allowed the Catholic and Jewish religious groups to flourish.

Present-Day Religious Affiliation

These historical events established the general profile of religion in America: (1) toleration of small sects and new religions and (2) the dominance of Catholicism, Protestantism, and Judaism. This dominance can be seen by reading membership figures reported in Table 2:

Table 2: Estimated Religious Composition in America

Religious Affiliation		Percent of Adult Population
Protestants		64
Baptists	20	
Methodists	14	
Lutherans	9	
Presbyterians	5	
Episcopalians	2	
Other Protestants	14	
Roman Catholics		26
Jews		3
Other		2
No Religious Affiliation Reported		5
Total		100

Note: The above table averages statements made by a sample of Americans between 1970 and 1975.

Source: Gallup Opinion Index (1971, p. 71, 1976, pp. 34–37. Reprinted by permission.

As can be seen, America is predominately Protestant. The Catholic church, however, represents the single largest cult structure since Protestants are split into a number of separate denominations. Jews constitute a very small proportion of the total religious population.

If we break religious membership down into more groups and report estimates of their total membership (as opposed to the percent of the total, as shown Table 2), we get a better idea of the diversity of religious activity in the United States.

Table 3: Religious Affiliation

Religious Affiliation	Total Number
Roman Catholic	48,215,000
Baptist	25,001,000
Methodist	11,221,000
Lutheran	8,574,000
Jewish	5,870,000
Episcopalian	3,286,000
Mormon	2,037,000
United Church of Christ	1,961,000
Greek Orthodox	1,950,000
African Methodist Episcopal	1,166,000
Assembly of God	1,065,000
Presbyterian	958,000
Seventh-Day Adventist	420,000
Jehovah's Witnesses	389,000
Salvation Army	327,000
Unitarian	265,000
Black Muslim	250,000
Pentecostal	115,000
Mennonite	89,000

Source: *Yearbook of American Churches,* (1972). Reprinted by permission.

By reporting religious affiliation in this way, we can see that Catholics represent a large, single cult of 48 million, with the largest Protestant church being the Baptists with 25 million members. Jews now rank fifth with almost 6 million members. Also, we can see the diversity of affiliation, with a sizable number of smaller cult structures, such as the Black Muslims, Unitarians, Pentecostal Church of God, Salvation Army, and Jehovah's Witnesses.

Social Characteristics of Religious Members

Max Weber (1957) was perhaps the first sociologist to explore the relationship between religious activity and people's place in society. For example, he noted that urban artisans and shopkeepers of the eighteenth and nineteenth centuries were inclined to view the nature of the world much differently than farmers in the European countryside. The market economy and its emphasis on the exchange of goods, contract, and meeting one's financial obligations led urbanites to seek religious doctrines that emphasized control of events, whereas the farmers' uncertain existence among the unpredictable forces of nature led them to rely upon magic and other appeals to supernatural realms.

This initial insight still concerns sociologists. What background factors influence people's religious affiliations? What are the social characteristics of those in different religious cults? Most research in this area is, unfortunately, much narrower than Weber's original analysis. In American sociology emphasis has been placed upon the occupational, income, educational, familial, political and ethnic/racial correlates of religious affiliation. We can briefly summarize the findings of this research in the following manner.[3]

Religion and Occupation. In general Jews and Protestants are more likely to have greater career success than Catholics. They are more likely to be upwardly mobile to new, more prestigious occupations.

---

[3]The generalizations in the following sections were drawn from the following sources: Demerath (1965); Gallup Index (1969, pp. 22 and 32); Gallup Poll (1968); Glenn and Hyland (1967); Gockel (1969); O'Dea (1970); and Schneider (1952, p. 228).

Religion and Income. Income levels reveal a more complex picture than job classifications of religious groups. There is wide variation among Protestant religious groups, thus making comparisons among Jews, Catholics, and Protestants difficult. In general, Jews are overrepresented in comparison to their numbers in the general population in higher income groups than Catholics; and on the whole, Catholics do better than Protestants. But when Protestant groups are broken down, Episcopalians, Presbyterians, and Lutherans have higher average income levels than Catholics (but still less than Jews), whereas Baptists and Methodists earn less, on the average, than Catholics.

Religion and Education. Because of the connection between income and education, the data on religion and education show much the same pattern as those for income and religion. Jews are overrepresented in comparison to their numbers in the general population among college graduates, whereas Catholics and Protestants are just under the national average for college graduates. However, when Protestant groups are broken down and examined, Episcopalians and Presbyterians are well above the national average. Lutherans and Methodists are just under the average at about the same level as Catholics; and Baptists are considerably under the national average.

Religion and Family. Religion appears to influence the selection of marriage partners. People tend to choose marriage partners whose religious beliefs and affiliations are close to their own. Divorce is influenced by religion: intermarriage across religious lines is more likely to result in divorce (Barron 1972, p. 44), and rates for each religious group tend to vary, with Protestants more likely to end marriage than either Catholics or Jews (Lenski, 1963). Remarriage after divorce is higher among Protestants than Catholics.

Religion and Politics. The relationship between religion and politics is somewhat confounded by social class. Protestants are about equally split between the Democratic and Republican parties, but the wealthier Protestants—the Episcopalians and Presbyterians, for example—are much more likely to be Republican, whereas poorer memberships, such as Southern Baptists, are more likely to be Democratic. Catholics, who are predominately of ethnic origin and blue-collar, have clear preferences for the Democratic party. Jews present an inverse relationship between class and party affiliation. Although more likely to be affluent, they vote Democratic. Thus, we can see that there is some independent influence of religion upon political orientations.

Race, Ethnicity, and Religion. In general, the largest, single group of black Americans are Baptist, attesting to their southern roots. Blacks, however, have a wide variety of smaller church organizations that do not affiliate with the Baptist church. Brown-skinned minorities, such as Mexican-Americans and Puerto Ricans, are overwhelmingly Catholic. Oriental Americans tend to affiliate with churches corresponding to their class position, and since this group is predominately in the middle-class category, their affiliations tend to be Protestant. White ethnics, who migrated to the United States in the early part of this century are overwhelmingly Catholic since they come from southern and eastern Europe. Many from eastern Europe, of course, are Jewish. Most German, Swedish, Norwegians, and Danish immigrants are Protestant.

Strength of Religious Ties in America

Data on religious affiliation and on the social characteristics of church members do not inform us of the degree of "religiosity" or "religious commitment" of these members. It is one matter to assert that "I'm a Catholic," but another to guide your life by such affiliation. Indeed, we can belong to a church, but never attend, except at Christmas, or we can avoid church membership but be profoundly religious. Thus, in order to get a picture of religion in America, we must know what religious affiliations mean to people. This is no easy matter to determine, however. But we should review what data are available.

Church Attendance. We can get an initial picture of "religiosity" in America by examining church attendance. Church attendance appears to have dropped and now leveled off. The Gallup Poll, for example, reports the following results on church attendance for the years 1955, 1960, 1965, 1970, and 1973. The figures show that the proportion of people who report attending church weekly has dropped for Catholics and Protestants (Gallup 1974):

Year	Catholics	Protestants
1955	72%	40%
1960	74%	44%
1965	67%	38%
1970	60%	38%
1973	55%	37%

Catholic attendance appears to have suffered more than Protestant. This fact is buttressed by other data on Catholics' performance of ritual activities. For example, Andrew Greeley (*Personal Communication*) and his associates have reported that the percentage of Catholics performing rituals such as daily prayer, making a Day of Recollection, and reading spiritual works has declined. However, the percentage receiving weekly communion has increased.

Protestant religiosity is more difficult to assess. Protestant churches, in general, have placed less emphasis on ritual activity. Attendance at church has often been the only required ritual, with individuals making "their own peace with God." Similarly, Jews' attendance at the synagogue has never been an accurate sign of religiosity, since attendance is highly variable. Performance of rituals outside the temple has often been given much more emphasis, and it appears that many of these rituals are still performed by Jews in the home.

Thus, church attendance does not provide clear information about people's religious commitment. Protestants and Jews have traditionally tended to be more individualistic than Catholics, emphasizing only a few key rituals. Catholics now appear to be approximating this pattern—lower attendance, but increased participation in such important rituals as taking communion. Yet, these conclusions tell us little about people's beliefs. Do they still believe in God? Do they interpret their dogmas literally? Do sacred objects still evoke powerful emotions and sentiments? It is difficult to assess the intensity of people's emotions, but sociologists Charles Glock and Rodney Stark (1965) attempted to provide at least some answers to

Table 4: Beliefs about God

Religious Groups	God exists	Some doubts, but believe God exists	Sometimes believe in God, other times not	No personal God, but there is a higher power	Don't know and no way to know if God exists	No God
Catholics	81%	13%	1%	3%	1%	—
Protestants	71%	17%	2%	7%	1%	—
Congregationalists	41%	34%	4%	16%	2%	1%
Episcopalians	63%	19%	2%	12%	2%	—
Disciples of Christ	76%	20%	—	—	—	—
Presbyterians	75%	16%	1%	7%	1%	—
American Baptists	78%	18%	—	2%	—	—
Southern Baptists	99%	1%	—	—	—	—
Sects	96%	2%	—	1%	—	—

Source: Glock and Stark (1965, p. 91). Adapted from Glock and Stark, *Religion and Society in Tension* (Chicago: Rand McNally, 1965). Reprinted by permission.

the question of the nature of people's religious beliefs for Protestants, Catholics, and smaller sects. Their results are summarized in Table 4.

We can see, then, that the vast majority of Protestants and Catholics claim to believe in God. Yet, there is considerable variation among Protestant churches. Thus, we can only conclude that people in America are religious to the extent that most believe in God, a large majority belong to an organized cult structure, about 35% to 55% go to church weekly, and an even higher proportion perform important rituals.

Just whether there is a decline or increase in religiosity in American society is difficult to assess. We might conclude, however, with a brief examination of those people for whom religion does appear to be growing in influence and importance.

The Appearance of New Sects in America

In different parts of the country, we can observe an increased intensity of religious beliefs. Certain religious groups appear to be growing. These all share one thing in common: a religious fundamentalism in which the Bible or some other text is given literal interpretation, and ritual activities that are invested with high emotion. Groups such as the Assemblies of God, Pentecostalists, Evangelicals, and the Southern Baptist Convention are growing rapidly. Other, more traditional church cults, such as the Mormons and Seventh-Day Adventists, are also expanding, apparently because

they offer the individual total religious involvement and life-style dominated by the church.

The evidence on this religious revival in the midst of an industrial, urban society guided by the scientific ethic and technology is, to say the least, an interesting occurrence. The evidence indicates that such a society can be highly alienating and impersonal. As we noted earlier, it can create new sources of tension and anxiety in people. Religion can provide a place to go, a sense of personal involvement, a path of action, and a set of guiding beliefs for many of these who suffer such experiences.

The Jesus people—or "Jesus Freaks" as they are often called by traditionalists—provide an example of these forces at work. A number of studies have been conducted on these groups, but we will examine the results of only one (Adams & Fox 1972). These investigators began by attending the nondenominational congregation of Jesus people in Orange County, California—probably the most suburban and conservative county in the state. Over a thousand persons attend services, which consist of rock music and exhortations by young, charismatic lay preachers. Most in attendance are under 20 and a high proportion are young girls. Songs are sung; prayers are offered; testimonials from those who have been "saved" and "cured" were given, the Bible is read, and about 100 are presented for confirmation. The authors conclude that these teen-agers seek peer approval and resolution of adolescent identity crises through this religious involvement. As we noted in our discussion of socialization in Chapter 7 and in our analysis of the family in the last chapter, adolescence can prove extremely stressful, particularly for middle-class teen-agers who will often be forced to prolong their nonadult status into their early 20s. Religious fervor and peer group activity can help alleviate much of the stress and anxiety associated with this prolonged adolescence.

The investigators also ventured outside Orange County in an effort to contact older members of this religious group. They found them in communes scattered along the California coast. Most were drop-outs from the drug culture, seeking to "clear their heads" and to "get in touch" with people again. The communes had strict segregation of the sexes and traditional male/female division of labor (men worked outside, women did the domestic chores). Moreover, the virtues of traditional marriage were emphasized by leaders and members. These communes, then, provided an emotional sanctuary for obviously distraught people, while reinforcing traditional family norms for those who had "dropped out."

These Jesus people emphasize the functions of religion for people in modern societies. Religion can still provide support for many who have experienced anxieties and tensions and left dominant institutions. In the midst of a highly secular society, then, the Jesus people offer testimony to the functions of religion in society.

The Jesus Movement can provide a sense of involvement for some young people in America.

SUMMARY AND PREVIEW

In this chapter we have examined the institution of religion. Religion was one of humans' earliest inventions and it is still a universal feature in human societies, having these certain common elements: (1) a notion of the sacred and supernatural, (2) beliefs and values, and (3) cult organization and ritual activity. Throughout the course of human evolution, and even in modern, secular societies, religion has served at least two functions: (1) reinforcing norms and (2) alleviating anxiety and tension.

We have sought to understand the diversity of religious forms and the general trends in religious evolution. In general, religious development is somewhat curvilinear; that is, it moves from simplicity to great complexity, and then, in more modern times, it becomes more simplified in its beliefs and values, while remaining bureaucratically complex.

We examined the American religious system in some detail. Religion in America is a congerie of small, sectlike cults that exist alongside three dominant cult organizations: Catholicism, Protestantism, and Judaism. Religion still exerts some influence on people's jobs, income levels, education, marriage patterns, and political references. Religious affiliations also vary with race and ethnicity. Although it is difficult to assess people's religiosity, Americans are still religious but less likely to adhere strictly to ritual activities. Among many Americans, particularly some of the young, religiosity and conformity to rituals appears to be very strong. Religion, then, still appears to serve its traditional functions for many segments of the population.

We have now completed an analysis of two human institutions: kinship and religion. Implicit in much of this analysis has been the hidden power and force of economic institutions; much of what occurs to kinship and religion is the result of economic forces. Under the impact of industrialization, a society becomes more secular, altering the profile of religion to a monotheism with simplified rituals and changing the family to a conjugal form with less emphasis on descent and residence norms. We are now ready to examine this basic institution. It is one of the prime movers of the human system. We could not understand much about a society—the structure of its institutions and other forms of social organization, such as groups, organizations, classes, communities—without knowledge of economic processes. Therefore, we will discuss this basic social institution in the next chapter.

Key Terms

Sacred: objects, persons, and places that are the stimulus to emotional arousal and that are believed to possess special powers and significance

Supernatural: a belief in a special realm, beyond everyday life, where the forces, spirits, powers, and beings, seen as influencing the operation of the world, reside

Religious Beliefs: people's shared conceptions of what is to be seen as sacred and what is to be defined as the supernatural realm

Pantheon: a complex of supernatural beings who are seen to have specific relationships with each other

Religious Values: conceptions that people hold about what the sacred and supernatural define as good and bad, appropriate and inappropriate

Ritual: stereotyped role behaviors directed toward the sacred and supernatural

Cult: the social unit in which religious rituals are performed and which provides a place of membership for those who share religious beliefs

Review Questions

1. What are the basic elements of all religions?

2. What are the universal functions of religion in society?

3. What are some of the prominent trends in religions throughout the world?

4. How did the circumstances of America's history influence contemporary religious organization in the United States?

5. How are job, income, education, politics, and family patterns related to religion?

Suggested Readings

Adams, J. ed. *A Readers Guide to the Great Religions.* New York: The Free Press, 1965.

Bellah, Robert N. *Beyond Belief: Essays on Religion in a Post-Traditional World.* New York: Harper & Row, 1970.

Glock, Charles, and Stark, Rodney. *Religion and Society in Tension.* Chicago: Rand McNally, 1965.

Herberg, Will. *Protestant-Catholic-Jew: An Essay in American Religious Sociology.* New York: Doubleday, 1955.

O'Dea, Thomas. *Sociology and the Study of Religion.* New York: Basic Books, 1970.

———. *The Sociology of Religion.* Englewood Cliffs, N.J.: Prentice-Hall, 1966.

Wallace, Anthony F. C. *Religion: An Anthropological View.* New York: Random House, 1966.

Wilson, Bryan. *Religion in Secular Society.* Baltimore: Penguin Books, 1969.

Yinger, Milton J. *The Scientific Study of Religion.* London: Macmillan, 1970.

THE ECONOMY

PROLOGUE

Guiding Questions: What must a species do to survive? What is an economy? How does it help humans survive? In what ways has the economy changed? How does the economy now control our lives?

Chapter Topics

The most basic issue facing all species is getting enough to eat. We cannot survive without food. Moreover, since we have thin and unprotected skin, we often require clothing and shelter in many parts of the world. The quest for food, clothing, and shelter is, as we will come to see in this chapter, an economic activity. Much of what our hominid ancestors did in their small bands and kinship units was economic. They gathered berries, roots, and nuts; they stole meat from other animals or took what was left over; and they eventually learned to hunt. These activities were carried on for millions of years. The human and prehuman economy was thus simple, for it yielded only subsistence levels of nourishment.

Perhaps it is difficult for us to view the world this way. We live in a society of large-scale and mechanized agriculture, mass industrial production, and conspicuous consumption of goods and services. If we hunt, it is for pleasure, and to gather roots would be beneath the dignity of most of us. Yet, agriculture was discovered only 10,000 years ago, and industrial production began a mere 250 years ago.

This rapid change in our economic system has, of course, brought far-reaching changes to the human system. We have already seen some of these changes in previous chapters: the proliferation of bureaucracy, the growth of urban regions, the high incidence of collective behavior, the attenuation of kinship, and the alteration of religion. We will see more changes in later chapters. It is clear, then, that we cannot truly understand the human system in its present form or in its past forms without examining the institution of the economy. So much of what occurs in society, in culture, and to individuals is influenced by the basic institution; therefore, we must understand its operation.

In this chapter we will first discuss the elements that all economies have in common. Then we will examine the universal functions of the economy. Next, we will try to understand the diversity of economic forms and some of the trends that they reveal. Finally, we will explore the American economy, an institution that profoundly influences all of our lives.

BASIC ELEMENTS OF ECONOMIC LIFE

Western economists consider the basic elements of an economy to be **land, labor, capital,** and **entrepreneurship.** Sociologists and anthropologists often consider **technology,** as a fifth element. Although these elements are often used to describe Western industrial capitalism, they can also be used to describe the economies of very simple hunters/gatherers as well as those of communist and socialist nations. Let us briefly define each of these five elements. (Turner 1972, pp. 18–20).

Land

This concept denotes more than real estate. It is used to describe the natural resources available to a society—oil, timber, coal, animals, agricultural acreage, lumber, uranium, minerals, gas, and the like. Societies differ tremendously in their access to various resources. Some are simple and cannot gain access to such resources as fossil fuels and key minerals. Although other societies have the ability to gain access, they do not have indigenous resources and must seek them in other societies. Thus, the question of resources is not one of how much a society has in, or beneath, its soil, but rather, the issue is the degree of access that a society has to its own resources or those of other societies.

Labor

Labor is the expenditure of human energy or effort. How much and what kind of labor exists in a society is, of course, influenced by many factors. For example, when people only know how to farm, labor will be directed toward agricultural activities. When people are concentrated into urban areas composed of factories, then labor will be much different. Labor varies in terms of such matters as (1) the knowledge and skill of workers, (2) their motivation to assume, and the ability to play, certain economic roles, (3) the degree to which labor is concentrated or dispersed, and (4) the nature and kinds of economic roles available to labor.

Capital

This concept denotes the nature and type of tools used to perform economic tasks. Sometimes capital is extremely simple and involves a digging stick or bow and arrow. In other societies it is very complex and includes factories, machines, and money to buy machines and equipment.

Entrepreneurship

This is an illusive term, because it has so many connotations. Our usage will be restricted: entrepreneurship refers to the way, manner, and degree of organization among such economic elements as land, labor, technology, and capital. In some societies this organization occurs through factories, offices, corporations, and other ways of organizing economic activity. In more simple societies the kinship system is a source of entrepreneurship, since kinship norms determine how the other economic elements are to be organized.

Technology

This concept denotes knowledge about how to control and manipulate the environment. There is wide variability in the knowledge in the culture of a society. Sometimes the cultural storehouse, as we termed it in Chapter 4, contains limited knowledge about the roots, berries, and animals available in different seasons and of how one goes about securing these resources from the environment with digging sticks and spears. In societies like ours, technology is vast; we know how to control, manipulate, and even destroy the environment.

Thus, economies vary in terms of the level of, and organization among, technology, labor, capital, and land. A given level of technology or knowledge allows for certain types of capital formation which, in turn, influences the composition of labor. All together, they become organized in certain ways, thereby allowing for a certain level of access to resources or land. The elements of the economy combine in ways that give each society its own distinctive economy. But as we will see, economies can be grouped or classified into certain distinct types. (Cole 1969). Before we examine how technology, capital, labor, entrepreneurship, and land combine to form distinctive types of economies, however, we must discover what an economy actually is and what it does for the human system. We will be in a position to define the institution of the economy after we review its functions or what it accomplishes for the human system.

Technologies and the use of tools can be exceedingly simple or complex. Here hunter-gatherers use digging sticks while two men work the coke ovens of a giant steel plant.

THE FUNCTIONS OF THE ECONOMY

In order to survive, humans must gather raw materials from their environment. They must convert these materials into usable nourishment and shelter, and they must have some way of sharing or distributing what they produce. Species of prehumans that could not do these things did not survive. Those that were able to gather resources, produce usable materials, and distribute them to group members were more likely to survive and reproduce themselves.

These processes describe the basic functions of the economy: (1) **gathering** resources, (2) **producing** usable goods and services, (3) **distributing** these goods and services, and (4) **servicing** these other economic processes in complex economies.

Gathering

We must gather resources from the environment to survive. Just what we gather and how we do so are determined by basic economic elements: technology, capital, labor, and entrepreneurship. In a society with little knowledge or technology about how to extract resources, there is likely to be only a rudimentary level of capital formation—perhaps digging sticks, spears, bows and arrows. More developed societies might have ox-drawn plows, a system of irrigation, and crude milling tools. Highly advanced societies have mechanized farms, high-yield mines, drilling, and other extractive machinery.

Organization of labor, technology, and capital for resource extraction will vary, of course. Simple societies will be organized around kinship, and the labor pool will be groups of kin

Gathering resources can be extremely complex and costly, as is the case for extracting oil.

who are skilled in various economic activities. In more developed agrarian and industrial societies, new principles of organization will become evident. Tenant farms, farms with wage labor, or a system of unionized wage earners who work with complex machines are likely to emerge, thus decreasing the reliance upon kinship as a means of organizing labor, technology, and capital in the gathering of resources.

*Gathering resources can also be simple, as is
illustrated by the use of the camel-drawn plow.*

Producing

What is gathered often must be converted into usable goods. As with gathering, the nature of production will vary in societies with different technologies, types of capital, labor skills, and entrepreneurship. A society with limited knowledge of available resources, with spears, grinding stones, and crude cookwear, bone needles, and knives, with a labor force limited to the use of such tools, and with organization of labor and other economic elements by kinship, will be limited in what it can produce: cooked food, ground roots, animal-skin clothing, and temporary shelters. In contrast, a society with vast knowledge of resources, with new sources of energy such as oil, coal, and uranium, with vast capital in the form of facto-

Distributing functions can be both simple and complex. The simple market pictured at the right is vastly different from the modern department store, and yet, both are examples of distributing functions of the economy.

ries, with urban labor forces ready to enter a labor market, and with market and bureaucratic principles of organization will be able to produce vast quantities and varieties of goods. Our own experiences in American society can attest to this fact. For most of human history, however, production has been highly limited, yielding little beyond a subsistence level of existence.

Distributing

What is produced must be distributed. We are so accustomed to modern market processes, with all the advertising, high-pressure sales, and easy flow of money and credit, that it is easy to forget that many societies do not have a market. Rather, goods are distributed equally, or by rank, within kinship units. There is no advertising, haggling, bargaining, credit, money, or any of the other items that we associate with the modern market. In fact, except for occasional trading among tribes,

markets did not become a prominent feature of the human system until the beginning of agriculture—a mere 10,000 years ago.

Thus, we can see that the basic economic elements of technology, capital, labor, land or resources, and entrepreneurship can influence how goods are distributed. When little surplus can be produced because of limited technology, capital, and resources and when kinship is the major societal unit, distribution remains very simple. When a surplus is produced, when labor is freed from kinship, and when technology, capital, and entrepreneurship allow for more elaborate gathering-and-producing activities, then an entirely new system of distribution must occur. New marketing technologies become essential; new kinds of labor skills in advertising, selling, and merchandising, become prominent; new forms of capital formation, such as warehouses, transportation systems, and retail outlets, become a necessity; and new forms of organizing exchanges of goods—markets, money, credit, banks, insurance, and the like—come to prominence.

Servicing

We noted earlier that something called services are often produced and distributed. Services are not hard goods or products, but they are essential in developing economies. Services are difficult to define in the abstract, but we might call them those skills that are produced and distributed to facilitate the operation of the other basic economic processes: gathering, producing, and distributing. Imagine, for example, a modern economy without bankers, insurance, bookkeeping, data processing, market forecasting, salespeople, personnel officers, managers, and the myriad of roles necessary to operate an economy. Services in very simple societies are performed by kin. But in societies with markets and with greater volumes of goods, new roles, such as bookkeeping and sales, emerge. The small shopkeepers and artisans of Egypt, Rome, or feudal Europe could perform these roles themselves, or members of their family could perform them. But they marked the beginning of a "servicing revolution" in which machines do much of the gathering and producing; and people increasingly perform services for each other and for maintaining the society.

Thus, although the first humans did not require service roles to survive, modern societies have so expanded their needs and expectations about what constitutes "subsistence" that society could not "survive" without service positions and organizations. At least, it could not exist as we have come to know it. Services, then, become one of the major "products" that are produced and distributed in human economic systems. We will come to appreciate this fact even more as we proceed with our discussion.

DEFINING THE ECONOMY AS AN INSTITUTION

We can now define the economy as a social institution. We have seen that economies are composed of five elements and that there are four basic economic processes. These elements and processes are related: the technology, capital, labor, access to resources (land), and organizational principles (entrepreneurship) of a society influence the way that statuses, roles, and norms will be organized around gathering, producing, distributing, and servicing.

Like all social forms, the economy is a structure composed of status positions, normative regulations, and enacted role behaviors. Clustering these into any social form—from a small kinship group to a large multinational corporation—that is involved in gathering resources, producing goods and services, and distributing these goods and services, has an economic aspect. We can thus define the economy as "all of those interrelated statuses, norms, and roles that are organized into various social forms and that are related to gathering resources, producing goods and services, and distributing these goods and services . . . " (Turner 1972, p. 22). With this definition in hand, and with an understanding of what it entails, we can proceed to examine different types of economies and to compare them to the American economy.

Tool Use Among Chimpanzees

Here, a Chimpanzee fashions a reed to use in termite gathering. In so doing, the Chimpanzees make and use tools—a capacity that was once thought to be solely the ability of humans.

We ordinarily do not think of the eating activities of animals as economic behavior; but such activities can be considered economic. They involve gathering and distributing food. For example, many animals hunt collectively and share their catch. What supposedly separated humans from other animales is that we use tools—or in economic terms, capital—in our gathering activities. It is this capacity to use tools that, as we observed in Chapter 3, accelerated the development of the human system. We now know, however, that our closest relative can also make tools—or capital.

Chimpanzees enjoy eating termites, which are a delicacy, but they are hard to get at. They live in mounds and hills, and if an animal just tears the hill apart, it will not get many termites. They will scatter all over the landscape. Picking up and eating a single termite is not likely to prove very satisfying. Chimpanzees were once spurred to invention. They now make a tool for eating termites. Much like our ancestors millions of years ago, necessity, or in this case, luxury, was a stimulus to the creation and use of tools. It is, of course, this capacity that makes economic systems as we know them possible.

Chimps learned that if they shaped a reed or long piece of grass in a certain way, they could insert it into termite holes. Termites would then walk along the inserted reed (now a tool). As the termites walk and fill up the reed, the chimp pulls the reed carefully from the hole and enjoys a nice treat of termites, neatly lined up on this tool.

This act of tool-making presupposes a certain brain size and complexity. The chimp must be capable of imagining the act of tool use in its mind. It must then find the right raw material, shape it in just the right way, insert it, and know what the termites will do. Only chimps can do this. Baboons have watched chimps catch and eat termites in this way, but they cannot "grasp" the complex operations. They never make tools, and even though they also like termites, they are not able to enjoy them in quantity because they persist in trying to catch them with their "bare hands."

Tool use—the basis of our economy—is thus the result of certain cognitive capacities. Our ancestors probably had about the same capacities as the chimpanzee, but as they encountered the hostile world of the savannah, tool use had selective value. Tool use was needed not to just secure luxuries like termites, but to survive. It is out of this selection process that the institution of the economy was born.

Source: Lancaster (1975).

TYPES OF ECONOMIC ORGANIZATION

Hunting-and-Gathering Economies[1]

For most of our existence as a species, we were gatherers. We also hunted small game, but most of a society's food came from gathering. Even with the advent of big-game hunting, day-to-day subsistence came from plant foods. Contrary to many stereotypes about the difficulty and hardships faced by gatherers and hunters, the people of these simple societies have been able to secure ample food. Even contemporary bands, who have been pushed onto the least desirable land by industrial and agrarian people, are able to survive without great effort. It is only recently, with the prolonged African drought, that such people have suffered severe malnutrition.

Although these economies have many unique features, they also have a number of common characteristics. First, there is a sexual division of labor—men hunt and women gather. This means that the labor of women is of more value in securing food than that of men. Second, women perform most of the domestic chores—caring for children, preparing food, and cooking meals. Men conduct hunts, usually alone but sometimes in small groups. Third, there is considerable free time for all. Women sit in groups and talk as they do their chores; men often gamble; and children

[1]For analyses of simple economic systems, see Belshaw (1965); Nash (1966); Service (1966); and Spier (1970).

play and rehearse the adult roles that they will assume. Fourth, economic activity is organized by kinship, with small groups of kin, rarely numbering over 50 persons, wandering over territories. Life is nomadic, but it is relaxed except during a drought or other unusual conditions. Fifth, there is little inequality in these societies, for there is not much to distribute unequally. Although they play different roles, men and women are equals, with the most noticeable inequalities existing between adults and children.

Hunting and gathering societies thus have a simple technology; little capital except digging sticks, cookwear, spears, and perhaps bows and arrows; limited access to resources; and kinship as the means for organizing economic activity. It is from such economic forms that more elaborate economic systems have evolved.

Agrarian Economies

About 10,000 years ago, a revolution occurred—a revolution in technology that forever changed the nature of the human system. This revolution is termed the **Neolithic,** and it revolved around the discovery of agriculture. For the first time, people learned how to cultivate, plant, and derive their food from the conscious manipulation of the soil. They also learned how to herd animals. Thus, rather than hunt and seek plant foods through gathering, humans could remain in one place, plant their food, and herd animals. Life assumed new dimensions heretofore impossible. First, agricultural pro-

duction generated more food, thus allowing societies to grow in size. Second, both men and women often performed the same economic roles, although men typically left much of the work to women. Third, kinship in the first agrarian economies remained the major organizing principle, although it became more elaborate since there were larger populations to coordinate (see Chapter 16 on kinship). Fourth, new principles of organization began to appear. Stable communities were possible, setting into motion a more urban way of life. Political leaders often emerged as one kin group came to dominate others. Markets where goods, labor, and services were traded expanded and became a major mechanism of distribution. Money came into use as a means for determining the value of goods, labor, and services. Inequality and stratification became more pronounced as some hoarded more resources than others. Warfare became a more frequent event as stable communities fought each other for territory, resources, and power.

Agrarian economies have enormous variation. The first were small and simple. The most elaborate, such as Egypt, Greece, the Roman Empire, and the preindustrial states of Europe had large populations, large cities, state governments, elaborate religions, vast inequalities, and perpetual warfare and internal conflict. Thus, agriculture allowed for the emergence and elaboration of many of the social forms

There are vast differences in the way tools are used in agrarian and industrial economies.

discussed in the chapters of the previous section: state and church bureaucracies, urban communities, and stratification.

Today, there are still many agrarian societies in Africa, Asia, and South America. Yet, they are doomed to pass from the world system under the impact of industrialization. Agriculture will, of course, remain a vital component of any economy, but its organization will be mechanized and most of a society's population will assume other economic roles.

Industrial Economies

Around 250 years ago, another technological revolution occurred—the industrial revolution. New technologies allowed for the use of new sources of power—water, steam, and eventually oil, coal, and uranium—to be harnessed to new forms of capital—machines. Increasingly, machines became concentrated in factories, setting into motion a dramatic series of events. The population became highly urbanized as it located near factories (Smelser 1959). Money markets for labor, goods, and services completely replaced kinship as the distributing mechanism (Belshaw 1965). Bureaucracies and factories organized economic activity. The state and government regulated economic and social life. (Reagan 1963). Today inequalities remain, although not as vast as in advanced agrarian societies. Kinship becomes less pervasive, loses many functions, and assumes primarily mating, social support, and socialization functions. New socialization structures, such as education, extend to the masses in an effort to train labor. Warfare remains prominent, but with the capacity to destroy the species. For the first time, agricultural, industrial, and urban pollution pose a severe threat to the world ecosystem.

Postindustrial Economies

Industrial economies revolve around machines and factories. Postindustrial economies mechanize and automate many gathering and production functions. Hence, economic roles increasingly revolve around distributing and servicing functions (Bell 1973; Fuchs 1966). People increasingly assume jobs that involve market and service activities: selling, advertising, banking, investing, insuring, administering, managing, repairing, and other nonfactory and nonagricultural jobs.

Postindustrial economies extend the trends stimulated by industrialization, such as the use of money and markets, bureaucratization, urbanization, and extension of educational institutions, the growth of the state and government, inequality between classes, and the limitation of kinship functions. It also increases people's material well-being and their leisure time. Social life becomes dominated by material consumption and the use of leisure. We are all familiar with these trends, of course, because we are experiencing them in the United States—the most postindustrial country of the world's economic system.

In just a short time period, then, the human system has undergone dramatic changes. From simple hunting-and-gathering societies, the institution of the economy has dramatically changed. New technologies, massive capital formation, unbelievable access to land or resources, a diversified and highly specialized labor force, and markets and bureaucracies as entrepreneurial tools have dramatically altered all social forms and all social institutions.

Since *Homo erectus* first revealed more truly humanlike qualities some one million years ago (see Chapter 3), our ancestors have been gatherers and hunters until a mere 10,000 years ago. We evolved as a species in response to a much simpler way of life, and thus, it is not surprising that we often have difficulty coping psychologically with the pace and tempo of a postindustrial society. Our social and cultural development have occurred at a fast rate, whereas biologically we remain not much different than our ancient ancestors. The contrasts between the lives of hunters and gatherers on the one hand and our daily lives as Americans on the other underscore the changes in the human system, between what we were and what we have become.

MODERNIZATION AND SOCIAL LIFE[2]

The process of social change stimulated by the progress of the economy from an agricultural to industrial form, and then, from an industrial to postindustrial profile, is termed **modernization.** The process of modernization, however, involves much more than economic change. Alteration in a society's economy influences change of the social and cultural fabric, as well as the personality of individuals. However, we must remember that although changes in the economy probably initiate major changes in society, culture, and individuals, alterations in the personality of individuals, in basic social forms, in cultural beliefs, values, and norms, and in basic institutions feed back upon the economy and influence events in the economy. Our concern now, however, is with what occurs to the rest of the human system with the development of an industrial economy.

Changing Culture

Basic values and beliefs are altered with industrialization. Beliefs become secular and stress the importance of scientific, rational, and efficient activity. Similarly, values increasingly emphasize achievement, progress, and mastery of nature.

Changing Personality

Although each individual possesses a unique personality, there are similarities in how individuals in modernizing societies are likely to behave. Modernization influences people's motives, their internal directives, the standards that they use for self-evaluation, and their role-playing style. People become more achievement motivated; they are guided by a desire to master and control their environment; they assess themselves in terms of their accomplishments and progress in the occupational world; and they assume a more impersonal and neutral style in many social contexts.

Changing Social Forms

With industrialization, large-scale bureaucracy becomes a major principle of social organization. Much of our daily life is spent in proliferating bureaucracies. Yet, we still seek emotional refuge in primary groups, such as the family, friendships, and informal work groups. Stratification is increasingly along occupational lines, as people's income, prestige, and power are determined by the nature of their jobs. Great inequalities persist, but there is some redistribution of income. Moreover, the use of ascribed criteria, such as race, birth place, religion, and family, for placing people in society declines, as emphasis is placed upon achievement and performance. Community forms become increasingly urban, as the small village and town give way to the large city which, in turn, becomes surrounded by the suburbs that form the metropolis and urban region. Ethnic and racial groups frequently become solidified with early industrialization, as groups become associated with certain occupations. But through increasing contact,

---

[2]For basic references on modernization, see Etzioni and Etzioni (1964); Hoselitz and Moore (1963); Hunter (1969); Moore (1974); Moore (1955); and Parsons (1966).

conflict, and assimilation, many barriers separating ethnic and racial groups begin to break down during postindustrialization. Finally, social organization becomes more fluid as all forms of collective behavior—fads, fashion, crazes, panics, crowds, and movements—become more prominent.

Changing Institutions

As one of the basic social forms, institutions also undergo change with modernization. The family is perhaps the most profoundly affected; it becomes nuclear, no longer performing production and many of its functions. Religious beliefs become simplified and secular, although churches remain bureaucratized. Formal education, as we will see in a later chapter, expands and assumes many functions that were previously performed by the family. Government becomes increasingly centralized and comes to regulate many diverse activities.

Changing Population

With industrialization, death rates decline with the spread of medical facilities. Yet, birth rates remain high for a period, thereby precipitating a sudden leap in the size of the population. But over time, birth rates decline and reach a zero rate of growth in postindustrial systems (we will explore these issues in Chapter 22).

Changing the Ecosystem

The production and consumption of wide varieties and larger numbers of goods creates pollution problems for all industrializing societies and for the global ecosystem. Natural flows and cycles that maintain the air, water, and soil are disrupted, and the potential for profound ecological problems escalates dramatically (see Chapter 21).

As we can see, modernization shatters old social forms, old beliefs and values, old ways of thinking and acting. Such is the power of the economy to shape and influence our lives in the human system.

Figure 1: Percentage of Labor Force in Different Types of Economic Roles
Source: ILO, Yearbook of Labor Statistics (Geneva, 1972).

Agricultural Societies

India

Bolivia

Industrial

USSR

Industrializing

Poland

Postindustrial Societies

USA

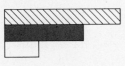

France

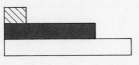

```
  0  10  20  30  40  50  60  70  80  90  100
```
Percentages of Work Force
in Agriculture, Industry, or Service

Agriculture   Industry   Service

THE AMERICAN ECONOMY

The American economy has arrived at a postindustrial stage. High levels of technology and massive expenditures of money on machines have decreased the proportion of the labor force involved in gathering and producing. This trend is emphasized by the increasing proportion of white-collar to blue-collar and farm workers as shown in Figure 1. The composition of the labor force thus changes with postindustrialization. It becomes better educated and concentrated around distribution and servicing functions of the economy.

These changes in the composition of the labor force produced by new technologies and machines are paralleled by dramatic changes in the way economic activity is organized. This is what we have termed the entrepreneurial element of the economy. Economic life in America has become increasingly controlled by large corporations, large labor unions, and big government. It is in the interaction of government, labor organizations, and corporations that most of the dynamics of the American economic system unfold. (Williams 1970, pp. 183–188). Thus, we should examine a number of trends in (1) corporate organization, (2) organization of labor, and (3) involvement of government in economic affairs.

Corporations

The **corporation** in the American economy is one of the primary means by which capital, technology, labor, and resources (land) are organized for economic activity. By issuing stocks to the public, money, or "liquid capital," is secured. This money is then used to buy technologies, "permanent capital," such as machines and equipment, necessary materials or resources, and labor. Corporations tend to concentrate on one of the basic economic processes: gathering, producing, distributing, or servicing. Gathering corporations sell their materials to producing companies that produce new forms of materials, such as steel from iron ore, which are then bought by other producing corporations, such as appliance companies, that make consumer goods. These goods are then marketed by separate distributing companies, such as retail department stores. Each corporation is likely to have its own servicing personnel—managers, bookkeepers, and others who keep the corporation running. But new service corporations also expand to provide needed services—banks, insurance firms, and computer companies, for example.

However, as we will see, the American economy is becoming dominated by large corporations. One result of this fact is that large corporations control more than one economic process. Thus, oil companies extract, refine, and distribute oil. Automobile companies produce and control much of the distribution of cars through "dealer networks."

Thus, the corporation is the basic economic unit in America. It is through the organization or entrepreneurship provided by corporations that other economic elements are brought together. If we are to understand the American economy, therefore, we must examine trends in corporate America (Turner 1976; pp. 22–28). Three such trends are most noteworthy: (1) monopoly and oligopoly, (2) intercorporate control, and (3) multinationalization.

Monopoly and Oligopoly. The basic assumption of the American economic system is that open competition among corporations and companies in the marketplace is the most efficient form of economic organization. In competing with each other in response to the demands in the market, corporations are presumed to have incentive to be efficient and to meet the priorities of the population. In actual practice, however, successful corporations can come to control the market. Once they have control, they can keep competitors out of their market, dictate prices to their suppliers and buyers, remain unresponsive to market demands, and become less efficient. For example, Standard Oil once dominated the oil industry to such a degree that no other company could compete. Only after this corporation was broken up under antitrust legislation did some degree of competition in the oil industry exist, although Exxon (Standard Oil of New Jersey) still disproportionately influences the market.

A **monopoly** is the control and domination of a market by one company. When several corporations control a market, this can be termed an **oligopoly.** The oil industry is an oligopoly in which less than ten companies control 99% of the market. In Table 1, we can observe this kind of oligopolistic control in other industries.

Table 1: Monopoly Power in Selected Industries, 1963

Industry	Percent of sales made by four largest firms
Automobiles	99
Aluminum	96
Flat glass	94
Steam engines and turbines	93
Light bulbs	92
Cigarettes	80
Copper	78
Metal cans	74
Soap and detergents	72
Tires and inner tubes	70
Blast furnaces and steel mills	50

Source: F. M. Scherer, *Industrial Market Structure and Economic Performance* U.S. Senate Judiciary Committee, subcommittee on Antitrust and Monopoly, Washington, D.C., 1964.

Table 2: Percent of Manufacturing Assets Held by the Largest 100 Firms

Year	Percent held by largest 100 firms
1925	35.1
1931	42.3
1939	42.4
1948	40.1
1955	43.8
1960	46.0
1965	47.6
1971	48.9

Source: *Studies by the Staff of the Cabinet Committee on Price Stability,* Washington, D.C., 1969, pp. 45, 92; *Statistical Abstract of the United States 1973,* p. 483.

Trends toward oligopoly indicate that large corporations are driving smaller ones out of business. The American economy is thus becoming increasingly controlled by a comparatively few corporations. For example, when one considers that there are close to 200,000 manufacturing companies in America and that the 100 largest control one-half of all manufacturing capital assets, then the trend toward larger and larger corporations controlling greater and greater shares of markets is clear. The trend from 1925 to the present decade is reported in Table 2.

Intercorporate Control. Not only are large corporations becoming prominent, there are many patterns of intercorporate control among them. Probably the most evident trend is for one corporation to own other corporations. Thus, Mobil Oil owns Wards, Bell Telephone owns Western Electric, General Motors owns Frigidaire, and in general, large corporations own many smaller corporations. The control of the economy by one corporation can extend well beyond its own market into other markets.

Who Owns the Large Corporations?

Tables 1 and 2 show the extent to which large corporations dominate the market. But who owns these large corporations? Who owns the stock? How concentrated is the stock in the hands of the rich? Can the "little guy" also share in ownership? Using data from Internal Revenue Service files, three researchers from the University of Pennsylvania have just completed a study of stock ownership of American corporations for the year 1971. Results: 1% of the nation's families—that is, those with incomes over $50,000 in 1971—own 51% of the stock and collect 47% of the dividends. The 53% of American families with incomes of less than $10,000 in 1971 owned less than 10% of the stock and collected about 11% of the dividends.

Source: *Newsweek,* December 18, 1974.

Multinationalization. Because corporations try to maximize profits, they will look for resources and labor where they are cheapest. They will also attempt to avoid governmental regulations and taxation policies that lower profits; and in their drive for profits, corporations will enter all markets in all parts of the world. It is not surprising, then, that America's large corporations are now multinational. They have plants, hire labor, and sell goods not just in the United States but everywhere that they can make profits.

This situation often creates economic difficulties in the domestic market, because major suppliers and producers are increasingly acting in regard to world markets. Thus, efforts to develop national economic policies often run into conflict with the worldwide interests and goals of America's large multinational corporations.

The American economy, then, is increasingly under the control of big, interlocking, and multinational corporations. This trend is inevitable in capitalist economies such as that in the United States. It will continue unless, of course, government decides to reverse the trend through new waves of antitrust legislation. Big corporations amass and organize technology, resources, capital, and labor. In response to the size and power of corporations, labor has sought to provide countervailing power: the power that large-scale unions can provide. Large-scale employee organizations have emerged in other contexts to protect the interests of labor in the face of large corporations and big government.

America's corporations are increasingly becoming multinational, extending their influence over the world.

*The union movement in America has moved from
frequent violence and confrontation to amicable
negotiation among large scale organizations,
one representing the owners and managers and the
other pursuing the interests of workers.*

The Organization of Labor

Before the Great Depression in the 1930s, very
few workers belonged to labor unions. Government had not been sympathetic to the cause,
and in a desire to keep their labor costs low,
corporations were much against the union
movement. Yet, as corporations began to grow
in size and dominance, workers began to actively, and often violently, protest their wage
and working conditions. In the face of civil
unrest the federal government passed legislation facilitating labor organization and media-
tion between corporations and workers.

The emergence of labor unions is one of the
best examples, then, of a social movement (see

Chapter 12). Dissatisfaction, structural conduciveness, emerging beliefs, and precipitating
incidents initially led to mass protests, strikes,
and often violent confrontations. Overtime
workers developed leadership, clear goals, political clout, and success in achieving union
representation. Today, the union movement is
at its institutional stage: large unions such as
the Teamsters and United Auto Workers and
confederations of smaller unions like the AFL-
CIO are accepted features of the economic
system. Relations with corporations are now
regularized and clear procedures for bargaining have been established.

Table 3: Union Membership from 1930 to 1972

Year	Total union membership	Percentage of total labor force
1930	3,401,000	6.8
1931	3,310,000	6.5
1932	3,050,000	6.0
1933	2,689,000	5.2
1934	3,088,000	5.9
1935	3,584,000	6.7
1936	3,989,000	7.4
1937	7,001,000	12.9
1938	8,034,000	14.6
1939	8,763,000	15.8
1940	8,717,000	15.5
1941	10,201,000	17.7
1942	10,380,000	17.2
1943	13,213,000	20.5
1944	14,146,000	21.4
1945	14,322,000	21.9
1946	14,395,000	23.6
1947	14,787,000	23.9
1948	14,319,000	23.1
1949	14,282,000	22.7
1950	14,267,000	22.3
1951	15,946,000	24.5
1952	15,892,000	24.2
1953	16,948,000	25.5
1954	17,022,000	25.4
1955	16,802,000	24.7
1956	17,490,000	25.2
1957	17,369,000	24.9
1958	17,029,000	24.2
1959	17,117,000	24.1
1960	17,049,000	23.6
1961	16,303,000	22.3
1962	16,586,000	22.6
1963	16,524,000	22.2
1964	16,841,000	22.2
1965	17,299,000	22.4
1966	17,940,000	22.7
1967	18,367,000	22.7
1968	18,916,000	23.0
1969	19,036,000	22.6
1970	19,381,000	22.6
1971	19,211,000	22.1
1972	19,435,000	21.8

Source: Handbook of Labor Statistics (1974, p. 366).

The overall trend in union membership can be seen in Table 3 which reports the percentage of the total labor force belonging to unions. As can be seen, union membership more than doubled in the 1930s, then rose to a peak in the early 1950s, and has now declined to about 22% of all workers.

Several trends have been evident in this union movement. First, unions have grown as the size of corporations has increased. Second, workers tend to be organized on a national and industrywide basis—the United Mine Workers, United Auto Workers, United Steel Workers are examples of prominent industrywide unions. Third, smaller unions have become consolidated into union confederations like the AFL-CIO or into large umbrella unions like the Teamsters. Fourth, white-collar workers have, in recent years, been willing to join unions as they see the benefits that they can bring. Fifth, public employees, from the police and fire departments to city managers and state employees, are now becoming unionized and willing to go on strike.

Thus, much of labor in America has become organized, especially the segment that works in large corporations and more recently, in large-scale government. The dynamics of the American economy often reside in the combative, and yet regularized, relations between labor and its employer.

Government and the Economy

Government has been drawn inexorably into the American economy. Periodic recessions and the depression of the 1930s forced government action. Mobilization of industry for war has been another force drawing the government into the economy, and the demands by many segments of the population for "equal opportunities" has further stimulated intervention. The government—whether at the federal, state, or local level—is now the single most important economic force. There are a number of ways to document this fact: (1) the government is the largest employer, (2) the government is the single largest purchaser of goods—from freeways to missiles, and (3) the taxing and regulatory powers of government allow it to manipulate exports, imports, interest rates, demand in the market, and if needed, prices and wages.

Government responds, at least to some degree, to political pressures from diverse sources: the public, large corporations, executive agencies such as the Defense Department which purchases billions in goods each year, and organized labor. Thus, governmental intervention in the economy is rarely as purposeful as in more centralized states. Too many competing interests must be reconciled. Moreover, government has sought to avoid direct intervention, such as price, wage, and rent controls, although such intervention occurred during World War II and the early 1970s. Rather, government has sought indirect intervention that can influence the market: tax cuts to stimulate demand, alterations in federal re- serve requirements to lower or raise interest rates, large government purchases of either goods or services, and similar market manipulation policies are the most frequent. The government does, however, directly regulate industries through such agencies as the Food and Drug Administration, the Civil Aeronautics Board, the Department of Agriculture, and the Justice Department to assure product safety, to reduce fraud and misrepresentation, and to coordinate certain activities.

In sum, the American economy reveals three distinct trends: (1) the growth of corporations and their dominance of key markets, (2) the stabilization of labor/employer relations through unionization, and (3) the increasing intervention of government into all phases of economic life.

SUMMARY AND PREVIEW

In this chapter we have attempted to understand one of the most basic structures in any society—the economy. Much of what occurs in the human system is influenced by the economy. Many of the social processes and forms that we have discussed in previous chapters exhibit the form that they do under pressures from the economy.

We first sought to understand just what an economy is. We saw that economies have five basic elements: land, labor, capital, technology, and entrepreneurship. The economy resolves the basic problems of gathering resources from the environment, producing goods and services, and distributing these to the members of a society. Unless these functions are performed, the human species could not survive.

We then analyzed diverse types of economies: hunting and gathering, agrarian, industrial, and postindustrial. Finally, we turned to an examination of the American economy as an example of a postindustrial economy. Three trends were found to be prominent: the growing size and dominance of large corporations, the organization of the labor force, and the expansion of government's intervention into economic affairs.

The expansion of government reminds us of the emergence and dominance of another fundamental human institution: government. As people discover new and improved ways to gather, produce, and distribute goods and services, political problems become more acute. Who is to make decisions? Who is to protect people's growing number of possessions? How is order to be maintained? As societies grow, kinship becomes inadequate to these tasks, and thus, government comes to dominate the human system. It is to the understanding of this process that we turn in the next chapter.

Key Terms

Land: the natural resources that a society uses in economic activity

Labor: human energy and effort expended in economic tasks

Capital: the tools and equipment, as well as the money to buy them, that are used in economic activity

Entrepreneurship: the manner and degree of organization of land, labor, capital, and technology in the economy

Technology: knowledge about how to manipulate and control the environment

Gathering: the basic economic process whereby resources are extracted from the environment

Producing: the basic economic process whereby resources are converted into usable goods and commodities

Distributing: the basic economic process whereby goods and services are made available to the members of a society

Servicing: skills that are produced and distributed in order to facilitate the operation of all basic economic processes

Neolithic Revolution: the discovery and application of agricultural technology, about 10,000 years ago

Modernization: the process of economic change from an agrarian to industrial and postindustrial profile, which alters the basic structure of the human system

Corporation: the primary unit in capitalist economic systems that organizes capital, technology, labor, and land for economic activity

Monopoly: that situation in which one corporation controls the market for a given good or service

Oligopoly: that situation in which a small number of corporations control the market for a given good or service

Intercorporate Control: those processes in which corporations form liaisons and patterns of cooperation and ownership that allow them to control diverse markets in the economy

Multinationalization: that situation in which a corporation does business and has invested capital in many different countries

Review Questions

1. How will differences in the basic elements of an economy influence the gathering, producing, distributing and servicing functions of the economy?

2. What has been the general trend in the economy throughout history?

3. What trends are evident in the American economy?

4. In what ways is the American economy an example of a postindustrial economy?

5. How does economic organization influence other aspects of the human system?

Suggested Readings

Bell, Daniel. *The Coming of Post-Industrial Society.* New York: Basic Books, 1973.

Etzioni, Amitai, and Etzioni, Eva. *Social Change: Sources, Patterns, and Consequences.* New York: Basic Books, 1964.

Moore, Wilbert E. *Social Change.* Englewood Cliffs, N.J.: Prentice-Hall, 1974.

——.*Economy and Society.* New York: Random House, 1955.

Nash, Manning. *Primitive and Peasant Economic Systems.* San Francisco: Chandler, 1966.

Service, Elman R. *The Hunters.* Englewood Cliffs, N.J.: Prentice-Hall, 1966.

Smelser, Neil J. *The Sociology of Economic Life.* Englewood Cliffs, N.J.: Prentice-Hall, 1963.

GOVERNMENT

PROLOGUE

Guiding Questions: How do societies make decisions and regulate their affairs? How does power become organized? Why does government emerge? What are its forms? What trends in government are evident?

Chapter Topics

BASIC ELEMENTS OF GOVERNMENT

In any society decisions must be made about what people are to do and how affairs are to be conducted. But who is to make such decisions, and why should those who make them be obeyed? Answers to these fundamental questions lead us to topics of power, politics, and government.

In our discussion of stratification we examined power. Recall that **power** is the capacity to realize goals even against active resistance. Individuals often have personal power, but our concern in this section on human institutions is how power becomes organized in a society and used to make decisions about what is to occur. This organization of decision-making is what we call **government,** and the processes occurring within government and between government and those subject to its decisions are usually termed *politics.* Our goal in this chapter is to understand power, politics, and government. They are among the most interesting and important facets of the human system.

Leaders and Decisions

A society without the capacity to decide what it will, must, or should do is vulnerable. It will have difficulty dealing with the contingencies of social life. A basic element of all governments, then, is **decision-making.** Of course, somebody, or some group of people, must make decisions. Thus, another element of government is **leadership.**

Leadership is often very simple, however. Among the traditional Eskimo, for example, there were no permanent leaders. People cooperated and survived without the need for "city hall," "politicians," and "politics." In a crisis, or on a hunt, leaders who possessed special skills or insight might emerge but no one was compelled to follow their decisions.

But as the human system increases in complexity, leadership becomes more formal and decision-making is more constraining. The simple life of the traditional Eskimo may give us a clue to our past, but our present involves the other key elements of government: power, and authority.

Power and Authority

As societies grew, people developed the ability to apply coercion. They could hire people to physically force others to do what they wanted. Ultimately, government relies upon the capacity to exert force. However, as the British reactionary, Edmund Burke, once proclaimed, "no nation is ruled which must be perpetually conquered." If one must physically coerce compliance, then collective revolt and other unpleasant outcomes are likely. Government

*Ultimately, the power of government
rests on its coercive power.*

must rely upon more than coercion and force, or the threat of these. It must be given the right by those who will be affected to make decisions. When a majority of a population bestows this right on leaders, then **authority** exists. Authority is simply legitimated power; it is a situation where people feel it proper that leaders make decisions. Coercion and authority are thus the extremes of power; one is power through force and the other is power by consent. Government usually involves elements of both.

These elements—leadership, decision-making, and power—are the basis for government. As we will come to see, they have been elaborated into many diverse forms. But all of these forms have certain common consequences, or functions, for society (Turner 1972).

THE FUNCTIONS OF GOVERNMENT

Establishing Goals for a Society

Societies typically have goals. They seek to meet certain ends, such as full employment, world dominance, "peace with honor," energy self-sufficiency, "equality for all," and many other goals. Government establishes goals and priorities among them. Decision-making leaders use their authority, and if necessary, their coercive power, to map out plans for the society. These plans are sometimes very clear, as has been the case with various "Five-Year Plans" in the Soviet Union; or they can be vague and vacillating as is the case with American society's commitments to social equality, world peace, full-employment, and energy self-sufficiency. Nevertheless, the existence of goals and their priorities are important determinants of what will occur in other institutional spheres, for as those with power seek to realize goals, they will use their power to allocate and mobilize a society's resources.

Allocating and Mobilizing a Society's Resources

Government mobilizes and allocates human and natural resources to meet goals and priorities. During wartime this capacity of government is dramatically evident as soldiers are recruited, industries convert to wartime production, and scarce resources, such as oil and metal, are rationed; but even during less stressful periods, government uses its power to mobilize and allocate resources. In America, for example, the amount of credit and money available, the extent of educational opportunities, the nature and amount of work that can be found, the prices of food and energy resources are, to a great extent, subject to much control by the federal government. Depending upon goals, the supplies of money, credit, education, jobs, energy, and food will vary.

Distributing Scarce and Valuable Resources

From our earlier discussion of stratification (see Chapter 14), we know that power is unequally distributed and that those with power can more readily secure other resources. From Karl Marx's and Max Weber's analyses, we know that the state, or government, is largely responsible for who gets what resources. As government allocates and mobilizes resources, it also bestows power and privilege on some segments of the society. For example, stockholders, managers, and employees of America's major corporations are often given varying degrees of money when the government gives a contract for a new weapons system. If government chooses to keep welfare payments low and to implement work requirements for those receiving aid, then it imposes poverty on certain sectors of the society. If the government decides to strive for energy self-sufficiency and gives oil companies tax incentives to explore for oil, it bestows income and profits for those in the oil industry. Government, then, is intimately connected with the unequal distribution of scarce and valuable resources in a society (Turner & Starnes 1976).

DEFINING THE INSTITUTION OF GOVERNMENT

Maintaining Social Order and Control

As the seat of power in a society, government is involved in maintaining conformity to key norms and values. Government can use its powers of **coercion;** it can manipulate public opinion through the restriction of information; it can control socialization in schools; and it creates and controls a system of courts for adjudicating disputes between private parties or between the state and private parties.

The social control functions are most evident in societies where leaders do not enjoy great legitimacy. Under these conditions, coercion by the police, persecution of dissidents, propagandism in schools, and manipulation of the media are likely to be evident. In more stable political systems, where leaders enjoy widespread legitimacy, social control is less coercive and restrictive. The state seeks to maintain the laws and to provide channels for parties to redress their grievances. But even in these societies, civil disorders will be met with coercion and the temporary suspension of civil liberties.

In sum, then, government has four major consequences, or functions, for society: (1) establishing goals, (2) allocating and mobilizing resources, (3) distributing scarce resources, and (4) maintaining social order. Since these activities have implications for almost everything that people do, it is little wonder that government is always the subject of controversy in a society.

All institutions are composed of statuses, norms, and role behaviors, and it is usually complexes of these elements that are organized into diverse social forms and that have certain common functions for society. So it is with government.

We have seen that the basic elements of government are leadership, decision-making, and power, and we now know that government is involved in four crucial functions. With this understanding, we can define the institution of **government** as that complex of statuses, roles, and norms organized into diverse social forms that have a monopoly on the use of coercive power to enforce decisions of leaders and that have important consequences for establishing goals, allocating and mobilizing resources, distributing scarce resources, and maintaining social order (Turner 1972, p. 266).

With this general understanding of government, we are now ready to explore this most basic institution further. Our discussion will be organized into several sections. First, we will explore the emergence of government. Then, we will discuss its variations. Next, we will review certain trends in the form of government. Finally, we will explore the structure and processes of government in the United States.

The Political Order of Baboons

We have commented upon the formal organization of baboon troops on the African savannah (see Chapter 11). Such organization shows a well-developed political order. One male usually dominates all others, although several high-ranking males may form an alliance to prevent the dominant male from pushing them around excessively. The threat or use of physical coercion—in our terms, power—is the basis for this male's domination. He threatens, and if necessary, attacks subordinates to achieve compliance. Over time, authority emerges because the decisions of the dominant male are given and accepted without great fanfare. The dominant male leads the troop in its daily movements, decides where to settle, and coordinates collective attacks and defenses of the troop. He uses other high-ranking males as a kind of "administrative staff" to help coordinate action among females, the young, and low-ranking males.

Why did this kind of political order emerge? As we have noted before, baboons are the only other primate besides humans to seek a niche on the hostile savannah. The key to the baboon's survival, unlike that of humans, was aggressiveness and tight organization. They move as a troop, sleep as a troop, and collectively defend themselves. This kind of coordination of tasks requires the concentration of power and authority in the absence of genetic programming to perform these tasks. The creation of dominance hierarchies of power and authority are the way baboons have dealt with this problem. Humans used tools, loose and flexible organization, and the cunning provided by their large brains to survive. It was only when populations of humans became concentrated that we began to develop political structures like those among baboons. Was this development simply the result of a need for social order, or was it also in our primate heritage?

Source: Kummer (1971).

THE EMERGENCE AND ELABORATION OF GOVERNMENT

The Earliest Leaders

The emergence of government is buried in the dust of our ancestors. We know that present-day hunting-and-gathering bands do not have well-developed governmental structures. Leaders emerge through their skill or charisma, and they have no power to enforce their decisions. Small bands of families—rarely more than 50—simply wander over their territories. Each family collects what it must, and for larger projects such as gathering berries and roots or big-game hunting, people cooperate and share the fruits of their labor. Those with skill and expertise are likely to lead, but they enjoy no power. Only increased honor and prestige go to these leaders. So it was, we suspect, for at least 30,000 of our 40,000 years as a distinct species (Carneiro 1970; Lenski 1966; Service 1962).

Chiefdoms

With the discovery of agriculture—the Neolithic revolution as we termed it in the last chapter—the nature of government underwent profound changes (Lenski 1966; Turner 1972). With a surplus, settled communities, and more elaborate forms of kinship (see Chapters 16 and 18), new possibilities for consolidating power developed. It is not known why people settled and began to domesticate animals and plant life. Hunters and gatherers eat as well as agriculturalists, and they usually have to work less. But once people settled and used agriculture, they could support larger populations. With larger populations, new principles and forms of social organization became necessary (Carneiro 1968; Spooner 1972).

Initially, kinship principles can organize expanding communities. In such societies chiefdoms become the major form of government. **Chiefdoms** are a political system in which people become ranked in terms of the share of resources that individuals can control. Leaders of kin groups who usually inherit leadership positions in accordance with descent norms do not enjoy great power. They have more possessions, but they are also required to give much of what they have to others. In this way they are accorded honor and prestige. For example, among the Trobriand Islanders, village chiefs receive presents of yams from various members of their kindred. The chief thus accumulates a large stockpile of yams. But the problem with yams is that one cannot coerce people with them. Yams are to be eaten, and it is a rare chief who could eat all of his yams. Moreover, the chief has obligations that do not fall upon others. He must cater feasts to which all his relatives are invited, and he is required to store yams in case of famine. The chief, then, is a custodian of the society's resources. In being the custodian, he is bestowed honor and prestige, but little coercive power (Pasternak 1976, p. 18).

The Emergence of the State

Chiefdoms, then, were probably the first political form to evolve with the use of agriculture. They represented a way for peoples with a surplus and a larger, settled population to organize themselves. But as populations grew and as economic productivity increased, a new form of political organization began to emerge: the **state.**

In state-based societies political leaders own more, and they are not required to give it away. They use their property to buy power—that is, control over others. They secure animals, land, water, control over irrigation, and other resources. They "hire" others to guard their privileges, and they are likely to mobilize armies not only to protect their resources but to gain control of other society's resources. War and conquest thus become more prominent in the human system.

The initial state societies were very simple; most likely, one kin group, such as a clan, gained control of a vital resource, such as water. It then pressed its advantage to gain control of other resources. Kinship rules determined access to power, and the state resembled a kind of large extended family. However, as the size of the state society grew and the tasks in which it became involved expanded, nonelite kinspeople were recruited for military duty and for civil works. Egypt, Rome, and much of feudal Europe represented such early state societies, with leaders inheriting power and recruiting nonkin to perform critical administrative and military roles.

But as the history of these societies documents, those nonelites who get close to power through their military or civil accomplishments often crave power and take power. If this occurs sufficiently often, kinship and inheritance decrease as a means for passing power to new leaders.

Warfare has traditionally been an important impetus to the growing power of the state. Pictured: warfare in the early states of India promoted the expansion of government.

Modern States

Modern state governments, with their elaborate armies, civil service bureaucracies, and wide-ranging projects, are the products of the industrial revolution. The vastly increased productive power of industrial economies enables people to hoard resources and to buy power. Moreover, the growth of the population and urban centers, as well as other changes associated with industrialization, create considerable civil unrest. Revolutions are common during early industrialization—as was the case in France, Russia, the United States, China, Mexico, Cuba, and elsewhere. A strong state, frequently with dictatorial powers, thus tends to emerge; and even without the threat of revolution, the complexities of social life require a central power to set goals, allocate resources, distribute resources, and maintain order. Eventually, as humans coped with the problems created by industrialization, they came to recognize the necessity for a large state form of government with coercive power, a large civil service bureaucracy, and hopefully, a fair justice system for redressing grievances.

With advanced industrialism, and the social stability that ensues, states become increasingly democratic. Leaders are elected; limits are imposed upon the use of coercive power; and citizens enjoy rights, privileges, and channels for redressing grievances against each other and against the state. Some societies, such as England and the United States, achieved political democracy early in the process of industrialization. Others, such as France,

Germany, and most Western European countries, developed democracy somewhat later. Still others, such as Russia and Eastern European countries, have achieved some degree of democracy, but still rely upon extensive coercion. Most Third World nations that are initiating industrialization are totalitarian states.

We can see, then, that the emergence of government is a mixed blessing. Simple hunting-and-gathering bands and early agricultural societies did not have a state with coercive power. More developed agricultural societies, with large populations, developed the political form that we have called the state (Fried 1960). State forms of government allow for better control and regulation of large populations, but they also grant coercive power and privilege to the few. During industrialization this power increases, although political democracy and citizen freedoms increase with advanced industrialization and postindustrialization.

VARIATIONS IN THE FORM OF GOVERNMENT

Table 1 shows the changes in the nature of government. This table can also let us see variations in government in the world today, since examples of hunters and gatherers, simple agrarian, advanced agrarian, early industrial, and advanced industrial can be found in various parts of the world. On the left side of the table, a number of points for comparison are listed. The "locus of government" pertains to who in the society is invested with decision-making. The "degree of coercive power" denotes the capacity of decision-makers to impose their will. The "sphere of government" specifies just who is subject to decisions by political leaders. The "structure of government" indicates how decision-making statuses are organized. The "acquisition and transfer of power and authority" highlights how new leaders are selected or how they emerge. The "degree of freedom" addresses the issue of how much freedom from political constraint people enjoy. By reading down each column of the table, we can get a quick profile of governance in various types of societies, and by reading from left to right across the table, we can appreciate the general trends in structure and form of government.

Table 1: The Changing Forms of Government

POINTS OF COMPARISON	TYPE OF SOCIETY				
	Hunting and Gathering	Simple Agrarian	Advanced Agrarian	Early Industrial	Advanced Industrial
The Locus of Government	individuals with expertise or charisma	chiefs	state: one kin group controls others	state: unrelated to kinship	large state
Degree of Coercive Power	none	none	some	great	great
Sphere of Government	limited: only those who choose to follow	limited: confined to kin groups	limited to those who can be induced or coerced to follow	established geo-political boundaries	established geo-political boundaries
Structure of Government	none: leaders emerge as needed, then recede	coextensive with descent rule in kinship	state dominated by kin; some recruitment from population	bureaucratic	bureaucratic
Acquisition and Transference of Authority or Power	no procedures	inherited in terms of kinship rules	inheritance and capture	capture	democratic elections
Degree of Freedom	great; limited by kinship	great; limited by kinship and obligations to chief	little	little	great; limited by law

TRENDS IN GOVERNMENTAL ORGANIZATION

As can be seen, the trend is toward a large, bureaucratic state with great coercive power within clear national boundaries. Leaders increasingly tend to be democratically elected and people enjoy considerable political freedom and have channels for redressing their grievances.

We should hasten to emphasize, however, that a minority of the world's peoples live under such forms of government. The vast majority live in agricultural and industrializing societies with repressive state governments. Moreover, even in the most democratic of societies, freedom is not total or complete. Government limits options; it distributes resources unequally; and it is, at times, coercive.

The information in Table 1 points to the prominence of certain political trends. We should highlight some of these so that we can view our own government within a broader perspective. We can view at least four general trends in political organization among the world's societies (Turner 1972, pp. 279–285): (1) increasing size of government, (2) bureaucratization of government, (3) centralization of government, and (4) democratization of government.

The Growing Size of Government

We have seen that primitive governments are small. With increased economic production, however, power and authority are concentrated first in the hands of kin leaders and groups, and then, in a civil state. Once power becomes concentrated, it is used to regulate, control, organize, allocate, and mobilize. To perform all these tasks requires that government grow in size; it takes more people to wield power. Thus, a cycle is set into motion: power is used to regulate; to regulate requires more people in governmental positions; with people in positions of authority, more power can be consolidated; hence, government expands to include more people to carry out and enforce the use of this expanded base of power.

Power thus generates its own imperatives. Its use necessitates new organization for carrying out and enforcing policies. The army, taxing powers, administrative apparatus of leaders, the courts, and many other structures expand as the government seeks to do more in a society.

The Growth of Bureaucracy

At present, humans use formal organizations, or bureaucracies, to carry out large-scale administrative tasks. We reviewed why this should be so in Chapter 11 on formal organizations. Although the initial consolidation of power occurs within kinship, it soon becomes necessary to recruit nonkindred if power is to be used and expanded. Army officers and soldiers must be recruited; civil servants must be recruited to tax, to run courts, to keep records, to give advice, and to carry out other tasks. With these civil servants and an army, government can grow and extend its influence, resulting in a greater need for an army, police, and civil servants to maintain this extended base of power.

Bureaucracy thus grows as the number and complexity of governmental statuses increase. Armies and civil service positions become bureaucratically organized. Early bureaucratization is often a far cry from Weber's ideal type of rational authority hierarchies of clear rules and objective criteria for promotion and advancement. Nepotism, ascription, and irrationality often dominate.

Yet, there is an organizational imperative toward rationality and efficiency—as Max Weber clearly recognized. Large-scale tasks require some degree of competence among those who carry them out. To assure that competent people are involved in the implementation of military or civil activities, objective criteria for evaluating and rewarding performance are likely to emerge. Large-scale tasks also require efficient organization. To assure efficient organization, clear rules and lines of authority become necessary; otherwise, armies lose battles, police are rendered impotent, taxes go uncollected, and civic projects remain uncompleted. Bureaucracy becomes the major organizational form of government as it grows in size and expands its functions.

Centralization

Power is, by definition, a capacity to realize one's will or goals. Those with power develop organizations that allow this capacity, even against resistance. Bureaucratic organizations tend to be authority hierarchies, concentrating increasing authority in positions at the top. Political decision-makers use these organizations to carry out their will; in using them, power becomes concentrated. Efficiently organized armies and police seek to remove "dissidents," especially those who possess any capacity for coercion. Through taxation and the use of tax monies to create and use large organizations, governments usurp much control and initiative from other organizations in society.

Power becomes concentrated and government becomes centralized. Governments always seek to eliminate counterbases of power, and as they increasingly expand their functions, they come to control and regulate more and more activities. Decision-making is difficult, time-consuming, and inefficient when performed by many people and many organizations. As social welfare, economic stability, national defense, and other activities are undertaken by government, decisions affecting these arenas are concentrated in the hands of chief executives, even in political democracies with large, representative bodies. Totalitarian dictatorships are obvious examples of total control of decision-making by chief executives who stand at the helm of military and civil service bureaucracies. But political democracies also show a trend toward concentration of decision-making in the hands of presidents and prime ministers. We will see why this occurs in our more detailed analysis of the American political system in the next section.

The Trend toward Democracy

Democracy is difficult to define, but we might offer a general definition. **Democracy** is that form of government in which those who are governed are able to freely elect those who are to make decisions on their behalf. There is, of course, no perfect democracy, only degrees of democracy. Political development is initially away from democratic government. Primitive people choose whom they will follow, and they give honor and prestige to those with leadership skills. They can choose new leaders when old ones can no longer deliver valuable services. But with advanced agriculture and the emergence of kin-based states and then with bureaucratic states, government becomes decidedly undemocratic. Elites make decisions and use the army, police, courts, and administrative bureaucracy to enforce them.

However, there is a built-in countervailing force in these societies. As competence is required in governmental positions and as skilled workers are needed in industrializing econo-

mies, education is extended to the masses. Literate populations are able to communicate ideas more effectively, especially as they are concentrated into urban/industrial regions and exposed to the mass media. Totalitarian governments seek to use the media and educational system to repress the masses, but urban and literate people are able to question policies, to codify beliefs about the fairness of policies, and to communicate these codes effectively. They can thus exert pressures through the threat of civil disorder for a greater voice in governmental affairs. At times, revolution casts aside a government as people seek to influence the decisions affecting their lives. Although repression, censorship, and manipulation by government remain prominent in all societies, there is a trend toward growing involvement of the people in political decisions. Public opinion is consulted; elites usually rise through the political ranks from the general population; and representative bodies are typically established to influence the decisions of chief executives.

These four trends are merely tendencies, not firm ends. Growing size, bureaucratization, and centralization are strong tendencies, whereas democratization is a more ambiguous tendency. Yet, if we look at the world's political systems, we can see movement—fluctuating and often uncertain—toward democracy. Perfect democracy, where the population influences all decisions, has never existed. The closest humans have ever come to this state is in their hunting-and-gathering stage—an epoch that will soon be a part of human history. There are only *degrees* of democracy, and compared to their advanced agrarian and early industrial stage of development, societies that have reached an advanced industrial stage have considerably more democracy.

GOVERNMENT IN AMERICA

The Overall Structure of Government

American government is divided into three branches: the executive, legislative, and judiciary. The **executive branch** embraces the administrative bureaucracy of the state, the **legislative** branch houses the elected representatives of the people, and the **judiciary** provides a system of courts. This tripartite division is replicated at a number of different levels: the federal, state, county, and city. At the federal level, the tripartite division is represented by the president and executive agencies, the Congress, and the federal court system. At the state level, the governor and state offices, the legislature or assembly, and state court system reflect this division of powers. At the city level, the mayor or city manager, council, and municipal courts maintain this division. At the county level, there is more variability, but the board of supervisors, county administrative staff, and county courts approximate these three branches of government.

Processes of Decision-Making

Sociologists are in disagreement over how political decisions are actually rendered, whether at the local community level or at the federal level of government. This disagreement revolves around the issue of how much power economic elites exert on political decisions. We briefly touched upon this issue in our discussion of stratification and the distribution of power. We should return to this controversy here, since it stands at the heart of how government operates in America.

Most studies of political power and decision-making have been conducted either at the community or national level. State and county decision-making has received comparatively little attention. In general, one of two positions is argued: (1) a power elite dominates decision-making or (2) diversified interest groups check and balance each other in influencing political decisions, thus making the political process pluralistic. We must examine, then, both **power elite** and **pluralism** as concepts of decision-making at the national and community level.

The Pluralist Viewpoint. Pluralists argue that power is dispersed rather than concentrated. Power is concentrated into the hands of diverse **interests,** but these groups often have different interests. Moreover, their power is limited to the capacity to "veto" or stop those political decisions that might hurt their interests. At the national level, such diverse interests as labor, oil, coal, steel, auto manufacturers, environmentalists, and national associations such as the American Medical Association, National Rifle Association, and the like are organized to bring pressures on the president, chiefs of executive agencies, and members of Congress on a particular issue that affects them (Kornhauser 1961; Rose 1967). At times, when there is no opposition from other interest groups to a piece of legislation or an executive decision, it is likely that a decision favoring that interest will be made.

For example, the auto industry may not want to meet federal air pollution standards, and thus, they lobby to have them weakened or delayed. Oil interests, labor, steel manufacturers, and coal interests have no direct con-

Figure 1: The Power Elite and Pluralist Viewpoints

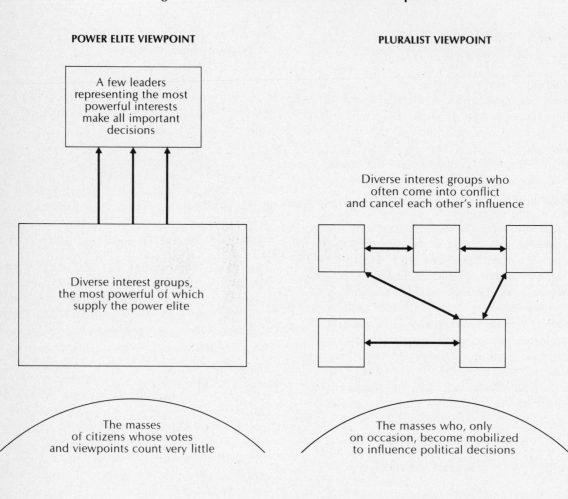

POWER ELITE VIEWPOINT

A few leaders representing the most powerful interests make all important decisions

Diverse interest groups, the most powerful of which supply the power elite

The masses of citizens whose votes and viewpoints count very little

PLURALIST VIEWPOINT

Diverse interest groups who often come into conflict and cancel each other's influence

The masses who, only on occasion, become mobilized to influence political decisions cern with this issue, and thus, they are unlikely to exercise an informal "veto" through counterlobbying. Consequently auto manufacturers face opposition only from environmentalists, with the result that they can overcome this opposition and realize a weakening, or delaying, of auto emission standards. Similar processes occur for other interests when there is no major concern at stake. But interests often clash, as is the case with strip miners and coal interests, on the one hand, and environmentalists on the other. In this instance the interests are more evenly matched, and in fact, the environmentalists may be able to exert more influence on Congress than coal interests. The result is a standoff, compromise legislation, or no action.

At the community level, the same view prevails. Decision-making reflects the interaction of the well-organized, but diverse, interests: the chamber of commerce, large local manufacturers, the local building industry, community leaders, and environmental groups, for example. Robert Dahl (1961) in a classic study on New Haven, Connecticut, discovered that decision-making was influenced primarily by diverse segments of the middle-class population who could exert pressures on issues affecting them, but their power to initiate decisions that went against the interests of other groups was limited.

Thus, the pluralist viewpoint sees political decision-making as influenced by well-organized and well-heeled interests. These interests, however, can come into conflict. Few have the power to initiate decisions that go against the interests of other powerful groups. However, the pluralist view does recognize, along with the elitist perspective, that the public exerts much less influence than interests. Only when their sentiment is aroused—and this is rare—does the unorganized public come to exert significant political pressures. In the day-to-day decisions of government, the interactions of government with organized interests are the most important.

The Power Elite Viewpoint. In the 1950s, the late sociologist C. Wright Mills (1959) codified the elitist point of view by postulating a *power elite* at the national level of government. Mills visualized three interlocking elites that have common interests in what he called military capitalism. These three elites included top military personnel, executives of large corporations, and powerful members of Congress. The power elite is thus drawn from three sectors of the society—military, economic, and political.

Mills argued that the interests of these elites converged, rather than diverged. For example, top military personnel have an interest in a large defense establishment; America's large corporations enjoy doing business with the Pentagon through lucrative defense contracts; politicians enjoy contributions from executives of corporations and profit from the prosperity created by military installations and defense industries in their districts.

More than common interest is involved, Mills argued. These elites circulate and establish many informal contacts. For instance, retired generals often go to work for defense contractors. Politicians become corporate lobbyists or executives. Administrators on regulatory agencies and cabinet officers go back and forth between government and industry. These elites thus know and come to depend upon each other, and as a result, they are able to exert enormous political influence. Decisions in government, Mills argued, reflect the common interests and informal liaisons of these power elites.

Other scholars such as William Domhoff (1967) have sought to extend Mills' analysis by exploring the way a small group of elites maintains its political power. For example, Domhoff has sought to document how the social, economic, and political lives of the elite are interwoven. Marriage patterns, club memberships, common directorships on corporate boards, and residential proximity all operate, he argues, to maintain the privilege of an upper elite who, in his words, "rules America."

At the community level, a number of studies have questioned Dahl's findings about a pluralistic community decision-making process. Domhoff (1978), for example, reanalyzed Dahl's data on New Haven and found extensive networks of elite interaction and the concerted influence that these elites have on decision-making. In the 1950s Floyd Hunter (1953) examined Atlanta, Georgia and concluded that a group of about 40 "influentials," operating behind the scenes, influenced political decisions.

When we compare the elitist and pluralist viewpoints, then, we get two different images of political decision-making in America. Which

is correct? It is difficult to know. Power is illusive and hard to measure, and by measuring power in different ways, different conclusions emerge. Moreover, at the community level there are probably great variations from community to community in how decisions are made (Rossi 1960). Depending upon what type of community is studied, an investigator might draw different conclusions about community power. At the national level the diversity of opinion is hard to reconcile. It often appears that if a researcher is morally and intellectually committed to either an elitist or pluralist position, then investigations will confirm these commitments. Depending on whether an investigator defines elites loosely or tightly or whether specific instances of conflicting interests or general affinities of interests are examined, a varying picture of power and decision-making emerges.

Trends in American Government

We noted earlier that a number of trends are evident in government throughout the world. America is no exception to these trends. We should, therefore, review the directions of change in the structure of government (Turner 1976).

The Growing Size of Government. The framers of the American Constitution held a "housekeeping" vision of American government. Government was to be in charge of defense and security, the coinage of money, and the regulation of trade. Government was thus to be small. However, this conception of government could not endure in the face of growing societywide problems, such as the needs to plan programs (from a highway system to monetary policy), to extend citizenship rights to all citizens, to stimulate the economy, and to maintain a vast defense establishment. To deal with these unforeseen changes associated with industrialization, the world political situation, and the increase in the size of the population required a larger governmental system.

The Bureaucratization of Government. We know from our earlier discussion that the larger the tasks to be performed, the more likely are those positions charged with performing these tasks to become organized bureaucratically. As the problems associated with transportation, defense, commerce, taxation, housing, health, education, and welfare, land use, resources, energy, and other concerns of an industrial society grew, so did the administrative bureaucracies charged with meeting these problems. As a result, government in America, as in other modern societies, became highly bureaucratized in the administration of policies set by the president and Congress. However, once large administrative and regulatory bodies exist and are given power to create and enforce rules, they become a political force in their own right. The civil service personnel of these bureaucracies can selectively implement laws, and extend their powers to new areas independently of the president and Congress. The result is that a considerable amount of power resides in high-level, career bureaucrats who command the day-to-day operation of the federal bureaucracy.

The Centralization of Government. Despite strong beliefs to the contrary, government in America is becoming centralized. Originally, power was to be decentralized and spread among the states and local communities. But over time the concentration of power into the hands of the federal government has increased. Within the federal government, power is increasingly concentrated in the presidency, despite the checks-and-balances concepts of our forefathers.

The reason for this trend resides in the growing needs for planning and for regulation. A complex urban, industrial society cannot function with each community and state enforcing its own unique regulations. Transportation, commerce, welfare, education, housing, energy, pollution, economics, and other areas of concern are national in scope, hence, they require national policies. Yet, even in the face of pressures for national planning, American society remains the most decentralized in the modern world.

Planning requires decisions. Congress is often unable to make definitive and rapid decisions because it is a collective body. As a result, the president has increasingly been held responsible for initiating key programs and legislation over the years. Congress has thus become more of a reactive force—responding to budgetary, defense, and domestic initiatives of the president. Thus, the presidency has gained considerably more power than originally envisioned by the framers of the Constitution.

Extensions of Political Democracy. American society is considerably more democratic than it was 60 years ago. Women can now vote—a right that they were denied until 1920. Many minority groups that had been excluded from voting now have the right as well as the opportunity to vote. Young adults can now vote. With the Supreme Court's "one person, one vote" ruling, Congressional representation more accurately reflects the distribution of the population.

We should note, of course, that democracy is a relative state. Both the elitist and pluralist viewpoints discussed earlier emphasize, to varying degrees, that the sentiments of the public, or majority of citizens, are less important than either those of elites or organized interests. Political decisions, therefore, do not always reflect public sentiment, even though many of these decisions are made, or reviewed, by the elected representatives of the public.

However, Americans do enjoy much personal freedom. They can sue each other and the government in court; they can express their views; the media are relatively free. However, freedom is also relative. The level of citizens' affluence, for example, increases their freedom, since the poor rarely can sue each other, much less the government. As protestors of the Vietnam War often learned, free speech and civil liberties can be suspended. As recent revelations have emphasized, key agencies such as the IRS, FBI, CIA, and Pentagon can break the law and violate people's civil liberties.

Yet, people today probably influence the political process and enjoy more freedoms than their counterparts 100 years ago. The trend is toward more democracy, but a trend is not the same as complete and unabridged freedom.

SUMMARY AND PREVIEW

In this chapter we have examined how power becomes institutionalized—that is, how it becomes organized into governmental structures. We first defined the key elements of government: decision-making, leadership, power, and authority. We then reviewed the principal functions of government: establishing goals, allocating and mobilizing, distributing scarce resources, and maintaining order.

We examined the emergence and development of government from simple hunting-and-gathering forms to the complex state forms of advanced industrial societies. In this development we noted a number of prominent trends: the increasing size, bureaucratization, centralization, and democratization of government.

We then reviewed some of the prominent features of American government. We noted that American government is a tripartite system operating at four levels: city, county, state, and federal. Decision-making is unclear, and depending upon the point of view, it is either pluralistic or elitist. American government also manifests trends toward growth, bureaucratization, centralization, and democratization.

In the first four chapters of this section we have studied four basic institutions: family, religion, economy, and government. We have seen how government changes with economic development. Another basic institution emerges and elaborates with economic and political development: education. It is to this last major human institution that we now turn.

Key Terms

Power: the capacity to realize goals or paths of conduct even in the face of active resistance

Government: the organization of decision-making in society

Decision-making: the process by which options are sorted out and paths of conduct are selected

Leadership: those who make decisions for others

Authority: power and leadership that is accepted as legitimate by those who are affected by decisions of leaders and their exercise of power

Coercion: the use of, or capacity to use, physical force

Government: those positions in a society that are invested with power, leadership, authority, and decision-making rights and obligations

Chiefdom: that form of government in which descent rules of kinship determine who is to be leader and possess authority for the larger kin group or groups in a territory

State: that form of government in which leaders possess coercive power and an administrative bureaucracy to help make and carry out decisions

Democracy: the situation in which those who are governed have some choice as to who is to govern them

Executive Branch: that part of government in which the chief executive of the state bureaucracy operates

Legislative Branch: that branch of government where elected representatives meet and engage in decision-making

Judiciary: that part of government in which procedures for resolving disputes among citizens and for redressing grievances against government are implemented

Power Elite: the view of government that argues that a comparatively few people make political decisions in a society and set the goals of the society

Pluralism: the situation in which multiple groups exert pressures on decision-makers in government

Interests: groups that have certain common goals and that press for decisions to help them meet these goals

Review Questions

1. What are the differences among power, authority, and coercion?

2. What are the functions of government? How does meeting these functions influence other aspects of a society?

3. When does the state emerge? Why?

4. Why are certain trends in government necessary?

5. What are the elitist and pluralist positions on decision-making in America? How can they be reconciled?

Suggested Readings

Domhoff, William G. *Who Really Rules?* Santa Monica, Ca.: Goodyear, 1978.

Keller, Suzanne. *Beyond the Ruling Class: Strategic Elites in Modern Society.* New York: Random House, 1963.

Milbraith, Lester W. *The Washington Lobbyists.* Chicago: Rand McNally, 1963.

Mills, C. Wright. *The Power Elite.* New York: Oxford University Press, 1959.

Olsen, Marvin E., ed. *Power in Societies.* New York: Macmillan, 1970.

Rose, Arnold M. *The Power Structure.* New York: Oxford University Press, 1967.

EDUCATION

PROLOGUE

Guiding Questions: Why does education occupy such a central place in human affairs? What has caused the educational explosion? What trends are evident in education? What problems persist?

Chapter Topics

20

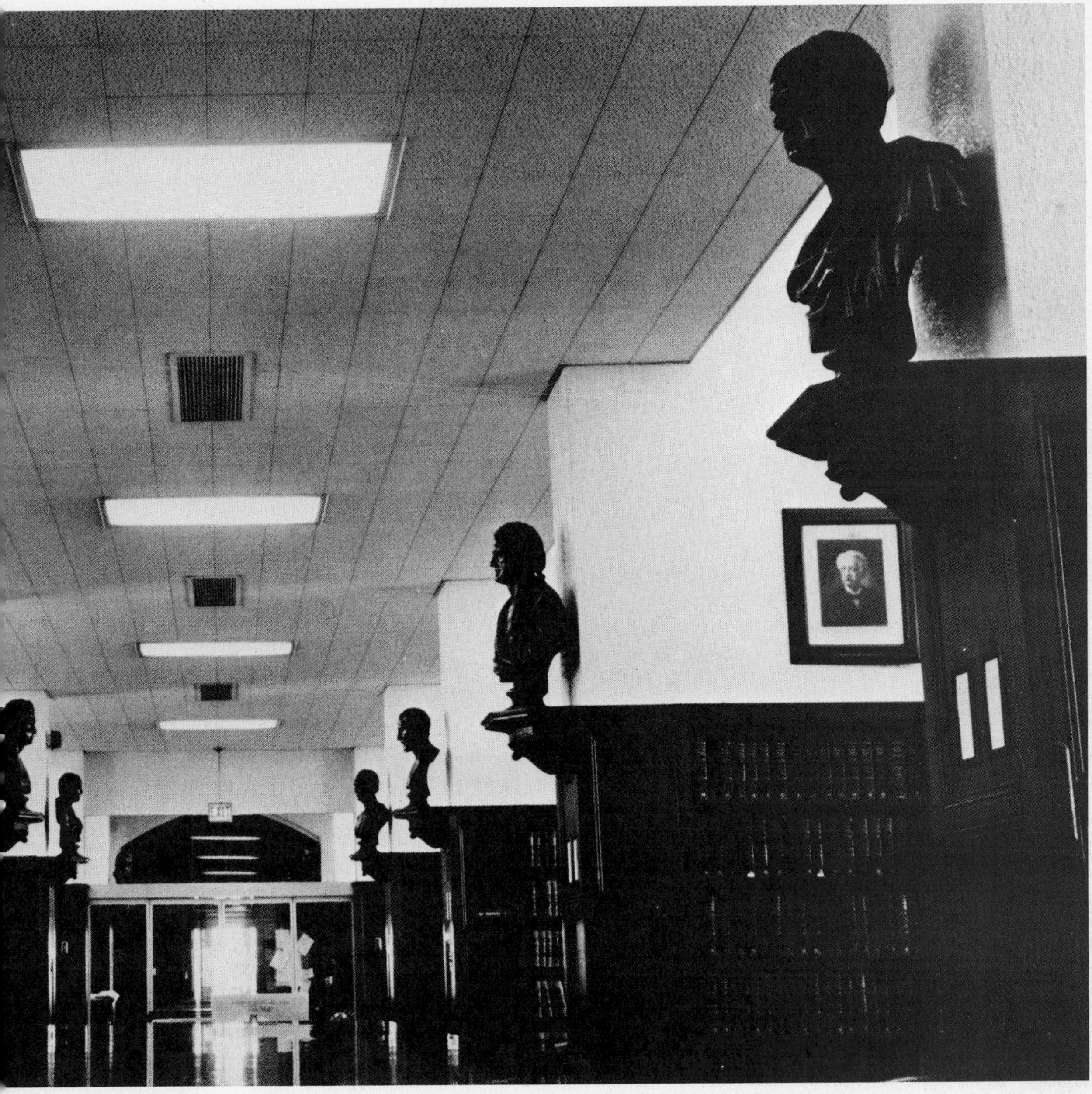

THE FUNCTIONS OF EDUCATION

Reading this page emphasizes our involvement in educational structures. We may not feel like reading today, but our eyes pass over the page; words are underlined; mental notes are made. Such is the power of the educational system in which we have all been involved. It organizes much of a person's life until adulthood, and as we will see, it has profound consequences for what happens to all people for the rest of their lives.

This power is recent. Education, as we have come to know it, has only recently expanded its influence. For most of human history, formal education was unnecessary. Children learned what was necessary in their kinship units or in play with other children. But as the economic life of a society changes, kinship becomes inadequate to the task of imparting all those skills necessary for participation in the society. Education becomes formal and increasingly expands to a larger proportion of the population. And in highly modern societies, such as the United States, we spend many of our earliest and best years in formal educational structures.

It is appropriate, therefore, that we come to understand this institution. Why did it emerge? What are its consequences for society and the individual? We would do well to have answers to such questions. For as you read this page, education is shaping your life.

As education emerges as a separate institution, its consequences for the individual and society expand. Once established, the institution of education begins to have at least five major consequences, or functions, for the human system: (1) **cultural storage,** (2) **cultural expansion,** (3) socialization, (4) **social placement,** and (5) social change.

Cultural Storage

As we already know, humans live in a world of symbols. We use many of these symbols, such as technologies, values, beliefs, and norms, to guide and organize our daily affairs. We store these symbols in our minds; they direct and guide us from within. But as societies become more complex, it is not possible to keep all of the cultural heritage in a single mind, or in the minds of groups of people. Written language allows for the elaboration of culture to a point where it must be stored by specialists. Education serves this function in modern societies. It keeps, maintains, and preserves the cultural system of a society.

Cultural Expansion and Change

As only a repository of culture, educational structures might resemble a "museum of symbols"; but in actual practice educational structures are usually involved in cultural innovation. Research is a major task in universities and colleges. New technologies, new insights, new interpretations of the present, past, and future are part of the goals of many structures of higher education. More indirectly, students are being taught to think, to reflect, to ponder, and hopefully to create new insights at all levels of the educational system. Thus, one of the goals of primary and secondary schools, as well as of colleges and universities, is to impart the skills that will enable people to expand the cultural storehouse in a wide variety of adult roles.

Socialization

In Chapter 7 we discussed in detail how socialization shapes personality and prepares the individual to assume key statuses and play roles. Education increasingly becomes a major agent of socialization. We learn in schools not only the substantive knowledge but also the skills necessary to play roles in the society at large. Moreover, we learn more than intellectual substance and technique. We also learn how to participate in formal organizations, how to live with impersonality, how to compete, how to subject ourselves to just and unjust evaluations. In other words, we learn many of the interpersonal skills and psychological dispositions necessary to participate in modern society. Thus, "slipping in the back door" is an entirely hidden curriculum: learning how to play the game of life as it is played in modern, industrial societies (Drucker 1959).

Social Placement

In societies without formal education, placement as adults in the broader society occurs in terms of kinship rules. Sex, birth order, and the rank of a family determine what children will become and do as adults. In more developed societies where a wide variety of alternative jobs exists, education assumes enormous importance in placing people into social and economic niches. The "credentials" acquired in the system of education become the main mechanism for hiring and promoting people. Education thus becomes "society's gatekeeper," sorting and allocating people to different places and rungs in the broader society.

Social Change

As a set of structures involved in storing and expanding culture, in socializing skills and attributes, and in placing or allocating people to social niches, education can be used as a vehicle for change. It grips the minds of the young and it possesses the power to decide what they learn, how they learn, and for what purposes this knowledge will be used. Aside from any innovations that the educational system may generate, then, education can be used for political purposes. It can be used to create a "new citizen," to undermine traditions of kinship or religion, or to generate a work force with new skills. Therefore, it is no coincidence that totalitarian states often use education to mold the

population in certain directions; nor is it surprising that governments—totalitarian or otherwise—often initiate their economic and social development through the creation of new schools oriented to the masses. Even in developed societies, such as the United States, education is used to foster change by industry and government. Integration of schools, the creation of federal land-grant colleges, the proliferation of junior colleges, or the endowments of private universities by corporate interests all document efforts to change the society in certain directions through the educational system.

DEFINITION OF THE INSTITUTION OF EDUCATION

We are now in a position to define education as a major social institution. As with all institutions, education must serve certain functions or have important consequences, which we have just reviewed. Like all structures in the human system, the institution of education is composed of statuses, norms, and roles. We have also used the term **formal** in our discussion, indicating that the institution of education is composed of statuses, norms, and roles that are formally organized. The institution of education can thus be defined as all those formally organized statuses, roles, and norms that increasingly come to have consequences for cultural storage, cultural expansion, socialization, social placement, and social change (Turner 1972, p. 148). With this definition we can now explore further the institution of education.

In the late 1960s, college students sought to use colleges and universities as vehicles of social change.

THE EMERGENCE OF EDUCATION

Probably the first beginnings of the institution of education occurred with the emergence of organized religious activity. Shaman, witch doctors, and other religious practitioners may have selected pupils for religious instruction. Much of the lore, tradition, and sacred customs of a society were imparted to these students who would, in turn, pass them on to other selected students.

Education was expanded with the emergence of state forms of governance (see Chapter 19). Such governments require administrative specialists—people to do the book-keeping, to organize state affairs, to wage war, to collect taxes, and the like. Although early political leaders relied upon kin to conduct governmental affairs, the need to recruit and train specialists increased as governments grew. Such growth usually depends upon an economic surplus created by an agrarian economy. Thus, formal education of specialists did not occur until 10,000 years ago. There were no governments sufficiently large to support or need administrative labor. Yet, the Egyptians of 4000 B.C. certainly had formal education not only for elites but also for selected peasants who showed "promise" and the ability to assist in the administration of government. Canals, irrigation, sewage disposal, the pyramids, tombs, and cities of this early state government could not have been designed and built without some degree of formal education of non-elites.

Formal education may also have been acquired by the crafts- and tradespeople as well as the shopkeepers of early cities. The creation of the larger trading centers of all the early empires probably required formal education to train people in keeping records and in administering other aspects of economic transactions. Yet, for significant periods of history in Asia and Europe, political unification and economic trade often disintegrated. For example, the Dark Ages are "dark" not because nothing occurred but because there were few, except isolated religious practitioners, to keep records. Similarly in Asia, literacy from formal education appears to have increased, and then decreased, depending upon political and economic trends (Turner 1972, pp. 149–150).

Even under the best conditions, however, education was a recessive institution. It reached only elites and few of the masses. But with the industrial revolution, the need for literacy and specialized skills increased dramatically. Schools were established to educate industrial workers, tradespeople, and increasingly, administrative specialists in industry and government. With industrialization, then, education became a prominent institution, serving the full range of functions outlined earlier. Yet, we should remember that despite its power and pervasiveness in all parts of the world today, the institution of education has only recently assumed its full proportions. It is one of the more recent creations of the human system.

THE STRUCTURE OF MODERN EDUCATION

Levels of Education

Most contemporary systems of education are divided into three levels: (1) **primary schools,** (2) **secondary schools,** and (3) **higher education.** Although there are wide variations in just how primary education is conducted, most societies have developed a primary school system for a majority of those between the ages 6 and 12. In poor nations this schooling is all the formal education that people will receive, and thus, the effort is to impart rudimentary reading, writing, and arithmetic skills. Political socialization that will make the masses loyal to the existing government is also a goal of the primary system.

In more affluent nations primary schools prepare students for participation in the secondary schools that will occupy their energies through adolescence. In most societies a secondary school education is the last phase of the educational process. Only a few will go further, and it is only in America that almost one-half of the college-aged population will seek education beyond secondary school. Part of this difference between American schools and those of other advanced societies is due to differences in the structure of secondary schools. Most societies have what is termed a **multiple track** system as opposed to the **single track** system in the United States. The differences between these two systems are shown in Figure 1 (Havighurst & Neugarten 1967, p. 90).

Figure 1: Multiple and Single Track School Systems

Source: Turner (1972:153). Adapted from Havighurst & Neugarten 1967.

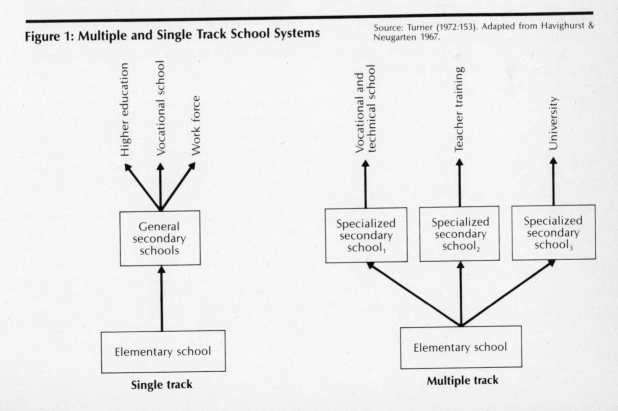

In the multiple track system, secondary schools train people for specialized jobs, different schools usually specializing in different types of training. As a result, much of what is taught in professional and trade schools in America is collapsed into the secondary curriculum in other societies. In contrast, the American system has one school track, for all must go to primary and secondary schools. Within the secondary school there are **lanes** for sorting out students—"vocational" and "college prep" lanes, for example. Lanes have many of the same consequences as tracks in the multiple track system: they sort and circumscribe the options that will be available to students upon graduation.

In most societies higher education is reserved for the sons and daughters of elites or for those who have shown exceptional ability in primary and secondary schools. The vast majority of citizens do not attend college, although it must be remembered that their secondary education is likely to have involved considerable specialized training.

World Trends in Education

The similar structure of formal education is due to certain pervasive educational trends. In response to economic and political pressures, education is undergoing a common transformation in all developing and developed nations (Turner 1972, pp. 162–169).

Massification and Democratization. In response to an industrializing economy's need for a literate labor force and a political regime's desire to maintain a loyal citizenry, education is currently being extended to all members of a population (Clark 1962). Primary schools are the first to be extended to all students; then secondary schooling becomes universal; and finally, there are trends in some countries, such as the United States, for the extension of higher education to the mass public.

Sometimes the creation of a mass educational system is symbolic: it can give the appearance that progress in the general social conditions of a society is occurring and that life for the average person is getting better. Yet, there is an inherent dilemma in the creation of a literate and skilled populace. What happens when they cannot realize their expectations about a better life? To be a literate peasant is probably much more frustrating than being an illiterate one. Thus, to have job skills but no job can pose severe problems of civil unrest in many developing nations. Even developed nations, such as the United States, have this problem during economic recessions. College graduates suddenly have difficulty finding jobs commensurate with their skills and expectations.

The extension of education to the masses is related to political and social democracy. By giving all at least some opportunity to develop their skills, people have a better chance to move up the stratification ladder. Moreover, a literate population is better able to perceive totally unjust policies and practices; and thus, over the long run, an educated population exerts pressures for increased political democracy.

As we know from our discussion of stratification in Chapter 14, however, opportunities to do well can be more illusionary than real. Family socialization, crushing poverty, and subtle forms of discrimination can work against lower class children in schools. We will examine this process in more detail for American schools, but the generalization is universally true. Children of the already educated are at an advantage in school competition with children of the uneducated. Moreover, political democracy can also be more illusionary than real. Highly educated populations in eastern Europe and China, for example, exist in and accept totalitarian political regimes. However, these regimes are more democratic than their predecessors, since the average citizen does have more opportunity to become a political or economic elite.

Bureaucratization. We already have emphasized the fact that the institution of education involves formality—that is, the creation of a bureaucratic structure. With growing numbers participating in the schools of a society, the sheer magnitude of the task of educating large numbers of students forces *increased* reliance on formal organizations. Schools and school systems become bureaucratic. Statuses become clearly defined and hierarchically arranged; performance and achievement in roles are emphasized; role behaviors are carried out more impersonally; and classes, schools, and school districts begin to show bureaucratic relations.

Centralization. Partly as a result of bureaucratization, schools and school systems become more centralized. They are increasingly controlled and regulated by central authorities. The United States is probably the only mass educational system that is not centralized—a situation that will occupy our attention shortly. Centralization also stems from political imperatives. Governments that are using education for specific purposes—whether these be economic, political, or social—are likely to desire control of the schools. Coordinating educational programs with economic growth requires coordination and control of schools. Using the schools to indoctrinate a "new citizenry" also requires political control; even in systems, such as the one in the United States, there are pressures for centralization as schools are used to achieve such goals as equality of opportunity for blacks and other minorities. To people in other societies, the intense resistance in America to federal control in the name of "community control" would be incomprehensible.

These general trends toward massification, democratization, bureaucratization, and centralization mark educational development all over the world. As the institution of education emerges and expands its functions, it tends to follow these trends. It is in the context of these worldwide trends that the American educational system presents an interesting paradox. It is massified, democratized, and bureaucratized, but it remains highly decentralized. It is thus an educational system worthy of further investigation.

EDUCATION IN AMERICA

No institution in America is subject to more public feeling than education. Of course, people are concerned about other institutions; they object to governmental abuses, and they do not like unemployment and economic recessions. But in the day-to-day politics of any community, the school often stands at the center of controversy. Not only are local schools an issue, but higher education is the subject of youths' aspirations and parents' hopes for their children's future. In our discussion of American education, then, we must analyze not just its properties, but also the reasons behind its position the public's eye. Thus, we will divide our discussion into two parts. First, we will review the general structure of American education, and then we will review some of the basic dilemmas or controversies in American education.

The Structure of American Education

Mass Education. Virtually every American receives a primary school education and close to 90% graduate from high school. Illiteracy is now below 3%. Even college enrollments have increased dramatically, with close to 50% of the population initiating some form of higher education and over 30% of those in the graduate-age population actually receiving four-year college degrees. Education thus extends to all segments of the population. Mass education is a fact of social life in America.

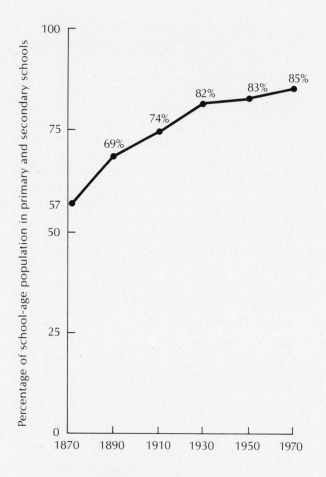

Figure 2: The Extension of Education in the United States, 1870–1970

Source: HEW, *Statistics of State School Systems* (Washington, D.C.: U.S. Government Printing Office, 1974).

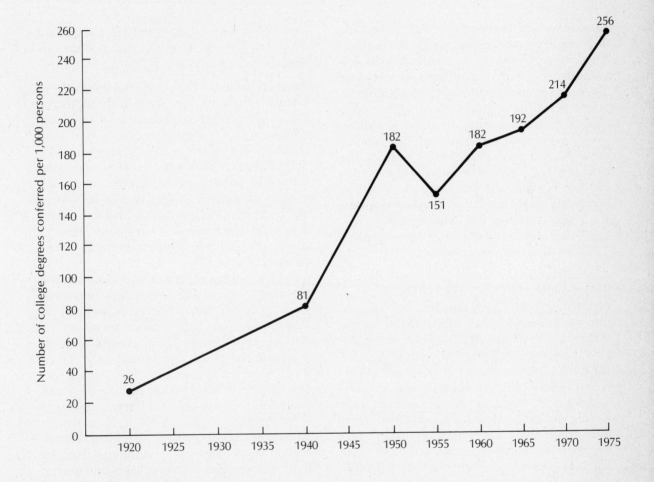

**Figure 3: The Extension of College
Education, 1900–1975**

Source: Bureau of the Census, *Statistical Abstracts of the United
States*, 97th ed., 1976, p. 140, Table 231.

Education and Democracy. Mass education does not necessarily mean an equal education. The quality of schools in America varies between rural/urban areas, urban and suburban cities, and from state to state. For example, to attend school in a rural area of a poor state assures that the quality of education will be less than the rural area of a wealthier state, or the suburban area of any state. Thus, to the extent that educational democracy means educational equality, there is far from complete democracy in the educational system in America. We will return to this issue shortly, for it is at the heart of many dilemmas confronting the educational system in America.

Bureaucratization. American schools have a unique pattern of bureaucratization. Each individual school is highly bureaucratized and is part of a larger district bureaucracy, which usually encompasses all the schools in a given city or county. All districts are part of a state-wide board of education, but as we will examine shortly, districts enjoy considerable autonomy. At the higher education level, both private and state colleges or universities have a high degree of bureaucratization—as any student reading this book knows. Most state colleges and universities are part of a larger, statewide bureaucracy.

Bureaucratization has increased with growing enrollments, and although enrollments at all educational levels are beginning to stabilize somewhat, the sheer volume of students requires extensive bureaucratization. As we will explore in the next section, this fact has created dilemmas for the American educational system.

Decentralization. The American educational system is the least centralized in the industrial world. At the lower educational level individual schools enjoy some autonomy from each other, but are subject to the district's authority. School districts have some autonomy from the state and federal administration, and each state establishes its own educational system within vague and general guidelines established by the federal government. Table 1 shows this pattern of influence and control (Turner 1972, p. 176).

As you can see in Table 1, American schools are subject to strong community pressures. Local property taxes finance a majority of school functions; school board members are elected; and strong "local-control" beliefs dominate the American consciousness. American lower education is thus highly decentralized with very little coordination and control at the national level (Pierce 1964).

At the higher educational level, a similar pattern of decentralization is evident. Private schools enjoy considerable autonomy from the federal government. State colleges and universities are administratively separate, although each is subject to budgetary and policy constraints of a statewide administration. Junior colleges are usually a part of the lower educational school district or a separate junior college district and are thus subject to some pressures by a school board and local community. Yet, in contrast to the "state institutes" of other nations, and their coordination by "ministries of education," higher education in America remains highly decentralized.

Table 1: Decentralization in American Schools

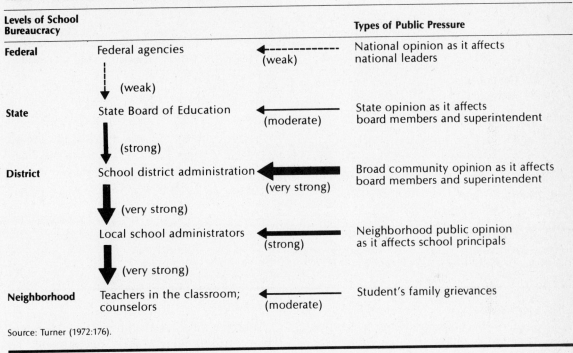

Levels of School Bureaucracy

Federal — Federal agencies ← - - - - - - - (weak) — National opinion as it affects national leaders

(weak) ↓

State — State Board of Education ← (moderate) — State opinion as it affects board members and superintendent

(strong) ↓

District — School district administration ← (very strong) — Broad community opinion as it affects board members and superintendent

(very strong) ↓

Local school administrators ← (strong) — Neighborhood public opinion as it affects school principals

(very strong) ↓

Neighborhood — Teachers in the classroom; counselors ← (moderate) — Student's family grievances

Types of Public Pressure

Source: Turner (1972:176).

These general structural characteristics of American education provide a backdrop for visualizing certain chronic dilemmas facing the educational system. Areas of controversy stem from problems built into a mass, bureaucratized, and decentralized system having clear inequalities. We are now in a position to explore these in more detail (Turner 1976, 1977).

The Enduring Dilemma of Lower Education: Educational Inequality

In the words of Thomas Jefferson, schools were to ". . . bring into action that mass of talents which lies buried in poverty in every country for want of means of development. . . ." There can be little doubt that mass public education has increased the skills of many Americans. Yet, the educational system does not do so equally. This fact has important

Table 2: Percentage of People with Different Levels of Education in Different Types of Occupations

Occupational Category	Did Not Graduate from High School		High School Graduate		1 to 3 Years of College		4 Years of College or More	
	Male	Female	Male	Female	Male	Female	Male	Female
Professional and technical	0.9	1.0	6.3	1.6	17.1	22.5	54.1	71.1
Managers and administrators	5.5	2.9	15.5	5.2	24.2	7.7	26.3	6.8
Clerical workers	2.9	6.5	8.3	19.0	10.0	46.8	3.1	13.5
Sales workers	1.3	3.7	5.9	7.4	10.6	5.0	8.3	3.0
Craft and kindred workers	25.4	2.7	29.4	3.0	18.7	1.2	3.9	0.5
Operatives	29.7	35.1	19.3	27.9	8.9	4.4	1.1	1.3
Service workers	10.6	42.9	7.3	33.0	6.4	11.0	1.6	3.1
Farmers and farm managers	5.7	0.5	3.2	0.2	1.6	0.3	1.0	0.3
Farm laborers and supervisors	4.7	3.5	0.6	1.1	0.4	0.4	0.2	0.2
Laborers, except farm	13.4	1.4	4.2	1.5	2.2	0.7	0.4	0.0

Source: U.S. Bureau of the Census, *Current Population Reports,* Series P-20, No. 274, December 1974, p. 6.

consequences. Because we live in a "credentialed society," people's chances for success are the result of their educational credentials. Although educational credentialing is a convenient way to determine the abilities of masses of potential workers, it forces the educational system to be the society's gatekeeper. People who can conform to the system's requirements will be well credentialed. But if people have personal, cultural, and socioeconomic handicaps, and have difficulty conforming, they are less likely to receive credentials and get well-paying jobs. The relationship between job and education is reported in Table 2.

Although differences in people's intellectual ability will influence their performance in schools, equally important are factors that have little to do with a student's intellect. For example, certain ethnic groups consistently do not go as far in school as others. This tendency is not related to differences in intelligence or innate ability among ethnics but to their social background, economic situation, and discrimination in the schools. Table 3 shows these differences in ethnic groups in terms of whether or not a group is above or below the national average for educational attainment. Similar differences exist for children from middle, working, and poverty classes, regardless of their ethnicity.

Table 3: Education Among Selected Ethnic Groups: Their Deviation from the National Average (10.9 years of school)

Ethnic Group	How Much Deviation from the National Average
Blacks	−1.2 years
Spanish-speaking	−1.6 years
Jews	+2.4 years
Protestant Irish	−0.3 years
Catholic Irish	+1.3 years
Italian	−0.2 years
Polish	−0.9 years

Source: Adapted from Greeley (1974, p. 65).

What data such as these indicate is that children from different ethnic and class backgrounds do not have an equal chance to achieve in school. It is this situation that presents the educational system with one of its most enduring dilemmas. The problems of the schools in providing an equal opportunity have been attributed to two forces: (1) the structure of American public education, particularly the lower educational system; and (2) the cultural and personal traits with which lower class children, especially minority poor, enter school.

It now appears that some of the bureaucratic features of public schools—emphasis on control, order, plans, schedules, and the like—can inadvertently discriminate against non-middle-class children. The formality of schools, for example, with their concern with silence, the lesson plan, the schedule, and the control of movement, can work to the disadvantage of some children from the lower classes, where physical assertiveness, noise, and spontaneity are more likely to be valued (Miller 1958). In middle-class-oriented schools, then, lower class children are more likely to become alienated.

Another source of discrimination comes from the teachers in public schools. Most are from the middle classes; as a result, they can communicate a subtle attitude or expectation that lower class or minority students will have learning problems. By expecting less of lower class students, teachers can potentially and unintentionally convince the students that they have "learning problems" (Rosenthal & Jacobson 1968; Silberman 1970, pp. 83–86).

Seemingly objective and fair tests represent yet another form of discrimination against lower class children. IQ tests, national achievement exams, or inclass quizzes are competitive and timed. Such tests favor students from middle-class backgrounds because the importance of test taking and competition is more likely to have been stressed. Moreover, most tests are written in standard English and this fact gives middle-class students, whose parents are more verbal than those in the lower classes, a competitive advantage. In addition, national achievement and IQ tests typically portray a world that is more familiar to middle-class students. A typical question from a standarized

IQ test, for example, reads as follows (Havighurst & Neugarten 1967, pp. 78–79).

A symphony is to a composer as a book is to what? ( ) paper ( ) sculptor ( ) author ( ) musician ( ) man

Symphonies, sculptors, authors, and musicians are probably more familiar to the young from middle classes; hence, they will perform better on these tests than youth from the lower classes. Such measuring instruments carry much weight. Scores on national achievement and IQ tests serve as guidelines that are used to channel students into college preparatory or vocational programs (Cicourel & Kitsuse 1963). Moreover, we can infer from our earlier examination of personality that experiences on tests are likely to shape young students' educational self-concept. They will come to define themselves as good, bad, or mediocre students. In turn, children's self-concepts will influence their performance and aspirations and the process of test taking can convince lower-class students that they cannot compete with middle-class students or meet the academic standards of the middle classes.

These kinds of experiences in schools appear to have more influence than the actual facilities of the schools on student achievement. In turn, just what a student experiences is a reflection of what traits they bring into the school (Coleman 1966; Jencks 1969).

In general, since schools are run and taught by middle-class personnel and because texts and tests are written by middle-class professionals, schools are more likely to reward those

Middle class teachers with their concern for order and silence often operate to discriminate against lower class students in America.

students from the middle classes. This situation is compounded by the experiences of many lower class children: poverty, parental frustration, hunger, and adult resignation. Some lower class homes and environments are not conducive to success in schools. Under these conditions the schools have a difficult problem in knowing how to reach and help these students. Funds are usually limited, and there is little consensus about what programs are useful.

Thus, the school system in America faces a difficult dilemma: how to equalize educational opportunities, and thereby, enable all students to realize their full potential. This dilemma will be one of the centers of controversy in the American educational system for many decades to come.

Problems of Higher Education

Size and Scope. There are over 2,500 institutions of higher education in America and about seven million students are enrolled in four-year colleges. Another two million attend two year colleges (Parker 1973). The scope and size of higher education is but another indication of the degree to which America is a "credentialed" society. To get a "good job," higher educational credentials are increasingly considered necessary (see Table 2). Now, almost one-half of college-age youths have entered the "credentials race." College enrollments have begun to level off but there are problems inherent in the size of higher education.

Increases in size of college campuses has increased the degree of bureaucratization and, hence, the specialization and neutralization of

Does a College Education Increase Income?

Although some college graduates may have trouble getting jobs, there is still a strong relationship between amount of income and education. However, women receive less income than comparably educated men, and college-educated women receive less than men who have not completed high school. In the table below, these facts are highlighted:

Years of School Completed	Average Yearly Income in 1974 for:	
	Men	Women
Completed Elementary School	$ 7,676	$3,114
Some High School	$ 9,626	$3,883
High School Diploma	$11,770	$4,777
Some College	$13,275	$5,576
College Diploma	$16,191	$6,873
Five or More Years of College	$18,404	$9,075

Source: U.S. Bureau of the Census, *Current Population Reports*, Series P–60, no. 101, January 1976, Table 58.

college life. The need to process masses of students has forced less personal instruction and larger classes. However, increases in volume of students have facilitated the development of better libraries, improved laboratories, and greater numbers of skilled faculties. Reconciling these advantages with the impersonality accompanying escalated bureaucratization will continue to be a dilemma for America's large state and private universities (Sewell 1971).

The Job Market. College enrollments emphasize students' belief that they must have a college education if they are to "get a good job." However, as more people receive a college degree, it begins to lose its significance. Many more people now have a degree and it is less discriminating. Many college-educated students must now often take "lesser jobs" which, ironically, they could probably have secured without a college degree. Table 2 emphasizes the fact that a college education still offers advantages to those who have one, but this degree may "mean less" in the future.

An emerging problem for higher education is: should the "credentials race" among greater numbers of students who will be less marketable be encouraged? The answer may come from employers rather than university administrations. Employers may decide that college degrees no longer discriminate among prospective employees, and thus, new measures of ability and motivation will have to be developed. Of course, this transformation is not likely in the near future. Yet, the problems of an educated population, which will encounter employment problems, are likely to increase in the future.

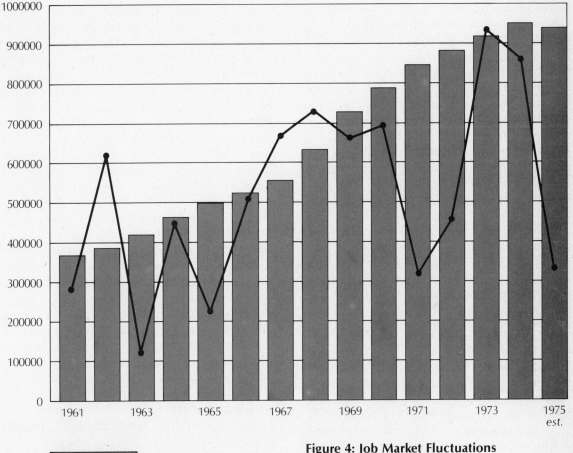

Figure 4: Job Market Fluctuations and College Graduates

College graduates

Employment in "college-level" jobs *(year-to-year change)*

The figure above reports the fluctuating job market for college graduates in relation to the increasing numbers of college graduates. As can be seen, the job market has decreased in relation to those with college degrees seeking "college-level" jobs.

Source: From Walter Guzzardi, "The Uncertain Passage From College," *Fortune*, January, 1976; (C) 1976 Time Inc.

Research vs. Teaching. Large universities are charged with a dual task of imparting existing knowledge to students and of developing new knowledge through research. Promoting research requires the expenditure of funds on research facilities, the accumulation of a large graduate student population that can assist in research, and the diversion of professors' energies away from undergraduate teaching. On the other hand, to emphasize undergraduate instruction necessitates more teaching effort from professors, decreased concern with graduate education, and the expenditure of funds for undergraduate programs.

There presently appears no easy solution to this dilemma. Currently, universities appear to have become differentiated in terms of their emphasis on research or teaching, and there are very few college campuses that are not in considerable turmoil over which should be given more or less emphasis.

Institutional Cooptation. The federal government increasingly funds research at all colleges and universities. This funding has allowed universities to increase their graduate student populations, to create excellent faculties, to construct large-scale and expensive research facilities, from computers to whole buildings, and to help finance many non-research activities. There are problems in these financial liaisons, however (Maccoby 1974; Orlans 1962). First, government-financed research is also government controlled, and it is possible that such control will limit research activities. This

situation violates one of the purposes of university research: to expand knowledge in all spheres of human endeavor. Second, by accepting research funds from the federal government, the current ranking of national priorities is tacitly supported. As a place of free inquiry, the university is established to examine neutrally social conditions. Under government control of research, however, researchers can become reluctant to express their professional views and conclusions for fear of losing lucrative and prestigious research contracts.

In addition to direct federal funding of research, the university maintains many other financial liaisons. Universities own stock in corporations; universities are often large landholders and, in some instances, slum lords; they compete for lucrative research contracts, much like business corporations; their faculty members often act as consultants for both government and business; and members of their boards of trustees are usually prominent businesspersons, frequently from companies with whom the universities do business (Ridgeway 1968). Of course, these kinds of liaisons are necessary to maintain the universities' solvency. To sever them completely would require a drastic increase in tuition at private universities and an increase in taxes for state-supported campuses.

This financial dependency of the university poses a perplexing problem. What kinds of institutional connections should universities have? Which ones could corrupt free inquiry? Which liaisons could and should be severed? These questions will continue to be a source of conflict and dialogue within universities.

SUMMARY AND PREVIEW

In this chapter we have attempted to understand the institution of education. We first examined the functions of education: cultural storage, cultural expansion, socialization, social placement, and social change. We saw that education is a recent institution in the human system and that it serves all its functions with industrialization. Presently, education is a dominant institution, showing several trends: massification, democratization, and centralization.

We also examined the American educational system, its structure and enduring dilemmas. Although the system reaches the masses and is highly bureaucratized, it has a highly decentralized profile. At the lower educational level, the problem of educational equality poses the most enduring problem. At the higher educational level, a number of dilemmas persist: size and scope, education for jobs, research vs. teaching, and institutional cooptation.

We have now completed our review of basic human institutions. We have examined kinship, religion, economy, polity, and the emergence and elaboration of the last great human institution, education. As we noted at the outset of this institutional analysis, social institutions are those broad congeries of structures dealing with basic problems facing humans and their organization. They are the most encompassing of social forms, since they are constructed of groups, formal and fluid patterns of organization, strata, and community forms. They represent one of the most interesting ways that basic elements of the human system—culture, interaction, social organization, and socialization—have been elaborated.

We are now in a position to review the human system, to see it in a broad perspective. In the next section we will provide an overview of how the human system has developed and how it is now structured. We will briefly present the trends of the human system and the ultimate problems it now faces.

Key Terms

Cultural Storage: the process by which the symbolic world created by humans is maintained over long periods of time

Cultural Expansion: the process by which new symbolic components are created and added to the cultural storehouse

Social Placement: the process of allocating individuals to positions in the broader social structure

Formal: social structures that have explicit and specialized statuses, unambiguous norms, clear authority relations, and an emphasis on impersonal role performance

Primary Schools: those school structures involved in educating students 5 to 12 years of age

Secondary Schools: those school structures involved in educating students during their early and middle adolescence

Higher Education: those school structures involved in educating graduates of secondary schools

Multiple Track: a system of secondary schools that is differentiated in terms of the kind of training that each school provides

Single Track: a system of secondary schools in which all schools provide the same educational programs

Lanes: different educational programs for students of varying abilities and orientation within a single track system

Massification: the process of extending access to education to all members of a society

Democratization: the process of seeking to use schools to provide equal opportunities for success

Bureaucratization: the process of creating formal organization

Centralization: the process of creating hierarchies and concentrating authority in those at the top of the hierarchy

Cooptation: the process of gaining control of a structure by increasing its dependence on another for basic resources

Review Questions

1. What are the functions of education in society?

2. What forces have stimulated the growth of education?

3. What are the current world trends in education?

4. How does American education compare with that in other societies?

5. What forces prevent schools from providing equal opportunities to all students?

6. What dilemmas do American colleges and universities face?

Suggested Readings

Berg, Ivar. *Education and Jobs: The Great Training Robbery.* New York: Praeger, 1970.

Friedenberg, Edgar Z. *Coming of Age in America: Growth and Acquiescence.* New York: Vintage Books, 1965.

Goslin, David A. *The School in Contemporary Society.* Chicago: Scott Foresman, 1965.

Havighurst, Robert J., and Neugarten, Bernice. *Society and Education.* Boston: Allyn & Bacon, 1968.

Jackson, Philip W. *Life in the Classroom.* New York: Holt, Rinehart and Winston, 1968.

Jencks, Christopher. *Inequality: A Reassessment of the Effect of Family and Schooling in America.* New York: Basic Books, 1972.

Katz, Michael B. *Class, Bureaucracy, and Schools: The Illusion of Educational Change in America.* New York: Praeger, 1971.

Rosenthal, Robert, and Jacobson, Lenore. *Pygmalion in the Classroom.* New York: Holt, Rinehart and Winston, 1968.

Sexton, Patricia Cayo. *The American School: A Sociological Analysis.* Englewood Cliffs, N.J.: Prentice-Hall, 1967.

Silberman, Charles E. *Crisis in the Classroom: The Remaking of American Education.* New York: Vintage Books, 1971.

CHALLENGE AND CHANGE IN THE HUMAN SYSTEM

CONTENTS

PREVIEW

In the previous sections we have explored the beginnings and the subsequent development of the human system. We have discussed the basic elements of this system and then shown how they have been elaborated into diverse social forms, from small groups to societywide institutions. In this last section we will view this human system as a whole. What is the relationship of the human system to the environment? How does the size, profile, movement, and growth of populations in a society and in the world influence the human system, and vice versa? What trends in humans' life on earth have been evident?

In Chapter 21 we will explore the implications of the fact that humans are

V

dependent upon other species and the inorganic environment for survival. Chapter 22 will address the issue of population characteristics and dynamics. In both of these chapters we will be concerned with the challenges that adaptation to the ecosystem and the rapid proliferation of our numbers pose for the continuity of the human system. Finally, in Chapter 23 we will summarize the trends and future prospects of the human system.

ECOLOGY AND THE HUMAN SYSTEM

PROLOGUE

Guiding Questions: In what ways are humans and nature united as one? What constraints does nature place on the human system? What have humans done to nature?

Chapter Topics

THE SCIENCE OF ECOLOGY

Humans now appear to dominate the animal species, and although a cynic once observed that in the long run, "the smart money is on the insects," we tend to forget that we, too, are a species. We saw in Chapter 3 how precarious our existence, and that of our ancestors, may have been thousands of years ago on the African savannah. Ecological forces constrained humans. Our population was kept small because we could not support ourselves in great numbers. Yet, these facts of our existence can sometimes appear to be behind us. We are ascendant. Our elaborate social forms are no longer subject to the constraints of the ecosystem.

Nothing could be further from the truth, for ultimately, humans are merely one of many species that inhabit the earth. Although our culture and elaborate social forms make us unique, we are like all animal species in our dependence upon air, water, and the sustenance provided by the soil and other animals.

A Definition of Ecology

When we think of **ecology,** what associations come to mind? Perhaps most commonly the word conjures up thoughts of the ecological reform movement that became prominent in the mid-1960s. The discipline of scientific ecology has, in fact, existed since the turn of the century. As near as can be determined, the word *ecology,* which, like *economy,* has its origins in the Greek word *oikos,* (a house or place to live) was first used by the German plant biologist Ernst Haeckel in 1868. The beginning of the formal study of ecology is marked by the publication of F. E. Clements' *Research Methods in Ecology* in 1905, his *Plant Physiology and Ecology* in 1907, and Eugenus Warming's *Ecology of Plants* in 1909 (Hawley 1950, p. 3).

Amos Hawley's *Human Ecology* (1950) is a landmark in sociology. In this work, Hawley sets down the definition of ecology as "The study of the relation of organisms or groups of organisms to their environment." Hawley's definition stresses the relationship between organisms and their environment. The interaction of an organism with its environment is known as behavior (Hawley 1950, p. 18). But ecology is not interested in behavior as we normally understand it. Notice that our definition refers to "organisms or groups of organisms." All terms in this phrase are specifically plural, and this designation of plurality should be taken literally. Ecologists are not interested in the behavior of single organisms; they are interested in the behavior of populations.

Sociologists and ecologists, alike, characterize the varieties of collective actions in terms of their *organization*. To make our distinction more clear, we can think of the "web of life"—a metaphor first proposed by Charles Darwin in *The Origin of Species* (1859). Studying this web, ecologists are not interested in the material or substance of the web. Rather, they are interested in patterns of organization in the web. Ecologists attempt to find significance in the intricacies of the web, its constant features, its idiosyncracies, and the processes that both keep the web whole and threaten to tear it apart.

The Elementary Principles of Ecology

Scientific ecology is greatly indebted to Charles Darwin (1859). It was Darwin who first articulated many of the basic principles of ecological research. Darwin's web-of-life conception is fundamental to the ecological point of view. Darwin is largely responsible for the important ecological principles of (1) organic life as an essential struggle and (2) the primacy of adaptation as a mechanism for community survival. These two basic ecological principles need to be explored further.

Struggle and Competition. It is generally accepted that the structure and tensions of the web of life are direct results of struggle. **Struggle** is a word that seems evaluative; it seems to imply a purely hostile approach to survival. "Red of tooth and claw" and "survival of the fittest" are often used as catch phrases to describe the totality of Darwin's theories. Unfortunately, these phrases seem to connote

Charles Darwin codified the theory of evolution which provides the science of ecology with its basic principle.

violence or at least a lack of cooperation. Neither the findings of Darwin nor the results of more modern ecological research point to a purely violent quality in the struggle of organic life. Certainly, violence of various sorts is constantly occurring in the natural world. Habitats themselves are often brutally indifferent, even to the needs of their natural inhabitants. However, struggle includes cooperation and creation as well as competition and destruction. In fact, the vast majority of actions undertaken in the struggle for existence contain both destructive and creative elements. The lioness and the high grasses of the plains cooperate to create a

situation wherein an antelope will fall to the predator. Dense fresh-water vegetation cooperates with the cottonmouth moccasin to create a very dangerous situation for bullfrogs. The violent, often fatal competition of stags during the mating season keeps weaker elks from passing their traits on to the next generation, thereby allowing the species to enjoy a more healthy and prosperous existence. Beavers, as well as humans, destroy trees to create shelters.

Adaptation and Survival. Those traits of organisms that facilitate adaptation to the environment are likely to be retained since they will promote the survival of the species. The large brain of humans is but one example of a trait that facilitated adaptation and survival. It allowed for the development of the tools and patterns of social organization that enabled our primate ancestors, and the first humans, to survive on the African savannah.

All species must continuously adapt to their environment if they are to survive. Environments rarely remain stable; hence, new traits must often emerge if the species is to survive. Even humans, who have drastically altered their environment with urban/industrial patterns of social organization, may have to alter these patterns if they are to adapt to the very changes in the environment that they have precipitated.

An ecological perspective on the world, then, alerts us to the fact that life is a struggle for all species—a struggle that always involves patterns of competition and cooperation—and

The ecosystem is a constant process of struggle and adaptation.

that life is a continuous process of adaptation to the environment—species must change if they are to survive. These are facts for *all* life—micro-organic, plant, or human.

Appreciating these facts gives us a new view of ourselves. We can see ourselves as but one of millions upon millions of species that are engaged in continuous struggle and that continuously seek to adapt to the environment. Ecologists employ additional concepts to help us visualize this situation more clearly: (1) habitat, (2) niche, (3) biotic community, and (4) genetic and somatic adaptations. In many ways, these concepts are extensions of the basic principles of struggle and adaptation.

Habitat. In ecology habitat refers to the *inorganic* elements, such as minerals, gases, water, topography, and climate that constitute the abode or home of a species. We usually consider our home, or habitat, to include surrounding trees, vegetation, and local wildlife. However ecologists consider these as members of other species in the struggle for life. They are never considered elements of a habitat.

Niche. The struggle for life is not without discernible and reasonable goals. Perhaps the most fundamental of these goals is the establishment of a niche, or functional role, in the larger ecosystem. If a species relates to the habitat in a manner that accommodates the species to the habitat, the species attains an ecological niche. Thereafter, this niche is characterized by what the species does in the habitat.

Biotic Community. The establishment of a niche does not guarantee the perpetuation of a species. Once a niche has been established, the continuing survival of the species depends on

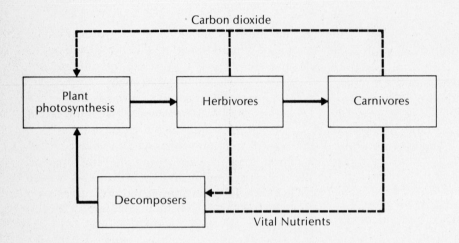

Figure 1: Fundamental Cycles of the Ecosystem

Source: Turner (1976, p. 254).

its relationship with other members of the biotic community. A biotic community is a complex of niches. The biotic community shares a common habitat and is considered to be "organized" because the functional action of each member species influences the activities of the other member species. Of course, once niches are established in a particular habitat, the foundation of a biotic community is not automatically assured. Yet, once various species come together to establish themselves at the level of the biotic community, interdependencies begin to become increasingly obvious.

These ecological interdependencies can be visualized as *chains, flows,* or *cycles* (Turner 1976, p. 253). A *chain* form of interdependence describes the manner in which any one species

of organism becomes food for another species which, in turn, becomes food for yet another species, and so forth. We commonly hear of food chains, for example. At one extreme of the food chain are tiny organisms, not immediately identifiable as either animal or vegetable in character, that feed solely and directly upon the energy provided by the sun (solar energy). At the other extreme we find humankind, which can, whether by choice or necessity, feed upon practically everything in the biological world, as well as upon a wide range of inorganic materials.

The *cycle* form of interdependency is well known to students of biology. A cycle is simply a chain process that folds back upon itself. For example, a very fundamental cycle involves energy from the sun, vegetative life, animal respiration, and the gaseous composition of the atmosphere. In this cycle, vegetative life

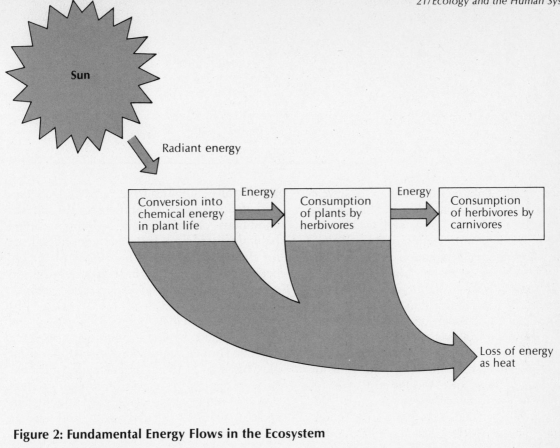

Figure 2: Fundamental Energy Flows in the Ecosystem

Source: Turner (1976, p. 255).

absorbs solar energy, which it uses in a direct manner to maintain itself through a process called photosynthesis. The chemistry of plant photosynthesis requires water and atmospheric nitrogen in addition to solar energy and, as a by-product of plant maintenance, oxygen is expelled into the atmosphere. Atmospheric oxygen is a basic requirement for animal life. Conversely, animal life expels carbon dioxide— essential to all plant life—into the air.

Some animals (herbivores) also maintain themselves by eating plants directly, whereas others (carnivores) subsist on the plant-eating animals. In turn, the solid wastes and dead carcasses of animals and plants are decomposed by fungi and other microorganisms. In this process, critical nutrients are recycled back through the ecosystem.

The chain and cycle forms mesh with a third major form of ecological interdependence called a *flow*. A *flow* is a more general form of ecological action than a chain or a cycle. By far, the most important flow is from the sun to the vast majority of living things, both animal and vegetable. Wind and tidal energies are major components of lesser, though nevertheless important, ecological flows.

The details of the complexity of interrelationships we have just briefly described are not fully understood. However, it is evident that life forms are closely dependent upon one another. No single species can ascend above its dependency on other life forms and the environment. Therefore, the capacity for life within the ecological community is reduced when the chains, cycles, and flows of nature are interrupted or out of balance.

Genetic and Somatic Adaptations. The vast and intricate network of niches, habitats, biotic communities, chains, flows, and cycles is a moment-to-moment reflection of the adaptive process in nature. Adaptation refers specifically to the life struggle and implies a coming to terms not only with the inorganic habitat but also with the organic world in general. For the various species, the fruit of adaptation is the security and control over their environment.

In a strictly biological sense, adaptation can be either genetic or somatic in nature. If an individual member of a species adjusts of its own accord to a changing environment, the adjustment is called a somatic adaptation. Somatic adaptations are usually limited to the life span of a single organism. Genetic adaptations, on the other hand, shape all members of a species. Moreover, they are passed from one generation to another. Genetic adaptations are almost always necessary before a species can attain an enduring niche in a habitat. Ecologists are interested in genetic adaptations because they are what influence the adaptation of a species to its environment.

Once a species has secured a niche in a biotic community, individual somatic adaptations become interesting to the ecologist. This interest evolves from the knowledge that activity or behavior is more readily adaptable than is the basic structure of a life form. Hidden changes in a habitat are often signaled by noticeable somatic adaptations on the part of one or more members of an affected resident species. The ecological importance of somatic adaptations is especially apparent in the human species.

Historically, humans have initiated and perpetuated dramatic adaptations to the current conditions of their biotic communities and habitats; yet none of these adaptations (at least for thousands of years) have been of the genetic type. Instead, they have been cultural and social in nature or, in ecological terms, somatic in nature.

From an ecological point of view, then, the human species has both common and unique aspects. Human populations exist within complex patterns of social organization, and their survival depends primarily on somatic adaptations of culture and social organization. Other species manifest themselves as more simple collectivities whose survival depends primarily on genetic adaptations. Yet all species share in common a crucial involvement with the cycles, chains, and flows of nature.

The heavy reliance of humans on culture and social organization for survival has stimulated a branch of social science known as "human ecology." We are a unique species, but we are still subject to basic ecological processes.

HUMAN ECOLOGY

The Emergence of Human Ecology

To this point we have become familiar with some of the basic terms and principles of the science of ecology. Today, ecology is separated into three fields of study: plant ecology, animal ecology, and human ecology. As we know, ecology had its beginnings at the turn of the century. At that time the study of ecology was almost exclusively devoted to plant life. Because of their docility and their relative lack of mobility, plants were obvious and convenient objects of scientific observation. Also, according to the biological understandings of the day, plants were far removed from us in the realm of the organic kingdom, and so their ecological functions were correspondingly amenable to objectification without fear of bias. Because the animal kingdom is composed of species more complex and more numerous than the species of the plant kingdom and because animal life is often both admirably mobile and far from docile, the beginnings of animal ecology came somewhat later.

The first attempts to give the human community a serious look from an ecological perspective were undertaken by a group of scientists (the Chicago School discussed in Chapter 13) who viewed their subject—the urban community—as "unnatural." Scientists ventured into the arena of human ecology because their curiosity was impelled by a newly appreciated possibility: perhaps human social activity could be described in terms of ecological processes known to be occurring in the plant and animal kingdoms. During the 1920s and 1930s the Chicago School was the vanguard of explorations of human ecology, although human ecology was not recognized as a distinct field of study at the time. The empirical and theoretical thrust of the Chicago School was greatly influenced by the work of early plant and animal ecologists and by Darwin's basic notions of struggle and adaptation. Ernest Burgess' concentric zone theory of urban segregation called attention to the possibility that the adaptation mechanisms of human populations could be generalized according to the effects of the competitive struggle for survival. A similar influence resulted from the Chicago School's studies of population concentration and dispersion. The Chicago School's conscientious study of neighborhood invasion and succession cycles was also innovative and similarly based on notions of the struggle for community survival.

As ecologists ventured further into the study of human populations, however, they soon discovered dramatic differences between human and other ecological niches. The mechanisms of population stability that operate to check the growth of other species seemed to be ineffective in human populations. Many complex human communities were seen to be "clumsy" in their interactions with the ecosystem; they often interfered with ecological processes that were tangential, at best, to human survival. Human populations were discovered to be exceptionally capable of adaptation to a wide variety of habitats, in all of which they seemed both determined and able to establish dominance.

The Study of Human Ecology

In common with plant ecology and animal ecology, **human ecology** also seeks to understand the forms and modes of development of relationships among groups of organisms and their environment. Of course, human ecology stresses the particular relationships of the human species with other species and various habitats. In addition, human ecology seeks in some ways to understand the forms and modes of development of relationships *within* the human species as well, which distinguishes it from plant and animal ecology. Plant ecology does not concern itself with relationships within a particular species of plant, nor does animal ecology concern itself (except in isolated cases) with relationships within a particular animal species.

Thus, the principal distinguishing feature of human ecology is its concern with the form and development of cultural and social activity *within* the human population. For only by understanding these cultural and social relationships within the human population can the relationships *between* humans and the environment be understood. The thrust of human ecology, then, is to visualize the general dynamics of what is termed "the human community" and then to analyze the relationship between this community and the environment.

In human ecology, four factors are given emphasis: (1) population characteristics, (2) organization, (3) environment, and (4) technology. An acronym for these factors—POET—is commonly used and easily remembered. The abbreviation POET will be used in our text when we refer to all four factors as a group. The four (POET) factors influence one another in complex, circular ways. Cultural components such as values, beliefs, and technology have effects on the characteristics of social organization and the population—number, age, and sex proportions, for example. Reciprocally, patterns of social organization have direct effects on the culture, the population, and the technologies within it. Population characteristics act in the same manner. These three factors—which for the ecologist make up the human community—act together upon the environment and vice versa. Although technology is an integral part of society's culture (being basically a system of knowledge about how to manipulate the environment), it is represented separately in this case because it is becoming increasingly pervasive and influential in human affairs. These relationships are outlined in Figure 3.

The POET Factors

Population. The various aspects that together compose a population both affect and are affected by other factors in the human ecological milieu. For instance, a highly concentrated population requires more advanced and intense forms of governmental, farming, educational, and other technologies. A relatively dispersed population, as exists in farming communities, demands fewer technologies and tolerates a less intense involvement with technology. A concentrated population is also more likely to effect dramatic alterations of the local environment than is a more dispersed population.

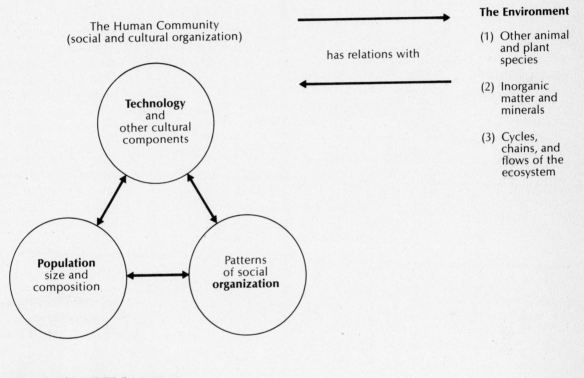

The Human Community
(social and cultural organization)

Technology
and
other cultural
components

Population
size and
composition

Patterns
of social
organization

has relations with

The Environment

(1) Other animal
and plant
species

(2) Inorganic
matter and
minerals

(3) Cycles,
chains, and
flows of the
ecosystem

Figure 3: The POET Factors

Organization. The nature of community, stratification, formal organization, and basic institutions, such as the economy and government, profoundly influences other POET factors—technology, population, and environment. For example, *industrial economic organization* is the product of technological breakthroughs, but once created, industrialization encourages new technologies, new values and beliefs, population concentrations, and pollu-tion of the environment. In contrast, a hunting-and-gathering economy dictates entirely different values, beliefs, technologies, social organization, and relationships with the environment.

Environment. The characteristics of the environmental factor can influence the other POET factors in various ways. Three major environmental characteristics are (1) climate, (2) available resources, and (3) nature of the terrain. Severe extremes of climate limit the

range and sophistication of technologies, and also limit community population size. Available resources act in much the same way. The nature of the terrain can be a direct factor in the determination of the relative concentration or dispersal of community populations. For example, a mountainous terrain with many hills and valleys promotes the formation of small pockets of dense population, whereas rolling farmland or flatlands allow a more dispersed population.

Technology. The numbers and kinds of available technologies have wide-ranging effects on the other factors. A powerful and advanced agricultural technology drastically alters the environment, as do mining and other engineering technologies, and, of course, we are becoming increasingly aware of the effects that industrial technologies can have on the environmental factor as well as on the population factor.

Otis Dudley Duncan (1969), has viewed the development of smog in the Los Angeles basin as an example of the interrelations among the POET factors. As Duncan describes it, a large influx of people and industries into the Los Angeles area occurred during World War II because of its strategic military location. Industrial waste and heavy automobile emissions were kept in the basin by an unfortunate and unavoidable combination of natural environmental characteristics in the area. Smog became prevalent, and when the smog was sufficiently dense, it promoted the spread of Los Angeles into even wider areas as people attempted to escape it. This migration led, in

The application of modern technology has created profound pollution problems. Here, the extension of airports has exposed a community to noise pollution.

turn, to an increased reliance on the automobile, which contributed to further accumulations of smog, and so on.

The process of interaction among the POET factors has been continuous throughout human history. In prehistory, environment was by far the most powerful of these four factors (see Chapter 3). Eventually other factors became more prominent. In response to the environmental factor, our ancestors evolved into social beings developing new patterns of social organization and cultural components, including technology. In turn, these new patterns of social organization and cultural factors, particularly technologies, have allowed for dramatic alteration of the environment. It is only now, with an energy shortage and massive ecological disruption, that the environmental factor is beginning to alter patterns of social organization, industrial technologies, and people's values and beliefs. We can visualize the impact of the POET factors in Figure 4.

Column 2 in Figure 4 highlights the interrelationships among technology, cultural values, patterns of social organization, and population characteristics. The operation of advanced technologies, values emphasizing production and consumption, and organization into an urban/industrial profile create great demand for energy resources and cause the discharge of waste residues. These are dumped into the basic renewable resources—air, soil, and water—upon which all life depends. As these renewable resources receive waste residues, the basic cycles, flows, and chains that rejuvenate these renewable resources are disrupted. With sufficient disruption of these chains, cycles, and flows, the ecosystem upon which humans depend is disrupted. For example, the life that produces 80% of our oxygen—the ocean's phytoplankton—is being invaded by chemicals that are running off into the oceans. The soil upon which we depend is becoming saturated with chemical fertilizers and pesticides. Humans now stand at a threshold: to use technologies and patterns of social and cultural organization in ways that do not cause further environmental disruption, or to continue the disruption of the ecosystem. The first human ecologists did not visualize this prospect of massive environmental disruption. But the threat it poses gives new urgency to the study of human ecology—an important area of sociological inquiry.

Figure 4: Society and Ecological Disruption

Source: Turner (1976)

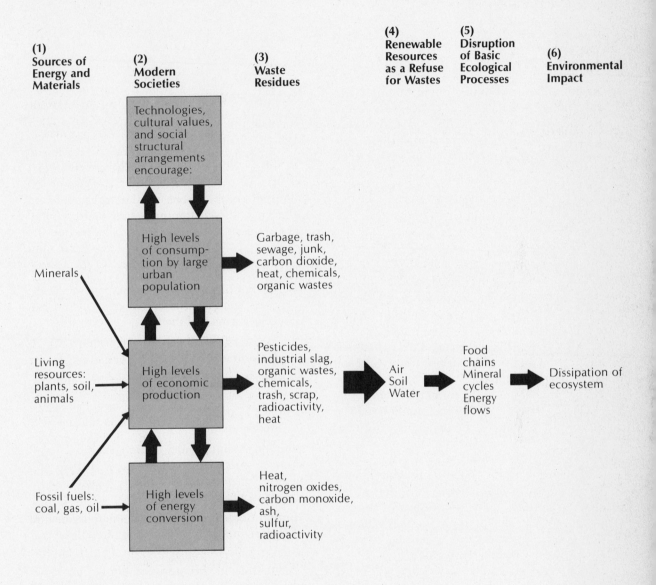

SUMMARY AND PREVIEW

In this chapter we have sought to emphasize that humans, like all other species, must adapt to their environment. This recognition has come late in sociological inquiry, but it is now clear that the elementary principles of ecology—struggle, competition, adaptation, habitat, niche, biotic community, and genetic or somatic adaptations—all have relevance to the study of the human species.

Yet, humans are unique in their creation of culture and patterns of social organization. Thus, the study of human ecology has focused on what is termed the POET factors—population, organization, environment, and technology. Increasingly, it is evident that human culture and patterns of organization pose a severe threat to the ecosystem. Basic processes that create and sustain the air, water, and soil have been disrupted in ways that may force dramatic changes in the human system.

One of the POET factors is population. The size, composition, distribution, and movement of a society's population influence other processes within the society and between a society and its environment. Since the human population has grown dramatically, it is one of the most important trends in the human system. Therefore, we will examine the way that sociologists study this most important force in the human system in the next chapter.

Key Terms

Ecology: the study of the relationship of organisms to their environment

Struggle: the competitive and cooperative processes among organisms in an environment

Adaptation: the processes by which species achieve a life-sustaining relationship to the environment

Habitat: the relationship of a species to the inorganic components of the environment

Niche: that place in the environment in which a species achieves functional relationships to other life forms and the inorganic components in the environment

Biotic Community: a complex of niches

Genetic Adaptation: permanent and inheritable alterations in the structure of the organisms of a species that facilitate adjustment to the environment

Somatic Adaptations: noninheritable alterations of structure, and behaviors, in the organisms of a species that facilitate adjustment to the environment

Human Ecology: the study of the relationship of humans to their environment

POET: the acronym used to refer to four important factors in the study of human ecology: population, organization, environment, and technology

Review Questions

1. In what ways are we like all other species? In what ways are we different?

2. What does human ecology study? What new concepts does it introduce?

3. What does POET mean? What implications does this term have for studying the human system?

4. What ecological problems does the human system now face?

Suggested Readings

Carson, Rachael. *The Silent Spring*. Boston: Houghton Mifflin, 1962.

Duncan, Otis Dudley, and Schnore, Arthur. "The Eco-system." In *Handbook of Sociology*, edited by E. A. Faris. Chicago: Rand McNally, 1964.

Hawley, Amos. *Human Ecology*. New York: Ronald Press, 1950.

Kormondy, E. J. *Concepts of Ecology*. Englewood Cliffs, N.J.: Prentice-Hall, 1969.

Scientific American, The Biosphere. San Francisco: W. H. Freeman, 1970.

Turner, Jonathan H. "The Eco-system." In *Understanding Social Problems*, edited by D. Zimerman and S. Zimerman. New York: Praeger, 1976.

POPULATION AND THE HUMAN SYSTEM

PROLOGUE

Guiding Questions: How does the number of individuals in a society influence its organization? Conversely, how is the character and movement of the population influenced by social forces? What trends in populations of the world are evident?

Chapter Topics

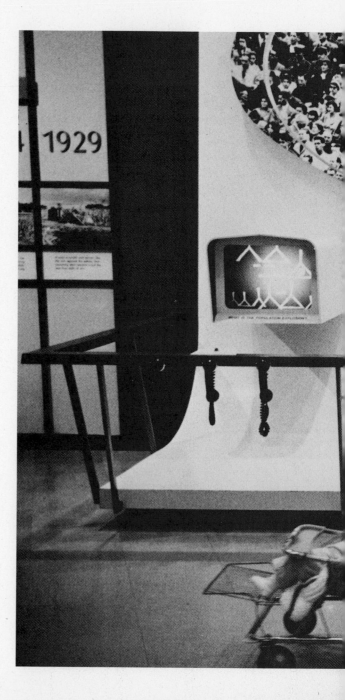

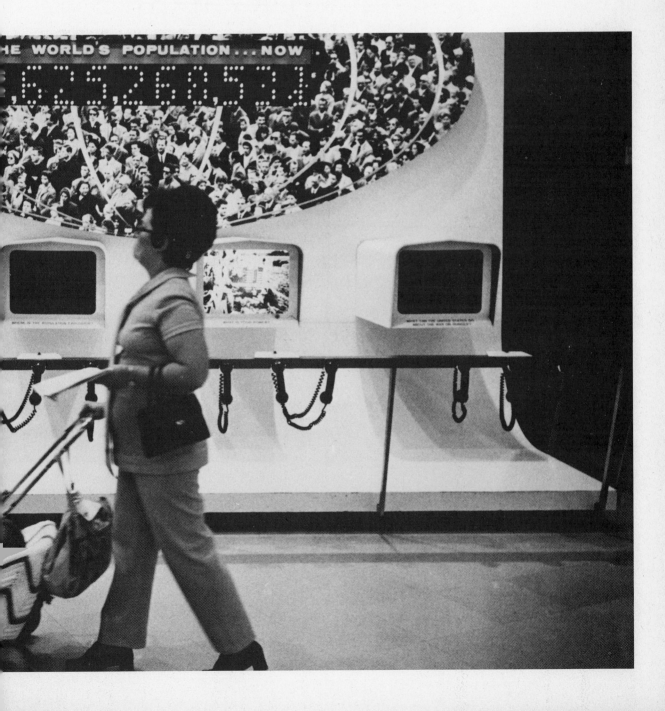

POPULATION COMPOSITION AND CHARACTERISTICS

As we become urbanized, it is hard not to notice the mass of humanity around us. The world seems crowded and congested. We also hear about a "population explosion" in other parts of the world and about imminent famine and starvation. We also note that in our society the elderly are more numerous and that a "baby boom" has come and gone. These and other events point to the importance of studying the population of the human system. We could not fully understand our world without some insight into the characteristics and trends in our own population and in that of the rest of the world.

The science of **demography** is the study of populations. In general, demographers study populations from three perspectives: (1) population composition and characteristics, (2) population movements, and (3) population trends. Our discussion in this short chapter will be organized from these three perspectives.

Just what a demographer studies depends upon the population to be examined. A United Nations demographer, for example, may be interested in any number of different populations, including the population of the world as a whole. A demographer for the U.S. Bureau of the Census, on the other hand, is interested only in the population of the United States or isolated populations within the United States.

Within any given population the characteristics most commonly studied by the demographer are: (1) size or number, (2) age composition, (3) sex ratios, and (4) birth (fertility) and death (mortality) rates. We will enhance our appreciation of the human system if we examine each of these areas of data collection.

Size

Demographers seek to determine the simple number of people in almost every survey population. This is done by a simple "head count." Knowledge of **population size** allows the demographer, over time, to determine the *rate of growth* of population. However, statistics concerning rates of growth require supplementation with information on migration patterns, birth rates, and death rates.

Age Composition

Demographers are interested in the distribution of age groups in a population. Usually, such data are grouped into age ranges that fit the interests and needs of those surveying a population. For example, for some purposes, data on age groups in the United States is categorized as follows: above or below 65 (retirement age), 21 (voting age), 18 (military draft or entrance into the working world), and 1 (infancy). This particular grouping yields considerable insight about the **age composition** within a society. For instance, government may be interested in how many new workers will be entering the economy or in what proportion of the population has reached retirement age. Gross imbalance between the retired and working populations can call for compensatory actions on the part of government.

Sex Ratio

Demographers typically collect information that allows them to determine the **sex ratio** within the survey population. The sex ratio, or SR, is the total number of men in a population, divided by the total number of women, and then multiplied by 100. For instance, if there are 2 men and 1 woman in the survey population, then the SR is 200; if there are 100 men and 200 women in the population, then its SR is 50. Often the SR is determined for particular age groups rather than for the population as a whole. This compartmentalization of the SR into age groups frequently yields meaningful information. In this manner, it has been determined that in the United States the SR is consistently a bit above 100 (usually between 105 and 110) in the age groups of newborns. This SR steadily decreases as age increases until it reaches about 70 among those 70 years of age or older. The SR is usually very close to 100, but it can be significantly shifted in either direction by various factors. Geographic frontier populations, for example, usually have SRs well above 100. Because of cultural values perhaps, men are more willing to undertake frontier settlements than are women. War and occupational hardships can lower the SR of a population quickly and sharply.

Fertility and Mortality

Demographers use the term **fertility** to denote the rate of births in a population. Birth rates are almost always broken down into more specific statistical categories. The most basic category is the *crude birth rate,* or the number of births per 1,000 people per year. Birth rates are influenced by cultural and social factors. For example, birth rates are typically higher among Catholic populations than they are among Protestant populations. It has been widely reported in recent years that the birth rate drops among advanced industrial and postindustrial populations, because of the sophistication of birth control technology and changing values. In cultures where children are viewed as useful laborers rather than as big expenses, birth rates remain high.

Mortality, or death rates, are computed in a manner similar to that used for determining birth rates. The *crude death rate* is an indication of the number of deaths per 1,000 base population per year. The death rate is often used as a rough measure of societal affluence, since in affluent societies, mortality is lessened because of better living conditions and medical care.

The Census, Registrations, and Surveys

The *census* is by far the most widespread and most important tool of demographic research. Census taking is often met with resistance, however. For example, Petersen (1969) reports that the first census undertaken by Nigeria, in 1962, met a wide variety of obstacles, some of which were seriously damaging. Data gatherers were often physically beaten or kidnapped, and local officials commonly inflated the head count in their area in order to justify more tax money from the central government for the public welfare and local economic development.

Today the census is largely disassociated from tax policies, at least in the United States and other highly developed nations. Tax determinations and fiscal projections still benefit from the census, but the most important uses of the census include scientific research into the nature of society, the coordination and determination of federal and state planning in transportation, farming, commerce, and other areas of concern.

A census is a project of vast proportions that demands extensive funding and personnel. In the United States we take for granted that a systematic, accurate census will be conducted every ten years. Even in the United States, however, the simple head count alone is in error by at least 3%, according to the best estimates.

The first census in the United States was conducted in 1790; since then, a census has been conducted every 10 years without fail. In the past, the U.S. census has been conducted on a door-to-door basis and with a nationally standardized questionnaire. In 1970 for the first time, census questionnaires in some areas were received by mail.

In addition to the standardized national questionnaire, representative sample populations are questioned more extensively concerning many aspects of occupation, housing, and education. The results are then treated statistically to attain national estimates. The accuracy of the census itself is tested by means of the Post-Enumeration Survey, in which a population sample is surveyed extensively. The resulting data is then treated statistically to determine the accuracy of the larger census.

The extensive demographic information supplied periodically by the census is complemented by the continuous stream of information supplied by *registrations*. Automobile registrations, birth certification, marriage licensing and registration, death certification, and business registrations are among the most common forms of registration. Information gathered from registrations is consistently broken down according to various categories by local, state, and federal agencies and is readily available for research purposes to all interested parties.

Surveys, or polls, provide a third source of demographic information. The most commonly known surveyors are George Gallup and Louis Harris, but surveys are undertaken by many people or agencies and for a wide variety of reasons. Social scientists often conduct independent surveys when a unique combination of demographic information is required for their research purposes.

POPULATION MOVEMENTS

A major concern in understanding a population is **migration.** Migration is simply the movement of people from one area to another. William Petersen, in his book *The Politics of Population* (1964), describes the various kinds of migration.

Controlled Migration

This form of migration involves movement from nation to nation. Controlled migration is marked by quotas that limit the number of migrants from various nations. Very few nations in the world today allow unrestricted immigration. Most prefer controlled immigration, or in some cases, no immigration at all. Controlled immigration appears to operate in various ways, according to the interests of the nation that sets the quota. The United States, for example, determines the fate of prospective immigrants primarily on the basis of the applicants' technical skills and family ties. Those candidates for immigration who have valuable work skills or who claim family ties in the United States are favored by being considered especially desirable immigrants.

Impelled Migration

People who migrate from one area to another because of the presence of extremely adverse conditions in their homeland are undertaking *impelled migration*. Examples of impelled migration can be found in the Jewish migrations from the Soviet Union and Nazi Germany. It can be seen in the contemporary emigrations of Europeans from Rhodesia, Uganda, and the Union of South Africa. The Irish were also forced to migrate in the Great Potato Famine. In a limited way we also see this type of migration today among Soviet nationals, as well as among nationals of other nations who suffer under certain types of political regimes.

Primitive Migration

Peoples who wander freely over territories hunting and foraging for food are exercising *primitive migration*. This type of migration exists in many parts of the world, as it always has. The aborigines of Australia are a prominent example of this type of migration, as are the nomadic tribes of the Sahara region and Afghanistan. Today, social forces work very strongly against this type of migration, however. In the middle and latter parts of the nineteenth century, for instance, native tribes in America were confined to governmentally controlled reservations. Otherwise, the great majority of native American tribes would still provide a dramatic illustration of primitive migration. The same restrictions are now being imposed upon many African hunting-and-gathering societies.

Free Migration

This form of migration may be thought of as the unhindered movement of peoples from one place to another and of their own free will, for reasons which are their own.

Forced Migration

This type of migration involves the movement of peoples from one nation or region to another with no regard for their individual will. Such migration is much less prominent today than previously; and in fact, the period of slavery and slave trade was the last epoch of mass forced migration.

In sum, then, migrations are one of the three most immediate determinants of population composition, the others being fertility and mortality. By studying and combining the analyses of these three factors, demographers achieve a richer understanding of population composition and fluctuation, and it is through the analysis of these three factors that demographers try to foresee the future and to project trends.

POPULATION TRENDS

Demographers share with all social scientists an interest in social trends: Will populations continue to grow? Will populations enter into a general period of numerical decline? What factors are going to influence birth and death rates? Will migration continue to be a major component of population dynamics? And if so, what forces act as major determinants of migration?

Social scientists know that attempts to project population trends into the future are difficult. Often projections based on known data have been foiled by sudden and unpredictable turns of events. Forty years ago, for example, many social scientists presumed to foretell the future on the basis of their knowledge of the recent past. Social projections of a declining population during the Great Depression were unexpectedly rendered inaccurate by the "baby boom" immediately following World War II. Yet, scientists also appreciate that attempts to anticipate the future are important, or at least unavoidable.

The Demographic Transition

Despite the problems of prediction, one major trend that has helped projections is the **demographic transition.** Figure 1 illustrates the problems posed by the demographic transition. With the introduction of medical technologies—hospitals, doctors, medicines—death rates in a modernizing society decline dramatically. This is particularly true for infant mortality. However, birth rates do not initially

Third World countries, which have experienced the demographic transition, now experience severe over-crowding.

undergo a corresponding drop in such societies. Changes in the values, beliefs, and social structural arrangements associated with industrialization usually must occur first. People must want fewer children. They must become involved in nonfamily structures. They must view children as an economic liability.

They must seek birth control, and governments must actively seek population control. This is what has happened in the recent history of contemporary modern societies.

During the period between the drop in death rates and the decline in birth rates, a population explosion occurs. This is what is now happening in Asia and Latin America. Death rates have declined, but birth rates have not dropped to a point where stability in the growth rate has been, or will soon be, reached. It is this fact that has led some to ponder the prospects of an overpopulated world.

Figure 1: Dynamics of the Transition

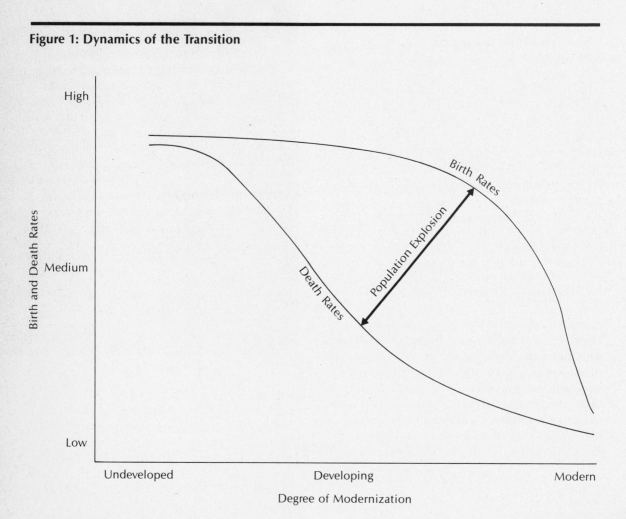

The Population Bomb

The world's population is expanding rapidly. These circumstances have led some, most notable among them being Paul Ehrlich (1971), to sound the alarm. They warn of the possible dire results of worldwide population trends. Ehrlich has dramatized these concerns by hypothesizing a "population bomb."

The problem of the "population bomb" hinges on two assumptions: (1) the world population is increasing at such a rapid pace that there will result a world community of so many people that the application of food technologies will not be able to supply the people with basic sustenance, and (2) the intense application of food technologies in response to a rapidly increasing need for basic nutrition will cause a massive disruption of the world ecosystem (see Figure 4 in Chapter 21). This argument has a basis in ecological fact. It is indeed feasible that a massive application of our food technology—chemical fertilizers and pesticides, for example—would so disrupt the world ecological system that recovery would be impossible.

However, there are also problems with this argument. It may lay blame at the wrong doorstep. Although we can imagine the massive demands of a growing Third World population coming into contact with industrially wrought conveniences for the first time, we must keep in mind the present demands of the societies that are already "developed." Al-though Western birth rates are "low," although Western populations are growing "slowly," and although the gross population of the Western industrial world is "small" in proportion to the world population, the Western industrialized nations are still at the core of the world ecological problem. The vision of Ehrlich and others has merit; their long-range concerns are realistic. But the present problem is with the modern nations with small populations. The demands of Western industrialized societies are met with massive applications of agricultural and industrial technologies that deposit great quantities of residues onto the environment while disrupting the flows, cycles, and chains that are necessary to renew the air, soil, and water (see Figure 4, Chapter 21). This process is harmful enough, but the problems of the future will make those of the present fade in comparison if what seems inevitable should actually happen: that current individual societies should serve as the technological model and servant for an expanded population base throughout the world. From this point of view the frightening aspects of the "Americanization" of the Third World can be more fully appreciated (Miles 1970; Stockwell 1968; Turner 1976).

Population Growth: Signs of Hope?

Just a decade ago, demographers were predicting that by the year 2050 the earth's population would have tripled, creating a planet suffocated in its own humanity and down to its last natural resources. Now, due to a plummeting birth rate in many nations and a sharp rise in deaths in some others, that grim prediction apparently will not come true. A new study shows that the world's population growth is tapering off, and that the threat of an eventual world population of 12 billion has now faded.

Already, four countries have reached zero population growth—East and West Germany, Austria and Lux-embourg—and Britain and Belgium are expected to reach birth-death equi-librium by the end of this year. The most dramatic change of all has been in China, which harbors one-fifth of mankind but now seems to have slowed its birth rate more rapidly than any country in history.

In the study, Lester Brown, direc-tor of Worldwatch Institute, reports that the world growth rate fell from 1.9 per cent in 1970 to 1.64 per cent in 1975. Dr. R.T. Ravenholt, population director of the U.S. Agency for Inter-national Development (AID), projects that the growth rate will fall below 1 per cent by 1985.

What these figures mean is that the earth's present population of 4 billion should go to only 5.4 billion by the end of the century—not to the 6.3 billion predicted in 1970. The shortfall of 900 million is equivalent to the populations of North America, Latin America and Western Europe combined. Moreover, the 1 per cent growth rate forecast by 1985 could decline even further, and the experts will no longer estimate what the population may be by 2050.

Many factors have combined to bring about the unprecedented decline in births. The chief cause is increased use of such contraceptive devices as the Pill, IUD's and the condom, along with publicly supported family-plan-ning clinics. Two more recent factors are a sharp rise in male sterilization and the liberalization of abortion laws. The Worldwatch study shows that in 1971, 38 per cent of the world's people live in countries where abortions were legal. Today the figure is 64 per cent.

Women: In the U.S., the population growth rate declined by 33 per cent between 1970 and 1975. The attrition was due largely to a drop in the mar-riage rate and growth in female employment: women now make up 40.7 percent of the labor force. The effect of working women on birth rates, says Brown, can be seen in East Germany. Largely because of its push for female employment, East Germany in 1969 became the first country to reach zero population growth.

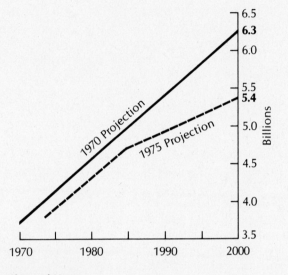

Signs of Hope

Experts used to fear that the world population would hit 6.3 billion by the year 2000 and continue to soar. Now they think that by then it may stabilize near 5.4 billion

Source: Lester R. Brown, Worldwatch Institute

Malthusian influences ranging from food shortages to a loss of natural resources and consumer goods have also contributed to the diminishing population rate. A housing shortage in the Soviet Union, for example, has discouraged many couples from starting their families. In Mexico, where unemployment is soaring, women are lining up for sterilization. Outright

starvation has added 2 million to the death rolls since 1972.

The largest drop in births has been in China. "You cannot begin to understand world population figures," says Ravenholt, "until you understand China." That is difficult, since nobody outside of China can do more than guess at its population and birth rate—or at the methods used to lower them. For what it's worth, Mao, three years before his death, told a visitor: "I am not sure that we are 800 million. I doubt even if we have reached 700 million." AID estimates that by making the Pill readily available and imposing severe social constraints on people who marry too young or have too many children, China lowered the number of births per thousand people from 35.5 in 1964 to 14.0 in 1975. If that is true, China represents family planning's greatest success story.

Among open societies, the most drastic measures to halt population growth have been taken in India. The government recently stated that no person with more than two children may get a government job, and in the Indian state of Maharashtra a new law will require compulsory sterilization of all males with three or more living children and compulsory abortion of any pregnancy that would result in a fourth child. This draconian measure may eventually be adopted throughout the country.

Myths: The latest population figures also shatter two favorite demographic theories: that fertility drops only when a country reaches a high standard of living, and that birth-control methods require a certain level of educational sophistication. "There is no place where family planning has been made available that fertility has not decreased," says Dr. Joseph Speidel, chief of research for the Office of Population.

Demographers are pleased and surprised by the declining fertility rates, though they admit that compulsory measures used to control population are violations of basic human rights. Brown finds one other dark blotch on the bright new statistics: that portion of the decline in population growth that is due to a rise in death rates resulting from starvation. But if the attrition in births should continue throughout this century, Brown is hopeful that governments will have more time to solve the problems of food and fuel shortages, to upgrade their economies and to make real improvements in the quality of their citizens' lives.

SUMMARY AND PREVIEW

In this chapter we have briefly reviewed how social scientists study population. This science of populations is known as demography. We have focused our attention on those three aspects of populations that are usually studied by demographers: population composition, movements, and trends. Each is vital to understanding the structure and dynamics of a society, per se, but increasingly, sociologists recognize the connection of population and its organization to broader ecological processes.

In this and the previous chapter we have discussed the broad parameters of the human system: ecology and population. We have delayed this discussion until we had examined the basic elements, forms, and institutions of the human system. The reason for this delay is simply that trends in the population of a society and in its adaptation to the environment reflect cultural values and beliefs as well as patterns of social organization. Conversely, the size and composition of a population and the nature of the ecosystem impose constraints on how far certain cultural and social elaborations can proceed. Human societies may soon reach their maximum size and may exceed the "carrying capacity" of the ecosystem, forcing the development of new social forms. Just whether these changes are needed, or possible, cannot be known. But in the past, as we saw in chapter 3 and throughout our analysis of social forms and institutions, humans have made the necessary adjustments. We might do well, therefore, to close this book with a short chapter on how humans have elaborated their system and on what trends for the future are likely.

Key Terms

Demography: the study of populations

Population Size: the number of people in a population

Age Composition: the distribution of age groups in a population

Sex Ratio: the proportion of males to females in a population

Fertility: the rate of births in a population

Mortality: the rate of deaths in a population

Migration: the movement of populations from one geographical area to another

Demographic Transition: the period during which death rates in a population initially decline, while birth rates remain high, leading to dramatic increases in a population's size until that point when birth rates also decline

Review Questions

1. Why do social scientists study population?
2. What aspects of population do demographers study?
3. How do population characteristics, cultural values, and social organization mutually influence each other?
4. How are the study of population and ecology related?

Suggested Readings

Ehrlich, Paul. *The Population Bomb.* New York: Ballantine, 1971

Falk, Richard. *This Endangered Planet.* New York: Random House, 1971

Petersen, William. *The Politics of Population.* New York: Doubleday, 1964

Wrong, Dennis H. *Population and Society.* New York: Random House, 1961

CONTINUITIES IN THE HUMAN SYSTEM

PROLOGUE

Guiding Questions: What have humans created? What are the long-term trends in the human system? What are the ultimate challenges? And what are the prospects for *Homo sapien sapien?*

Chapter Topics

WAR, REVOLUTION, AND EVOLUTION

For 22 chapters we have reviewed, in broad strokes, how sociologists study the human system. This review is only an introduction. Hopefully, it has whet your appetite. In our overview of sociology we have gained some appreciation for a ubiquitous social fact: change. Humans are creative animals. They constantly restructure their world, and although these creations have form or comparatively stable structures, the social world has undergone profound changes. In this chapter we will examine the dynamics in the human system.

As Marx emphasized over 100 years ago, conflict over resources is the basic dynamic of human systems. Marx's analysis was more limited than necessary. No doubt, humans have fought each other since their first beginnings. They have competed for resources on the African savannah; they have engaged in full-scale wars; they have revolted within a society against their oppressors. Human action is thus potentially volatile. In Chapter 12 we reviewed some of the general conditions leading to outbursts within societies. What drives entire societies to engage in warfare is, of course, still somewhat of a mystery. Many factors are usually involved: needs or desires for more resources, the internal unity that comes from an external enemy, historical animosities buried in the recesses of history, and perhaps, the greed and hunger for power of potential leaders.

Yet, in addition to these more violent eruptions, some long-term trends in the human system have occurred. War, conflict, and revolution are often the instigators of events which, over time, become a part of an evolutionary trend. We should never underestimate the impact of violence in changing the profile of the human system. At the end of our review of the human system, however, we might do well to abstract above the particular forces causing change and look at what has occurred to *Homo sapiens sapiens*. We have evolved as a biological species, and more importantly, we have elaborated culture and social forms. What has been the trend in this elaboration? Where have humans come from, and where are they going? These are the kinds of questions that we will address in this last chapter.

War and violence have been prominent
features of the human system.

THE CREATION OF THE HUMAN SYSTEM

In Chapter 3 we speculated about the emergence of humans as a species. We saw how the African savannah presented problems of adaptation that encouraged first the development of bipedalism and crude tool use and then the evolution of larger brains as our ancestors came to rely more upon language and social organization for their survival. With larger brains and language, the world of symbols—or culture—was opened. Our ancestors like *Homo erectus* and the Neanderthals could increasingly regulate their affairs with values, beliefs, norms, expanded technologies, and perhaps religious dogmas. With culture more extensive and elaborate interactions were possible; hence, more complex patterns of social organization became viable. Without the capacity to create culture and to use it for elaborating social organization, the human system could not have emerged.

With increasing reliance upon culture and with more complex patterns of social organization, socialization of personality becomes a critical social process. Large-brained organisms must be born early and are highly dependent upon their mothers for survival. When this large brain must be filled with culture and taught interpersonal and technical skills, socialization becomes the life line of the society. People must be taught what to value and believe; they must be trained how to perform essential tasks; they must learn how to interact with each other; and they must acquire a desire to become involved in crucial social activities.

By the time *Homo sapiens sapiens* emerged some 40,000 years ago, these basic elements—culture, symbolic interaction, the rudiments of social organization, and the extensive reliance upon socialization—were clearly evident. This is why we called them "the basic elements" in Part II. They are what make humans unique.

The human system consisted of small, kinship-based bands wandering over territories. As the young were born, they were socialized into this simple system. For 30,000 years, human life on earth showed few dramatic changes. Then suddenly, and for reasons that are not understood, the pace of change in the human system accelerated, and social life would never be the same again.

ELABORATION OF THE HUMAN SYSTEM

The Neolithic Revolution

As we noted in the chapters on community and economy, the discovery of agricultural technology was a revolution. We termed this revolution, the **Neolithic revolution.** It is difficult to know how or why this new technology was discovered and used about 10,000 years ago. But once developed, agriculture stimulated the elaboration of the human system.

The first noticeable elaboration was kinship. For it is in agricultural societies that we find the most extensive systems of descent, family authority, and marriage rules. The reason is that the first agricultural societies could not have elaborate governments, corporations, and other social forms to regulate and organize the society. As we saw in Chapter 16, kinship became a major organizing principle.

Agricultural activity required a stable relationship to the land. People ceased moving about in a nomadic way. They settled down in their kin groups, and they formed the beginnings of community. They organized their houses, paths among them, the disposal of sewage, the securing of water, and other facets of community life. Once community existed, it created pressures for change: it provided a place for trade; it attracted migrants to settle; it was subject to raids and required a defense. Defense, trade, and population growth, in turn, demanded new methods of organization. Some kin leaders became the first political leaders who governed and regulated a territory and actions in that territory.

As communities grew, as government expanded, as trade and commerce accelerated, and as new agricultural technologies increased productivity, social inequality and stratification became more pronounced. Hunters and gatherers had highly egalitarian systems, but the existence of a surplus and the dominance of political elites encouraged hoarding of wealth and the subjugation of those landless peasants who migrated to the city to perform labor. In between these elites and propertyless masses were the artisans and merchants. The resources of parents now began to influence people's chances in life and their access to scarce resources. In a word, stratification had become a dominant social form in the human system.

Religion has always been a part of the human, and probably the prehuman, systems. With a stable community and economic surplus, the organization of religion could become more extensive. Permanent buildings, altars, and other religious structures were built with the labor of peasants. A religious elite could be supported with the surplus, and these elites could begin to organize religion and to extend its influence to larger numbers of people. We saw how this occurs in Chapter 17.

Political and religious organization stimulated the beginnings of another distinctive social form, formal organizations. We studied these in Chapter 11. Once large-scale tasks—from the building of a pyramid to the waging of war—are undertaken, formal organization becomes a part of the human system. In communities with a surplus, filled with peasant labor, and ruled by political and religious elites, large-scale tasks become possible, and thus, the early beginnings of bureaucracy were evident.

Large, urban agricultural societies also evidenced the beginnings of formal education.

Such education was restricted to elites for their cultural enrichment or to a small number of well-qualified nonelites who became the "bureaucrats" of the emerging bureaucracies. But education was still a recessive institution, reaching only a handful of the population.

Urban societies with vast inequalities also are subject to revolts and riots by the impoverished masses. Privilege and poverty are highly conducive to conflict and the venting of frustrations and hostilities. The human system thus became subject to new and varied patterns of fluid organization: fads, rumors, crazes, crowds, and even revolutions.

The Neolithic revolution thus changed the nature of economic production which, in turn, allowed for the elaboration of basic social forms: institutions, communities, formal organizations, stratification, and fluid organization. The exact profile of this elaboration ebbed and flowed with the patterns of conquest and political decay that marked the world from 10,000 B.C. to just a few hundred years ago. Egypt, Greece, the Roman Empire, feudal Europe and Asia, and the other periods of human history have differed in the content of their social form. But they all evidenced the expansion of the basic human elements—culture, interaction, social organization, and socialization—into basic social forms—formal organizations, fluid organizations, communities, strata, and varied social institutions. However, these elaborations were limited by the resources that an agricultural economy could provide. It took another technological revolution, translated into new modes of economic production, for further elaboration of the basic forms of the human system. This was, of course, the industrial revolution.

The Industrial Revolution

With the discovery of how to use new sources of power to run machines, the human system was dramatically altered. Less than 300 years ago, this **industrial revolution** stimulated the further development of basic social forms into their present profile.

The hallmark of the maturing industrial revolution was the factory system in which workers were concentrated around machines. Once workers leave their family units to work, kinship is dramatically altered. Factories and other economic units, rather than descent and authority rules in kinship, organize and pool productive labor. Instead of being tied to the land, labor is often asked to move as new resources are uncovered and as additional factories are built. The result is for residence rules and the extended family to break up, since rules restricting mobility prevent movement to work and since large families are costly to move.

Another institution, which had been recessive for thousands of years, now became prominent. Formal education of the population increases dramatically with industrialization. Literacy is a necessary skill for many workers, and thus, schools are built to provide the labor force with this basic capacity. The need for other skills—accounting, managing, advertising, banking, insuring, marketing, and the like—also escalates with industrialization. More than mere literacy is required; hence, higher education is gradually extended to an ever-increasing proportion of the population.

The factory system was the hallmark of the industrial revolution, dramatically altering social forms in the human system.

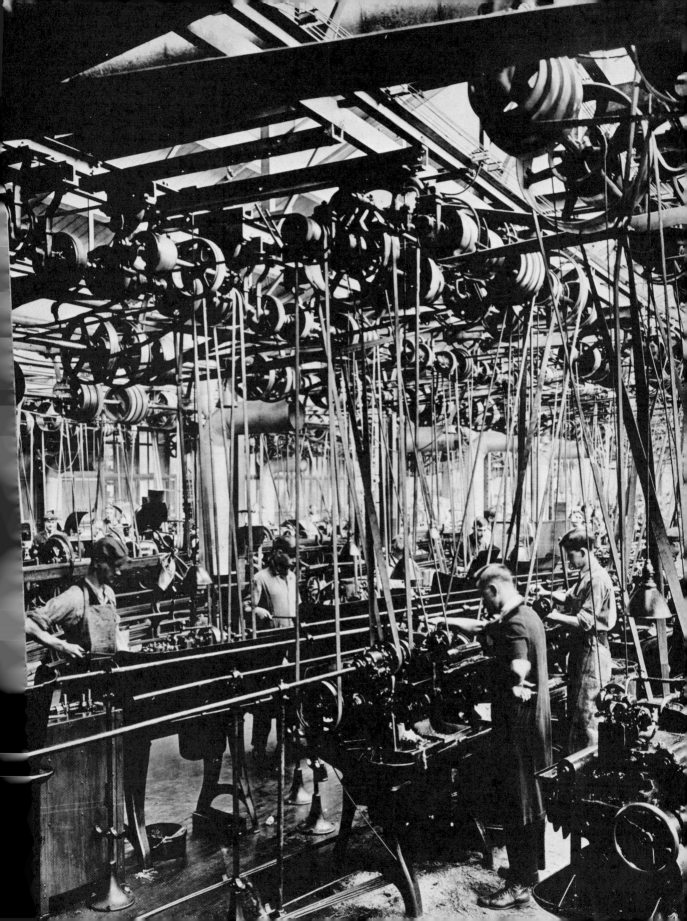

Government also undergoes changes. Governments in advanced agricultural societies tend to be despotic with some form of feudal nobility controlling societal activity. With industrialization concentrated and literate masses of workers represent a potential or actual source of revolt. Whether through actual revolt—as in France, China, and Russia, for example—or potential revolution—as in England, for example—government is forced to change. It becomes more responsive to people's needs and allows at least some "common people" access to key decision-making processes.

The community is forever altered with industrialization. Factories and the administrative bureaucracies of government and industry draw people to urban areas. As a result, cities increase in size, forcing increasing governmental regulation of key services such as police, fire, health, and important facilities, such as roads, garbage, sewage, schools, and housing. As we saw in Chapter 13, core cities are first to grow; then, people spill out into the suburbs; and as the suburbs of major cities begin to merge, giant urban corridors are created.

Industrialization, the growth of formal education and government, and urbanization are all possible by virtue of the expansion and extension of another social form: formal organization. Education is a bureaucratic form designed to impart knowledge and skills to large numbers of people. Government is a giant administrative bureaucracy coordinating such diverse functions as maintaining a military and collecting and allocating taxes. Industry is a bureaucratic form. Factories are a formal organization for coordinating machines and people, and as the economies grow, purely administrative economic forms emerge to coordinate the services—banking, insuring, accounting, marketing, and the like. Thus, formal organization becomes the major means by which many of the dramatic changes associated with the industrial revolution are made possible.

Religion, as we saw in Chapter 17, changes with industrialization. It becomes increasingly segregated from government and economy, which are run on rational bureaucratic principles. Yet, it continues to provide a place of security and relief for many who experience the tensions and frustrations of urban life. Although organized religion was perhaps the first social unit to approximate a bureaucratic form, this bureaucracy is now altered to approximate that in government and industry. The supernatural realm becomes simplified; rituals are truncated; and the church seeks to expand its membership and to maintain many nonspiritual activities—schools, recreation programs, social work, land and stock investments, and other diversified involvements.

The degree of inequality in industrializing societies decreases somewhat (Lenski 1966). Yet, inequality in the distribution of money, power, and prestige is still great—just less than that of advanced agricultural societies (Turner & Starnes 1975). Social classes now revolve around occupation and income. The rather small middle class of artisans and shopkeepers of the preindustrial city is dramatically increased with the expansion of the white-collar middle classes. Blue-collar working classes also expand; and as the income differentials between blue-collar and lower white-collar occupations decrease, class distinctions become more pronounced—use of leisure, speech patterns, prestige of job, and the like. A small upper elite, however, still hoards much of the total wealth in industrial societies and still commands, to a degree not proportionate to their small numbers, considerable political power.

The existence of inequality, the concentration of people into urban areas, the ability of people to read and become aware of this situation, and the instant and incessant exposure to the media all create a constant conduciveness for collective behavior. Crazes, fads, and fashions are the products of people in media-dominated urban societies. Public opinion is also the product of media coverage of mass behaviors and of political elites' desire to know what people think. Riots and other forms of crowd behavior also increase as people become aware of their mutual plight and are better able to communicate their grievances to each other. Indeed, revolution has often accompanied initial industrialization—Russia, France, and China being the most obvious examples. In lieu of revolution, long-term social movements, sprinkled with incidences of crowd behavior, force social change; the union movement and the women's movement represent prominent examples in the United States. Thus, patterns of fluid organization, creating constant pressures for change, are elaborated with industrialization and the changes in the human system that it stimulates.

We can see, then, how the forms of the human system—formal and fluid organization, community, stratification, and social institutions—have been altered with the two great technological revolutions: agriculture and industry. Other such revolutions may be in our future, or perhaps we are in the middle of one now but are too close to see it. What is critical for our understanding of the human system is the recognition that the basic elements of the first human system—culture, symbolic interaction, rudimentary social organization, and the reliance of socialization—have become elaborated. The major changes in the human system have involved the creation of, and then the change in, basic social forms.

We have yet to address the first and most basic social form, the group. It is probably the least subject to change of all human forms. Although our involvement in larger, more impersonal groups that we termed secondary (see Chapter 10) has certainly increased, primary group involvement is still the basis for our emotional and psychological stability. Wherever we look, we see primary group organization emerging and existing within other social forms: organizations, social strata, community, education, government, family, religion, and the economy. Primary groups were probably the first social form, our first pattern of social organization. They are basic to human needs; and although humans have created and elaborated diverse and complex social structures, groups are still the basic social form. Of course, all of us can participate for a time in a nongroup world. We can go to a class where we do not know anyone. We shop in a crowded store. We can drive on a freeway. But few humans can remain divorced from groups. They seek refuge in groups, and they try to create groups if they are forced to participate together for a period. Thus, within the dramatic changes that have occurred in the human system, there is a continuity in our reliance, as humans with needs for personal ties and relationships, upon groups.

TRENDS IN THE HUMAN SYSTEM

The elaboration of the human system shows certain trends. General patterns of organization can be discerned, and perhaps we should close our review of the human system by noting some of these trends. In many ways, we are making an odyssey back to our sociological forefathers—Comte, Spencer, Durkheim, Weber, and Marx. They were all concerned with the broad social trends occurring around them. What is the direction of society? Where did we come from and where are we going to?

Differentiation and Complexity

The human system has increasingly become differentiated. Herbert Spencer and Émile Durkheim emphasized this fact of social life. Humans have created new social forms, and their lives involve participation in a wide variety of contexts: family, work, play, travel, church, and so on. Each of us, to use a concept from our earlier analysis of status and role, have wide status sets and role sets. We occupy many positions and are required to play many roles, some of which come into conflict. The world is, in a word, differentiated.

Durkheim recognized that **differentiation** opened new options and gave people more freedom to choose. But differentiation of social life into so many varied structures also creates a problem of coordination and control. How are all the groups, organizations, social classes, and different institutions to be regulated and coordinated? Modern societies often have difficulties in this area. Economic corporations

and government often come into conflict. Students are educated for nonexistent jobs. Social classes fight each other for resources. Union organizations battle corporate organizations. Differentiation, and the companion problem of integration, thus represent a clear trend.

The present response to these integrative problems also reveals a trend: (1) the reliance upon law and courts to mediate conflicts and (2) the extension and expansion of governmental powers of planning and control. Thus, we can expect the extension of governmental involvement in the human system. At present, humans have little knowledge of how else to mitigate potential conflicts and points of malintegration in the human system.

Impersonality

For the participants in modern societies, the social world often seems impersonal. We do not know people well or intimately. It is not hard to see why this **impersonality** exists. We participate in many secondary groups; we work in, and must deal with, formal organizations; and in all likelihood, we live in a large urban area. We maintain our psychological well-being through involvement in primary groups, but much of our waking life is spent outside such groups.

This trend of nonprimary group participation is not likely to abate in the near future. Our hunting-and-gathering ancestors, if thrust into such an impersonal world as many African tribes and native Americans have been, would have difficulty adjusting. Most of our life on earth as a species has involved participation in primary relationships. Yet, we now organize

Social distance between, and compartmentalization of, people is a prominent feature of contemporary human systems.

the human system and much of our lives with impersonal structures. We may have become conditioned to this existence, or it may continue to extract a toll on our primate nature.

Rationality

As humans have attempted to cope with their environment, they increasingly sought to make their world predictable and efficient. We have relied less upon prayer to the supernatural in our daily lives and more on our organization into structures that can manipulate the environment and coordinate social affairs. Formal organizations represent the present mode for this **rationality.** Humans set goals—whether they be increased economic productivity, implementation of social services, education of the masses, or the planning of cities—and use economic, political, educational, civic, and other organizations to reach these goals. Although these efforts are not always successful, there is a presumption that they can be achieved with efficient organizational effort.

Cultural values and beliefs are increasingly oriented toward rational and efficient pursuit of goals, and our attempts at creating better organizations both reflect, and contribute to, this emphasis. Much of the human system is thus predicated on rationality and this trend is likely to continue. In the future, humans will continue to strive for more efficiency and rationality in crucial activities. Traditional, emotional, and religious orientations are now confined to delimited spheres—Sunday worship, family support, ritual holidays, and the like—for much of what occurs in the human system concerns planning, control, and manipulation of exigencies, which, only a few thousand years ago, were considered beyond our mastery.

Precarious Mastery

There is an irony to human efforts at control and manipulation. As we increase economic productivity, concentrate our populations in urban areas, and consume vast quantities of goods, we also discharge into the ecosystem enormous amounts of waste residues. These residues, as we saw in Chapter 21, pose threats to vital chains, cycles, and flows in the ecosystem. Our rationality has, in a sense, been selective, for it is possible that we could disrupt the very processes upon which all life depends.

There is, then, only a precarious mastery of the world. Nature appears to no longer control our existence, as it did for prehumans and early human societies, and yet, we could have altered nature to such a degree that we may be more at the mercy of environmental forces than the first humans. Whatever our fate, there can be little doubt that the trend toward escalated environmental disruption will increase in the near future.

Population Growth

As we have achieved a sense of control over our existence, we have multiplied our numbers. Human **population growth** may soon reach the carrying capacity of the ecosystem, for, indeed, food and other resources are increasingly in short supply. It is endemic to humans, or any species, to propagate their numbers. The survival of any species depends upon this tendency, and yet, like many other species that multiply beyond their food supplies, there is inevitable starvation, famine, and death. The world's population will reach 5 to 6 billion in the year 2000. Just whether we can increase food supplies without the massive environmental disruption that would make all human life precarious is an open question. Whether we can create new values and new living patterns that stem, and perhaps reverse, the exponential population growth is also an unknown. But there is a clear trend for growth—a growth that, in a few generations, will exceed the carrying capacity of the earth.

These are the broad trends now evident in the human system: complexity, impersonality, rationality, precarious mastery, and overpopulation. They pose difficult problems of adjustment for a species that has inhabited the earth for less than 100,000 years. They will test the flexibility and adaptability of the human system to the same degree that the vicissitudes of the African savannah tested our earliest ancestors.

SUMMARY AND CONCLUSION

We are now at the end of our introduction to sociology. In this chapter we have reviewed the creation and elaboration of the basic elements studied in Part II into the diverse social forms examined in Parts III and IV of this book. We have attempted to abstract and isolate the general trends, with an eye to the ultimate challenges that they pose for our species. We have saved these questions until the end because they require an accumulation of facts about people and their creation, the human system. Hopefully, we have acquired a sense for what this system is, how it operates, and how sociologists approach its study.

As we conclude our analysis, we are in a position to appreciate the social world in which we live. But we must also remember, as we have emphasized through the preceding chapters, that humans are only one species inhabiting the earth. We are, of course, a unique and fascinating species, and it is this uniqueness that has stimulated the emergence of sociology as the science of the human system. Sociology offers much to the student who is interested in the social world, and our goal has been to stimulate this interest and invite you to invest more of your time and intellect in the study of sociology.

Key Terms

Neolithic Revolution: the discovery and application of agricultural technology to economic production

Industrial Revolution: the coupling of nonhuman and nonanimal power to machines in economic production

Differentiation: the splitting of status roles formerly encompassed within one structure to separate structures

Impersonality: the decreasing incidence of personal and emotionally involving interaction

Rationality: the pursuit of specified goals in the most efficient manner available or possible

Population Growth: the increasing numbers of a given species

Review Questions

1. What are the basic elements of the human system?

2. How have these become elaborated during the Neolithic and industrial revolutions?

3. What broad trends are evident in the human system?

4. What are the prospects for *Homo sapiens sapiens?*

GLOSSARY

Abstractness: the situation where a statement is not tied to specific referents in a particular time and place

Achieved Status: positions that people assume by virtue of effort and performance

Adaptation: the processes by which species achieve a life-sustaining relationship to the environment

Adjusted Responses: actions of individuals that occur after role-taking and imaginative rehearsal and that lead to cooperation among actors

Age Composition: the distribution of age groups in a population

Agents Of Socialization: those persons, groups, organizations, media, and other social forces that are involved in shaping the emergence, persistence, and change in a person's personality

Alienation: that process whereby actors cease depositing emotional energy in their roles

Anatomy: those factors pertaining to the bodily structure of humans

Anomie: a state where norms are unclear, nonexistent, or in conflict

Apes: a species of the primate order that emerged after monkeys and from which humans evolved

Ascribed Status: positions that individuals inherit at birth

Australopithecus: a hominid that emerged some 5 million years ago and that was the first member of the genus *Homo*

Authority: power and leadership that is accepted as legitimate by those who are affected by decisions of leaders and their exercise of power

Beliefs: ideas or conceptions that people hold about what should exist or what *actually does exist* in a *particular* social situation or context

Bilateral: a descent norm, which indicates that both sides of a couple's family are to be treated equally

Biological Heritage: all those genetic characteristics with which a person is born

Biotic Community: a complex of niches

Bourgeoisie: Karl Marx's term for those who own the means of production in capitalist societies

Bureaucracy: another term to designate formal organizations

Bureaucratization: the process of creating formal organization

Capital: the tools and equipment, as well as the money to buy these, that are used in economic activity

Censorship: the withholding of information from the public

Centralization: the process of creating hierarchies and concentrating authority in those at the top of the hierarchy

Chiefdom: that form of government in which descent rules of kinship determine who is to be leader and possess authority for the larger kin group or groups in a territory

Cities: communities in which a comparatively large and concentrated population lives and works, engaging in extensive trade of goods and services with each other and with the surrounding environment

Class: Max Weber's and Karl Marx's term for rankings based on one's relationship to economic forces

Client-Centered Organizations: those organizations that provide services and benefits for individuals outside the organization

Coercion: the use of, or capacity to use, physical force

Coercive Organizations: those formal organizations in which membership is involuntary

Collective Behavior: those social forms that reveal less structure, evidence less predictable profiles, endure for shorter periods of time than most social forms, while often consuming their incumbents' emotional energies

Commonwealth Organizations: those public or governmental organizations that provide services and benefits to the society as a whole

Community: those patterns of action and interaction that are shaped by people's daily activities in a relatively permanent place of residence

Concept: statements that isolate, point to, or denote some feature of the world

Conjugal Family: family units composed of only a husband and wife

Constructive Conformity: that adaptation in a formal organization in which workers conform to the rules, maintain knowledge of organizational goals, evidence personal initiative, and keep their personal integrity

Control Group: the group in an experimental design that is unexposed to a stimulus of interest to the researcher

Conurbation, or Megalopolis: the merger of two or more urban regions

Corporation: the primary unit in capitalist economic systems that organizes capital, technology, labor, and land for economic activity

Correlations: statistical techniques that summarize the relationships among variables

Cooptation: the process of gaining control of a structure by increasing its dependence on another for basic resources

Counterculture: a group of people whose behavior and culture rejects that of the dominant society and culture

Crazes: obsessive emotional behavior in which people hold in abeyance many of their routine activities

Cro-Magnons: the first modern humans who emerged about 40,000 years ago

Crowds: temporary gatherings of people reacting to a common stimulus

Cult: the social unit in which religious rituals are performed and which provides a place of membership for those who share religious beliefs

Cultural Directives: the process in which cultural symbols guide and direct a person's perceptions, feelings, and actions

Cultural Expansion: the process by which new symbolic components are created and added to the cultural storehouse

Cultural Pluralism: that situation in which ethnic groups retain their uniqueness but are still given equal opportunities

Cultural Relativity: the scientific recognition that the values, beliefs, and other systems of symbols and patterns of behavior of a culture and society must be assessed in their own terms and that scientists must not impose their own values, beliefs, and other cultural components when examining a society

Culture: a system of meaningful symbols that people in a society create, store, and use to organize their affairs

Culture of Poverty: the concept used to describe the transmission of cultural values and beliefs among the poor that will inhibit their ability to perform well in crucial social spheres, and hence, to take advantage of opportunities for upward social mobility

Culture Storage: the process by which the symbolic world created by humans is maintained over long periods of time

Decision-making: the process by which options are sorted out and paths of conduct are selected

Definitions: statements that indicate what is or exists in the world and that are used to formulate concepts.

Democracy: the situation in which those who are governed have some choice as to who is to govern them

Democratization: the process of seeking to use schools to provide equal opportunities for success

Demographic Transition: the period during which death rates in a population initially decline, while birth rates remain high, leading to dramatic increases in a population's size until that point when birth rates also decline

Demography: the study of populations

Deviance: behavior which violates important social norms

Deviant Act: a distinct unit of behavior that violates a norm

Deviant Groups and Organizations: those situations where individuals are organized collectively to pursue deviance

Deviant Habit: persistent behavior that violates a social norm and that interferes with conformity to other norms

Deviant Personalities: deviance that appears to be caused by disorders of personality

Deviant Subcultures: a population whose distinctive cultural traits violate, and are at odds with, those of the majority in a society

Differential Association: the ratio of definitions favoring deviance or conformity that a person receives in interaction with others

Differential Fertility: the term used to describe the fact that different social classes have varying birth rates

Differentiation: the splitting of status roles formerly encompassed within one structure to separate structures

Discrimination: a type of interaction in which the rights and privileges enjoyed by most are denied to others

Distributing: the basic economic process whereby goods and services are made available to the members of a society

Division of Labor: the differential allocation of tasks and functions to different members of society

Downward Mobility: the process in which individuals move from a higher to lower social position in a system of rankings

Ecology: the study of the relationship of organisms to their environment

Egalitarian: a norm of family authority specifying that a family unit is to share authority

Ego: Sigmund Freud's concept used to describe those processes which reconcile situational expectations, a person's motives, impulses, and cultural values and beliefs in ways that allow the person to act in the social world

Empirical Beliefs: conceptions that people hold about what actually *does exist in a particular* social situation or context

Endogamy: marriage norms indicating that marriage partners must be chosen within defined kin or other units

Entrepreneurship: the manner and degree of organization of land, labor, capital, and technology in the economy

Ethnic Group: a population that is distinguished socially and that has its own distinctive cultural and social patterns

Ethnocentrism: the practice of viewing other societies and cultures in terms of the standards of one's own culture

Evaluative Beliefs: ideas or conceptions that people hold about what *should exist* in a *particular* social situation or context

Executive Branch: that part of government in which the chief executive of the state bureaucracy operates

Exogamy: marriage rules specifying that marriage partners must be found outside a defined kin or other unit

Experimental Design: the procedure by which at least two matched groups are used to collect data. One is exposed to a stimulus, whereas the other remains unexposed to the stimulus

Experimental Group: the group in an experimental design that is exposed to a stimulus of interest to the researcher

Expulsion: the removal of a minority from a society through force or incentives

Extended Family: large families that include many relatives within the household unit

Extermination: the killing of members of a minority population

Fads, Fashion: the pursuit of a particular interest, usually done capriciously and briefly, often with an exaggerated sense of devotion or zeal

Fertility: the rate of births in a population

Formal: social structures that have explicit and specialized statuses, unambiguous norms, clear authority relations, and an emphasis on impersonal role performance

Formal Organization: the organization of status, roles, and norms in ways that involve explicit relations among status positions, clear norms, and highly standardized role performances

Formal Sanctions: patterned and organized ways that rewards and punishments are bestowed

Gathering: the basic economic process whereby resources are extracted from the environment

Gender: the general term used to denote masculine and feminine, or male and female, distinctions made by members of a society

Generalize: the practice of viewing specific events as instances of more generic processes

Genetic: those factors pertaining to genetic structure of humans, particularly to the alignment of genes or chromosomes

Genetic Adaptation: permanent and inheritable alterations of the structure in the organisms of a species that facilitate adjustment to the environment

Genocide: the extermination of an entire ethnic population

Gestures: signs or signals—verbal, facial, bodily—that people emit and use as a basis for interpreting others' dispositions and intentions

Government: the organization of decision-making in society; those positions in a society that are invested with power, leadership, and authority

Group Pressure: the process whereby people perceive group expectations to exert pressures for conformity

Groups: those relatively small social units, composed of few statuses and clear norms, in which individuals enact roles

Habitat: the relationship of a species to the inorganic components of the environment

Higher Education: those school structures involved in educating graduates of secondary schools

Hominids: that order of apes who are humanlike and who can be classified as the ancestors, or close relative of the ancestors, of humans

Homo erectus: the first true humans who emerged 1.3 million years ago and who belonged to the family of *H. sapiens*

Homo sapien sapien: modern humans

Horizontal Mobility: the process in which individuals move from one position to another without going to a higher or lower position in a system of rankings

Hormone: chemical substances secreted into the circulatory system that influence bodily functions

Human Ecology: the study of the relationship of humans to their environment

The Human System: the entire complex of social relationships created by humans

Hypothesis: a proposition that states an expected relationship among events in a particular research setting

Id: Sigmund Freud's concept to describe the energy and motives that drive individuals to act in certain ways

Ideal Type: Weber's strategy of analytically accentuating the most salient features of a social pattern.

Imaginative Rehearsal: G. H. Mead's term for describing the process of imagining the consequences of alternative lines of conduct

Impersonality: the decreasing incidence of personal and emotionally involving interaction

Incest Taboo: rules that restrict sexual and marriage relations among specific members of the family

Income Distribution: the term used to describe the distribution of total income in a society for a given year to various percentages of income earners

Income Fifth: a statistical category for describing 20% of income earners in a given year

Industrial Revolution: the coupling of nonhuman and nonanimal power to machines in economic production

Informal Sanctions: sanctions emitted in the ordinary course of interaction

Informal System: those more personal, informal, and affective ties that develop among individuals in formal organizations

In-group: those groups in which individuals perceive themselves as like-minded in relation to external events and forces

Institutionalization: the patterning of social interaction in ways that reduce the possibility for tension, conflict, and deviance

Integration: that situation in which members of ethnic groups have equal access to the same roles as nonethnics

Interaction: the process whereby individuals (and other types of social units) mutually influence each other and, in so doing create, maintain, change, or terminate a pattern of joint action

Intercorporate Control: those processes in which corporations form liaisons and patterns of cooperation and ownership that allow them to control diverse markets in the economy

Interests: groups that have certain common goals and that press for decisions to help them meet these goals

Iron Law of Oligarchy: that process whereby a small clique perpetuates its control of an organization

Judiciary: that part of government in which procedures for resolving disputes among citizens and for redressing grievances against government are implemented

Kinship: those normatively specified statuses created by marriage and blood lines that reveal still other norms for regulating role behaviors with respect to the functions of sex and mating, biological support, social reproduction, social support, and social placement

Labeling: the process of an act being designated as deviant by those with whom one interacts

Labor: human energy and effort expended in economic tasks

Land: the natural resources that a society uses in economic activity

Lanes: different educational programs for students of varying abilities and orientation within a single track system

Leadership: those who make decisions for others

Legislative Branch: that branch of government where elected representatives meet and engage in decision-making

Looking-glass Self: Charles Horton Cooley's concept to describe the process whereby people use other people as a frame of reference for viewing and evaluating themselves

Mass: a relatively large number of persons, spatially dispersed and anonymous, reacting to one or more of the same stimuli but acting individually without regard for one another

Mass Behavior: those behaviors that are unstructured, unorganized, and individually selected

Massification: the process of extending access to education to all members of a society

Matriarchal: a norm of family authority specifying that the wife's relatives, usually her brother, is to have most of the authority in the family unit

Matrilineal: a descent norm in which the mother's side of the family is defined as most important, with authority and inheritance being calculated through the female side of the family

Matrilocal: a rule of residence specifying that a husband must live near or with his wife's relatives

Meaning: what is capable of interpretation and over which a grouping of humans share common interpretations

Methods: the procedures used to examine the events of the world

Migration: the movement of populations from one geographical area to another

Mind: the capacity of humans to designate each other, mentally construct alternative lines of conduct, inhibit inappropriate responses, and select a desired response

Minority Group: ethnic groups that are the victims of discrimination by the majority in a society

Modernization: the process of economic change from an agrarian to industrial and postindustrial profile, which alters the basic structure of the human system

Monkeys: a species of the primate order that evolved for life in the jungle forest after the prosimians

Monopoly: that situation in which one corporation controls the market for a given good or service

Mortality: the rate of deaths in a population

Motives: those processes within individuals that "energize" and propel them to act in certain ways

Multinationalization: that situation in which a corporation does business and has invested capital in many different countries

Multiple Track: a system of secondary schools that is differentiated in terms of the kind of training that each school provides

Mutual Benefit Organizations: those organizations that are established and run to provide benefits and services for their members

Natural Selection: the process whereby those traits that facilitate adaptation to the environment are retained in a species, because members possessing those traits are more likely to survive and reproduce

Neanderthals: the last early relative of humans who lived up to about 100,000 years ago

Neolithic Revolution: the discovery of agricultural technology, about 10,000 years ago and its application to economic production

Neolocal: a rule of residence specifying that newly married couples are free to live where they choose

Niche: that place in the environment in which a species achieves functional relationships to other life forms and the inorganic components in the environment

Norms: expectations about what people are supposed to do, or how they are supposed to behave, in a particular social position or situation

Nuclear Family: family units composed of husband, wife, and their children

Observation: the research technique in which the researcher collects data through personal observation of events

Oligopoly: that situation in which a small number of corporations control the market for a given good or service

Organizational Confinement: the segregation and isolation of deviants in specialized organizations

Out-groups: those groups in which individuals perceive themselves to be nonmembers

Panics: behavior in which people behave hysterically, either to escape or approach some stimulus

Pantheon: a complex of supernatural beings who are seen to have specific relationships with each other

Participant Observation: the research technique in which the researcher actually participates in, and then observes, the events that are being studied

Party: Max Weber's term for rankings based on the possession of power

Patriarchal: a norm of family authority specifying that husbands are to have most of the authority within the family unit

Patrilineal: a rule of descent in which the father's side of the family is defined as most important, with authority and inheritance residing in the male side of the family

Patrilocal: a rule of residence specifying that a wife must live near or with her husband's relatives

Personality: all people's traits and characteristics that organize their feelings about themselves, their orientations to situations, and their tendencies to act

The Peter Principle: that process in formal organizations whereby people are promoted to, and then frozen in, those positions in which their level of competence is exceeded by the demands of the position

Pluralism: the situation in which multiple groups exert pressures on decision-makers in government

POET: the acronym used to refer to four important factors in the study of human ecology: population, organization, environment, and technology

Polygamous Family: families that involve plural marriages in which either the husband or wife takes on several marriage partners

Population Growth: the increasing numbers of a given species

Population Size: the number of people in a population

Power: the capacity of individuals or social units to realize goals or paths of conduct, and to impose their wills, even against active resistance by other individuals or social units

Power Elite: the view of government that argues that a comparatively few people make political decisions in a society and set the goals of the society

Prejudice: negative and hostile beliefs about others

Prestige: the bestowing of social honor to a person or social position

Primary Deviance: deviant acts that go unnoticed and unperceived by those emitting them as deviant

Primary Groups: those groups that are small and that involve frequent and intimate interaction

Primary Schools: those school structures involved in educating students 5 to 12 years of age

Primates: the order of mammals to which prosimians, monkeys, apes, and humans belong

Producing: the basic economic process whereby resources are converted into usable goods and commodities

Proletariat: Karl Marx's term for workers in capitalist societies

Propaganda: efforts by organizations to create a climate of public opinion favorable to their interests and goals

Proposition: a statement of relationship among events denoted by concepts or variables

Prosimians: mammal (premonkeys) who ascended the trees and became the first primate

Public: an aggregation, group, or other plurality of people who are focused on an issue or concern

Public Opinion: the assessment of a public's attitudes and other feelings or cognitions about particular issues

Race: the superficial biological differences among populations

Ramapithecus: the first hominid, it is believed, who lived on the savannah some 15 million years ago

Random Sample: a sample in which subjects are selected by chance, with all members of a population having an equal chance to be selected

Rationality: the pursuit of specified goals in the most efficient manner available or possible

Reference Groups: any group, social entity, or perspective that individuals use to assess themselves and guide their conduct

Religious Beliefs: people's shared conceptions of what is to be seen as sacred and what is to be defined as the supernatural realm

Religious Values: conceptions that people hold about what the sacred and supernatural define as good and bad, appropriate and inappropriate

Research Problem: a question about events that is to be the subject of scientific inquiry

Ritual: stereotyped role behaviors directed toward the sacred and supernatural

Ritualism: that process in formal organizations in which employees strictly adhere to formal rules, even if such conformity decreases flexibility and prevents attainment of organizational goals

Role: behavior that is manifested by persons occupying status positions

Role Conflict: a situation in which enactment of one role prevents, alters, or hinders the enactment of other roles

Role-playing Skills: the level of skill and the typical style with which a person plays roles in society

Role Strain: a situation in which a person has difficulty meeting the requirements of a role

Role-taking: the process whereby actors mutually interpret each others' gestures, putting themselves in each others' places and interpreting others' dispositions to act

Romantic Love Complex: norms of marriage selection indicating that a couple are to choose each other in terms of mutual compatibility and love

Sacred: objects, persons, and places that are the stimulus to emotional arousal and that are believed to possess special powers and significance

Sample: a smaller group of a larger population selected for study

Scarce Resources: any material or symbolic object that is valued by members of a population

Science: the use of theory and of objective and verifiable methods to test, or to create, generalizations about processes and events

Scientific Method: the established procedures of science by which accurate and verifiable data are collected and used to test or create theory

Scientific Questions: research problems that are designed to test or create theory

Secondary Deviance: deviant acts that have been labeled, with the labels further channeling actions into a deviant role

Secondary Groups: those groups that involve impersonal interaction and that do not reveal a high degree of intimacy or affect among their members

Secondary Schools: those school structures involved in educating students during their early and middle adolescence

Segregation: the confinement of a minority group to a limited range of roles

Self: the capacity to view oneself as an object and to develop attitudes, dispositions and feelings about oneself

Self-concept: that stable cluster of attitudes that people develop about themselves as objects

Servicing: skills that are produced and distributed in order to facilitate the operation of all basic economic processes

Sex: differences between males and females that have a biological or physiological basis

Sex Ratio: the proportion of males to females in a population

Sex Roles: those behaviors in a society that are assigned to, or assumed to be related to being either male or female

Sexual Dimorphism: differences in the size, strength, and other relevant features between males and females

Significant Other: a concept used by George Herbert Mead to denote those individuals who are particularly important in a child's, and later an adult's, social world

Single Track: a system of secondary schools in which all schools provide the same educational programs

Social Class: the concept used by contemporary sociologists to describe the existence of distinct populations who hold similar jobs, who share a given portion of scarce resources, and who evidence common experiences and life-styles

Social Control: those processes that attempt to maintain conformity to existing norms

Social Movement: persistent and often enduring efforts by people to effect or resist social change

Social Placement: the process of allocating individuals to positions in the broader social structure

Social Psychology: the study of the relationship between individuals and the human system

Social Relationships: social bonds that emerge among humans as they communicate and interact. These bonds can range from simple friendships to large urban regions and institutional complexes

Social Sanctions: actions on the part of others in a society that provide rewards for conformity and punishments for non-conformity

Social Structure: social relationships which reveal some degree of stability and continuity over time

Socialization: those interactive processes with others in society that lead to the acquisition of a personality

Sociobiology: the study of how human biology interacts with the way humans organize themselves in society

Sociology: the scientific study of social relationships—from their simplest to most complex forms

Somatic Adaptations: noninheritable alterations of structure, and behaviors, in the organisms of a species that facilitate adjustment to the environment

State: that form of government in which leaders possess coercive power and an administrative bureaucracy to help make and carry out decisions

Status: Max Weber's term for rankings based on prestige or social honor

Status: a social position within a larger network of positions

Stratification: the unequal distribution of scarce resources in such a way as to create enduring rankings of positions that can be distinguished in terms of their respective shares of scarce resources

Structural Mobility: the situation in which changes in people's social ranking can be explained by changes in the distribution of positions rather than by their attributes

Structure: relatively stable patterns of interaction among social units

Struggle: the competitive and cooperative processes among organisms in an environment

Subculture: a group of people who share certain common systems of symbols that distinguish them from the majority of people in a society

Suburb: a city, or group of cities, surrounding an even larger central city

Superego: Sigmund Freud's concept to describe the process whereby cultural values and beliefs shape and constrain a person's motives and action

Supernatural: a belief in special realm, beyond everyday life, where the forces, spirits, powers, and beings, seen as influencing the operation of the world, reside

Surveys: the research technique in which samples of subjects are asked to respond to prepared questions

Symbol: a sign that humans emit and use to represent ideas, objects, and others in their world

Systems of Symbols: symbols that are interrelated with each other and that give meaning and the capacity to interpret and make sense of objects or events

Tabulations: a means for presenting data on events in a table

Technology: knowledge about how to manipulate and control the environment

Theory: the use of abstract concepts, incorporated into propositions to understand and explain the events of the world

Upward Mobility: the process in which individuals move from a lower to higher social position in a system of rankings

Urban Metropolis, Region: a large central city surrounded by smaller cities

Utilitarian Organizations: those voluntary organizations in which membership is paid and induced by financial and other rewards

Values: ideas or conceptions that people in a society share about what is good and bad or appropriate and inappropriate

Variable: a type of concept that denotes the variable properties of phenomena in the world

Voluntary Organizations: those formal organizations in which membership is voluntary and unpaid

Wealth: all material possessions that are valued and viewed as assets

Wealth Distribution: the term used to describe the distribution of total wealth in a given year to various percentages of wealth holders

Wealth Fifth: a statistical category for describing 20% of the wealth holders in a given year

BIBLIOGRAPHY

Abrahamson, Mark. *Urban Sociology.* Englewood Cliffs, N.J.: Prentice-Hall, 1976.

Abrams, Charles. "The Housing Problem and the Negro." In *The Negro American,* edited by T. Parsons and K. Clark. Boston: Houghton Mifflin, 1966.

———. "Housing Policy—1937–1967." In *Shaping an Urban Future,* edited by B. J. Frieden and W. W. Nash. Cambridge, Mass.: M.I.T. Press, 1969.

Adams, J., ed. *A Reader's Guide to the Great Religions.* New York: The Free Press, 1965.

Adams, Robert L., and **Fox, Robert J.** "Maintaining Jesus: The New Trip." *Society* (1972):8–16.

Allen, R. F. and **Adair, C. H.** *Violence and Riots in Urban America.* Worthington, Ohio: C. A. Jones, 1969.

Aramoni, Ancieto. "Machismo." *Psychology Today* (January 1972): 69–72.

Asch, S. E. "Effects of Group Pressure upon the Modification and Distortion of Judgements." In *Readings in Social Psychology,* edited by E. E. Maccoby, T. M. Newcomb, and E. L. Hartley. New York: Holt, Rinehart and Winston, 1958.

Ash, Roberta. *Social Movements in America.* Chicago: Markham, 1972.

Asumi, Koya, and **Hage, Jerald.** *Organization Systems.* Boston: D. C. Heath, 1972.

Balswick, Jack O., and **Peek, Elizabeth.** "The Inexpressive Male: A Tragedy of American Society." *The Family Coordinator* 20 (October 1971): 363–368.

Bardwick, Judith, and **Douvan, Elizabeth.** "Ambivalence: the socialization of women." In *Women in Sexist Society,* edited by Vivian Gornick and Barbara K. Moran. New York: Basic Books, 1971.

Barron, Milton, ed. *The Blending American.* Chicago: Quadrangle, 1972.

Barzini, Luigi. *The Italians.* New York: Atheneum, 1964.

Beals, Ralph, and **Hoijer, Harry.** *An Introduction to Anthropology.* 3rd ed. New York: Macmillan, 1967.

de Beauvoir, Simone. *The Second Sex.* New York: Knopf, 1953.

Becker, Howard S. *Outsiders: Studies in the Sociology of Deviance.* New York: The Free Press, 1963.

———ed. *The Other Side: Perspectives on Deviance.* New York: The Free Press, 1964.

Bell, Daniel. *The Coming of Post-Industrial Society.* New York: Basic Books, 1973.

Bell, N. W., and **Vogel, E. F.,** eds. *A Modern Introduction to the Family.* New York: The Free Press, 1968.

Bell, Robert R. *Social Deviance: A Substantive Analysis.* Homewood, Ill.: The Dorsey Press, 1971.

Bell, Wendell. "Social Choice, Life Styles, and Suburban Residence." In *The Suburban Community,* edited by William M. Dobriner. New York: G. P. Putnam, 1958.

Bellah, Robert N. "Religious Evolution." *American Sociological Review* (1964):358–374.

———*Beyond Belief: Essays on Religion in a Post-Traditional World.* New York: Harper & Row, 1970.

Belshaw, C. S. *Traditional Exchange and Modern Markets.* Englewood Cliffs, N.J.: Prentice-Hall, 1965.

Bennis, Warren G. *American Bureaucracy.* Chicago: Aldine, 1970.

Benser, Arthur. "Economic Deprivation and Family Patterns." In *Low Income Life Styles,* edited by L. M. Irelan. Washington, D.C.: U.S. Government Printing Office, 1971.

Berelson, Bernard, and **Janowitz, Morris,** eds. *Reader in Public Opinion and Communication.* New York: The Free Press, 1966.

Berger, Bennett M. *Working-Class Suburb.* Berkeley: University of California Press, 1960.

Berger, Peter. "Religious Institutions." In *Sociology: An Introduction,* edited by Neil J. Smelser. New York: Wiley, 1967.

Bernard, Jessie. *Women and the Public Interest: An Essay on Policy and Protest.* Chicago: Aldine-Atherton, 1971.

Biddle, Bruce J., and **Thomas, Edwin J.** *Role Theory: Concepts and Research.* New York: Wiley, 1966.

Bird, Caroline. "The Invisible Bar." In *Up Against the Wall, Mother . . . ,* edited by Elsie Adams and May Louise Briscoe. Beverly Hills: Glencoe Press, 1971.

Bird, Caroline, with **Welles, Sara.** *Born Female.* New York: McKay, 1968.

Blake, Judith, and **Davis, Kingsley.** "On Norms and Values." In *Handbook of Modern Sociology,* edited by R. L. Faris. Chicago: Rand McNally, 1964.

Blau, Peter M. and **Duncan, Otis Dudley.** *The American Occupational Structure.* New York: Wiley, 1967.

Blau, Peter M., and **Meyer, Marshall.** *Bureaucracy in Modern Society.* New York: Random House, 1971.

Blau, Peter M., and **Scott, Richard.** *Formal Organizations: A Comparative Approach.* London: Routledge & Kegan, 1963.

Blauner, Robert T. *Racial Oppression in America.* New York: Harper & Row, 1972.

Blisten, D. R. *The World of the Family.* New York: Random House, 1963.

Blood, R. O., and **Hamblin, R. L.** "The Effects of Wives' Employment on Family Power." In *A Modern Introduction to the Family*, edited by N. Bell and E. Vogel. New York: The Free Press, 1968.

Blumenfeld, Hans. "The Modern Metropolis." In *Cities.* New York: Knopf, 1971.

Blumer, Herbert. "Public Opinion and Public Opinion Polling." *American Sociological Review* (1948):542–549.

——. "Collective Behavior." In *Principles of Sociology*, edited by A. M. Lee. New York: Barnes & Noble, 1957.

——. *Symbolic Interactionism: Perspective and Method.* Englewood Cliffs, N.J.: Prentice-Hall, 1969.

Bogaraz, Vladimir G. "The Chuckchee." *Memoirs of the American Museum of Natural History* II (1907):448–457.

Bonacich, Edna. "A Theory of Ethnic Antagonism: The Split Labor Market." *American Sociological Review* (1972):547–559.

Bowerman, Charles E., and **Kinch, John W.** "Changes in Family and Peer Orientation of Children between the Fourth and Tenth Grades." *Social Forces* (1959):201–211.

Brim, Orville G., Jr. "Adult Socialization." In *Socialization and Society*, edited by J. A. Clausen. Boston: Little, Brown, 1968.

Brim, Orville G., Jr., and **Wheeler, Stanton.** *Socialization after Childhood.* New York: Wiley, 1966.

Brody, Jane E. "More than 100,000 Persons a Year Are Reported Seeking Sterilization As a Method of Contraception." *The New York Times* (March 22, 1970):22.

Bronfenbrenner, Urie. "Socialization and Social Class Through Time and Space." In *Readings in Social Psychology*, edited by E. E. Maccoby et al. New York: Holt, Rinehart and Winston, 1958.

Brophy, W. A., and **Aberle, S. D.** *Indians: America's Unfinished Business.* Norman: University of Oklahoma Press, 1966.

Brown, Roger W. "Mass Phenomena." In *Handbook of Social Psychology*, edited by G. Lindzey. Reading, Mass.: Addison-Wesley, 1954.

——. "Feral and Isolated Man." In *Language*, edited by V. P. Clark et al. New York: St. Martin's Press, 1972.

Burgess, Ernest W. "The Growth of the City." In *An Introduction to the Science of Sociology*, edited by R. E. Park and E. W. Burgess. Chicago: University of Chicago Press, 1921.

Burma, John H. *Mexican-Americans in the United States.* Cambridge, Mass.: Schenkman, 1970.

Butler, Edgar B. *The Family and Its Emerging Alternatives.* New York: Harper & Row, in press.

Cantril, Hadley. "The Invasion from Mars." In *Readings in Social Psychology*, edited by E. Maccoby et al. New York: Holt, Rinehart and Winston, 1958.

——. *The Psychology of Social Movements.* New York: Wiley, 1963.

Caplow, Theodore. *Principles of Organizations.* New York: Harcourt Brace Jovanovich, 1964.

Carneiro, R. L. "The Transition from Hunting to Horticulture in the Amazon Basin." In *Man in Adaptation*, edited by Y. A. Cohen. Chicago: Aldine, 1968.

——. "A Theory of the Origin of the State." *Science* (1970):733–738.

Carroll, John B. *Language, Thought and Reality: Selected Writings of Benjamin Lee Whorf.* Cambridge, Mass.: M.I.T. Press, 1956.

Carter, H., and **Glick, P. C.** *Marriage and Divorce: A Social and Economic Study.* Washington, D.C.: Vital Health Statistics Monographs, APHA, 1970.

Cartwright, Dorwin. and **Zander, Alvin,** eds. *Group Dynamics.* 3rd ed. New York: Harper & Row, 1968.

Cavan, Ruth S. *The American Family.* New York: Crowell, 1969.

Chesler, Phyllis. *Women and Madness.* New York: Doubleday, 1972.

Childe, V. Gordon. *Man Makes Himself.* New York: New American Library, 1952.

Clark, B. R. *Educating the Expert Society.* San Francisco: Chandler, 1962.

Clausen, John A. "The Organism and Socialization." *Social Behavior* (1967):243–252.

Clausen, John A. et al. *Socialization and Society.* Boston: Little, Brown, 1968.

Clinard, Marshall B., ed. *Anomie and Deviant Behavior.* New York: The Free Press, 1964.

——. *The Sociology of Deviant Behavior.* 4th ed. New York: Holt, Rinehart and Winston, 1974.

Cloward, Richard A., and **Ohlin, Lloyd E.** *Delinquency and Opportunity.* New York: The Free Press, 1960.

Cohen, Albert K. *Deviance and Control.* Englewood Cliffs, N.J.: Prentice-Hall, 1966.

Cohen, Albert K., and **Hodges, Harold M.** "Lower Blue-Collar Characteristics." *Social Problems* (1963):303–334.

Cole, C. *The Economic Fabric of Society.* New York: Harcourt Brace Jovanovich, 1969.

Coleman, James S. *The Adolescent Society.* New York: The Free Press, 1961.

Coleman, J. S. et al. *Equality of Educational Opportunity.* Washington, D.C.: U.S. Government Printing Office, 1966.

Cooley, Charles Horton. *Social Organization.* New York: Charles Scribner's & Sons, 1909.

——. *Human Nature and the Social Order.* New York: Schocken, 1964.

Crime in the United States: Uniform Crime Reports. Washington, D.C.: U.S. Government Printing Office, 1975.

Crozier, Michael. *The Bureaucratic Phenomenon.* Chicago: University of Chicago Press, 1964.

Dahl, Robert A. *Who Governs? Democracy and Power in an American City.* New Haven: Yale University Press, 1961.

Dahlström, Edmund. "Analysis of the Debate on Sex Roles." In *The Changing Roles of Men and Women,* edited by Edmund Dahlström. Boston: Beacon Press, 1967.

Dahrendorf, Ralf. *Class and Class Conflict in Industrial Society.* Stanford: Stanford University Press, 1959.

D'Andrade, Roy G. "Sex Differences and Cultural Institutions." In *The Development of Sex Differences,* edited by E. E. Maccoby. Stanford: Stanford University Press, 1966.

Daniels, Roger, and **Kitano, Harry H. C.** *American Racism: Exploration of the Nature of Prejudice.* Englewood Cliffs, N.J.: Prentice-Hall, 1970.

Darwin, Charles. *On the Origin of Species.* London: Collins, 1859.

Davis, Kingsley. "Extreme Social Isolation of a Child." *American Journal of Sociology* (1940):554–564.

——. "A Final Note on a Case of Extreme Isolation." *American Journal of Sociology* (1947):432–437.

——. *Human Societies.* New York: Macmillan, 1948.

——. "The Origin and Growth of Urbanization." *American Journal of Sociology* (1955):431–442.

——. "The Urbanization of the Human Population." In *Cities.* New York: Knopf, 1971.

——. "The American Family in Relation to Demographic Change." In *Demographic and Social Aspects of Population Growth,* edited by C. F. Westoff and R. Parke. Washington, D.C.: U.S. Government Printing Office, 1972.

Davis, Kingsley, and **Moore, Wilbert.** "Some Principles of Stratification." *American Sociological Review* (1945):242–249.

Dawson, Carl A., and **Gettys, Warner E.** *An Introduction to Sociology.* New York: Ronald Press, 1935.

Demerath, N. J. *Social Class in American Protestantism.* Chicago: Rand McNally, 1965.

Demerath, N. J., and **Hammond, P. E.** *Religion in Social Context.* New York: Random House, 1969.

Dewey, John. *Human Nature and Human Conduct.* New York: Holt, Rinehart and Winston, 1922.

Dixon, Marlene. "Why Women's Liberation?" In *Up Against the Wall, Mother . . . ,* edited by Elsie Adams and Mary Louise Briscoe. Beverly Hills: Glencoe Press, 1971.

Dobzhansky, Theodosius. *Mankind Evolving: The Evolution of the Human Species.* New Haven: Yale University Press, 1962.

Domhoff, William G. *Who Rules America?* Englewood Cliffs, N.J.: Prentice-Hall, 1967.

———. *Who Really Rules?* Santa Monica, Ca.: Goodyear, in press.

Drucker, P. *Landmarks of Tomorrow.* New York: Harper & Row, 1959.

Duncan, Otis Dudley. "From Social System to Ecosystem." *Sociological Inquiry* 31 (Spring 1961):140–149.

Durkheim, Émile. *The Elementary Forms of Religious Life.* Translated by J. W. Swain. London: Allen & Unwin, 1912.

Duvall, E. M. "Conceptions of Parenthood." *American Journal of Sociology* (1946):193–203.

Dworkin, Anthony Gary, and **Dworkin, Rosalind J.** *The Minority Report: An Introduction to Racial, Ethnic and Gender Relations.* New York: Praeger, 1976.

Eaton, G. Gray. "The Social Order of Japanese Macaques." *Scientific American* (1976):97–107.

Ehrlich, Carol. "The Male's Socialization Burden: The Place of Women in Marriage and Family Texts." *Journal of Marriage and the Family* 33 (August 1971):421–430.

Ehrlich, Paul R. *The Population Bomb.* New York: Ballantine, 1971.

Eisenstadt, S. I. *From Generation to Generation.* New York: The Free Press, 1956.

Elkin, Frederick, and **Handel, Gerald.** *The Child and Society: The Process of Socialization.* 2nd ed. New York: Random House, 1972.

Ellis, Albert. "The Sexual Psychology of Human Hermaphrodites." *Psychosomatic Medicine* (1945): 108–125.

Erikson, Erik. *Childhood and Society.* New York: Norton, 1950.

Etzioni, Amitai. *A Comparative Analysis of Complex Organizations.* New York: The Free Press, 1961.

Etzioni, Amitai, and **Etzioni, Eva.** *Social Change: Sources, Patterns, and Consequences.* New York: Basic Books, 1964.

Eysenck, Hans J. *The Biological Basis of Personality.* Springfield, Ill.: Charles C. Thomas, 1970.

Farb, Peter. *Word Play.* New York: Knopf, 1973.

Faris, Ellsworth. "The Primary Group: Essence and Accident." *American Journal of Sociology* (1932):41–50.

Farley, Reynolds. "Suburban Persistence." *American Sociological Review* (1964):38–47.

Farley, Ronald, and **Taeuber, Karl E.** "Population Trends in Residential Segregation Since 1960." *Science* (1968):685–694.

Farrell, Warren. "Guidelines for Consciousness-Raising." *Ms.* (July 1972):163.

Fasteau, Marc. "Why aren't we talking?" *Ms.* (July 1972):163.

Field, Mark G., and **Flynn, Karin I.** "Worker, Mother, Housewife: Soviet Women Today." In *Sex Roles in Changing Society.* New York: Random House, 1970.

Firth, Raymond. *We, the Tikopia.* New York: American Book, 1936.

Flavell, John H. *The Developmental Psychology of Jean Piaget.* New York: van Nostrand, 1963.

Fouts, Roger S. "Language: Origins, Definitions and Chimpanzees." *Journal of Human Evolution* (1974):475–482.

Fox, Thomas, and **Miller, S. M.** "Intra-county Variations: Occupational Stratification and Mobility." *Studies in Comparative International Development* (1965):3–10.

Freud, Sigmund. *The Basic Writings of Sigmund Freud.* Translated and edited by A. A. Brill. New York: Modern Library, 1938.

Fried, M. H. "On the Evolution of Social Stratification and the State." In *Culture in History,* edited by S. Diamond. New York: Columbia University Press, 1960.

Friedan, Betty. *The Feminine Mystique.* New York: Dell, 1963.

———. "The problem that has no name." In *Up Against the Wall, Mother . . . ,* edited by Elsie Adams and Mary Louise Briscoe. Beverly Hills: Glencoe Press, 1971.

Fuchs, Victor. "The First Service Economy." *The Public Interest* (1966):894–902.

Furstenberg, F. F. "Industrialization and the American Family." *American Sociological Review* (1968):326–337.

Gallup, George. "Churchgoing Decline of Last Decade Result of Sliding Catholic Attendance." *The Gallup Poll,* January 13, 1974.

Gallup Opinion Index. *Religion in America,* 1976.

———. *Religion in America,* Report 70, 1971.

———. No. 44, 1969.

Gallup Poll. American Institute of Public Opinion, 764, June 1968.

——. *City Planning in America: A Sociological Analysis.* In *People and Plans.* New York: Basic Books, 1968.

——. *The Levittowners: Ways of Life and Politics in a New Suburb.* New York: Random House, 1967.

Gans, Herbert J. "Urbanism and Suburbanism as Ways of Life: A Re-evaluation of Definitions." In *Human Behavior and Social Process,* edited by A. M. Rose, Boston: Houghton Mifflin, 1962a.

——. *The Urban Villagers.* New York: The Free Press, 1962b.

Garn, Stanley M. "Culture and the Direction of Human Evolution." *Human Biology* (1963):1–13.

Gergen, John A. "Physiological Aspects of Sexual Behavior: Genetics, Hormones, and the Central Nervous System." In *Human Sexuality in Medical Education and Practice,* edited by Clark E. Vincent. Springfield, Ill.: Charles C. Thomas, 1968.

Gerstl, J. E., and **Rainwater, L.** "Persistence and Change in Working-Class Life Style." In *Blue Collar World,* edited by A. B. Shostak and W. Gomberg. Englewood Cliffs, N.J.: Prentice-Hall, 1964.

Gerth, Hans H. and **Wright Mills, C.,** eds. From *Max Weber: Essays in Sociology.* Oxford: Oxford University Press, 1946.

Gibbons, Don C., and **Jones, Joseph F.** *The Study of Deviance: Perspectives and Problems.* Englewood Cliffs, N.J.: Prentice-Hall, 1975.

Glenn, Norval D., and **Hyland, Ruth.** "Religious Preference and Worldly Success: Some Evidence from National Surveys." *American Sociological Review* (1967):73–75.

Glock, Charles Y., ed. *Religion in Sociological Perspective.* Belmont, Calif.: Wadsworth, 1973.

Glock, Charles Y. and **Stark, Rodney.** *Religion and Society in Tension.* Chicago: Rand McNally, 1965.

Gockel, Galen L. "Income and Religious Affiliation: A Regression Analysis." *American Journal of Sociology* (1969):632–646.

Goffman, Erving. *The Presentation of Self in Everyday Life.* New York: Doubleday, 1959.

——. *Interaction Ritual.* New York: Doubleday, 1967.

Goode, William J. *Religion Among the Primitives.* New York: The Free Press, 1951.

——. "A Theory of Role Strain." *American Sociological Review* (1960):483–496.

——. *World Revolution and Family Patterns.* New York: The Free Press, 1963.

——. *The Family.* Englewood Cliffs, N.J.: Prentice-Hall, 1964.

Gordon, Milton M. *Assimilation in American Life.* New York: Oxford University Press, 1964.

Gornick, Vivian, and **Moran, Barbara K.,** eds. *Women in Sexist Society: Studies in Power and Powerlessness.* New York: Basic Books, 1971.

Goslin, David A., ed. *Handbook of Socialization Theory and Research.* Chicago: Rand McNally, 1969.

Gove, Walter R., and **Tudor, Jeannette F.** "Adult Sex Roles and Mental Illness." In *Changing Women in a Changing Society,* edited by Joan Huber. Chicago: University of Chicago Press, 1973.

Greely, Andrew M. *Ethnicity in the United States: A Preliminary Reconnaissance.* New York: Wiley, 1974.

——. *Why Can't They Be Like Us?: America's White Ethnic Groups.* New York: Dutton, 1975.

Green, Richard. *Sexual Identity Conflict in Children and Adults.* New York: Basic Books, 1974.

Green, Richard, and **Money, John.** *Transsexualism and Sex Reassignment.* Baltimore, Md.: Johns Hopkins, 1969.

Greenberg, Selig. "Why Women Live Longer Than Men." *Harper's* 215 (October 1957).

Greer, Germaine. *The Female Eunuch.* New York: McGraw-Hill, 1971.

Greer, Scott. "Urbanism Reconsidered: A Comparative Study of Local Areas in a Metropolis." *American Sociological Review* (1956):19–25.

Gross, Edward C. "Some Functional Consequences of Primary Groups in Formal Organizations." *American Journal of Sociology* (1953):368–373.

Gross, Neal; Mason, W. S.; and **McEachern, A. W.,** *Explorations in Role Analysis.* New York: Wiley, 1958.

Gusfield, Joseph R. *Protest, Reform, and Revolt: A Reader in Social Movements.* New York: John Wiley, 1970.

Guzzardi, Walter. "The Uncertain Passage from College." *Fortune* (January 1976):18–24.

Hall, Edward T. *The Silent Language.* New York: Doubleday, 1959.

Hall, Peter. *The World Cities.* New York: McGraw-Hill, 1966.

Haney, C. C.; Banks, C.; and **Zimbardo, P. G.** "Interpersonal Dynamics in a Simulated Prison." *International Journal of Crime and Penology* (1973):69–97.

Hare, A. Paul. *Handbook of Small Group Research.* New York: The Free Press, 1962.

Hare, A. Paul; Bales, Robert F.; and **Borgatta, Edgar,** eds. *Small Groups.* New York: Knopf, 1965.

Harlow, Harry F. "Love in Infant Monkeys." *Scientific American* (1959):68–74.

Harlow, Harry F., and **Harlow, Margaret K.** "Social Deprivation in Monkeys." *Scientific American* (1962a):137–146.

——. "The Effect of Rearing Conditions on Behavior." *Bulletin of the Menninger Clinic* (1962b):213–224.

Harrington, Michael. *The Other America.* New York: Macmillan, 1962.

Harris, Chauncy D., and **Ullman, Edward L.** "The Nature of Cities." *Annals of the American Academy of Political and Social Science* (1945):789–796.

Hartley, Ruth. "A Developmental View of Sex Role Identifications." In *Role Theory: Concepts and Research.* New York: Wiley, 1966.

Hastrof, Albert H., and **Cantril, Hadley.** "They Saw a Game: A Case Study." *Journal of Abnormal and Social Psychology* (1954):129–134.

Hauser, Philip M. "The Chaotic Society: Product of the Social Morphological Revolution." *American Sociological Review* (1969): 1–12.

Havighurst, R. J., and **Neugarten, B. L.** *Society and Education.* 3rd ed. Boston: Allyn & Bacon, 1967.

Hawley, A. *Human Ecology.* New York: Ronald Press, 1950.

Heise, David R., ed. *Personality and Socialization.* Chicago: Rand McNally, 1972.

Herberg, Will. *Protestant–Catholic–Jew: An Essay in American Religious Sociology.* New York: Doubleday, 1955.

Hetzel, A. M., and **Cappetta, M.** "Teen-agers: Marriages, Divorces, Parenthood, and Mortality." *Vital Health Statistics,* series 21, no. 23. Washington, D.C.: National Center for Health Statistics, 1973.

Hewes, Gordon W. "Primate Communication and the Gestural Origin of Language." *Current Anthropology* (1973):5–24.

Hewitt, John P. *Self and Society: A Symbolic Interactionist Social Psychology.* Boston: Allyn & Bacon, 1976.

Hill, Jane. "On the Evolutionary Foundations of Language." *American Anthropologist* (1972):308–317.

Hodge, Robert W.; Siegel, Paul M.; and **Rossi, Peter H.** "Occupational Prestige in the United States: 1925–1963." *American Journal of Sociology* (1964):286–302.

Holter, Harriet. *Sex Roles and Social Structure.* Oslo: Universitets Forlaget, 1970.

Homans, George C. *The Human Group.* New York: Harcourt Brace Jovanovich, 1950.

——. "Group Factors in Worker Productivity." In *Readings in Social Psychology,* edited by E. E. Maccoby, T. M. Newcomb, and E. L. Hartley. New York: Holt, Rinehart and Winston, 1958.

Hopper, Rex D. "The Revolutionary Process: A Frame of Reference for the Study of Revolutionary Movements." *Social Forces* (1950):207–279.

Horner, Matina S. "Fail: Bright Women." *Psychology Today* 3 (November 1969): 36ff.

——. "Toward an understanding of achievement-related conflicts in women." *Journal of Social Issues* 28 (1972):157–175.

Hoselitz, Bert F., and **Moore, Wilbert E.,** eds. *Industrialization and Society.* Hague: UNESCO, 1963.

Hoult, Thomas Ford. *Dictionary of Modern Sociology.* New York: Littlefield, Adams, 1969.

Howard, John R. *The Cutting Edge: Social Movements and Social Change in America.* Philadelphia: Lippincott, 1974.

Howe, Irving, ed. *The World of the Blue-Collar Worker.* New York: Quadrangle, 1972.

Hoyt, Homer. *The Structure and Growth of Residential Neighborhoods in American Cities.* Washington, D.C.: FHA, 1939.

——. "The Structure of American Cities in the Post-War Era." *American Journal of Sociology* (1943): 475–492.

Huber, Joan, ed. *Changing Women in a Changing Society.* Chicago: University of Chicago Press, 1973.

Hughes, Helen MacGill, ed. *Racial and Ethnic Relations.* Boston: Holbrook Press, 1970.

Hunt, Chester L., and **Walker, Lewis.** *Ethnic Diversity.* New York: Dorsey Press, 1974.

Hunter, Floyd. *Community Power Structure.* Chapel Hill: University of North Carolina Press, 1953.

Hunter, Guy. *Modernizing Peasant Societies: A Comparative Study in Asia and Africa.* New York: Oxford University Press, 1969.

Irelan, L. M., ed. *Low Income Life Styles.* Washington, D.C.: HEW, Welfare Administration, no. 14, 1966.

Jencks, Christopher. "A Reappraisal of the Most Controversial Educational Document of Our Time." *New York Times Magazine* (August 10, 1969).

Jencks, Christopher et al. *Inequality: A Reassessment of the Effects of Family and Schooling in America.* New York: Basic Books, 1972.

Joffe, Carol. "Sex Role Socialization and the Nursery School: As the Twig Is Bent." *Journal of Marriage and the Family* 33 (August 1971):467–475.

Johnson, Donald M. "The Phantom Anesthetist of Matoon: A Field Study of Mass Hysteria." *Journal of Abnormal and Social Psychology* (1945):145–186.

Johnstone, Ronald J. *Religion and Society in Interaction.* Englewood Cliffs, N.J.: Prentice-Hall, 1975.

Kagan, Jerome. "Acquisition and Significance of Sex Typing and Sex Role Identity." In *Review of Child Development Research,* vol. 1, edited by M. Hoffman and L. W. Hoffman. New York: Russell Sage Foundation, 1964.

Kahl, Joseph. *The American Class Structure.* New York: Holt, Rinehart and Winston, 1961.

Kantrowitz, N. *Ethnic and Racial Segregation in the New York Metropolis.* New York: Praeger, 1973.

Karaguezian, Dikran. *Blow It Up.* Boston: Gambit, 1971.

Katz, Daniel; Cartwright, D.; Eldersveld, S.; and **Lee, A. M.,** eds. *Public Opinion and Propaganda.* New York: Holt, Rinehart and Winston, 1954.

Katz, Marlaine L. "Female Motive to Avoid Success." unpublished manuscript. Stanford: Stanford University School of Education.

Keith, Jeff. "My Own Men's Liberation." *Win* (September 1, 1971): 22–26.

Keller, Suzanne. "The Family in the Kibbutz: What Lessons for Us?" In *Israel—Social Structure and Change,* edited by Michael Curtis and Mordecai S. Chertoff. New Brunswick, N.J.: Transaction Books, 1973.

Kerckhoff, Alan C. *Socialization and Social Class.* Englewood Cliffs, N.J.: Prentice-Hall, 1972.

Kerner Report. *National Advisory Commission on Civil Disorders.* New York: Bantam Books, 1968.

Killian, Lewis M. "Social Movements: A Review of the Field." In *Social Movements: A Reader and Source Book,* edited by R. R. Evans. Chicago: Rand McNally, 1973.

Kitano, Harry H. L. *Japanese Americans: The Evolution of a Subculture.* Englewood Cliffs, N.J.: Prentice-Hall, 1971.

Knowles, Louis, and **Prewitt, Kenneth.** *Institutional Racism in America.* Englewood Cliffs, N.J.: Prentice-Hall, 1969.

Kohlberg, Lawrence. "Moral and Religious Education and the Public Schools." In *Religion and Public Education,* edited by T. Sizer. Boston: Houghton Mifflin, 1967.

Kohlberg, Lawrence, and **Gilligan, Card.** "The Adolescent as a Philosopher: The Discovery of the Self in a Postconventional World." *Daedalus* (1971):1051–1086.

Kohn, Melvin L. "Social Class and Parent-Child Relationships." *American Journal of Sociology* (1963):471–480.

———. *Class and Conformity.* Homewood, Ill.: Dorsey Press, 1969.

Komarovsky, Mirra "Cultural Contradictions and Sex Roles: The Masculine Case." In *Changing Women in a Changing Society,* edited by Joan Huber. Chicago: University of Chicago Press, 1973.

———.*Blue-Collar Marriage.* New York: Random House, 1964.

Kornhauser, W. " 'Power Elite' or 'Veto Groups'?" In *Culture and Social Character,* edited by S. M. Lipset and L. Lowenthal. Glencoe, Ill.: The Free Press, 1961.

Kramer, Judith R. *The American Minority Community.* New York: T. Y. Crowell, 1970.

Kroeber, A. L. *Anthropology.* New York: Harcourt, Brace & World, 1948.

Kroeber, A. L., and **Kluckhohn, Clyde.** *Culture: A Critical Review of Concepts and Definitions.* New York: Vintage Books, 1963.

Kroeber, A. L., and **Parsons, Talcott.** "The Concepts of Culture and of Social System." *American Sociological Review* (1958):582–583.

Kuhn, Manford H. "The Reference Group Reconsidered." *The Sociological Quarterly* (1964):6–21.

Kummer, Hans. *Primate Societies.* New York: Aldine, 1971.

Lancaster, June B. *Primate Behavior and the Emergence of Human Culture.* New York: Holt, Rinehart and Winston, 1975.

Landsberger, Henry A. *Hawthorne Revisited.* Ithaca, N.Y.: Cornell University Press, 1958.

Lang, Kurt, and **Lang, Gladys.** *Collective Behavior.* New York: T. Y. Crowell, 1961.

Leavitt, Ruby R. "Women in Other Cultures." In *Women in Sexist Society,* edited by Vivian Gornick and Barbara K. Moran. New York: New American Library, 1972.

Lederer, Wolfgang. *The Fear of Women.* New York: Harcourt Brace Jovanovich, 1968.

Lee, Richard B., and **DeVore, Irven,** eds. *Man the Hunter.* New York: Aldine, 1968.

Lemert, Edwin M. *Social Pathology.* New York: McGraw-Hill, 1951.

Lenski, Gerhard. *The Religious Factor: A Sociologist's Inquiry.* Garden City, N.Y.: Anchor, 1963.

———. *Power and Privilege: A Theory of Stratification.* New York: McGraw-Hill, 1966.

Leslie, Gerald R. *The Family in Social Context.* New York: Oxford University Press, 1976.

Lessa, W., and **Vogt, E.,** eds. *Reader in Comparative Religion.* Evanston, Ill.: Row, Peterson, 1958.

Lewis, Oscar. *La Vida.* New York: Random House, 1965.

———. *Five Families: Mexican Case Studies in the Culture of Poverty.* New York: New American Library, 1971.

Lieberson, Stanley, and **Silverman, Arnold R.** "The Precipitants and Underlying Conditions of Race Riots." *American Sociological Review* (1965):885–896.

Liebert, Robert M., and **Povlos, Rita W.** "TV for Kiddies—Truth, Goodness, Beauty, and a Little Bit of Brainwash." *Psychology Today* (November 1972):21–26.

Lifton, Robert Jay. *Thought Reform and the Psychology of Totalism.* New York: W. W. Norton, 1961.

Liljestrom, Rita. "The Swedish Model." In *Sex Roles in Changing Society,* edited by Georgene H. Seward and Robert C. Williamson. New York: Random House, 1970.

Linton, Ralph. *The Study of Man.* New York: Appleton-Century-Crofts, 1936.

Lipset, Seymour Martin, and **Bendix, Reinhard.** *Social Mobility in Industrial Society.* Berkeley: University of California Press, 1959.

Little, Roger W. "Buddy Relations and Combat Performance." In *The New Military,* edited by M. Janowitz. New York: Russell Sage, 1964.

Lowie, Robert H. *Primitive Religion.* New York: Boni & Liveright, 1948.

Maccoby, Eleanor E., ed. *The Development of Sex Differences.* Palo Alto, Ca.: Stanford University Press, 1966.

Maccoby, Eleanor, and **Jacklin, Carol.** *The Psychology of Sex Differences.* Palo Alto, Ca.: Stanford University Press, 1974.

Maccoby, M. "Government, Scientists, and the Priorities of Science." *Dissent* (Winter 1974):642–657.

Mailer, Norman. "Ego." *Life Magazine* 70 (March 19, 1971):18–36.

Malinowski, Bronislaw. *Magic, Science and Religion.* Garden City, N.Y.: Doubleday, 1925.

Manville, W. H. "The Locker Room Boys." *Cosmopolitan* 166 (November 1969):110–115.

March, James G., ed. *Handbook of Organizations.* Chicago: Rand McNally, 1965.

March, James G., and **Simon, Herbert A.** *Organizations.* New York: Wiley, 1958.

Marshall, L. A. *Men Against Fire.* New York: Morrow, 1947.

Marx, Karl, and **Engels, Friedrich.** *The Communist Manifesto.* New York: Appleton-Century-Crofts, 1955.

Mazur, Allan, and **Robertson, Leon S.** *Biology and Social Behavior.* New York: The Free Press, 1972.

McKinley, D. G. *Social Class and Family Life.* New York: The Free Press, 1964.

Mead, George Herbert. *Mind, Self and Society.* Chicago: University of Chicago Press, 1934.

———. *The Philosophy of the Act.* Chicago: University of Chicago Press, 1938.

Mead, Margaret. *Sex and Temperament in Three Primitive Societies.* New York: Dell, 1935.
——. *Male and Female.* New York: New American Library, 1950.
Merton, Robert K. "Social Structure and Anomie." *American Sociological Review* (1938):672–682.
——. "Discrimination and the American Creed." In *Discrimination and National Welfare,* edited by R. M. McIver. New York: Harper and Row, 1949.
——. *Social Theory and Social Structure.* New York: The Free Press, 1968.
Michels, Robert. *Political Parties.* New York: Hearst, 1915.
Miles, R. E. "Whose Baby Is the Population Bomb?" *Population Bulletin* (February 1970):38–49.
Milgram, Stanley, and **Toch, Hans.** "Collective Behavior: Crowds and Social Movements." In *Handbook of Social Psychology,* edited by G. Lindzey and E. Aronson. Reading, Mass.: Addison-Wesley, 1968.
Miller, Walter B. "Lower-class Culture as a Generating Milieu of Gang Delinquency." *Journal of Social Issues* (1958):5–19.
Mills, C. Wright. *The Power Elite.* New York: Oxford University Press, 1959.
Mills, Theodore M. *The Sociology of Small Groups.* Englewood Cliffs, N.J.: Prentice-Hall, 1967.
Moberg, D. O. *The Church as a Social Institution.* Englewood Cliffs, N.J.: Prentice-Hall, 1962.
Money, John. *Sex Research, New Developments.* New York: Holt, Rinehart and Winston, 1965.

Money, John, and **Ehrhardt, Anke.** *Man and Woman, Boy and Girl.* Baltimore, Md.: Johns Hopkins Press, 1972.
Moody, Paul Amos. *Genetics of Man.* New York: Norton, 1967.
Moore, Joan W., and **Cuéllar, A.** *Mexican Americans.* Englewood Cliffs, N.J.: Prentice-Hall, 1970.
Moore, Wilbert E. *Economy and Society.* New York: Random House, 1955.
——. *Social Change.* Englewood Cliffs, N.J.: Prentice-Hall, 1974.
Morgan, Robin. *Sisterhood is Powerful.* New York: Vintage, 1970.
Moynihan, Daniel Patrick, ed. *On Understanding Poverty.* New York: Basic Books, 1969.
Mumford, Lewis. *The City in History.* New York: Harcourt, Brace & World, 1961.
Murdock, George. "Comparative Data on the Division of Labor by Sex." *Social Forces* 15 (May 1935):548–556.
——. *Our Primitive Contemporaries.* New York: Macmillan, 1936.
Murphy, Raymond J. "Postscript on the Los Angeles Riots." In *Problems and Prospects of the Negro Movement,* edited by R. J. Murphy and H. Elinson. Belmont, Calif.: Wadsworth, 1966.

Napier, John, and **Napier, P. H.** *Handbook of Living Primates.* New York: Academic Press, 1962.
Nash, Manning. *Primitive and Peasant Economic Systems.* San Francisco: Chandler, 1966.

National Center for Health Statistics, Department of Health, Education, and Welfare. *Summary Report: Final Divorce Statistics.* Washington, D.C.: U.S. Government Printing Office, 1974.
National Council of Churches. *Yearbook of American and Canadian Churches.* Nashville, Tenn.: Abingdon Press, 1975.
Neiman, Lionel J., and **Hughes, James W.** "The Problem of the Concept of Role: A Resurvey of the Literature." *Social Forces* (1951):141–149.
Neumann, Erich. *The Great Mother.* Bollingen Series, 67. New York: Pantheon, 1963.
Niebuhr, R. *The Social Sources of Denominationalism.* Cleveland: World Publishing, 1957.
Nimkoff, M. F., ed. *Comparative Family Systems.* Boston: Houghton Mifflin, 1965.
Norbeck, E. *Religion in Primitive Society.* New York: Harper & Row, 1961.
Novak, Michael. *The Rise of the Unmeltable Ethnics.* New York: Macmillan, 1972.
Nye, F. I., and **Berardo, F. M.,** eds. *Emerging Conceptual Frameworks in Family Analysis.* New York: Macmillan, 1966.

Oberschall, Anthony. *Social Conflict and Social Movements.* Englewood Cliffs, N.J.: Prentice-Hall, 1973.
O'Dea, Thomas. *The Sociology of Religion.* Englewood Cliffs, N.J.: Prentice-Hall, 1966.
——. *Sociology and the Study of Religion.* New York: Basic Books, 1970.

Olmsted, Michael S. *The Small Group.* New York: Random House, 1959.

Olsen, Marvin E. *The Process of Social Organization.* New York: Holt, Rinehart and Winston, 1968.

Orlans, H. *The Effects of Federal Programs on Higher Education.* Washington, D.C.: Brookings Institute, 1962.

Orrick, William H. *Shut It Down.* National Commission on Causes and Prevention of Violence, 1969.

Ossowska, Maria. *Social Determinants of Moral Ideas.* Philadelphia: University of Pennsylvania Press, 1970.

Park, Robert E.; Burgess, Ernest W.; and **McKenzie, Roderick D.** *The City.* Chicago: University of Chicago Press, 1925.

Parker, G. G. "Survey of College Enrollments." *Intellect* (February and April, 1973).

Parsons, Talcott. *The Social System.* New York: The Free Press, 1951.

——. "The Kinship System of the Contemporary United States." In *Essays in Sociological Theory.* New York: The Free Press, 1954.

——. "The School Class as a Social System." In *Social Structure and Personality.* New York: The Free Press, 1964.

——. *Societies: Evolutionary and Comparative Perspectives.* Englewood Cliffs, N.J.: Prentice-Hall, 1966.

Parsons, Talcott, and **Bales, Robert Freid,** eds. *Family Socialization and Interaction Process.* New York: The Free Press, 1955.

Pasternak, B. *Introduction to Kinship and Social Organization.* Englewood Cliffs, N.J.: Prentice-Hall, 1976.

Pavenstedt, E. "A Comparison of the Childrearing Environments of Upper-Lower and Very Lower Class Families." *American Journal of Orthopsychiatry* (1965):89–98.

Peter, Laurence F., and **Hull, Raymond.** *The Peter Principle.* New York: Morrow, 1969.

Petersen, William. *The Politics of Population.* New York: Doubleday, 1964.

——. *Japanese Americans: Oppression and Success.* New York: Random House, 1971.

Petras, John W. *Sex: Male/Gender: Masculine.* Port Washington, N.Y.: Alfred Publishing Co., 1975.

Pfeiffer, John E. *The Emergence of Man.* New York: Harper & Row, 1969.

Piaget, Jean. *The Moral Judgement of the Child.* London: Kegan Paul, 1932.

Pierce, T. M. *Federal, State, and Local Government in Education.* Washington, D.C.: Center for Applied Research in Education, 1964.

Pilbeam, David. *The Ascent of Man.* New York: Macmillan, 1972.

Pinkney, Alphonso. *Black Americans.* Englewood Cliffs, N.J.: Prentice-Hall, 1969.

Pleck, Joseph. "Male Sex Role and Personality: Toward a Research and Clinical Perspective." Paper given at Harvard University, February, 1972.

Prescott, D. "Efficacy-related imagery, education, and politics." Unpublished honor thesis, Harvard University, 1971.

Presthus, Robert. *The Organizational Society: An Analysis and a Theory.* New York: Random House, 1962.

Rainwater, Lee. *And the Poor Get Children.* Chicago: Quadrangle, 1960.

Reagan, Michael D. *The Managed Economy.* London: Oxford University Press, 1963.

Reuben, David. *Any Woman Can.* New York: McKay, 1972.

Reynolds, Vernon. *The Biology of Human Action.* San Francisco: W. H. Freeman, 1976.

Rheingold, Harriet L. "The Social and Socializing Infant." In *Handbook of Socialization Theory and Research,* edited by D. A. Goslin. Chicago: Rand McNally, 1969.

Ridgeway, J. *The Closed Corporation: American Universities in Crisis.* New York: Ballantine Books, 1968.

Robbins, Lillian and **Edwin,** letter. *The New York Times Magazine.* (February 4, 1973):56.

Roberts, Ron E., and **Kloss, Robert M.** *Social Movements: Between the Balcony and the Barricade.* St. Louis: Mosby, 1974.

Rogers, Carl C. *On Encounter Groups.* New York: Harper & Row, 1970.

Rose, Arnold M. *The Power Structure: Political Process in America.* New York: Oxford University Press, 1967.

Rosen, Marjorie. *Popcorn Venus.* New York: Coward, McCann, and Geoghegan, 1973.

Rosenberg, Morris. *The Logic of Survey Analysis.* New York: Basic Books, 1968.

Rosenthal, Robert, and **Jacobson, Lenore.** *Pygmalion in the Classroom.* New York: Holt, Rinehart & Winston, 1968.

Ross, H. Lawrence. "Uptown and Downtown: A Study of Middle Class Residential Areas." *American Sociological Review* (February, 1965).

Rossi, Alice S. "Equality Between the Sexes: An Immodest Proposal." *Daedalus* 93 (Spring 1964):607–652.

Rossi, Peter H. "Power and Community Structure." *Midwest Journal of Political Science* (1960):396–401.

Rossi, Peter H., and **Blum, Zahava D.** "Class, Status and Poverty." In *On Understanding Poverty,* edited by D. P. Moynihan. New York: Basic Books, 1969.

Salisbury, W. S. *Religion in American Culture.* Homewood, Ill.: Dorsey Press, 1964.

Sapir, Edward. "Fashion." In *Encyclopedia of the Social Sciences.* New York: Macmillan, 1937.

Sarbin, Theodore R. "Role Theory." In *Handbook of Social Psychology,* edited by G. Lindzey. Reading, Mass.: Addison-Wesley, 1954.

Scarf, Maggie. "He and She: The Sex Hormones and Behavior." *The New York Times Magazine* (May 7, 1972):30ff.

Schaller, George B. "Mountain Gorilla Displays." *Field Studies in Natural History.* New York: Van Nostrand Reinhold, 1970.

Schlesinger, A. "The City in American History." In *Reader in Urban Sociology,* edited by P. Hatt and A. Reiss. New York: The Free Press, 1951.

Schneider, Herbert. *Religion in 20th Century America.* Cambridge, Mass.: Harvard University Press, 1972.

Sears, Robert R.; Maccoby, Eleanor E.; and **Levin, Harry.** *Patterns of Child-Rearing.* Evanston, Ill.: Row, Peterson, 1957.

Seeley, John R. "The Slum: Its Nature, Use, and Users." In *Neighborhood, City, and Metropolis,* edited by R. Guttman and D. Popenoe. New York: Random House, 1970.

Sennet, Richard, and **Cobb, Jonathan.** *The Hidden Injuries of Class.* New York: Knopf, 1972.

Service, Elman R. *Primitive Social Organization.* New York: Random House, 1962.

——. *The Hunters.* Englewood Cliffs, N.J.: Prentice-Hall, 1966.

Sewell, W. H. "Students and the University." *American Sociologist* (1971):34–39.

Shapiro, Harvey D. "I.B.M. and the Dwarfs: Think, Sell, Grow." *New York Times Magazine* (July 23, 1973).

Shaw, Clifford R., and **McKay, Henry D.** *Delinquency Areas.* Chicago: University of Chicago Press, 1929.

Shepard, Clovis R. *Small Groups: Some Sociological Perspectives.* New York: Intext, 1964.

Shibutani, Tamotsu. "Reference Groups as Perspectives." *American Journal of Sociology* (1955):562–569.

——. *Society and Personality.* Englewood Cliffs, N.J.: Prentice-Hall, 1961.

Shils, Edward A., and **Janowitz, Morris.** "Cohesion and Disintegration in the Wehrmacht in World War II." *Public Opinion Quarterly* (1948):280–315.

Shostak, Arthur B. *Blue-Collar Life.* New York: Random House, 1969.

Silberman, Charles E. *Crisis in the Classroom: The Remaking of American Education.* New York: Vintage Books, 1971.

Simmel, Georg. *Conflict and the Web of Group Affiliations.* Glencoe, Ill.: The Free Press, 1955. Originally published in 1908.

Simon, W., and **Gagnon, John.** In *Life Styles: Diversity in American Society,* edited by S. Feldman and G. W. Thiebar. Boston: Little, Brown, 1972.

Simpson, George E., and **Yinger, J. Milton.** *Racial and Cultural Minorities: An Analysis of Prejudice and Discrimination.* 4th ed. New York: Harper & Row, 1972.

Simpson, George Gaylord. *The Meaning of Evolution.* New Haven: Yale University Press, 1952.

Singer, Milton. "The Concept of Culture." *International Encyclopedia of the Social Sciences,* vol. 3. New York: Macmillan, 1968.

Sjoberg, Gideon. *The Preindustrial City.* New York: The Free Press, 1960.

——. "The Origin and Evolution of Cities." In *Cities.* New York: Knopf, 1971.

Slater, Philip. *The Pursuit of Loneliness.* Boston: Beacon Press, 1970.

Smelser, Neil J. *Social Change in the Industrial Revolution.* Chicago: University of Chicago Press, 1959.

——. *The Sociology of Economic Life.* Englewood Cliffs, N.J.: Prentice-Hall, 1963a.

——. *A Theory of Collective Behavior.* New York: The Free Press, 1963b.

Spectorsky, A. C. *The Exurbanites.* Philadelphia: Lippincott, 1955.

Spencer, Metta. *Foundations of Modern Sociology.* Englewood Cliffs, N.J.: Prentice-Hall, 1976.

Spier, R. F. G. *From the Hand of Man: Primitive Preindustrial Technologies.* Boston: Houghton Mifflin, 1970.

Spooner, B. *Population Growth.* Cambridge: M.I.T. Press, 1972.

Stark, Rodney, and **Glock, Charles.** *American Piety: The Nature of Religious Commitment.* Berkeley: University of California Press, 1968.

Stein, Maurice R. *The Eclipse of Community.* New York: Harper & Row, 1964.

Stephens, W. N. *The Family in Cross-Cultural Perspective.* New York: Holt, Rinehart and Winston, 1963.

Stockwell, E. G. *Population and People.* Chicago: Quadrangle, 1968.

Stoddard, Ellwyn. *Mexican Americans.* New York: Random House, 1973.

Stoller, Robert. *Sex and Gender.* New York: Science House, 1968.

Strauss, Anselm L. *Images of the American City.* New York: The Free Press, 1961.

Stryker, Sheldon. "Role-Taking Accuracy and Adjustment." *Sociometry* (1961):286–296.

Sullerot, Evelyn. *Women, Society, and Change.* New York: McGraw-Hill, 1971.

Sumner, William Graham. *Folkways.* Boston: Ginn, 1906.

Sutherland, Edwin H. *Principles of Criminology.* Philadelphia: Lippincott, 1939.

Swanson, Guy E. *The Birth of the Gods.* Ann Arbor: University of Michigan Press, 1960.

Taueber, Karl, and **Taueber, Alma.** *Negroes in Cities.* Chicago: Aldine, 1965.

Theodore, Athena, ed. *The Professional Woman.* Cambridge, Mass.: Schenkman, 1971.

Tobias, Philip V. *The Brain in Hominid Evolution.* New York: Columbia University Press, 1971.

Toch, Hans. *The Social Psychology of Social Movements.* Indianapolis: Bobbs-Merrill, 1965.

Tresemor, David. "Fear of Success: Popular but Unproven." *Psychology Today* 7 (March 1974):82–85.

Tumin, Melvin M. "Some Principles of Stratification: A Critical Analysis." *American Sociological Review* (1953):387–393.

——. *Social Stratification: The Forms and Functions.* Englewood Cliffs, N.J.: Prentice-Hall, 1967.

Turner, Jonathan H. *American Society: Problems of Structure.* New York: Harper & Row, 1972a.

——. *Patterns of Social Organization.* New York: McGraw-Hill, 1972b.

——. *American Society: Problems of Structure.* 2nd ed. New York: Harper & Row, 1976a.

——. "The Ecosystem." in D. Zimmerman, et al., *Understanding Social Problems.* New York: Praeger, 1976b.

——. *Social Problems in America: The Cultural and Structural Basis.* New York: Harper & Row, 1977.

Turner, Jonathan H., and **Singleton, Royce.** "A Theory of Racial Oppression." *Social Forces,* in press.

Turner, Jonathan H., and **Starnes, C. E.** *Inequality: Privilege and Poverty in America.* Santa Monica, Calif.: Goodyear, 1976.

Turner, Ralph H. "Role-taking: Process vs. Conformity." In *Human Behavior and Social Processes,* edited by A. Rose. Boston: Houghton Mifflin, 1962.

——. "Role: Sociological Aspects." *International Encyclopedia of the Social Sciences,* vol. 13. New York: Macmillan, 1968.

Turner, Ralph H., and **Killian, Lewis.** *Collective Behavior.* Englewood Cliffs, N.J.: Prentice-Hall, 1972.

U.S. Bureau of the Census. *1970 Census of Population, U.S. Summary.* Washington, D.C.: U.S. Government Printing Office, 1970.

——. *Detailed Characteristics.* Washington, D.C.: U.S. Department of Commerce, 1972.

——. *Current Population Reports.* Series P-20, No. 274. Washington, D.C.: U.S. Government Printing Office, 1974.

——. "Estimates of Population of Metropolitan Areas, 1973 and 1974 and Components of Change Since 1970." *Current Population Reports,* Series P-25, No. 618, January 1976.

van den Berghe, Pierre, ed. *Intergroup Relations: Sociological Perspectives.* New York: Basic Books, 1972.

Vander Zanden, James W. *American Minority Relations: The Sociology of Racial and Ethnic Groups.* 3rd ed. New York: Ronald Press, 1972.
van Lawick-Goodall, Jane. "Cultural Elements in a Chimpanzee Community." *Symposia of the Fourth International Congress of Primatology,* vol. I. Basel: Karger, 1973.
Vernon, Glenn M. *Sociology of Religion.* New York: McGraw-Hill, 1962.
Vidich, Arthur J., and **Bensman, Joseph.** *Small Town in Mass Society.* Princeton, N.J.: Princeton University Press, 1958.

Wallace, Anthony F. C. *Religion: An Anthropological View.* New York: Random House, 1966.
——. *Culture and Personality.* 2nd ed. New York: Random House, 1970.
Wallerstein, James S., and **Wyle, Clement J.** "Our Law-Abiding Law Breakers." *Probation* (1947):107–114.
Warner, Lloyd W. *A Black Civilization.* New York: Harper & Row, 1937.
——. *American Life: Dream and Reality.* Chicago: University of Chicago Press, 1962.
Warner, Lloyd W, et al. *Social Class in America.* Chicago: Social Research, 1949.
Warner, Lloyd W., and **Lunt, Paul S.** *The Social Life of a Modern Community.* New Haven: Yale University Press, 1941.

Warriner, Charles K. "Groups are Real: A Reaffirmation." *American Sociological Review* (1956):549–554.
——. *The Emergence of Society.* Englewood Cliffs, N.J.: Prentice-Hall, 1970.
Weber, Max. *The Protestant Ethic and the Spirit of Capitalism.* London: Allen & Unwin, 1904.
——. *The Theory of Social and Economic Organization.* New York: The Free Press, 1947.
Weitzman, Lenore J., and **Eifler, Deborah.** "Sex Role Socialization in Picture Books for Preschool Children." *American Journal of Sociology* 77 (May 1972):1125–1144.
Westley, William A. "Secrecy and the Police." *Social Forces* (1956): 254–257.
Whitehurst, Carol. *Women in America: The Oppressed Majority.* Santa Monica, Ca.: Goodyear Publishing, 1977.
Whorf, Benjamin Lee. *Language, Thought and Reality.* New York: Wiley, 1940, 1956.
Whyte, William Foote. *The Organization Man.* Garden City, N.Y.: Doubleday, 1957.
Williams, Robin M., Jr. *Strangers Next Door.* Englewood Cliffs, N.J.: Prentice-Hall, 1964.
——. "Individual and Group Values." In *Social Intelligence for America's Future,* edited by B. M. Gross. Boston: Allyn & Bacon, 1969.
——. *American Society: A Sociological Interpretation.* New York: Knopf, 1970.
Wilson, Bryan. *Religion in Secular Society.* Baltimore: Penguin Books, 1969.
Wilson, John. *Introduction to Social Movements.* New York: Basic Books, 1973.

Winch, Robert F. *The Modern Family.* New York: Holt, Rinehart and Winston, 1971.
Wirth, Louis. "Urbanism as a Way of Life." *American Journal of Sociology* (1938):46–63.
——. "The Problem of Minority Groups." In *The Science of Man in the World Crisis,* edited by Ralph Linton. New York: Columbia University Press, 1945.
Wollstonecraft, Mary. *A Vindication of the Rights of Women (1792).* New York: Norton, 1967.

Yearbook of American Churches. New York: National Council Press, 1959–1973.
Yinger, Milton J. "Contraculture and Subculture." *American Sociological Review* (1960):625–635.
——. *The Scientific Study of Religion.* London: Macmillan, 1970.
Yorburg, Betty. *Sexual Identity: Sex Roles and Social Change.* New York: Wiley, 1974.
Yuan, D. Y. "Voluntary Segregation: A Study of New York Chinatown." *Phylon* (1963):255–265.

NAME INDEX

SUBJECT INDEX

PHOTO CREDITS

THE SCIENCE OF SOCIETY

Why do we study the human system? The answer is that we are curious about ourselves and the social world. We want to know more, and we want to understand and comprehend as much as we can. But how are we to know, understand, and comprehend? How do we learn about the social world? How do we accumulate knowledge?

Such questions led to the development of *science*. Science is a way of accumulating knowledge about *why* events occur. Speculation about the social world has gone on for millennia, but only recently have the procedures and tools of science been applied to the study of the human system.

Science involves two related activities: (1) accumulating knowledge and (2) collecting data or information. These two activities are usually termed *theory* and *methods*, respectively. **Theory** is how we accumulate knowledge and make sense of the world. **Methods** are procedures for looking at the world. The two are inseparable; methods are involved in the collection of data, or information, that needs interpretation, or theory.

The Relationship of Theory, Methods, and the Real World to Each Other

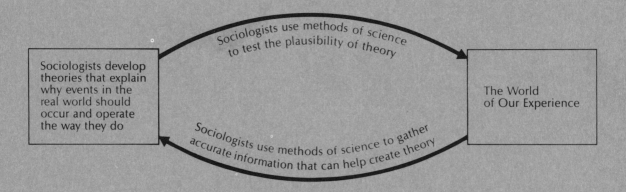

Sociologists develop theories that explain why events in the real world should occur and operate the way they do

Sociologists use methods of science to test the plausibility of theory

Sociologists use methods of science to gather accurate information that can help create theory

The World of Our Experience